파고다 토익 LC RC 실전 1000제

초판 1쇄 인쇄	2020년 1월 2일
초판 1쇄 발행	2023년 5월 18일
초판 7쇄 발행	2024년 7월 9일

지 은 이	파고다교육그룹 언어교육연구소
펴 낸 이	박경실
펴 낸 곳	PAGODA Books 파고다북스
출판등록	2005년 5월 27일 제 300-2005-90호
주 소	06614 서울특별시 서초구 강남대로 419, 19층(서초동, 파고다타워)
전 화	(02) 6940-4070
팩 스	(02) 536-0660
홈페이지	www.pagodabook.com

저작권자	ⓒ 2020 파고다아카데미

이 책의 저작권은 저자와 출판사에 있습니다. 서면에 의한 저작권자와 출판사의 허락 없이 내용의 일부 혹은 전부를 인용 및 복제하거나 발췌하는 것을 금합니다.

Copyright ⓒ 2020 by PAGODA Academy

All rights reserved. No part of this publication may be reproduced, stored in a retrieval system, or transmitted, in any form, or by any means, electronic, mechanical, photocopying, recording or otherwise, without the prior written permission of the copyright holder and the publisher.

ISBN 978-89-6281-837-6 (13740)

파고다북스	www.pagodabook.com
파고다 어학원	www.pagoda21.com
파고다 인강	www.pagodastar.com
테스트 클리닉	www.testclinic.com

▌낙장 및 파본은 구매처에서 교환해 드립니다.

파고다 토익
LC RC

실전 1000제
R

이 책의 구성과 100% 활용법

파고다 토익 실전 1000제 LC+RC는 최근에 출제되었던 토익 문제를 분석하여 가장 최고의 문제만 골라 만든 실전에 가까운 토익 모의고사 문제집입니다. 최신 경향에 맞는 문제를 풀어 보시고, 원하는 점수 꼭 달성하기 바랍니다.

5회의 문제집을 풀고 채점하면서 본인의 점수 상승률을 기록해 두면서 실제 시험에서의 예상 점수까지 알아보세요. 실제 시험장에서 너무나도 낯익은 문제들이 많아 깜짝 놀랄 겁니다.

▶▶ 목차

MP3 파일 무료 다운로드: www.pagodabook.com

문제집		해설지 (별책)	
TEST 1	16	TEST 1	2
TEST 2	60	TEST 2	44
TEST 3	104	TEST 3	89
TEST 4	148	TEST 4	132
TEST 5	190	TEST 5	176
OMR 카드	233		

▶▶ 부가 학습 자료

1타 선생님의 무료 해설 강의
해설서를 봐도 알쏭달쏭 이해가 잘 안 되는 어려운 문제들! 파고다 1타 토익 선생님들의 무료 강의로 어려운 문제도 완전히 이해하고 넘어 가세요. 선생님들의 자세한 해설 강의가 무료로 제공됩니다.

편리한 모바일 해설서
무거운 해설서가 그대로 내 스마트폰으로! 해설서를 들고 다니지 않아도 언제 어디서나 스마트폰으로 볼 수 있는 모바일 해설서가 있습니다. 모바일 해설서를 통하여 LC 문제 MP3 파일도 들을 수 있고, 무료 동영상 강의도 볼 수 있습니다.

토익에 관한 모든 질문! 파고다 토익 카페
https://cafe.naver.com/pagodatoeicbooks
혼자 공부하는 혼공족들! 더 이상 외로운 혼공족이 아니다! 모르는 게 있어도, 해설지를 봐도 도저히 이해가 안가는 경우, 누구한테 질문할 수 있을까요? 파고다 토익 카페에 오시면 파고다 어학원의 1타 선생님들과 토익 R&D 전문가들의 실시간 답변을 들을 수 있습니다.

LC/RC 파트별, 유형별 문제 무료 다운로드
토익 어휘만 공부하실 건가요! 토익 시험의 파트별 연습 문제를 무료로 다운로드 받아 연습해 보세요. 토익 전문가들이 파트별 문제 유형을 분석하여 만든 엄청난 양의 문제를 다운로드 받으세요. <파고다 토익-부가자료 → 공용 LC 자료실 / 공용 RC 자료실>

토익 모의고사 2회분 무료 다운로드
토익 전문가들이 만든 실제 시험과 유사한 토익 모의고사 2회분을 무료로 다운로드 받을 수 있습니다. 문제지, 해설지, 무료 동영상 강의까지! 토익 시험 전 마무리 모의고사 놓치지 마세요! <파고다 토익-부가자료 → 온라인 실전 모의고사>

핵심만 쏙쏙 뽑은 핵심 동영상 강의

핵심 동영상 강의를 촬영해 주신 파고다 어학원의 대표 1타 선생님들을 소개합니다.

	LC	RC
TEST 1	강남 파고다 **켈리정** 선생님	강남 파고다 **유나 신** 선생님
TEST 2	강남 파고다 **강솔아** 선생님	강남 파고다 **이지후** 선생님
TEST 3	종로 파고다 **유호영** 선생님	종로 파고다 **초강욱** 선생님
TEST 4	신촌 파고다 **HONEY 이** 선생님	신촌 파고다 **JAMIE 오** 선생님
TEST 5	신촌 파고다 **RACHEL 문** 선생님	신촌 파고다 **윤지성** 선생님

토익 시험의 모든 것

›› 토익 시험의 구성

파트		시험 형태	문항 수	시간	배점
듣기 (LC)	1	사진 묘사	6	약 45분	495점
	2	질의 응답	25		
	3	짧은 대화	39		
	4	짧은 담화	30		
읽기 (RC)	5	단문 공란 메우기	30	75분	495점
	6	장문 공란 메우기	16		
	7 독해	단일 지문 (10개 지문)	29		
		이중 지문 (2개 지문)	10		
		삼중 지문 (3개 지문)	15		
			200	120분	990점

›› 토익 시험 접수와 성적 확인

- 시험 접수는 www.toeic.co.kr에서 온라인 접수가 가능합니다.
- 두 달 후의 시험까지 접수 가능하고 정기 접수는 시험일로부터 2주 전까지 마감되지만, 시험일의 3일 전까지 추가 접수할 수 있는 특별 접수 기간이 있습니다. (응시료 4,000원 추가)
- 성적은 시험일로부터 16~18일 후에 인터넷이나 ARS(060-800-0515)를 통해 확인할 수 있습니다.
- 성적표는 온라인으로 발급이 가능하고 유효 기간 내에 홈페이지에서 본인이 직접 1회에 한해 무료 출력할 수 있습니다. 토익 성적은 시험일로부터 2년간 유효합니다.

›› 시험 당일 준비물

시험 당일 준비물은 규정 신분증, 연필, 지우개입니다. 허용되는 규정 신분증은 토익 공식 웹 사이트에서 확인하기 바랍니다. 필기구는 연필이나 샤프펜만 가능하고 볼펜이나 컴퓨터용 사인펜은 사용할 수 없습니다. 수험표는 출력해 가지 않아도 됩니다.

›› 시험 진행 안내

오전 시험

오전 9:30~9:45	오전 9:45~9:50	오전 9:50~10:05	오전 10:05~10:10	오전 10:10~10:55	오전 10:55~12:10
15분	5분	15분	5분	45분	75분
답안지 작성 관련 오리엔테이션	휴식시간	신분증 확인 (감독 교사)	문제지 배부 파본 확인	듣기 평가(LC)	읽기 평가(RC) 2차 신분증 확인

오후 시험

오후 2:30~2:45	오후 2:45~2:50	오후 2:50~3:05	오후 3:05~3:10	오후 3:10~3:55	오후 3:55~5:10
15분	5분	15분	5분	45분	75분
답안지 작성 관련 오리엔테이션	휴식시간	신분증 확인 (감독 교사)	문제지 배부 파본 확인	듣기 평가(LC)	읽기 평가(RC) 2차 신분증 확인

파트별 토익 소개

파트 1 PHOTOGRAPHS (사진 문제)

문항 수	6문항 (1번~6번)
DIRECTION 소요 시간	약 1분 30초
문제를 들려주는 시간	약 20초
다음 문제까지의 여유 시간	약 5초
문제 유형	1인 사진 / 2인 이상 사진 / 인물·사물 혼합 사진 / 사물·풍경 사진

▶▶ 문제 유형
- **1인 사진 문제:** 한 사람이 등장, 인물의 동작과 옷차림 등의 상태 묘사
- **2인 이상 사진 문제:** 두 사람 이상 등장, 인물의 공통 동작, 상호 동작, 개별 동작 및 상태 묘사
- **인물·사물 혼합:** 사진 인물과 사물이 함께 등장하여 동시에 혼합적으로 묘사
- **사물·풍경 사진:** 사람이 등장하지 않고 사물과 풍경 중심, 사물의 위치나 전체적 풍경 묘사

▶▶ 출제 포인트
- 인물 중심 사진에서 인물의 동작이 아니라 상태를 묘사하는 정답이 더 자주 출제되고 있다.
- 인물 중심 사진이더라도 사람 주변의 사물이나 배경을 묘사하는 정답도 출제된다.
- 사물·풍경 사진을 현재형 일반동사로 묘사하는 정답이 출제된다.

▶▶ PART 1 이렇게 대비하자
- Part 1에 자주 출제되는 사진의 상황별 빈출 표현들을 정리하여 암기한다.
- Part 1에서는 정답을 찾기보다 오답을 소거해야 한다. 평소 문제 풀이를 하면서 오답 보기들이 왜 정답이 될 수 없는지를 완벽하게 이해한다.
- 문제 풀이에서 틀린 문제들을 중점적으로 반복 청취하면서 문장 단위로 받아쓰기 연습을 하고, 듣고 따라 말하는 (shadowing) 청취 훈련이 필요하다.

시험지에 인쇄되어 있는 모양	스피커에서 들리는 음성
	Number 1. Look at the picture marked number 1 in your test book. (A) They're writing on a board. (B) They're taking a file from a shelf. (C) They're working at a desk. (D) They're listening to a presentation.

정답 (C)

파트 2 QUESTION-RESPONSE (질의응답)

문항 수	25문항 (7번 ~ 31번)
DIRECTION 소요 시간	약 25초
문제를 들려주는 시간	약 15초
다음 문제까지의 여유 시간	약 5초
문제 유형	의문사 의문문 / 부정 의문문 / 부가 의문문 / 평서문 / 선택 의문문 / 제안·제공·요청문 / BE동사·조동사 의문문 / 간접 의문문

▶▶ 문제 유형
- **의문사 의문문:** Who, When, Where, What, Which, How, Why
- **일반(Yes/No) 의문문:** Be동사 의문문, 조동사 의문문(Have, Do, Can, Will 등)
- **특수 의문문:** 부정 의문문, 부가 의문문, 선택 의문문, 요청문(제안·제공·요청), 간접 의문문, 평서문

▶▶ 출제 포인트
- 단답형으로 응답하는 의문문의 비중은 줄고, 다양한 응답이 가능한 평서문과 부가 의문문의 비중이 커지고 있다.
- 모르겠다, 아직 정해지지 않았다 등의 우회적인 응답이나 되묻는 응답의 비중 역시 직접 응답의 비중과 비슷한 수준으로 출제된다.

▶▶ PART 2 이렇게 대비하자
- Part 2에 자주 출제되는 질문·응답 유형 및 필수 표현을 정리한다.
- 질문은 알아듣기 쉽지만, 응답은 알아듣기 어려운 토익 Part 2는 질문의 핵심 키워드에 어울리지 않는 오답을 소거해 나가는 연습이 필요하다.

시험지에 인쇄되어 있는 모양	스피커에서 들리는 음성
7. Mark your answer on your answer sheet. (A) (B) (C)	**Number 7.** How was the English test you took today? (A) I took the bus home. (B) I thought it was too difficult. (C) I have two classes today.

정답 (B)

파트 3 SHORT CONVERSATION (짧은 대화)

문항 수	13개 대화문, 39문항 (32번 ~ 70번)
DIRECTION 소요 시간	약 30초
문제를 들려주는 시간	약 30~40초
다음 문제까지의 여유 시간	약 8초
질문 유형	- 전체 내용 관련 문제: 주제·목적, 인물, 장소 문제 - 세부사항 문제: 문제점, 이유·방법, 핵심어 정보 찾기 - 제안·요청 문제 / 앞으로 할 일 문제 / 유추·추론 문제 - 맥락상 화자의 의도 파악 문제 / 시각 정보 연계 문제

›› 대화 주제
- 회사 생활 | 사내외 업무, 일정, 인사 업무, 기기·사무용품
- 일상생활 | 상점, 식당, 여행·여가활동, 주거·편의시설
→ 3인 대화문: 주고받는 대화 수 증가 / 실생활에서 사용하는 회화 표현(구어체)의 증가

›› 출제 포인트
- 대화의 주제·목적을 묻는 문제보다 세부 사항을 묻는 문제의 비중이 높다.
- 짧은 대화가 빠른 속도로 진행되는 3인 이상의 대화와 주고받는 대화 수가 5턴 이상으로 늘어난 대화가 출제된다.

›› PART 3 이렇게 대비하자
3인 이상의 화자가 등장하는 대화는 전반적인 내용은 이해하기 쉬우나 대화 중간에 말의 속도가 매우 빠른 부분들이 섞여 나오기 때문에 체감 대화 속도가 매우 빠르다. 평소 빠르게 듣는 훈련이 필요하다.

시험지에 인쇄되어 있는 모양	스피커에서 들리는 음성
32. What is the conversation mainly about? (A) Changes in business policies (B) Sales of a company's products (C) Expanding into a new market (D) Recruiting temporary employees 33. Why does the woman say, "There you go"? (A) She is happy to attend a meeting. (B) She is frustrated with a coworker. (C) She is offering encouragement. (D) She is handing over something. 34. What do the men imply about the company? (A) It has launched new merchandise. (B) It is planning to relocate soon. (C) It has clients in several countries. (D) It is having financial difficulties.	**Questions 32-34** refer to the following conversation with three speakers. **A:** How have you two been doing with your sales lately? **B:** Um, not too bad. My clients have been ordering about the same amount of promotional merchandise as before. **C:** I haven't been doing so well. But I do have a meeting with a potential new client tomorrow. **B:** There you go. I'm sure things will turn around for you. **A:** Yeah, I hope it works out. **B:** It's probably just temporary due to the recession. **C:** Maybe, but I heard that the company may downsize to try to save money. **A:** Actually, I heard that, too.

정답 32. (B) 33. (C) 34. (D)

파트 4 SHORT TALK (짧은 담화)

문항 수	10개 담화, 30문항 (71번 ~ 100번)
DIRECTION 소요 시간	약 30초
문제를 들려주는 시간	약 30~40초
다음 문제까지의 여유 시간	약 8초
질문 유형	- 전체 내용 관련 문제: 주제·목적, 인물, 장소 문제 - 세부사항 문제: 문제점, 이유·방법, 핵심어 정보 찾기 - 제안·요청 문제 / 앞으로 할 일 문제 - 맥락상 화자의 의도 파악 문제 / 시각 정보 연계 문제

▶▶ 담화 유형

공지·안내방송(Announcement) / 전화·녹음 메시지(Telephone·Recorded message) / 연설·강연(Speech·Lecture)
방송·뉴스·보도(Broadcast·News report) / 광고(Advertisement) / 인물 소개(Introduction) /
기타 담화(Talk)공지·안내방송(Announcement) / 전화·녹음 메시지(Telephone·Recorded message) /
연설·강연(Speech·Lecture) / 방송·뉴스·보도(Broadcast·News report) / 광고(Advertisement) /
인물 소개(Introduction)

▶▶ 출제 포인트
- 담화의 주제·목적을 묻는 문제보다 세부 사항을 묻는 문제의 비중이 높다.
- 직접적인 질문보다는 정답을 유추해야 하는 문제가 증가하고 있다.
- 지문에 등장하는 정답의 단서가 질문이나 정답에는 다른 표현으로 제시되는 Paraphrasing의 빈도와 수준이 높아지고 있다.

▶▶ PART 4 이렇게 대비하자

Part 4 화자 의도 파악 문제는 담화문의 주요 흐름을 파악하면서 화자가 한 말의 앞뒤 문장을 집중해서 듣고, 문맥상 그 말의 실제 의미 또는 의도를 찾아야 한다. 평소 단순 듣기에서 벗어나 담화의 전반적인 흐름을 이해하는 훈련이 필요하다.

시험지에 인쇄되어 있는 모양	스피커에서 들리는 음성
71. Where most likely is the speaker? (A) At a trade fair (B) At a corporate banquet (C) At a business seminar (D) At an anniversary celebration 72. What are the listeners asked to do? (A) Pick up programs for employees (B) Arrive early for a presentation (C) Turn off their mobile phones (D) Carry their personal belongings 73. Why does the schedule have to be changed? (A) A speaker has to leave early. (B) A piece of equipment is not working. (C) Lunch is not ready. (D) Some speakers have not yet arrived.	**Questions 71-73** refer to the following talk. I'd like to welcome all of you to today's employee training and development seminar for business owners. I'll briefly go over a few details before we get started. There will be a 15 minute break for coffee and snacks halfway through the program. This will be a good opportunity for you to mingle. If you need to leave the room during a talk, make sure to keep your wallet, phone, and …ah… any other valuable personal items with you. Also, please note that there will be a change in the order of the program. Um… Mr. Roland has to leave earlier than originally scheduled, so the last two speakers will be switched.

정답 71. (C) 72. (D) 73. (A)

파트 5 INCOMPLETE SENTENCE (단문 빈칸 채우기)

>> **문항 수** 30문항 (101번 ~ 130번)

>> **출제 포인트**
- 문법적 지식과 어휘력을 동시에 묻는 문제들이 증가하고 있다.
- 두 가지 이상의 문법 포인트를 묻는 문제들이 출제되고 있다.
- 다양한 품사의 선택지로 구성된 문제들이 출제되고 있다.

>> **PART 5 문제 유형별 문제 풀이 접근법**

어형 문제	아래 문제처럼 한 단어의 네 가지 형태가 선택지로 나오는 문제를 어형 문제 또는 자리 찾기 문제라고 한다. 어형 문제는 빈칸이 [주어, 동사, 목적어, 보어, 수식어] 중에 어떤 자리인지를 파악해서 선택지 중 알맞은 품사나 형태를 고르는 문제이다. **101.** Billy's Auto Repair has ------- with 15 different parts suppliers. (A) contracting　　(B) contracts　　(C) contractor　　(D) contract 빈칸은 이 문장의 목적어 자리로 명사가 들어갈 자리인데 명사가 보기에 (B), (C), (D) 이렇게 세 개나 나와 있다. 이런 문제들은 자리만 찾는 것으로 끝나지 않고 한 단계 더 나아가 명사의 특성을 알고 있어야 풀 수 있는 문제이다. 한정사 없이 가산 단수 명사는 쓸 수 없으므로 복수명사 (B)가 답이 되는 문제이다.
어휘 문제	아래 문제처럼 같은 품사의 네 가지 다른 단어가 선택지로 나오는 문제를 어휘 문제라고 한다. 한 어휘 문제는 최소한 빈칸 주변을 해석해야만 풀 수 있고, 어려운 문제의 경우에는 가산/불가산 명사의 구분, 자/타동사의 구분과 같은 문법 사항까지 같이 포함되어 출제되기도 한다. **102.** I have enclosed a copy of my résumé for your ------- and look forward to hearing from you soon. (A) explanation　　(B) participation　　(C) reference　　(D) consideration 빈칸은 전치사 FOR의 목적어 자리에 어떤 명사 어휘를 넣으면 가장 자연스러운지를 고르는 문제인데 '당신의 고려를 위해 제 이력서를 첨부합니다' 정도는 해석해야만 정답 (D)를 고를 수 있는 문제로 어형 문제보다는 훨씬 난이도가 높다.
문법 문제	아래 문제처럼 종속접속사, 등위접속사, 전치사, 부사 등이 선택지에 같이 나오는 문제를 문법 문제라고 한다. 문법 문제는 그 문장의 구조를 파악하여 구와 절을 구분하고 절이라면 여러 가지 절 중 어떤 절인지를 파악해야 하는 어려운 문제들로 대부분 해석까지도 필요하다. **103.** We need more employees on the production line ------- production has increased by 60 percent. (A) although　　(B) since　　(C) because of　　(D) so 빈칸은 전치사 두 개의 절을 연결하는 종속 접속사자리이다. 전치사인 (C)와 등위접속사인 (D)는 답이 될 수 없고, 접속사 (A)와 (B) 중에서 '생산이 증가했기 때문에 추가직원을 고용해야 한다'는 의미에 맞는 (B)를 답으로 고르는 문제이다.

정답 101. (B)　102. (D)　103. (B)

파트 6 TEXT COMPLETION (장문 빈칸 채우기)

>> **문항 수** 4개 지문, 16문항 (131번 ~ 146번)

>> **지문 유형** 편지·이메일, 기사, 공지, 지시문, 광고, 회람, 설명서, 발표문, 정보문 등

>> **출제 포인트**
- 파트 5는 명확한 시제힌트가 나오는 반면 파트 6는 앞뒤 문맥을 통해 시제를 결정하는 문제의 출제 비중이 높다.
- 두 문장을 자연스럽게 이어주는 접속부사를 선택하는 문제가 많이 출제된다.
- 맥락상으로 파악해야 하는 대명사의 인칭 일치 문제, 수 일치 문제가 출제된다.
- 어휘는 그 문장만 보고는 문제를 풀 수 없고 앞뒤 문맥을 파악하여 고르는 문제가 출제된다.

>> **PART 6 문제 유형별 문제 풀이 접근법**

Questions 143-146 refer to the following article.

Jakarta, INDONESIA (5 June) - An Indonesian steelmaker, Irwan Steel Company, announced that it had named Maghfirah Baldraf its new Chief Operating Officer of the Java Division effective 1 September. His 30 years of experience in the **143.** ------- made him the obvious choice for the position. Baldraf majored in metal engineering at the National University of Indonesia. After graduation, he then **144.** ------- his career in the quality control department at Putirai Metal. 15 years ago, he joined Irwan Steel Company. **145.** -------. Baldraf will go to Java to oversee the daily operations of Irwan Steel Company **146.** ------- its inauguration on September 1.

1. 어휘 문제

143. (A) license   (B) industry   (C) outset   (D) program

이 문제에서는 '그 산업 분야에서의 30년 경력 때문에 그가 그 자리에 확실한 선택이었다'라는 의미를 파악해서 (B)를 골라야 한다. Part 6의 어휘 문제는 파트 5와는 달리 전체적인 맥락을 파악해야 하며, 특히 앞뒤 문장에서 힌트를 찾아야 한다.

2. 어형 문제

144. (A) started   (B) had started   (C) was starting   (D) will start

이 문제는 동사의 시제를 고르는 문제로 문맥상 이 사람이 처음으로 직장 생활을 시작한 것을 이야기하고 있으므로 과거 시제인 (A)가 답이 되며, then도 힌트가 될 수 있다. Part 5에서는 시제를 고를 수 있는 부사 또는 부사구의 힌트가 명확하게 주어지는 경우가 많지만 Part 6에서는 전체적인 맥락을 파악해서 풀어야 한다.

3. 문장 고르기 문제

145. (A) The company also has a division in Singapore.
(B) He has been interested in engineering since he was young.
(C) Most recently, he has served as Vice President of Development of Irwan Steel Company.
(D) As soon as Baldraf is appointed, the company will go through a major restructuring.

이 문제에서는 대학교 졸업 후부터 이 사람의 경력을 나열하고 있으므로 (C)가 답이 된다.

4. 문법 문제

143. (A) by the time   (B) as soon as   (C) when   (D) after

이 문제에서는 빈칸 뒤에 명사구가 있으므로 명사를 목적어로 취하는 전치사가 답이 되어야 하는데 보기 중에 전치사로 쓰일 수 있는 것이 (D)뿐이다.

정답 143. (B) 144. (A) 145. (C) 146. (D)

파트 7 TEXT COMPLETION (장문 빈칸 채우기)

▶▶ 문항 수 54문항 (147번 ~ 200번)
단일 지문: 10개 지문, 19문항
이중 지문: 2개 지문, 10문항
삼중 지문: 3개 지문, 15문항

▶▶ 지문 유형
편지, 이메일, 광고, 공지, 회람, 기사, 안내문, 웹 페이지(회사나 제품소개, 행사 소개, 고객 사용 후기), 청구서 또는 영수증, 문자, 온라인 채팅 대화문 등

▶▶ 문제 유형

- 주제·목적 문제   - 세부 사항 문제   - 암시·추론 문제   - 사실 확인 문제
- 동의어 문제   - 화자 의도 파악 문제   - 문장 삽입 문제

▶▶ PART 7 문제 유형별 문제 풀이 접근법

Questions 158-160 refer to the following Web page.

---
http://www.sdayrealestate.com/listing18293

Looking for a new home for your family? This house, located on 18293 Winding Grove, was remodeled last month. It features 2,500 square feet of floor space, with 5,000 square feet devoted to a gorgeous backyard. Also included is a 625 square feet garage that can comfortably fit two mid-sized vehicles —[1]—. Located just a five-minute drive from the Fairweather Metro Station, this property allows for easy access to the downtown area, while providing plenty of room for you and your family. —[2]—. A serene lake is just 100-feet walk away from the house. —[3]—. A 15 percent down payment is required to secure the property. —[4]—. For more detailed information or to arrange a showing, please email Jerry@sdayrealestate.com.

---

1. 세부 사항 문제

158. How large is the parking space?
(A) 100 square feet   (B) 625 square feet   (C) 2,500 square feet   (D) 5,000 square feet

주차장의 면적을 묻는 세부사항 문제이다. included is a 625 square feet garage라고 하였으므로 정답은 (B)이다. 지문의 garage가 문제*에서는 parking space로 패러프레이징된 점을 간파해야 한다.

2. 사실 확인 문제

159. What is NOT stated as an advantage of the property?
(A) It has a spacious design.   (B) It has been recently renovated.
(C) It is in a quiet neighborhood.   (D) It is near public transportation.

remodeled last month

3. 문장 삽입 문제

160. In which of the positions marked [1], [2], [3], and [4] does the following sentence best belong?
"A smaller amount may be accepted, depending on the buyer's financial situation."
(A) [1]   (B) [2]   (C) [3]   (D) [4]

정답 158. (B) 159. (C) 160. (D)

TEST 01

MP3 바로 듣기

1타 강사 강의듣기

준비물: OMR 카드, 연필, 지우개, 시계
시험시간: LC 약 45분 / RC 75분

나의 점수

	LC	RC
맞은 개수		
환산 점수		

총점: _____ 점

TEST 1	TEST 2	TEST 3	TEST 4	TEST 5
_____점	_____점	_____점	_____점	_____점

점수 환산표

LC		RC	
맞은 개수	환산 점수	맞은 개수	환산 점수
96-100	475-495	96-100	460-495
91-95	435-195	91-95	425-490
86-90	405-475	86-90	395-465
81-85	370-450	81-85	370-440
76-80	345-420	76-80	335-415
71-75	320-390	71-75	310-390
66-70	290-360	66-70	280-365
61-65	265-335	61-65	250-335
56-60	235-310	56-60	220-305
51-55	210-280	51-55	195-270
46-50	180-255	46-50	165-240
41-45	155-230	41-45	140-215
36-40	125-205	36-40	115-180
31-35	105-175	31-35	95-145
36-30	85-145	36-30	75-120
21-25	60-115	21-25	60-95
16-20	30-90	16-20	45-75
11-15	5-70	11-15	30-55
6-10	5-60	6-10	10-40
1-5	5-60	1-5	5-30
0	5-35	0	5-15

LISTENING TEST

In the Listening test, you will be asked to demonstrate how well you understand spoken English. The entire listening test will last approximately 45 minutes. There are four parts, and directions are given for each part. You must mark your answers on the separate answer sheet. Do not write your answers in your test book.

PART 1

Directions: For each question in this part, you will hear four statements about a picture in your test book. When you hear the statements, you must select the one statement that best describes what you see in the picture. Then find the number of the question on your answer sheet and mark your answer. The statements will not be printed in your test book and will be spoken only one time.

Statement (B), "A man is pointing at a document," is the best description of the picture, so you should select answer (B) and mark it on your answer sheet.

1.

2.

GO ON TO THE NEXT PAGE

3.

4.

5.

6.

GO ON TO THE NEXT PAGE

PART 2

Directions: You will hear a question or statement and three responses spoken in English. They will not be printed in your test book and will be spoken only one time. Select the best response to the question or statement and mark the letter (A), (B), or (C) on your answer sheet.

7. Mark your answer on your answer sheet.
8. Mark your answer on your answer sheet.
9. Mark your answer on your answer sheet.
10. Mark your answer on your answer sheet.
11. Mark your answer on your answer sheet.
12. Mark your answer on your answer sheet.
13. Mark your answer on your answer sheet.
14. Mark your answer on your answer sheet.
15. Mark your answer on your answer sheet.
16. Mark your answer on your answer sheet.
17. Mark your answer on your answer sheet.
18. Mark your answer on your answer sheet.
19. Mark your answer on your answer sheet.
20. Mark your answer on your answer sheet.
21. Mark your answer on your answer sheet.
22. Mark your answer on your answer sheet.
23. Mark your answer on your answer sheet.
24. Mark your answer on your answer sheet.
25. Mark your answer on your answer sheet.
26. Mark your answer on your answer sheet.
27. Mark your answer on your answer sheet.
28. Mark your answer on your answer sheet.
29. Mark your answer on your answer sheet.
30. Mark your answer on your answer sheet.
31. Mark your answer on your answer sheet.

PART 3

Directions: You will hear some conversations between two or more people. You will be asked to answer three questions about what the speakers say in each conversation. Select the best response to each question and mark the letter (A), (B), (C), or (D) on your answer sheet. The conversations will not be printed in your test book and will be spoken only one time.

32. What does the man need assistance with?

    (A) Exchanging a product
    (B) Unloading some packages
    (C) Renewing a store membership
    (D) Finding some merchandise

33. What is the cause of the problem?

    (A) A warehouse closed early.
    (B) A manager is not available.
    (C) A shipment was damaged.
    (D) A price tag was incorrect.

34. Where does the woman instruct the man to go?

    (A) To the cashier
    (B) To the help desk
    (C) To a different aisle
    (D) To a storage room

35. What event are the speakers planning?

    (A) A film festival
    (B) A birthday party
    (C) An awards ceremony
    (D) A holiday celebration

36. What does the man say he will do?

    (A) Prepare a snack
    (B) Arrange some transportation
    (C) Order a delivery
    (D) Revise a schedule

37. What does the woman offer to do?

    (A) Contact another department
    (B) Confirm a reservation
    (C) Ask for a discount
    (D) Purchase some supplies

38. What did the woman buy online?

    (A) A computer
    (B) A television
    (C) A camera
    (D) A phone

39. What error did the woman make?

    (A) She provided an incorrect phone number.
    (B) She did not submit the entire payment.
    (C) She chose the wrong size.
    (D) She forgot to apply a discount.

40. What does the man inform the woman about?

    (A) A promotional event
    (B) A product feature
    (C) A delivery service
    (D) An extra charge

41. Why is the woman at the theater?

    (A) To interview an actor
    (B) To celebrate an anniversary
    (C) To apply for a job
    (D) To perform an inspection

42. Why is the woman disappointed?

    (A) An entrance fee has increased.
    (B) She could not find parking.
    (C) A performance was canceled.
    (D) The lead actor has retired.

43. What does the man offer the woman?

    (A) Some headphones
    (B) A program guide
    (C) A business card
    (D) Reduced rates

GO ON TO THE NEXT PAGE

44. What are the speakers planning to do next month?

(A) Visit a client
(B) Start a new project
(C) Go on vacation
(D) Attend a conference

45. Why has Brad NOT booked accommodations yet?

(A) There are no affordable hotels available.
(B) A corporate credit card must be used.
(C) He would like to get some feedback.
(D) A promotion begins next week.

46. What does the woman offer to do?

(A) Call a vehicle rental agency
(B) Install an application
(C) Print a restaurant menu
(D) Order some tickets

47. Why did the man contact the woman?

(A) To confirm travel arrangements
(B) To postpone a consultation
(C) To change a meeting place
(D) To request an invoice

48. What does the woman ask about?

(A) Completing some paperwork
(B) Conducting an interview
(C) Extending a deadline
(D) Meeting another lawyer

49. Why does the woman say a location is convenient?

(A) It is situated in downtown.
(B) It is open late.
(C) It is close to a subway station.
(D) It is near her workplace.

50. What will the listeners learn about?

(A) Entering customer data
(B) Uploading expense reports
(C) Installing a program
(D) Repairing a device

51. What does the woman offer to do?

(A) Find a different seat
(B) Bring new equipment
(C) Provide her notes
(D) Give a presentation

52. What will the listeners probably do next?

(A) Complete a survey
(B) Test a product
(C) Download an update
(D) Review a file

53. Where most likely do the speakers work?

(A) At a hotel
(B) At a landscaping firm
(C) At a magazine
(D) At a construction company

54. Why does the man say, "She won it last year"?

(A) To express admiration
(B) To confirm a detail
(C) To refuse a recommendation
(D) To suggest a solution

55. What do the speakers decide to do?

(A) To cancel a meeting
(B) To ask for staff opinions
(C) To extend working hours
(D) To take a training course

56. What does the woman ask for?

(A) A parking permit
(B) A local guide
(C) A bus pass
(D) A product catalog

57. What does the man say about an art gallery?

(A) It changed owners.
(B) It has free admission.
(C) It features famous paintings.
(D) It was recently renovated.

58. What event will be held on Sunday?

(A) A concert
(B) A park opening
(C) A sports competition
(D) A parade

59. Where is the conversation taking place?

(A) At a bakery
(B) At a restaurant
(C) At a farm
(D) At a supermarket

60. What does the man imply when he says, "I came at the right time, then"?

(A) He was able to arrive at an event on time.
(B) He is eager to sample some items.
(C) He is available to help the woman.
(D) He was able to meet a project deadline.

61. What is the woman looking forward to?

(A) A revised packaging process
(B) The hiring of more employees
(C) A seasonal sales event
(D) The addition of a produce section

Gasoline Type	Price Per Gallon
Unleaded	$1.10
Super	$1.20
Supreme	$1.35
Diesel	$1.55

62. What does the man ask for?

(A) A password
(B) A receipt
(C) A guide
(D) A refund

63. Look at the graphic. Which type of gasoline did the man select?

(A) Unleaded
(B) Super
(C) Supreme
(D) Diesel

64. What will the man receive with his fuel purchase?

(A) A movie ticket
(B) A beverage
(C) A gift certificate
(D) A car accessory

Macmore's Flooring
Special Discount Event!
(Offer Valid Until June 30)

Ceramic Tile Installation: 40% off

Porcelain Tile Installation: 30% off

Stone Tile Installation: 20% off

Marble Tile Installation: 10% off

Mayertown Cooking Contest
May 25 Schedule

Time / Location	Cuisine
2:00 P.M. / Elk Arena	Chinese
3:00 P.M. / Elk Arena	Italian
4:00 P.M. / Remo Arena	Mexican
5:00 P.M. / Remo Arena	Greek

65. Why does the man want to install new floor tiles?

(A) To replace old flooring
(B) To match the living room wallpaper
(C) To accommodate more floor space
(D) To sell his home

66. Look at the graphic. How much will most likely be discounted from the man's order?

(A) 10%
(B) 20%
(C) 30%
(D) 40%

67. What does the woman emphasize about the floor tiles?

(A) They are lightweight.
(B) They are durable.
(C) They are eco-friendly.
(D) They are affordable.

68. What does the woman suggest doing?

(A) Exchanging seats
(B) Meeting early
(C) Sharing a ride
(D) Ordering a meal

69. Look at the graphic. What is the man's favorite kind of food?

(A) Chinese
(B) Italian
(C) Mexican
(D) Greek

70. What does the woman remind the man to do?

(A) Reserve a table
(B) Wear warm clothing
(C) Submit a form
(D) Bring an umbrella

PART 4

Directions: You will hear some talks given by a single speaker. You will be asked to answer three questions about what the speaker says in each talk. Select the best response to each question and mark the letter (A), (B), (C), or (D) on your answer sheet. The talks will not be printed in your test book and will be spoken only one time.

71. What service is being advertised?

(A) Event planning
(B) Interior designing
(C) Digital marketing
(D) Product packaging

72. What advantage does the advertisement mention?

(A) Express delivery
(B) Quality merchandise
(C) Affordable pricing
(D) Flexible hours

73. Why should the listeners check a Web site?

(A) To contact a representative
(B) To view previous projects
(C) To download a program
(D) To complete a registration form

---

74. Where does the listener most likely work?

(A) At a software development firm
(B) At a bookstore
(C) At a publishing company
(D) At a graphic design agency

75. What is the speaker's supervisor worried about?

(A) A publication deadline
(B) A shipment date
(C) A local law
(D) A price estimate

76. What does the speaker imply when he says, "Ms. Yoon needs to review it by the end of the day"?

(A) A document contains some errors.
(B) His manager is going on vacation.
(C) He is unable to complete a task alone.
(D) A request should be handled quickly.

77. What type of business did the woman most likely call?

(A) A furniture store
(B) A café
(C) A painting company
(D) A library

78. Why did the woman call?

(A) To inquire about a missing item
(B) To look into operating hours
(C) To request a discount
(D) To reschedule an appointment

79. What does the woman say she will do tonight?

(A) Pick up a client
(B) Call another location
(C) Work extra hours
(D) Check out a business

---

80. Who is Mr. Barnes?

(A) A school teacher
(B) A journalist
(C) A government worker
(D) An artist

81. What will happen in the summer?

(A) A museum will be renovated.
(B) An internship program will be held.
(C) Local officials will be elected.
(D) Award winners will be announced.

82. According to the speaker, what will be distributed in August?

(A) Some survey forms
(B) Some parking passes
(C) Some concert tickets
(D) Some cash payments

GO ON TO THE NEXT PAGE

83. What is the subject of the convention?

    (A) Hiring qualified employees
    (B) Developing better products
    (C) Reducing operating expenses
    (D) Building brand awareness

84. What does the speaker imply when he says, "we invite experts from across the world"?

    (A) The listeners will learn from a variety of speakers.
    (B) The listeners will have to pay a bigger fee this year.
    (C) He thinks convention tickets will sell out fast.
    (D) He believes more translators are needed for an event.

85. How can the listeners receive a discount?

    (A) By recommending a presenter
    (B) By organizing a group package
    (C) By contacting a coordinator
    (D) By registering early

---

86. What is the purpose of the meeting?

    (A) To review some job candidates
    (B) To organize an event
    (C) To develop an evaluation form
    (D) To introduce some employees

87. According to the speaker, what is an objective this year?

    (A) To expand a business
    (B) To improve productivity
    (C) To combine teams
    (D) To lower operating costs

88. What does the speaker instruct the listeners to do?

    (A) Move to another room
    (B) Turn on some laptops
    (C) Hold group discussions
    (D) Sign some paperwork

89. What is the message mainly about?

    (A) Springtime programs
    (B) Roadside construction
    (C) A sports competition
    (D) A location change

90. According to the speaker, what can be accessed on a Web site?

    (A) Directions
    (B) Photographs
    (C) A registration form
    (D) An events calendar

91. How can listeners borrow some sports equipment?

    (A) By submitting an ID card
    (B) By completing an application
    (C) By paying a fee
    (D) By reserving it online

---

92. What is the speaker's company planning to do this fall?

    (A) Attend an exposition
    (B) Conduct a seminar
    (C) Hire some interns
    (D) Launch a Web site

93. What does the speaker mean when he says, "it's completely different from what I've seen in the past"?

    (A) He is upset with an outcome.
    (B) He is satisfied with some designs.
    (C) He needs help moving some tools and supplies.
    (D) He is unsure about following a suggestion.

94. What does the speaker request?

    (A) A cost estimate
    (B) A phone number
    (C) A size measurement
    (D) A sample catalog

COURSE MAP

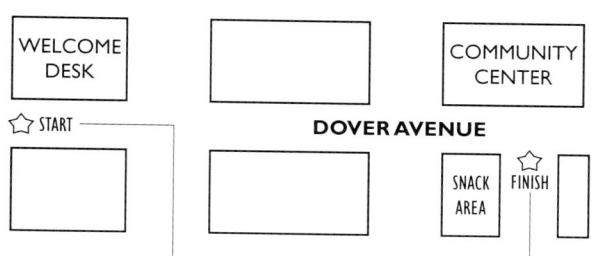

95. What event are the listeners probably attending?

    (A) A guided tour
    (B) A clean-up initiative
    (C) An athletic contest
    (D) A street parade

96. According to the speaker, what should the listeners pick up?

    (A) A permit
    (B) A drink
    (C) A towel
    (D) A hat

97. Look at the graphic. Where will the listeners take a group photo?

    (A) At the welcome desk
    (B) At the starting line
    (C) At the snack area
    (D) At the community center

Five-Alarm Chili Recipe

2 onions
5 red peppers
6 tomatoes
7 cloves of garlic
1 cup of shredded cheese
1 can of beans
500g beef

98. What event did the speaker attend last Monday?

    (A) A culinary competition
    (B) A corporate anniversary party
    (C) A new employee luncheon
    (D) A store opening

99. Look at the graphic. Which amount does the speaker suggest changing?

    (A) 2
    (B) 5
    (C) 6
    (D) 7

100. Where did the speaker get the recipe from?

    (A) An article
    (B) A friend
    (C) A TV show
    (D) A cookbook

GO ON TO THE NEXT PAGE →

READING TEST

In the Reading test, you will read a variety of texts and answer several different types of reading comprehension questions. The entire Reading test will last 75 minutes. There are three parts, and directions are given for each part. You are encouraged to answer as many questions as possible within the time allowed.

You must mark your answers on the separate answer sheet. Do not write your answers in your test book.

PART 5

Directions: A word or phrase is missing in each of the sentences below. Four answer choices are given below each sentence. Select the best answer to complete the sentence. Then mark the letter (A), (B), (C), or (D) on your answer sheet.

101. After Ms. Park's film, viewers are encouraged to stay for a short -------.

(A) participation
(B) discussion
(C) attendance
(D) concurrence

102. Ms. Guelph ------- the seminar with the results of the latest marketing survey.

(A) concluding
(B) will conclude
(C) was concluded
(D) conclude

103. Takagawa Co. renovated the building by constructing a ------- outside dining area.

(A) beautifully
(B) beautiful
(C) beautify
(D) beauty

104. ------- 5,000 people visited Kowloon Finance's Web site yesterday.

(A) Over
(B) Well
(C) Any
(D) Other

105. The broadly advertised technology convention at the National Exhibition Center is ------- a large audience.

(A) calling
(B) suggesting
(C) happening
(D) attracting

106. Dr. Muniz is ------- to see the patient on Thursday at 5:15 P.M.

(A) comfortable
(B) probable
(C) available
(D) possible

107. According to GHM Corp.'s regulations, all staff must ------- request reimbursement within two months of a business trip.

(A) formalize
(B) formally
(C) formality
(D) formal

108. ------- this morning's team meeting, Mr. Insel acknowledged the need for further research regarding international business practices.

(A) Upon
(B) Across
(C) With
(D) During

109. In order to make its servers instantly -------, the restaurant chain hired a well-known fashion designer to create stylish uniforms for its employees.

(A) identify
(B) identifying
(C) identifiable
(D) identification

110. The owner of the Mountaindell Bed and Breakfast ------- responds to all reviews that visitors post on the Internet.

(A) slightly
(B) personally
(C) approximately
(D) recklessly

111. Eighty percent of doctors ------- that General Department's antibacterial hand wash is better than the competitors'.

(A) favor
(B) assure
(C) confess
(D) agree

112. ------- the annual inspection has been completed, the warehouse crew can begin installing the additional shelving units.

(A) With that
(B) In order that
(C) In that
(D) Now that

113. Mr. Griffon examined the applications for ------- who could handle the redesign project with a limited budget.

(A) him
(B) ours
(C) himself
(D) anyone

114. The laboratory manager is required to ensure proper ------- of all chemicals.

(A) store
(B) storable
(C) stores
(D) storage

115. Seeing that your rent is now two weeks -------, you must pay an additional late fee as stated in the contract.

(A) valuable
(B) remaining
(C) overdue
(D) owed

116. Ms. Pangchorn will answer her e-mails when she ------- from her trip on Wednesday.

(A) return
(B) returning
(C) returns
(D) had returned

117. The Sultan Financial Group's Web site will be inaccessible ------- the hours of 2 A.M. and 4 A.M.

(A) in
(B) since
(C) among
(D) between

118. Ms. O'Driscoll has a speaking ------- on Friday, October 13.

(A) recruitment
(B) term
(C) topic
(D) engagement

119. The appliances included in the sale were assembled at different factories, so they arrived -------.

(A) separately
(B) separates
(C) separating
(D) separate

120. All customer -------, no matter how minor, should always be answered promptly and politely.

(A) inquiries
(B) inquiring
(C) inquiry
(D) inquired

GO ON TO THE NEXT PAGE

121. The company's sanitation standards for their production line extend ------- those of most other companies'.

(A) far
(B) even
(C) more
(D) beyond

122. The legal guarantee period for the BMV convertible is five years ------- 300 thousand kilometers, whichever takes place first.

(A) plus
(B) or
(C) but
(D) to

123. Due to a lack of time, the company's programmers have not updated the mobile application -------.

(A) continually
(B) shortly
(C) firmly
(D) recently

124. Many manufacturers are producing more energy-efficient air conditioners ------- stricter government regulations.

(A) prior to
(B) inasmuch as
(C) as a result of
(D) further from

125. Randit Corporation's history of 30 years of ------- service is unique in the industry.

(A) reliable
(B) relied
(C) relying
(D) rely

126. Budget changes impacting employee incentives ------- to the CEO right away.

(A) should be submitted
(B) will be submitting
(C) may have submitted
(D) has been submitted

127. The city of Morrison is inviting public ------- on its plan to put up a new commemorative plaque celebrating the city's centennial.

(A) arrangement
(B) interest
(C) comment
(D) order

128. Mr. Ponchartrain, ------- is away on business, left Ms. Hyun in charge of the Carter account.

(A) which
(B) whose
(C) that
(D) who

129. For safety reasons, visitors to the Militech plant must be ------- while on site.

(A) consulted
(B) escorted
(C) presented
(D) supported

130. Duchene Investment Firm provides free consultations to help ------- business owners apply for loans.

(A) inexperienced
(B) indisputable
(C) unwilling
(D) unfamiliar

PART 6

Directions: Read the texts that follow. A word, phrase, or sentence is missing in parts of each text. Four answer choices for each question are given below the text. Select the best answer to complete the text. Then mark the letter (A), (B), (C), or (D) on your answer sheet.

Questions 131-134 refer to the following advertisement.

Are you looking for the latest fashions?

Do you care about the environmental impact of your choices?

If so, you need to visit Eka's Boutique. -------. This includes recycled cotton, wool, and
                                          131.
three types of silk. We guarantee you'll like what you see!

We at Eka's Boutique always care ------- our products' sources. This is ------- we only
                                 132.   **133.**
offer clothing made in verified manufacturing facilities. To learn more and view our -------
                                                                                    134.
catalogue, please go to our Web site, www.ekasboutique.co.uk.

131. (A) Our boutique recently signed a contract with the local textile factory.
(B) We have dresses, jackets, and other fashionable items made from sustainable fabrics.
(C) Our boutique is conveniently located in Fashion Valley.
(D) We are open from 10:00 A.M. to 8:00 P.M., seven days a week.

132. (A) to
(B) on
(C) along
(D) about

133. (A) why
(B) where
(C) how
(D) when

134. (A) completed
(B) complete
(C) completely
(D) completeness

Questions 135-138 refer to the following article.

Safeguards and Precautions

The National Sculpture Gallery (NSG) makes every effort to protect the priceless works on display by carefully -------- the environment of the exhibits. Works made of wood are
           135.
vulnerable to hot and dry conditions. --------, the gallery does not keep any pieces in
                                       136.
rooms with sunlight or other potentially damaging lighting. Nor does it display pieces outside during the summer months due to the -------- caused by the rainy season. --------.
                                                                               137.   **138.**
By making this effort to guard our priceless collection, we hope to preserve the history and genius of our nation far into the future.

135. (A) conducting
(B) securing
(C) promoting
(D) monitoring

136. (A) Accordingly
(B) Previously
(C) Surprisingly
(D) Finally

137. (A) humidity
(B) humidify
(C) humid
(D) humidly

138. (A) Additionally, please refrain from touching any of the pieces on display.
(B) These will be exhibited again once they are returned to the gallery this fall.
(C) Sadly, some sculptures have been removed for emergency repairs.
(D) Some of the artworks are over 300 years old.

Questions 139-142 refer to the following notice.

Notice to all Auto-Smart Customers:

When you have car windows replaced, you will notice an extra fee of $10 per window (or windshield) replaced. This fee is to cover the cost of auto glass disposal. ------- you indicate otherwise, we will go ahead and take care of the windows for you.
139.

The combination of glass and plastic in car windows is tricky to work with, and improper disposal causes significant environmental damage. The good news is that these materials are perfect for carpet backing and insulation, as long as the windows are correctly -------. Just $10 covers this important process.
140.

This payment is -------. You are free to take the old windows with you and handle everything yourself, in which case, we will not charge you. -------.
141. **142.**

139. (A) Because
(B) While
(C) Unless
(D) Although

140. (A) recycles
(B) recycled
(C) recycling
(D) recyclable

141. (A) frequent
(B) expensive
(C) final
(D) voluntary

142. (A) We are confident that you will be very pleased with your new windows.
(B) Just remember to deal with the process in an eco-friendly way.
(C) If you notice cracks or other damages, you should contact customer service immediately.
(D) Yearly inspections are not required, but they are highly recommended.

Questions 143-146 refer to the following letter.

January 5

Dana Wilkinson
12654 Salmon River Road
San Diego, CA 92129

Dear Ms. Wilkinson,

This letter is to remind you that your membership at the Golf and Tennis Club (GTC) expired last month. If you do not plan to continue your membership, please let ------- know so that we may update our records. However, if you would like to extend, I should mention that we are currently offering a 30 percent discount on membership renewals. This means that for just $2,000, you would have one more year of full membership including ------- of GTC's swimming pool. -------. To renew your membership, ------- submit the application form enclosed here.

We look forward to keeping you as a valued member here at GTC.

Sincerely,

Kelso Montburg
Director of Membership Services

ENCLOSURE

---

143. (A) her
(B) him
(C) them
(D) us

144. (A) use
(B) uses
(C) used
(D) using

145. (A) Please reply by January 10 to take advantage of this deal.
(B) You can ignore this letter if you have already paid your bill.
(C) We offer personal instruction sessions twice a week.
(D) A confirmation e-mail regarding your membership cancellation will be sent to you shortly.

146. (A) extremely
(B) simply
(C) clearly
(D) apparently

PART 7

Directions: In this part you will read a selection of texts, such as magazine and newspaper articles, e-mails, and instant messages. Each text or set of texts is followed by several questions. Select the best answer for each question and mark the letter (A), (B), (C), or (D) on your answer sheet.

Questions 147-148 refer to the following invitation.

We are honored to invite you to this year's
David Conrad Memorial Marketing Seminar

Hosted by
James Nakamoto
Business Advisor at the Toronto Small Business Center (TSBC)
and owner of Alpine Grill

Subject: Digital Marketing
Time: June 28, 1:00 – 3:00 P.M.
Place: The Grand Hotel Conference Room

This seminar is available to all entrepreneurs in the Toronto area. All attendees must present a copy of their business registration certificate when signing up. Please call the TSBC for more information.

---

147. For whom is the invitation most likely intended?

(A) Marketing specialists
(B) Business owners
(C) Financial advisors
(D) Hotel managers

148. What are interested individuals asked to do?

(A) Provide a certificate
(B) Arrange a seminar room
(C) Call Mr. Nakamoto's restaurant
(D) Look over an event schedule

GO ON TO THE NEXT PAGE

Questions 149-150 refer to the following form.

RK Co.

Client: Top Ten Electronics
Address: 446 Cleveland Rd.
Attn: Angela Martin

Thank you again for your business. You'll find the bill for your October 30th service below. If you have any issues, don't hesitate to call Gerry Martin at (555) 212-9891.

Service/Product	Amount	Price Per Unit	Price
Fittings	x20 Faucets (Brass)	$20	$400
Pipe Installation	x10 Type L Piping (Copper)	$25	$250
Fixture Replacement	x4 Sinks (Porcelain)	$40	$160
Labor	35 hours	$25/hr	$875
			Total $1,685

149. What most likely is RK Co.?

(A) An electrical company
(B) A plumbing business
(C) A hardware store
(D) A metal manufacturer

150. What information was NOT included?

(A) The contact representative of RK Co.
(B) The number of workers involved
(C) The kind of pipes that were purchased
(D) The length of a project

Questions 151-152 refer to the following e-mail.

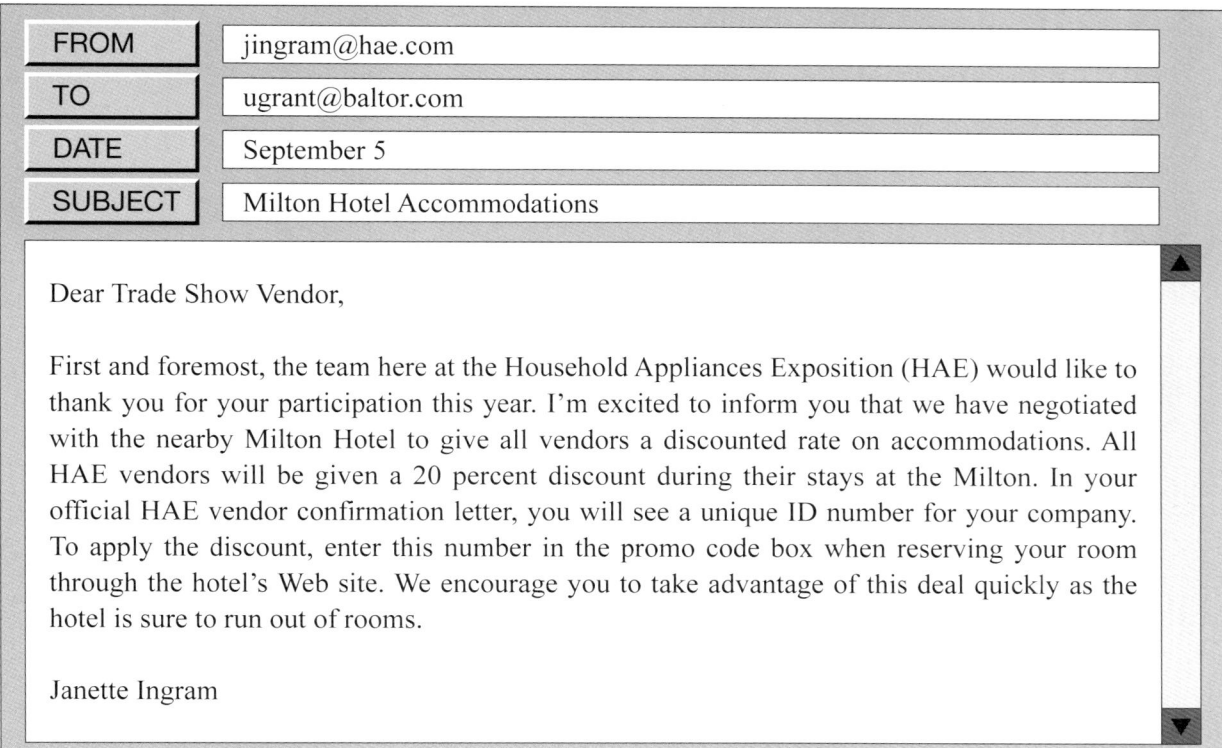

FROM	jingram@hae.com
TO	ugrant@baltor.com
DATE	September 5
SUBJECT	Milton Hotel Accommodations

Dear Trade Show Vendor,

First and foremost, the team here at the Household Appliances Exposition (HAE) would like to thank you for your participation this year. I'm excited to inform you that we have negotiated with the nearby Milton Hotel to give all vendors a discounted rate on accommodations. All HAE vendors will be given a 20 percent discount during their stays at the Milton. In your official HAE vendor confirmation letter, you will see a unique ID number for your company. To apply the discount, enter this number in the promo code box when reserving your room through the hotel's Web site. We encourage you to take advantage of this deal quickly as the hotel is sure to run out of rooms.

Janette Ingram

151. Who most likely is Janette Ingram?

(A) A hotel manager
(B) A travel agent
(C) An event coordinator
(D) A business owner

152. How can an ID number be used?

(A) To enter a facility
(B) To receive a price reduction
(C) To purchase an appliance
(D) To access a membership account

Questions 153-154 refer to the following text message chain.

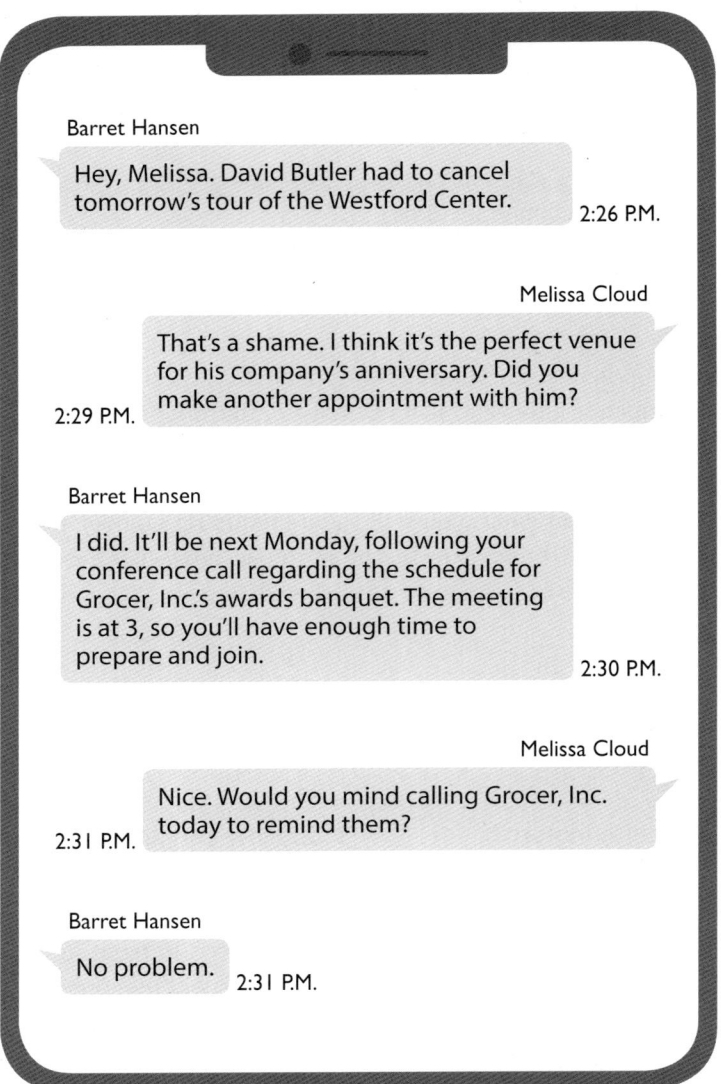

153. What most likely is Ms. Cloud's profession?

(A) Maintenance worker
(B) Restaurant manager
(C) Event planner
(D) Personnel director

154. At 2:31 P.M., what does Ms. Cloud most likely mean when she writes, "Nice"?

(A) She is eager to visit a facility.
(B) She is excited to call Mr. Butler.
(C) She is pleased with the progress of a project.
(D) She is satisfied with Mr. Hansen's work.

Questions 155-157 refer to the following announcement.

SAVE THE REEF

The Australian Department of the Environment and Energy (ADEE) is holding a global fundraiser to save the Great Barrier Reef. —[1]—. A goal of $10 million (AUD) by the end of the month has been set, and friends from all over the world are encouraged to contribute to help preserve one of the great natural wonders of the world. —[2]—. Money raised will be applied towards research on how to better protect the Reef from threats such as rising sea temperatures and the increased frequency of severe weather events. —[3]—.

To learn more about what you can do to save the Reef, visit www.environment.gov.au/savethereef. —[4]—.

Show your support today!

---

155. Why was the announcement written?

(A) To explain a new energy plan
(B) To advertise a monthly deal
(C) To request a donation
(D) To report on a new research finding

156. What is implied about the Great Barrier Reef?

(A) It is home to various sea creatures.
(B) It is being affected by climate change.
(C) It is Australia's biggest tourist attraction.
(D) It is closed to the public.

157. In which of the positions marked [1], [2], [3], and [4] does the following sentence best belong?

"In addition, some of it will be used to help improve the water quality in the surrounding area."

(A) [1]
(B) [2]
(C) [3]
(D) [4]

Questions 158-160 refer to the following memo.

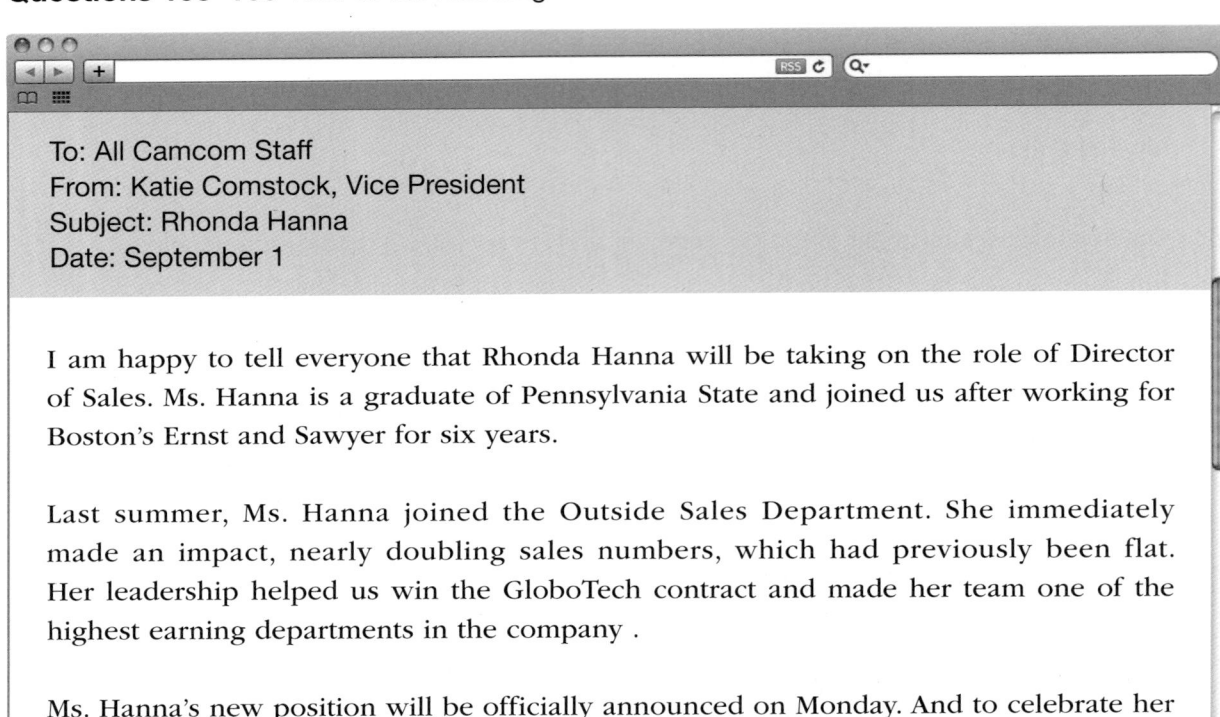

To: All Camcom Staff
From: Katie Comstock, Vice President
Subject: Rhonda Hanna
Date: September 1

I am happy to tell everyone that Rhonda Hanna will be taking on the role of Director of Sales. Ms. Hanna is a graduate of Pennsylvania State and joined us after working for Boston's Ernst and Sawyer for six years.

Last summer, Ms. Hanna joined the Outside Sales Department. She immediately made an impact, nearly doubling sales numbers, which had previously been flat. Her leadership helped us win the GloboTech contract and made her team one of the highest earning departments in the company .

Ms. Hanna's new position will be officially announced on Monday. And to celebrate her promotion, I've booked the private banquet room at Dorsia this Thursday. I've heard from many of you about their famous lobster stew, so I can't wait to try it. Seating is limited, so make sure to email Terry Wright by this afternoon if you plan on coming.

158. Why was the memo posted?

(A) To announce the signing of a contract
(B) To advertise a job opening
(C) To introduce a new coworker
(D) To publicize a staff member's promotion

159. What is mentioned about the Outside Sales Department?

(A) It has given its members a pay raise.
(B) Its employees will regularly attend training sessions.
(C) Its revenue has increased significantly.
(D) It will relocate to the Boston branch.

160. What is implied about Dorsia?

(A) It is popular with Camcom personnel.
(B) It has very limited hours.
(C) It does not have private seating.
(D) It serves only seafood.

Questions 161-164 refer to the following e-mail.

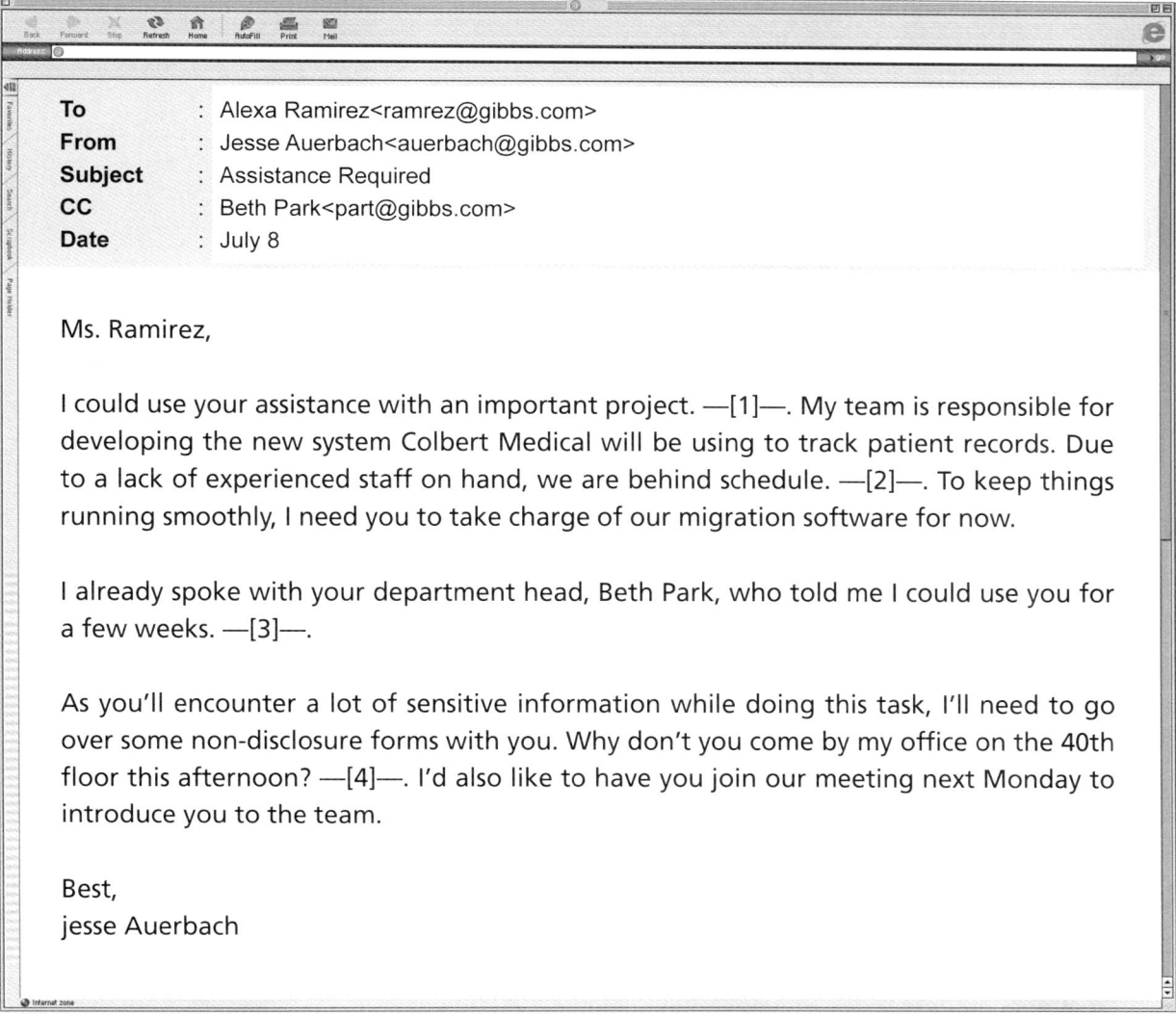

To: Alexa Ramirez<ramrez@gibbs.com>
From: Jesse Auerbach<auerbach@gibbs.com>
Subject: Assistance Required
CC: Beth Park<part@gibbs.com>
Date: July 8

Ms. Ramirez,

I could use your assistance with an important project. —[1]—. My team is responsible for developing the new system Colbert Medical will be using to track patient records. Due to a lack of experienced staff on hand, we are behind schedule. —[2]—. To keep things running smoothly, I need you to take charge of our migration software for now.

I already spoke with your department head, Beth Park, who told me I could use you for a few weeks. —[3]—.

As you'll encounter a lot of sensitive information while doing this task, I'll need to go over some non-disclosure forms with you. Why don't you come by my office on the 40th floor this afternoon? —[4]—. I'd also like to have you join our meeting next Monday to introduce you to the team.

Best,
jesse Auerbach

161. What most likely is Ms. Ramirez's profession?

(A) Construction manager
(B) Medical doctor
(C) Job recruiter
(D) Computer programmer

162. What has Mr. Auerbach asked for?

(A) Additional funds for a project
(B) A collection of patient records
(C) The temporary help of an employee
(D) The floor plan of a vacant office

163. Why does Mr. Auerbach want to meet with Ms. Ramirez?

(A) To provide some training
(B) To discuss some forms
(C) To introduce a new product
(D) To hold an evaluation

164. In which of the positions marked [1], [2], [3], and [4] does the following sentence best belong?

"She said her department would be fine without you this month."

(A) [1]
(B) [2]
(C) [3]
(D) [4]

Questions 165-168 refer to the following online chat discussion.

Mayumi Ohta [10:15 A.M.]
Mr. Young and Ms. Olson, I have a quick update. Two more companies have signed up to participate in the RFT Technology Convention. We should have enough vendors now.

Eric Young [10:16 A.M.]
That's good news. Which companies?

Mayumi Ohta [10:18 A.M.]
Natural Power will be demonstrating the efficiency of their latest solar panels, and Aperture, Inc. will introduce their newest line of cameras for beginners.

Ingrid Olson [10:19 A.M.]
That sounds promising. I've actually been meaning to get into photography.

Mayumi Ohta [10:21 A.M.]
Same here. So, Natural Power has confirmed for June 5, while Aperture, Inc. will contact me soon with their preferred date. I'm on my way to the store to pick up some supplies, but I should return by noon. I'll let you know if I hear from them.

Ingrid Olson [10:23 A.M.]
Alright. Once we get confirmation, I'll email the complete convention schedule to everyone on our mailing list.

Mayumi Ohta [10:24 A.M.]
Remember to include directions to the venue.

Ingrid Olson [10:25 A.M.]
I will. Thanks for the reminder!

Eric Young [10:26 A.M.]
Actually, Ms. Olson, hang on a moment before you email that out. More people have signed up for our newsletter, and I need to include their addresses to the list.

Ingrid Olson [10:27 A.M.]
Not a problem!

Mayumi Ohta [10:29 A.M.]
I'm going to be driving for a bit. Talk to you guys soon.

165. Why did Ms. Ohta contact her colleagues?

(A) To notify them of some recent registrations
(B) To explain the arrangement of some display booths
(C) To update them on an upcoming purchase
(D) To inquire about the location of a venue

166. At 10:19 A.M., what does Ms. Olson most likely mean when she writes, "That sounds promising"?

(A) She believes that many people want solar panels.
(B) She is excited to meet a famous photographer.
(C) She has recently purchased a new camera.
(D) She is looking forward to a presentation.

167. Where will Ms. Ohta most likely be in the afternoon?

(A) At a clinic
(B) At a convention center
(C) At a camera shop
(D) At her office

168. What does Mr. Young instruct Ms. Olson to do?

(A) Delay the sending of an e-mail
(B) Book a conference room
(C) Include some addresses to a list
(D) Contact a local supplier

Questions 169-171 refer to the following instructions.

Sparkle Again

First, make sure to absorb and wipe away excess residue from the spill with a paper towel. Then, apply a small amount of the solution to the fabric. Gently rub the Sparkle Again solution in a circular motion. The stain will begin to lighten and disappear. Reapply if the stain is still visible.

Sparkle Again uses all-natural ingredients to keep your clothes from discoloring. For best results, apply it immediately after a spill. It is highly recommended that you only apply Sparkle Again to non-delicate fabrics, as it may ruin clothes made from other materials.

To get more information and for videos on how to use Sparkle Again, visit our Web site at www.sparkleagain.com/howto. If you'd like to talk to one of our friendly customer support agents directly, please call +(41) 555-8274 or email us at cs@sparkleagain.com.

169. What is the purpose of Sparkle Again?

(A) To polish surfaces
(B) To lighten colors
(C) To eliminate stains
(D) To prevent odors

170. According to the instructions, what is important to do when using the product?

(A) Avoid using it on delicate fabrics
(B) Avoid applying it multiple times
(C) Allow it to dry once on the clothing
(D) Allow it to absorb all of the liquid

171. What is indicated about Sparkle Again?

(A) The product contains synthetic ingredients.
(B) The company provides tutorials on its Web site.
(C) The product can be purchased online or in stores.
(D) The company will reimburse customers for damaged clothing.

Questions 172-175 refer to the following Web page.

Italia Soleggiata

509 E Main
Libertyville, IL 60049
219-999-2218
Hours: 12:00 P.M. to 11:00 P.M. Daily (excluding specific holidays)

86% Recommended

To reserve a table, visit the restaurant's Web site (www.italiasoleggiata/reservations). For special events or arrangements, call during regular business hours. For big parties (up to 30 guests), you can reserve the East Dining Room, but you must pay a security deposit.

| **Reviews** | Menu | Show on map |

Barry Evans *would recommend*
I'd heard a lot about this place, and it really lived up to expectations. Aside from the long wait for the table, I had a lovely dining experience. I wasn't sure what to order, but our waiter was very thoughtful and made helpful recommendations. The Greek salad was superb, and we even got a complimentary plate of olives with our meal. What a welcoming place!

Kim Gordon *would recommend*
The food was delicious, and there were a surprisingly large number of vegetarian options. They really should update the decorations, though. They're quite old-fashioned.

Sheila Rajneesh Jr. *wouldn't recommend*
Great quality food but not as special as everyone says. The location is far from downtown, and most of the menu items are unoriginal. Not worth the long trip, and certainly not worth the price.

Dave Lynch *would strongly recommend*
A top-notch place. It's not cheap, but it was a perfect location for my birthday party. Everyone was impressed with how beautiful the East Dining Room was. Whatever you order, you won't regret it. The entire menu is fantastic.

Paul Mulhouse *would recommend*
Terrific meal. The restaurant provided food to our office Christmas event. And while they were here, the staff really took care of us, serving our whole group quickly and feeding us some of the best Italian cuisine in the area.

172. What did Barry Evans like the most about Italia Soleggiata?

(A) The restaurant's interior
(B) The variety of vegetarian options
(C) The good customer service
(D) The discount coupons

173. What is most likely true about the reservation made by Dave Lynch?

(A) It required a security deposit.
(B) It was made on a Web site.
(C) It was made after 11 P.M.
(D) It qualified for a discount.

174. What is indicated about Italia Soleggiata?

(A) It offers a catering service.
(B) It will open a downtown location.
(C) It operates every day of the year.
(D) It serves Italian food exclusively.

175. On what aspect of the restaurant do all the reviewers agree?

(A) The taste of the dishes
(B) The quality of the decorations
(C) The spacious parking lot
(D) The affordable menu items

Questions 176-180 refer to the following Web page and e-mail.

www.alphalumenstar.co.uk/review/LU-X/ad52d

Huntsdale Botanical Garden Guide

Thanks for visiting! Just a short walk from Grand Central Station and our city's most popular hotels and restaurants, the Huntsdale Botanical Garden offers guests a great way to relax and explore the beauty of nature without having to leave the city. Tours are also available for those who would like to get the most from their visit. There's plenty of on-site parking for both cars and bicycles. And why not stay for lunch at our own Garden Buffet salad bar?

Prices:

Admission Level	Price	Access
General	$5	Main Garden and Greenhouse
Deluxe	$10	General Admission + Japanese Garden Tour
Executive	$15	Deluxe Admission + Organic Farm Tour
VIP	$25	Executive Admission + Wildlife Show

Wildlife Shows:
Meet a Cheetah: Big Cats in the Big City (January–March)
Coyote Beautiful: Coyotes, Foxes, and Wolves (April–June)
The Great Escape: Gorillas, Chimpanzees, and the Orlando Orangutan (July–September)
The Park After Dark: Nocturnal Animals of the Desert (October–December)

To: HPers@huntsdalegarden.org
From: Damian@indioschools.edu
Date: November 6
Subject: Planned visit

Dear Mr. Pers,

I am Leticia Damian, organizer of the Indio Middle School Nature Club (IMSNC). As you might guess from the name, our club seeks to increase young students' awareness of the natural world and ecological issues that face it.

We plan to visit your botanical garden on November 22. At this time, we know that at least 20 members plan to attend, and those individuals have expressed interest in touring the Japanese Garden and the on-site Organic Farm.

I wanted to confirm that we would have access to these areas as part of the tour we arrange. We also hope to see the current wildlife show, if one is scheduled. Please advise which type of ticket we should purchase to ensure that these conditions are met.

Best Regards,

Leticia Damian
Faculty Mentor, IMSNC

176. What is implied about the Huntsdale Botanical Garden?

(A) It has recently opened a restaurant.
(B) It offers discounts for large groups.
(C) It is in a convenient location.
(D) It allows bicycle tours.

177. What is the purpose of the e-mail?

(A) To inquire about tour options
(B) To announce the founding of a club
(C) To reschedule a visit
(D) To explain Ms. Damian's role as a faculty mentor

178. According to Ms. Damian, what is IMSNC?

(A) An entertainment program
(B) A government department
(C) A student exchange agency
(D) An environmental education group

179. Which type of admission will IMSNC most likely choose?

(A) General
(B) Deluxe
(C) Executive
(D) VIP

180. Which show will the IMSNC members most likely see?

(A) Meet a Cheetah
(B) Coyote Beautiful
(C) The Great Escape
(D) The Park After Dark

Questions 181-185 refer to the following press release and e-mail.

Press Release
Contact: media@ropavieja.com

Phoenix, March 15 – Ropavieja Retailers announced that next week, they will launch a spring recruitment drive in hopes of placing 700 new employees in its 80 branches by June 1. Ropavieja is looking to add salespeople and cashiers in all of its locations. The retail chain is known for its excellent compensation, as well as benefits such as tuition assistance and daycare.

Ropavieja branches in select cities will also hold information sessions, led by regional managers, on every Wednesday evening of April. Those who attend will have a chance to ask questions about the company and discuss career opportunities in individual interviews. To reserve a spot for a session, send an e-mail to recruit@ropavieja.com by March 22. Visit www.ropavieja.com for a complete list of job openings.

Ropavieja started out as a small shop in downtown Tucson 20 years ago. These days, it has branches all over North America, and is set to open one more in El Centro, California, in the coming weeks.

To	Steve Henry <shenry@bkmail.com>
From	Brad Narukawa <narukawa@ropavieja.com>
Subject	Details
Date	April 10

Dear Mr. Henry,

It was nice meeting you last Wednesday night. Based on our meeting, I would like to meet again to discuss a possible opportunity to work as a sales manager for us in Southern California. Letty Cantu, our Director of Sales, will also be at the interview.

Are you free on April 12 in the afternoon? Please give me a call at (505) 555-1212 to confirm.

Best Regards,

Brad Narukawa

181. According to the press release, what will Ropavieja Retailers begin soon?

(A) A new product promotion
(B) A major hiring campaign
(C) A company merger
(D) An executive board election

182. What is implied about Ropavieja Retailers?

(A) Its president will be resigning.
(B) Its budget will be decreased.
(C) Its first store is in California.
(D) Its business is growing.

183. What should people interested in a Wednesday evening event do?

(A) Make a reservation
(B) Download some forms
(C) Visit a company's head office
(D) Research information about tuition

184. What is the purpose of the e-mail?

(A) To promote a new service
(B) To discuss a project timeline
(C) To announce an upcoming sale
(D) To arrange an appointment

185. What is suggested about Brad Narukawa?

(A) He was born in El Centro.
(B) He was recently hired at Ropavieja Retailers.
(C) He is a regional manager.
(D) He is relocating to a new branch.

Questions 186-190 refer to the following notice, article, and e-mail.

Attention Bradbury Art Museum Patrons:

From time to time, during Pioneer City's upcoming renovations on 41st Street, the museum's entrance will be blocked. Unfortunately, this means that the museum will sometimes have to close. Please visit the museum's Web site for the most up-to-date information regarding this schedule.

Please remember that there are other museums downtown, such as the Museum of Modern History or the Stamp Museum. The renovations are expected to be completed by July 31. We're sorry for the disruptions this will cause.

Pioneer City Observer

(September 2)—After nearly two months of renovations that carried over until late August, work on 41st Street has finally finished. Bradbury Art Museum can finally breathe easy, as it saw its visitor numbers significantly drop during this period. In addition to resuming its normal schedule, the museum will soon unveil a new addition. Thanks to funding from the City Council, the museum was finally able to finish its own construction project of a scenic courtyard that has a stage reserved for live concerts and shows.

To celebrate, Bradbury Art Museum will host a free music festival in the new courtyard on October 20. Acts that are scheduled to attend include Charles Liou's Jazz Messengers and saxophonist Ann Sandman. All attendees will be entered into a raffle for gifts.

In the event of inclement weather, the event may be rescheduled for October 22. Check www.bradburymuseum.org/events for more details.

From:	terrygreen@bradburymuseum.org
To:	charlesliou@messengers.net
Subject:	Congratulations
Date:	October 23

Dear Mr. Liou,

I just wanted to thank you for your performance yesterday afternoon. I'm glad the weather cleared up so that the city could hear your band's excellent performance. It was great to see such an enthusiastic crowd. Everyone I know is still talking about the show!

Please come back to Pioneer City soon.

Best,

Terry Green

186. What is the notice mainly about?

(A) An upcoming building closure
(B) Increased membership fees
(C) A museum job opening
(D) Customer service policies

187. What is implied about the street renovation project?

(A) It began in August.
(B) It required more funds.
(C) It was overseen by Mr. Green.
(D) It took longer than anticipated.

188. According to the article, what was constructed at the museum?

(A) A parking lot
(B) An entertainment area
(C) A gift shop
(D) An indoor theater

189. What does the article state as one feature of the festival?

(A) A food sampling event
(B) A new art exhibition
(C) A prize drawing
(D) An auction

190. What is suggested about the festival?

(A) It had to be postponed.
(B) It was only open to local residents.
(C) It will be held every year.
(D) It did not attract many attendees.

GO ON TO THE NEXT PAGE

Questions 191-195 refer to the following article, e-mail, and online review.

Sherbrooke Gazette

March 9 – A new skating rink is being created in downtown Sherbrooke between Rue Papineau and Rue Eymard. Construction of Leopold Arena started six months ago. Steven Fontaine, who works in the Quebec branch of the French company, Ayoub, is the mastermind behind the Arena's unique design.

Ayoub has built sports complexes in both North America and Western Europe. Because of concerns that construction of the rink would run into delays, Ayoub CEO Jean-Baptiste Charpentier has offered a cash incentive to all Canadian staff if Leopold Arena is finished in time to host the Bantam Sherbrooke International Hockey Tournament. The tournament is scheduled for the end of next January.

People who back the creation of the new arena believe that it will give the area's economy a much-needed boost. Ayoub is employing more than 100 Sherbrooke residents to help build the facility. And City Councilor Yvette Sevigny points out that ice hockey will be a long-term revenue source. In addition to ticket sales, local businesses are sure to benefit as fans purchase food, lodging, and souvenirs in Sherbrooke.

To: Steven Fontaine <fontaine@ayoub.ca>
From: David Harrachi <harrachi@ayoub.fr>
Date: January 12
Subject: Update

Hi Steven,

Just a quick note to congratulate you on having Leopold Arena ready for the big tournament. I'm sure all the Canadian staff are delighted, as is Mr. Charpentier, who is looking forward to meeting with you again during your next visit to corporate headquarters.

Sincerely,

David Harrachi
Executive Assistant

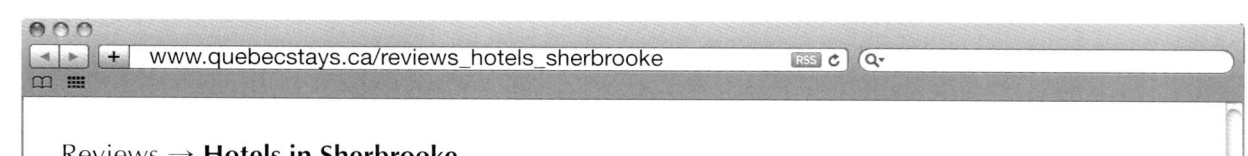

Reviews → **Hotels in Sherbrooke**

Hotel Caméléon

Feb 19 by Armand Boucher

My favorite hockey team made it to the finals at the Bantam Sherbrooke International Tournament, so of course, I had to come here and cheer them on. Such an exciting time!

Hotel Caméléon was very welcoming to all the hockey fans in town for the event, and a great place to celebrate afterwards. I was especially impressed with the special "victory dinner" that the hotel's restaurant prepared on the last night of the tournament. We came to attend the hockey games, but honestly, it would be worth a trip back to Sherbrooke just to have that food again. The place is a little noisy, since it's located right next to a busy shopping and entertainment district. But overall, Hotel Caméléon has been a great place to stay, and I would highly recommend it.

191. Why was the article written?

(A) To compare construction companies
(B) To discuss a decline in tourists
(C) To introduce a building project
(D) To advertise a rental property

192. In the article, the word "back" in paragraph 3, line 1, is closest in meaning to

(A) reverse
(B) support
(C) assist
(D) turn

193. What is suggested in the e-mail?

(A) Employees in Canada will receive a bonus.
(B) Mr. Charpentier will visit the Quebec region.
(C) Ayoub will sponsor some hockey players.
(D) Mr. Fontaine will be offered a promotion.

194. What is probably true about Armand Boucher?

(A) He knows Mr. Charpentier.
(B) He works near Sherbrooke.
(C) He has visited Leopold Arena.
(D) He used to be a professional athlete.

195. What did Mr. Boucher especially like about Hotel Caméléon?

(A) The fitness facilities
(B) The spacious rooms
(C) The souvenir store
(D) The evening meal

GO ON TO THE NEXT PAGE

Questions 196-200 refer to the following e-mail, flyer, and schedule.

Date	April 30
From	Julian Kojima<julian@maddux.com>
To	Christine Walters<christine@maddux.com>
Subject	Team-building Event

Dear Christine,

I trust that you're doing well. I know it can be rather challenging to keep track of everything at first, but I'm certain you will get the hang of it soon. Every year, around this time, our administrative coordinator organizes a company-wide event. I believe we discussed it when you interviewed in February. In past years, we have gone to soccer games and taken hikes in the national park, among other things. It's a great chance to get to know one another outside of work.

This year, I think it would be nice to go to a concert. Many employees are big music fans and have been talking about the outdoor concert series in Leeper Pavilion. It would need to be a concert on a weekday, and it should be a jazz show. We have $400 budgeted for this year. And, after a quick look at the pricing, it looks like that will be sufficient to get every employee a ticket.

If you need any help, Scott can help you with this. He has helped organize the event in the past.

Regards,

Julian Kojima
President, Maddux Industries

Join us for an evening to remember
at Leeper Pavilion

Concert tickets are available at reduced rates for large groups. Savings start when you buy 12 or more, and the more, the merrier! As a bonus, your group will be admitted to the venue early, receive complimentary refreshments, and will be entered into a contest to win VIP access to the backstage area to meet the artists.

Group Rates
- 12 tickets for $240
- 25 tickets for $375
- 50 tickets for $650
- 100 tickets for $1,200

Call or text 219-555-5040 if you have any questions.

Springtime in Leeper Pavilion
May Concert Schedule

Performer	Date	Day	Genre	Time
Merrion-Clark Ensemble	May 11	Saturday	Jazz	4:30 P.M.
Hill Street Seven	May 16	Thursday	Jazz	7:00 P.M.
Marcia Barton Quintet	May 26	Sunday	Classical	2:00 P.M.
Elkhart Philharmonic	May 29	Wednesday	Classical	8:00 P.M.

Tickets are now on sale at **www.leeperpavilion.gov/concertseries**

196. What was the main reason Mr. Kojima emailed Ms. Walters?

(A) To invite her on a team-building hike
(B) To introduce a new filing protocol
(C) To instruct her to arrange an outing
(D) To inform her of his upcoming vacation

197. What does the e-mail suggest about Ms. Walters?

(A) She was recently hired at Maddux.
(B) She will be relocating to work on a new project.
(C) She has attended a performance at Leeper Pavilion.
(D) She is a fan of jazz music.

198. According to the flyer, what is an advantage of buying tickets in bulk?

(A) Lower ticket prices
(B) VIP seating
(C) Discounted concessions
(D) Gift bags

199. How many employees does Maddux Industries most likely have?

(A) 12
(B) 25
(C) 50
(D) 100

200. On what date will Maddux Industries hold their event?

(A) May 11
(B) May 16
(C) May 26
(D) May 29

Stop! This is the end of the test. If you finish before time is called, you may go back to Part 5, 6, and 7 and check your work.

TEST 02

MP3 바로 듣기

1타 강사 강의듣기

준비물: OMR 카드, 연필, 지우개, 시계
시험시간: LC 약 45분 / RC 75분

나의 점수		
	LC	RC
맞은 개수		
환산 점수		

총점: _____ 점

TEST 1	TEST 2	TEST 3	TEST 4	TEST 5
_____점	_____점	_____점	_____점	_____점

점수 환산표

LC		RC	
맞은 개수	환산 점수	맞은 개수	환산 점수
96-100	475-495	96-100	460-495
91-95	435-195	91-95	425-490
86-90	405-475	86-90	395-465
81-85	370-450	81-85	370-440
76-80	345-420	76-80	335-415
71-75	320-390	71-75	310-390
66-70	290-360	66-70	280-365
61-65	265-335	61-65	250-335
56-60	235-310	56-60	220-305
51-55	210-280	51-55	195-270
46-50	180-255	46-50	165-240
41-45	155-230	41-45	140-215
36-40	125-205	36-40	115-180
31-35	105-175	31-35	95-145
36-30	85-145	36-30	75-120
21-25	60-115	21-25	60-95
16-20	30-90	16-20	45-75
11-15	5-70	11-15	30-55
6-10	5-60	6-10	10-40
1-5	5-60	1-5	5-30
0	5-35	0	5-15

LISTENING TEST

In the Listening test, you will be asked to demonstrate how well you understand spoken English. The entire listening test will last approximately 45 minutes. There are four parts, and directions are given for each part. You must mark your answers on the separate answer sheet. Do not write your answers in your test book.

PART 1

Directions: For each question in this part, you will hear four statements about a picture in your test book. When you hear the statements, you must select the one statement that best describes what you see in the picture. Then find the number of the question on your answer sheet and mark your answer. The statements will not be printed in your test book and will be spoken only one time.

Statement (B), "A man is pointing at a document," is the best description of the picture, so you should select answer (B) and mark it on your answer sheet.

1.

2.

3.

4.

5.

6.

GO ON TO THE NEXT PAGE

PART 2

Directions: You will hear a question or statement and three responses spoken in English. They will not be printed in your test book and will be spoken only one time. Select the best response to the question or statement and mark the letter (A), (B), or (C) on your answer sheet.

7. Mark your answer on your answer sheet.
8. Mark your answer on your answer sheet.
9. Mark your answer on your answer sheet.
10. Mark your answer on your answer sheet.
11. Mark your answer on your answer sheet.
12. Mark your answer on your answer sheet.
13. Mark your answer on your answer sheet.
14. Mark your answer on your answer sheet.
15. Mark your answer on your answer sheet.
16. Mark your answer on your answer sheet.
17. Mark your answer on your answer sheet.
18. Mark your answer on your answer sheet.
19. Mark your answer on your answer sheet.
20. Mark your answer on your answer sheet.
21. Mark your answer on your answer sheet.
22. Mark your answer on your answer sheet.
23. Mark your answer on your answer sheet.
24. Mark your answer on your answer sheet.
25. Mark your answer on your answer sheet.
26. Mark your answer on your answer sheet.
27. Mark your answer on your answer sheet.
28. Mark your answer on your answer sheet.
29. Mark your answer on your answer sheet.
30. Mark your answer on your answer sheet.
31. Mark your answer on your answer sheet.

PART 3

Directions: You will hear some conversations between two or more people. You will be asked to answer three questions about what the speakers say in each conversation. Select the best response to each question and mark the letter (A), (B), (C), or (D) on your answer sheet. The conversations will not be printed in your test book and will be spoken only one time.

32. What kind of business do the speakers work for?
    (A) A clothing retailer
    (B) An advertising agency
    (C) A construction firm
    (D) A grocery store

33. What does the man recommend?
    (A) Providing a discount
    (B) Displaying a sign
    (C) Hiring a company
    (D) Adjusting a budget

34. What does the man say Kay is skilled at?
    (A) Selling products
    (B) Designing graphics
    (C) Making Web sites
    (D) Training new employees

35. What does the man say he did?
    (A) Moved a meeting time
    (B) Visited a client's office
    (C) Arranged a delivery
    (D) Revised a presentation

36. What does the woman decide to do?
    (A) Go on a business trip
    (B) Order more supplies for a lounge
    (C) Change a catering menu
    (D) Allow employees to leave early

37. According to the man, what will happen in the evening?
    (A) A parking lot will close.
    (B) A machine will be fixed.
    (C) An area will be renovated.
    (D) A system will restart.

38. What did the woman recently do?
    (A) She delivered a package.
    (B) She met with a supervisor.
    (C) She moved to a new home.
    (D) She bought some supplies.

39. What is the reason for the woman's call?
    (A) To submit a payment
    (B) To make a complaint
    (C) To purchase extra items
    (D) To schedule a consultation

40. What does the man request?
    (A) Some personal information
    (B) A coupon code
    (C) A store map
    (D) Some product samples

41. What is June's job?
    (A) Computer programmer
    (B) Accounting clerk
    (C) Office administrator
    (D) Financial officer

42. What will June most likely do next?
    (A) Complete an assignment
    (B) Meet a manager
    (C) Read an article
    (D) Visit a Web site

43. What does June say about some software?
    (A) It is widely used in the industry.
    (B) She downloaded it on her computer.
    (C) She is already familiar with it.
    (D) It is from another country.

GO ON TO THE NEXT PAGE

44. What did the man receive a reward for?

(A) Designing a successful product
(B) Cutting operating expenses
(C) Overseeing a project overseas
(D) Attracting many customers

45. What does the man plan to do next week?

(A) Participate in a sports competition
(B) Meet some family members
(C) Attend a performance
(D) Host a company banquet

46. What does the man say he might do with his reward?

(A) Give it to a colleague
(B) Sell it online
(C) Use it later
(D) Put it in a frame

47. What are the speakers mainly discussing?

(A) A malfunctioning machine
(B) An upcoming conference
(C) A room reservation
(D) A delivery fee

48. Why does the woman say, "We use this room frequently for meetings"?

(A) To describe why a request is important
(B) To change the location of a meeting
(C) To recommend purchasing more furniture
(D) To indicate that an area is too small

49. What will the man do next?

(A) Explain a process
(B) Issue a refund
(C) Revise a report
(D) Contact a store

50. Where do the women work?

(A) At a formal clothing retailer
(B) At a textile factory
(C) At a fashion magazine publisher
(D) At a laundry business

51. Why is the man visiting the business?

(A) To sign an agreement
(B) To receive a refund
(C) To apply for a job
(D) To pick up an item

52. What does the man agree to do?

(A) Return at another time
(B) Provide some comments
(C) Take a special tour
(D) Pay in cash

53. Who most likely is the woman?

(A) An event organizer
(B) A professional photographer
(C) A news reporter
(D) A computer technician

54. What does the man's friend make?

(A) Speakers
(B) Laptops
(C) Digital cameras
(D) Mobile programs

55. What does the man give to the woman?

(A) A conference schedule
(B) A visitor's badge
(C) Some application forms
(D) Some contact information

56. What is the main topic of the conversation?

(A) A landscaping project
(B) A price estimate
(C) A vacant property
(D) A gardening tool

57. What does the man mention about some fountains?

(A) They are not working properly.
(B) They will be installed tomorrow.
(C) They are too heavy.
(D) They look outdated.

58. What does the man imply when he says, "This patio area is larger than I thought"?

(A) It will take a while to finish a task.
(B) A manager's approval is required.
(C) Additional supplies need to be ordered.
(D) He would like to request more workers.

59. Where do the speakers work?

(A) At a supermarket
(B) At a café
(C) At a farm
(D) At a bottling plant

60. According to the man, what has recently happened?

(A) The price of a product has increased.
(B) A contract was terminated.
(C) The owner of a business has changed.
(D) A sales event was held.

61. What does the woman say she will do tomorrow?

(A) Call a new supplier
(B) Speak with an applicant
(C) Conduct a survey
(D) Hold a meeting

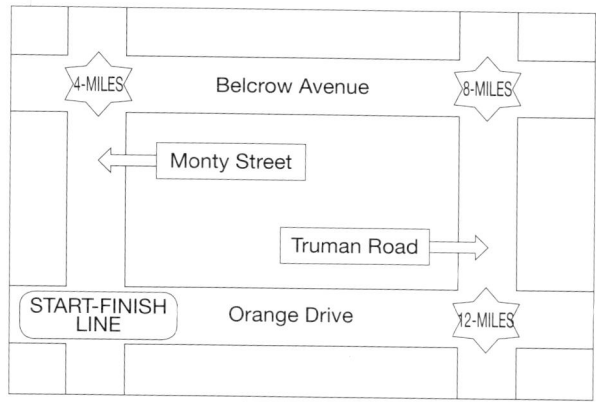

62. What will the woman do at the marathon?

(A) Take some pictures
(B) Direct some traffic
(C) Provide some beverages
(D) Interview some participants

63. Look at the graphic. Which intersection will the woman go to?

(A) Monty Street and Belcrow Avenue
(B) Belcrow Avenue and Truman Road
(C) Truman Road and Orange Drive
(D) Orange Drive and Monty Street

64. What is the woman instructed to do after the marathon?

(A) Clean up an area
(B) Hand out some prizes
(C) Fill out a survey
(D) Share some photos

GO ON TO THE NEXT PAGE

Upcoming Spring Seminars	
March 12	Eating for Energy
March 29	Starting Yoga
April 3	Creating a Jogging Program
April 16	Keeping a Training Journal

65. Why is the woman able to participate in free seminars?

(A) She is a local resident.
(B) She is a fitness trainer.
(C) She purchased a membership.
(D) She completed early registration.

66. Look at the graphic. On which date will the woman attend an event?

(A) March 12
(B) March 29
(C) April 3
(D) April 16

67. What will Brianne Pyle introduce?

(A) A nutrition plan
(B) A fitness machine
(C) An exercise routine
(D) A health book

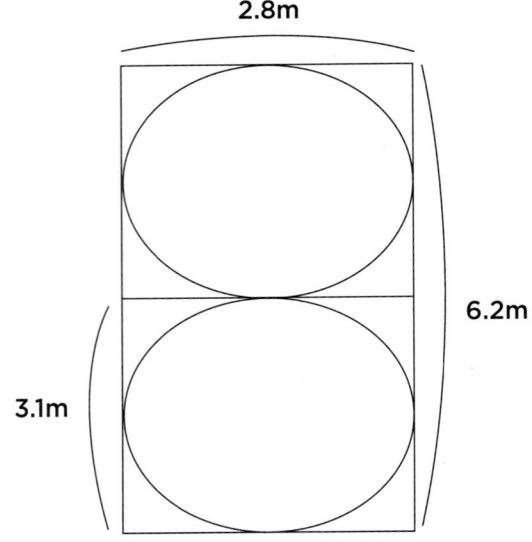

68. What kind of business does the man own?

(A) A storage facility
(B) A coffee shop
(C) An employment agency
(D) An art gallery

69. Look at the graphic. Which dimension does the man want to change?

(A) 2.8 meters
(B) 3.1 meters
(C) 4.3 meters
(D) 6.2 meters

70. What will the woman probably do next?

(A) Calculate a price
(B) Measure some material
(C) Provide a sample
(D) Contact a manufacturer

PART 4

Directions: You will hear some talks given by a single speaker. You will be asked to answer three questions about what the speaker says in each talk. Select the best response to each question and mark the letter (A), (B), (C), or (D) on your answer sheet. The talks will not be printed in your test book and will be spoken only one time.

71. What type of businesses does the company own?
    (A) Stationery stores
    (B) Food services
    (C) Wholesale markets
    (D) Car rentals

72. What will the businesses begin doing?
    (A) Arranging automatic payments
    (B) Offering time-based discounts
    (C) Extending their business hours
    (D) Providing delivery of items

73. What does the speaker ask José Alvarez to do?
    (A) Send out an e-mail
    (B) Describe an action plan
    (C) Pass out a schedule
    (D) Call a caterer

74. Where is the announcement probably being heard?
    (A) On a train
    (B) On a bus
    (C) On an airplane
    (D) On a ferry

75. What problem does the speaker mention?
    (A) Inclement weather
    (B) A shortage of staff
    (C) A faulty system
    (D) Road work

76. What are the listeners instructed to do?
    (A) Remain in their seats
    (B) Pick up a discount voucher
    (C) Take their belongings
    (D) Contact their family members

77. What kind of business is being advertised?
    (A) A home landscaping company
    (B) An interior design service
    (C) A photography studio
    (D) An art gallery

78. How can the listeners receive a complimentary gift?
    (A) By mentioning an advertisement
    (B) By posting a review
    (C) By submitting a photo
    (D) By completing a survey

79. What does the speaker say the listeners can do during a phone call?
    (A) Order a picture frame
    (B) Get some directions
    (C) Schedule an appointment
    (D) Receive some advice

80. Where is the introduction being held?
    (A) At an awards ceremony
    (B) At an international convention
    (C) At an anniversary party
    (D) At an employee luncheon

81. What does the speaker say Benedict Freeman is known for?
    (A) His travel books
    (B) His work for endangered species
    (C) His problem-solving skills
    (D) His illustrated guides of plants

82. What are the listeners encouraged to do?
    (A) Welcome a guest speaker
    (B) Fill out a questionnaire
    (C) Go on a tour
    (D) Make a donation

GO ON TO THE NEXT PAGE

83. What kind of business do the listeners most likely work for?

    (A) A staffing agency
    (B) An auto repair shop
    (C) An electronics store
    (D) A marketing firm

84. What does the speaker mean when he says, "Now, we've added a section on our Web site"?

    (A) A new product will be introduced.
    (B) An employee has been hired.
    (C) A layout will be changed.
    (D) An issue has been resolved.

85. What does the speaker plan to do on Mondays?

    (A) Compile some comments
    (B) Talk to some customers
    (C) Check some inventory
    (D) Send some packages

86. What department does the speaker most likely work in?

    (A) Payroll
    (B) Information Technology
    (C) Sales
    (D) Research and Development

87. What does the speaker mean when she says, "we already have your information from the last job you did for us"?

    (A) The listener was able to recover a file.
    (B) The listener does not have to make a visit.
    (C) The speaker has another assignment.
    (D) The speaker does not have a phone number.

88. What does the speaker recommend the listener do soon?

    (A) Create a new account
    (B) Retrieve some documents
    (C) Inquire about another job
    (D) Email a résumé

89. Who most likely is the speaker?

    (A) A repair technician
    (B) A plant supervisor
    (C) A program developer
    (D) A car salesperson

90. According to the speaker, what is being replaced this week?

    (A) Some software
    (B) Some machinery
    (C) Some name tags
    (D) Some storage units

91. What are the listeners asked to do?

    (A) Register for a training session
    (B) Wear safety gear
    (C) Prepare for an upcoming inspection
    (D) Suggest some ideas

92. Where do the listeners work?

    (A) At a dairy farm
    (B) At a grocery store
    (C) At a bakery
    (D) At a restaurant

93. How did the company find out about Web Maestros?

    (A) From a TV commercial
    (B) From a current employee
    (C) From a former client
    (D) From a newspaper advertisement

94. Why does the speaker say, "Web Maestros will designate a qualified technician to us"?

    (A) A project will be delayed.
    (B) A contract needs to be reviewed.
    (C) The listeners do not have to be concerned.
    (D) The listeners should interview a job applicant.

Productivity Challenge	
WEEK 1	Organize your life and your work
WEEK 2	Energize with physical activity
WEEK 3	Update your technical skills
WEEK 4	Improve your public speaking

95. What reward will some staff members receive?

(A) A cash prize
(B) An extra vacation day
(C) A discount voucher
(D) A free meal

96. Look at the graphic. When will a seminar take place?

(A) Week 1
(B) Week 2
(C) Week 3
(D) Week 4

97. What should listeners who want to attend a seminar do?

(A) Contact an event organizer
(B) Go to an information session
(C) Pay a deposit
(D) Fill out a registration form

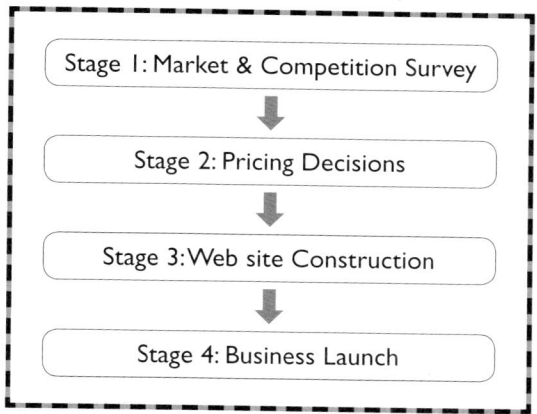

98. What industry do the listeners work in?

(A) Information Technology
(B) Food Service
(C) Healthcare
(D) Tourism

99. Look at the graphic. Which stage will a guest speaker discuss?

(A) Stage 1
(B) Stage 2
(C) Stage 3
(D) Stage 4

100. According to the speaker, what can the listeners do on the first floor?

(A) Attend another seminar
(B) Address some concerns
(C) Access a computer program
(D) Check out a map

READING TEST

In the Reading test, you will read a variety of texts and answer several different types of reading comprehension questions. The entire Reading test will last 75 minutes. There are three parts, and directions are given for each part. You are encouraged to answer as many questions as possible within the time allowed.

You must mark your answers on the separate answer sheet. Do not write your answers in your test book.

PART 5

Directions: A word or phrase is missing in each of the sentences below. Four answer choices are given below each sentence. Select the best answer to complete the sentence. Then mark the letter (A), (B), (C), or (D) on your answer sheet.

101. Meilee Zhang was nominated for a promotion for her many ------- as contract negotiator.

(A) competitors
(B) contributions
(C) computations
(D) considerations

102. The concert organizers ------- planned to hold the event at Dartmoor College, but it was deemed too remote.

(A) evenly
(B) originally
(C) relatively
(D) excellently

103. Amount charged after the 20th of every month will be reflected on the ------- month's statement.

(A) developing
(B) incoming
(C) following
(D) accompanying

104. HR team members may use the Marketing Department's photocopier while ------- is being repaired.

(A) them
(B) their
(C) they
(D) theirs

105. Unless you are using a virtual private network, ------- changing your password is advised.

(A) regularized
(B) regulation
(C) regularly
(D) regular

106. You are welcome to catch us at this spring's West Music Festival, ------- our newest song will be performed for the first time.

(A) thus
(B) together
(C) where
(D) resulting

107. Min-hee Park transformed her research on the ------- effects of physical exercise into a popular nonfiction film.

(A) favor
(B) favorable
(C) favorably
(D) favored

108. The schedule ------- in the chart is only an estimate, as the arrival time is subject to change depending on traffic conditions.

(A) show
(B) showing
(C) shown
(D) are shown

109. The warehouse manager told the order fillers that ------- more employees relocated, they would have to work additional hours.

(A) whenever
(B) once
(C) until
(D) even

110. Mr. Watson is responsible for accepting all produce or meat shipment when they ------- after regular business hours have ended.

(A) are delivered
(B) will deliver
(C) deliver
(D) are delivering

111. As our local supplier did not have the raw materials we required on site, we ordered them from a larger provider -------.

(A) alike
(B) rather
(C) though
(D) instead

112. As a result of Marie Speer's able leadership, the Smartphone Department has achieved rapid -------.

(A) growth
(B) grower
(C) growing
(D) grow

113. To gain a new perspective, Ellerton Security is conducting an ------- search for a new director of human resources.

(A) available
(B) external
(C) alternating
(D) organized

114. Builders must wear hard hats at all times ------- on the construction site.

(A) while
(B) regrettably
(C) forward
(D) before

115. Top Post Stationery offers a range of ------- created greeting cards and gifts.

(A) tremendously
(B) neglectfully
(C) thoughtfully
(D) considerably

116. Because of missing permits, Ms. Cheung ------- the application to construct a new building on the property.

(A) rejected
(B) reject
(C) was rejected
(D) will be rejected

117. ------- the rising cost of petroleum, the merchandising team is being advised to decrease the availability of free shipping.

(A) Of
(B) For
(C) Upon
(D) Given

118. Mr. Briggs' program manual should prove ------- to customers who are unfamiliar with the new software.

(A) instructed
(B) instructions
(C) instructive
(D) instructively

119. Hancock Financial Services never ------- client information to other parties without the account holder's authorization.

(A) locates
(B) manages
(C) collects
(D) discloses

120. If all of your paperwork is -------, the temporary working visa should take less than a week to issue.

(A) on call
(B) in order
(C) on duty
(D) in advance

GO ON TO THE NEXT PAGE

121. ------- in the Belknap Association is open to amateur as well as professional scientists.

(A) Allowance
(B) Endorsement
(C) Certification
(D) Membership

122. ------- our Legal Department manager, Mr. Belfort has just been appointed Director of Legal Affairs.

(A) Exclusively
(B) Candidly
(C) Formerly
(D) Exactly

123. Ms. Romanov became a valued resource at Robertson Ltd. ------- increasing its distribution network.

(A) therefore
(B) from
(C) by
(D) along

124. While the auditor has valued the artwork at $50,000, the owner may be willing to ------- if you can pay by wire transfer.

(A) diminish
(B) negotiate
(C) include
(D) contradict

125. The manufacturing plant in Toronto reported that production figures reached their ------- rate ever in the last week of September.

(A) highness
(B) highest
(C) highly
(D) high

126. The training ------- have turned in their final evaluations of the recently hired interns for official approval.

(A) supervision
(B) supervisory
(C) supervisors
(D) supervisor

127. Many people find the wait before seeing the dentist for their routine checkup almost -------.

(A) unbearable
(B) irresistible
(C) inexplicable
(D) unbeatable

128. Cornwall Barriers is ------- a week-long shutdown of its production facilities so that they may be inspected for safety.

(A) generating
(B) implementing
(C) inducing
(D) arbitrating

129. ------- interest in the seminar series on ancient Egyptian art failed to meet expectations, it was quickly cancelled.

(A) Unless
(B) Obviously
(C) Since
(D) Due to

130. The Southeast Asian Education Initiative believes that continued ------- between educators and families is critical.

(A) competence
(B) assistance
(C) compliance
(D) collaboration

PART 6

Directions: Read the texts that follow. A word, phrase, or sentence is missing in parts of each text. Four answer choices for each question are given below the text. Select the best answer to complete the text. Then mark the letter (A), (B), (C), or (D) on your answer sheet.

Questions 131-134 refer to the following notice.

Attention Wyandotte County Residents

Please note that Wyandotte County Public Works (WCPW) will be resurfacing major roads and highways in the county throughout the month of May in accordance with our annual maintenance schedule. Road resurfacing is planned for every Monday of this month between 3 A.M. and 5 A.M. -------. Also, in the days following the completion
                                                            131.
of resurfacing, the pavement will be soft, so slower driving speeds are recommended. This is ------- but cannot be avoided. County residents ------- longer commute times for
        132.   133.
about six weeks. WCPW will send out a similar announcement ------- the next yearly
                                                              134.
maintenance period, which normally occurs in late spring. Please contact WCPW at 555-1212 with any questions or concerns.

131. (A) During these times, motorists are prohibited from accessing these roads.
(B) The revised schedule will be posted as quickly as possible.
(C) As an alternative, county officials may choose to fund a bus route.
(D) Most businesses are closed between midnight and 6 A.M.

132. (A) ideal
(B) complete
(C) temporary
(D) cautious

133. (A) expecting
(B) have expected
(C) should expect
(D) expects

134. (A) since
(B) while
(C) against
(D) before

Questions 135-138 refer to the following e-mail.

To: vasquez@watertown.gov
From: shenderson@bryantconsulting.com
Subject: Web site feedback
Date: December 3
Attachment: Analysis

Ms. Vasquez,

I have compiled a summary of my colleagues' thoughts on your city's municipal Web site in the space below.

Overall, they thought it was not as ------- as it could be. It would be helpful to streamline
135.
the design, simplifying its appearance for ease of use. They also noticed some bugs appearing persistently ------- the site, causing pages to load very slowly.
136.

They also recommended supplementing the photos used on the front page. -------.
137.
Accordingly, it would be a good use of resources to post some brief, professional-looking videos that guide users on how to use the Web site. -------, they have
138.
recommended adding a live chat feature which allows users to ask for help in real time.

Let me know if you have any questions.

Sincerely,

Spencer Henderson

---

135. (A) effectively
(B) effective
(C) effecting
(D) effectiveness

136. (A) throughout
(B) forward
(C) over
(D) against

137. (A) These photos need to be posted in higher resolution.
(B) Without a proper file-naming protocol, the image files become disorganized.
(C) The photos don't look like they were taken by a professional photographer.
(D) It is difficult to keep users engaged with images alone.

138. (A) To be clear
(B) As a result
(C) Nonetheless
(D) In addition

Questions 139-142 refer to the following product description.

DB Mallex's new "Anywhere" dress shirt is made of lightweight, odor-absorbing organic cotton perfect for traveling wherever you need to go. -------(139.)-------. Our special set-in design on the -------(140.)------- allows for greater mobility and comfort. The combination of stylish fit and breathability make it perfect whether you're in a meeting or on a hiking trail. This shirt comes with a reversible collar flap -------(141.)------- provides an extra degree of versatility. Every purchase -------(142.)------- from our headquarters in Wharton and is guaranteed to arrive anywhere in the country within 48 hours of ordering.

139. (A) This high-tech fabric stays wrinkle-free and never needs ironing.
(B) A hidden pocket is perfect for storing important items.
(C) The lightweight cotton pillow case stays cool throughout the night.
(D) Its stylish design goes well with any style of shirt.

140. (A) buttons
(B) sleeves
(C) brim
(D) packaging

141. (A) still
(B) then
(C) such
(D) that

142. (A) have shipped
(B) had shipped
(C) were shipped
(D) will be shipped

Questions 143-146 refer to the following article.

Escondido (October 5) – Sleek Mobile (SM) and Bexmont Cellular Services (BCS) ------- into one organization. The business merger is expected to be completed by December 1. The newly ------- firm will be known as West Coast Telecommunications. SM has over 150 locations in California, and BCS has 100 locations spread across Washington and Oregon. -------. During a joint press conference, Sheena Kim, CEO of SM, and Timothy Rogers, President of BCS, stated that there will not be any changes to their current services. ------- also indicated that all staff members will be able to keep their jobs.

143. (A) have merged
(B) are merged
(C) have been merging
(D) will be merging

144. (A) formed
(B) acquired
(C) admitted
(D) remedied

145. (A) Both firms are known to be leaders in their own industry.
(B) The exact terms will be announced after this week's shareholder meeting.
(C) The telecommunications field is crucial to the West Coast's economy.
(D) Both firms are planning to expand into other countries.

146. (A) It
(B) They
(C) He
(D) We

PART 7

Directions: In this part you will read a selection of texts, such as magazine and newspaper articles, e-mails, and instant messages. Each text or set of texts is followed by several questions. Select the best answer for each question and mark the letter (A), (B), (C), or (D) on your answer sheet.

Questions 147-148 refer to the following form.

Kurtz BBQ and Wings

Thanks for stopping by Kurtz BBQ and Wings. We'd appreciate it if you took a moment to fill out the survey below.

	Vasquez	Neutral	Disagree
The food looked and tasted great.		X	
The food was reasonably priced.	X		
I didn't have to wait too long.		X	
The service was friendly and helpful.	X		
The restaurant was exceptionally clean.		X	
The lighting and music were set to proper levels.			X

Name and contact info:
Gerald Brunswick
555 032-4592

Comments:
The restaurant was packed, but I was impressed with the service. Despite having a small staff, all our items arrived quickly and were prepared properly. It would have been better if the restaurant wasn't so dim. Some overhead fixtures would really help brighten up the place.

147. What did Mr. Brunswick indicate about his dining experience?

(A) The menu items were a good value for the price.
(B) His order was delayed for a few minutes.
(C) Some items arrived at the table cold.
(D) The portion sizes were large.

148. What improvement does Mr. Brunswick suggest?

(A) Additional staff should be hired.
(B) A loyalty card should be offered.
(C) Menu items should be better presented.
(D) More lighting should be installed.

GO ON TO THE NEXT PAGE

Questions 149-150 refer to the following notice.

**Remington Lawn Masters:
For Your Lawn Mowing and Gardening Needs**

Thanks for purchasing the Lawn Master MM2500d. If you keep the following information in mind, your machine should work well for many years.

- Make sure to drain the tank of gasoline at the end of the mowing season. Old fuel can make the engine hard to start after a long winter.

- Clean the bottom of the mower regularly to prevent buildup. The blades can be filled with grass and dirt over time, causing malfunction.

- Replace the sparkplug every year. By changing this inexpensive, easy-to-replace component, you'll prevent the need for more expensive repairs.

- Get a periodic tune-up. A good way to ensure your machine lasts a long time is to take it into a repair shop regularly so that a professional can inspect it.

149. What is indicated about the blades of the Lawn Master MM2500d?

(A) They can become blocked.
(B) They are expensive to replace.
(C) They are only available from Remington.
(D) They can cut any type of grass.

150. What is NOT mentioned as a tip for lawnmower maintenance?

(A) Emptying the gas tank
(B) Using a specific cleaning product
(C) Buying a new part annually
(D) Visiting a specialist

Questions 151-152 refer to the following notice.

Haynes Apparel Grand Re-Opening

Construction on our beautiful, modern facility at 2117 East Highway is complete. So after two months of absence, we're pleased to announce that Haynes Apparel will be relocating to the Tri-state Area on April 1.

The East Highway location will be in the heart of downtown. This will mean that the store will be more accessible to customers throughout the metro region.

To celebrate Haynes Apparel's re-opening, we will be holding a special event on the first of April. The first 50 customers to arrive when the store opens at 10:00 A.M. will be entered in a raffle. We will draw the names of two lucky winners who will be rewarded with $500 gift cards. Come on down! This is an event you won't want to miss!

And don't forget to check out our online store at www.haynesapparel.com.

151. According to the notice, why is Haynes Apparel relocating?

(A) To be situated in a more convenient area
(B) To attract a different group of customers
(C) To offer a wider range of clothing items
(D) To provide a faster delivery service

152. How will Haynes Apparel celebrate its re-opening on April 1?

(A) By giving online discounts
(B) By opening earlier than usual
(C) By revealing a new product
(D) By distributing some prizes

GO ON TO THE NEXT PAGE

Questions 153-154 refer to the following text message chain.

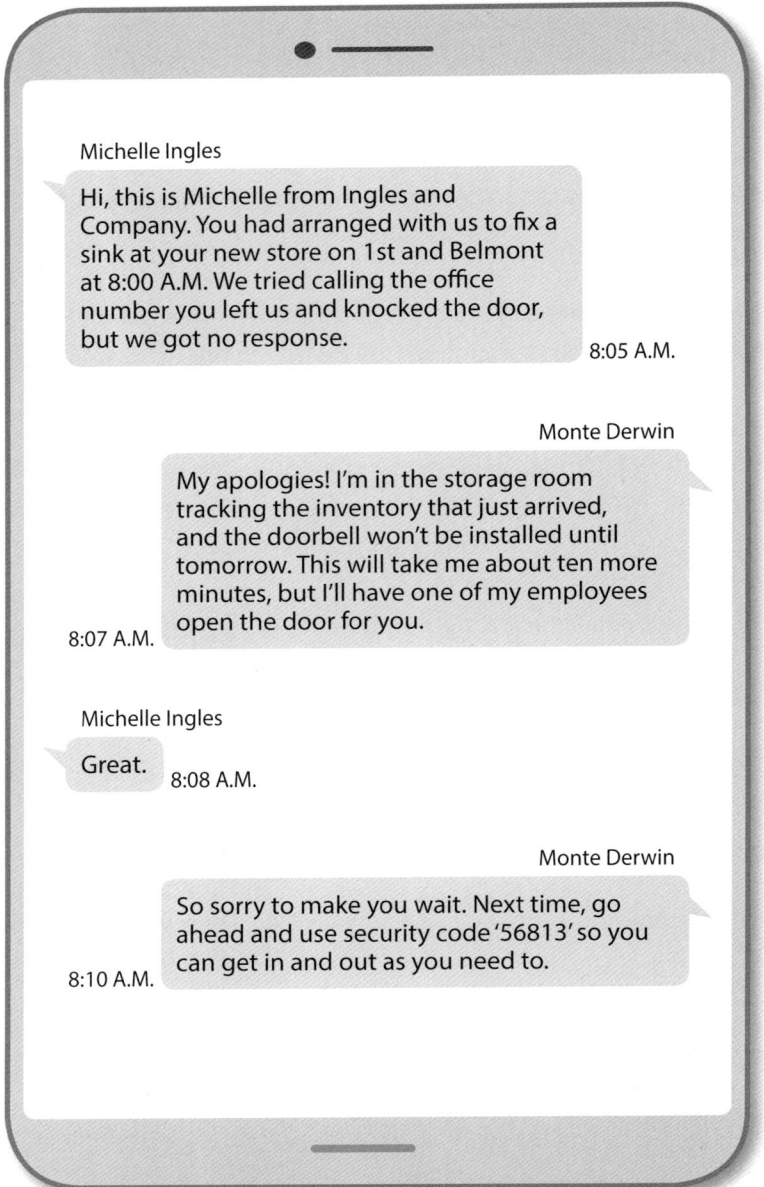

153. What was scheduled at 8:00 A.M.?

(A) An inventory meeting
(B) A doorbell installation
(C) A plumbing repair
(D) A product delivery

154. At 8:07 A.M., why most likely does Mr. Derwin write, "My apologies!"?

(A) He forgot a store could not be accessed.
(B) He is unsure when he can help Ms. Ingles.
(C) He thought Ms. Ingles would come the next day.
(D) He expected an employee to share a security code.

Questions 155-157 refer to the following e-mail.

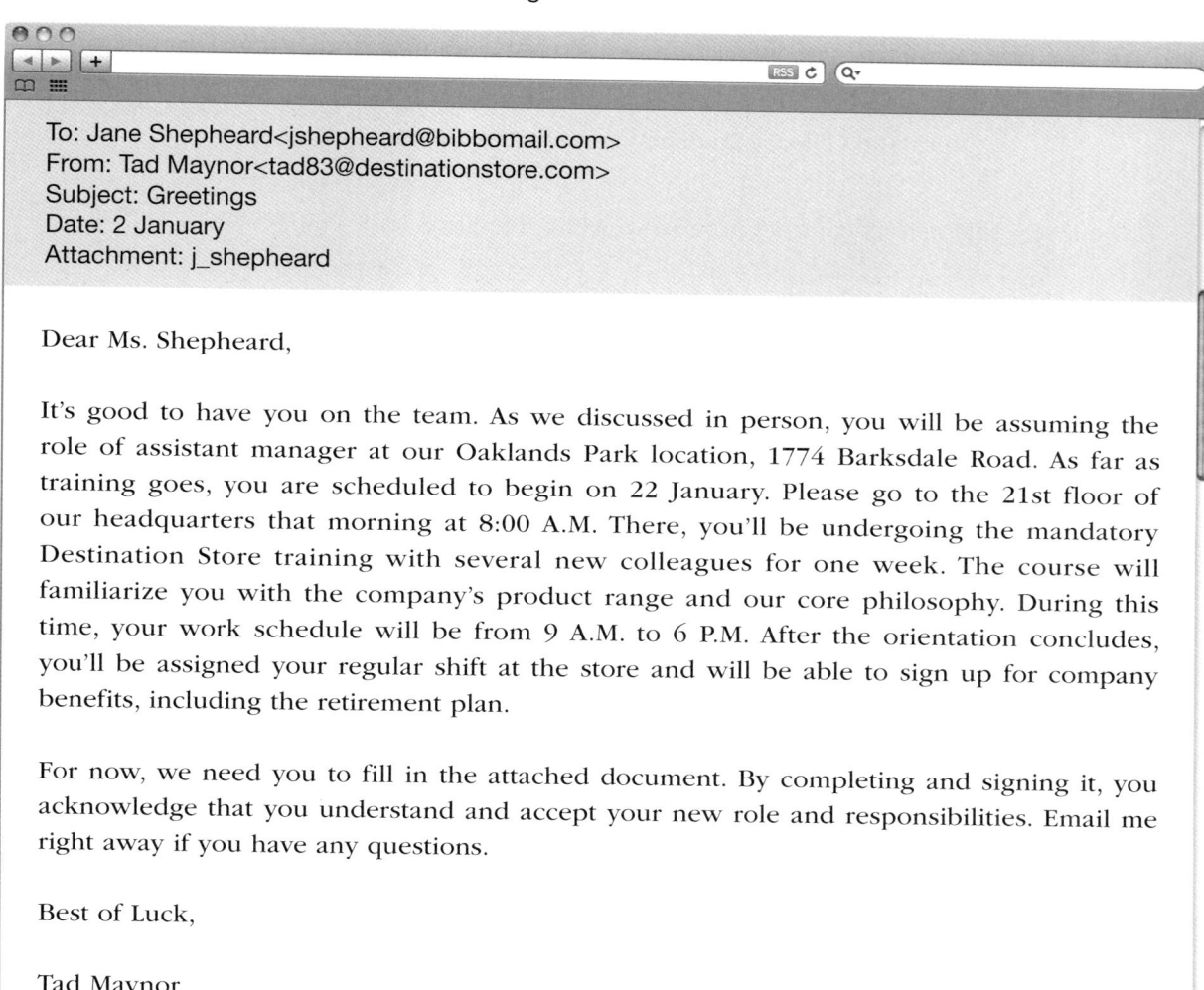

To: Jane Shepheard<jshepheard@bibbomail.com>
From: Tad Maynor<tad83@destinationstore.com>
Subject: Greetings
Date: 2 January
Attachment: j_shepheard

Dear Ms. Shepheard,

It's good to have you on the team. As we discussed in person, you will be assuming the role of assistant manager at our Oaklands Park location, 1774 Barksdale Road. As far as training goes, you are scheduled to begin on 22 January. Please go to the 21st floor of our headquarters that morning at 8:00 A.M. There, you'll be undergoing the mandatory Destination Store training with several new colleagues for one week. The course will familiarize you with the company's product range and our core philosophy. During this time, your work schedule will be from 9 A.M. to 6 P.M. After the orientation concludes, you'll be assigned your regular shift at the store and will be able to sign up for company benefits, including the retirement plan.

For now, we need you to fill in the attached document. By completing and signing it, you acknowledge that you understand and accept your new role and responsibilities. Email me right away if you have any questions.

Best of Luck,

Tad Maynor
Personnel Director

155. Why did Mr. Maynor write the e-mail?

(A) To discuss plans for a store promotion
(B) To explain a retirement policy
(C) To give details about a position
(D) To reschedule a meeting

156. According to Mr. Maynor, what will probably happen after one week?

(A) Ms. Shepheard will attend a celebration.
(B) Ms. Shepheard's wages will be increased.
(C) Ms. Shepheard will relocate to a different city.
(D) Ms. Shepheard's work hours will be adjusted.

157. What did Mr. Maynor include in the e-mail?

(A) An agreement form
(B) An insurance brochure
(C) An orientation agenda
(D) A product catalog

GO ON TO THE NEXT PAGE

Questions 158-160 refer to the following advertisement.

Auckland Culinary Students' Test Kitchen Is Open for Dinner

Do you want that perfect gourmet experience without the usual price tag? —[1]—.

The Auckland Culinary School would like to make you dinner for just $10. For one full week at the beginning of every month, our students cook meals for the general public. The experience of running our Test Kitchen gives the students valuable experience in their field. —[2]—. To make sure your dining experience is up to our high standards, one of our top instructors will be in the kitchen to oversee the service.

Reservations for the Test Kitchen can be made in the last week of each month, but book quickly. Our location only has eight tables. —[3]—. You can use the Fork and Knife app to get a table before they run out.

Be aware that the student may require a little longer to get your dish exactly right. It should also be noted that the students are required to follow Test Kitchen recipes, so no substitutions or special requests will be taken. —[4]—.

---

158. What is indicated about instructors at the Auckland Culinary School?

(A) They work one week per month.
(B) They decide which students will cook.
(C) They supervise service at the Test Kitchen.
(D) They give students safety training.

159. What is NOT mentioned about the Test Kitchen?

(A) It can be reserved through an application.
(B) It has an outdoor dining area.
(C) It does not have much space for customers.
(D) It might take some time to serve dishes.

160. In which of the positions marked [1], [2], [3], and [4] does the following sentence best belong?

"Because of this, make sure to check the menu carefully if you have any dietary restrictions."

(A) [1]
(B) [2]
(C) [3]
(D) [4]

Questions 161-163 refer to the following invitation.

Sunday, April 10 from Noon to 4 P.M.

Come Commemorate 200 years of Chesterton at the Civic Heritage Museum!

This year is our town's bicentennial anniversary. To honor 200 years of history, the museum is presenting a commemorative event that celebrates the unique culture and heritage of our community over the years. All donors who have supported the Civic Heritage Museum are invited to come for an afternoon of film, fine dining, and a first look at our newest exhibit. Enjoy presentations and panel discussions featuring noted scholars, with a keynote speech by Professor Chloe Emmerich of Chesterton University. And you won't want to miss the screening of acclaimed director Geoffrey Maxwell's documentary film *From Frontier to Front Yard*. Lunch and beverages will be provided by Twin Rivers Pub. All profits from ticket and food sales will go to the town's Future Filmmakers project.

To reserve a ticket, visit www.chestertonCHM.com/bookings. Keep in mind that they must be purchased at least 48 hours in advance, and only a limited number are available.

---

161. For whom is the invitation most likely intended?

(A) History professors
(B) Chesterton town officials
(C) Past contributors
(D) Film students

162. The word "over" in paragraph 1, line 3, is closest in meaning to

(A) above
(B) more
(C) beyond
(D) through

163. What is true about the event?

(A) It will only sell a certain number of tickets.
(B) It features a free lunch.
(C) It will include a speech on film history.
(D) It is held on an annual basis.

Questions 164-167 refer to the following online chat discussion.

Tony Gandolfini [7:45 P.M.]
Hey, everyone. I'm new to the neighborhood, and I heard this was a good place to ask questions. Have any of you tried installing your own windows?

Sam Rockwell [7:47 P.M.]
Welcome to the Glenview neighborhood chat, Tony. Are you planning on doing the job yourself? I put in new windows in my attic last year. I'm not sure I would do it again, though.

Tony Gandolfini [7:48 P.M.]
From my research, it looks like you can save a lot of money by doing it yourself. But I admit I've never done anything like this.

Deidre Stapleton [7:52 P.M.]
If you are good at this kind of thing, it's possible to install windows after seeing someone do it a few times. But you need to be very precise. It's easy to damage certain parts of the windows if you make a mistake.

Sam Rockwell [7:53 P.M.]
When I did it, I visited www.yourhouseproj.com to read a lot of online resources and watched how-to videos first. But I will probably hire a professional next time.

Sam Rockwell [7:54 P.M.]
Deidre, have you worked on many of these projects? Would you advise Tony to do the job by himself?

Tony Gandolfini [7:54 P.M.]
That's very helpful. I'm grateful for the input.

Deidre Stapleton [7:55 P.M.]
I operate a windows and siding business. Whether I would advise it would depend on a few things. Tony, will you be fitting a new window, or will you have to remove the old one? Also, are you sure you have all the right tools?

Tony Gandolfini [7:55 P.M.]
I was thinking of replacing just one window, but it sounds like something a new homeowner would have trouble doing. Deidre, can I get your company's phone number?

Deidre Stapleton [7:57 P.M.]
We'd be happy to help. My office number is 555-4220. Just mention that you spoke to me.

164. For whom is the chat room intended?

(A) People who will go on vacation together
(B) People who work in the same office
(C) People who take the same course
(D) People who live in the same area

165. At 7:47 P.M., what does Mr. Rockwell most likely mean when he writes, "I'm not sure I would do it again, though"?

(A) He regrets not hiring a professional.
(B) He thought a project cost too much money.
(C) He purchased some unreliable materials.
(D) He needs to redecorate his home.

166. What is most likely true about Ms. Stapleton?

(A) She works with Mr. Gandolfini.
(B) She is experienced with window installations.
(C) She regularly uploads videos to www.yourhouseproj.com.
(D) She is a new homeowner.

167. What will Mr. Gandolfini probably do next?

(A) Exchange a damaged window
(B) Watch an instructional video
(C) Call a business
(D) Review a price estimate

Questions 168-171 refer to the following e-mail.

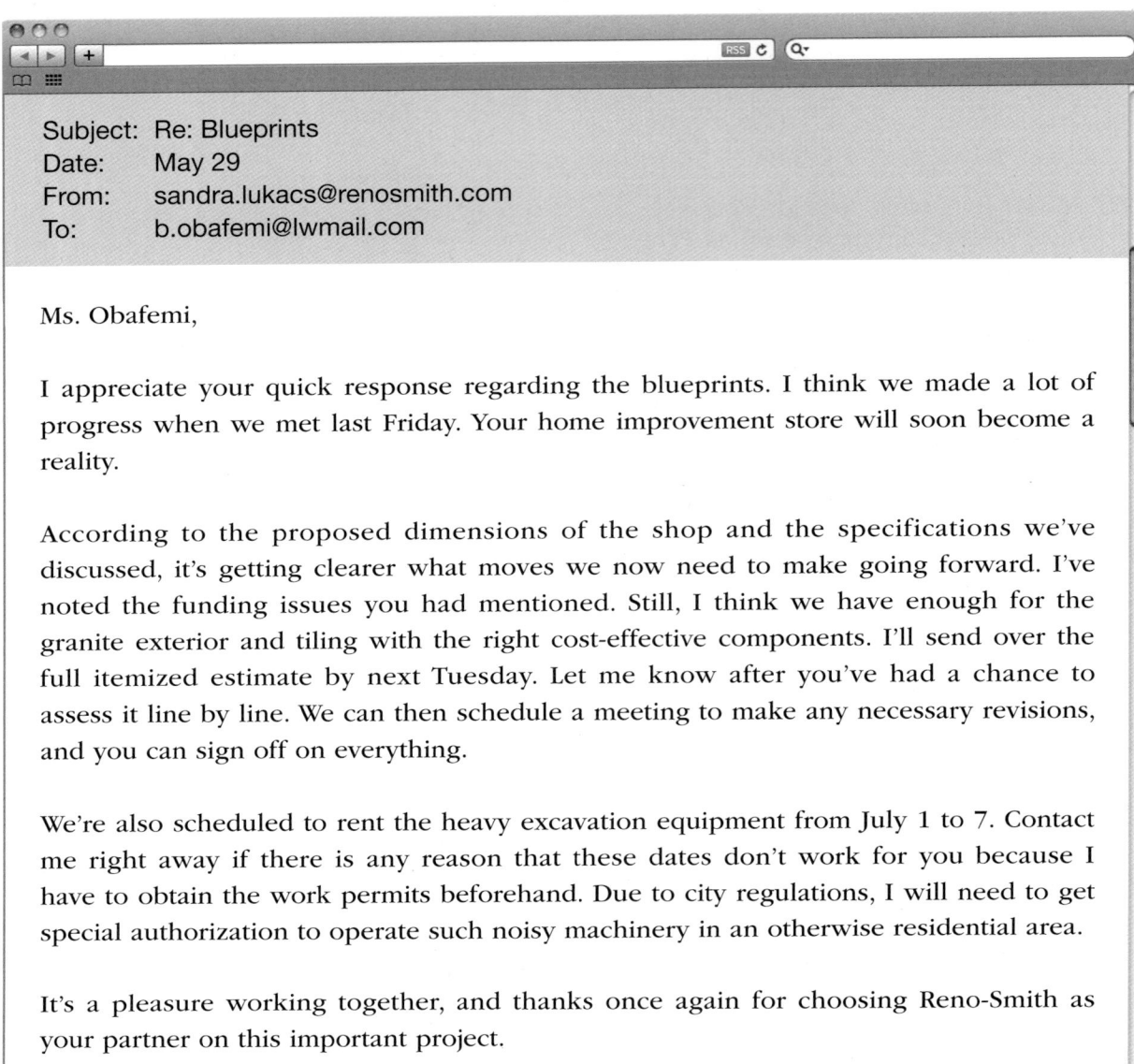

Subject: Re: Blueprints
Date: May 29
From: sandra.lukacs@renosmith.com
To: b.obafemi@lwmail.com

Ms. Obafemi,

I appreciate your quick response regarding the blueprints. I think we made a lot of progress when we met last Friday. Your home improvement store will soon become a reality.

According to the proposed dimensions of the shop and the specifications we've discussed, it's getting clearer what moves we now need to make going forward. I've noted the funding issues you had mentioned. Still, I think we have enough for the granite exterior and tiling with the right cost-effective components. I'll send over the full itemized estimate by next Tuesday. Let me know after you've had a chance to assess it line by line. We can then schedule a meeting to make any necessary revisions, and you can sign off on everything.

We're also scheduled to rent the heavy excavation equipment from July 1 to 7. Contact me right away if there is any reason that these dates don't work for you because I have to obtain the work permits beforehand. Due to city regulations, I will need to get special authorization to operate such noisy machinery in an otherwise residential area.

It's a pleasure working together, and thanks once again for choosing Reno-Smith as your partner on this important project.

Sincerely,
Sandra Lukacs

168. What is the purpose of the e-mail?

(A) To request the approval of some documents
(B) To detail the next stage of a project
(C) To explain some additions to a plan
(D) To outline the total cost of a project

169. What is suggested about Ms. Obafemi?

(A) She owns a successful store.
(B) She has a restricted budget.
(C) She needs to apply for a permit.
(D) She wants to relocate her business.

170. According to the e-mail, what should Ms. Obafemi do to prepare for the next meeting?

(A) Create a blueprint
(B) Review some figures
(C) Purchase some materials
(D) Sign a contract

171. Why does Ms. Lukacs mention heavy equipment?

(A) To confirm that it will be available on requested dates
(B) To make sure that she has a large enough construction crew
(C) To make sure that regulations are being followed
(D) To confirm that it will fit in the building's dimensions

Questions 172-175 refer to the following article.

UNLIMITED VACATION?

Greg Waiters, Staff Writer

Workers often dream about going on vacations to get away from the stresses of their work. Unfortunately, a limited number of vacation days may not allow employees to get the rest and relaxation they need. —[1]—. Some companies, however, have begun offering their employees unlimited paid leave. Even though this policy may seem to put companies at a disadvantage, it has been shown to have a positive impact. Companies have noticed that their employees work harder, they are able to recruit and retain top talent, and they don't need to pay out unused vacation time, since there is no fixed number of days to be taken.

Before implementing such measures, employers must ensure that the policy is well-understood and that expectations are realistic. —[2]—. This includes educating your company's employees on how the policy will benefit the company overall, as well as emphasizing that unlimited time off does not translate to any reduction in responsibility for getting their share of work done. Employees should also be clear on the proper procedure for taking days off of work. —[3]—. Employers should check on this regularly to make sure there are no issues. —[4]—.

172. For whom is the article mainly intended?

(A) Magazine writers
(B) Legal experts
(C) Travel agents
(D) Company executives

173. What is NOT stated as a benefit of unlimited vacation?

(A) It keeps a company from losing employees.
(B) It allows a company to save money.
(C) It increases productivity levels.
(D) It offers employees a telecommuting option.

174. According to the article, what should happen periodically?

(A) A review of a procedure
(B) A change in management
(C) A training seminar
(D) A discussion of job duties

175. In which of the positions marked [1], [2], [3], and [4] does the following sentence best belong?

"For instance, employees may need to request time off in advance if taking an extended holiday."

(A) [1]
(B) [2]
(C) [3]
(D) [4]

Questions 176-180 refer to the following flyer and letter.

Are you between the ages of 18 and 42, living in the Chicago area, and in need of some extra cash? Then, contact Mercer Research!

We at Mercer Research are looking for people to participate in paid focus group sessions, so we can obtain valuable input for our clients. If you are interested in any of the listings below, please visit www.mercerresearch.com/focusgroups to sign up. You will need to complete a questionnaire to confirm that you are a suitable candidate.

#G918 – Music lovers are wanted to give their opinions on a local band's new album. Participants will earn $75 for the 90-minute listening session.

#G929 – Electronics enthusiasts are wanted to test and review a brand-new tablet PC for two hours. After completing a short survey, attendees will earn $125 for their time.

#G951 – Parents of children under the age of five are invited to take part in a two-day focus group on toys. Meetings will last for three hours on each day, and participants will earn $300 for their time.

#G996 – Sports fans are needed to give their opinions on the local professional baseball team. Both new and old fans are encouraged to sign up to attend a pair of one-hour discussions. In return, participants will receive $50 and two tickets to the next home game.

October 3

Jacob Tambor
1912 Farland Way
Chicago, IL 60606

Mr. Tambor,

You have been accepted to participate in session #G996. As our Web page states, you will be asked to attend two one-hour meetings set for August 18 at 12 P.M. and August 20 at 1 P.M. I will lead both of the sessions. Since time is limited, we ask that you watch a short video and fill out a survey before attending the session. This should allow for a more productive discussion.

Our building is currently undergoing a renovation project, so we will not be meeting at our main office. Instead, we have reserved a workspace in the city center (directions can be found our Web site). Also, enclosed, you'll find a pass that will give you access to the building's parking garage.

In the event that you are unable to attend your session, it is important that you let us know as quickly as you can. This will allow us to notify an alternative candidate.

We appreciate your help and time.

Nathaniel Olsen

Nathaniel Olsen
Mercer Research

Enclosure

176. What is the purpose of the flyer?

(A) To hire qualified research assistants
(B) To promote a new marketing firm
(C) To list upcoming athletic competitions
(D) To advertise a discussion opportunity

177. How much will Mercer Research most likely pay Mr. Tambor?

(A) $50
(B) $75
(C) $125
(D) $300

178. What is implied about Mr. Olsen?

(A) He needs to purchase a tablet PC.
(B) He organizes focus groups.
(C) He has a part-time job.
(D) He works at a sports stadium.

179. What is included with the letter?

(A) A building map
(B) An application form
(C) A parking pass
(D) A meal coupon

180. What will Mercer Research do if Mr. Tambor cancels his appointment?

(A) Contact another applicant
(B) Send an information packet
(C) Reschedule a meeting
(D) Issue a full reimbursement

Questions 181-185 refer to the following Web page and e-mail.

Adventure Excursions: South America
FAQ: Self-driving tours

Are visas required?
For EU citizens, you will be able to travel freely without a special visa, as long as your passport is current. For citizens of other countries, please confirm the latest entry requirements with the relevant government authorities. Every traveler should be ready to present their passport on the first day of the tour for a photocopy. Subsequently, remember to keep it on hand to display whenever we pass through border security. An international driver's license and car insurance plan are also required.

Where do I pick up my vehicle, and where do I drop it off?
We will send our drivers to the airport when you arrive. From there, you can drive yourself or rest in the support car. On your way out of the country, you can simply leave the vehicle with us at the airport. If you are not flying out immediately, you will need to organize your own means of transport to the airport.

What information do I need to be aware of?
Each excursion will be equipped with heavy-duty 4-wheel-drive vehicles capable of passing over rough terrain. Thirty days prior to your excursion, we will send an e-mail information on the exact make and model, along with a final itinerary with expected travel times, road conditions, and planned accommodations.

What should I pack?
It is important to bring versatile clothing. You will experience both humid jungles near sea level and snow-capped peaks at high altitudes. Pack accordingly.

DATE: 22 April
To: jorge_montero@adventureexcursions.com
FROM: moira_oriordan@iemail.com
SUBJECT: Self-driving tour

I booked a self-driving trip last week, which is due to run from August 7 to August 19. I've explored some pretty remote parts of Alaska, but I've never been to South America. As I'm taking a long flight over, I would like to see some additional sites after the excursion ends. If possible, I'd love to end my tour near Huascaran National Park and adjust the route around that. Also, could I ask you to help plan a backpacking trip there? I might need to rent some extra equipment for a few days. I understand the Cordillera Blanca mountains are quite beautiful. I'm open to suggestions, but I'd like to figure out the plan before I get there.

Best Regards,

Moira O'Riordan

181. What is implied about Adventure Excursions: South America's self-driving tours?

(A) They allow visitors to see more sites than a traditional tour.
(B) They are meant for people traveling in large groups.
(C) They go through predominately cool weather locations.
(D) They involve traveling to multiple countries.

182. According to the Web page, what should travelers do before the tour?

(A) Organize transportation to the tour office
(B) Fax a copy of their international driver's license
(C) Determine if a visa is necessary
(D) Get special travel vaccines

183. What will Ms. O'Riordan need to do if she changes her travel plans as described in her e-mail?

(A) Adjust a flight time
(B) Rent a different model
(C) Pay an additional service fee
(D) Arrange a trip to the airport

184. What is likely to happen in July?

(A) Ms. O'Riordan will receive detailed tour information.
(B) Mr. Montero will lead a tour of the Cordillera Blanca mountains.
(C) Mr. Montero will copy some travel documents.
(D) Ms. O'Riordan will rent a vehicle in Alaska.

185. In the e-mail, the phrase "figure out" in line 8 is closest in meaning to

(A) infer
(B) evaluate
(C) accept
(D) clarify

Questions 186-190 refer to the following e-mail, form, and article.

Date: 13 February
Subject: Emerging Leaders Initiative
To: All
From: HR Team
Attachment: Application Form

Any staff member who has been with JTB Motors for less than two years is invited to sign up for a new leadership initiative, which will pair a select group of 20 junior workers with some of the most experienced staff members at the company. The program aims to provide junior staff with an opportunity to refine their skill sets and build networks, preparing them for the next step in their careers. Participants will be matched with mentors solely based on their area of expertise and professional responsibilities. From April, each pair will meet up regularly for at least an hour every week.

To be selected for this program, fill out the attachment and email it to the Emerging Leaders Initiative coordinator, Daria Donnelly by 25 February. Selected applicants will receive an acceptance e-mail from Ms. Donnelly on 3 March.

**Emerging Leaders
Application Form**

Name: Ned Griffin
Department: Product Development
Staff ID: N_Griffin

Career Goals and Professional Focus
I want to learn more about the process of designing products localized for international markets and how to better present those ideas to my managers in an appealing way. Any career advice would be welcome.

Availability
Afternoons from Wednesday through Friday

JTB Motors Quarterly

Emerging Leaders Initiative Bears Fruit

Veteran creative director Phillip Jackson was curious to see what would happen when the human resources team reached out last spring to see if he would mentor one of the company's younger employees. He was hopeful, but he did not expect it to be so rewarding. "After working with Mr. Griffin, I feel happier coming into work every day knowing that I am helping an up-and-coming employee. My only regret is that I did not have someone giving me advice when I started here all those years ago," said Jackson.

For his part, Mr. Griffin says, "I was looking for someone to show me how to pitch my design ideas." Since joining the program, he says several of his designs have been put to use, including an integral part of an electric engine. He is more confident and now knows what it takes to rise in the ranks of JTB Motors. "I have never had clearer goals, nor have I been more fulfilled in the office, and it is all thanks to Mr. Jackson."

The program will be expanding. If you would like to participate, reach out to Daria Donnelly in Human Resources.

---

186. What does the e-mail suggest about the initiative?

(A) There will be a limited number of participants.
(B) It is intended for Product Development staff.
(C) It was requested by the company's newer employees.
(D) Participants will be required to attend a networking event.

187. How will junior staff members most likely be chosen?

(A) They will be recommended by their supervisors.
(B) They will be interviewed by potential mentors.
(C) They will be selected based on their education background.
(D) They will be assessed by Ms. Donnelly.

188. What is suggested about Mr. Griffin?

(A) He has been transferred to Mr. Jackson's department.
(B) He has submitted his design proposal to overseas clients.
(C) He has worked at JTB Motors for less than three years.
(D) He has recently earned a new promotion.

189. What is most likely true about Mr. Jackson?

(A) He has been a mentor for several employees.
(B) He works in the Human Resources Department.
(C) He is one of the company's longest-serving employees.
(D) He has international Product Development experience.

190. How have both Mr. Griffin and Mr. Jackson benefited from the initiative?

(A) More defined goals
(B) Pay increases
(C) Improved job fulfillment
(D) Better job security

Questions 191-195 refer to the following advertisement, e-mail, and information sheet.

MeiHua Bamboo

MeiHua Bamboo is proud to celebrate 25 years of offering top-quality bamboo products to China and the world!

Bamboo houses and furniture have been popular for thousands of years in Asia due to their beauty and durability. As a building material, it has many notable features:

1. **Lightweight:** Bamboo is much lighter than other building materials. This means it requires less labor to transport, store, and install most bamboo products.
2. **Strength:** Bamboo is far stronger than wood. In fact, it can withstand more pressure than concrete and almost as much tension as steel.
3. **Easy Maintenance:** Bamboo is quite durable and is more water-resistant than most woods. Therefore, it is not difficult to clean bamboo. For example, if you spill something on a bamboo floor, all you need to do is use a dry towel to clean it up.
4. **Versatility:** Despite its strength, bamboo is easy to cut and form into various shapes. That means we can work with you to custom-design just about anything you'd like to add to your home or business, from floors, to cabinets, and even curtains!
5. **Eco-Friendly:** Bamboo is a completely renewable, non-polluting resource. Any left over materials can be easily recycled or safely discarded.

To: Giuseppine Nieddu
From: Earl Doherty
Subject: Bamboo Countertops
Date: June 27

Dear Ms. Nieddu,

Thank you for meeting with me and showing me your design proposal for custom bamboo countertops. The countertops are different from anything I've ever seen, and I believe they will be a perfect addition to DDD's new chain of donut and coffee shops in Canada.

My company's management team is of the same opinion, but they do have one question. We will be preparing and serving food and beverages on these countertops. Can you suggest a proper chemical solution to protect the surfaces? Naturally, we need to apply a solution that will keep the counters clean and attractive for a long time, but most importantly provide the safest possible environment for food preparation and consumption.

Thanks in advance,

Earl Doherty
Doherty's Donut Domain (DDD), Inc.

Finishing Options for Bamboo Products

Finishing is the last step in the manufacture of bamboo items. Finishing simply involves covering the surface of the item with a chemical solution that only absorbs a small amount of water, dirt, and oil particles. When the solution dries, it protects the original surface from moisture and bacteria during use. Depending on how and where the product will be used, one of the following finishing products should be chosen.

Material	Durability	Food-Safe?
Natural wax	Poor	Always
Water-based varnish	Excellent	Usually
Oil-based varnish	Very good	Never
Mineral oil	Very good	Always

191. What is mentioned about MeiHua?

(A) It is based in Canada.
(B) It can create customized merchandise.
(C) It will open this year.
(D) It makes furniture cleaning products.

192. Why did Mr. Doherty write the e-mail?

(A) To delay a delivery
(B) To schedule a meeting
(C) To request a recommendation
(D) To revise an order

193. Which feature of MeiHua's bamboo building materials did Ms. Nieddu and Mr. Doherty discuss?

(A) Feature 2
(B) Feature 3
(C) Feature 4
(D) Feature 5

194. According to the information sheet, what does finishing require?

(A) A smooth surface
(B) A cloth made of special material
(C) A cool environment
(D) A solution with low absorbency

195. Which finishing product will DDD, Inc. most likely choose?

(A) Natural wax
(B) Water-based varnish
(C) Oil-based varnish
(D) Mineral oil

GO ON TO THE NEXT PAGE

Questions 196-200 refer to the following Web page and e-mails.

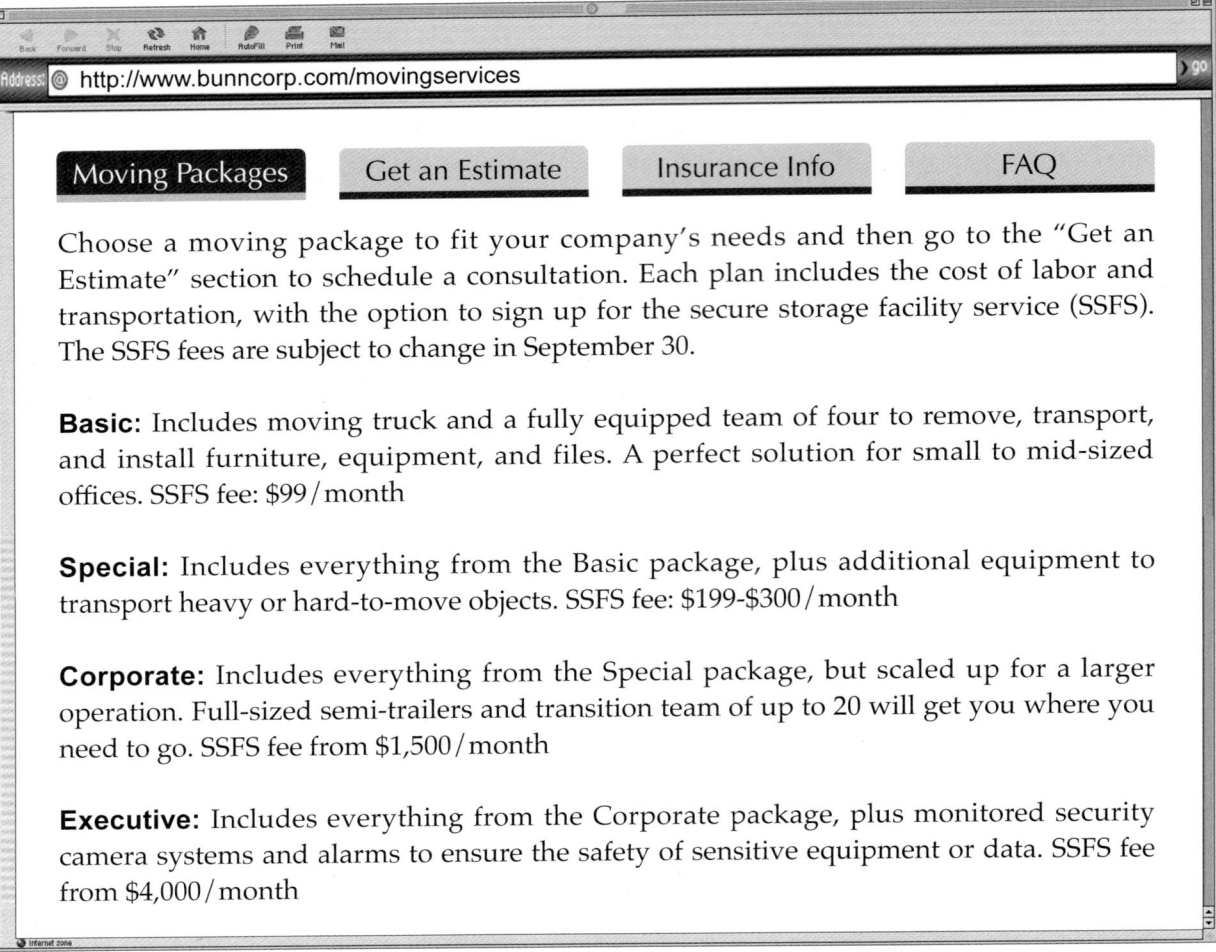

http://www.bunncorp.com/movingservices

Moving Packages | Get an Estimate | Insurance Info | FAQ

Choose a moving package to fit your company's needs and then go to the "Get an Estimate" section to schedule a consultation. Each plan includes the cost of labor and transportation, with the option to sign up for the secure storage facility service (SSFS). The SSFS fees are subject to change in September 30.

Basic: Includes moving truck and a fully equipped team of four to remove, transport, and install furniture, equipment, and files. A perfect solution for small to mid-sized offices. SSFS fee: $99/month

Special: Includes everything from the Basic package, plus additional equipment to transport heavy or hard-to-move objects. SSFS fee: $199-$300/month

Corporate: Includes everything from the Special package, but scaled up for a larger operation. Full-sized semi-trailers and transition team of up to 20 will get you where you need to go. SSFS fee from $1,500/month

Executive: Includes everything from the Corporate package, plus monitored security camera systems and alarms to ensure the safety of sensitive equipment or data. SSFS fee from $4,000/month

---

To BMoore@kraussfinancial.com
From BBunn@bunncorp.com
Date July 2
Subject First Phase of Relocation: Done

Dear Mr. Moore,

This is to confirm that our workers have successfully moved all of your company's equipment into our large storage warehouse on 2000 Huxley Drive. As agreed upon during our meeting last week and in accordance with your SSFS, the items will be stored there until July 31. And at approximately 10 A.M. on that day, we will transport them into your new office in the Crytech Building on 19724 Brookhurst Street.

Should you need to use the SSFS beyond July 31, you will have to give us prior notice at least five days before. Furthermore, you will be assessed a fee for every month that your items remain in our warehouse. The charge will be reflected in your bill on the first date of each month.

Sincerely,
Bradley Bunn
Bunn Corp

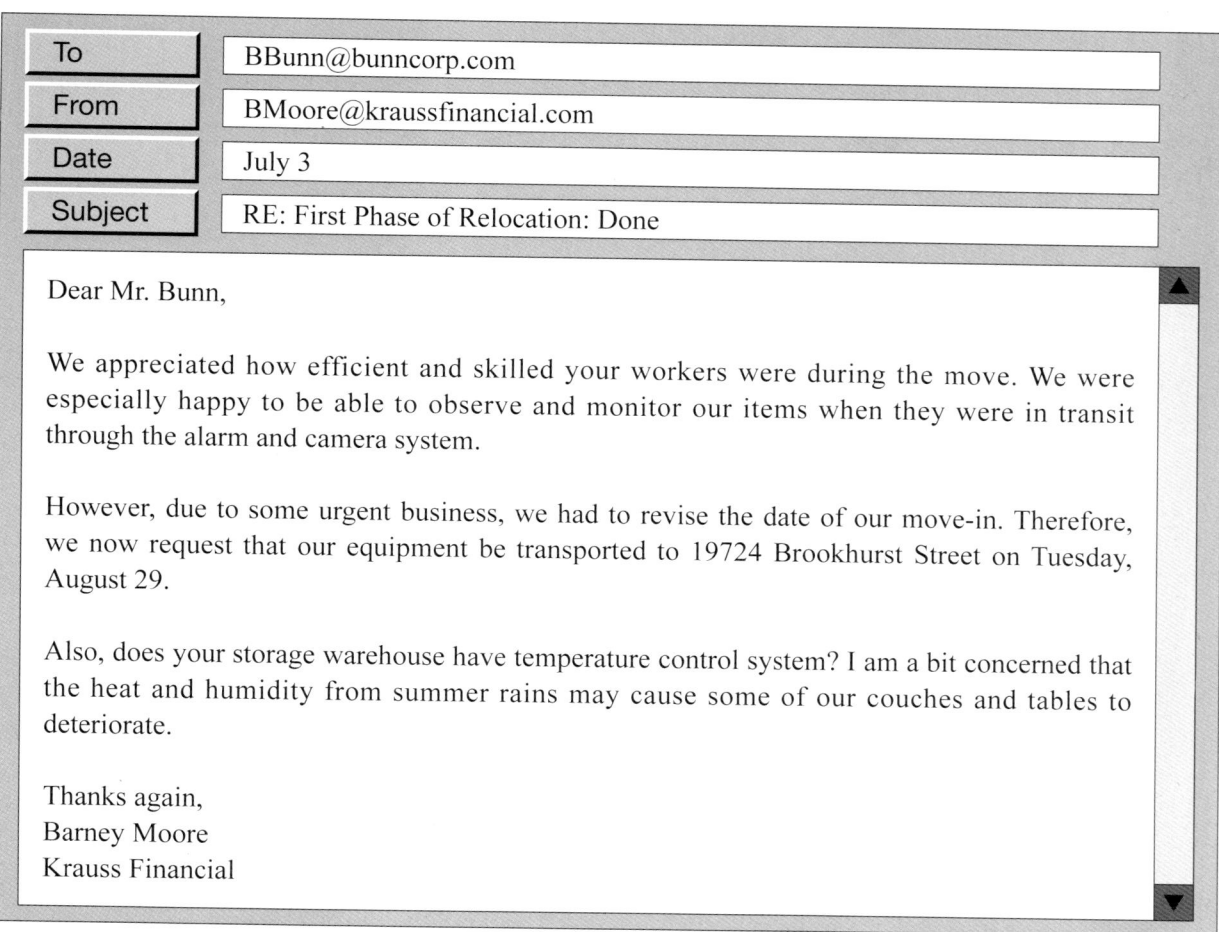

To: BBunn@bunncorp.com
From: BMoore@kraussfinancial.com
Date: July 3
Subject: RE: First Phase of Relocation: Done

Dear Mr. Bunn,

We appreciated how efficient and skilled your workers were during the move. We were especially happy to be able to observe and monitor our items when they were in transit through the alarm and camera system.

However, due to some urgent business, we had to revise the date of our move-in. Therefore, we now request that our equipment be transported to 19724 Brookhurst Street on Tuesday, August 29.

Also, does your storage warehouse have temperature control system? I am a bit concerned that the heat and humidity from summer rains may cause some of our couches and tables to deteriorate.

Thanks again,
Barney Moore
Krauss Financial

196. According to Bunn Corp.'s Web page, what is true about the secure storage facility services?

(A) They are currently being discounted.
(B) Their prices vary by the moving package.
(C) They must be paid for in advance.
(D) Their fees are updated every six months.

197. What is the purpose of the first e-mail?

(A) To discuss a billing mistake
(B) To respond to a client's inquiry
(C) To ask for a deposit
(D) To provide an update on a project

198. What moving package did Mr. Moore probably select?

(A) Basic
(B) Special
(C) Corporate
(D) Executive

199. According to the second e-mail, what is Mr. Moore worried about?

(A) Revised contract conditions
(B) Damages to some furniture
(C) Increased fuel costs
(D) Access to a building

200. What is suggested about Bunn Corp.?

(A) Its head office will relocate to the Crytech Building.
(B) It will not be able to move additional equipment.
(C) It will charge Krauss Financial an extra fee on August 1.
(D) Its employees have received awards for their work.

Stop! This is the end of the test. If you finish before time is called, you may go back to Part 5, 6, and 7 and check your work.

TEST 03

MP3 바로 듣기

1타 강사 강의듣기

준비물: OMR 카드, 연필, 지우개, 시계
시험시간: LC 약 45분 / RC 75분

나의 점수		
	LC	RC
맞은 개수		
환산 점수		

총점: _____ 점

TEST 1	TEST 2	TEST 3	TEST 4	TEST 5
_____ 점	_____ 점	_____ 점	_____ 점	_____ 점

점수 환산표

LC		RC	
맞은 개수	환산 점수	맞은 개수	환산 점수
96-100	475-495	96-100	460-495
91-95	435-195	91-95	425-490
86-90	405-475	86-90	395-465
81-85	370-450	81-85	370-440
76-80	345-420	76-80	335-415
71-75	320-390	71-75	310-390
66-70	290-360	66-70	280-365
61-65	265-335	61-65	250-335
56-60	235-310	56-60	220-305
51-55	210-280	51-55	195-270
46-50	180-255	46-50	165-240
41-45	155-230	41-45	140-215
36-40	125-205	36-40	115-180
31-35	105-175	31-35	95-145
36-30	85-145	36-30	75-120
21-25	60-115	21-25	60-95
16-20	30-90	16-20	45-75
11-15	5-70	11-15	30-55
6-10	5-60	6-10	10-40
1-5	5-60	1-5	5-30
0	5-35	0	5-15

LISTENING TEST

In the Listening test, you will be asked to demonstrate how well you understand spoken English. The entire listening test will last approximately 45 minutes. There are four parts, and directions are given for each part. You must mark your answers on the separate answer sheet. Do not write your answers in your test book.

PART 1

Directions: For each question in this part, you will hear four statements about a picture in your test book. When you hear the statements, you must select the one statement that best describes what you see in the picture. Then find the number of the question on your answer sheet and mark your answer. The statements will not be printed in your test book and will be spoken only one time.

Statement (B), "A man is pointing at a document," is the best description of the picture, so you should select answer (B) and mark it on your answer sheet.

1.

2.

3.

4.

5.

6.

PART 2

Directions: You will hear a question or statement and three responses spoken in English. They will not be printed in your test book and will be spoken only one time. Select the best response to the question or statement and mark the letter (A), (B), or (C) on your answer sheet.

7. Mark your answer on your answer sheet.
8. Mark your answer on your answer sheet.
9. Mark your answer on your answer sheet.
10. Mark your answer on your answer sheet.
11. Mark your answer on your answer sheet.
12. Mark your answer on your answer sheet.
13. Mark your answer on your answer sheet.
14. Mark your answer on your answer sheet.
15. Mark your answer on your answer sheet.
16. Mark your answer on your answer sheet.
17. Mark your answer on your answer sheet.
18. Mark your answer on your answer sheet.
19. Mark your answer on your answer sheet.
20. Mark your answer on your answer sheet.
21. Mark your answer on your answer sheet.
22. Mark your answer on your answer sheet.
23. Mark your answer on your answer sheet.
24. Mark your answer on your answer sheet.
25. Mark your answer on your answer sheet.
26. Mark your answer on your answer sheet.
27. Mark your answer on your answer sheet.
28. Mark your answer on your answer sheet.
29. Mark your answer on your answer sheet.
30. Mark your answer on your answer sheet.
31. Mark your answer on your answer sheet.

PART 3

Directions: You will hear some conversations between two or more people. You will be asked to answer three questions about what the speakers say in each conversation. Select the best response to each question and mark the letter (A), (B), (C), or (D) on your answer sheet. The conversations will not be printed in your test book and will be spoken only one time.

32. Where does the woman work?
    (A) At a public university
    (B) At a travel agency
    (C) At an art gallery
    (D) At a newspaper company

33. Why is the woman calling?
    (A) To request access to some equipment
    (B) To file a complaint about a purchase
    (C) To express interest in using a picture
    (D) To order some copies of a publication

34. What does the man ask the woman for?
    (A) A name of an item
    (B) An e-mail address
    (C) A proof of identification
    (D) A product code

35. Why is the man meeting with the woman?
    (A) To check out available office space
    (B) To participate in a job interview
    (C) To inquire about a service
    (D) To negotiate a contract

36. Why does the man mention his sister?
    (A) To discuss a well-known author
    (B) To explain where he learned a skill
    (C) To request a special price
    (D) To describe how he found out about a firm

37. What area does the man want to concentrate on?
    (A) Software programming
    (B) Book editing
    (C) Client relations
    (D) Web design

38. What is the man trying to do?
    (A) Book a table
    (B) Purchase a train ticket
    (C) Check into a room
    (D) Submit a cover letter

39. What is the man missing?
    (A) His photo ID
    (B) His discount voucher
    (C) His mobile phone
    (D) His confirmation code

40. What does the woman offer to do?
    (A) Call a colleague
    (B) Browse a system
    (C) Send a work request
    (D) Review an invoice

41. What did the man recently find out?
    (A) The date of a CEO's visit has changed.
    (B) An employee has been promoted.
    (C) The location of a meeting has been moved.
    (D) A magazine will report on the company.

42. What do the speakers have to do?
    (A) Update some software
    (B) Meer with some candidates
    (C) Finish a report
    (D) Respond to a customer

43. What does the woman suggest to the man?
    (A) Revising a sales report
    (B) Taking a break for lunch
    (C) Participating in a conference call
    (D) Letting a coworker handle a task

GO ON TO THE NEXT PAGE

44. Who most likely is the woman?

(A) A hotel clerk
(B) A flight attendant
(C) A travel agent
(D) A fitness trainer

45. What do the men inquire about?

(A) Purchasing airplane tickets
(B) Enrolling in some classes
(C) Upgrading some equipment
(D) Touring a facility

46. What does the woman offer to do?

(A) Reduce a price
(B) Print out an invoice
(C) Contact a supervisor
(D) Provide a map

47. Where are the speakers?

(A) At a clothing retailer
(B) At a department store
(C) At a construction firm
(D) At an elementary school

48. What does the woman say has happened?

(A) A building has been remodeled.
(B) A marketing campaign has been launched.
(C) Some new workers have been hired.
(D) Some new policies have been adopted.

49. What does the woman imply when she says, "I know we adjusted some of the brands that we carry"?

(A) The man will like some merchandise.
(B) The man should speak to a team manager.
(C) The man needs to walk to another building.
(D) The man might not find what he is looking for.

50. Where is the conversation taking place?

(A) At a train station
(B) At a bus terminal
(C) At an airport gate
(D) At a ferry port

51. What problem does the woman mention?

(A) A payment cannot be processed.
(B) A computer is not working.
(C) Some seats are unavailable.
(D) Some documents are missing.

52. What does the woman suggest that the man do?

(A) Download an application
(B) Purchase a membership
(C) Go to a restaurant
(D) Print out a voucher

53. What will happen in the first week of August?

(A) Some new instructors will be recruited.
(B) An awards ceremony will take place.
(C) Some machines will be replaced.
(D) A director will visit the Chicago area.

54. What will be offered to the students?

(A) A free device
(B) A refund
(C) An discount
(D) An online consultation

55. What will the man most likely do next?

(A) Inspect some computers
(B) Teach a class
(C) Design a Web site
(D) Speak with some students

56. What are the speakers discussing?

    (A) Creating a financial plan
    (B) Completing a company merger
    (C) Attending a musical performance
    (D) Organizing a retirement party

57. What information does Chelsea need?

    (A) A list of food preferences
    (B) An approval of a budget proposal
    (C) A supplier's contact information
    (D) An agenda for a presentation

58. What does the man suggest doing as soon as possible?

    (A) Changing a reservation
    (B) Confirming some responses
    (C) Placing an order
    (D) Sending a payment

59. Where are the speakers?

    (A) At a ski resort
    (B) At a hardware store
    (C) At a manufacturing plant
    (D) At a landscaping firm

60. Why does the man say, "it's going to be winter soon"?

    (A) To point out an upcoming deadline
    (B) To indicate that he is excited about traveling
    (C) To show that he is interested in a service
    (D) To order some new products

61. What does the woman give to the man?

    (A) A project portfolio
    (B) A work schedule
    (C) A sample contract
    (D) An information pamphlet

Leon's Wednesday Schedule	
8:00 A.M.	Department Meeting
9:00 A.M.	
10:00 A.M.	Videoconference Session
11:00 A.M.	
12:00 P.M.	Team Luncheon
1:00 P.M.	
2:00 – 5:00 P.M.	Client Meetings

62. According to the woman, what will happen on Thursday?

    (A) She will leave for vacation.
    (B) Some clients will visit an office.
    (C) She will record a video.
    (D) Some software will be installed.

63. Look at the graphic. What time will the speakers probably meet?

    (A) 8:00 A.M.
    (B) 10:00 A.M.
    (C) 11:00 A.M.
    (D) 1:00 P.M.

64. What does the man say he will do next?

    (A) Update a system
    (B) Edit a document
    (C) Email a coworker
    (D) Reserve a room

GO ON TO THE NEXT PAGE

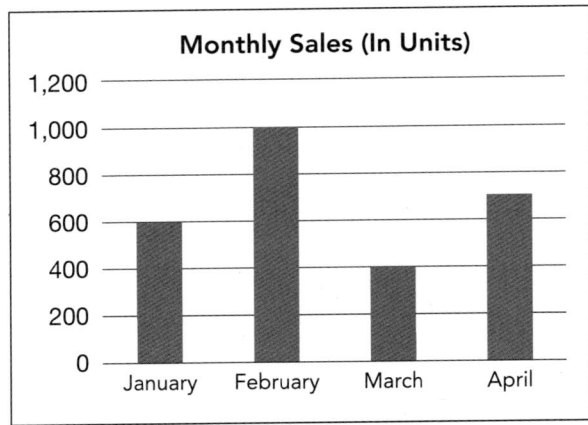

Statesville Technology Convention
[Morning Sessions]

	Diamond Hall	Star Room	Emerald Lounge	Crystal Auditorium
7:30 – 9:30 A.M.	Using Social Media	Future of Internet		
9:40 – 11:40 A.M.		Tablets and Smartphones		Online Payment Platforms

65. What kind of business do the speakers most likely work for?

(A) An office supply store
(B) A car dealership
(C) An electronics producer
(D) A sporting goods retailer

66. Look at the graphic. Which sales number is the man surprised about?

(A) 600
(B) 1,000
(C) 400
(D) 500

67. Who is Catherine Burke?

(A) A marketing specialist
(B) A financial consultant
(C) An IT supervisor
(D) A HR recruiter

68. What was the woman concerned about?

(A) Not bringing an ID
(B) Losing an important packet
(C) Being unable to sign up
(D) Going to an incorrect location

69. Look at the graphic. Where will Baymox, Inc. give their product demonstration?

(A) In the Diamond Hall
(B) In the Star Room
(C) In the Emerald Lounge
(D) In the Crystal Auditorium

70. Why does the man apologize?

(A) There are no more complimentary pens.
(B) A guide contains some wrong information.
(C) A presentation has been delayed.
(D) The woman's credit card cannot be processed.

PART 4

Directions: You will hear some talks given by a single speaker. You will be asked to answer three questions about what the speaker says in each talk. Select the best response to each question and mark the letter (A), (B), (C), or (D) on your answer sheet. The talks will not be printed in your test book and will be spoken only one time.

71. Where does the speaker probably work?

(A) At a clothing manufacturer
(B) At a sports stadium
(C) At a marketing firm
(D) At an accounting company

72. What is the speaker mainly discussing?

(A) A service fee
(B) A new company policy
(C) An event venue
(D) A schedule change

73. What does the speaker ask the listeners to do?

(A) Arrange a delivery
(B) Submit a report
(C) Work additional hours
(D) Contact their clients

74. Why did the speaker leave the message?

(A) To explain a schedule
(B) To report a problem
(C) To arrange a meeting
(D) To apologize for an error

75. What has the speaker already done?

(A) Talked to a business owner
(B) Paid for a service
(C) Reserved some tables
(D) Checked some equipment

76. What does the speaker say she will do today?

(A) Conduct an inspection
(B) Send some photos
(C) Renovate a store
(D) Visit an office

77. What is the main topic of the broadcast?

(A) An automotive conference
(B) A corporate merger
(C) Current shopping trends
(D) Revised hiring procedures

78. According to the speaker, who is Terry Logan?

(A) A Web designer
(B) A news reporter
(C) A construction supervisor
(D) An executive officer

79. According to the speaker, what will WIE Motors do next year?

(A) Move its headquarters
(B) Build a manufacturing facility
(C) Launch a new product
(D) Make financial donations

80. What is being discussed?

(A) A high-tech sports watch
(B) A wireless audio device
(C) A digital camera
(D) A portable heater

81. According to the speaker, what is special about the item?

(A) It is energy-efficient.
(B) It is wearable.
(C) It is water-resistant.
(D) It is inexpensive.

82. What does the speaker recommend doing?

(A) Reserving a product online
(B) Watching a tutorial
(C) Purchasing an extended warranty
(D) Picking up a package in person

GO ON TO THE NEXT PAGE

83. What is the speaker's department working on?

(A) Client questionnaire replies
(B) A cunstomer service process
(C) A new mobile phone
(D) Some computer software

84. Why did Tony recommend the listener?

(A) She has technical knowledge.
(B) She has worked with a company before.
(C) She can lead a training workshop.
(D) She can recommend an outside vendor.

85. Why does the speaker say, "Most of my teammates are at a seminar until Friday"?

(A) To ask that an event be postponed
(B) To explain the need for assistance
(C) To suggest a deadline extension
(D) To order some more supplies

86. According to the speaker, what has just arrived today?

(A) An air conditioner
(B) A laptop
(C) A photocopier
(D) A label maker

87. What does the speaker emphasize about the product?

(A) It is easy to use.
(B) It is the best-selling model.
(C) It is long-lasting.
(D) It is environmentally friendly.

88. Why does the speaker say, "But keep in mind that they're pretty busy this time of year"?

(A) To ask that listeners be patient
(B) To request that more employees be recruited
(C) To point out an unreasonable project timeline
(D) To recommend contacting a manufacturer

89. Where do the listeners most likely work?

(A) At a news station
(B) At a library
(C) At a bookstore
(D) At a publishing company

90. What was the questionnaire designed to find out about?

(A) Security policies
(B) Newly launched products
(C) Reader satisfaction
(D) Subscription prices

91. What incentive was offered for completing the questionnaire?

(A) A service upgrade
(B) A discount voucher
(C) A complimentary bag
(D) A cash prize

92. What is the main topic of the program?

(A) A town parade
(B) A street construction project
(C) A public transit service
(D) A job opportunity

93. What does the speaker mean when she says, "this kind of thing takes a lot of time"?

(A) A deadline is difficult to meet.
(B) The results of a project are impressive.
(C) A budget should be increased.
(D) More volunteers are needed for an assignment.

94. According to the speaker, what will Mr. Rames do?

(A) Read some reviews
(B) Interview a resident
(C) Introduce a director
(D) Give some advice

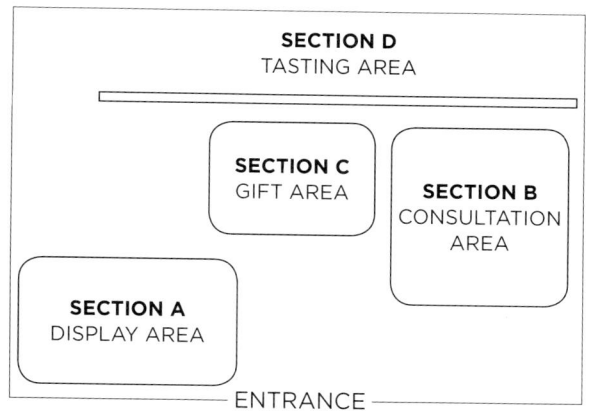

95. What most likely is the speaker's occupation?

    (A) Event planner
    (B) Head chef
    (C) Interior designer
    (D) Computer technician

96. What does the speaker say about the pasta sauces?

    (A) They must be stored in a cool area.
    (B) They can be sold at reduced prices.
    (C) They are going to be distributed as gifts.
    (D) They will be located in the front.

97. Look at the graphic. Which section was added?

    (A) Section A
    (B) Section B
    (C) Section C
    (D) Section D

98. Where most likely is the meeting taking place?

    (A) At a community center
    (B) At an amusement park
    (C) At a department store
    (D) At a health club

99. Why does the speaker thank the listeners?

    (A) For assisting with a task
    (B) For signing up for a magazine
    (C) For attending a orientation session
    (D) For purchasing a membership

100. Look at the graphic. Which amount has changed?

    (A) $25
    (B) $30
    (C) $50
    (D) $90

GO ON TO THE NEXT PAGE

READING TEST

In the Reading test, you will read a variety of texts and answer several different types of reading comprehension questions. The entire Reading test will last 75 minutes. There are three parts, and directions are given for each part. You are encouraged to answer as many questions as possible within the time allowed.

You must mark your answers on the separate answer sheet. Do not write your answers in your test book.

PART 5

Directions: A word or phrase is missing in each of the sentences below. Four answer choices are given below each sentence. Select the best answer to complete the sentence. Then mark the letter (A), (B), (C), or (D) on your answer sheet.

101. Because the Internet connection at the office was not fast -------, employees could not watch the live video feed of the CEO's speech.
    (A) either
    (B) enough
    (C) around
    (D) almost

102. Ali Gallery determines artwork for exhibition mainly by ------- of patron donations.
    (A) petitions
    (B) expenses
    (C) means
    (D) regards

103. Thanks to her 10-year experience at SKG Accounting, Mrs. Ho has a ------- understanding of business tax consulting.
    (A) prospective
    (B) preliminary
    (C) thorough
    (D) misleading

104. The caterers will evaluate all of the produce suppliers' bids and select ------- that suits their menu.
    (A) few
    (B) each
    (C) one
    (D) several

105. Whole Grains Grocery Store ------- résumés and cover letters for the cashier position until the end of the day next Friday.
    (A) accepted
    (B) acceptable
    (C) has been accepting
    (D) will be accepting

106. The president of Rocket Bikes sent an e-mail to his factory workers ------- them for the rapid production run.
    (A) advancing
    (B) substituting
    (C) distributing
    (D) complimenting

107. Pyreen kitchen appliances will help your restaurant operate ------- no matter what cuisine you serve.
    (A) smooth
    (B) smoothed
    (C) smoothing
    (D) smoothly

108. With its new health facilities nearing -------, Fitness First is changing its focus to hiring qualified personal trainers.
    (A) conception
    (B) completion
    (C) compilation
    (D) competition

109. Ms. Salina's flight may not arrive on time ------- the wind shifts sooner than predicted.

    (A) despite
    (B) except
    (C) since
    (D) unless

110. The conversation with Mr. Davidson was ------- Biznet Magazine's best interview of the year.

    (A) easy
    (B) easiest
    (C) easily
    (D) easing

111. The Canberra Photographers Association is a prominent group with very ------- members.

    (A) lenient
    (B) anonymous
    (C) fundamental
    (D) accomplished

112. When requesting a reimbursement, employees must fill out this form and provide receipts for the ------- purchases.

    (A) exposed
    (B) forwarded
    (C) gained
    (D) listed

113. Papillion, Inc. will enter ------- a business contract with Lunae Corporation once they renegotiate some of the finer points of the document.

    (A) that
    (B) quite
    (C) into
    (D) through

114. Jun Lin loved to travel around the world but ------- imagined he would found his own international resort chain.

    (A) after
    (B) whereas
    (C) never
    (D) therefore

115. The Builders Safety Group will examine the blueprints and provide ------- to the architects.

    (A) opinion
    (B) reaction
    (C) feedback
    (D) knowledge

116. Owing to the ------- pipe burst, businesses within 200 meter radius were forced to close when raw sewage flowed into the streets.

    (A) appropriate
    (B) sudden
    (C) impending
    (D) immediate

117. The top five candidates for the marketing officer position will be contacted ------- they are chosen.

    (A) as soon as
    (B) along with
    (C) rather than
    (D) on behalf of

118. The Costa Sol Produce Company announced a record-high crop yield of avocados ------- an unusually wet spring and summer.

    (A) apart from
    (B) caused by
    (C) depending on
    (D) exempt from

119. Mr. Zhukov replaced his car remote since it had not been working -------.

    (A) deliberately
    (B) actively
    (C) properly
    (D) moderately

120. Notwithstanding the initial -------, the Covington City Festival was a popular event.

    (A) critic
    (B) criticized
    (C) criticizing
    (D) criticism

GO ON TO THE NEXT PAGE

121. A few alterations in the garment's design ------- the manufacturer thousands of euros.

(A) saved
(B) examined
(C) intended
(D) prevented

122. The Arcadia National Bank restorations are ------- to resume within the next three months.

(A) yet
(B) almost
(C) expected
(D) relevant

123. After a sample group described Route 1 Shoes' current commercial as -------, the company decided to film a new version.

(A) forgot
(B) forgetful
(C) forgettable
(D) forgetting

124. Ms. Chun was instructed to pick ------- she concluded was the best security firm.

(A) if
(B) anything
(C) whichever
(D) that

125. Although she ------- the complete sales report, Ms. Orrin was still satisfied with the results of the recent online promotion.

(A) has not seen
(B) had not seen
(C) was not seen
(D) is not seeing

126. ------- and unit price were factored equally in selecting ABM Computers for our new notebooks.

(A) Accommodation
(B) Estimation
(C) Reliability
(D) Dependency

127. No one at Shackleton Incorporated lobbied ------- for the construction of the company parking lot than Garrett Nguyen.

(A) eagerly
(B) more eagerly
(C) more eager
(D) eager

128. Mr. Ramirez assured the directors that he would revise the document ------- by noon.

(A) ourselves
(B) themselves
(C) itself
(D) himself

129. ------- the expansion of the street is not complete, please use the rear entrance.

(A) In the event that
(B) Overall
(C) In response to
(D) Nevertheless

130. Barrow Road, Inc. ------- that its heaters are the most energy-efficient in the industry.

(A) compares
(B) claims
(C) features
(D) inquires

PART 6

Directions: Read the texts that follow. A word, phrase, or sentence is missing in parts of each text. Four answer choices for each question are given below the text. Select the best answer to complete the text. Then mark the letter (A), (B), (C), or (D) on your answer sheet.

Questions 131-134 refer to the following article.

TRA, Inc. Appoints New Director

Tokyo (10 March) – In a press conference this morning, a TRA representative announced that Hiro Musashi will take over as Director of Client Relations. Mr. Musashi will manage a department ------- business relationships with domestic and international companies.
                                                131.

TRA President Aiko Ogawa stated, "We look forward to working with Mr. Musashi, and we know he will ------- us to expand into different regions and create new partnerships."
                                132.

-------. When he was the business relations manager at Wango Solutions, he helped
133.
increase annual sales by an average of 5 percent every year.

TRA offers ------- for commercial computer networks in major cities across Japan. It
              134.
also services other areas in Asia and Europe.

---

131. (A) develops
(B) that develops
(C) its development
(D) is developing

132. (A) enable
(B) discern
(C) inform
(D) profit

133. (A) Mr. Musashi will be transferring to the headquarters in Tokyo.
(B) Mr. Musashi was previously the president of Wango Solutions.
(C) Mr. Musashi will be welcomed at a corporate party.
(D) Mr. Musashi joins TRA with nearly 20 years of industry experience.

134. (A) content
(B) support
(C) gifts
(D) courses

Questions 135-138 refer to the following e-mail.

To: Eric Bollman <ebollman@leihouma.com>
From: Nancy Jensen <njensen@leihouma.com>
Subject: Water Issue
Date: Monday, September 10

Welcome to Leihouma's San Francisco branch. I am in charge of ensuring that you adjust well to this new location.

------- . I am sorry that your bathroom sink is not working. I have arranged for a technician to come by your place tomorrow at 7 A.M., but this can be canceled if the issue is resolved before -------; please advise if this is the case. Also, be sure to present your company ------- when the technician visits your home.

I ------- you again to follow up and make sure that everything is working properly tomorrow morning.

Best Regards,

Nancy Jensen
HR Representative

135. (A) Ichiro Plumbing Co.'s representative can meet with you next Friday at 3 P.M.
(B) The water delivery service will be complimentary for the first month only.
(C) The quality of our drinking water has greatly improved.
(D) I got your message that you need to call for a plumber.

136. (A) early
(B) fast
(C) then
(D) there

137. (A) status
(B) identification
(C) video
(D) permit

138. (A) email
(B) had emailed
(C) will email
(D) would have emailed

Questions 139-142 refer to the following notice.

Lab Equipment: Glass Beaker Protocols

Due to its superior reusability, most of our lab equipment is made out of glass rather than plastic. -------, dissimilar to plastic, glass is quite fragile. As a result, special precautions need to be taken when performing experiments using tools composed of glass. In particular, when loading and unloading glass containers from the centrifuge, perform a brief check to ensure they are not chipped, scratched, or otherwise compromised. -------. While we are in the process of removing all equipment that does not meet the highest tolerance standards, including flasks ------- of soda-lime glass, some do remain in circulation. Should you come across one, do not attempt to use it. It is unlikely to be properly calibrated. Just remember to carefully wrap it in paper and place it in the green recycling box, instead of the receptacle for normal -------.

139. (A) In short
(B) On the other hand
(C) In this case
(D) Presumably

140. (A) This is one notable advantage that plastic containers have over glass.
(B) Glass beakers must be allowed to fully dry before use.
(C) They will need to be stored separately in the future.
(D) Before doing so, read all of the safety guidelines first.

141. (A) made
(B) make
(C) making
(D) makes

142. (A) process
(B) amount
(C) waste
(D) arrangement

Questions 143-146 refer to the following Web page.

Conveniently located next to City Hall in Lawrence, Kansas, the Coscia Foreign Studies Institute (CFSI) offers individual and group lessons to learners of all ages and nationalities. -------. **143.**

At present, CFSI offers individual classes in a variety of -------. You'll have a choice **144.** of Spanish, French, German, Arabic, and Chinese. ------- teach every skill for total **145.** competency, including listening, writing, reading, and of course, speaking. To find out about this month's special events and facility tours, call 785-555-1212. And remember to check out our instructor section, www.cosciafsi.edu/biographies, to learn ------- our **146.** teachers.

143. (A) Our instructors will ensure you receive the best education possible.
(B) The institute's registrar office closes earlier on Fridays.
(C) Your invoice lists all of your enrolled classes.
(D) The facility will undergo renovations next month.

144. (A) features
(B) languages
(C) advantages
(D) students

145. (A) Its
(B) You
(C) I
(D) We

146. (A) on
(B) about
(C) around
(D) to

PART 7

Directions: In this part you will read a selection of texts, such as magazine and newspaper articles, e-mails, and instant messages. Each text or set of texts is followed by several questions. Select the best answer for each question and mark the letter (A), (B), (C), or (D) on your answer sheet.

Questions 147-148 refer to the following online article.

---

http://www.yeoviltribune.co.uk/local

HELP US CROWN THE WINNER:
The Annual Yeovil's Best Poll

For the third year running, we're asking locals to help us select the very best businesses in the region. This year, all Yeovil residents can take part—not just subscribers.

Our staff has put together a list of nominees for best retail shop, café, restaurant, and inn. In each category, the top six were nominated based on a customer satisfaction survey. To see the survey results, click **here**.

To make your favorite candidate a winner, visit one of our many participating businesses this month and fill out a ballot. By taking part, you'll be helping promote the establishments that make our area special. Don't wait too long: voting ends on 9 May at 11:00 A.M.

---

147. What was the main purpose of this article?

(A) To ask businesses to donate money
(B) To encourage readers to make a choice
(C) To promote a new magazine subscription
(D) To name the winners of a contest

148. What is indicated about the Yeovil's Best Poll?

(A) It can be taken online.
(B) It offers a cash incentive to participants.
(C) It has six categories.
(D) It is conducted at several locations.

Questions 149-150 refer to the following text-message chain.

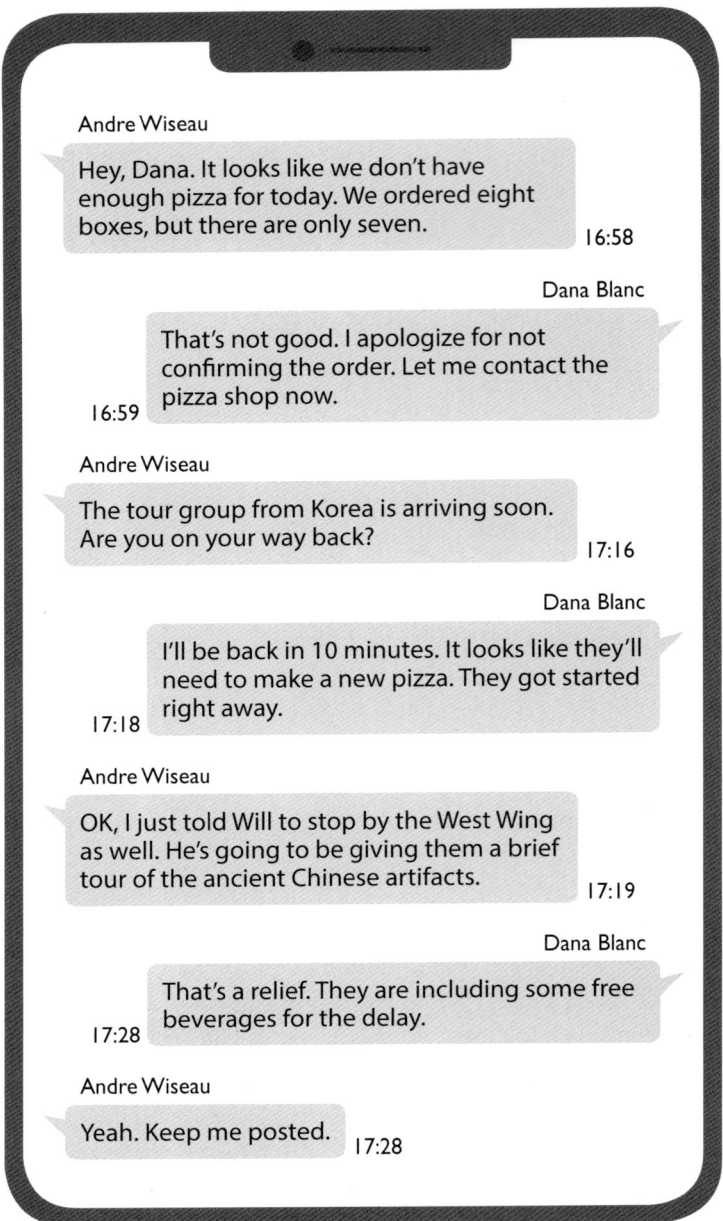

149. What is probably true about Mr. Wiseau?

(A) He is overseeing a tour group.
(B) He is skilled at making pizzas.
(C) He is employed at a history museum.
(D) He is going to purchase some beverages.

150. At 17:18, what does Ms. Blanc mean when she writes, "They got started right away"?

(A) Some drinks are being refilled.
(B) A new tour group just arrived.
(C) Some guests have begun eating a meal.
(D) An order is being handled quickly.

Questions 151-152 refer to the following advertisement.

The Supreme Multi-Tool – Everything You Need, Right In Your Pocket
$50.00

TOOLS

Needle-nose Pliers – Great for reaching into compact spaces and holding small objects

Wire Stripper – Safely strip the plastic coating around all types of wires

Knife – Made with high-carbon stainless steel that can cut through tough materials

Spring-action Scissors – Springs assist the cutting action and reduce hand strain

Can and Bottle Opener – Easily open canned goods or bottled drinks

Medium Screwdriver – Loosen or tighten any flathead screw

Includes a leather case for easy carrying in your pocket

---

151. What is mentioned about the needle-nose pliers?

(A) They can be used in tight areas.
(B) They cut through different types of materials.
(C) They tighten loose screws.
(D) They open metal containers.

152. What is indicated about The Supreme Multi-Tool?

(A) It comes in many colors.
(B) It comes with an accessory.
(C) It has a lifetime warranty.
(D) It has an easy-to-read manual.

GO ON TO THE NEXT PAGE

Questions 153-154 refer to the following e-mail.

From	Thomas Satoranksy
To	Antonia Montoya
Subject	Satoransky's Dealership
Date	June 2

Dear Ms. Montoya,

I met with Ronnie at your shop the other day to talk about my vintage sports car. I was impressed since I didn't know anyone could get old parts such as chrome bumpers these days. According to Ronnie, a plastic attachment to hold the hood ornament is coming in from California next week. When that's put on, the vehicle will be fully restored.

As I mentioned before, I'll need to have the automobile dropped off by June 10. On June 11, my dealership will hold its 20th anniversary celebration. This sports car is my business' main attraction. It's featured in our logo and all other promotional materials. The hood ornament is not needed to drive the car, but it would definitely make the vehicle look nicer.

Best,
Thomas

153. What is indicated about the sports car?

(A) It has an unreliable engine.
(B) It was made 20 years ago.
(C) It represents Santoransky's Dealership.
(D) It was created by Thomas Santoransky.

154. What is implied about the plastic attachment?

(A) It cannot be repaired.
(B) It is not required to operate a vehicle.
(C) It will no longer be produced in California.
(D) It is covered by a warranty.

Questions 155-157 refer to the following invoice.

DeLaurentis Security Systems

Billing Number: AHD84-1113
Appointment Date: March 25
Billed to: Antonia Brown (Due March 31)

On-Site Consultation (2 hours, $35/hour)	$70.00
Out-of-Area Service Request	$50.00
Subtotal	$120.00
Referral Code (25% off)	$24.00
Total Amount Due	$96.00

Let us know what you thought about your appointment! Send us feedback on Sonya Young's service via our mobile app, DL Secure, today. If you have any concerns or need more information regarding our billing procedure, contact Thomas Nwamba at tnwamba@delaurentissecuritysys.com.

---

155. What is indicated on the bill?

(A) It was issued on March 31.
(B) A fee was charged for at-location service.
(C) A consultation price was recently raised.
(D) It was given to a private corporation.

156. Why most likely did Ms. Brown get a discount?

(A) She has purchased products from the company before.
(B) Her order was placed during a March promotion.
(C) Her consultation took less than three hours.
(D) A previous customer recommended the service to her.

157. Who most likely provided the consultation?

(A) Ms. Brown
(B) Mr. DeLaurentis
(C) Ms. Young
(D) Mr. Nwamba

GO ON TO THE NEXT PAGE

Questions 158-160 refer to the following notice.

Douglas EasyBooks

Congratulations on purchasing the Douglas EasyBooks accounting program. Our application will save you time, allowing you to focus on being the best business you can be.

With your purchase, your business is eligible for a training seminar, free of charge. This three-part online training series is a great way to educate your staff on how to use the software effectively.

These brief but helpful sessions are conducted by trainers who have utilized our product to simplify practices at their own firms. To reserve your training seminar, log on to Douglaseasybooks.com/training today.

158. What is a purpose of the notice?

(A) To recruit some trainers
(B) To advertise a new book
(C) To explain some fees
(D) To describe a service

159. According to the notice, what qualification do the trainers possess?

(A) They have a graduate degree in economics.
(B) They have been employed at Douglas' EasyBooks for a long time.
(C) They helped develop the accounting program.
(D) They have experience using the accounting program.

160. The word "focus" in paragraph 1, line 2, is closest in meaning to

(A) concentrate
(B) direct
(C) adjust
(D) adopt

Questions 161-163 refer to the following e-mail.

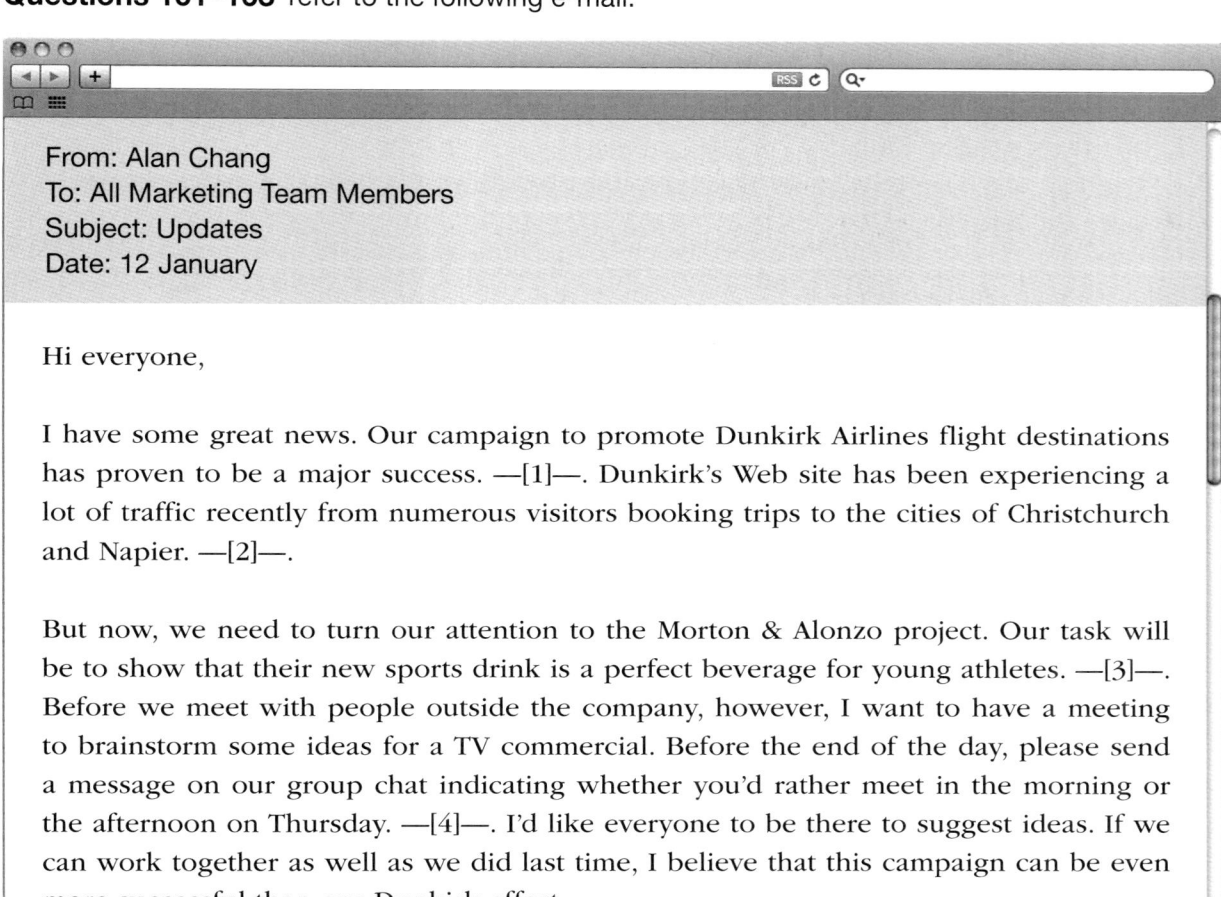

From: Alan Chang
To: All Marketing Team Members
Subject: Updates
Date: 12 January

Hi everyone,

I have some great news. Our campaign to promote Dunkirk Airlines flight destinations has proven to be a major success. —[1]—. Dunkirk's Web site has been experiencing a lot of traffic recently from numerous visitors booking trips to the cities of Christchurch and Napier. —[2]—.

But now, we need to turn our attention to the Morton & Alonzo project. Our task will be to show that their new sports drink is a perfect beverage for young athletes. —[3]—. Before we meet with people outside the company, however, I want to have a meeting to brainstorm some ideas for a TV commercial. Before the end of the day, please send a message on our group chat indicating whether you'd rather meet in the morning or the afternoon on Thursday. —[4]—. I'd like everyone to be there to suggest ideas. If we can work together as well as we did last time, I believe that this campaign can be even more successful than our Dunkirk effort.

Best regards,

Alan Chang
Director of Marketing

161. What is indicated as evidence that the Dunkirk Airline campaign was a success?

(A) An increase in membership subscriptions
(B) The number of positive customer testimonials
(C) The volume of vacation bookings
(D) A decrease in airline fares

162. What does Mr. Chang request that the marketing employees do?

(A) Develop a survey
(B) Confirm their availability
(C) Contact a travel agency
(D) Read a consumer report

163. In which of the positions marked [1], [2], [3], and [4] does the following sentence best belong?

"For this purpose, we plan to interview both athletes and nutritional consultants."

(A) [1]
(B) [2]
(C) [3]
(D) [4]

Questions 164-167 refer to the following online chat discussion.

Edith Crawley (12:38 P.M.)
Hey, Joan and Dave. Have either of you seen the latest data on the FPX-2220 air conditioner we're about to release?

Joan Mitchell (12:39 P.M.)
Just did. I was surprised that it could cool faster while also being more energy-efficient.

Dave Edison (12:40 P.M.)
I know! It's a shame I won't be able to show it at my meeting with Baez Systems.

Joan Mitchell (12:40 P.M.)
I emailed a copy to everyone in the department.

Edith Crawley (12:42 P.M.)
That's scheduled for 3:30, though. You should have enough time to pick out the most pertinent graphs and put them into a slideshow.

Dave Edison (12:44 P.M.)
The problem is I'm giving a training seminar at 1:00, and I'll have to drive out to the Baez's new main office immediately after. It's almost 30 miles away now.

Edith Crawley (12:45 P.M.)
I'd take care of it for you, but I'm already on my way to the airport.

Joan Mitchell (12:46 P.M.)
I'm on it. I'll make a file with the best charts and put it on a flash drive. Just make sure to pick it up from my desk before you go.

Edith Crawley (12:48 P.M.)
I hope the meeting is a success. If Baez agrees to a major purchase, it will definitely be worth celebrating.

Dave Edison (12:51 P.M.)
I appreciate your support!

164. What most likely is Mr. Edison's profession?

(A) Computer programmer
(B) Project manager
(C) Sales agent
(D) Repair technician

165. What will happen at 3:30 P.M.?

(A) A flight will take off.
(B) An application will be submitted.
(C) A meeting will be held.
(D) An award will be given.

166. What is implied about Baez Systems?

(A) It will soon release a new product.
(B) Ms. Crawley has many clients there.
(C) Mr. Edison was once employed there.
(D) Its headquarters was recently relocated.

167. At 12:46 P.M. what does Ms. Mitchell most likely mean when she writes, "I'm on it"?

(A) She will conduct a training session.
(B) She will send an e-mail.
(C) She will gather some data.
(D) She will create some visual aids.

Questions 168-171 refer to the following article.

Filling Up A Plate
At Cheesman Park

Eldorado, July 7 – Hayward's took home the award for Best Tasting Food at the Backyard Cook-off at Cheesman Park last Friday. It won first place among 11 contestants.

The Backyard Cook-off is a popular event, drawing participating restaurants and spectators from all over the greater Eldorado area. After a short introduction from the event organizer, Malcolm Jones, cooks from all the establishments began smoking and grilling meats all around the park. Attendees were given the opportunity to sample different types of barbecue from each restaurant. They were then asked to rate the food they had sampled. Later that night, after all the ratings were reviewed, everyone gathered for the awards presentation.

Hayward's continued its string of successes at this year's event. Last year, their smoky pulled pork came in second, and the year before, their spicy chicken took third place. Be sure to try both when you visit their restaurant.

Hayward's recently celebrated its 10th anniversary in Eldorado. During its first year of business, Hayward's was just a barbecue smoker and a couple of picnic tables outside a local supermarket. Now, they operate in a space that fits up to 40 families.

Before Hayward's received their prize, the winners for second place and third place were announced. Rattlesnake Barbecue took home the latter honor, while Joe's Smokehouse won second for their brisket.

168. What kind of event is mentioned in the article?

(A) The opening of a new location in south Eldorado
(B) A food sale to collect donations for charity
(C) A celebration for a newly-elected government official
(D) A cooking competition featuring local businesses

169. According to the article, what probably happened on Friday night?

(A) Rattlesnake Barbecue moved to a new location.
(B) Joe's Smokehouse bought a new grill.
(C) Hayward's was given an award.
(D) Cheesman Park closed early for the day.

170. What is true about Hayward's?

(A) It raises its own chickens.
(B) It was recognized in two previous Backyard Cook-offs.
(C) It sells its products to supermarkets in the Eldorado area.
(D) It is owned by Malcolm Jones.

171. What is suggested about Rattlesnake Barbecue?

(A) It got lower ratings than Joe's Smokehouse.
(B) It was started by a chef who was previously employed at Hayward's.
(C) It is a family-run business.
(D) It is famous for its brisket dish.

GO ON TO THE NEXT PAGE

Questions 172-175 refer to the following Web page.

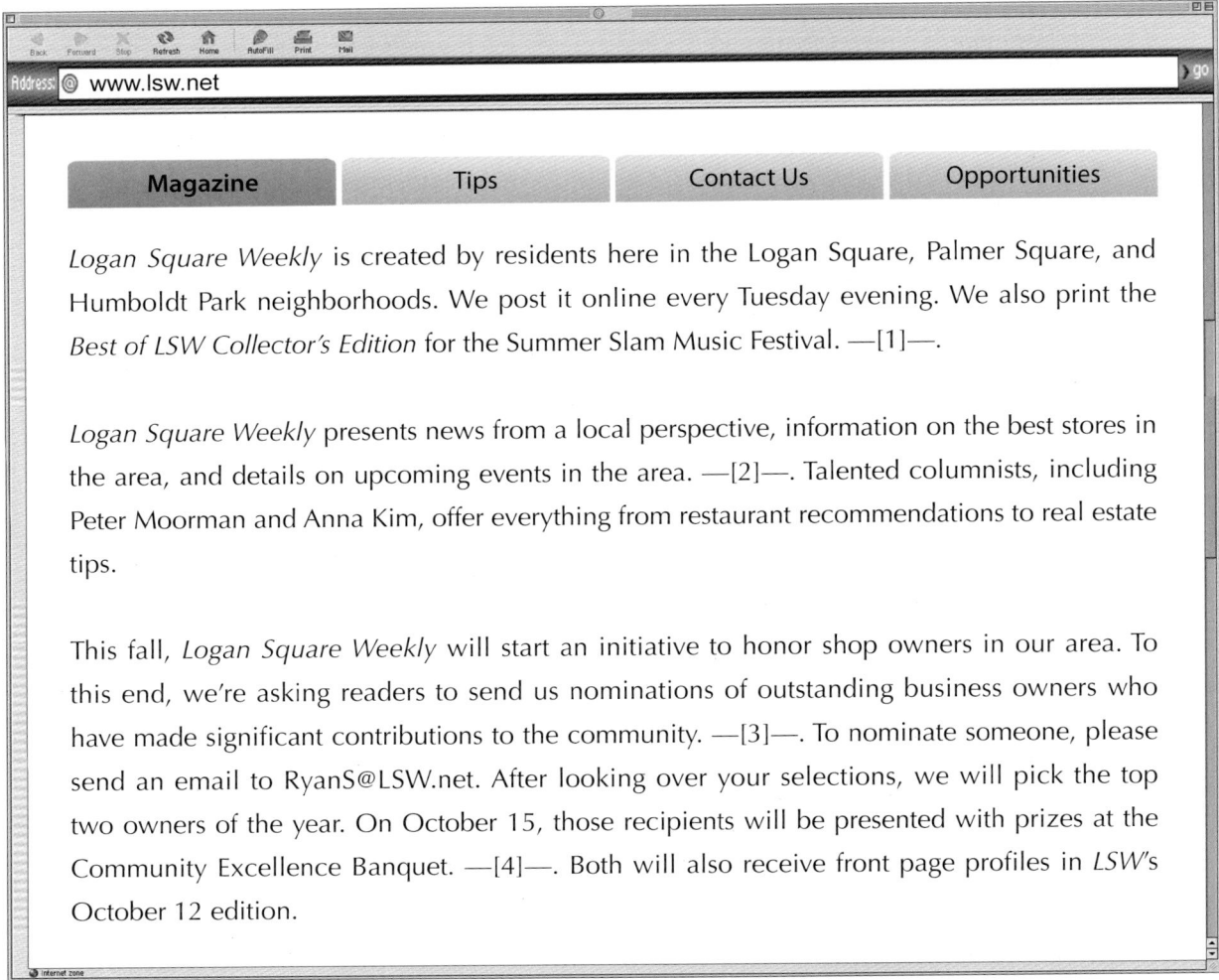

| Magazine | Tips | Contact Us | Opportunities |

Logan Square Weekly is created by residents here in the Logan Square, Palmer Square, and Humboldt Park neighborhoods. We post it online every Tuesday evening. We also print the *Best of LSW Collector's Edition* for the Summer Slam Music Festival. —[1]—.

Logan Square Weekly presents news from a local perspective, information on the best stores in the area, and details on upcoming events in the area. —[2]—. Talented columnists, including Peter Moorman and Anna Kim, offer everything from restaurant recommendations to real estate tips.

This fall, *Logan Square Weekly* will start an initiative to honor shop owners in our area. To this end, we're asking readers to send us nominations of outstanding business owners who have made significant contributions to the community. —[3]—. To nominate someone, please send an email to RyanS@LSW.net. After looking over your selections, we will pick the top two owners of the year. On October 15, those recipients will be presented with prizes at the Community Excellence Banquet. —[4]—. Both will also receive front page profiles in *LSW*'s October 12 edition.

172. What is the purpose of the Web page?

(A) To advertise a community publication
(B) To describe a restaurant opening
(C) To explain a local election
(D) To announce a concert schedule

173. What new feature is being announced?

(A) A new column for financial advice
(B) A Web chat service
(C) A plan to recognize store owners
(D) A property listing page

174. What will happen on October 15?

(A) An article will be published.
(B) City officials will be appointed.
(C) A new shop will open.
(D) Prizes will be distributed.

175. In which of the positions marked [1], [2], [3], and [4] does the following sentence best belong?

"As always, it will be available for purchase for $1 throughout the event."

(A) [1]
(B) [2]
(C) [3]
(D) [4]

Questions 176-180 refer to the following advertisement and e-mail.

Chanthavong Thai Boxing Academy
12856 Salmon River Road
San Diego, CA 92129
858-555-1212

Thank you for your interest in Chanthavong Thai Boxing Academy. We are now accepting students for the coming year. Memberships will be effective from January 1 through December 31.

Class Levels:
- Just for Kicks (JFK): JFK students will get an introduction to kickboxing training Wednesday and Friday nights from 7:00 to 8:00 P.M. The class emphasizes conditioning and etiquette. Students will also learn three basic punches and two basic kicks.

- High Beginner Class (HBC): HBC students continue their study of Thai boxing on Monday and Wednesday nights from 7:30 to 8:30 P.M. Students will work mainly on the heavy bag ("sandbag"), and a variety of punching and kicking combinations will be introduced.

- Intermediate Boxing Training (IBT): IBT students will focus heavily on training with a partner. Sparring is encouraged but not mandatory. Class meets on Tuesday and Thursday nights from 6:00 P.M. to 7:00 P.M.

- Nak Muay Thai (NMT): NMT students are the Academy's competition team. Participation in the Academy's Winter Tournament and Summer Tournament is required, as is attendance at five weekly practices: Monday through Thursday from 8:00 P.M. to 9:00 P.M., and Saturdays from 4:00 P.M. to 6:00 P.M.

No classes are held on Sundays, but the Academy is open from 9:00 A.M. to 7:00 P.M. for independent practice.

All members get an academy T-shirt, free tickets to the semi-annual tournaments, and a 20 percent discount on gloves and other training supplies.

To	Diana Langley <dlangley@ujjp.com>
From	Sakda Khongsawatwaja <s.khongsawatwaja@ctba.com>
Date	December 12
Subject	Next year's memberships
Attachment	form.doc

Dear Ms. Langley,

We are very glad to have your son, Tony, and your daughter, Josephine, as students this coming year. We will start Tony out in the Just for Kicks (JFK) class—we're sure he'll love it and advance quickly!

Josephine, on the other hand, is qualified for our competition team. Since this involves hard training and full-contact sparring, we do require a special consent form from participants' parents. Please sign and return the attached form at the information session for parents on December 20.

Best Regards,

Sakda Khongsawatwaja
Head Instructor,
Chanthavong Thai Boxing Academy

176. What is NOT stated as a benefit for a Chanthavong Thai Boxing Academy membership?

(A) A free clothing item
(B) Complimentary admission to tournaments
(C) Reduced rates on personal instruction
(D) Discounted training equipment

177. What is mentioned about Chanthavong Thai Boxing Academy?

(A) It has morning classes.
(B) Its instructors are former professional athletes.
(C) It provides weekly practice opportunities.
(D) Its facility was recently expanded.

178. Why did Mr. Khongsawatwaja write to Ms. Langley?

(A) To announce her children's placements
(B) To ask that she pay her children's membership fee
(C) To advertise new merchandise at the academy
(D) To explain a new registration process

179. On what day will both of Ms. Langley's children most likely be at the academy?

(A) Monday
(B) Tuesday
(C) Wednesday
(D) Thursday

180. What will Josephine most likely do next year?

(A) Work part-time at a sports stadium
(B) Enter two competitions
(C) Participate in an information session
(D) Advance to the High Beginner Class

GO ON TO THE NEXT PAGE

Questions 181-185 refer to the following Web page and e-mail.

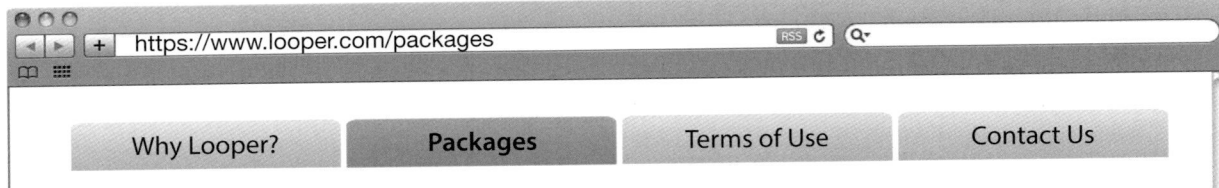

| Why Looper? | Packages | Terms of Use | Contact Us |

Looper is an online platform perfect for both startups and large corporations. Our project management software will maximize your company's efficiency and productivity by keeping your employees connected and informed on your company's daily activities.

STARTUP PACKAGE
Ideal for startups with fewer than 100 employees. Use our mobile and desktop versions with built-in messaging and file sharing functions, group calendars, and 10 GB of cloud storage for each team member.

PREMIUM PACKAGE
Recommended for businesses with fewer than 500 employees. In addition to all the features from the Startup Package, gain access to features such as the discussion board, portfolio management, project status tracking, and 20 GB of cloud storage for each team member.

CORPORATE PACKAGE
Perfect for companies with up to 800 staff members. On top of the features from the Premium Package, enjoy activity feeds, the ability to send out surveys and feedback, and one-on-one video conferencing, as well as 35 GB of cloud storage for each team member.

MULTINATIONAL PACKAGE
This plan is for companies with over 1,000 employees. In addition to all of the features from the Corporate Package, enjoy audio and video conferencing with up to 20 participants with interactive screen sharing, 24/7 customer support help, synchronized editing for documents, and 50 GB of storage for each employee.

Sign up for a free one-month trial. By the end of your trial, you'll see why some of the largest and most successful companies in the world choose our software over the competitors'. For more information on which package is right for you, click on the Contact Us tab to speak with our sales associate.

FROM p.malkin@capsun.ca
TO a.crosby@looper.com
DATE May 19
SUBJECT Looper Packages

Dear Ms. Crosby,

My name is Paul Malkin, and I'm the Chief Strategy Officer at Capsun Industries. We have been using Looper for the past five years, and I can't stress enough how important your software has been to our growth. We've recently finalized plans to expand, and we will soon have over 1,300 staff members across Canada. We've made good use of the cloud storage that your company offers, but we're going to be needing more than 35 GB per employee now, as well as a better way to track work progress. Do you have anything that is tailored to this?

I look forward to your response.

Paul Malkin
Chief Strategy Officer
Capsun Industries

---

181. How would Looper software most likely be used?

(A) For hiring new employees
(B) For advertising goods online
(C) For providing assistance to clients
(D) For improving staff productivity

182. What is true about Looper?

(A) Its products are used by major companies.
(B) It has merged with Capsun Industries.
(C) Its first line of software was released five years ago.
(D) It has over 200 employees.

183. What is the purpose of the e-mail?

(A) To confirm the purchase of an item
(B) To get advice on selecting a product
(C) To complain about some program issues
(D) To request an updated user manual

184. Which product will Ms. Crosby most likely recommend?

(A) The Startup Package
(B) The Premium Package
(C) The Corporate Package
(D) The Multinational Package

185. In the e-mail, the word "stress" in paragraph 1, line 2, is closest in meaning to

(A) anticipate
(B) worry
(C) emphasize
(D) pressure

Questions 186-190 refer to the following e-mails and rate sheet.

From: Maggie Jones<maggiejones@albanytours.ca>
To: David Davis<daviddavis@orourkeschools.edu>
Subject: April Tournament Estimate
Date: 6 March
Attachment: ORourke_April.pdf; EntertainmentOptions.pdf

Hi David,

We really enjoyed putting together the school trip this past December, and we appreciate the opportunity to make arrangements for the Edmonton Bears for this month's Provincial Hockey Playoffs. We were able to find a hotel near the venue to meet your request for an open-ended reservation, which I understand is required since the duration of the team's stay will be determined by the stage they reach in the competition.

You'll find an attachment that details the rates below. I've also included some pamphlets describing local tourist attractions and recommended activities.

I appreciate your continued business.

Best,
Maggie B. Jones

The Alpine Inn, Richview

Check-in Date: 21 April
Guests: Edmonton Bears (student-athletes, team managers, and coaches)
Contact Person: David Davis (818) 555-3143

Competition Round	Total Length of Stay	Total Room Rate Per Round
Round 1	5 nights	$10,000
Round 2	4 nights	$8,000
Round 3	3 nights	$6,000
Finals	2 nights	$4,000
Charges are due at the end of each stage. Your daily group rate is $2,000 per night.		

From: David Davis<daviddavis@orourkeschools.edu>
To: Maggie Jones<maggiejones@albanytours.ca>
Date: 27 April
Subject: April Event

Maggie,

Thanks for sending over the updated itemized bill for the team trip. My assistant visited your office earlier in the afternoon and dropped off a check for $6,000 as agreed. Regarding the trip, I want to thank you. Everything went very smoothly with lodging, food, and transportation, and we especially loved the horse-riding tour you suggested. The team had so much fun taking photos with the animals afterwards.

I'll let you know about our next trip soon. It will likely be in October, but I'll fill you in when I get the details.

David Davis

---

186. Who most likely is Ms. Jones?

(A) A hockey coach
(B) A hotel employee
(C) A school official
(D) A travel agent

187. What is true about the room rates sent to Mr. Davis?

(A) They do not change by the length of stay.
(B) They include a free morning meal.
(C) They are only provided to sports teams.
(D) They have increased recently.

188. According to the second e-mail, what is indicated about Mr. Davis' payment?

(A) It was paid in person.
(B) It was made in installments.
(C) It was higher than expected.
(D) It was made for an October trip.

189. What did Mr. Davis most likely do with the pamphlets Ms. Jones sent?

(A) He updated the information.
(B) He distributed them to the Edmonton Bears.
(C) He requested that more copies be made of them.
(D) He emailed them to a colleague.

190. What was the last round of the competition that the Edmonton Bears participated in?

(A) Round 1
(B) Round 2
(C) Round 3
(D) Finals

Questions 191-195 refer to the following article, Web page, and online order form.

BROOKLYN (September 25) — A recently launched app is changing the way people eat in the Williamsburg neighborhood. Thrive Fresh is a food delivery app started by a local Jason Vernon. The app gives users access to detailed nutritional and sourcing information on hundreds of menu items from a diverse range of local kitchens. For a monthly fee, it can also track users' orders and make dietary recommendations based on their needs and preferences.

Mr. Vernon got the idea when he noticed how greasy the food from traditional delivery services tended to be. "Whenever my former coworkers and I stayed late at work—which was quite often—we would order food, but it hardly ever had any fresh ingredients. Most of us tried to watch what we ate, but when it came to delivery, we were in the dark."

In response, Mr. Vernon developed a system that promoted transparency and wellness. Thrive Fresh works with local food providers that exclusively sell organic dishes. Its wide variety of healthy options and affordable prices have helped the service build a large and loyal customer base. The app still only delivers to users in the Williamsburg area but will expand to the rest of New York City in December.

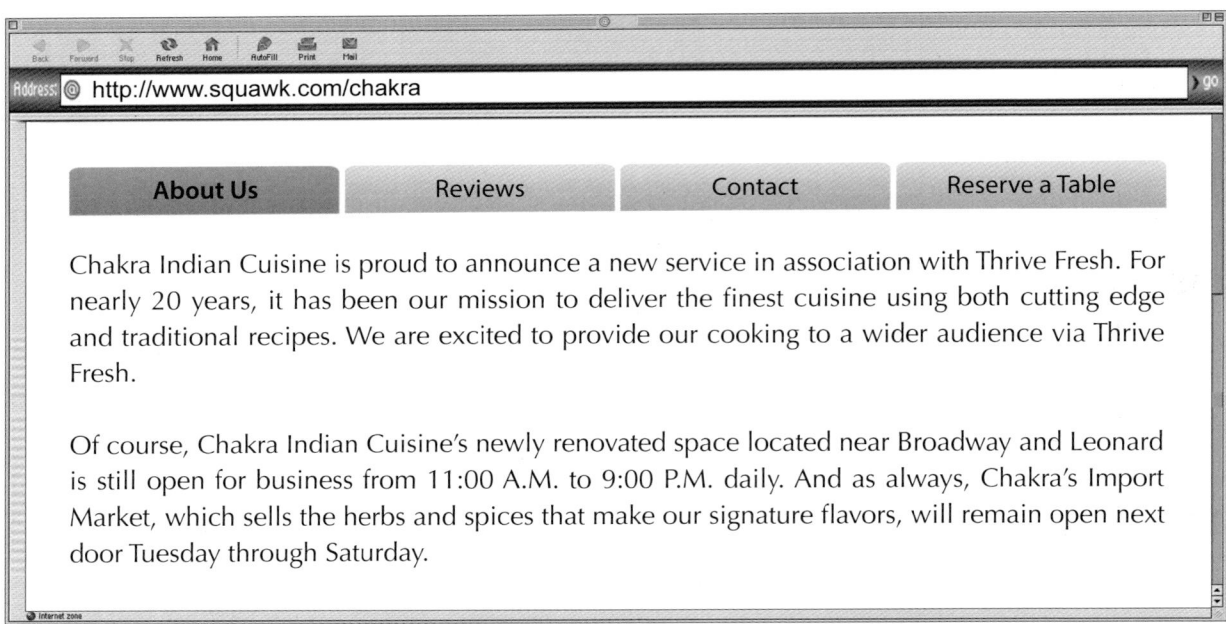

http://www.squawk.com/chakra

| About Us | Reviews | Contact | Reserve a Table |

Chakra Indian Cuisine is proud to announce a new service in association with Thrive Fresh. For nearly 20 years, it has been our mission to deliver the finest cuisine using both cutting edge and traditional recipes. We are excited to provide our cooking to a wider audience via Thrive Fresh.

Of course, Chakra Indian Cuisine's newly renovated space located near Broadway and Leonard is still open for business from 11:00 A.M. to 9:00 P.M. daily. And as always, Chakra's Import Market, which sells the herbs and spices that make our signature flavors, will remain open next door Tuesday through Saturday.

Thrive Fresh Order Confirmation

Order:
Manpasand Quinoa Salad	$7.00
Spinach Kofta Curry	$12.00
Dal Makhani	$13.00
Food	$32.00
Membership Discount	-$3.20
Tax	$1.06
Total	**$30.05**

(Payment at the door via credit card)

Name: Jill Klein
Address: 169 Lynch St., Apartment 3B
Phone: 718-555-9922
Delivery Time: Between 14:35-14:50, September 29

---

191. What is the article mainly about?

(A) What diet plan will help readers lead a healthy lifestyle
(B) Where inexpensive groceries can be bought
(C) How a meal service app was founded
(D) Why a restaurant became successful

192. According to the article, what is one reason Thrive Fresh is popular?

(A) Its quick delivery times
(B) Its high-quality user interface
(C) Its 24-hour availability
(D) Its reasonable prices

193. What is announced on Chakra Indian Cuisine's Web page?

(A) A new location
(B) A business partnership
(C) Some job openings
(D) Some upcoming renovations

194. What is most likely true about Chakra Indian Cuisine?

(A) It only sells organic dishes.
(B) It is only available through Thrive Fresh.
(C) It has been open for 20 years.
(D) It has multiple locations.

195. What is implied about Ms. Klein?

(A) She follows a strict nutritional plan.
(B) She is one of Mr. Vernon's colleagues.
(C) She lives in Williamsburg.
(D) She is hosting an event on September 29.

GO ON TO THE NEXT PAGE

Questions 196-200 refer to the following online form, e-mail, and Web page.

---

www.nguyensportswear.vn/service

Please fill out the information below, followed by your detailed feedback. Thank you for allowing us to serve you better.

Name: Hassina Boulmerka
E-mail: hassina.b@elwatan.vn
Phone number: 514-555-1212

Feedback:
I've been purchasing items from Nguyen Sportswear ever since you had your original offline shop in Ho Chi Minh City, and I have always been satisfied. For that reason, I was surprised and disappointed by my most recent order. Once the sweatshirt arrived, it was clear right away that it was made from a cheaper—and less comfortable—material than before. To make matters worse, after I had worn it just a couple of times, the fabric in the sleeve near the elbow wore down and tore open!

To:	hassina.b@elwatan.vn
From:	ggruber@nguyensportswear.vn
Date:	23 May
Subject:	Your feedback

Dear Ms. Boulmerka,

I am sorry to find out that your most recent experience was not positive. In hopes of providing the quality our clients require at even lower prices, we recently outsourced some of our manufacturing operations to another firm. Since our standards have not been met, we are re-evaluating our current arrangement.

We are sending you a voucher for an amount equal to that of your original purchase, and we would also like to offer you one of our popular 495-Z sweatshirts, free of charge, as an apology and a token of our appreciation. This item, created from our special durable fabric, is guaranteed to endure extreme conditions and last for a long time. Simply reply to this e-mail with your desired size and color.

We hope you will continue to do business with us in the future.

Best Regards,

Glenn Gruber
Client Service Associate

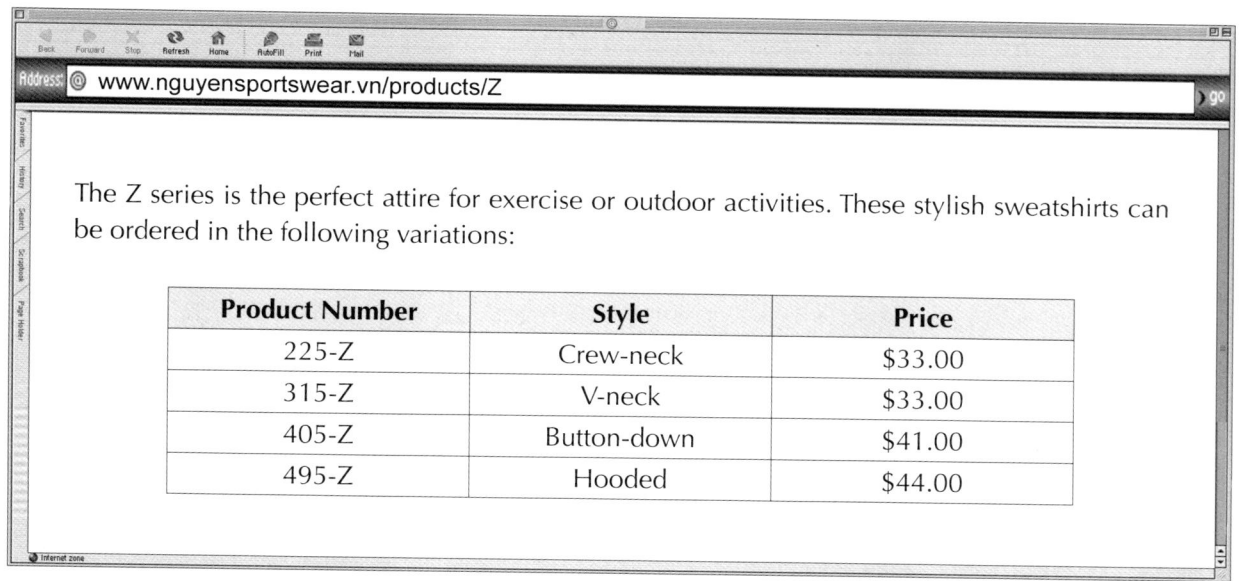

196. What is Ms. Boulmerka's main problem?

(A) Some prices have increased.
(B) The quality of an item has declined.
(C) An order was delivered late.
(D) A Web site did not work.

197. What is implied about some of Nguyen Sportswear's merchandise?

(A) They have been sold at a lower price than other product lines.
(B) They have been produced by another company.
(C) They are not designed for athletes.
(D) They are currently not in stock.

198. What is indicated about the Z series?

(A) It wears out more quickly than other items.
(B) It was manufactured in Ho Chi Minh City.
(C) It is made of a unique material.
(D) It recently added some new options.

199. What is Ms. Boulmerka asked to do?

(A) Provide her order preferences
(B) Drop by a store
(C) Use a different credit card
(D) Return some clothing items

200. What type of sweatshirt does Mr. Gruber offer to Ms. Boulmerka?

(A) Crew-neck
(B) V-neck
(C) Button-down
(D) Hooded

Stop! This is the end of the test. If you finish before time is called, you may go back to Part 5, 6, and 7 and check your work.

TEST 04

MP3 바로 듣기

1타 강사 강의듣기

준비물: OMR 카드, 연필, 지우개, 시계
시험시간: LC 약 45분 / RC 75분

나의 점수		
	LC	RC
맞은 개수		
환산 점수		

총점: _____ 점

TEST 1	TEST 2	TEST 3	TEST 4	TEST 5
_____점	_____점	_____점	_____점	_____점

점수 환산표

LC		RC	
맞은 개수	환산 점수	맞은 개수	환산 점수
96-100	475-495	96-100	460-495
91-95	435-195	91-95	425-490
86-90	405-475	86-90	395-465
81-85	370-450	81-85	370-440
76-80	345-420	76-80	335-415
71-75	320-390	71-75	310-390
66-70	290-360	66-70	280-365
61-65	265-335	61-65	250-335
56-60	235-310	56-60	220-305
51-55	210-280	51-55	195-270
46-50	180-255	46-50	165-240
41-45	155-230	41-45	140-215
36-40	125-205	36-40	115-180
31-35	105-175	31-35	95-145
36-30	85-145	36-30	75-120
21-25	60-115	21-25	60-95
16-20	30-90	16-20	45-75
11-15	5-70	11-15	30-55
6-10	5-60	6-10	10-40
1-5	5-60	1-5	5-30
0	5-35	0	5-15

LISTENING TEST

In the Listening test, you will be asked to demonstrate how well you understand spoken English. The entire listening test will last approximately 45 minutes. There are four parts, and directions are given for each part. You must mark your answers on the separate answer sheet. Do not write your answers in your test book.

PART 1

Directions: For each question in this part, you will hear four statements about a picture in your test book. When you hear the statements, you must select the one statement that best describes what you see in the picture. Then find the number of the question on your answer sheet and mark your answer. The statements will not be printed in your test book and will be spoken only one time.

Statement (B), "A man is pointing at a document," is the best description of the picture, so you should select answer (B) and mark it on your answer sheet.

1.

2.

3.

4.

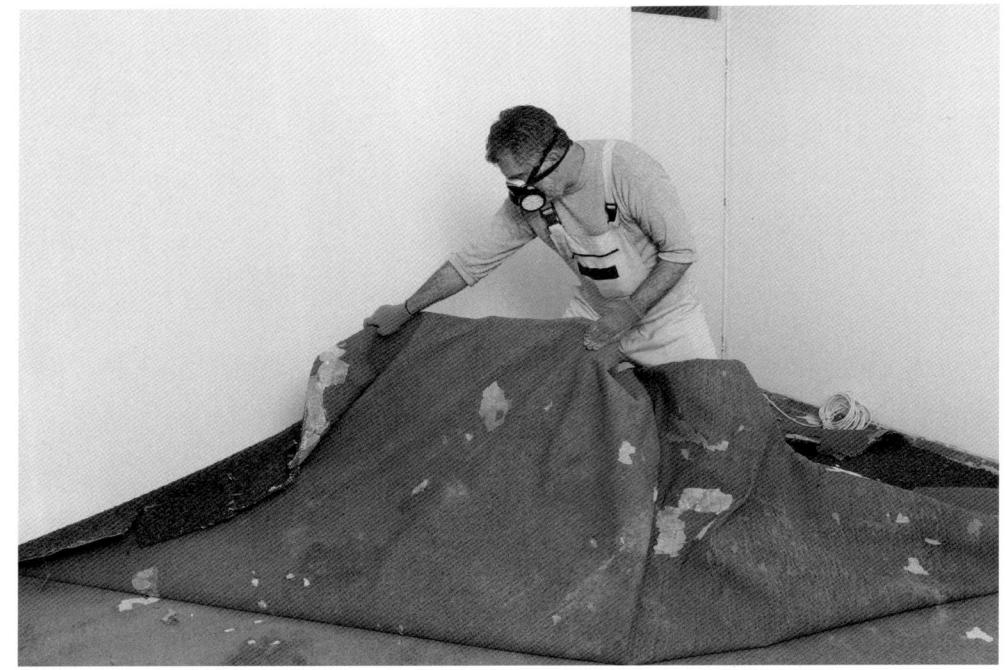

5.

6.

PART 2

Directions: You will hear a question or statement and three responses spoken in English. They will not be printed in your test book and will be spoken only one time. Select the best response to the question or statement and mark the letter (A), (B), or (C) on your answer sheet.

7. Mark your answer on your answer sheet.
8. Mark your answer on your answer sheet.
9. Mark your answer on your answer sheet.
10. Mark your answer on your answer sheet.
11. Mark your answer on your answer sheet.
12. Mark your answer on your answer sheet.
13. Mark your answer on your answer sheet.
14. Mark your answer on your answer sheet.
15. Mark your answer on your answer sheet.
16. Mark your answer on your answer sheet.
17. Mark your answer on your answer sheet.
18. Mark your answer on your answer sheet.
19. Mark your answer on your answer sheet.
20. Mark your answer on your answer sheet.
21. Mark your answer on your answer sheet.
22. Mark your answer on your answer sheet.
23. Mark your answer on your answer sheet.
24. Mark your answer on your answer sheet.
25. Mark your answer on your answer sheet.
26. Mark your answer on your answer sheet.
27. Mark your answer on your answer sheet.
28. Mark your answer on your answer sheet.
29. Mark your answer on your answer sheet.
30. Mark your answer on your answer sheet.
31. Mark your answer on your answer sheet.

PART 3

Directions: You will hear some conversations between two or more people. You will be asked to answer three questions about what the speakers say in each conversation. Select the best response to each question and mark the letter (A), (B), (C), or (D) on your answer sheet. The conversations will not be printed in your test book and will be spoken only one time.

32. What sort of merchandise are the speakers discussing?

    (A) A vehicle
    (B) A mobile phone
    (C) Some fitness equipment
    (D) Some office furniture

33. What still needs to be decided?

    (A) A name
    (B) A marketing campaign
    (C) A launch date
    (D) A price

34. What does the man recommend doing?

    (A) Speaking with coworkers
    (B) Scheduling a meeting
    (C) Revising a deadline
    (D) Modifying some features

35. What is the subject of the conversation?

    (A) The expansion of a business
    (B) Responses to a questionnaire
    (C) An annual budget
    (D) Potential job candidates

36. What does the woman say is the main problem?

    (A) An application is difficult to use.
    (B) A team is understaffed.
    (C) Some expenses are too high.
    (D) Some employees are not motivated.

37. What does the man recommend doing?

    (A) Upgrading some hardware
    (B) Talking to a security officer
    (C) Posting an explanation
    (D) Redesigning a Web site

38. Why is the man calling?

    (A) To discuss an extra charge
    (B) To purchase some supplies
    (C) To register for a business conference
    (D) To follow up on a renovation project

39. What did the woman recently do?

    (A) She sold her company.
    (B) She published a book.
    (C) She came back from a trip.
    (D) She designed a new product.

40. What will happen in the first week of March?

    (A) Some prices will be finalized.
    (B) Some interviews will take place.
    (C) A workshop will be held.
    (D) A client will visit.

41. In which department does the man work?

    (A) Design
    (B) Sales
    (C) Finance
    (D) Editorial

42. What does the man say is the cause for a change in consumer habits?

    (A) The availability of better technology
    (B) Improved economic conditions
    (C) The need for a cleaner environment
    (D) Increased fuel costs

43. What do the speakers agree on?

    (A) Hosting an online workshop
    (B) Discontinuing a service
    (C) Hiring a new marketing agency
    (D) Renovating an office

GO ON TO THE NEXT PAGE

44. What are the speakers mainly discussing?

(A) A county event
(B) A recent transaction
(C) Monthly salaries
(D) New laws

45. What does the woman suggest?

(A) Contacting a government worker
(B) Providing some training
(C) Working extra hours
(D) Reviewing some forms

46. What does the woman say some accountants will be doing on Friday?

(A) Visiting some banks
(B) Participating in a convention
(C) Going to another branch
(D) Meeting with some clients

---

47. Where does the conversation most likely take place?

(A) At a clothing accessory store
(B) At an antique shop
(C) At a sporting goods retailer
(D) At a baseball stadium

48. What is Baton Co. known for?

(A) Selling affordable products
(B) Hiring qualified employees
(C) Operating for a long time
(D) Receiving a prize

49. What additional benefit does an item have?

(A) It includes a cleaning tool.
(B) It comes with a large carrying bag.
(C) It includes a 10-year warranty.
(D) It comes with an online discount voucher.

50. What feature of the shoes is the man pleased about?

(A) The comfortable soles
(B) The eco-friendly materials
(C) The cost
(D) The patterns

51. Why does the man say, "Tina told me not to make design changes to the boots"?

(A) To mention that a budget is limited
(B) To report that Tina will revise a sketch
(C) To point out that a product is selling well
(D) To give a reason for not doing a task

52. What will the woman send to Tina?

(A) Some sales data
(B) Some new designs
(C) A guest list
(D) A project proposal

---

53. Where do the speakers probably work?

(A) At a law firm
(B) At a publishing company
(C) At a high school
(D) At a broadcasting agency

54. What is the main topic of the conversation?

(A) A revised contract
(B) Some award nominees
(C) A retiring employee
(D) Some budget figures

55. Why is the man relieved?

(A) A project will get additional funding.
(B) A client is pleased with some work.
(C) He will receive more help with an assignment.
(D) He has enough time to make a selection.

56. Who most likely is the woman?

(A) A realtor
(B) An engineer
(C) An office manager
(D) A maintenance worker

57. Why is the man disappointed?

(A) A schedule cannot be adjusted.
(B) Some locations are too pricey.
(C) Some fixtures are broken.
(D) An employee is not available.

58. What will the speakers do on Thursday?

(A) View a property
(B) Set a deadline
(C) Review a budget
(D) Attend a conference

---

59. Why does the man say, "Samantha, you've been here a long time, right"?

(A) To ask for assistance
(B) To compliment a colleague
(C) To accept a recommendation
(D) To request approval

60. What did the man do yesterday?

(A) He revised a document.
(B) He participated in a workshop.
(C) He downloaded an update.
(D) He met with a customer.

61. What will the man most likely do next?

(A) Sign up for a training session
(B) Check out a Web site
(C) Book a meeting room
(D) Contact the IT Department

Business Proposal

Section 1	Description of Business
Section 2	Location and Facilities
Section 3	Industry Trends
Section 4	Profit Forecast
Section 5	Marketing

62. What type of business does the woman want to start?

(A) A travel agency
(B) A fitness center
(C) A market research company
(D) A financial planning firm

63. According to the woman, what did she learn from her last business?

(A) How to choose an ideal location
(B) How to design effective ads
(C) How to establish a loyal customer base
(D) How to obtain a business license

64. Look at the graphic. According to the man, which section of the business proposal should be revised?

(A) Section 2
(B) Section 3
(C) Section 4
(D) Section 5

GO ON TO THE NEXT PAGE

Invoice	
Work Description	Price
Oil change	$30
Windshield repair	$70
Battery replacement	$120
Tire installation	$600

65. Why is the woman calling?

(A) To set up a maintenance inspection
(B) To inquire about a special deal
(C) To purchase some supplies
(D) To receive help with a program

66. Look at the graphic. Which price will be changed?

(A) $30
(B) $70
(C) $120
(D) $600

67. What does the man recommend that the woman do next time?

(A) Pay with a credit card
(B) Use an online communication service
(C) View a video tutorial
(D) Check some customer testimonials

Geller's Grocery Store
Recognizing Achievements

- 5 years rated as Top Small Business
- 20 years run by the current owner
- 50 years in the same location
- 80 years in operation

68. Where does the man most likely work?

(A) At a delivery company
(B) At a grocery store
(C) At a convention center
(D) At a printing business

69. Look at the graphic. Which achievement is the man amazed by?

(A) Years rated as Top Small Business
(B) Years run by the current owner
(C) Years in the same location
(D) Years in operation

70. What will the woman have to pay extra for?

(A) On-site installation
(B) Express shipping
(C) A rental vehicle
(D) Special supplies

PART 4

Directions: You will hear some talks given by a single speaker. You will be asked to answer three questions about what the speaker says in each talk. Select the best response to each question and mark the letter (A), (B), (C), or (D) on your answer sheet. The talks will not be printed in your test book and will be spoken only one time.

71. Where will the tour take place?

(A) At a crafts workshop
(B) At a research laboratory
(C) At an art gallery
(D) At a photo studio

72. What should the listeners avoid doing?

(A) Talking to the designers
(B) Using their mobile phones
(C) Bringing food with them
(D) Wandering away from the group

73. What does the speaker request the listeners to do?

(A) Provide some feedback
(B) Browse a souvenir store
(C) Sign up for a membership
(D) Enter a competition

74. What business most likely created the message?

(A) An employment agency
(B) An insurance company
(C) A doctor's office
(D) A law firm

75. What is mentioned about the business?

(A) It is being remodeled.
(B) It will be relocating.
(C) It will have new business hours.
(D) It is closed due to a holiday.

76. What does the speaker instruct the listeners to do?

(A) Go to a Web site
(B) Leave a message
(C) Call at another time
(D) Submit some forms

77. Why does the speaker thank the listeners?

(A) For working extra hours
(B) For meeting a sales target
(C) For subscribing to a magazine
(D) For responding to a survey

78. What has the company decided to do?

(A) Update some software
(B) Postpone an event
(C) Revise a company policy
(D) Expand office space

79. According to the speaker, what will the listeners probably do next month?

(A) Participate in performance evaluations
(B) Work from other locations
(C) Meet new personnel
(D) Attend a trade show

80. Why was the listener's application most likely rejected?

(A) She does not have enough work experience.
(B) She does not know a specific language.
(C) She is not able to work on weekends.
(D) She is not able to move to another city.

81. What does the speaker imply when he says, "they've already started interviewing people"?

(A) Action should be taken soon.
(B) Interviews cannot be rescheduled.
(C) A department has already hired someone.
(D) A job is more difficult than expected.

82. What does the speaker offer to do?

(A) Book a room
(B) Forward a document
(C) Visit an office
(D) Call an applicant

GO ON TO THE NEXT PAGE

83. Who most likely is the talk intended for?

(A) Automotive mechanics
(B) Factory employees
(C) Sales associates
(D) Computer technicians

84. What does the speaker imply when he says, "They probably have limited knowledge about it"?

(A) The listeners should explain a topic clearly.
(B) The listeners should show a video.
(C) The listeners should attend a seminar.
(D) The listeners should meet with an expert.

85. What does the speaker remind the listeners about?

(A) Hiring staff members
(B) Meeting a quota
(C) Printing out a document
(D) Cutting some costs

86. What is the talk mainly about?

(A) Safety procedures
(B) Training schedules
(C) Employee benefits
(D) Vacation policies

87. According to the speaker, what can the listeners get discounts on?

(A) Medicine
(B) Airfare
(C) Phone plans
(D) Office supplies

88. What will the speaker do next?

(A) Answer some questions
(B) Hand out some information
(C) Introduce some guests
(D) Demonstrate some equipment

89. What is the main topic of the talk?

(A) Ingredients of some dishes
(B) Changes to a menu
(C) Renovations to a restaurant
(D) Locations of some food

90. What special event is probably being held?

(A) A welcome reception
(B) An awards dinner
(C) A grand opening
(D) A retirement party

91. What will the speaker check?

(A) The sizes of some tables
(B) The details of a reservation
(C) The availability of a room
(D) The prices of some items

92. What will a mobile application allow users to do?

(A) Find businesses
(B) Play games
(C) Upload pictures
(D) Bank online

93. What does the speaker mean when she says, "it has over 25,000 downloads"?

(A) A program is popular.
(B) A marketing campaign is needed.
(C) A server needs to be upgraded.
(D) A site is malfunctioning.

94. What can some users participate in?

(A) A raffle contest
(B) A trial period
(C) A research study
(D) An athletic race

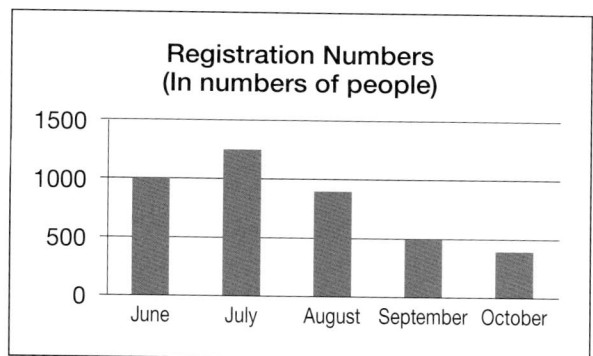

95. Where does the speaker most likely work?

(A) At an educational institute
(B) At a department store
(C) At a delivery company
(D) At a conference center

96. Look at the graphic. In what month did the online program start?

(A) June
(B) July
(C) August
(D) September

97. What will probably happen next?

(A) Listeners will access a Web site.
(B) Listeners will divide into groups.
(C) Some interviews will be conducted.
(D) Some questionnaire data will be presented.

A-Z Commercial Cleaning Service

400 to 600 Square Feet = $45
600 to 800 Square Feet = $65
800 to 1,000 Square Feet = $85
1,000 to 1,200 Square Feet = $105

98. Where did the caller get the listener's phone number?

(A) From a television commercial
(B) From a neighbor
(C) From a newsletter
(D) From a city guide

99. Look at the graphic. How much will the service cost?

(A) $45
(B) $65
(C) $85
(D) $105

100. Why is the caller unavailable this morning?

(A) He is visiting a doctor's office.
(B) He is meeting with a client.
(C) He is presenting at a company workshop.
(D) He is going to the bank.

READING TEST

In the Reading test, you will read a variety of texts and answer several different types of reading comprehension questions. The entire Reading test will last 75 minutes. There are three parts, and directions are given for each part. You are encouraged to answer as many questions as possible within the time allowed.

You must mark your answers on the separate answer sheet. Do not write your answers in your test book.

PART 5

Directions: A word or phrase is missing in each of the sentences below. Four answer choices are given below each sentence. Select the best answer to complete the sentence. Then mark the letter (A), (B), (C), or (D) on your answer sheet.

---

101. The Silvercove Resort is easily accessible and has ------- own shuttle bus service.

(A) each
(B) one
(C) other
(D) its

102. Due to its ------- location in the province, Martenville has the largest train switch yard.

(A) center
(B) centering
(C) central
(D) centrally

103. Mr. Coulson will organize the ceremony and press conference for the ------- of the new headquarters.

(A) openness
(B) opening
(C) opener
(D) open

104. Push firmly ------- the bar with your hands to release emergency door's locking mechanism.

(A) on
(B) at
(C) by
(D) up

105. The administrator of this office will remove any advertisements that ------- do not conform to the regulations of the university.

(A) clearing
(B) clearly
(C) clear
(D) cleared

106. The Marchand Choir stands out because the singers know ------- to blend their individual singing styles.

(A) this
(B) many
(C) how
(D) after

107. To receive a complimentary beverage at the theater café, guests must present a ------- admission ticket.

(A) moderate
(B) valid
(C) plausible
(D) determined

108. The customer survey results indicate that most people ------- Milkmade's strawberry drinking yogurt very satisfying.

(A) enjoy
(B) find
(C) sense
(D) correspond

109. Regardless of ------- a proposal is selected for a project, all submissions are kept in the database for two years.

(A) which
(B) even
(C) any
(D) whether

110. Ms. Sawyer's train arrived ------- late for her to participate in the luncheon.

(A) very
(B) quite
(C) so
(D) too

111. There is ------- more essential to preserving good nutrition than drinking 2 liters of water daily.

(A) nothing
(B) whenever
(C) other
(D) either

112. The Maynard Fine Art Museum requires that the ------- of recording devices be limited to the lobby and reception areas.

(A) category
(B) usage
(C) capacity
(D) period

113. ------- the final contract had been signed, Ms. Cheng thanked the negotiators for their time and effort.

(A) Soon
(B) After
(C) If
(D) While

114. ------- its membership rewards program, Tesseract Communcations' service rates are regarded as exorbitant by many.

(A) Thanks to
(B) Far from
(C) Despite
(D) During

115. Over the next few months, the company executive ------- to see the profits predicted by the Corporate Strategy Department.

(A) hoping
(B) hopefully
(C) hopes
(D) hoped

116. An early novel draft by Scottish author Giles Fitzpatrick was purchased by a private collector today ------- an unknown amount.

(A) to
(B) for
(C) over
(D) out

117. The Gensian range and oven combo is Albi Kitchenwares' most ------- priced configuration.

(A) reasonably
(B) definitely
(C) sparsely
(D) approximately

118. Wednesday's seminar will help regional managers ------- their ability to efficiently hire, manage, and encourage employees.

(A) evaluate
(B) protect
(C) assemble
(D) progress

119. Guests are invited ------- the newly opened ancient Greek-Roman wing of the Montcrew Museum.

(A) tours
(B) having toured
(C) to tour
(D) touring

120. The guest speaker insisted that addressing employee complaints ------- was one vital element for retaining staff.

(A) largely
(B) similarly
(C) consistently
(D) immensely

121. After a careful probe of the artist's replica alongside the original, the critic was able to classify the ------- attributes of both.

    (A) distinguish
    (B) distinguished
    (C) distinguishes
    (D) distinguishing

122. The estimate for the hotel renovation will be sent this afternoon ------- we receive the contractor's measurements before noon.

    (A) besides
    (B) as long as
    (C) predicting
    (D) if not

123. This announcement is to inform passengers of ------- on carry-on luggage for international flights.

    (A) limitations
    (B) limit
    (C) limiting
    (D) limited

124. ------- the Tyson Center for Business Research, allowing employees to choose a flexible schedule improves work performance.

    (A) Except for
    (B) According to
    (C) In regard to
    (D) Because of

125. Ms. Fontaine had a conflict with the conference since she was ------- required to be present at a meeting on that date.

    (A) yet
    (B) already
    (C) rather
    (D) not

126. The research and development department at the Helvetica Corp. rewards employee -------.

    (A) innovatively
    (B) innovation
    (C) innovative
    (D) innovator

127. Considering the ------- call volumes on Monday mornings, contacting our customer services may take longer than expected.

    (A) multiple
    (B) noisy
    (C) heavy
    (D) extended

128. Employees attending the convention in Houston were directed to make ------- for transportation, keep their receipts, and file reimbursement requests after they return.

    (A) pay
    (B) to pay
    (C) paying
    (D) payments

129. Following the Web design workshop, participants stated that their site traffic was ------- higher.

    (A) severely
    (B) considerably
    (C) necessarily
    (D) willingly

130. The Flagstone Café ------- breakfast promotions on Sundays for the last decade.

    (A) will be offering
    (B) would have been offering
    (C) has been offering
    (D) is offering

PART 6

Directions: Read the texts that follow. A word, phrase, or sentence is missing in parts of each text. Four answer choices for each question are given below the text. Select the best answer to complete the text. Then mark the letter (A), (B), (C), or (D) on your answer sheet.

Questions 131-134 refer to the following letter.

A message to our loyal customers:

Bullseye Appliances strives ------- high-quality products at affordable prices. In addition to our competitive costs, our tremendous customer service has made us the most trusted chain of appliance retailers in the province. Bullseye's five locations have served Ontarians ------- a collective total of 60 years.

To enable us to provide you with the best possible service, we will close the Kitchener location from May 8 to May 29 for remodeling. -------. Throughout this time, the store in neighboring Cambridge will remain open during regular business -------. Let us know any questions or comments you might have. As always, we value your time and your business.

Thank you,

Pablo Guaido
Owner and Founder, Bullseye Appliances

131. (A) to be offered
 (B) to offer
 (C) offered
 (D) offering

132. (A) by
 (B) within
 (C) for
 (D) between

133. (A) The store will remain open an hour later until May 31.
 (B) All feedback will receive a response within 48 hours.
 (C) This guarantee will be available for a limited time only.
 (D) We would like to apologize in advance for any bother this causes.

134. (A) recruitment
 (B) owners
 (C) evaluations
 (D) hours

Questions 135-138 refer to the following information.

Many of the ------- to *The Natural World* are veteran biologists who have collaborated
         135.
with our publication over an extended period. -------, we are always interested in
                                                136.
promoting the work of aspiring scientists. For every issue, we aim to feature at least one
to two submissions from a new researcher, but with our quarterly publishing schedule,
it is difficult to include every worthy article. Before you submit your work, it is essential
to familiarize yourself with our publication guidelines (available at naturalworld.com/
submissions), which detail our citation and formatting rules. -------.
                                                                  137.

Keep in mind that we make every effort to respond to all correspondence we receive,
but due to the high volume of submissions, we cannot always do so quickly. Because of
this, we have to ask you to be -------.
                                138.

135. (A) contributing
(B) contributes
(C) contributors
(D) contribution

136. (A) In contrast
(B) Even so
(C) In this case
(D) For example

137. (A) Most of our subscribers are university professors and graduate students.
(B) This month's issue will be delivered within the next two weeks.
(C) We're impressed by your approach, but we require more statistical evidence.
(D) This will improve the chances that your work is chosen.

138. (A) minor
(B) concise
(C) meticulous
(D) patient

Questions 139-142 refer to the following advertisement.

TBD Financial's new Endeavor card rewards you for investing in yourself.

TBD Financial is excited to offer a rewards credit card for business owners that lets you accrue points from day to day business expenses, ranging from ordering inventory to buying new office furniture. Now, you can start saving up for that next vacation while you work. Why ------- for a card that only rewards you for dining out at restaurants or
     139.
going to the movies? ------- the Endeavor card turns 1.5 percent of every purchase into
                     140.
points, it provides double that for key business expenses, such as office supplies, gas, and mobile services. It's the best choice for ------- individuals whose main priority is
                                                   141.
their own business. Sign up with TBD Financial today to take advantage of our special $500 signing bonus. -------.
                    142.

139. (A) settling
(B) settled
(C) settle
(D) settlement

140. (A) Moreover
(B) Despite
(C) While
(D) Then

141. (A) they
(B) those
(C) this
(D) that

142. (A) This amazing offer expires March 1, so don't wait.
(B) The Endeavor card does not offer bonus points for restaurant expenses.
(C) Expenses related to transportation do not generate points.
(D) Each person you refer will also receive the introductory gift.

Questions 143-146 refer to the following e-mail.

From: Amanda Nguyen
To: staff@hbcentertainment.com
Subject: Jakob Bernal's new position
Date: 21 November

Good morning,

I'm both deeply proud and a little sad to inform you all that Jakob Bernal will be moving on from HBC Entertainment to join Etten Media as Vice President of Operations. His ------- day here will be Thursday, January 31.
       143.

Throughout Jakob's time at our company, he has been a big part of the production team. Especially over the course of the last two years, he has guided some of our biggest and most successful projects. In that time, he ------- strong and lasting friendships with so
                                           144.
many of us at HBC Entertainment. His passion and leadership have been something we could count on. -------.
                145.

If you can make the time over the next few days, please reach out to Jakob. I think we should all wish him good luck and ------- success in his new position.
                                        146.

Best,

Amanda Nguyen
CEO

143. (A) next
(B) nearest
(D) latest
(D) last

144. (A) formed
(B) should form
(C) forms
(D) will form

145. (A) He developed a program in collaboration with Khepri Faried.
(B) HR conducted an extensive search for a qualified candidate.
(C) He previously worked in the media and design team at DeBrunye, Inc.
(D) I'm sure we'll all miss his quick wit, good humor, and dedication.

146. (A) continued
(B) continue
(C) continuation
(D) continues

PART 7

Directions: In this part you will read a selection of texts, such as magazine and newspaper articles, e-mails, and instant messages. Each text or set of texts is followed by several questions. Select the best answer for each question and mark the letter (A), (B), (C), or (D) on your answer sheet.

Questions 147-148 refer to the following information.

To All Electric Avenue Listeners!

Now, our listeners can access the show on all major online streaming platforms.

- Stream our content any time
- Play our entire catalogue free of charge

Search "Electric Avenue" on your music subscription service.

Or tune in to WCCRB to hear us live from 8 P.M. to midnight.

147. What is the main purpose of the information?

(A) To announce a new streaming platform
(B) To publicize a special live event
(C) To advertise a new option for fans
(D) To attract new listeners to a radio station

148. What is indicated about the streaming service?

(A) Listeners can access the show 24 hours a day.
(B) It requires listeners to pay a monthly fee.
(C) It is only available to certain listeners.
(D) Listeners need to activate an account via e-mail.

GO ON TO THE NEXT PAGE

Questions 149-150 refer to the following article.

Turner Institute Wants You

The Turner Institute is looking for research assistants who have a deep knowledge of agricultural sciences and a background in farm management. Go to www.turnercropinitiative.org to find out more about the requirements for the project and to apply online. Or, if you want to apply in person, visit the institute, located on 2425 Lyndale Road, and ask for Nicole Sessions.

The institute, founded by Dr. Jackson Sparrow, aims to feed the whole world by creating, testing, and promoting open-source seeds that will grow wholesome, pest-resistant crops.

149. What is the purpose of this article?
- (A) To explain a farming method
- (B) To request volunteers for market testing
- (C) To celebrate a scientist's retirement
- (D) To announce some job openings

150. Who most likely is Ms. Sessions?
- (A) A graduate student
- (B) An institute employee
- (C) An agriculture professor
- (D) A local journalist

Questions 151-152 refer to the following instructions.

Thank you for choosing Rison Electronics! To register your product, please complete the following steps:

1. Visit our Web site at www.risonelectronics.com/product_registration.
2. Log in using the temporary ID and password included inside the product box.
3. Complete the form including your name and e-mail address. You will also need to input the purchase date and the original country of purchase. Afterward, enter your product's serial number, which can be found on the back page of your instruction manual.
4. You will then be asked to make your own personal ID and password. Please use this information whenever you need to access your account.
5. Once everything is filled out, click on the "Submit" button. Your product is now registered under our warranty service.

RISON ELECTRONICS

151. For whom are the instructions most likely intended?

(A) Rison Electronics employees
(B) Product developers
(C) First-time customers
(D) Quality-control inspectors

152. What is the reader asked to do?

(A) Extend a warranty
(B) Update some log-in details
(C) Download some files
(D) Complete a survey

Questions 153-154 refer to the following text message chain.

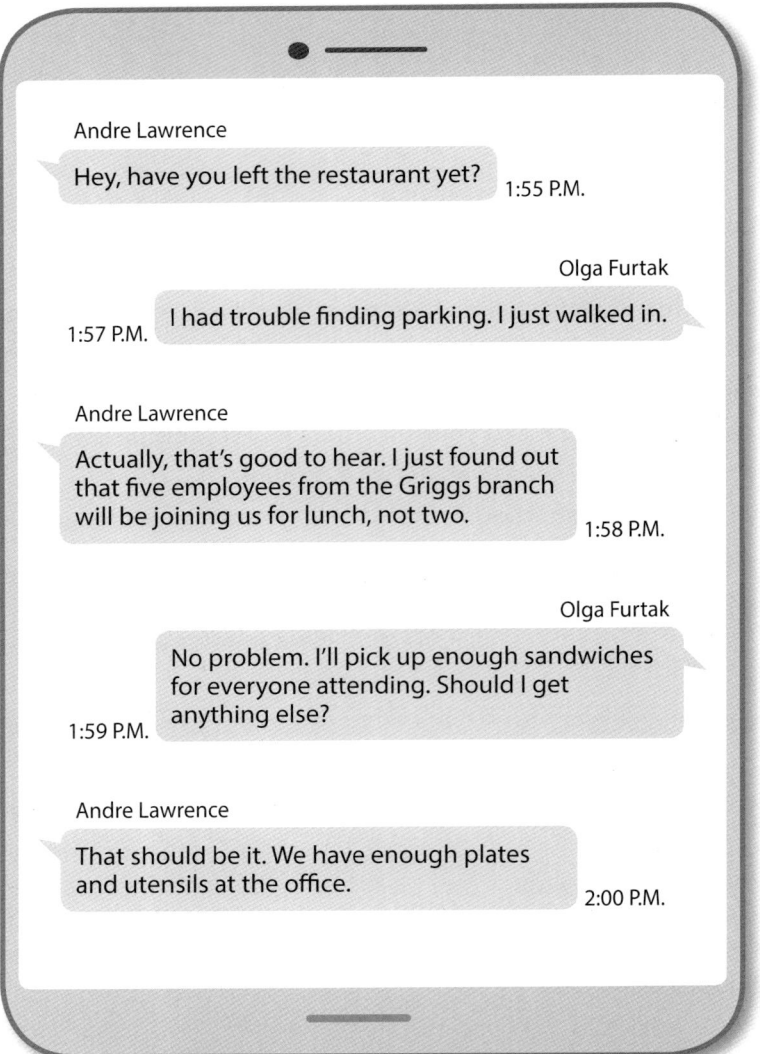

153. At 1:58 P.M., what does Mr. Lawrence most likely mean when he writes, "Actually, that's good to hear"?

(A) He is satisfied with some menu options.
(B) He thinks a restaurant is a good meeting place.
(C) He contacted Ms. Furtak in time to provide some information.
(D) He is happy that Ms. Furtak is transferring to the Griggs branch.

154. What will Ms. Furtak probably do next?

(A) Buy plates and utensils
(B) Visit a different business
(C) Order additional food
(D) Contact a supervisor

Questions 155-157 refer to the following e-mail.

From: JohnRothko@updikehomestore.com
To: JiwooP@flash.net
Subject: Issue with Delivery
Date: March 15

Ms. Park,

Your copy of Updike Home Store's fall catalog was sent out last week. However, the package was given back to us with a note saying "Return to Sender."

We want you to have the catalog so that you don't miss out on this fall's exclusive offers. Given the purchases you've made in the past, you may want to know about our new range of patio chairs and tables. Please provide us with your current home address so that we can mail you the catalog again as well as a discount voucher worth $50.

In addition, we have improved our customer support services. Now, instead of calling, you have the option of using our new online chat feature to talk with our representatives. Of course, you can still call our support center at 555-3093 with any issues you have about your order.

We are looking forward to hearing from you.

John Rothko
General Manager, Updike Home Store

---

155. Why was the e-mail sent?

(A) To request new contact information
(B) To follow up on a job application
(C) To apologize for a damaged item
(D) To describe a revised refund policy

156. What is indicated about Ms. Park?

(A) She has moved to another city recently.
(B) She has bought furniture from Updike Home Store before.
(C) She requested a discount voucher.
(D) She used an old catalog to purchase a product.

157. What is a change Updike Home Store recently made?

(A) The support center is now available 24 hours a day.
(B) Home installation fees have been lowered.
(C) Some unpopular product lines have been discontinued.
(D) Customer inquiries can be addressed through a chat service.

Questions 158-160 refer to the following e-mail.

Subject	Order #234-19887
Date	April 2
To	emacpherson@naismith.org
From	Carl@customizedcookwarehouse.com

Mr. Macpherson,

This e-mail is in reference to your recent order. —[1]—. Unfortunately, the item listed below has already sold out:

"Customized Kitchen" Professional Ceramic Non-Stick Fry Pan Set, $150

We would like to apologize for the confusion this may cause. —[2]—. We strive to provide a seamless user experience; however, we do occasionally run into issues. —[3]—. Our last remaining set was purchased by another customer a few hours ago. Due to a delay in processing their payment, our inventory system was not properly updated to reflect that the item was out of stock. This is a rare, but unfortunate error, which we are working to address.

We have refunded the points used to make the purchase to your Cookwarehouse.com account. Please verify that these appear on our Web site, but do allow two to six hours for the reimbursement to process. —[4]—.

Best Regards,

Carl Weizen
Customized Cookwarehouse, Customer Relations

---

158. What is the main purpose of this e-mail?

(A) To mention an item cannot be purchased
(B) To report that an order will be delayed
(C) To promote a sale on a certain product
(D) To confirm that a shipment has been delivered

159. What is Mr. Macpherson asked to do?

(A) Provide a new form of payment
(B) Check an online account
(C) Email the customer relations team
(D) Use a special discount code

160. In which of the positions marked [1], [2], [3], and [4] does the following sentence best belong?

"This has occurred in your case."

(A) [1]
(B) [2]
(C) [3]
(D) [4]

Questions 161-163 refer to the following e-mail.

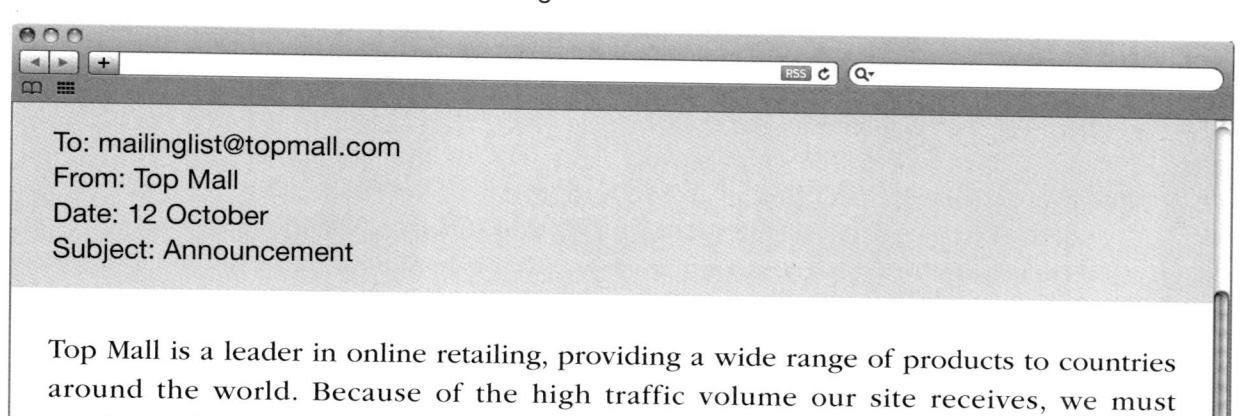

To: mailinglist@topmall.com
From: Top Mall
Date: 12 October
Subject: Announcement

Top Mall is a leader in online retailing, providing a wide range of products to countries around the world. Because of the high traffic volume our site receives, we must continuously upgrade our servers to ensure a pleasant shopping experience.

Therefore, on 15 October, from 3 A.M. to 11 A.M. GMT, our Web site will be down to perform these upgrades. During this time, users will not be able to browse our inventory, access their shopping carts, or make changes to their orders. Our customer service agents, however, will be available to answer your questions and concerns in English, Chinese, and Spanish. Unfortunately, some account information may not be available during this process. We appreciate your understanding.

After 15 October, we will be even better able to assist you with all of your shopping needs. Top Mall will also start offering our customers a weekly newsletter with information on special offers and promotions. Sign up online to have it sent directly to your e-mail, and we will also send you a discount voucher good for 15 percent off your next purchase.

161. Why was the e-mail sent?

(A) To confirm an order
(B) To introduce a new product
(C) To announce a system upgrade
(D) To provide a shipping update

162. What is indicated about the Top Mall?

(A) Its Web site is easy to use.
(B) Its staff can speak several languages.
(C) It has offices in several countries.
(D) It was highly rated by customers.

163. How can readers receive a coupon?

(A) By upgrading an online service
(B) By subscribing to a newsletter
(C) By spending over a certain amount
(D) By calling a customer service agent

Questions 164-167 refer to the following article.

NEW YORK (April 2) — Yesterday afternoon, Judge John Reinsdorf ruled that a merger between the nation's two leading accounting firms could go ahead despite objections from some experts. This means that Markkanen & Associates and Donovan ELX are now free to form what will be the country's largest accounting company, with over 300,000 employees.

"We're excited about what will happen when these two companies join forces," said Spencer Mitchell of Markkanen, who will most likely become CEO of the new firm to be known as Markkanen-Donovan. "We have a tremendous amount of know-how and two amazingly diverse client portfolios. This move will not only let us keep our New York and Los Angeles branches, but also make it possible to increase our reach worldwide. We're looking at setting up a new office outside of the U.S. in Singapore in the next year."

Mitchell has drawn the attention of press agencies around the country for his charity work, especially his efforts to promote small businesses in developing countries through microloans.

Mitchell said that Markkanen-Donovan plans to retain the entire staff of each company. "Every department has vital skills to bring to the table," he explained.

164. What is the main purpose of this article?

(A) To explain new tax regulations
(B) To report on the combining of two firms
(C) To discuss a legal case
(D) To advertise an accounting service

165. What does Markkanen-Donovan plan to do?

(A) Borrow some money
(B) Hold an executive board election
(C) Close one of its New York branches
(D) Expand to a new country

166. What is suggested about Mr. Mitchell?

(A) He is nationally recognized.
(B) He used to be a banker.
(C) He is based in Los Angeles.
(D) He owns a small business.

167. The word "reach" in paragraph 2, line 11, is closest in meaning to

(A) length
(B) arrival
(C) influence
(D) extension

Questions 168-171 refer to the following article.

Compared to other music instructors, Herbert McGraw is truly unique. After spending most of his career as a successful attorney with Roth & Stein Associates, he suddenly turned his attention to music. —[1]—. McGraw struggled to keep up as an elementary school student. But starting in middle school, his school's music program caught his interest. His passion for music also helped him improve his focus on academic studies. So, when he learned that the school district from his hometown had cut all of the music programs from its budget, he knew he had to do something. —[2]—. That "something" became his music studio, To the Beat.

The music studio is located in the heart of the city, making it easily accessible to students in the area. Best of all, McGraw provides everything to the students for free.

—[3]—. McGraw's studio is stocked with instruments of nearly every kind imaginable, and students are encouraged to pick them up and play. Every day, To the Beat offers kids the opportunity to discover their talents and express themselves through music. "I was upset when I heard that the schools in my hometown were getting rid of their music programs," said McGraw. "I know from experience that music teaches important skills for school and for life. I just hope that I can find a way to finance this for the long term—that part won't be easy." —[4]—.

The award-winning band, The Jamming Camels, heard about McGraw's efforts to help these kids. To show their support, they have donated an undisclosed amount to McGraw and To the Beat music studio.

---

168. Where did Herbert McGraw start his professional life?

(A) In the advertising business
(B) In the legal field
(C) In the music industry
(D) In the education sector

169. What has changed in Herbert McGraw's hometown?

(A) The amount of tourists
(B) The number of school programs
(C) The costs of some properties
(D) The size of the community's population

170. What is true about To the Beat?

(A) It recently hired Roth & Stein Associates.
(B) It has received some funding from The Jamming Camels.
(C) It will donate supplies to a local school district.
(D) It will record an album with an award-winning band.

171. In which of the marked [1], [2], [3], and [4] does the following sentence best belong?

"Now, however, help has arrived from an unexpected source."

(A) [1]
(B) [2]
(C) [3]
(D) [4]

Questions 172-175 refer to the following online chat discussion.

Kevin Johnson [10:33 A.M.]
Good morning, everyone. I know we have to go over some details regarding the ad campaign Harper Marketing Agency is creating for us, but I just received some big news. Our spring line of men's clothes will be on display at next month's Global Fashion Show.

Aviva Feldman [10:35 A.M.]
That's amazing! I'm really proud of the work we did for that project.

Udom Haslam [10:36 A.M.]
Me, too. This will definitely help generate more revenue next quarter.

Aviva Feldman [10:38 A.M.]
I think so, too. There will be many potential clients at this show.

Kevin Johnson [10:40 A.M.]
We should thank Fodesi for another job well done.

Udom Haslam [10:41 A.M.]
Yes, they are a big reason why we've been so successful.

Kevin Johnson [10:43 A.M.]
Fodesi was especially cooperative this time considering that we asked them to use new materials. We opted for mesh fabrics rather than traditional cotton, and the shirts came out just the way we wanted them.

Aviva Feldman [10:44 A.M.]
And the quality is still great.

Kevin Johnson [10:45 A.M.]
Alright, let's continue on to today's main topic. Udom, did Amit Mathur from Harper have any suggestions on the ad campaign?

Udom Haslam [10:45 A.M.]
He did. I'll email them to you right now.

172. What did Kevin Johnson share with his colleagues?

(A) An exciting event for their firm
(B) An announcement about a company merger
(C) Data from a sales report
(D) Responses from a recent survey

173. At 10:38 A.M., what does Ms. Feldman most likely mean when she writes, "I think so, too"?

(A) It is necessary to discuss ideas with coworkers.
(B) It was a pleasure to work with talented people.
(C) The company's products are popular in many countries.
(D) The company will earn more money.

174. What most likely is Fodesi?

(A) A textile producer
(B) A fashion magazine
(C) An advertising agency
(D) A law office

175. What will Mr. Haslam do next?

(A) Send some suggestions from a marketing agency
(B) Call Mr. Mathur to adjust a timeline for a campaign
(C) Book tickets to the Global Fashion Show
(D) Purchase some additional shirts

Questions 176-180 refer to the following flyer and e-mail.

Idalou Urban Market
Invites all Craftspeople

The Idalou Urban Market is returning to Skyline Park this June 12-15. Craftspeople will have the chance to show off their talents and products. Every year we have seen the number of visitors increase, and we expect the same this year. In previous years, only Texas-based artisans were eligible to participate, but we have modified the rules to include everyone regardless of the state they live in.

To apply, please do the following:

1. Go to www.idaloumarket.com/register and fill out the form. For those planning to share a stand, one form can be used for both parties. However, the $35 registration fee still applies to both sellers.

2. Upload no more than 10 photos of the items you plan to display at the market. Please name the files as such: item description_seller name.

The final day to submit the necessary documents is April 20. If you have been approved, an e-mail will be sent to you by May 2. These people will need to pay the remaining stand management fee of $525 by May 16. This fee includes four five-foot-long tables to be used as you wish. The images that you provide will be displayed on our Web site under the "Exhibitors" tab along with a link to your homepage.

FROM: rin.takai@takaisupply.com
TO: e.orville@idaloumarket.com
CC: henry.reiss@reissphotos.net
SUBJECT: Urban Market
DATE: May 9

Hello,

I, along with my stall partner, Henry Reiss, received the approval e-mails, and we are thrilled to be a part of this year's festivities. We have sent the payment for our shared stand via bank transfer using the account number on your Web site. We can't wait to hear more about this year's event.

I had the chance to partake in the event last year, and I really enjoyed the tutorials that some artisans provided. Will there be something similar to that this year? Please let us know if there is because I would love to show the audience how we produce some of our crafts.

Sincerely,

Rin Takai

176. When will approval e-mails be sent?

(A) April 20
(B) May 2
(C) May 16
(D) June 12

177. What does the flyer indicate about the Idalou Urban Market?

(A) It offers complimentary parking for all attendees.
(B) Its online page promotes the participating craftspeople.
(C) It is being held for the first time.
(D) It does not charge for admission.

178. What is suggested about Ms. Takai and Mr. Reiss?

(A) They filled out different forms.
(B) They will need extra tables.
(C) They both paid a $35 fee.
(D) They offer video tutorials.

179. What is probably true about Ms. Takai?

(A) Her crafts were popular last year.
(B) Her work was featured in a magazine.
(C) She does not have an online page.
(D) She resides in Texas.

180. In the e-mail, what does Ms. Takai ask about?

(A) The possibility of demonstrating some skills
(B) The dimensions of her stall
(C) Contact information of other artists
(D) Acceptable forms of payment

Questions 181-185 refer to the following notice and e-mail.

QMC Construction Solutions, Inc.
Contreras Work Study Program

QMC Construction Solutions, Inc., based in Rancho Cucamonga, is looking for 15 promising students for the Contreras Work-Study Program (CWSP). Program participants will work in one of QMC's three facilities: San Bernardino, Riverside, or Rancho Cucamonga. For consideration, students should send a cover letter and CV to CWSP@qmcconstruction.com. Those selected for the program will be featured in a special article in *Inland Empire Business Journal* next month.

About the Program:
CWSP is the creation of Anthony Contreras, who wanted to commemorate the work of Guillermo M. Contreras, the original owner of QMC Construction Solutions. The program is designed to foster young architecture students to follow Guillermo Contreras' example, exploring and developing more effective solutions to design and construction problems. After completing his Master's degree in architecture, Guillermo Contreras opened QMC Construction Solutions, Inc. in partnership with his brother Edwin. As the years passed, he grew the small company into one of the most respected construction firms in Southern California. After leading the company for 35 years, he stepped down earlier this year to let his nephew, Anthony, take charge.

To:	Jerry Skakal <JSkakal@desertcollege.edu>
From:	Deanna Rogers <rogers@qmcbuilders.com>
Date:	July 14
Subject:	Details

Dear Mr. Skakal,

Congratulations on your acceptance to the Contreras Work Study Program. You will receive your official letter of acceptance and contract in the next few days. Concerning your question about accommodations, I certainly understand that you'd prefer not to make a 2-hour drive from your home in San Diego every day, but I'm afraid that we are unable to arrange housing for program participants. However, Rodrigo Carvalho, the program coordinator for the Riverside office, would be a good person to talk to about this. He was born and raised in Riverside, and he will probably have some suggestions for low-cost lodging there.

Once again, congratulations, and we look forward to working with you.

Best Regards,

Deanna Rogers
HR Specialist
QMC Construction Solutions, Inc.

181. Why was the notice posted?

(A) To promote a corporate program
(B) To seek a new company president
(C) To report on a construction project
(D) To advertise a magazine article

182. Who is Anthony Contreras?

(A) A university administrator
(B) The founder of a company
(C) The leader of a business
(D) A student intern

183. What is one purpose of Ms. Rogers' e-mail?

(A) To discuss Mr. Skakal's contract
(B) To recommend a real estate agency
(C) To ask about an issue
(D) To respond to a inquiry

184. What is true about Mr. Skakal?

(A) He studies architecture.
(B) He has met Mr. Carvalho before.
(C) He will relocate to another office.
(D) He wants to hire QMC Construction Solutions.

185. Where will Mr. Skakal work?

(A) In San Bernardino
(B) In Riverside
(C) In Rancho Cucamonga
(D) In San Diego

Questions 186-190 refer to the following e-mail, advertisement, and note.

From	Lew Burns (Flotech UK)
To	Ashraf Bhagat (Flotech Pakistan)
Date	December 5
Subject	Awad Engineering

Hi Ashraf,

I've just heard that you are preparing for a visit from Awad Engineering. The UK branch of Flotech Consulting has been working with Awad Engineering for many years here in London, and they are looking forward very much to a good relationship with the Flotech Pakistan team as well. I think you will find them very easy to work with.

Concerning the meal you are planning for them on January 12, I should mention that several of the engineers have rather strict dietary restrictions. You'll want to keep this in mind when making arrangements.

Give me a call if you have any questions.

Thanks,

-Lew

Darbar Catering
Karachi

When you want to plan the perfect event, Darbar Catering is at your service. Our company has delighted clients in Karachi since 1955, providing the finest food and beverages for both corporate and family gatherings.

Why Darbar? Well, this is what makes us stand out:
*Customized decorations, including your company's logo
*A global menu featuring Western, South Asian, and Chinese favorites
*Special menus that can be created to suit a variety of food preferences
*Dance floor setup and music entertainment services available on request

Our services are available daily, noon to 10 P.M.

For more details, please give us a call at (92) 0213-555-1212.

Bilal Resort
An Avaricor Group Hotel

January 12

Dear Mr. Opfel,

Welcome to Pakistan: I hope you had a pleasant flight form London! My team and I would be honored if you would join us at 12:30 P.M. for a special luncheon in Rainbow Hall on the second floor of this resort. We're looking forward to getting to know you a bit over some good food before heading out to the construction site.

In the meantime, please give me a call at (92) 0304-551-2522 if I may be of assistance.

Yours Faithfully,

Ashraf Bhagat

186. Why was the e-mail sent?

(A) To discuss the terms of a new contract
(B) To cooperate with another branch about a client
(C) To recommend a candidate for an engineering position
(D) To reschedule a client lunch meeting

187. What feature of Darbar Catering makes it the most suitable vendor for the event?

(A) Its affordable services
(B) Its large venues
(C) Its customized menus
(D) Its entertainment choices

188. According to the advertisement, what type of event would Darbar Catering be least likely to assist with?

(A) An awards dinner
(B) A corporate breakfast
(C) A holiday celebration
(D) A graduation party

189. Where does Mr. Opfel most likely work?

(A) Awad Engineering
(B) Darbar Catering
(C) Flotech Consulting
(D) Avaricor Group

190. Where was Mr. Opfel most likely given the note?

(A) At the front desk of a resort
(B) At a social gathering hosted by Flotech
(C) At the departure gate of the London airport
(D) At the head office of Awad Engineering

GO ON TO THE NEXT PAGE

Questions 191-195 refer to the following e-mails and event information.

From	XiaoHui Huang
To	Joseph Lucchese
Date	July 12
Subject	August 12 Poster
Attachment	Poster Content

Hi Joseph,

Per our conversation, here is the content to be displayed on the poster. We'll need at least 100 copies to post around various locations at each of our branches. After reviewing the template you provided, I think we should go with "hot pink" for the background and "baby blue" for the majority of the lettering. But also, let's use a fancy font for the lecturers' names so that they catch people's attention.

To make sure that management is on the same page, let's make sure to show them a sample far in advance of the celebration. Do you think you can have one ready by next week?

Thanks,

XiaoHui Huang,
Program Organizer

ErgoBuff Laboratories

35th Year of Recognizing Excellence

Overlook Hotel, August 12, 7-10 P.M.

7:00P.M.-7:15P.M. – Opening remarks by CEO Tony Bibbo
7:15P.M.-8:15P.M. – Dinner and Musical Performance by Juan Talavera
8:15P.M.-8:45P.M. – Special Lecture 1: *"The Gym" as a Way of Life* by Roger Severen, Vice President of Marketing, Silver's Gym.
8:45P.M.-9:15P.M. Special Lecture 2: *The Future of the Nutritional Supplement Industry* by Professor Ernest Jung of Tamaulipas University.
9:15P.M.-9:45P.M. Presentations
9:45P.M.-10:00P.M. Closing remarks

Recipients:
Philip Bain – Outstanding Business Development
Shruti Chandrashekar - Top Sales
Rebecca Wilson – Silver Anniversary
Eileen Vogel - Best New Idea

From	Eric Eilenberger
To	XiaoHui Huang
Date	July 19
Subject	Content for August 12 Poster

Hi XiaoHui,

I reviewed the proposed design for the poster, and it looks good overall. With the bright background and font colors, it certainly has a more cheerful feel to it than the posters we've put up in past years! From their job titles, the guest lecturers certainly look impressive as well.

Just one note: The recipient for the Silver Anniversary is given to someone who has been with the company for more than 25 years. Most likely, this individual is in a senior management position. Aside from that, the current order is fine. Before you finalize anything though, be sure to get Mr. Bibbo's approval. In addition, confirm that every name on the poster is written correctly. It is a special event after all.

The print shop we use is usually very busy during this time of year. Therefore, it is crucial that you maintain frequent contact with the shop. Two years back, the program organizer took too long to place the order that the posters came on the day of the event.

Eric Eilenberger
HR Manager

191. Whose name will most likely be shown in a special style in the poster?
(A) Tony Bibbo's
(B) Ernest Jung's
(C) Juan Talavera's
(D) Eileen Vogel's

192. In the first e-mail, the word "far" in paragraph 2, line 1, is closest in meaning to
(A) distant
(B) long
(C) deep
(D) stretched

193. What event will be held on August 12?
(A) An awards ceremony
(B) A managers' conference
(C) A branch opening
(D) A product launch

194. What is suggested about Ms. Wilson?
(A) She will provide entertainment at the August 12 event.
(B) She has been employed at ErgoBuff for over 25 years.
(C) She used to work as an event organizer.
(D) She supervises the Human Resources Department.

195. What does Mr. Eilenberger ask Ms. Huang to do?
(A) Choose a different vendor
(B) Order more supplies
(C) Check that some information is correct
(D) Modify the color of a background

Questions 196-200 refer to the following invoice and e-mails.

Ronzone's Suppliers

435 Harrison Avenue
Elkhart, IN 46516

(574) 555-1212
www.ronzonesuppliers.com

Date: May 15
Customer: Michele's Italian Restaurant

Product Number	Product Name	Quantity	Price/unit	Amount
255X	Olive Oil	30	$5.25/bottle	$157.50
136B	Pickled Garden Vegetable Mix	25	$3.15/jar	$78.75
119Z	Red Wine	50	$10.60/bottle	$530
364D	Tomato Paste	100	$2.25/can	$225.00

Your total ($991.25) is due upon delivery.

From	Michele Ciaramitaro
To	Greg Ronzone
Date	May 18
Subject	May 15 Order

Hi Greg,

I'm afraid there are a few issues with my May 15 order. I got just 15 jars of the garden vegetable mix, and 10 of the wine bottles were visibly scratched. Have you made changes to your operation?

I've been very happy with your services since you got started 20 years ago, so I never expected to have this kind of thing happen. Furthermore, I think I should mention that my friend Sanjiv Saini, general manager of Beaugard Culinary Institute, had similar problems when he ordered from you this month as well.

In any case, please let me know what you will do to correct this situation. It's our busy season, so I really need these supplies.

Thank you,

Michele Ciaramitaro

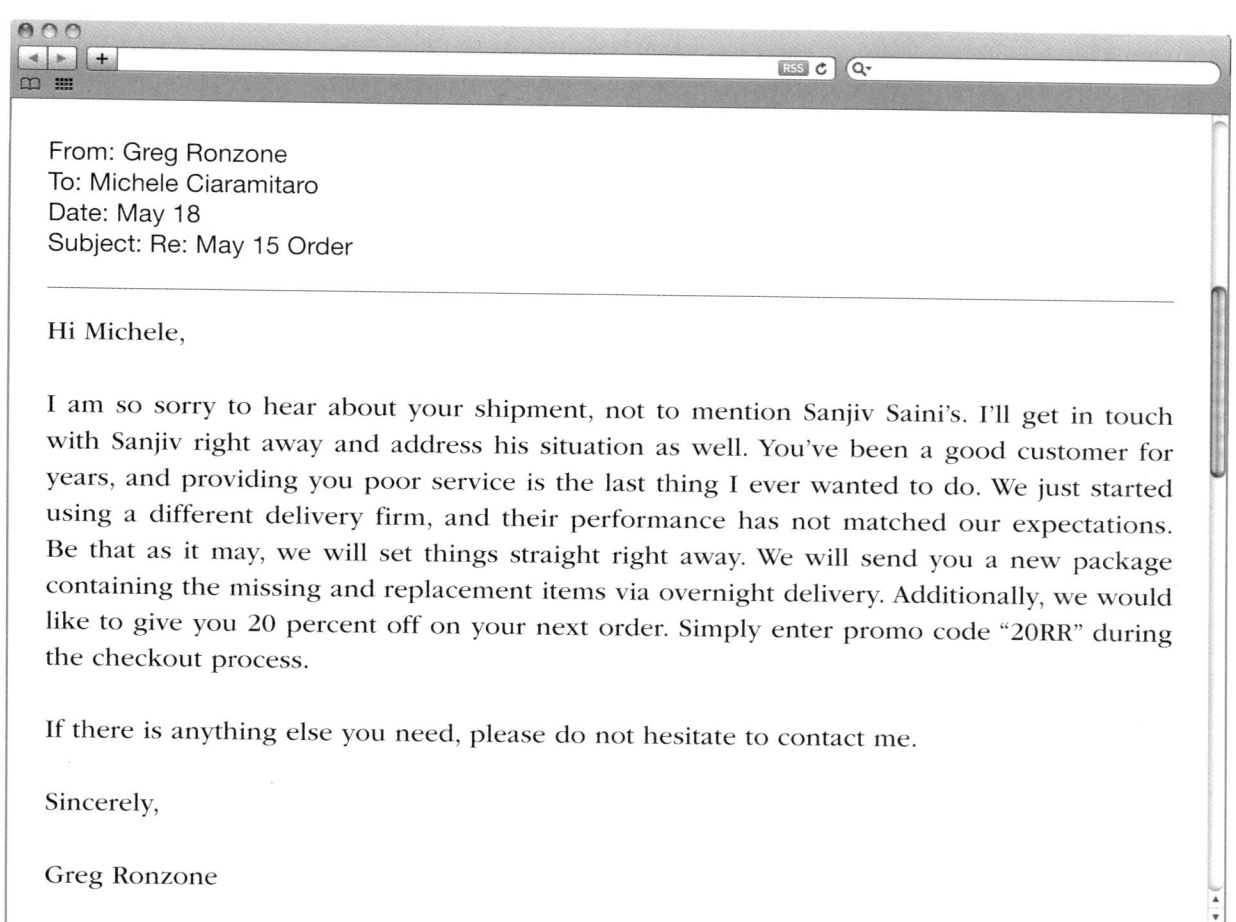

From: Greg Ronzone
To: Michele Ciaramitaro
Date: May 18
Subject: Re: May 15 Order

Hi Michele,

I am so sorry to hear about your shipment, not to mention Sanjiv Saini's. I'll get in touch with Sanjiv right away and address his situation as well. You've been a good customer for years, and providing you poor service is the last thing I ever wanted to do. We just started using a different delivery firm, and their performance has not matched our expectations. Be that as it may, we will set things straight right away. We will send you a new package containing the missing and replacement items via overnight delivery. Additionally, we would like to give you 20 percent off on your next order. Simply enter promo code "20RR" during the checkout process.

If there is anything else you need, please do not hesitate to contact me.

Sincerely,

Greg Ronzone

196. What was the purpose of the first e-mail?

(A) To update an order
(B) To introduce a customer
(C) To request that an issue be resolved
(D) To respond to a survey

197. What product was delivered damaged?

(A) 255X
(B) 136B
(C) 119Z
(D) 364D

198. In the second e-mail, the word "address" in paragraph 1 line 2 is closest in meaning to

(A) locate
(B) direct
(C) handle
(D) mail

199. What is NOT mentioned about Ronzone Suppliers?

(A) They are updating their product list.
(B) They sell their items to cooking schools.
(C) They recently hired a new company.
(D) They have been in business for 20 years.

200. What will Ronzone Suppliers give Mr. Ciaramitaro?

(A) Some additional olive oil bottles
(B) Samples of some new merchandise
(C) A discount on a future purchase
(D) A delivery fee waiver

Stop! This is the end of the test. If you finish before time is called, you may go back to Part 5, 6, and 7 and check your work.

TEST 05

MP3 바로 듣기

1타 강사 강의듣기

준비물: OMR 카드, 연필, 지우개, 시계
시험시간: LC 약 45분 / RC 75분

나의 점수		
	LC	RC
맞은 개수		
환산 점수		

총점: _____ 점

TEST 1	TEST 2	TEST 3	TEST 4	TEST 5
_____점	_____점	_____점	_____점	_____점

점수 환산표

LC		RC	
맞은 개수	환산 점수	맞은 개수	환산 점수
96-100	475-495	96-100	460-495
91-95	435-195	91-95	425-490
86-90	405-475	86-90	395-465
81-85	370-450	81-85	370-440
76-80	345-420	76-80	335-415
71-75	320-390	71-75	310-390
66-70	290-360	66-70	280-365
61-65	265-335	61-65	250-335
56-60	235-310	56-60	220-305
51-55	210-280	51-55	195-270
46-50	180-255	46-50	165-240
41-45	155-230	41-45	140-215
36-40	125-205	36-40	115-180
31-35	105-175	31-35	95-145
36-30	85-145	36-30	75-120
21-25	60-115	21-25	60-95
16-20	30-90	16-20	45-75
11-15	5-70	11-15	30-55
6-10	5-60	6-10	10-40
1-5	5-60	1-5	5-30
0	5-35	0	5-15

1.

2.

3.

4.

5.

6.

GO ON TO THE NEXT PAGE

PART 2

Directions: You will hear a question or statement and three responses spoken in English. They will not be printed in your test book and will be spoken only one time. Select the best response to the question or statement and mark the letter (A), (B), or (C) on your answer sheet.

7. Mark your answer on your answer sheet.
8. Mark your answer on your answer sheet.
9. Mark your answer on your answer sheet.
10. Mark your answer on your answer sheet.
11. Mark your answer on your answer sheet.
12. Mark your answer on your answer sheet.
13. Mark your answer on your answer sheet.
14. Mark your answer on your answer sheet.
15. Mark your answer on your answer sheet.
16. Mark your answer on your answer sheet.
17. Mark your answer on your answer sheet.
18. Mark your answer on your answer sheet.
19. Mark your answer on your answer sheet.
20. Mark your answer on your answer sheet.
21. Mark your answer on your answer sheet.
22. Mark your answer on your answer sheet.
23. Mark your answer on your answer sheet.
24. Mark your answer on your answer sheet.
25. Mark your answer on your answer sheet.
26. Mark your answer on your answer sheet.
27. Mark your answer on your answer sheet.
28. Mark your answer on your answer sheet.
29. Mark your answer on your answer sheet.
30. Mark your answer on your answer sheet.
31. Mark your answer on your answer sheet.

PART 3

Directions: You will hear some conversations between two or more people. You will be asked to answer three questions about what the speakers say in each conversation. Select the best response to each question and mark the letter (A), (B), (C), or (D) on your answer sheet. The conversations will not be printed in your test book and will be spoken only one time.

32. Why did the woman visit Roy's room?

(A) To return an item
(B) To fix some equipment
(C) To discuss a budget proposal
(D) To submit some documents

33. Why is Roy unavailable?

(A) He is meeting with an executive.
(B) He is leaving for the airport soon.
(C) He is conducting a customer survey.
(D) He is participating in a convention.

34. What will the woman do next?

(A) Contact a manager
(B) Read a user guide
(C) Give an office tour
(D) Download a program

35. Where do the speakers probably work?

(A) At a fabric store
(B) At a newspaper company
(C) At a library
(D) At a factory

36. What do the speakers believe is most important?

(A) Hiring knowledgeable employees
(B) Expanding product lines
(C) Maintaining good client relations
(D) Creating high-quality materials

37. What will the man send the woman?

(A) A bonus payment
(B) A sample contract
(C) A job summary
(D) A product list

38. Who most likely is the man?

(A) A university professor
(B) A museum manager
(C) A famous artist
(D) A conference organizer

39. What is the main topic of the conversation?

(A) Sculpture exhibits
(B) Traffic conditions
(C) Membership benefits
(D) Photo submissions

40. What does the woman ask about?

(A) Buying a gift
(B) Renting a device
(C) Storing a bag
(D) Paying a fee

41. What industry do the speakers probably work in?

(A) Appliance sales
(B) Automobile manufacturing
(C) Food production
(D) Computer programming

42. What problem is being discussed?

(A) Some equipment keeps turning off.
(B) A manager is not available.
(C) Some customers have made complaints.
(D) An inventory list is incorrect.

43. What does the man recommend?

(A) Choosing a new vendor
(B) Ordering a replacement part
(C) Offering a coupon
(D) Delaying a shipment

GO ON TO THE NEXT PAGE

44. What kind of business does the man own?

(A) A restaurant
(B) A trading corporation
(C) An IT firm
(D) A taxi service

45. What do the speakers like about the auditorium?

(A) It has a place to buy food.
(B) It has plenty of space.
(C) It is convenient for travelers.
(D) It is in a scenic location.

46. How is the computer network used at the man's business?

(A) To calculate expenses
(B) To process orders
(C) To create schedules
(D) To inspect merchandise

---

47. What is the man calling about?

(A) Completing an order
(B) Recruiting temporary workers
(C) Arranging some furniture
(D) Finding a bigger venue

48. What does the woman imply when she says, "the client made a specific request for this"?

(A) The man should contact the client.
(B) A price has already been set.
(C) A modification cannot be made.
(D) The man has to fix an error.

49. What does the man offer to do?

(A) Contact local businesses
(B) Provide a discount
(C) Expedite a delivery
(D) Set up some equipment

50. What is the purpose of the man's call?

(A) To apply for a position
(B) To ask for a refund
(C) To report a problem
(D) To extend a membership

51. Why does the woman apologize?

(A) The man was given incorrect instructions.
(B) An invoice included an extra charge.
(C) The man does not qualify for a discount.
(D) A credit card cannot be processed.

52. What does the woman offer to do?

(A) Update some contact information
(B) Revise an order
(C) Provide a free item
(D) Call another branch

---

53. Where most likely are the speakers?

(A) At a vehicle rental agency
(B) At a conference hall
(C) At a tourist office
(D) At a city bus terminal

54. Why does the woman say, "I've never been to this city"?

(A) To request a tour guide
(B) To ask for a suggestion
(C) To describe a problem
(D) To inquire about transportation

55. Why does the man encourage the woman to order online?

(A) A discount will be available.
(B) There is no additional fee.
(C) There is no wait time.
(D) A Web site has more items.

LISTENING TEST

In the Listening test, you will be asked to demonstrate how well you understand spoken English. The entire listening test will last approximately 45 minutes. There are four parts, and directions are given for each part. You must mark your answers on the separate answer sheet. Do not write your answers in your test book.

PART 1

Directions: For each question in this part, you will hear four statements about a picture in your test book. When you hear the statements, you must select the one statement that best describes what you see in the picture. Then find the number of the question on your answer sheet and mark your answer. The statements will not be printed in your test book and will be spoken only one time.

Statement (B), "A man is pointing at a document," is the best description of the picture, so you should select answer (B) and mark it on your answer sheet.

56. Where do the speakers most likely work?

(A) At a marketing firm
(B) At a clothing retailer
(C) At a legal office
(D) At a production agency

57. What does the woman suggest?

(A) Moving to a bigger location
(B) Signing up for a seminar
(C) Consulting with a lawyer
(D) Working additional hours

58. What does the man offer to do?

(A) Process some payments
(B) Schedule a meeting
(C) Pick up a client
(D) Review some job applications

59. Why is the man at Watscorp Publishers?

(A) To discuss a new book project
(B) To lead a company workshop
(C) To conduct an inspection
(D) To interview for a position

60. According to the man, what is his biggest accomplishment?

(A) Making educational materials
(B) Starting his own business
(C) Receiving a national award
(D) Becoming an R&D manager

61. What does the man like about Watscorp?

(A) It publishes famous novels.
(B) It cares about its workers.
(C) It is an industry leader.
(D) It recently expanded its offices.

Train Number	Destination	Departure Time / Status
230	Rochester	8:20 A.M. On Schedule
231	Buffalo	9:15 A.M. Delayed 60 minutes
232	Albany	10:30 A.M. On Schedule
233	Syracuse	11:00 A.M. Delayed 45 minutes

62. What is the man's problem?

(A) He will arrive late.
(B) He could not reserve a ticket.
(C) He left his notes at home.
(D) He is unable to find parking.

63. Look at the graphic. Which train will the speakers board?

(A) 230
(B) 231
(C) 232
(D) 233

64. What does the man request the woman do?

(A) Give a speech
(B) Send a message
(C) Review a presentation
(D) Make a payment

GO ON TO THE NEXT PAGE

Rack 1	Apples
Rack 2	Oranges
Rack 3	Peaches
Rack 4	Strawberries

65. What problem does the man report?

   (A) A storage room has to be cleaned.
   (B) Some items must be restocked.
   (C) Some food has expired.
   (D) A delivery was damaged.

66. Look at the graphic. Which rack is the woman working on?

   (A) Rack 1
   (B) Rack 2
   (C) Rack 3
   (D) Rack 4

67. What does the man instruct the woman to do?

   (A) Discard some boxes
   (B) Repair a device
   (C) Call a business
   (D) Handle a customer inquiry

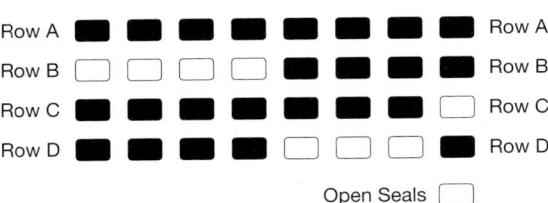

68. What has recently happened at the performing arts center?

   (A) A new manager was hired.
   (B) The dates of a show were changed.
   (C) The renovation of a facility was finished.
   (D) A parking lot was constructed.

69. Look at the graphic. Which row will the woman most likely buy tickets for?

   (A) Row A
   (B) Row B
   (C) Row C
   (D) Row D

70. What does the woman say she would like to do?

   (A) Use a voucher
   (B) Become a member
   (C) Receive electronic tickets
   (D) Upgrade her seats

PART 4

Directions: You will hear some talks given by a single speaker. You will be asked to answer three questions about what the speaker says in each talk. Select the best response to each question and mark the letter (A), (B), (C), or (D) on your answer sheet. The talks will not be printed in your test book and will be spoken only one time.

71. What is the topic of the convention?

    (A) Renewable energy
    (B) Computer engineering
    (C) Waste recycling
    (D) Textile production

72. According to the speaker, what did Jonathan Matthews do this year?

    (A) He invented a machine.
    (B) He received an award.
    (C) He founded a company.
    (D) He wrote a new book.

73. What does the speaker remind the listeners to do?

    (A) Write down questions
    (B) Sample a product
    (C) Attend a demonstration
    (D) Wear a name tag

74. Where does the speaker most likely work?

    (A) At a computer manufacturer
    (B) At an Internet service provider
    (C) At a home repair company
    (D) At a broadcasting station

75. What is the cause of the problem?

    (A) There was a technical error.
    (B) Some work was left unfinished.
    (C) Some machines were damaged.
    (D) There was severe weather.

76. What should the listeners do if the problem continues?

    (A) Submit some paperwork
    (B) Replace some equipment
    (C) Call again later
    (D) Visit a business

77. What is the theater celebrating?

    (A) A film premiere
    (B) A showroom opening
    (C) A building renovation
    (D) An anniversary

78. What will the listeners do first?

    (A) Watch a video
    (B) Go on a tour
    (C) Take some pictures
    (D) Answer some questions

79. What will the listeners receive?

    (A) A concession stand voucher
    (B) A movie display prop
    (C) A free entrance ticket
    (D) A show time schedule

80. What is the speaker preparing?

    (A) A research presentation
    (B) A client visit
    (C) An anniversary party
    (D) A holiday

81. Who most likely is the listener?

    (A) A ship captain
    (B) A travel agent
    (C) A resort manager
    (D) An exhibition coordinator

82. What does the speaker mean when she says, "I'm told that the Mediterranean is breathtaking during that season"?

    (A) She is dissatisfied with a service.
    (B) She agrees with a recommendation.
    (C) She believes a purchase may be worth the price.
    (D) She wants the listener to accompany her.

GO ON TO THE NEXT PAGE

83. Why is the speaker interested in the Glenmoore community?

(A) It is near a recreation center.
(B) It has a security gate.
(C) It has a good school district.
(D) It is affordable.

84. What does the speaker want in his home?

(A) A home theater
(B) A garden area
(C) A furnished living room
(D) A large basement

85. What does the speaker say he will do tonight?

(A) Purchase some instruments
(B) Meet with a band
(C) Speak to his landlord
(D) Go on a business trip

---

86. Where is the announcement taking place?

(A) At a bus terminal
(B) At a railway station
(C) On a boat
(D) On an airplane

87. What caused a problem?

(A) Inclement weather
(B) Broken equipment
(C) Some late passengers
(D) A lack of staff

88. What will the listeners receive?

(A) A parking permit
(B) A meal voucher
(C) A magazine
(D) A refund

89. What is the speaker preparing for?

(A) An anniversary event
(B) A training session
(C) A sales conference
(D) A charity fundraiser

90. What does the speaker imply when he says, "the employees from the overseas branch are also coming"?

(A) More food should be ordered.
(B) A bigger venue will be required.
(C) A guest list should be updated.
(D) Some documents will be translated.

91. Why does the speaker want to meet with the woman?

(A) To select menu options
(B) To discuss a budget
(C) To review a contract
(D) To choose a speaker

---

92. What does the speaker emphasize about the museum?

(A) Its staff
(B) Its history
(C) Its size
(D) Its location

93. Why does the speaker say, "the museum does rely on financial donations from our guests"?

(A) To respond to guest complaints
(B) To explain a membership plan
(C) To ask for contributions
(D) To announce a revised policy

94. According to the speaker, what is prohibited?

(A) Taking photographs
(B) Leaving a group
(C) Bringing a bag
(D) Touching artifacts

Reward Tier	Amount of Sales	Reward
Tier A	Over $3,000	Free round-trip airfare
Tier B	$2,000 to $3,000	$300 Gift Certificate
Tier C	$1,000 to $2,000	Set of Steak Knives
Tier D	Under $1,000	Pair of Headphones

95. What kind of business does the speaker most likely work for?

(A) A mobile phone company
(B) A car dealership
(C) A clothing store
(D) An advertising agency

96. Look at the graphic. Which reward tier did most of the staff members achieve?

(A) Tier A
(B) Tier B
(C) Tier C
(D) Tier D

97. Why does the speaker say Henry Manning will travel to Vermont next month?

(A) To see his family
(B) To attend a marketing seminar
(C) To receive a prize
(D) To compete in a contest

Product #75 Chocolate Box ($25)
Product #82 Wallet ($55)
Product #79 Sunglasses ($70)
Product #95 Wireless Charger ($40)

98. Who most likely are the listeners?

(A) Airline passengers
(B) Concert attendees
(C) Resort customers
(D) Shopping mall visitors

99. What does the speaker offer to do?

(A) Provide a beverage
(B) Turn off the lights
(C) Store some belongings
(D) Refund some money

100. Look at the graphic. Which item is no longer available?

(A) The chocolate box
(B) The wallet
(C) The sunglasses
(D) The wireless charger

GO ON TO THE NEXT PAGE

READING TEST

In the Reading test, you will read a variety of texts and answer several different types of reading comprehension questions. The entire Reading test will last 75 minutes. There are three parts, and directions are given for each part. You are encouraged to answer as many questions as possible within the time allowed.

You must mark your answers on the separate answer sheet. Do not write your answers in your test book.

PART 5

Directions: A word or phrase is missing in each of the sentences below. Four answer choices are given below each sentence. Select the best answer to complete the sentence. Then mark the letter (A), (B), (C), or (D) on your answer sheet.

101. The company executives are grateful ------- all the hard work and effort from all staff members.

    (A) with
    (B) much
    (C) that
    (D) for

102. Lisa Chen proofread the press release ------- prior to its publication.

    (A) caution
    (B) cautioned
    (C) cautious
    (D) cautiously

103. Having started only a week ago, Ms. LaPointe had a difficult time keeping ------- with the other physician's assistants.

    (A) line
    (B) track
    (C) pace
    (D) control

104. For decades, Margate College has been ------- in supporting local youth organizations through annual fundraising events.

    (A) activities
    (B) activists
    (C) actively
    (D) active

105. Kaiser Media and Gaulish Press have ------- an agreement to merge at the beginning of the fiscal year.

    (A) emerged
    (B) criticized
    (C) reached
    (D) acclaimed

106. Devon International is pleased to announce the expansion ------- its east training center.

    (A) over
    (B) as
    (C) from
    (D) of

107. Diners can try ------- dishes all year round at the newly opened Merchant Bistro.

    (A) dominant
    (B) abundant
    (C) exceptional
    (D) excessive

108. The Van Tassel Media is rather small in comparison to other production companies, but its documentary films are ------- among the best in the country.

    (A) argued
    (B) arguable
    (C) argument
    (D) arguably

109. Duoyi's most popular fitness tracker ------- a state-of-the-art GPS system.

(A) exercises
(B) challenges
(C) features
(D) contends

110. The office space will be cleaned ------- the workers remove the furniture.

(A) all
(B) or
(C) only
(D) once

111. Harper Wallpaper is sold in a wide variety of patterns ------- any home.

(A) is suiting
(B) to suit
(C) suited
(D) suit

112. Thanks to its ------- design, the new Strom smartphone can comfortably fit in the user's pocket.

(A) compact
(B) vague
(C) rigid
(D) significant

113. Hiroko Mifune, ------- financial support has made the new city park possible, will give a speech at the dedication ceremony.

(A) whose
(B) whoever
(C) who
(D) whom

114. After Ms. Kitigoe inspects the assembly line, ------- will suggest ways to make it run more efficiently.

(A) her
(B) herself
(C) she
(D) hers

115. Students ------- in attending the annual job fair should complete a registration form.

(A) interests
(B) interest
(C) interested
(D) interesting

116. Visitor numbers at the Natural History Museum increased ------- following the opening of the new dinosaur exhibit.

(A) strictly
(B) exactly
(C) rapidly
(D) closely

117. ------- the building supplies were delivered late, the construction staff worked quickly and kept the project on schedule.

(A) Not all
(B) Also
(C) Contrary to
(D) Although

118. At Kraven Law School, six months of legal internship ------- for certification as a graduate student.

(A) require
(B) will require
(C) are required
(D) has required

119. The graphic designer made ------- to the company's logo for the ad campaign.

(A) duplications
(B) revisions
(C) installations
(D) complications

120. Calumet Construction's proposal to remodel the Rotherton Museum received ------- by the management this morning.

(A) obedience
(B) decision
(C) approval
(D) reaction

GO ON TO THE NEXT PAGE

121. Your clothing items should be delivered ------- 48 hours, but it may take up to four business days.

(A) next
(B) into
(C) within
(D) plus

122. Utilities companies have ------- been offering online bill paying services to make the process more convenient.

(A) increased
(B) increasingly
(C) increases
(D) increasing

123. Stowaway Storage Center apologized for the ------- difficulties that renters had with its electronic locking system.

(A) occasionally
(B) occasion
(C) occasioned
(D) occasional

124. Dr. Rangit will be in his office for short ------- from 1 P.M. to 6 P.M. on Thursday.

(A) consulting
(B) consultants
(C) consultant
(D) consultations

125. In spite of recent uncertainty in the rubber industry, demand for vehicle tires has remained fairly -------.

(A) unpredictable
(B) complacent
(C) stable
(D) strict

126. The demonstration of Feder Corporation's new consumer electronics line ------- a lot of attention at the technology expo.

(A) generate
(B) generating
(C) is generated
(D) has generated

127. The Titanium series of Duratek laptops can be dropped from 2 meters without losing -------.

(A) functioned
(B) functional
(C) functionally
(D) functionality

128. Sales soared after the promotional event, ------- the store manager will consider offering more special deals.

(A) only if
(B) as though
(C) however
(D) so

129. The parking garage is owned and regulated -------, but convention visitors receive tickets to use the space.

(A) independently
(B) unintentionally
(C) steadily
(D) automatically

130. The packages of office supplies arrived just as the receptionist ------- for home.

(A) has been leaving
(B) has left
(C) was leaving
(D) leaves

PART 6

Directions: Read the texts that follow. A word, phrase, or sentence is missing in parts of each text. Four answer choices for each question are given below the text. Select the best answer to complete the text. Then mark the letter (A), (B), (C), or (D) on your answer sheet.

Questions 131-134 refer to the following memo.

To: drivers@canberratransport.gov.au

From: Harold Strahan

Subject: Vehicle assessment

Date: 7 May

To All Drivers,

As I mentioned last week, representatives from the mayor's office ------- an assessment of our bus fleet. They plan to determine ------- motor coaches and transport vans should be replaced in the coming year.
131.   132.

It would be helpful if you assist us in this -------. When you have time, inform us of any problems that have persistently occurred when operating your vehicle. Please send this information to the management team via e-mail at mgmt@canberratransport.gov.au. -------. We need only the vehicle's registration number, model year, and a short summary of the issue.
133.   134.

We always appreciate your dedication.

---

131. (A) was administering
(B) administer
(C) will have administered
(D) will be administering

132. (A) some
(B) each
(C) whom
(D) which

133. (A) tour
(B) model
(C) matter
(D) space

134. (A) We were surprised by the extent of the damage reported.
(B) An exact technical explanation is not necessary.
(C) The repairs will be performed as swiftly as possible.
(D) You will receive a $100 bonus if the person you referred is hired.

GO ON TO THE NEXT PAGE

Questions 135-138 refer to the following e-mail.

From: Curtis Branson <branson@edental.com>
To: Dominic Powell <dpowell@iu.edu>
Subject: Patient alerts
Date: October 27

Dear Mr. Powell,

In hopes of ------- our patients as efficiently and conveniently as possible, we have
      135.
started offering the opportunity to receive notifications and reminders by using a mobile
application. Currently, we send you updates to your e-mail address. -------. If you would
                                                                         136.
like to try using the app or wish to discuss your ------- for notifications from us, please
                                                      137.
give us a call at 858-555-1212.

------- aim is to provide patients with timely and helpful information about all aspects of
138.
dental care and to ensure an optimal patient experience at all times.

Curtis Branson
Office Manager
Elite Dental Clinic of Lenexa

135. (A) allowing
(B) serving
(C) improving
(D) thanking

136. (A) We believe that our clinic is the best in the area.
(B) Remember to schedule at least one yearly visit.
(C) E-mail alerts first became available last year.
(D) No changes will be made if you are satisfied with this arrangement.

137. (A) opted
(B) options
(C) optional
(D) optionally

138. (A) My
(B) Its
(C) Our
(D) Your

Questions 139-142 refer to the following letter.

July 16

Derek Hunter
Personnel Department
Milltek Systems, Inc.

Dear Mr. Hunter,

I would like to inquire about the engineering manager opening recently posted on your Web site. I am confident that I would be a valuable addition to Milltek Systems' engineering ------- as a supervisor.
                   139.

-------. I am presently employed as a project manager at Tappco Machinery, and I have
140.
designed agricultural and industrial sorting machinery for nearly a decade. ------- to this,
                                                                              141.
I worked at AgroTec Engineering, where I developed computerized processes for milling and baking applications.

I have attached a copy of my CV, which ------- more information about my experience
                                        142.
and qualifications. If you agree that these are a good match for your organization, I would love to meet and discuss it further.

Best Regards,

Edwin Dearing
Enclosure

139. (A) design
(B) quality
(C) proposal
(D) team

140. (A) I have many years of experience in relevant industries.
(B) You mentioned that an engineering degree is required for this job.
(C) You should have received several e-mails from my former coworkers.
(D) Please let me know if a more suitable position becomes available.

141. (A) Following
(B) Prior
(C) Similar
(D) Considering

142. (A) provide
(B) provides
(C) provided
(D) is providing

Questions 143-146 refer to the following article.

Yuccaville (August 9) – Row upon row of rooftop solar panels attest to the fact that Yuccaville has taken an interest in renewable energy. In fact, 5 percent of the power generated in the Yuccaville comes from solar energy these days, and that number is rising at a ------- rate. To a certain degree, this is because of the town's significant tax
143.
------- granted to solar panel owners. According to Brian Alvarez, CEO of Yuccaville
144.
Renewable Energy Solutions, more efficient batteries and easy-to-install panels have ------- made the technology more attractive. Mr. Alvarez anticipates that the number of
145.
solar panels in Yuccaville will increase dramatically in the future. -------.
146.

143. (A) temporary
(B) limited
(C) steady
(D) potential

144. (A) reduce
(B) reduced
(C) reducing
(D) reduction

145. (A) ever
(B) soon
(C) also
(D) much

146. (A) As a matter of fact, he believes that within a decade, almost all buildings will have solar panels.
(B) He believes this is one reason that fewer businesses have been opening in the Yuccaville.
(C) He worries about how the increased cost will affect sales.
(D) Furthermore, he has been very happy with the quality of the panels that he purchased last year.

PART 7

Directions: In this part you will read a selection of texts, such as magazine and newspaper articles, e-mails, and instant messages. Each text or set of texts is followed by several questions. Select the best answer for each question and mark the letter (A), (B), (C), or (D) on your answer sheet.

Questions 147-148 refer to the following voucher.

Luigi Angelo's

We at Luigi Angelo's are pleased to announce that the remodeling of our Chester Park location is now complete. Please join us at 196 Yosemite Way as we reopen our doors to the public. Bring this voucher any time between March 3 and March 9 to receive a complimentary garden salad when ordering a fountain drink and one of our homemade pasta dishes. Limit one coupon per table.

---

147. What is true about Luigi Angelo's?

(A) It has a vegetable garden.
(B) It will open a new location in March.
(C) It makes its own pasta.
(D) It recently expanded its menu offerings.

148. What is implied about the voucher?

(A) It can be applied to delivery orders.
(B) All Luigi Angelo's locations will accept it.
(C) Diners will receive a free drink with it.
(D) It is only valid for one week.

Questions 149-150 refer to the following Web page.

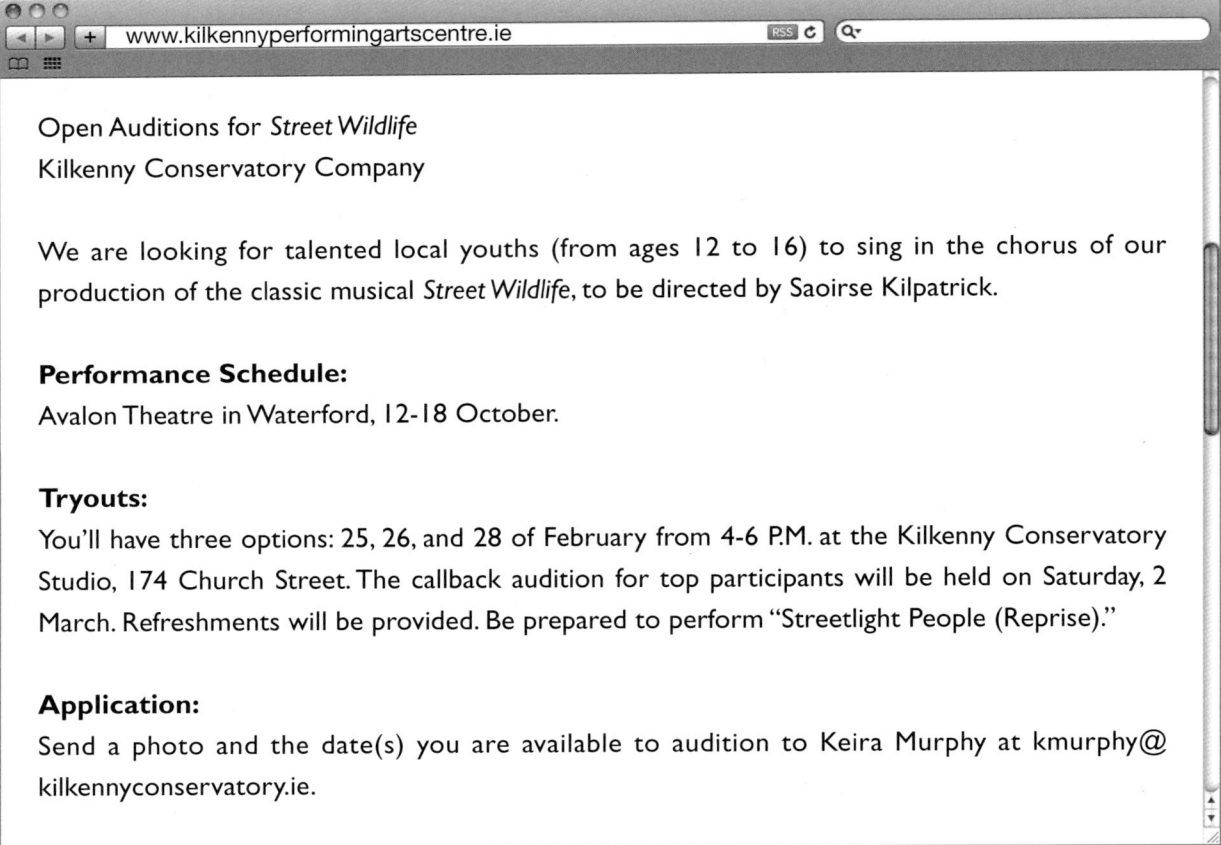

Open Auditions for *Street Wildlife*
Kilkenny Conservatory Company

We are looking for talented local youths (from ages 12 to 16) to sing in the chorus of our production of the classic musical *Street Wildlife*, to be directed by Saoirse Kilpatrick.

Performance Schedule:
Avalon Theatre in Waterford, 12-18 October.

Tryouts:
You'll have three options: 25, 26, and 28 of February from 4-6 P.M. at the Kilkenny Conservatory Studio, 174 Church Street. The callback audition for top participants will be held on Saturday, 2 March. Refreshments will be provided. Be prepared to perform "Streetlight People (Reprise)."

Application:
Send a photo and the date(s) you are available to audition to Keira Murphy at kmurphy@kilkennyconservatory.ie.

149. According to the Web page, who should get in touch with Ms. Murphy?

(A) Singers
(B) Models
(C) Directors
(D) Artists

150. What is suggested about *Street Wildlife*?

(A) It was written by Ms. Kilpatrick.
(B) It was originally performed in Waterford.
(C) It will be performed in October.
(D) It will be performed three times.

Questions 151-152 refer to the following text message chain.

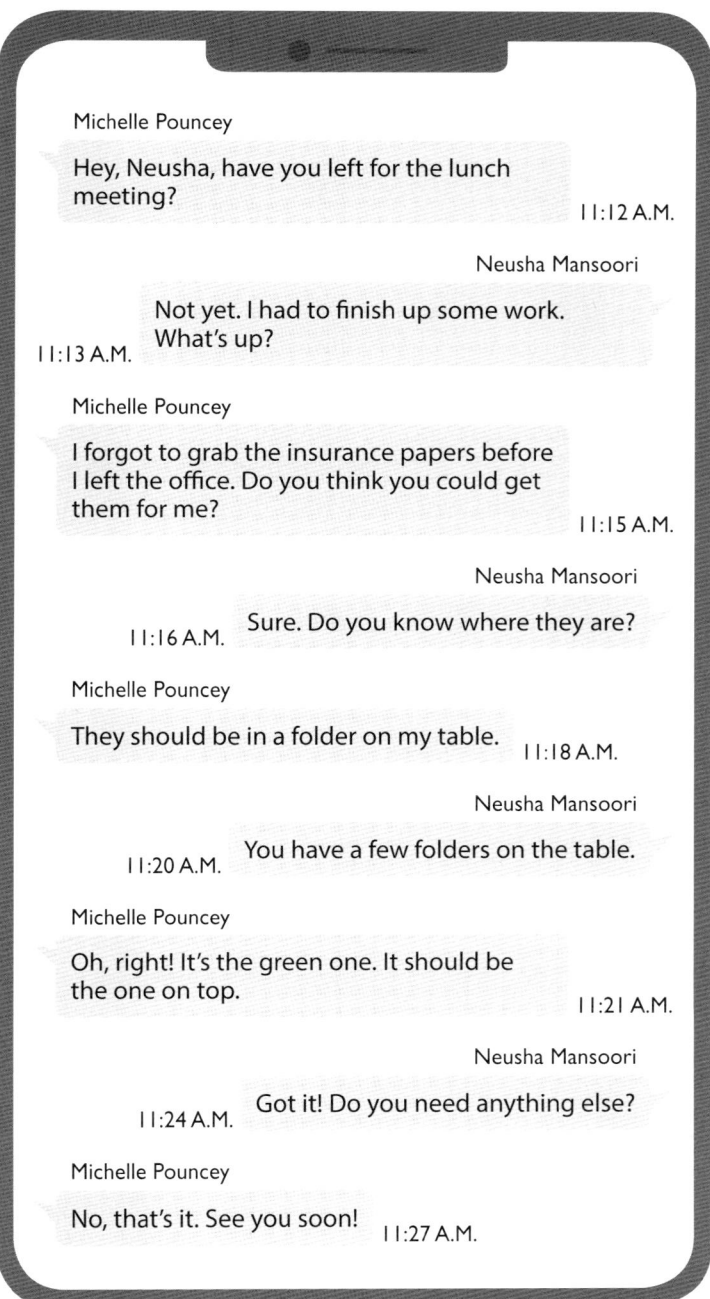

151. What problem does Ms. Pouncey mention?

(A) She needs help finding a location.
(B) She did not bring some documents.
(C) She is late for a meeting.
(D) She forgot to pay her insurance bill.

152. At 11:20 A.M., what does Ms. Mansoori imply when she writes, "You have a few folders on the table"?

(A) She needs additional information.
(B) She has to order more office supplies.
(C) Ms. Pouncey needs a bigger table.
(D) Ms. Pouncey should organize her workspace.

Questions 153-154 refer to the following e-mail.

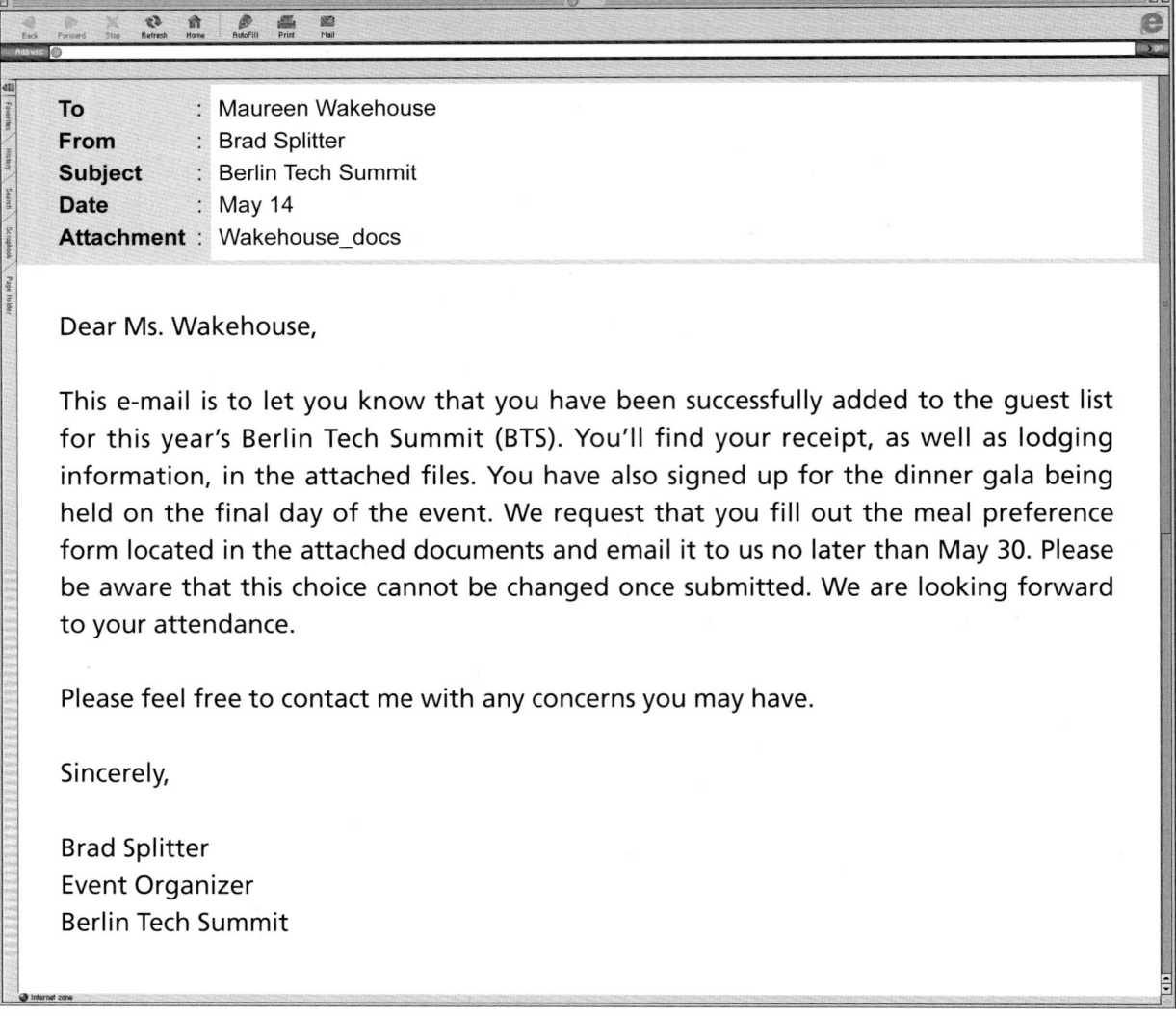

To : Maureen Wakehouse
From : Brad Splitter
Subject : Berlin Tech Summit
Date : May 14
Attachment : Wakehouse_docs

Dear Ms. Wakehouse,

This e-mail is to let you know that you have been successfully added to the guest list for this year's Berlin Tech Summit (BTS). You'll find your receipt, as well as lodging information, in the attached files. You have also signed up for the dinner gala being held on the final day of the event. We request that you fill out the meal preference form located in the attached documents and email it to us no later than May 30. Please be aware that this choice cannot be changed once submitted. We are looking forward to your attendance.

Please feel free to contact me with any concerns you may have.

Sincerely,

Brad Splitter
Event Organizer
Berlin Tech Summit

153. Why did Mr. Splitter send the e-mail?
(A) To inform Ms. Wakehouse of a schedule change
(B) To highlight the BTS's accomplishments
(C) To confirm a registration
(D) To recommend a hotel

154. What is Ms. Wakehouse advised to do?
(A) Update her contact information
(B) Reply by a specific date
(C) Arrive at a dinner party early
(D) Print out a map

Questions 155-157 refer to the following form.

CONTRACTOR INVOICE

PABLO'S PROFESSIONAL SIGN SERVICES (PPSS)

PHONE: 613-555-7899
E-MAIL: pablo@ppss.ca
HOMEPAGE: http://www.ppss.ca

BILL TO: Raphael Boucher
WORK SITE: 1350 Golden Line Road, Ottawa, Ontario
TYPE OF WORK: Store Sign
SCHEDULED INSTALLATION DATE:
21 August, 11:00 A.M.
ESTIMATED COMPLETION TIME: 4:00 P.M.

DESCRIPTION OF WORK AND SERVICES	AMOUNT
Design and create custom sign	$499.99
Delivery and installation of sign	$245.95
Quarterly maintenance visits	$150.50

TOTAL: $896.44
DOWN PAYMENT (received on 2 August): $300
AMOUNT DUE (upon completion): $596.44

---

155. What is indicated about the project?

(A) It will be completed over two days.
(B) It offers a service periodically.
(C) It was paid for all at once.
(D) It requires special lighting equipment.

156. Where will the project take place?

(A) At a sports stadium
(B) At a bus stop
(C) At PPSS's main office
(D) At Mr. Boucher's business location

157. How much will PPSS receive on August 21?

(A) $245.95
(B) $300.00
(C) $499.99
(D) $596.44

GO ON TO THE NEXT PAGE

Questions 158-160 refer to the following job advertisement.

Museum Curator Job Opening

POSITION
Montreal National Art Museum is in need of an experienced individual for its Ancient Art Department. Responsibilities of the curator include acquiring artifacts, care and display of collections, as well as educating and informing visitors of the exhibits.

QUALIFICATIONS
Candidates need at least two years of work experience in a museum or gallery setting. In addition, successful candidates will have the ability to speak French fluently. Candidates must also hold a university degree or equivalent in a subject such as fine arts or art history. Although a graduate degree is not necessary, it is an added bonus.

HOW TO APPLY
Visit our Web site at www.montrealart.com/jobs/ancientart to fill out an application.

CONTACT
If you have any questions, or would like to learn more about the position, please email our HR manager at janlopez@montrealart.com.

---

158. What is a necessary qualification for the job?

(A) A graduate degree
(B) Strong communication skills
(C) Proficiency in a specific language
(D) Experience in teaching fine arts

159. The word "bonus" in paragraph 2, line 4, is closest in meaning to

(A) prize
(B) advantage
(C) commission
(D) compensation

160. How can more information about the job be acquired?

(A) By attending a career fair
(B) By contacting an employee
(C) By going to a museum
(D) By visiting a home page

Questions 161-163 refer to the following press release.

PRESS RELEASE
Leonard Osgard
PR Director, Windermere Partners
losgard@windermerep.com

Marina (February 15) – Windermere Partners proudly announces the opening of its brand new shopping area, Marina Square. —[1]—. Although many of the commercial units have been sold, 10 retail spaces are still up for sale.

All retail spaces come with an open floor plan for you to design to your liking with the option to add on extra features such as shelving, countertops, and partitions. —[2]—. In addition, all stores will be able to take advantage of the shopping center's free wireless Internet, security patrols to keep your business safe day and night, and on-site cleaning and maintenance assistance, along with many other conveniences.

Marina Square is more than just a shopping center; it's also a great entertainment destination. —[3]—. With multiple fine dining options and plenty of activities for the whole family to take part in, Marina Square is set to become the new hot spot in town.

Feel free to stop by Marina Square and have a look around. —[4]—. For an individual consultation, call 710-555-6214 to arrange an appointment.

161. What kind of business most likely is Windermere Partners?

(A) A public relations company
(B) A construction materials manufacturer
(C) A private security company
(D) A commercial property developer

162. What is indicated about the retail spaces?

(A) They include storage rooms.
(B) They have access to several services.
(C) They are designed to be environmentally friendly.
(D) They can be leased for a short period.

163. In which of the positions marked [1], [2], [3], and [4] does the following sentence best belong?

"We have showings every day beginning at 11 A.M. and ending at 5 P.M."

(A) [1]
(B) [2]
(C) [3]
(D) [4]

Questions 164-167 refer to the following online chat discussion.

David Villa [1:02 P.M.]
Hey, guys. I need to ask for a favor. I'm supposed to work the night shift tonight, but I'm not feeling too well. Would it be possible to swap shifts with anyone?

Allison Costello [1:04 P.M.]
I wouldn't mind taking the hours, but I won't be able to make it to the hotel until 9. I have a dinner appointment at 7 in downtown Haverford. If Ms. Wahlberg is fine with me starting the shift a bit later, I can cover for you.

Lamar Jackson [1:06 P.M.]
I'd help you out, David, but I already purchased tickets to the evening showing of that new film, *Halfway There*. Hopefully, someone else can help.

David Villa [1:08 P.M.]
Allison, that's not a bad idea, but I'm worried Ms. Wahlberg would reject it. She's really serious about having enough people at the front desk at all times of day.

Allison Costello [1:09 P.M.]
True. David, why don't you contact Ms. Wahlberg and check if someone who is already there can work a little longer?

Jessica Choi [1:12 P.M.]
Hi, all, I would've replied earlier, but we got really busy. I'll be happy to stay later and wait until Allison gets here.

Allison Costello [1:14 P.M.]
That sounds like a good plan. Do you think it will be OK with Ms. Wahlberg?

David Villa [1:18 P.M.]
I just got off the phone with her. Ms. Walhberg doesn't mind at all. Thanks for your support, everyone.

Allison Costello [1:19 P.M.]
Sure thing. See you later, Jessica.

164. Where do the writers work?

(A) At a theater
(B) At a hospital
(C) At a restaurant
(D) At a hotel

165. What is probably true about all the writers?

(A) They work for the same supervisor.
(B) They will have dinner together.
(C) They regularly watch movies.
(D) They all live in Haverford.

166. At 1:18 P.M., what does Mr. Villa mean when he writes, "Ms. Walhberg doesn't mind at all"?

(A) She does not like a plan.
(B) She can pick him up.
(C) She will cover his shift for one week.
(D) She is fine with a scheduling change.

167. Who will end work later than originally intended this evening?

(A) David Villa
(B) Lamar Jackson
(C) Allison Costello
(D) Jessica Choi

Questions 168-171 refer to the following e-mail.

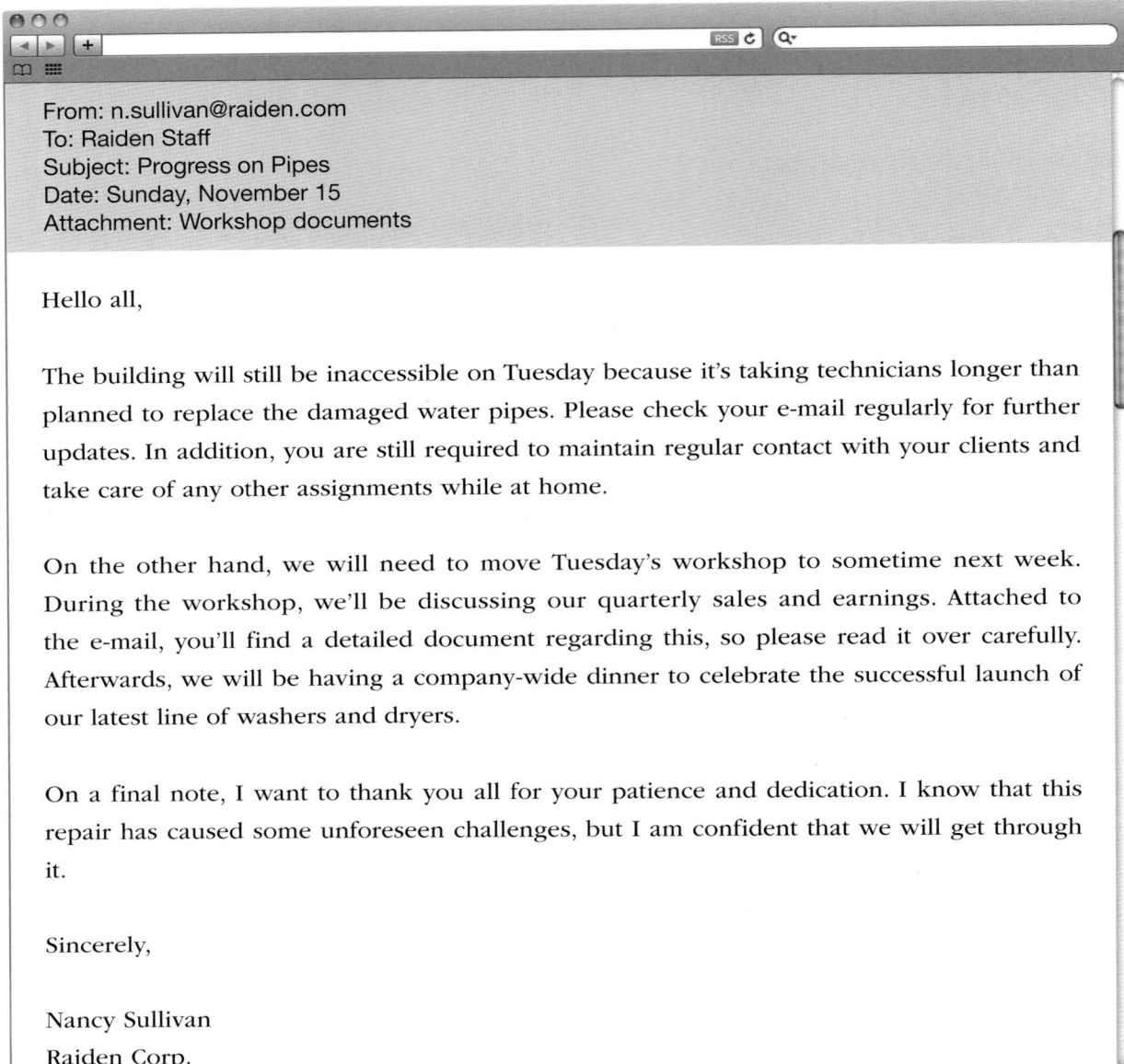

From: n.sullivan@raiden.com
To: Raiden Staff
Subject: Progress on Pipes
Date: Sunday, November 15
Attachment: Workshop documents

Hello all,

The building will still be inaccessible on Tuesday because it's taking technicians longer than planned to replace the damaged water pipes. Please check your e-mail regularly for further updates. In addition, you are still required to maintain regular contact with your clients and take care of any other assignments while at home.

On the other hand, we will need to move Tuesday's workshop to sometime next week. During the workshop, we'll be discussing our quarterly sales and earnings. Attached to the e-mail, you'll find a detailed document regarding this, so please read it over carefully. Afterwards, we will be having a company-wide dinner to celebrate the successful launch of our latest line of washers and dryers.

On a final note, I want to thank you all for your patience and dedication. I know that this repair has caused some unforeseen challenges, but I am confident that we will get through it.

Sincerely,

Nancy Sullivan
Raiden Corp.

168. What is mentioned about some water pipes?

(A) They are expensive to repair.
(B) They were initially inspected by Ms. Sullivan.
(C) They have been leaking for weeks.
(D) They will take more time to replace.

169. What are staff members expected to do on Tuesday?

(A) Work out of another location
(B) Visit some businesses
(C) Use a vacation day
(D) Come to the office later

170. What did Nancy Sullivan include with the e-mail?

(A) A dinner menu
(B) A client contact list
(C) An event calendar
(D) A financial report

171. What kind of business most likely is Raiden Corp.?

(A) A property management firm
(B) A home appliance producer
(C) A plumbing company
(D) An accounting business

GO ON TO THE NEXT PAGE

Questions 172-175 refer to the following article.

SINDRI COMES TO MANITOBA

(March 19)—Sindri, the Canadian manufacturer known for making personal electronics, is moving its main production facility. Most of its production in Quebec will cease when the new state-of-the-art plant opens in Manitoba next July. —[1]—. The relocation coincides with Sindri's announcement of a new range of models, including a tablet PC.

"Our original model, the Sindri Book laptop, was tremendously popular when it came out seven years ago," said Claude McCleod, the company's founder and CEO. "Since we started selling our all-in-one desktop three years ago, we've received feedback from our customers that they were interested in something more portable," he continued. While sales of existing models remain strong, McCleod is confident that the new tablet will draw new demographics of customers to the company's products. —[2]—.

Sindri has distinguished itself by offering high-quality products without the usual steep price tags. —[3]—. Sindri has grown as demand for affordable consumer electronics has taken off and has been particularly strong in countries with developing economies. The company's internal polling suggests that the top reasons customers chose Sindri over their competitors were its products' warranty and reputation for reliability, and their high price-performance ratio across all models. —[4]—. Find out more about the company's new line of products at their Web site sindri.com.

172. What does the article suggest about Sindri?

(A) It has manufacturing plants in multiple countries.
(B) It will operate two factories in Manitoba.
(C) It makes personal devices.
(D) It has been in business for over a decade.

173. What was the first product sold by Sindri?

(A) A smart watch
(B) A desktop
(C) A tablet
(D) A laptop

174. What is indicated about Sindri customers?

(A) They are concerned about pricing.
(B) They are environmentally-conscious.
(C) They prefer tablets to other products.
(D) They mostly live in developed countries.

175. In which of the positions marked [1], [2], [3], and [4] does the following sentence best belong?

"Younger people, and students in particular, are likely customers."

(A) [1]
(B) [2]
(C) [3]
(D) [4]

GO ON TO THE NEXT PAGE

Questions 176-180 refer to the following e-mail and notice.

FROM: Petra Stojakovic <petras@bellingercorp.com>
TO: employees@bellingercorp.com
SUBJECT: Reallocation of parking spaces
DATE: 22 April

Attention Staff:

This e-mail is to remind you that construction of the new Bellinger Corp. R&D Facility will commence on 29 April.

Starting 27 April, parking lots J and K will be inaccessible until 9 July, the estimated date of completion. Employees allocated to lots J and K will receive a temporary "visitor" parking permit allowing them to park their vehicles in the visitor garage. The Facilities Management Department will deliver these permits to your desk by noon tomorrow. Please place the permits on the passenger side of your front windshield.

The street leading up to parking lots J and K will be closed off due to the creation of a construction access road. In addition, the main entrance to the security office and flower garden will be closed. An alternate entry point will be available for both locations.

In order to reduce the number of incoming cars, we urge everyone to avoid these areas unless you have urgent business. Remember, when using the temporary entrance, please use the painted walkway only.

Thank you for your cooperation.

Best regards,

Petra Stojakovic
Facilities Management

WELCOME TO BELLINGER CORP.
BUILDING INFORMATION DESK

IMPORTANT NOTICE:
PARKING LOTS J & K WILL BE CLOSED UNTIL 1 AUGUST

Employees who are assigned to these lots but have not been given a temporary permit must visit the security office as soon as possible. An employee ID badge and a vehicle registration form are necessary.

Vehicles parked near designated work zones, such as the construction site or loading areas, are subject to be towed. Cars that are parked in lots without the proper permit will be issued a $30 penalty per day.

Staff members are on hand to help you.

176. Why are some parking lots being closed?

(A) They will only be available for visitors.
(B) They are being cleaned and repainted.
(C) Some construction work is starting soon.
(D) A company is using them for an event.

177. According to the e-mail, who will receive a temporary parking permit?

(A) People who normally park in lots J and K
(B) People who are touring the R&D Facility
(C) People who are interviewing for a job at Bellinger Corp.
(D) People who register for one with the Facilities Department

178. Why should employees try to avoid visiting the security office?

(A) So that guests can access an information desk
(B) So that security personnel can perform an inspection
(C) So that they can enjoy the garden
(D) So that there will be less traffic

179. What changed after the e-mail was sent on April 22?

(A) Which parking lots are inaccessible
(B) How long some parking lots will be inaccessible
(C) When employees will receive their parking permits
(D) Where parking permits should be placed

180. According to the notice, why might a staff member's vehicle be towed?

(A) If it is parked in the garage after July 9
(B) If it is parked next to a loading area
(C) If it does not have a parking permit
(D) If it is parked in the guest lot

GO ON TO THE NEXT PAGE

Questions 181-185 refer to the following questionnaire and e-mail.

QUESTIONNAIRE

Thank you for taking a moment to fill out our questionnaire. By doing so, you are helping us to better serve you here at Barkley's. In the form below, please check the box that indicates your level of satisfaction with each aspect.

(1=Poor, 2=Fair, 3=Average, 4=Good, 5=Excellent)

	1	2	3	4	5
How would you rate the store's atmosphere and cleanliness?	☐	☐	☐	■	☐
How would you rate the freshness of the ingredients used in your dish?	☐	☐	☐	☐	■
How would you rate your satisfaction compared to how much you paid for the food?	☐	☐	☐	■	☐
How would you rate the speed of the service you received?	☐	☐	☐	☐	■
How would you rate the staff's ability to answer your questions?	■	☐	☐	☐	☐
How would you rate your overall impression of Barkley's?	☐	☐	☐	■	☐

- How much did you spend today?: $75
- Age (optional):
  14-21 ☐ / 22-29 ■ / 30-37 ☐ / 38-45 ☐ / 46-54 ☐ / 55+ ☐
- Name (optional): Miguel Nunez
- E-mail (optional): mnunez1@penmail.co.nz

TO: Miguel Nunez <mnunez1@penmail.co.nz>
FROM: Support Services <ss@barkleys.co.nz>
SUBJECT: QUESTIONNAIRE
DATE: Tuesday, 4 August, 11:25 A.M.
ATTACHMENT: coupon

Dear Mr. Nunez,

We would like to thank you for taking the time to fill out our questionnaire about Barkley's. We received feedback from a lot of people, and we value all of your opinions. This information provides us with an opportunity to learn and serve you better.

We are glad to see that your overall rating of Barkley's was satisfactory. We were, however, disappointed to see that the majority of the responses we received expressed negative impressions regarding the same aspect that you were unhappy with. I want to assure you that we are taking the necessary steps to correct this problem. A new employee education program will be starting in the near future.

To show our appreciation for your feedback, we would like you to have a coupon (attached to this e-mail) for 20 percent off your next purchase at any Barkley's location in the nation. As always, we thank you for your business.

Best,

Yasiel Sanders

181. What kind of business most likely is Barkley's?

(A) An electronics store
(B) A supermarket
(C) A restaurant
(D) A marketing agency

182. Which statement about Barkley's would Mr. Nunez most likely agree with?

(A) It is reasonably priced.
(B) It has a wide range of services.
(C) It is in a convenient location.
(D) It has experienced employees.

183. In the e-mail, the word "value" in paragraph 1, line 2, is closest in meaning to

(A) calculate
(B) appreciate
(C) profit
(D) emphasize

184. What most likely is Barkley's planning to do?

(A) Clean the workplace more frequently
(B) Lower prices on some of its merchandise
(C) Offer a coupon to every customer who participates in a questionnaire
(D) Train workers to be more knowledgeable about its products

185. What is implied about the questionnaire?

(A) It must be filled out on the Internet.
(B) Many customers have completed it.
(C) It is updated every two years.
(D) Mr. Sanders designed it.

GO ON TO THE NEXT PAGE

Questions 186-190 refer to the following planning guide, information, and comment card.

San Lorenzo: Getting the Most Out of Your Visit

Drop in for a couple of hours or stay a while. Either way, you'll fall in love with the city of San Lorenzo. Here are our recommendations to plan your stay.

Partial Day
Go to the San Lorenzo Visitor Center at 113 Main Street for a brief lecture on the city's history. Then, hop on the tour bus that picks up and drops off visitors at landmarks around the city.

Complete Day
On top of all the partial-day activities, check out Phoenix Palace right across from the Visitor Center. Guided tours of the palace and its botanical garden are available from noon to sundown daily. Be sure to visit the gift shop for some beautiful souvenirs.

Multi-Day (More than one day)
After doing all the activities listed above, discover more of San Lorenzo by taking a walking tour around the city and its surrounding area.

San Lorenzo Walking Trails

Rainbow Ridge (10.3km)
This 10.3-kilometer, mostly uphill hike takes you from the harbor, through downtown, to all the way up to the scenic bluffs of Rainbow Ridge Park. Perfect for the best views of the city, but demanding for novice hikers.

Borges Peninsula (6.1km)
This 6.1-kilometer trail takes you through the rolling hills near Borges Wildlife Reserve. The thick foliage means that the trail doesn't get much light, so head back before sundown.

The Old Church Route (1.7km)
Stroll the cobbled streets from St. Catherine's to St. Jessica's Churches, admiring the sights along the way. A flat, easygoing 1.7 kilometers.

Brilliant Boulevard (2.1km)
A popular route from the Museum District to Crimson Tower. Enjoy great shopping and dining options along the way. This 2.1-kilometer route can be a little hectic at night.

San Lorenzo Visitor Center
Comment Card

Name: Scottie Fitzgerald
Date(s) of Visit: August 1-2

Message:
My family loved our visit to San Lorenzo. Since we'd never visited the city, we followed the recommendations in the Visitor Center's planning guide exactly, and it really helped. We spent both Saturday and Sunday in town, and we saw a lot. The tour bus was well-worth the price. The only walking trail we didn't try out was the longest and most difficult one. Our children are still too young for something like that. However, I wish to try it soon—hopefully before my San Lorenzo transit card I bought on my first day expires on the last day of August.

186. What does the planning guide indicate about Phoenix Palace?

(A) It offers discounts to residents
(B) It does not charge an admission fee.
(C) It is located on Main Street.
(D) It is the oldest site in San Lorenzo.

187. According to the walking trail information, what is true about the Borges Peninsula trail?

(A) It provides views of the city.
(B) It is in a shaded area.
(C) It is very beautiful at night.
(D) It should not be used by beginners.

188. What did Mr. Fitzgerald probably do first when he visited the city?

(A) Board a tour bus
(B) Visit a palace
(C) Listen to a lecture
(D) Go on a hike

189. Which trail does Mr. Fitzgerald plan to hike in the future?

(A) Rainbow Ridge
(B) Borges Peninsula
(C) The Old Church Route
(D) Brilliant Boulevard

190. What does Mr. Fitzgerald suggest on his comment card?

(A) He didn't think the planning guide was very useful.
(B) He is a professional hiker.
(C) He purchased a one-month transportation card.
(D) He booked a hotel near the Visitor Center.

GO ON TO THE NEXT PAGE

Questions 191-195 refer to the following article, schedule, and e-mail.

Johnson County to Renovate Water Pipe Network

(March 12) - Throughout the month of April, Johnson County Water District intends to upgrade several miles of copper pipes with new polyvinyl chloride (PVC) pipes in order to ensure that the county's water system continues to function in an optimal manner.

"The ability of PVC pipes to withstand greater water pressure will allow for better operation of laundry machines, dishwashers, and a variety of other consumer devices," said Mr. Sohel Khan, Johnson County Water District Supervisor. "The new pipes will also pose fewer potential environmental hazards than the old copper ones."

Several roads in the county will be completely inaccessible for 24-hour periods while the renovation is taking place. Water District officials are consulting with local store owners in hopes of agreeing upon a timetable that will avoid causing unnecessary problems for businesses. Constant revisions will be made to the schedule, which can be found on the County Clerk's Web site. Residents may also address comments and concerns to the County Clerk.

---

www.johnsoncountyclerk.gov

Water Pipe Renovation Schedule:

Saturday, April 4	Antioch Street
Sunday, April 5	Corinth Avenue
Saturday, April 11	Jameson Lane
Sunday, April 12	Cherokee Drive

After the renovation has been completed, a Johnson County Water District employee will visit your home or business to check water pressure.

To Ed Haber <eddie@eddiesbakery.com>
From Anita Quackenbush <quackenbush@johnsoncountyclerk.gov>
Subject Inspection
Date April 1

Dear Mr. Haber,

As you may know, we will be renovating water lines on the street that runs along your store on Saturday, April 11. You should anticipate about 4 hours without running water that morning. We apologize for any inconvenience this may cause. A Water District technician is scheduled to visit your business the following day between 9 A.M. and 11 A.M. to confirm proper water pressure. If you need to arrange a different time, please notify us at 555-1212.

Best Regards,

Anita Quackenbush

191. According to the article, what is indicated about the new pipes?

(A) They are more affordable than copper pipes.
(B) They will make some equipment function better.
(C) They are going to be installed during the morning.
(D) They will be inspected on a frequent basis.

192. What does the article mention about the project schedule?

(A) It will be updated regularly.
(B) Mr. Khan created it.
(C) Some residents don't approve of it.
(D) It has some problems.

193. What will happen on April 4?

(A) A new county clerk director will be appointed.
(B) A road will be blocked.
(C) A business convention will be held.
(D) A city parade will take place.

194. What is implied about Mr. Haber's store?

(A) It has been closed for one week.
(B) It operates 24 hours a day.
(C) It is located on Jameson Lane.
(D) It has recently opened.

195. Who most likely is Ms. Quackenbush?

(A) A local business owner
(B) A construction worker
(C) A Water District technician
(D) A government employee

Questions 196-200 refer to the following brochure and e-mails.

Nevardo's

Just outside Palm Springs in the desert community of Cathedral City, Nevardo's provides a perfect location for any seminar, party, or ceremony. Situated at the edge of the gorgeous Indian Canyon Nature Preserve, it features breathtaking views from its spacious patio lounge.

Inside, the Coachella Room hosts groups of up to 150 people, and the Agua Caliente Hall can comfortably fit 250 attendees. For conferences, the Joshua Tree Room works well for groups of up to 75 participants, or larger turnouts can be accommodated in the newly restored Lucille Ball Auditorium, which can seat 100. The latter two are fully equipped with top-quality audio-visual equipment to ensure a successful presentation.

Our award-winning buffet, the Nopalitos Grill, serves up a fantastic array of Mexican and Southwestern dishes. Make sure to check out our special Cinco de Mayo menu on May 5!

For more information check out our Web site: www.nevardos.com.

We offer a special Local Partner discount of 30 percent to Coachella Valley businesses on certain days. For details, call 760-555-1212.

To	Dan Chan <dchan@charpentierfinancial.com>
From	Fadila Boumaza <fboumaza@charpentierfinancial.com>
Date	January 4
Subject	Merger Celebration Plan

Dear Mr. Chan,

I checked out that place, Nevardo's, you mentioned in Monday's meeting, and I think it would be perfect for our corporate merger party. The location's really scenic, and since we've got a lot of guests, now over 200, attending from out of town, it's a fine opportunity to show visitors the beauty of the desert. They have an appropriate space available on May 11, May 25, and May 27. The first date is when they offer a substantial discount for local companies like ours.

Please confirm with Accounting and let me know when they say it's okay to make the reservation. But we shouldn't wait too long. The place is already booked up through April, and these openings in May will probably fill up quickly, too.

Thanks,

Fadila

To	Fadila Boumaza <fboumaza@charpentierfinancial.com>
From	Dan Chan <dchan@charpentierfinancial.com>
Date	January 4
Subject	Re: Merger Celebration Plan

Fadila,

Thank you for the details regarding Nevardo's. After talking with the accounting manager, we decided to go with the date where we can receive a reduced rate. This will be good for our budget. Please call Nevardo's and book the venue.

Dan Chan
HR Director, Charpentier Financial

---

196. According to the brochure, what is true about Nevardo's?

(A) It plans to remodel an auditorium.
(B) It has recently updated its restaurant menu.
(C) It is in downtown Palm Springs.
(D) It is suitable for various kinds of events.

197. What does Ms. Boumaza indicate about the corporate merger party?

(A) It will be held on multiple dates.
(B) It requires approval from others.
(C) It will include a video presentation.
(D) It may be postponed.

198. Where will the corporate merger party most likely be held?

(A) In the Coachella Room
(B) In the Agua Caliente Hall
(C) In the Joshua Tree Room
(D) In the Lucille Ball Auditorium

199. Why is Ms. Boumaza worried?

(A) The price of a venue may increase.
(B) A location may be too inconvenient.
(C) Many guests have not confirmed their attendance.
(D) The most ideal room may become unavailable.

200. When will Charpentier Financial's party most likely take place?

(A) On May 5
(B) On May 11
(C) On May 25
(D) On May 27

Stop! This is the end of the test. If you finish before time is called, you may go back to Part 5, 6, and 7 and check your work.

ANSWER SHEET

TEST 01

LISTENING (Part I-IV)

NO.	ANSWER	NO.	ANSWER	NO.	ANSWER	NO.	ANSWER	NO.	ANSWER
	A B C D		A B C D		A B C D		A B C D		A B C D
1	Ⓐ Ⓑ Ⓒ Ⓓ	21	Ⓐ Ⓑ Ⓒ	41	Ⓐ Ⓑ Ⓒ Ⓓ	61	Ⓐ Ⓑ Ⓒ Ⓓ	81	Ⓐ Ⓑ Ⓒ Ⓓ
2	Ⓐ Ⓑ Ⓒ Ⓓ	22	Ⓐ Ⓑ Ⓒ	42	Ⓐ Ⓑ Ⓒ Ⓓ	62	Ⓐ Ⓑ Ⓒ Ⓓ	82	Ⓐ Ⓑ Ⓒ Ⓓ
3	Ⓐ Ⓑ Ⓒ Ⓓ	23	Ⓐ Ⓑ Ⓒ	43	Ⓐ Ⓑ Ⓒ Ⓓ	63	Ⓐ Ⓑ Ⓒ Ⓓ	83	Ⓐ Ⓑ Ⓒ Ⓓ
4	Ⓐ Ⓑ Ⓒ Ⓓ	24	Ⓐ Ⓑ Ⓒ	44	Ⓐ Ⓑ Ⓒ Ⓓ	64	Ⓐ Ⓑ Ⓒ Ⓓ	84	Ⓐ Ⓑ Ⓒ Ⓓ
5	Ⓐ Ⓑ Ⓒ Ⓓ	25	Ⓐ Ⓑ Ⓒ	45	Ⓐ Ⓑ Ⓒ Ⓓ	65	Ⓐ Ⓑ Ⓒ Ⓓ	85	Ⓐ Ⓑ Ⓒ Ⓓ
6	Ⓐ Ⓑ Ⓒ Ⓓ	26	Ⓐ Ⓑ Ⓒ	46	Ⓐ Ⓑ Ⓒ Ⓓ	66	Ⓐ Ⓑ Ⓒ Ⓓ	86	Ⓐ Ⓑ Ⓒ Ⓓ
7	Ⓐ Ⓑ Ⓒ	27	Ⓐ Ⓑ Ⓒ	47	Ⓐ Ⓑ Ⓒ Ⓓ	67	Ⓐ Ⓑ Ⓒ Ⓓ	87	Ⓐ Ⓑ Ⓒ Ⓓ
8	Ⓐ Ⓑ Ⓒ	28	Ⓐ Ⓑ Ⓒ Ⓓ	48	Ⓐ Ⓑ Ⓒ Ⓓ	68	Ⓐ Ⓑ Ⓒ Ⓓ	88	Ⓐ Ⓑ Ⓒ Ⓓ
9	Ⓐ Ⓑ Ⓒ	29	Ⓐ Ⓑ Ⓒ Ⓓ	49	Ⓐ Ⓑ Ⓒ Ⓓ	69	Ⓐ Ⓑ Ⓒ Ⓓ	89	Ⓐ Ⓑ Ⓒ Ⓓ
10	Ⓐ Ⓑ Ⓒ	30	Ⓐ Ⓑ Ⓒ Ⓓ	50	Ⓐ Ⓑ Ⓒ Ⓓ	70	Ⓐ Ⓑ Ⓒ Ⓓ	90	Ⓐ Ⓑ Ⓒ Ⓓ
11	Ⓐ Ⓑ Ⓒ	31	Ⓐ Ⓑ Ⓒ Ⓓ	51	Ⓐ Ⓑ Ⓒ Ⓓ	71	Ⓐ Ⓑ Ⓒ Ⓓ	91	Ⓐ Ⓑ Ⓒ Ⓓ
12	Ⓐ Ⓑ Ⓒ	32	Ⓐ Ⓑ Ⓒ Ⓓ	52	Ⓐ Ⓑ Ⓒ Ⓓ	72	Ⓐ Ⓑ Ⓒ Ⓓ	92	Ⓐ Ⓑ Ⓒ Ⓓ
13	Ⓐ Ⓑ Ⓒ	33	Ⓐ Ⓑ Ⓒ Ⓓ	53	Ⓐ Ⓑ Ⓒ Ⓓ	73	Ⓐ Ⓑ Ⓒ Ⓓ	93	Ⓐ Ⓑ Ⓒ Ⓓ
14	Ⓐ Ⓑ Ⓒ	34	Ⓐ Ⓑ Ⓒ Ⓓ	54	Ⓐ Ⓑ Ⓒ Ⓓ	74	Ⓐ Ⓑ Ⓒ Ⓓ	94	Ⓐ Ⓑ Ⓒ Ⓓ
15	Ⓐ Ⓑ Ⓒ	35	Ⓐ Ⓑ Ⓒ Ⓓ	55	Ⓐ Ⓑ Ⓒ Ⓓ	75	Ⓐ Ⓑ Ⓒ Ⓓ	95	Ⓐ Ⓑ Ⓒ Ⓓ
16	Ⓐ Ⓑ Ⓒ	36	Ⓐ Ⓑ Ⓒ Ⓓ	56	Ⓐ Ⓑ Ⓒ Ⓓ	76	Ⓐ Ⓑ Ⓒ Ⓓ	96	Ⓐ Ⓑ Ⓒ Ⓓ
17	Ⓐ Ⓑ Ⓒ	37	Ⓐ Ⓑ Ⓒ Ⓓ	57	Ⓐ Ⓑ Ⓒ Ⓓ	77	Ⓐ Ⓑ Ⓒ Ⓓ	97	Ⓐ Ⓑ Ⓒ Ⓓ
18	Ⓐ Ⓑ Ⓒ	38	Ⓐ Ⓑ Ⓒ Ⓓ	58	Ⓐ Ⓑ Ⓒ Ⓓ	78	Ⓐ Ⓑ Ⓒ Ⓓ	98	Ⓐ Ⓑ Ⓒ Ⓓ
19	Ⓐ Ⓑ Ⓒ	39	Ⓐ Ⓑ Ⓒ Ⓓ	59	Ⓐ Ⓑ Ⓒ Ⓓ	79	Ⓐ Ⓑ Ⓒ Ⓓ	99	Ⓐ Ⓑ Ⓒ Ⓓ
20	Ⓐ Ⓑ Ⓒ	40	Ⓐ Ⓑ Ⓒ Ⓓ	60	Ⓐ Ⓑ Ⓒ Ⓓ	80	Ⓐ Ⓑ Ⓒ Ⓓ	100	Ⓐ Ⓑ Ⓒ Ⓓ

READING (Part V-VII)

NO.	ANSWER	NO.	ANSWER	NO.	ANSWER	NO.	ANSWER	NO.	ANSWER
	A B C D		A B C D		A B C D		A B C D		A B C D
101	Ⓐ Ⓑ Ⓒ Ⓓ	121	Ⓐ Ⓑ Ⓒ Ⓓ	141	Ⓐ Ⓑ Ⓒ Ⓓ	161	Ⓐ Ⓑ Ⓒ Ⓓ	181	Ⓐ Ⓑ Ⓒ Ⓓ
102	Ⓐ Ⓑ Ⓒ Ⓓ	122	Ⓐ Ⓑ Ⓒ Ⓓ	142	Ⓐ Ⓑ Ⓒ Ⓓ	162	Ⓐ Ⓑ Ⓒ Ⓓ	182	Ⓐ Ⓑ Ⓒ Ⓓ
103	Ⓐ Ⓑ Ⓒ Ⓓ	123	Ⓐ Ⓑ Ⓒ Ⓓ	143	Ⓐ Ⓑ Ⓒ Ⓓ	163	Ⓐ Ⓑ Ⓒ Ⓓ	183	Ⓐ Ⓑ Ⓒ Ⓓ
104	Ⓐ Ⓑ Ⓒ Ⓓ	124	Ⓐ Ⓑ Ⓒ Ⓓ	144	Ⓐ Ⓑ Ⓒ Ⓓ	164	Ⓐ Ⓑ Ⓒ Ⓓ	184	Ⓐ Ⓑ Ⓒ Ⓓ
105	Ⓐ Ⓑ Ⓒ Ⓓ	125	Ⓐ Ⓑ Ⓒ Ⓓ	145	Ⓐ Ⓑ Ⓒ Ⓓ	165	Ⓐ Ⓑ Ⓒ Ⓓ	185	Ⓐ Ⓑ Ⓒ Ⓓ
106	Ⓐ Ⓑ Ⓒ Ⓓ	126	Ⓐ Ⓑ Ⓒ Ⓓ	146	Ⓐ Ⓑ Ⓒ Ⓓ	166	Ⓐ Ⓑ Ⓒ Ⓓ	186	Ⓐ Ⓑ Ⓒ Ⓓ
107	Ⓐ Ⓑ Ⓒ Ⓓ	127	Ⓐ Ⓑ Ⓒ Ⓓ	147	Ⓐ Ⓑ Ⓒ Ⓓ	167	Ⓐ Ⓑ Ⓒ Ⓓ	187	Ⓐ Ⓑ Ⓒ Ⓓ
108	Ⓐ Ⓑ Ⓒ Ⓓ	128	Ⓐ Ⓑ Ⓒ Ⓓ	148	Ⓐ Ⓑ Ⓒ Ⓓ	168	Ⓐ Ⓑ Ⓒ Ⓓ	188	Ⓐ Ⓑ Ⓒ Ⓓ
109	Ⓐ Ⓑ Ⓒ Ⓓ	129	Ⓐ Ⓑ Ⓒ Ⓓ	149	Ⓐ Ⓑ Ⓒ Ⓓ	169	Ⓐ Ⓑ Ⓒ Ⓓ	189	Ⓐ Ⓑ Ⓒ Ⓓ
110	Ⓐ Ⓑ Ⓒ Ⓓ	130	Ⓐ Ⓑ Ⓒ Ⓓ	150	Ⓐ Ⓑ Ⓒ Ⓓ	170	Ⓐ Ⓑ Ⓒ Ⓓ	190	Ⓐ Ⓑ Ⓒ Ⓓ
111	Ⓐ Ⓑ Ⓒ Ⓓ	131	Ⓐ Ⓑ Ⓒ Ⓓ	151	Ⓐ Ⓑ Ⓒ Ⓓ	171	Ⓐ Ⓑ Ⓒ Ⓓ	191	Ⓐ Ⓑ Ⓒ Ⓓ
112	Ⓐ Ⓑ Ⓒ Ⓓ	132	Ⓐ Ⓑ Ⓒ Ⓓ	152	Ⓐ Ⓑ Ⓒ Ⓓ	172	Ⓐ Ⓑ Ⓒ Ⓓ	192	Ⓐ Ⓑ Ⓒ Ⓓ
113	Ⓐ Ⓑ Ⓒ Ⓓ	133	Ⓐ Ⓑ Ⓒ Ⓓ	153	Ⓐ Ⓑ Ⓒ Ⓓ	173	Ⓐ Ⓑ Ⓒ Ⓓ	193	Ⓐ Ⓑ Ⓒ Ⓓ
114	Ⓐ Ⓑ Ⓒ Ⓓ	134	Ⓐ Ⓑ Ⓒ Ⓓ	154	Ⓐ Ⓑ Ⓒ Ⓓ	174	Ⓐ Ⓑ Ⓒ Ⓓ	194	Ⓐ Ⓑ Ⓒ Ⓓ
115	Ⓐ Ⓑ Ⓒ Ⓓ	135	Ⓐ Ⓑ Ⓒ Ⓓ	155	Ⓐ Ⓑ Ⓒ Ⓓ	175	Ⓐ Ⓑ Ⓒ Ⓓ	195	Ⓐ Ⓑ Ⓒ Ⓓ
116	Ⓐ Ⓑ Ⓒ Ⓓ	136	Ⓐ Ⓑ Ⓒ Ⓓ	156	Ⓐ Ⓑ Ⓒ Ⓓ	176	Ⓐ Ⓑ Ⓒ Ⓓ	196	Ⓐ Ⓑ Ⓒ Ⓓ
117	Ⓐ Ⓑ Ⓒ Ⓓ	137	Ⓐ Ⓑ Ⓒ Ⓓ	157	Ⓐ Ⓑ Ⓒ Ⓓ	177	Ⓐ Ⓑ Ⓒ Ⓓ	197	Ⓐ Ⓑ Ⓒ Ⓓ
118	Ⓐ Ⓑ Ⓒ Ⓓ	138	Ⓐ Ⓑ Ⓒ Ⓓ	158	Ⓐ Ⓑ Ⓒ Ⓓ	178	Ⓐ Ⓑ Ⓒ Ⓓ	198	Ⓐ Ⓑ Ⓒ Ⓓ
119	Ⓐ Ⓑ Ⓒ Ⓓ	139	Ⓐ Ⓑ Ⓒ Ⓓ	159	Ⓐ Ⓑ Ⓒ Ⓓ	179	Ⓐ Ⓑ Ⓒ Ⓓ	199	Ⓐ Ⓑ Ⓒ Ⓓ
120	Ⓐ Ⓑ Ⓒ Ⓓ	140	Ⓐ Ⓑ Ⓒ Ⓓ	160	Ⓐ Ⓑ Ⓒ Ⓓ	180	Ⓐ Ⓑ Ⓒ Ⓓ	200	Ⓐ Ⓑ Ⓒ Ⓓ

ANSWER SHEET

TEST 02

LISTENING (Part I-IV)

NO.	ANSWER	NO.	ANSWER	NO.	ANSWER	NO.	ANSWER
1	A B C D	21	A B C D	41	A B C D	61	A B C D
2	A B C D	22	A B C D	42	A B C D	62	A B C D
3	A B C D	23	A B C D	43	A B C D	63	A B C D
4	A B C D	24	A B C D	44	A B C D	64	A B C D
5	A B C D	25	A B C D	45	A B C D	65	A B C D
6	A B C D	26	A B C D	46	A B C D	66	A B C D
7	A B C D	27	A B C D	47	A B C D	67	A B C D
8	A B C D	28	A B C D	48	A B C D	68	A B C D
9	A B C D	29	A B C D	49	A B C D	69	A B C D
10	A B C D	30	A B C D	50	A B C D	70	A B C D
11	A B C D	31	A B C D	51	A B C D	71	A B C D
12	A B C D	32	A B C D	52	A B C D	72	A B C D
13	A B C D	33	A B C D	53	A B C D	73	A B C D
14	A B C D	34	A B C D	54	A B C D	74	A B C D
15	A B C D	35	A B C D	55	A B C D	75	A B C D
16	A B C D	36	A B C D	56	A B C D	76	A B C D
17	A B C D	37	A B C D	57	A B C D	77	A B C D
18	A B C D	38	A B C D	58	A B C D	78	A B C D
19	A B C D	39	A B C D	59	A B C D	79	A B C D
20	A B C D	40	A B C D	60	A B C D	80	A B C D

NO.	ANSWER
81	A B C D
82	A B C D
83	A B C D
84	A B C D
85	A B C D
86	A B C D
87	A B C D
88	A B C D
89	A B C D
90	A B C D
91	A B C D
92	A B C D
93	A B C D
94	A B C D
95	A B C D
96	A B C D
97	A B C D
98	A B C D
99	A B C D
100	A B C D

READING (Part V-VII)

NO.	ANSWER	NO.	ANSWER	NO.	ANSWER	NO.	ANSWER	NO.	ANSWER
101	A B C D	121	A B C D	141	A B C D	161	A B C D	181	A B C D
102	A B C D	122	A B C D	142	A B C D	162	A B C D	182	A B C D
103	A B C D	123	A B C D	143	A B C D	163	A B C D	183	A B C D
104	A B C D	124	A B C D	144	A B C D	164	A B C D	184	A B C D
105	A B C D	125	A B C D	145	A B C D	165	A B C D	185	A B C D
106	A B C D	126	A B C D	146	A B C D	166	A B C D	186	A B C D
107	A B C D	127	A B C D	147	A B C D	167	A B C D	187	A B C D
108	A B C D	128	A B C D	148	A B C D	168	A B C D	188	A B C D
109	A B C D	129	A B C D	149	A B C D	169	A B C D	189	A B C D
110	A B C D	130	A B C D	150	A B C D	170	A B C D	190	A B C D
111	A B C D	131	A B C D	151	A B C D	171	A B C D	191	A B C D
112	A B C D	132	A B C D	152	A B C D	172	A B C D	192	A B C D
113	A B C D	133	A B C D	153	A B C D	173	A B C D	193	A B C D
114	A B C D	134	A B C D	154	A B C D	174	A B C D	194	A B C D
115	A B C D	135	A B C D	155	A B C D	175	A B C D	195	A B C D
116	A B C D	136	A B C D	156	A B C D	176	A B C D	196	A B C D
117	A B C D	137	A B C D	157	A B C D	177	A B C D	197	A B C D
118	A B C D	138	A B C D	158	A B C D	178	A B C D	198	A B C D
119	A B C D	139	A B C D	159	A B C D	179	A B C D	199	A B C D
120	A B C D	140	A B C D	160	A B C D	180	A B C D	200	A B C D

ANSWER SHEET

TEST 03

LISTENING (Part I-IV)

NO.	ANSWER	NO.	ANSWER	NO.	ANSWER	NO.	ANSWER	NO.	ANSWER
1	A B C D	21	A B C	41	A B C D	61	A B C D	81	A B C D
2	A B C D	22	A B C	42	A B C D	62	A B C D	82	A B C D
3	A B C D	23	A B C	43	A B C D	63	A B C D	83	A B C D
4	A B C D	24	A B C	44	A B C D	64	A B C D	84	A B C D
5	A B C	25	A B C	45	A B C D	65	A B C D	85	A B C D
6	A B C	26	A B C	46	A B C D	66	A B C D	86	A B C D
7	A B C	27	A B C	47	A B C D	67	A B C D	87	A B C D
8	A B C	28	A B C	48	A B C D	68	A B C D	88	A B C D
9	A B C	29	A B C	49	A B C D	69	A B C D	89	A B C D
10	A B C	30	A B C	50	A B C D	70	A B C D	90	A B C D
11	A B C	31	A B C	51	A B C D	71	A B C D	91	A B C D
12	A B C	32	A B C	52	A B C D	72	A B C D	92	A B C D
13	A B C	33	A B C	53	A B C D	73	A B C D	93	A B C D
14	A B C	34	A B C	54	A B C D	74	A B C D	94	A B C D
15	A B C	35	A B C	55	A B C D	75	A B C D	95	A B C D
16	A B C	36	A B C	56	A B C D	76	A B C D	96	A B C D
17	A B C	37	A B C	57	A B C D	77	A B C D	97	A B C D
18	A B C	38	A B C	58	A B C D	78	A B C D	98	A B C D
19	A B C	39	A B C	59	A B C D	79	A B C D	99	A B C D
20	A B C	40	A B C	60	A B C D	80	A B C D	100	A B C D

READING (Part V-VII)

NO.	ANSWER	NO.	ANSWER	NO.	ANSWER	NO.	ANSWER	NO.	ANSWER
101	A B C D	121	A B C D	141	A B C D	161	A B C D	181	A B C D
102	A B C D	122	A B C D	142	A B C D	162	A B C D	182	A B C D
103	A B C D	123	A B C D	143	A B C D	163	A B C D	183	A B C D
104	A B C D	124	A B C D	144	A B C D	164	A B C D	184	A B C D
105	A B C D	125	A B C D	145	A B C D	165	A B C D	185	A B C D
106	A B C D	126	A B C D	146	A B C D	166	A B C D	186	A B C D
107	A B C D	127	A B C D	147	A B C D	167	A B C D	187	A B C D
108	A B C D	128	A B C D	148	A B C D	168	A B C D	188	A B C D
109	A B C D	129	A B C D	149	A B C D	169	A B C D	189	A B C D
110	A B C D	130	A B C D	150	A B C D	170	A B C D	190	A B C D
111	A B C D	131	A B C D	151	A B C D	171	A B C D	191	A B C D
112	A B C D	132	A B C D	152	A B C D	172	A B C D	192	A B C D
113	A B C D	133	A B C D	153	A B C D	173	A B C D	193	A B C D
114	A B C D	134	A B C D	154	A B C D	174	A B C D	194	A B C D
115	A B C D	135	A B C D	155	A B C D	175	A B C D	195	A B C D
116	A B C D	136	A B C D	156	A B C D	176	A B C D	196	A B C D
117	A B C D	137	A B C D	157	A B C D	177	A B C D	197	A B C D
118	A B C D	138	A B C D	158	A B C D	178	A B C D	198	A B C D
119	A B C D	139	A B C D	159	A B C D	179	A B C D	199	A B C D
120	A B C D	140	A B C D	160	A B C D	180	A B C D	200	A B C D

ANSWER SHEET

TEST 04

LISTENING (Part I-IV)

NO.	ANSWER A B C D	NO.	ANSWER A B C D	NO.	ANSWER A B C D	NO.	ANSWER A B C D
1	A B C	21	A B C D	41	A B C D	61	A B C D
2	A B C	22	A B C D	42	A B C D	62	A B C D
3	A B C	23	A B C D	43	A B C D	63	A B C D
4	A B C	24	A B C D	44	A B C D	64	A B C D
5	A B C	25	A B C D	45	A B C D	65	A B C D
6	A B C	26	A B C D	46	A B C D	66	A B C D
7	A B C	27	A B C D	47	A B C D	67	A B C D
8	A B C	28	A B C D	48	A B C D	68	A B C D
9	A B C	29	A B C D	49	A B C D	69	A B C D
10	A B C	30	A B C D	50	A B C D	70	A B C D
11	A B C	31	A B C D	51	A B C D	71	A B C D
12	A B C	32	A B C D	52	A B C D	72	A B C D
13	A B C	33	A B C D	53	A B C D	73	A B C D
14	A B C	34	A B C D	54	A B C D	74	A B C D
15	A B C	35	A B C D	55	A B C D	75	A B C D
16	A B C	36	A B C D	56	A B C D	76	A B C D
17	A B C	37	A B C D	57	A B C D	77	A B C D
18	A B C	38	A B C D	58	A B C D	78	A B C D
19	A B C	39	A B C D	59	A B C D	79	A B C D
20	A B C	40	A B C D	60	A B C D	80	A B C D

NO.	ANSWER A B C D
81	A B C D
82	A B C D
83	A B C D
84	A B C D
85	A B C D
86	A B C D
87	A B C D
88	A B C D
89	A B C D
90	A B C D
91	A B C D
92	A B C D
93	A B C D
94	A B C D
95	A B C D
96	A B C D
97	A B C D
98	A B C D
99	A B C D
100	A B C D

READING (Part V-VII)

NO.	ANSWER A B C D	NO.	ANSWER A B C D	NO.	ANSWER A B C D	NO.	ANSWER A B C D	NO.	ANSWER A B C D
101	A B C D	121	A B C D	141	A B C D	161	A B C D	181	A B C D
102	A B C D	122	A B C D	142	A B C D	162	A B C D	182	A B C D
103	A B C D	123	A B C D	143	A B C D	163	A B C D	183	A B C D
104	A B C D	124	A B C D	144	A B C D	164	A B C D	184	A B C D
105	A B C D	125	A B C D	145	A B C D	165	A B C D	185	A B C D
106	A B C D	126	A B C D	146	A B C D	166	A B C D	186	A B C D
107	A B C D	127	A B C D	147	A B C D	167	A B C D	187	A B C D
108	A B C D	128	A B C D	148	A B C D	168	A B C D	188	A B C D
109	A B C D	129	A B C D	149	A B C D	169	A B C D	189	A B C D
110	A B C D	130	A B C D	150	A B C D	170	A B C D	190	A B C D
111	A B C D	131	A B C D	151	A B C D	171	A B C D	191	A B C D
112	A B C D	132	A B C D	152	A B C D	172	A B C D	192	A B C D
113	A B C D	133	A B C D	153	A B C D	173	A B C D	193	A B C D
114	A B C D	134	A B C D	154	A B C D	174	A B C D	194	A B C D
115	A B C D	135	A B C D	155	A B C D	175	A B C D	195	A B C D
116	A B C D	136	A B C D	156	A B C D	176	A B C D	196	A B C D
117	A B C D	137	A B C D	157	A B C D	177	A B C D	197	A B C D
118	A B C D	138	A B C D	158	A B C D	178	A B C D	198	A B C D
119	A B C D	139	A B C D	159	A B C D	179	A B C D	199	A B C D
120	A B C D	140	A B C D	160	A B C D	180	A B C D	200	A B C D

ANSWER SHEET

TEST 05

LISTENING (Part I-IV)

NO.	ANSWER A B C D	NO.	ANSWER A B C D	NO.	ANSWER A B C D	NO.	ANSWER A B C D
1	Ⓐ Ⓑ Ⓒ Ⓓ	21	Ⓐ Ⓑ Ⓒ Ⓓ	41	Ⓐ Ⓑ Ⓒ Ⓓ	61	Ⓐ Ⓑ Ⓒ Ⓓ
2	Ⓐ Ⓑ Ⓒ Ⓓ	22	Ⓐ Ⓑ Ⓒ Ⓓ	42	Ⓐ Ⓑ Ⓒ Ⓓ	62	Ⓐ Ⓑ Ⓒ Ⓓ
3	Ⓐ Ⓑ Ⓒ Ⓓ	23	Ⓐ Ⓑ Ⓒ Ⓓ	43	Ⓐ Ⓑ Ⓒ Ⓓ	63	Ⓐ Ⓑ Ⓒ Ⓓ
4	Ⓐ Ⓑ Ⓒ Ⓓ	24	Ⓐ Ⓑ Ⓒ Ⓓ	44	Ⓐ Ⓑ Ⓒ Ⓓ	64	Ⓐ Ⓑ Ⓒ Ⓓ
5	Ⓐ Ⓑ Ⓒ Ⓓ	25	Ⓐ Ⓑ Ⓒ Ⓓ	45	Ⓐ Ⓑ Ⓒ Ⓓ	65	Ⓐ Ⓑ Ⓒ Ⓓ
6	Ⓐ Ⓑ Ⓒ Ⓓ	26	Ⓐ Ⓑ Ⓒ Ⓓ	46	Ⓐ Ⓑ Ⓒ Ⓓ	66	Ⓐ Ⓑ Ⓒ Ⓓ
7	Ⓐ Ⓑ Ⓒ Ⓓ	27	Ⓐ Ⓑ Ⓒ Ⓓ	47	Ⓐ Ⓑ Ⓒ Ⓓ	67	Ⓐ Ⓑ Ⓒ Ⓓ
8	Ⓐ Ⓑ Ⓒ Ⓓ	28	Ⓐ Ⓑ Ⓒ Ⓓ	48	Ⓐ Ⓑ Ⓒ Ⓓ	68	Ⓐ Ⓑ Ⓒ Ⓓ
9	Ⓐ Ⓑ Ⓒ Ⓓ	29	Ⓐ Ⓑ Ⓒ Ⓓ	49	Ⓐ Ⓑ Ⓒ Ⓓ	69	Ⓐ Ⓑ Ⓒ Ⓓ
10	Ⓐ Ⓑ Ⓒ Ⓓ	30	Ⓐ Ⓑ Ⓒ Ⓓ	50	Ⓐ Ⓑ Ⓒ Ⓓ	70	Ⓐ Ⓑ Ⓒ Ⓓ
11	Ⓐ Ⓑ Ⓒ Ⓓ	31	Ⓐ Ⓑ Ⓒ Ⓓ	51	Ⓐ Ⓑ Ⓒ Ⓓ	71	Ⓐ Ⓑ Ⓒ Ⓓ
12	Ⓐ Ⓑ Ⓒ Ⓓ	32	Ⓐ Ⓑ Ⓒ Ⓓ	52	Ⓐ Ⓑ Ⓒ Ⓓ	72	Ⓐ Ⓑ Ⓒ Ⓓ
13	Ⓐ Ⓑ Ⓒ Ⓓ	33	Ⓐ Ⓑ Ⓒ Ⓓ	53	Ⓐ Ⓑ Ⓒ Ⓓ	73	Ⓐ Ⓑ Ⓒ Ⓓ
14	Ⓐ Ⓑ Ⓒ Ⓓ	34	Ⓐ Ⓑ Ⓒ Ⓓ	54	Ⓐ Ⓑ Ⓒ Ⓓ	74	Ⓐ Ⓑ Ⓒ Ⓓ
15	Ⓐ Ⓑ Ⓒ Ⓓ	35	Ⓐ Ⓑ Ⓒ Ⓓ	55	Ⓐ Ⓑ Ⓒ Ⓓ	75	Ⓐ Ⓑ Ⓒ Ⓓ
16	Ⓐ Ⓑ Ⓒ Ⓓ	36	Ⓐ Ⓑ Ⓒ Ⓓ	56	Ⓐ Ⓑ Ⓒ Ⓓ	76	Ⓐ Ⓑ Ⓒ Ⓓ
17	Ⓐ Ⓑ Ⓒ Ⓓ	37	Ⓐ Ⓑ Ⓒ Ⓓ	57	Ⓐ Ⓑ Ⓒ Ⓓ	77	Ⓐ Ⓑ Ⓒ Ⓓ
18	Ⓐ Ⓑ Ⓒ Ⓓ	38	Ⓐ Ⓑ Ⓒ Ⓓ	58	Ⓐ Ⓑ Ⓒ Ⓓ	78	Ⓐ Ⓑ Ⓒ Ⓓ
19	Ⓐ Ⓑ Ⓒ Ⓓ	39	Ⓐ Ⓑ Ⓒ Ⓓ	59	Ⓐ Ⓑ Ⓒ Ⓓ	79	Ⓐ Ⓑ Ⓒ Ⓓ
20	Ⓐ Ⓑ Ⓒ Ⓓ	40	Ⓐ Ⓑ Ⓒ Ⓓ	60	Ⓐ Ⓑ Ⓒ Ⓓ	80	Ⓐ Ⓑ Ⓒ Ⓓ

NO.	ANSWER A B C D
81	Ⓐ Ⓑ Ⓒ Ⓓ
82	Ⓐ Ⓑ Ⓒ Ⓓ
83	Ⓐ Ⓑ Ⓒ Ⓓ
84	Ⓐ Ⓑ Ⓒ Ⓓ
85	Ⓐ Ⓑ Ⓒ Ⓓ
86	Ⓐ Ⓑ Ⓒ Ⓓ
87	Ⓐ Ⓑ Ⓒ Ⓓ
88	Ⓐ Ⓑ Ⓒ Ⓓ
89	Ⓐ Ⓑ Ⓒ Ⓓ
90	Ⓐ Ⓑ Ⓒ Ⓓ
91	Ⓐ Ⓑ Ⓒ Ⓓ
92	Ⓐ Ⓑ Ⓒ Ⓓ
93	Ⓐ Ⓑ Ⓒ Ⓓ
94	Ⓐ Ⓑ Ⓒ Ⓓ
95	Ⓐ Ⓑ Ⓒ Ⓓ
96	Ⓐ Ⓑ Ⓒ Ⓓ
97	Ⓐ Ⓑ Ⓒ Ⓓ
98	Ⓐ Ⓑ Ⓒ Ⓓ
99	Ⓐ Ⓑ Ⓒ Ⓓ
100	Ⓐ Ⓑ Ⓒ Ⓓ

READING (Part V-VII)

NO.	ANSWER A B C D	NO.	ANSWER A B C D	NO.	ANSWER A B C D	NO.	ANSWER A B C D	NO.	ANSWER A B C D
101	Ⓐ Ⓑ Ⓒ Ⓓ	121	Ⓐ Ⓑ Ⓒ Ⓓ	141	Ⓐ Ⓑ Ⓒ Ⓓ	161	Ⓐ Ⓑ Ⓒ Ⓓ	181	Ⓐ Ⓑ Ⓒ Ⓓ
102	Ⓐ Ⓑ Ⓒ Ⓓ	122	Ⓐ Ⓑ Ⓒ Ⓓ	142	Ⓐ Ⓑ Ⓒ Ⓓ	162	Ⓐ Ⓑ Ⓒ Ⓓ	182	Ⓐ Ⓑ Ⓒ Ⓓ
103	Ⓐ Ⓑ Ⓒ Ⓓ	123	Ⓐ Ⓑ Ⓒ Ⓓ	143	Ⓐ Ⓑ Ⓒ Ⓓ	163	Ⓐ Ⓑ Ⓒ Ⓓ	183	Ⓐ Ⓑ Ⓒ Ⓓ
104	Ⓐ Ⓑ Ⓒ Ⓓ	124	Ⓐ Ⓑ Ⓒ Ⓓ	144	Ⓐ Ⓑ Ⓒ Ⓓ	164	Ⓐ Ⓑ Ⓒ Ⓓ	184	Ⓐ Ⓑ Ⓒ Ⓓ
105	Ⓐ Ⓑ Ⓒ Ⓓ	125	Ⓐ Ⓑ Ⓒ Ⓓ	145	Ⓐ Ⓑ Ⓒ Ⓓ	165	Ⓐ Ⓑ Ⓒ Ⓓ	185	Ⓐ Ⓑ Ⓒ Ⓓ
106	Ⓐ Ⓑ Ⓒ Ⓓ	126	Ⓐ Ⓑ Ⓒ Ⓓ	146	Ⓐ Ⓑ Ⓒ Ⓓ	166	Ⓐ Ⓑ Ⓒ Ⓓ	186	Ⓐ Ⓑ Ⓒ Ⓓ
107	Ⓐ Ⓑ Ⓒ Ⓓ	127	Ⓐ Ⓑ Ⓒ Ⓓ	147	Ⓐ Ⓑ Ⓒ Ⓓ	167	Ⓐ Ⓑ Ⓒ Ⓓ	187	Ⓐ Ⓑ Ⓒ Ⓓ
108	Ⓐ Ⓑ Ⓒ Ⓓ	128	Ⓐ Ⓑ Ⓒ Ⓓ	148	Ⓐ Ⓑ Ⓒ Ⓓ	168	Ⓐ Ⓑ Ⓒ Ⓓ	188	Ⓐ Ⓑ Ⓒ Ⓓ
109	Ⓐ Ⓑ Ⓒ Ⓓ	129	Ⓐ Ⓑ Ⓒ Ⓓ	149	Ⓐ Ⓑ Ⓒ Ⓓ	169	Ⓐ Ⓑ Ⓒ Ⓓ	189	Ⓐ Ⓑ Ⓒ Ⓓ
110	Ⓐ Ⓑ Ⓒ Ⓓ	130	Ⓐ Ⓑ Ⓒ Ⓓ	150	Ⓐ Ⓑ Ⓒ Ⓓ	170	Ⓐ Ⓑ Ⓒ Ⓓ	190	Ⓐ Ⓑ Ⓒ Ⓓ
111	Ⓐ Ⓑ Ⓒ Ⓓ	131	Ⓐ Ⓑ Ⓒ Ⓓ	151	Ⓐ Ⓑ Ⓒ Ⓓ	171	Ⓐ Ⓑ Ⓒ Ⓓ	191	Ⓐ Ⓑ Ⓒ Ⓓ
112	Ⓐ Ⓑ Ⓒ Ⓓ	132	Ⓐ Ⓑ Ⓒ Ⓓ	152	Ⓐ Ⓑ Ⓒ Ⓓ	172	Ⓐ Ⓑ Ⓒ Ⓓ	192	Ⓐ Ⓑ Ⓒ Ⓓ
113	Ⓐ Ⓑ Ⓒ Ⓓ	133	Ⓐ Ⓑ Ⓒ Ⓓ	153	Ⓐ Ⓑ Ⓒ Ⓓ	173	Ⓐ Ⓑ Ⓒ Ⓓ	193	Ⓐ Ⓑ Ⓒ Ⓓ
114	Ⓐ Ⓑ Ⓒ Ⓓ	134	Ⓐ Ⓑ Ⓒ Ⓓ	154	Ⓐ Ⓑ Ⓒ Ⓓ	174	Ⓐ Ⓑ Ⓒ Ⓓ	194	Ⓐ Ⓑ Ⓒ Ⓓ
115	Ⓐ Ⓑ Ⓒ Ⓓ	135	Ⓐ Ⓑ Ⓒ Ⓓ	155	Ⓐ Ⓑ Ⓒ Ⓓ	175	Ⓐ Ⓑ Ⓒ Ⓓ	195	Ⓐ Ⓑ Ⓒ Ⓓ
116	Ⓐ Ⓑ Ⓒ Ⓓ	136	Ⓐ Ⓑ Ⓒ Ⓓ	156	Ⓐ Ⓑ Ⓒ Ⓓ	176	Ⓐ Ⓑ Ⓒ Ⓓ	196	Ⓐ Ⓑ Ⓒ Ⓓ
117	Ⓐ Ⓑ Ⓒ Ⓓ	137	Ⓐ Ⓑ Ⓒ Ⓓ	157	Ⓐ Ⓑ Ⓒ Ⓓ	177	Ⓐ Ⓑ Ⓒ Ⓓ	197	Ⓐ Ⓑ Ⓒ Ⓓ
118	Ⓐ Ⓑ Ⓒ Ⓓ	138	Ⓐ Ⓑ Ⓒ Ⓓ	158	Ⓐ Ⓑ Ⓒ Ⓓ	178	Ⓐ Ⓑ Ⓒ Ⓓ	198	Ⓐ Ⓑ Ⓒ Ⓓ
119	Ⓐ Ⓑ Ⓒ Ⓓ	139	Ⓐ Ⓑ Ⓒ Ⓓ	159	Ⓐ Ⓑ Ⓒ Ⓓ	179	Ⓐ Ⓑ Ⓒ Ⓓ	199	Ⓐ Ⓑ Ⓒ Ⓓ
120	Ⓐ Ⓑ Ⓒ Ⓓ	140	Ⓐ Ⓑ Ⓒ Ⓓ	160	Ⓐ Ⓑ Ⓒ Ⓓ	180	Ⓐ Ⓑ Ⓒ Ⓓ	200	Ⓐ Ⓑ Ⓒ Ⓓ

파고다 토익 LC RC

실전 1000제 R
해설서

파고다북스 외국어교육연구소 | 저

PAGODA Books

파고다 토익 LC RC

실전 1000제 R
해설서

TEST 01

PART 1					P. 16
1 (D)	2 (D)	3 (B)	4 (C)	5 (D)	6 (C)

PART 2					P. 20
7 (C)	8 (C)	9 (B)	10 (A)	11 (A)	12 (C)
13 (C)	14 (C)	15 (A)	16 (B)	17 (C)	18 (B)
19 (C)	20 (B)	21 (B)	22 (B)	23 (B)	24 (B)
25 (C)	26 (C)	27 (B)	28 (B)	29 (A)	30 (B)
31 (C)					

PART 3					P. 21
32 (D)	33 (C)	34 (B)	35 (D)	36 (A)	37 (D)
38 (B)	39 (C)	40 (D)	41 (B)	42 (C)	43 (D)
44 (C)	45 (C)	46 (B)	47 (B)	48 (D)	49 (D)
50 (A)	51 (C)	52 (D)	53 (C)	54 (C)	55 (B)
56 (B)	57 (D)	58 (A)	59 (D)	60 (C)	61 (D)
62 (B)	63 (A)	64 (B)	65 (A)	66 (D)	67 (B)
68 (C)	69 (B)	70 (B)			

PART 4					P. 25
71 (B)	72 (D)	73 (B)	74 (D)	75 (D)	76 (D)
77 (A)	78 (A)	79 (D)	80 (A)	81 (B)	82 (D)
83 (D)	84 (A)	85 (D)	86 (C)	87 (B)	88 (C)
89 (D)	90 (A)	91 (A)	92 (A)	93 (B)	94 (A)
95 (C)	96 (C)	97 (D)	98 (B)	99 (B)	100 (B)

PART 5					P. 28
101 (B)	102 (B)	103 (B)	104 (A)	105 (D)	106 (C)
107 (B)	108 (D)	109 (C)	110 (B)	111 (D)	112 (D)
113 (D)	114 (D)	115 (C)	116 (C)	117 (D)	118 (D)
119 (A)	120 (A)	121 (D)	122 (B)	123 (D)	124 (C)
125 (A)	126 (A)	127 (C)	128 (D)	129 (B)	130 (A)

PART 6					P. 31
131 (B)	132 (D)	133 (A)	134 (B)	135 (D)	136 (A)
137 (A)	138 (A)	139 (C)	140 (B)	141 (D)	142 (B)
143 (D)	144 (A)	145 (A)	146 (B)		

PART 7					P. 35
147 (B)	148 (A)	149 (B)	150 (B)	151 (C)	152 (B)
153 (C)	154 (D)	155 (B)	156 (C)	157 (C)	158 (D)
159 (C)	160 (D)	161 (D)	162 (C)	163 (B)	164 (C)
165 (A)	166 (D)	167 (D)	168 (A)	169 (C)	170 (A)
171 (B)	172 (C)	173 (A)	174 (A)	175 (A)	176 (C)
177 (A)	178 (D)	179 (D)	180 (D)	181 (B)	182 (B)
183 (A)	184 (B)	185 (C)	186 (A)	187 (D)	188 (B)
189 (C)	190 (A)	191 (C)	192 (B)	193 (A)	194 (C)
195 (D)	196 (C)	197 (A)	198 (A)	199 (B)	200 (B)

PART 1

P. 16

1 1인 중심   난이도 중

[미국]

(A) A sculpture is being washed with water.
(B) There's a parking area near the building.
(C) He's putting on a jacket.
(D) He's standing in front of a fountain.

(A) 조각상이 물에 씻기고 있다.
(B) 건물 근처에 주차장이 있다.
(C) 남자가 재킷을 입는 중이다.
(D) 남자가 분수 앞에 서 있다.

해설 (A) ✗ 사진에 없는 사물 (a sculpture)
(B) ✗ 사진에 없는 사물 (a parking area)
(C) ✗ 동작 묘사 오류 (is putting on)
(D) ○ 남자가 분수 앞에 서있는 모습을 적절히 묘사했으므로 정답

Key point
put on은 '입다, 착용하다'라는 의미의 동작을 나타내는 동사이므로 이 사진에서 (C)는 답이 될 수 없다. 남자가 재킷을 입고 있는 모습을 묘사하려면 착용하고 있는 상태를 나타내는 동사 wear를 사용하여 He is wearing a jacket. 이라고 해야 한다.

Possible Answer
A man is holding a phone. 남자가 전화기를 들고 있다.

어휘 sculpture n. 조각상 wash v. 씻다 parking area 주차장 put on ~을 입다 fountain n. 분수

2 2인 이상   난이도 상

[영국]

(A) One of the men is nailing some boards together.
(B) One of the men is tightening his utility belt.
(C) The men are removing some protective gear.
(D) The men are carrying some wooden planks.

(A) 남자들 중 한 명이 합판들을 못으로 박고 있다.
(B) 남자들 중 한 명이 그가 맨 다용도 벨트를 조이고 있다.
(C) 남자들이 보호 장구를 벗고 있다.

(D) 남자들이 나무 판자들을 나르고 있다.

해설 (A) ✗ 동작 묘사 오류 (is nailing)
(B) ✗ 동작 묘사 오류 (is tightening)
(C) ✗ 동작 묘사 오류 (are removing)
(D) ○ 두 작업자가 목재를 옮기는 모습을 적절히 묘사했으므로 정답

Possible Answer
They are working at a construction site. 그들은 공사장에서 일하고 있다.

어휘 **nail** v. 못으로 박다 **tighten** v. 단단히 조이다 **utility belt** 다용도 벨트 **protective gear** 보호 장구 **carry** v. 나르다, 옮기다 **wooden** adj. 나무로 만든 **plank** n. 널빤지, 판자

3 1인 중심 난이도 상

[미국]

(A) A man is bending over to tie his shoe.
(B) Benches line a walkway outdoors.
(C) A lamppost is being repaired by workers.
(D) Leaves are being swept off a path.

(A) 남자가 신발 끈을 묶기 위해 몸을 굽히고 있다.
(B) 벤치들이 야외에 있는 보도를 따라 늘어서 있다.
(C) 가로등 기둥이 작업자들에 의해 수리되고 있다.
(D) 낙엽들이 길 위에서 쓸어지고 있다.

해설 (A) ✗ 동작 묘사 오류 (is bending over)
(B) ○ 벤치들이 야외에 있는 보도를 따라 늘어선 모습을 적절히 묘사했으므로 정답
(C) ✗ 상태 묘사 오류 (is being repaired)
(D) ✗ 상태 묘사 오류 (are being swept off)

Possible Answer
A man is reading a book on a bench. 남자가 벤치에서 책을 읽고 있다.

어휘 **bend over** 몸을 굽히다 **tie** v. 묶다 **line** v. ~을 따라 늘어서다 **walkway** n. 보도 **outdoors** adv. 야외에서 **lamppost** n. 가로등 기둥 **repair** v. 수리하다 **sweep off** 쓸어내다

4 사물/풍경 난이도 상

[호주]

(A) A rug has been rolled up against the wall.
(B) A plant is being placed on a windowsill.
(C) Some tables have been set up for a meal.
(D) Some curtains are being draped across the window.

(A) 깔개가 둥글게 말려 벽에 기대어져 있다.
(B) 화분이 창턱에 놓이고 있다.
(C) 몇몇 테이블이 식사를 위해 준비되어 있다.
(D) 창문에 커튼이 드리워지고 있다.

해설 (A) ✗ 사진에 없는 사물 (a rug)
(B) ✗ 동작 묘사 오류 (is being placed)
(C) ○ 테이블에 식사가 준비된 모습을 적절히 묘사했으므로 정답
(D) ✗ 동작 묘사 오류 (are being draped)

Key point
(B)와 (D)의 현재 진행 수동태(be being p.p.)는 현재 "~되고 있다"는 진행 중인 동작을 나타내므로 사람이 없는 사진에서는 답이 될 수 없다. 창턱에 화분이 있는 모습을 묘사하려면 A plant has been placed on a windowsill. 과 같이 상태를 나타내는 현재 완료 수동태를 써야 한다.

Possible Answer
Some frames are hanging on a wall. 몇 개의 액자들이 벽에 걸려 있다.

어휘 **rug** n. 깔개 **roll up** (둥글게) 말다 **place** v. 놓다 **windowsill** n. 창턱 **set up** 준비하다 **drape** v. (천 등을 느슨하게) 씌우다 **frame** n. 틀, 액자 **hang** v. 걸리다

5 2인 이상 난이도 상

[영국]

(A) Computers are being assembled in the room.
(B) Documents are being cleared from a table.
(C) One of the men is handing out some papers.
(D) A woman is presenting at a meeting.

(A) 컴퓨터들이 방에서 조립되고 있다.
(B) 서류들이 테이블에서 치워지고 있다.
(C) 남자들 중 한 명이 서류를 나누어 주고 있다.
(D) 여자가 회의에서 발표를 하고 있다.

해설 (A) ✗ 동작 묘사 오류 (are being assembled)
(B) ✗ 동작 묘사 오류 (are being cleared)
(C) ✗ 동작 묘사 오류 (is handing out)
(D) ○ 여자가 회의에서 발표를 하는 모습을 적절히 묘사했으므로 정답

Possible Answer
Some people are seated in a conference room. 몇몇 사람들이 회의실에 앉아있다.

어휘 **assemble** v. 조립하다 **clear** v. 치우다 **hand out** (사람들에게 물건을) 나누어 주다 **present** v. 발표하다

6 사물/풍경 난이도 상

[미국]

(A) Some umbrellas are shading a balcony.
(B) A bridge leads to the ocean.
(C) Some chairs are facing a body of water.
(D) A cabin is located near the beach.

(A) 몇몇 파라솔들이 발코니에 그늘을 드리우고 있다.
(B) 다리가 바다로 이어져 있다.
(C) 몇몇 의자들이 수역을 향하고 있다.
(D) 오두막이 해변 근처에 위치해 있다.

TEST 01 3

해설 (A) ✗ 상태 묘사 오류 (are shading)
(B) ✗ 사진에 없는 사물 (a bridge)
(C) ◯ 의자들이 바다를 향해 있는 모습을 적절히 묘사했으므로 정답
(D) ✗ 사진에 없는 사물 (a cabin)

Possible Answer
Some chairs have been arranged on a beach. 몇몇 의자들이 해변에 배열되어 있다.

어휘 **umbrella** n. 파라솔 **shade** v. 그늘을 드리우다 **lead to** ~로 이어지다 **face** v. 향하다 **a body of water** (호수, 강, 바다 등의) 수역 **cabin** n. 오두막집 **be located in** ~에 위치해 있다

PART 2   P. 20

7 일반 의문문   난이도 중

미국 ↕ 영국

Did you see your doctor this morning?
(A) Some hospital employees.
(B) Can you pick up my prescription?
(C) No, I had to run some other errands.

오늘 오전에 진찰 받으셨어요?
(A) 몇몇 병원 직원들이요.
(B) 제 처방전 좀 받아 주시겠어요?
(C) 아니요, 다른 볼 일이 좀 있었거든요.

해설 (A) ✗ 연상 어휘 함정 (doctor – hospital)
(B) ✗ 연상 어휘 함정 (doctor – prescription)
(C) ◯ 'No'로 대답하고, 다른 볼 일이 있었다며 적절히 덧붙여 말했으므로 정답

Possible Answer
My appointment is on Tuesday. 제 예약은 화요일이에요.

어휘 **prescription** n. 처방전 **run an errand** 볼 일을 보다

8 Where 의문문   난이도 하

미국 ↕ 호주

Where can I get some flowers?
(A) Yes, I enjoy gardening.
(B) A floral arrangement.
(C) There's a shop on Bloor Road.

어디서 꽃을 좀 살 수 있을까요?
(A) 네, 저는 정원 가꾸기를 즐겨요.
(B) 꽃꽂이요.
(C) Bloor Road에 가게가 하나 있어요.

해설 (A) ✗ 의문사 의문문 Yes/No 응답 불가
(B) ✗ 유사 발음 함정 (flowers – floral)
(C) ◯ Bloor Road에 있다며 위치로 말했으므로 정답

Possible Answer
I actually bought some online. 사실 저는 온라인으로 샀어요.

어휘 **gardening** 정원 가꾸기 **floral arrangement** 꽃꽂이

9 평서문   난이도 중

영국 ↕ 미국

The air conditioner won't turn on.
(A) It was almost 30 degrees.
(B) I see. I'll have someone assist you.
(C) Some terms and conditions.

에어컨이 켜지지 않네요.
(A) 거의 30도였어요.
(B) 알겠습니다. 도와드릴 사람을 보내드리겠습니다.
(C) 일부 약관이요.

해설 (A) ✗ 연상 어휘 함정 (air conditioner – 30 degrees)
(B) ◯ 'I see'로 대답하고, 도와드릴 사람을 보내겠다며 적절히 덧붙여 말했으므로 정답
(C) ✗ 유사 발음 함정 (conditioner – conditions)

Possible Answer
Do you know what's wrong with it? 뭐가 잘못되었는지 아시겠어요?

어휘 **degree** n. (온도 단위인) 도 **terms and conditions** 약관, 계약조건

10 부가 의문문   난이도 중

영국 ↕ 미국

The advertisement campaign was very successful, wasn't it?
(A) Yes, our sales have increased.
(B) She's the marketing manager.
(C) The end of the quarter.

광고 캠페인이 매우 성공적이었어요, 그렇죠?
(A) 네, 매출이 증가했어요.
(B) 그녀는 마케팅 부장이에요.
(C) 분기 말이요.

해설 (A) ◯ 'Yes'로 대답하고, 매출이 증가했다며 적절히 덧붙여 말했으므로 정답
(B) ✗ 주어 불일치 함정 (it – she), 연상 어휘 함정 (advertisement campaign – marketing)
(C) ✗ 질문과 무관한 대답

Possible Answer
It exceeded our expectations. 우리의 기대를 뛰어넘었죠.

어휘 **quarter** n. 사분기(1년의 4분의 1인)

11 선택 의문문   난이도 중

호주 ↕ 영국

Are the subscription payments made monthly or yearly?
(A) On the first of every month.
(B) No, a weekly delivery.
(C) Cash or credit cards only.

구독료 납부는 한 달에 한 번 하나요, 일 년에 한 번 하나요?
(A) 매달 1일이에요.
(B) 아니요, 매주 배송이요.
(C) 현금이나 신용카드만요.

해설 (A) ◯ 매달 1일이라며 전자로 말했으므로 정답
(B) ✗ 연상 어휘 함정 (monthly, yearly – weekly)
(C) ✗ 연상 어휘 함정 (payments – cash or credit cards)

Possible Answer
The yearly option is cheaper. 연간 옵션이 더 저렴해요.

어휘 **make a payment** 납부하다 **monthly** adv. 한 달에 한 번

12 Which 의문문   난이도 상

호주 ↕ 미국

Which brands of automobiles do you sell at this shop?
(A) I just got a new car.
(B) At the auto body shop.
(C) We only do repairs here.

이 상점에서는 어느 자동차 브랜드를 판매하시나요?
(A) 새 차 산지 얼마 안 됐어요.
(B) 자동차 정비소에서요.
(C) 여기서는 수리만 해요.

해설 (A) ✗ 연상 어휘 함정 (automobiles – car)
(B) ✗ 유사 발음 함정 (automobiles – auto), 동어 반복 함정 (shop – shop)
(C) ◎ 여기서는 수리만 한다며 자동차를 판매하고 있지 않음을 우회적으로 말했으므로 정답

Possible Answer
We have German cars. 독일 차량을 판매합니다.

어휘 auto body shop 자동차 정비소 repair n. 수리작업

13 선택 의문문 난이도 하

Should we install the carpet on Wednesday or Thursday?
(A) Please read over the installation manual.
(B) I vacuumed the floor.
(C) Thursday would be more convenient.

카펫을 수요일에 설치할까요, 아니면 목요일에 할까요?
(A) 설치 매뉴얼을 꼼꼼히 읽어주세요.
(B) 진공청소기로 바닥을 청소했어요.
(C) 목요일이 더 편할 거예요.

해설 (A) ✗ 유사 발음 함정 (install – installation)
(B) ✗ 연상 어휘 함정 (carpet – floor)
(C) ◎ 목요일이 더 편하다며 후자로 말했으므로 정답

Possible Answer
I prefer Wednesday morning. 저는 수요일 오전이 더 좋습니다.

어휘 read over ~을 꼼꼼히 읽다 vacuum v. 진공청소기로 청소하다

14 제안/요청 난이도 중

Should I book the venue for the anniversary dinner?
(A) A guest list.
(B) Tomorrow afternoon around 2.
(C) The HR Department is in charge of that.

제가 기념일 만찬 장소를 예약할까요?
(A) 초대 손님 명단이요.
(B) 내일 오후 두 시쯤이요.
(C) 그건 인사부가 담당해요.

해설 (A) ✗ 연상 어휘 함정 (anniversary dinner – guest list)
(B) ✗ When 의문문에 어울리는 대답
(C) ◎ 인사부가 담당한다며 예약하지 않아도 됨을 우회적으로 말했으므로 정답

Possible Answer
Yes, I'd appreciate that. 네, 그렇게 해주시면 고맙겠습니다.

어휘 venue n. 장소 HR(Human Resources) Department 인사과 be in charge of ~을 담당하다

15 부정 의문문 난이도 중

Don't you want to watch the movie with us today?
(A) When does it start?
(B) Emma bought it last night.
(C) A documentary on birds.

오늘 저희와 영화 보지 않으시겠어요?
(A) 언제 시작하는데요?
(B) Emma가 어젯밤에 샀어요.
(C) 조류에 관한 다큐멘터리요.

해설 (A) ◎ 언제 시작하냐고 반문하며 질문에 적절하게 말했으므로 정답
(B) ✗ 연상 어휘 함정 (today – last night)
(C) ✗ 연상 어휘 함정 (movie – documentary)

Possible Answer
I'd like that. 그거 좋죠.

어휘 documentary n. 다큐멘터리

16 When 의문문 난이도 상

When are we going to have our salary negotiations?
(A) Almost 50 thousand dollars a year.
(B) The president is away on business this month.
(C) Yes, they offer excellent employee benefits.

임금협상은 언제 하나요?
(A) 매년 거의 5만 달러요.
(B) 이번 달에는 사장님께서 출장 중이시라 안 계세요.
(C) 네, 그들은 훌륭한 복리후생을 제공해요.

해설 (A) ✗ 연상 어휘 함정 (salary – fifty thousand dollars)
(B) ◎ 대표가 출장으로 없다며 이번 달에는 할 수 없음을 우회적으로 말했으므로 정답
(C) ✗ 의문사 의문문 Yes/No 응답 불가

Possible Answer
At the end of the month. 이달 말에요.

어휘 salary n. 급여 away adj. 부재의, 외출중의 on business 볼일이 있어, 업무로 employee benefits 복리후생

17 How 의문문 난이도 중

How did you learn about this position?
(A) Put your seat in an upright position.
(B) How can I get to the meeting room?
(C) I heard about it from a former coworker.

이 일자리에 대해 어떻게 알게 되셨나요?
(A) 좌석을 똑바로 세워 주기 바랍니다.
(B) 회의실에는 어떻게 갑니까?
(C) 예전에 함께 일했던 동료에게서 들었습니다.

해설 (A) ✗ 동어 반복 함정 (position – position)
(B) ✗ 동어 반복 함정 (how – how)
(C) ◎ 예전 동료에게 들었다며 질문에 적절히 말했으므로 정답

Possible Answer
Through an online job posting. 온라인 구인광고를 통해서요.

어휘 upright adj. 똑바로 세워 둔 former adj. 예전의

18 부가 의문문 난이도 중

We should hire a caterer for Ken's retirement party, shouldn't we?
(A) On a higher floor.
(B) Yes, that sounds great.
(C) Next Thursday evening.

Ken의 은퇴파티를 위해 출장 연회업체를 써야겠죠, 그렇죠?

(A) 더 높은 층에요.
(B) 네, 그게 좋겠네요.
(C) 다음 주 목요일 저녁에요.

해설 (A) ✖ 유사 발음 함정 (hire – higher)
(B) ◯ 'Yes'로 대답하고, 그게 좋겠다며 적절히 덧붙여 말했으므로 정답
(C) ✖ When 의문문에 어울리는 대답, 연상 어휘 함정 (retirement party – next Thursday)

Possible Answer
Don't worry. I already took care of it. 걱정하지 마세요. 제가 이미 처리했어요.

어휘 caterer n. 출장 연회업체

19 Why 의문문   난이도 중

영국↕미국

Why was the meeting postponed to later in the week?
(A) In conference room B.
(B) Good idea. Let's do that.
(C) Helen is out of the office.

회의가 왜 주 후반으로 연기되었나요?
(A) B 회의실에서요.
(B) 좋은 생각이에요. 그렇게 하죠.
(C) Helen이 출장 중이거든요.

해설 (A) ✖ 연상 어휘 함정 (meeting – conference)
(B) ✖ 질문과 무관한 대답
(C) ◯ Helen이 출장 중이라며 이유를 들어 말했으므로 정답

Possible Answer
You should ask the director. 이사님께 여쭤보세요.

어휘 postpone v. 연기하다 conference room 회의실

20 How 의문문   난이도 상

호주↕영국

How long does it take to walk to the subway station?
(A) It doesn't stop at this station.
(B) I ride the bus there.
(C) Usually by 8 A.M.

지하철역까지 걸어가는 데 얼마나 걸리나요?
(A) 이 역에는 정차하지 않아요.
(B) 저는 거기까지 버스로 가요.
(C) 보통 오전 8시까지요.

해설 (A) ✖ 동어 반복 함정 (station – station)
(B) ◯ 거기까지 버스로 간다며 지하철역에 걸어가는데 얼마나 걸리는지 모름을 우회적으로 말했으므로 정답
(C) ✖ When 의문문에 어울리는 대답

Possible Answer
A little more than 10 minutes. 10분 남짓 걸려요.

어휘 ride v. (승객으로 차량을) 타다[타고 가다]

21 일반 의문문   난이도 상

미국↕호주

Do you enjoy working as a computer engineer?
(A) No, I set up the software yesterday.
(B) Well, my pay is pretty competitive.
(C) The newest engine.

컴퓨터 기술자로 일하는 걸 즐기시나요?

(A) 아니요, 어제 소프트웨어를 설치했어요.
(B) 음, 급여가 꽤 높거든요.
(C) 최신 엔진이요.

해설 (A) ✖ 연상 어휘 함정 (computer engineer – set up the software)
(B) ◯ 급여가 꽤 높다며 질문에 긍정함을 우회적으로 말했으므로 정답
(C) ✖ 유사 발음 함정 (engineer – engine)

Possible Answer
It's a challenging field, but I enjoy it. 만만치 않은 분야이긴 하지만 재미있어요.

어휘 set up v. 설치하다 pay n. 급여 competitive adj. 경쟁력 있는 challenging adj. 힘든 field n. 분야

22 Where 의문문   난이도 상

미국↕영국

Where is the nearest stationery shop?
(A) A few notepads.
(B) There's a city map.
(C) No, it closes at 8 o'clock.

가장 가까운 문구점이 어디인가요?
(A) 메모장 몇 개요.
(B) 시내 지도가 있어요.
(C) 아니요, 8시에 문을 닫아요.

해설 (A) ✖ 연상 어휘 함정 (stationery shop – notepads)
(B) ◯ 시내 지도가 있다며 지도를 보고 확인하면 된다고 질문에 우회적으로 말했으므로 정답
(C) ✖ 의문사 의문문 Yes/No 응답 불가

Possible Answer
It's a ten-minute walk from here. 여기서부터 10분만 걸어가시면 됩니다.

어휘 stationery store 문구점 depart v. 떠나다, 출발하다

23 평서문   난이도 상

영국↕미국

We should get started so we won't run late.
(A) I start work on Monday.
(B) Nate will be here soon.
(C) We're running out of space.

우리가 늦지 않으려면 시작해야 해요.
(A) 저는 월요일에 근무를 시작해요.
(B) Nate가 금방 올 거예요.
(C) 자리가 점점 없어지고 있어요.

해설 (A) ✖ 동어 반복 함정 (started – start)
(B) ◯ Nate가 금방 올 거라며 조금 있다 시작해야 함을 우회적으로 말했으므로 정답
(C) ✖ 동어 반복 함정 (run – running)

Possible Answer
Sure. Let's begin in 5 minutes. 좋습니다. 5분 후에 시작합시다.

어휘 get started (어떤 일을 하기) 시작하다 run late 늦어지다 run out of ~이 없어지다

24 What 의문문   난이도 상

호주↕영국

What are we publishing on the front page of our newspaper tomorrow?
(A) No, Dylan is the editor.

(B) Let's figure it out after lunch.
(C) It will be published next month.

내일 우리 신문 1면에는 뭘 실을 거예요?
(A) 아니요, Dylan은 편집장이에요.
(B) 점심식사 후에 생각해봐요.
(C) 다음 달에 출간될 거예요.

해설 (A) ✗ 의문사 의문문 Yes/No 응답 불가, 연상 어휘 함정 (publishing, newspaper – editor)
(B) ○ 점심식사 후에 생각해보자며 질문에 적절하게 말했으므로 정답
(C) ✗ 유사 발음 함정 (publishing – published)

Possible Answer
It hasn't been decided yet. 아직 정해지지 않았습니다.

어휘 publish v. 게재하다, 싣다 front page (신문의) 제1면 editor n. 편집장 figure out 생각해 내다

25 부가 의문문   난이도 중

미국↑↓미국
I think Janelle will get promoted to account executive, don't you?
(A) An end-of-the-year sales promotion.
(B) I created a new user account.
(C) Most likely. She earned it.

제 생각에는 Janelle이 거래처 담당 임원으로 승진할 것 같아요, 안 그래요?
(A) 연말 판촉 행사요.
(B) 새 사용자 계정을 만들었어요.
(C) 그럴 것 같아요. 그녀라면 그럴만하죠.

해설 (A) ✗ 유사 발음 함정 (promoted – promotion)
(B) ✗ 동어 반복 함정 (account – account)
(C) ○ 아마도 그녀가 승진할 자격이 있다며 질문에 적절하게 말했으므로 정답

Possible Answer
Yes, and she'll do a great job. 맞아요, 그리고 그녀는 아주 잘 할 겁니다.

어휘 account executive 거래처 담당 임원 sales promotion 판촉 (활동) account n. (정보 서비스) 이용 계정 most likely 아마, 필시 earn v. (감사·보수 등을) 받을 만하다

26 Which 의문문   난이도 중

미국↑↓영국
Which radio program should we advertise our new product in?
(A) A 30-second commercial.
(B) I heard it at the broadcasting station.
(C) How about *The Morning Show*?

우리 신제품을 어느 라디오 프로그램에서 광고할까요?
(A) 30초짜리 광고요.
(B) 방송국에서 들었어요.
(C) <The Morning Show>는 어때요?

해설 (A) ✗ 연상 어휘 함정 (advertise – commercial)
(B) ✗ 연상 어휘 함정 (radio – broadcasting station)
(C) ○ <The Morning Show>는 어떠냐고 선택하며 말했으므로 정답

Possible Answer
The one with the highest ratings. 청취율이 가장 높은 거요.

어휘 commercial n. (텔레비전·라디오의) 광고 broadcasting station 방송국

27 Why 의문문   난이도 중

영국↑↓호주
Why wasn't the company newsletter sent out this month?
(A) That's great news!
(B) We had some mechanical issues.
(C) The last Friday of every month.

이번 달에는 왜 사보가 발송되지 않았나요?
(A) 그거 희소식이네요!
(B) 기계적인 문제가 좀 있었어요.
(C) 매월 마지막 금요일이요.

해설 (A) ✗ 유사 발음 함정 (newsletter – news)
(B) ○ 기계적인 문제가 있었다며 이유로 말했으므로 정답
(C) ✗ 동어 반복 함정 (month – month)

Possible Answer
Didn't you receive it in the mail? 우편 못 받으셨어요?

어휘 newsletter n. 소식지[회보] mechanical adj. 기계[엔진]와 관련된 issue n. 문제

28 부정 의문문   난이도 중

호주↑↓미국
Aren't you going to attend the client dinner with us?
(A) Can I have some water, please?
(B) I'm afraid I have a prior engagement.
(C) The deadline was extended.

고객 저녁 식사 자리에 저희와 함께 안 가세요?
(A) 물 좀 주시겠어요?
(B) 죄송하지만 선약이 있어요.
(C) 마감일이 연장됐어요.

해설 (A) ✗ 연상 어휘 함정 (dinner – water)
(B) ○ 선약이 있다며 우회적으로 거절한 대답이므로 정답
(C) ✗ 유사 발음 함정 (attend – extended)

Possible Answer
Actually, I already ate. 실은 제가 이미 식사를 했어요.

어휘 prior engagement 선약 deadline n. 기한, 마감시간 extend v. 연장하다

29 평서문   난이도 중

미국↑↓영국
The Finance Department recruited more staff this month.
(A) They won't have to work overtime now.
(B) Didn't Jason get a certificate in finance?
(C) She's a corporate banker.

회계부가 이번 달에 직원을 더 채용했어요.
(A) 그들은 이제 야근하지 않아도 되겠어요.
(B) Jason이 재무 자격증을 따지 않았나요?
(C) 그녀는 법인 담당 은행원이에요.

해설 (A) ○ 회계부가 이제 야근하지 않아도 되겠다며 적절히 답했으므로 정답
(B) ✗ 동어 반복 함정 (Finance – finance)
(C) ✗ 주어 불일치 함정 (The Finance Department – She), 연상 어휘 함정 (Finance – corporate banker)

Possible Answer
That's great news. 정말 좋은 소식이네요.

어휘 Finance Department 재무부 work overtime 시간 외 근무하다 certificate n. 자격증 corporate banker 법인 담당 은행원

30 Who 의문문　　　난이도 중

미국↑↓호주

Who is going to oversee the Berlin office when James moves?
(A) The IT team.
(B) They haven't made a decision yet.
(C) It has a great view.

James가 이동하면 누가 Berlin 지사를 관리하나요?
(A) IT팀이요.
(B) 그들이 아직 결정하지 않았어요.
(C) 그곳의 전망이 매우 좋아요.

해설　(A) ✗ 연상 어휘 함정 (office – IT team)
　　　(B) ◯ 아직 결정하지 않았다며 질문에 적절하게 말했으므로 정답
　　　(C) ✗ 연상 어휘 함정 (oversee – view)

Possible Answer
He'll be with us for a few more years. 그분은 저희와 몇 년 더 일 하실 거예요.

어휘　oversee v. 감독[관리]하다　decision n. 결정　view n. 전망

31 제안/요청　　　난이도 상

영국↑↓미국

Would you mind coming in to the store this weekend?
(A) The warehouse is full.
(B) Yes, I had an enjoyable weekend.
(C) Do you need me on both days?

이번 주말에 매장에 와주시겠어요?
(A) 창고가 가득 찼어요.
(B) 네, 즐거운 주말이었어요.
(C) 이틀 모두 제가 필요하신가요?

해설　(A) ✗ 연상 어휘 함정 (store – warehouse)
　　　(B) ✗ 동어 반복 함정 (weekend – weekend)
　　　(C) ◯ 이틀 모두 필요하냐고 반문하며 질문에 적절하게 말했으므로 정답

Possible Answer
I'll be out of town. 저는 다른 도시에 있을 거예요.

어휘　warehouse n. 창고　enjoyable adj. 즐거운

PART 3　　　P. 21

호주 ⇄ 영국

Questions 32-34 refer to the following conversation.

M: Excuse me, could you explain something? According to your store's Web site, **you're offering a 15 percent discount on the Cross Adventure hiking boots. But I don't see them in the footwear aisle.**(32)

W: Unfortunately, we are all out of those at the moment. **A new shipment did come in this morning, but it was damaged.** (33) We'll receive a new one tomorrow.

M: Ah, OK. Well, the Web site said the promotion was valid through today. Will you still offer the same deal tomorrow?

W: Yes. **Just visit our help desk,**(34) and an employee will give you a voucher to use when purchasing the boots.

32-34번은 다음 대화에 관한 문제입니다.

남: 저기요, 뭐 설명 좀 해주시겠어요? 상점 웹 사이트를 보면, **Cross Adventure 등산화가 15퍼센트 할인하고 있다고 나오는데요. 그런데 등산화가 신발 섹션에서 안 보여요.**(32)

여: 유감스럽게도, 현재 재고가 없어요. **새 배송품이 오늘 오전에 들어 왔는데, 파손이 되었어요.**(33) 내일 새 제품이 들어옵니다.

남: 아, 그렇군요. 웹 사이트에서는 그 프로모션이 오늘까지 유효하다 고 되어 있는데요. 내일도 동일하게 할인해 주시나요?

여: 네, **저희 안내 데스크에 방문하시면,**(34) 직원이 등산화를 구매하실 때 이용하실 쿠폰을 드릴 겁니다.

어휘　footwear n. 신발류　aisle n. 통로　at the moment 지금
　　　shipment n. 배송품　promotion n. 판촉 행사　valid adj. 유효한
　　　through prep. ~까지　voucher n. 상품권, 할인권

32 세부정보　　　난이도 중

해석　남자는 무엇에 도움이 필요한가?
(A) 제품을 교환하는 것
(B) 차에서 소포들을 내리는 것
(C) 상점 회원권을 갱신하는 것
(D) 상품을 찾는 것

해설　남자가 you're offering a 15 percent discount on the Cross Adventure hiking boots. But I don't see them in the footwear aisle. (Cross Adventure 등산화가 15퍼센트 할인하고 있다고 나오는 데요. 그런데 등산화가 신발 섹션에서 안 보여요.)라고 말했으므로 (D) 가 정답

Paraphrasing Cross Adventure hiking boots ➡ merchandise

33 세부정보　　　난이도 하

해석　문제의 원인은 무엇인가?
(A) 창고가 일찍 문을 닫았다.
(B) 관리자가 시간이 없다.
(C) 배송품이 파손되었다.
(D) 가격표가 잘못되었다.

해설　여자가 A new shipment did come in this morning, but it was damaged. (새 배송품이 오늘 오전에 들어왔는데, 파손이 되었어요.) 라고 말했으므로 (C)가 정답

34 요청/제의/제안　　　난이도 하

해석　여자는 남자에게 어디로 가라고 알려주는가?
(A) 계산대로
(B) 안내 데스크로
(C) 다른 통로로
(D) 창고로

해설　여자가 Just visit our help desk (저희 안내 데스크에 방문하시면)이 라고 말했으므로 (B)가 정답

미국 ⇄ 호주

Questions 35-37 refer to the following conversation.

W: Hey, Ron. **The office holiday party is coming up later this week.**(35) Let's review everything we're going to need for the ceremony. I suppose we'll need snacks, some beverages, and decorations.

M: Wait. Don't buy any snacks. **I'll make some more of my chocolate chip cookies instead.**(36) Everybody seemed to enjoy that at your birthday party last month.

W: That would be very helpful! OK, in that case, there are just a couple things left. **I can stop by the supermarket tomorrow and pick up some decorations.**(37)

35-37번은 다음 대화에 관한 문제입니다.

여: Ron. 사무실 홀리데이 파티가 이번 주 말이에요.(35) 행사에 필요한 것들을 전부 검토해봐요. 제 생각에는 간식과 음료, 그리고 장식품이 필요할 것 같아요.

남: 잠시만요. 간식은 아무것도 사지 마세요. 대신 제가 초콜릿 칩 쿠키를 좀 더 만들어 올게요.(36) 지난 달 당신 생일 파티에서 보니 모두 잘 먹는 것 같았거든요.

여: 그럼 많은 도움이 될 거예요! 알았어요, 그러면 몇 가지밖에 없네요. 제가 내일 슈퍼마켓에 들러서 장식품을 좀 사 올게요.(37)

어휘 review v. 검토하다 ceremony n. 식, 의식 suppose v. 생각하다, 추측하다 snack n. 간식 beverage n. 음료 decoration n. 장식품 instead adv. 그 대신 seem v. ~인 것 같다 helpful adj. 도움이 되는 stop by (잠시) 들르다

35 세부정보   난이도 하

해석 화자들은 어떤 행사를 계획하고 있는가?
(A) 영화제
(B) 생일 파티
(C) 시상식
(D) 홀리데이 기념행사

해설 여자가 The office holiday party is coming up later this week. (사무실 홀리데이 파티가 이번 주 말이에요.)라고 말했으므로 (D)가 정답

Paraphrasing party ➡ celebration

36 세부정보   난이도 중

해석 남자는 무엇을 할 거라고 말하는가?
(A) 간식을 준비할 거라고
(B) 교통편을 마련할 거라고
(C) 배달 주문을 할 거라고
(D) 일정을 변경할 거라고

해설 남자가 I'll make some more of my chocolate chip cookies instead. (대신 제가 초콜릿 칩 쿠키를 좀 더 만들어 올게요.)라고 말했으므로 (A)가 정답

Paraphrasing make ~ chocolate chip cookies ➡ prepare a snack

37 요청/제의/제안   난이도 중

해석 여자는 무엇을 하겠다고 제안하는가?
(A) 다른 부서에 연락하겠다고
(B) 예약을 확인해 주겠다고
(C) 할인을 요청하겠다고
(D) 물품들을 구매하겠다고

해설 여자가 I can stop by the supermarket tomorrow and pick up some decorations. (제가 내일 슈퍼마켓에 들러서 장식품을 좀 사 올게요.)라고 말했으므로 (D)가 정답

Paraphrasing pick up some decorations ➡ purchase some supplies

미국 ⇄ 미국

Questions 38-40 refer to the following conversation.

W: Hello, **I'm calling regarding a recent purchase I made from your Web site.**(38) The order number is XV7814.

M: Please give me a moment to check the system. Alright, **it's the Sirka HD television,**(38) right?

W: Yeah, but when I reviewed my invoice, I discovered that **I chose the 50-inch one by accident. I actually wanted to purchase the 55-inch model.**(39) Is it possible to revise my order?

M: Yes. Fortunately, your item hasn't been sent out yet, so I can update the order. And just so you know, **this model is more expensive, so your credit card will be charged an additional $70.**(40)

38-40번은 다음 대화에 관한 문제입니다.

여: 안녕하세요, 제가 웹 사이트에서 한 최근 주문건과 관련해서 전화 드려요.(38) 주문 번호는 XV7814이에요.

남: 시스템을 확인하는 동안 잠시만 기다려 주세요. 네, Sirka HD 텔레비전이네요,(38) 맞으세요?

여: 네, 그런데 제가 청구서를 검토하다 발견했는데 제가 실수로 50 인치 상품을 선택했어요. 실은 55 인치 모델을 구매하고 싶었거든요.(39) 제 주문을 수정하는 것이 가능할까요?

남: 네. 다행히, 귀하의 물품이 아직 발송되지 않아서, 주문을 업데이트해 드릴 수 있습니다. 그리고 아시다시피, 이 모델이 더 비싸서, 귀하의 신용카드로 70달러가 추가 청구될 거예요.(40)

어휘 regarding prep. ~에 관하여 make a purchase 구매하다 review v. 검토하다 invoice n. 청구서 revise v. 수정하다, 변경하다 expensive adj. 비싼 charge v. 청구하다

38 세부정보   난이도 하

해석 여자는 온라인으로 무엇을 사는가?
(A) 컴퓨터
(B) 텔레비전
(C) 카메라
(D) 전화기

해설 여자가 I'm calling regarding a recent purchase I made from your Web site. (제가 웹 사이트에서 한 최근 주문건과 관련해서 전화 드려요.)라고 하자, 남자가 it's the Sirka HD television (Sirka HD 텔

레비전이네요)라고 말했으므로 (B)가 정답

Paraphrasing purchase ➡ buy, Web site ➡ online

39 세부정보 난이도 중

해석 여자는 어떤 실수를 했나?
(A) 잘못된 전화번호를 제공했다.
(B) 전액을 지불하지 않았다.
(C) 크기를 잘못 선택했다.
(D) 할인 적용하는 것을 깜박했다.

해설 여자가 I chose the 50-inch one by accident. I actually wanted to purchase the 55-inch model. (제가 실수로 50인치 상품을 선택했어요. 실은 55인치 모델을 구매하고 싶었거든요.)라고 말했으므로 (C)가 정답

40 세부정보 난이도 하

해석 남자는 여자에게 무엇에 관하여 알려주는가?
(A) 판촉 행사
(B) 제품 기능
(C) 배송 서비스
(D) 추가 요금

해설 남자가 this model is more expensive, so your credit card will be charged an additional $70. (이 모델이 더 비싸서, 귀하의 신용카드로 70달러가 추가 청구될 거예요.)라고 말했으므로 (D)가 정답

Paraphrasing additional ➡ extra

호주 ⇄ 영국

Questions 41-43 refer to the following conversation.

M: Welcome to the Bailey Theater. How may I be of service?

W: Good afternoon. **It's our wedding anniversary today, and my husband and I wanted to celebrate it by watching a show here.**(41) But it looks like *Take Me Away* is not on today's list of plays.

M: Oh, I'm afraid **that play has been canceled for today**(42) because the lead actor is not feeling well.

W: Ah, **that's a shame. We really wanted to watch that play.** (42)

M: I'm so sorry. If you'd like, **I could give you a discount on tickets for another play tonight called *Sky Falling*.**(43) It's quite popular.

41-43번은 다음 대화에 관한 문제입니다.

남: Bailey 극장에 오신 것을 환영합니다. 어떻게 도와드릴까요?

여: 안녕하세요. 오늘이 저희 결혼기념일이라서, 남편과 제가 여기서 공연을 보면서 축하하고 싶었어요.(41) 그런데 <Take Me Away>가 오늘의 연극 목록에 없는 것 같네요.

남: 아, 안타깝게도 주연 배우의 컨디션이 좋지 않아서 **오늘 연극은 취소되었어요.**(42)

여: 아, 아쉽네요. 그 연극을 정말 보고 싶었거든요.(42)

남: 정말 죄송합니다. 원하신다면, **오늘 밤에 하는 <Sky Falling>이라는 다른 연극 티켓을 할인해드릴 수 있어요.**(43) 아주 인기 있어요.

어휘 **wedding anniversary** 결혼 기념일 **celebrate** v. 축하하다, 기념하다 **play** n. 연극 **afraid** adj. 유감스러운 **cancel** v. 취소하다 **lead actor** 주연배우 **feel well** 컨디션이 좋다 **give a discount on** ~에 할인을 해주다 **popular** adj. 인기 있는

41 주제/목적 난이도 하

해석 여자는 왜 극장에 있는가?
(A) 배우를 면접하기 위해
(B) 기념일을 축하하기 위해
(C) 일자리에 지원하기 위해
(D) 점검을 실시하기 위해

해설 여자가 It's our wedding anniversary today, and my husband and I wanted to celebrate it by watching a show here. (오늘이 저희 결혼기념일이라서, 남편과 제가 여기서 공연을 보면서 축하하고 싶었어요.)라고 말했으므로 (B)가 정답

42 세부정보 난이도 하

해석 여자는 왜 실망하는가?
(A) 입장료가 인상되었다.
(B) 주차할 곳을 찾을 수 없었다.
(C) 공연이 취소되었다.
(D) 주연 배우가 은퇴했다.

해설 남자가 that play has been canceled for today (그 연극은 오늘 취소되었어요.)라고 하자, 여자가 Ah, that's a shame. We really wanted to watch that play. (아, 그것 유감이네요. 그 연극을 정말 보고 싶었거든요.)라고 말한 것이므로 (C)가 정답

Paraphrasing play ➡ performance

43 요청/제의/제안 난이도 하

해석 남자는 여자에게 무엇을 제공하는가?
(A) 헤드폰
(B) 프로그램 가이드
(C) 명함
(D) 할인 요금

해설 남자가 I could give you a discount on tickets for another play tonight called *Sky Falling*. (오늘 밤에 하는 <Sky Falling>이라는 다른 연극 티켓을 할인해드릴 수 있어요.)라고 말했으므로 (D)가 정답

Paraphrasing a discount ➡ reduced rates

미국 ⇄ 호주 ⇄ 미국

Questions 44-46 refer to the following conversation with three speakers.

W: Brad, Tyler, I'm excited about our vacation next month. (44) I heard Seoul has a lot of great restaurants and entertainment options.

M1: I'm looking forward to it, too! **Have you booked the accommodations yet,**(45) Brad?

M2: Umm... **No. I've made a list of affordable hotels, but I want you two to review them before I choose.**(45) Also, should we rent a car to get around there?

M1: I'm not sure. Celia, you've been there before, right?

W: Yeah, **the public transportation system there is really great. I can install the mobile app for it on both of your phones.**(46)

M2: I'd appreciate that!

44-46번은 다음 세 화자의 대화에 관한 문제입니다.

여: Brad, Tyler, **저는 다음 달 휴가 갈 생각에 신나요.**(44) 서울에 훌륭한 레스토랑들과 즐길 거리가 많다고 들었거든요.

남1: 저도 기대하고 있어요! **숙박은 예약했나요,**(45) Brad?

남2: 음… 아니요. **가격이 적당한 호텔 목록을 만들었는데, 제가 고르기 전에 두 분이 검토해 주셨으면 해요.**(45) 그리고, 거기서 돌아다니려면 렌터카를 이용해야 할까요?

남1: 잘 모르겠어요. Celia, 거기 가본 적 있잖아요, 그렇죠?

여: 네, **거기 대중교통 시스템이 아주 훌륭해요. 제가 두 분 핸드폰에 모바일 앱을 설치해 드릴 수 있어요.**(46)

남2: 감사해요!

어휘 book v. 예약하다 accommodations n. 숙박 시설 affordable adj. (가격이) 알맞은 rental n. 임대 get around 돌아다니다 public transportation 대중교통

44 주제/목적 난이도 하

해설 화자들은 다음 달에 무엇을 하려고 계획 중인가?
(A) 고객을 방문하려고
(B) 신규 프로젝트를 시작하려고
(C) 휴가를 가려고
(D) 회의에 참석하려고

해설 여자가 Brad, Tyler, I'm excited about our vacation trip to Seoul next month. (Brad, Tyler, 저는 다음 달 서울로 휴가 갈 생각에 신나요.)라고 말했으므로 (C)가 정답

45 세부정보 난이도 중

해설 Brad는 왜 아직 숙소를 예약하지 않았는가?
(A) 적당한 가격대의 예약 가능한 호텔들이 없다.
(B) 법인 신용카드를 사용해야만 한다.
(C) 의견을 받고 싶어한다.
(D) 다음 주에 판촉행사가 시작된다.

해설 남자가 Have you booked the accommodations yet, Brad? (숙박은 예약했나요, Brad?)라고 하자, 남자가 No. I've made a list of affordable hotels, but I want you two to review them before I choose. (아니요. 가격이 알맞은 호텔들 목록을 만들었는데, 제가 고르기 전에 두 분이 검토해 주셨으면 해요.)라고 말했으므로 (C)가 정답

46 요청/제의/제안 난이도 하

해설 여자는 무엇을 하겠다고 제안하는가?
(A) 렌터카 대리점에 전화하겠다고
(B) 애플리케이션을 설치하겠다고
(C) 레스토랑 메뉴를 인쇄하겠다고
(D) 티켓을 주문하겠다고

해설 여자가 the public transportation system there is really great. I can install the mobile app for it on both of your phones. (거기 대중교통 시스템이 아주 훌륭해요. 제가 두 분 핸드폰에 그 모바일 앱을 설치해 드릴 수 있어요.)라고 말했으므로 (B)가 정답

Paraphrasing mobile app ➡ application

Questions 47-49 refer to the following conversation.

M: Hi, I'm Sal Guberman's assistant, and **I'm calling regarding your consultation on Thursday. Something has come up, and Mr. Guberman will have to be out of town for the rest of the week. If you're available next week, we'd like to arrange a new appointment for you.**(47)

W: Ah, well… My schedule is tight next week with meetings and projects. **Can I just meet with a different lawyer on Thursday?**(48)

M: Hmm… Violet Wakers is available at 5 P.M., but she works in our **Belford branch.**(49)

W: Oh, my office is in Belford so that should actually be less of a drive for me.(49) I'll do that.

47-49번은 다음 대화에 관한 문제입니다.

남: 안녕하세요, 저는 Sal Guberman의 비서인데요, **목요일에 있을 귀하의 상담과 관련하여 전화 드립니다. 일이 좀 생겨서, Mr. Guberman이 이번 주 내내 출장을 가셔야 합니다. 다음 주에 시간 괜찮으시면, 새로 예약을 잡아드렸으면 합니다.**(47)

여: 아, 음… 저는 다음 주에 회의와 프로젝트들로 일정이 빡빡해요. **그냥 목요일에 다른 변호사와 만날 수 있을까요?**(48)

남: 음… Violet Wakers가 오후 5시에 시간이 되시는데, Belford 지점에 계세요.(49)

여: 아, 제 사무실이 Belford에 있어서, 사실상 저로서는 운전을 덜 해도 되겠네요.(49) 그렇게 할게요.

어휘 assistant n. 비서, 조수 regarding prep. ~에 관하여 consultation n. 상담 come up 생기다[발생하다] available adj. 시간이 있는 arrange v. 정하다, 잡다 tight adj. 빡빡한 branch n. 지사, 분점

47 주제/목적 난이도 중

해설 남자는 왜 여자에게 연락했는가?
(A) 여행 준비를 확인하기 위해
(B) 상담을 연기하기 위해
(C) 회의 장소를 변경하기 위해
(D) 청구서를 요청하기 위해

해설 남자가 I'm calling regarding your consultation on Thursday. Something has come up, and Mr. Guberman will have to be out of town for the rest of the week. If you're available next week, we'd like to arrange a new appointment for you. (목요일에 있을 귀하의 상담과 관련하여 전화 드립니다. 일이 좀 생겨서, Mr. Guberman이 이번 주 내내 출장을 가셔야 합니다. 다음 주에 시간 괜찮으시면, 새로 예약을 잡아드렸으면 합니다.)라고 말했으므로 (B)가 정답

| 48 | 세부정보 | 난이도 하 |

해석 여자는 무엇에 관하여 묻는가?
(A) 서류 작업을 완료하는 것
(B) 면접을 진행하는 것
(C) 마감기한 연장하는 것
(D) 다른 변호사를 만나는 것

해설 여자가 Can I just meet with a different lawyer on Thursday? (그냥 목요일에 다른 변호사와 만날 수 있을까요?)라고 말했으므로 (D)가 정답

Paraphrasing different ➡ another

| 49 | 세부정보 | 난이도 중 |

해석 여자는 왜 장소가 편리하다고 말하는가?
(A) 시내에 위치해 있다.
(B) 늦게까지 문을 연다.
(C) 지하철역에서 가깝다.
(D) 자신의 직장 근처에 있다.

해설 남자가 Violet Wakers is available at 5 P.M., but she works in our Belford branch. (Violet Wakers가 오후 5시에 시간이 되시는데, Belford 지점에 계세요.)라고 하자, 여자가 my office is in Belford so that should actually be less of a drive for me. (제 사무실이 Belford에 있어서 사실상 저로서는 운전을 덜 해도 되겠네요.)라고 말했으므로 (D)가 정답

Paraphrasing office ➡ workplace

미국 ⇄ 호주 ⇄ 미국

Questions 50-52 refer to the following conversation with three speakers.

M1: I'd like to welcome everyone to this afternoon's training seminar. Please turn on the laptop in front of you. This afternoon, **you'll be learning how to input customer information into our new system.**(50) But before we start, does anyone have questions or comments about yesterday's session?

M2: I do. I was out sick yesterday. What do I…

W: Actually, Michael, **I can give you the notes I took yesterday.** (51)

M1: Thank you, Krista. OK. Now, **I'd like all of you to open the document labeled "System Instructions."**(52) It contains basic guidelines on how to use the program.

50-52번은 다음 세 화자의 대화에 관한 문제입니다.

남1: 오늘 오후 교육 세미나에 오신 모든 분들을 환영합니다. 여러분 앞에 있는 노트북을 켜주세요. 오늘 오후에는, **새로운 시스템에 고객 정보를 입력하는 방법을 배울 것입니다.**(50) 그런데 시작하기 전에, 어제 수업에 관해 질문이나 의견 있는 분 계신가요?

남2: 저요. 제가 어제 아파서 결석했거든요. 제가 무엇을 하면…

여: 어, Michael, **제가 어제 필기한 것을 줄 수 있어요.**(51)

남1: 고마워요, Krista. 좋습니다. 이제, **여러분 모두 "시스템 설명"이라고 되어 있는 문서를 열어 주세요.**(52) 거기에 프로그램 사용법에 관한 기본 가이드라인이 들어 있습니다.

어휘 input v. 입력하다 comment n. 의견, 논평 be out sick 아파서 결석[결근]하다 take notes 필기하다, 기록하다 instruction n. 설명 contain v. 들어 있다

| 50 | 주제/목적 | 난이도 하 |

해석 청자들은 무엇에 관해 배울 것인가?
(A) 고객 데이터를 입력하는 것
(B) 비용 보고서를 업로드하는 것
(C) 프로그램을 설치하는 것
(D) 기기를 수리하는 것

해설 남자가 you'll be learning how to input customer information into our new system .(새로운 시스템에 고객 정보를 입력하는 방법을 배울 것입니다.)라고 말했으므로 (A)가 정답

Paraphrasing input customer information ➡ enter customer data

| 51 | 요청/제의/제안 | 난이도 하 |

해석 여자는 무엇을 하겠다고 제안하는가?
(A) 다른 자리를 찾겠다고
(B) 새 장비를 가져오겠다고
(C) 자신의 필기를 제공하겠다고
(D) 발표를 하겠다고

해설 여자가 I can give you the notes (제가 어제 필기한 것을 줄 수 있어요.)라고 말했으므로 (C)가 정답

Paraphrasing give ➡ provide

| 52 | 다음 행동/계획 | 난이도 중 |

해석 청자들은 다음에 무엇을 하겠는가?
(A) 설문지를 작성할 것이다
(B) 제품을 테스트할 것이다
(C) 업데이트를 다운로드 할 것이다
(D) 파일을 검토할 것이다

해설 남자가 I'd like all of you to open the document (여러분 모두 "시스템 설명"이라고 되어 있는 문서를 열어 주세요.)라고 말했으므로 (D)가 정답

Paraphrasing document ➡ file

호주 ⇄ 영국

Questions 53-55 refer to the following conversation.

M: Hi, Julia. I'd like to talk to you about our company's anniversary banquet. **It's just six weeks away, so we need to decide who should be given the prize as Writer of the Year.**(53)/(54)

W: Let's see. How about Irina? **Her magazine articles are always highly rated in our reader surveys.**(53)/(54)

M: **She won it last year.**(54) And there are others who have helped increase our subscription recently.

W: You're right. Well, what if we took a vote among the employees and see who they think deserves it the most?(55)

M: I like that idea. I've always thought we should let everybody who works here vote on it.(55)

53-55번은 다음 대화에 관한 문제입니다.

남: 안녕하세요, Julia. 우리 회사 기념일 연회에 관해 얘기하고 싶어요. 6주밖에 안 남아서, 누가 <올해의 작가> 상을 받아야 할지 결정해야 해요.(53)/(54)

여: 어디 봅시다. Irina는 어때요? 그녀가 쓴 잡지 기사가 저희 독자 설문에서 항상 높은 평가를 받거든요. (53)/(54)

남: 그 분은 작년에 받았어요.(54) 그리고 최근에 구독을 늘리는 데 도움을 주신 분들이 있어요.

여: 그렇네요. 직원들끼리 투표를 해서 그들이 생각하기에 가장 받을만한 사람이 누구라고 생각하는지 알아보면 어떨까요?(55)

남: 그 아이디어 좋은데요. 여기서 일하는 사람들 모두가 투표를 해야 한다고 항상 생각했거든요.(55)

어휘 | anniversary n. 기념일 banquet n. 연회 rate v. 평가하다 subscription n. 구독 vote n. 투표 v. 투표하다 deserve v. ~을 받을 만하다

53 장소/근무지 난이도 중

해석 화자들은 어디서 일하겠는가?
(A) 호텔
(B) 조경 회사
(C) 잡지사
(D) 건설 회사

해설 남자는 It's just six weeks away, so we need to decide who should be given the prize as Writer of the Year. (6주밖에 안 남아서, <올해의 작가>로 누가 상을 받아야 할지 결정해야 해요.)라고 말했고, 여자는 Let's see. How about Irina? Her magazine articles are always highly rated in our reader surveys. (어디 봅시다. Irina는 어때요? 그녀가 쓴 잡지 기사가 저희 독자 설문에서 항상 높은 평가를 받거든요.)라고 말했으므로 (C)가 정답

54 화자 의도 파악 난이도 중

해석 남자는 왜 "그 분은 작년에 받았어요."라고 말하는가?
(A) 존경을 표하려고
(B) 세부사항을 확인하려고
(C) 추천을 거절하려고
(D) 해결책을 제안하려고

해설 남자가 It's just six weeks away, so we need to decide who should be given the prize as Writer of the Year. (6주밖에 안 남아서, <올해의 작가>로 누가 상을 받아야 할지 결정해야 해요.)라고 하자, 여자가 Let's see. How about Irina? Her magazine articles are always highly rated in our reader surveys. (어디 봅시다. Irina는 어때요? 그녀가 쓴 잡지 기사가 저희 독자 설문에서 항상 높은 평가를 받거든요.)라고 제안했는데, 남자가 She won it last year. (그 분은 작년에 받았어요.)라고 대답한 것이므로 (C)가 정답

55 다음 행동/계획 난이도 중

해석 화자들은 무엇을 하기로 결정하는가?
(A) 회의를 취소하기로
(B) 직원들의 의견을 구하기로
(C) 근무 시간을 연장하기로
(D) 교육을 받기로

해설 여자가 Well, what if we took a vote among the employees and see who they think deserves it the most? (직원들끼리 투표를 해서 그들이 생각하기에 가장 받을만한 사람이 누구라고 생각하는지 알아보면 어떨까요?)라고 하자, 남자가 I like that idea. I've always thought we should let everybody who works here vote on it. (그 아이디어 좋은데요. 여기서 일하는 사람들 모두가 투표를 해야 한다고 항상 생각했거든요.)라고 말했으므로 (B)가 정답

Paraphrasing employees ➡ staff

영국 ⇄ 호주

Questions 56-58 refer to the following conversation.

W: Hi, I just moved to this city. **Can I get a guide that lists local attractions and restaurants?**(56)

M: Of course. Take this one right here. By the way, **I highly suggest checking out the Pearl Art Gallery. It was remodeled last week.**(57)

W: Thank you for the recommendation! I'll read about it in the guide before I go.

M: Great. One more thing: **there will be live music performances on Sunday at Manitz Park.**(58) Admission is free, but you'll want to arrive early because parking spaces will fill up fast.

56-58번은 다음 대화에 관한 문제입니다.

여: 안녕하세요, 제가 최근에 이 도시로 이사 왔거든요. 지역 명소와 식당 목록이 있는 안내서를 받을 수 있을까요?(56)

남: 물론이죠. 여기 이거 가져가세요. 그나저나, 저는 Pearl 미술관에 가보시는 걸 강력히 추천합니다. 지난주에 리모델링을 했거든요.(57)

여: 추천 고맙습니다! 가기 전에 안내서에서 그곳에 관해 읽어볼게요.

남: 좋아요. 한 가지 더요: 일요일에 Manitz 공원에서 라이브 음악공연이 있어요.(58) 입장은 무료이지만, 주차장이 금세 다 차버리니까 일찍 가시는 게 좋을 거예요.

어휘 | list v. 열거하다 attraction n. 명소 admission n. 입장 fill up 가득 차다

56 세부정보 난이도 하

해석 여자는 무엇을 요청하는가?
(A) 주차권
(B) 지역 안내서
(C) 버스 탑승권
(D) 제품 카탈로그

해설 여자가 Can I get a guide that lists local attractions and restaurants? (지역 명소와 식당 목록이 있는 안내서를 받을 수 있을까요?)라고 말했으므로 (B)가 정답

57 세부정보 난이도 중

해석 남자는 미술관에 관하여 뭐라고 말하는가?
(A) 주인이 바뀌었다.
(B) 입장이 무료이다.
(C) 명화를 전시한다.
(D) 최근 개조되었다.

해설 남자가 I highly suggest checking out the Pearl Art Gallery. It was remodeled last week. (저는 Pearl 미술관에 가보시는 걸 강력히 추천합니다. 지난 주에 리모델링을 했거든요.)라고 말했으므로 (D)가 정답

Paraphrasing remodeled last week ➡ recently renovated

58 세부정보 난이도 중

해석 일요일에 어떤 행사가 열릴 것인가?
(A) 콘서트
(B) 공원 개장
(C) 스포츠 경기
(D) 퍼레이드

해설 여자가 there will be live music performances on Sunday at Manitz Park. (일요일에 Manitz 공원에서 라이브 음악 공연이 있어요.)라고 말했으므로 (A)가 정답

Paraphrasing live music performances ➡ a concert

호주 ⇄ 미국

Questions 59-61 refer to the following conversation.

M: Hey, Liz. I see that we've received a new shipment of produce. Did you begin entering the data into the supermarket's database yet?(59)

W: I was just about to. Are you free right now? If I do this alone, it'll take me the whole day.(60)

M: I came at the right time, then.(60) Oh, these are the items that we purchased for our store's new organic produce section.(61)

W: Yeah, I'm looking forward to this new addition.(61) A lot of customers have been interested in healthier products lately. Anyway, let's get started.

M: OK. Why don't we unpack the shipment and take out the boxes first?

59-61번은 다음 대화에 관한 문제입니다.

남: 저기, Liz. 보니까 새로운 농산물 배송품을 받았네요. 슈퍼마켓 데이터베이스에 데이터 입력을 시작했나요?(59)

여: 막 하려던 참이었어요. 지금 시간 있으세요? 제가 이걸 혼자 하려면, 온종일 걸릴 거예요.(60)

남: 그렇다면 제가 제때 왔네요.(60) 아, 이것들은 우리 매장의 새로운 유기농 농산물 코너용으로 구입한 제품들이네요.(61)

여: 네, 저는 이 새로 추가되는 코너가 기대돼요.(61) 최근에 많은 고객들이 건강에 더 좋은 제품들에 관심이 있으셨거든요. 어쨌든, 시작합시다.

남: 좋아요. 배송품을 풀어서 상자 먼저 꺼내는 게 어떨까요?

어휘 shipment n. 배송품 produce n. 농산물 enter v. 입력하다 be about to 막 ~하려고 하다 organic adj. 유기농의 look forward to ~을 고대하다 lately adv. 최근에 unpack v. (짐을) 풀다

59 장소/근무지 난이도 중

해석 대화는 어디에서 이루어지고 있는가?
(A) 제과점에서
(B) 레스토랑에서
(C) 농장에서
(D) 슈퍼마켓에서

해설 남자가 I see that we've received a new shipment of produce. Did you begin entering the data into the supermarket's database yet? (보니까 새 농산물 수송품을 받았네요. 슈퍼마켓 데이터베이스에 데이터 입력을 시작했나요?)라고 말했으므로 (D)가 정답

60 화자 의도 파악 난이도 상

해석 남자가 "그렇다면, 제가 제때 왔네요"라고 말할 때, 그가 내비친 것은?
(A) 그는 행사에 제시간에 도착할 수 있었다.
(B) 그는 어떤 제품을 맛보고 싶어한다.
(C) 그는 여자를 도와줄 시간이 있다.
(D) 그는 프로젝트 마감기한을 맞출 수 있었다.

해설 여자가 Are you free right now? If I do this alone, it'll take me the whole day. (지금 시간 있으세요? 제가 이걸 혼자 하려면, 온종일 걸릴 거예요.)라고 하자, 남자가 I came at the right time, then. (그렇다면 제가 제때 왔네요.)라고 말한 것이므로 (C)가 정답

61 세부정보 난이도 중

해석 여자는 무엇을 고대하고 있는가?
(A) 수정된 포장 절차
(B) 더 많은 직원 채용
(C) 시즌 할인 행사
(D) 농산물 코너의 추가

해설 남자가 these are the items that we purchased for our store's new organic produce section. (이것들은 우리 매장의 새로운 유기 농산물 코너용으로 구입한 제품들이네요.)라고 하자, 여자가 Yeah, I'm looking forward to this new addition. (네, 저는 이 새로 추가되는 코너가 기대돼요.)라고 말했으므로 (D)가 정답

미국 ⇄ 미국

Questions 62-64 refer to the following conversation and sign.

M: Hello. I just put gas in my car at pump 8, but the receipt wouldn't print. Can I get it here?(62)

W: Sure. Give me a second.

M: Of course. By the way, I'm surprised at how cheap your gas prices are. It was only $1.10 per gallon. I've paid a lot more at other gas stations.(63)

W: Yeah, a lot of customers say that. Anyway, here you go. Also, today, we're offering complimentary bottled water with every fuel purchase.(64)

Gasoline Type	Price Per Gallon
Unleaded	$1.10 (63)
Super	$1.20
Supreme	$1.35
Diesel	$1.55

62-64번은 다음 대화와 안내판에 관한 문제입니다.

남: 안녕하세요. 제가 방금 8번 펌프에서 차에 기름을 넣었는데, 영수증이 출력되지 않네요. 여기서 받을 수 있나요? (62)

여: 물론이죠. 잠깐만 기다려 주세요.

남: 네. 그런데 기름값이 너무 싸서 놀랐어요. 갤런당 1.10 달러밖에 안 하던데, 다른 주유소에서는 훨씬 더 많이 냈거든요. (63)

여: 네, 많은 고객이 그렇게 말씀하시죠. 자, 여기 있습니다. 그리고 오늘은 주유하시는 모든 분께 무료 생수를 제공해 드립니다. (64)

휘발유 종류	갤런당 가격
무연	1.10달러 (63)
고급	1.20달러
최고급	1.35달러
디젤	1.55달러

어휘 put gas in (차에) 기름을 넣다 print v. (어떤 상태로) 인쇄되다 per prep. ~당[마다] gas station 주유소 complimentary adj. 무료의 fuel n. 연료 purchase n. 구입 gasoline n. 휘발유 unleaded adj. 무연의 supreme adj. 최고의

62 세부정보 난이도 중

해석 남자는 무엇을 요청하는가?
(A) 비밀번호
(B) 영수증
(C) 안내서
(D) 환불

해설 남자가 I just put gas in my car at pump 8, but the receipt wouldn't print. Can I get it here? (제가 방금 8번 펌프에서 차에 기름을 넣었는데, 영수증이 출력되지 않네요. 여기서 받을 수 있나요?)라고 말했으므로 (B)가 정답

63 시각 정보 연계 난이도 상

해석 시각 자료를 보시오. 남자는 어떤 종류의 휘발유를 선택했는가?
(A) 무연
(B) 고급
(C) 최고급
(D) 디젤

해설 남자가 It was only $1.10 per gallon. I've paid a lot more at other gas stations. (갤런당 1.10 달러밖에 안 하던데, 다른 주유소에서는 훨씬 더 많이 냈거든요.)라고 말했고, 시각 자료에서 Unleaded (무연)이 $1.10 (1.10달러)임을 확인할 수 있으므로 (A)가 정답

64 세부정보 난이도 중

해석 남자는 연료 구입으로 무엇을 받을 것인가?

(A) 영화표
(B) 음료
(C) 상품권
(D) 자동차 액세서리

해설 여자가 Also, today, we're offering complimentary bottled water with every fuel purchase. (그리고 오늘은 주유하시는 모든 분께 무료 생수를 제공해 드립니다.)라고 말했으므로 (B)가 정답

Paraphrasing bottled water ➡ beverage

미국 ⇌ 호주

Questions 65-67 refer to the following conversation and advertisement.

W: You've reached Macmore's Flooring. This is Katie speaking.

M: Hello, I want to install new floor tiles in my living room. I haven't changed the current ones since I moved in here which was 40 years ago. (65)

W: You called the right place. And just so you know, we're offering discounts on our products right now. The price varies depending on what kind of floor tiles you want.

M: Hmm... The ones I have right now are stone, so this time I'd like to go with ceramic tiles. (66)

W: Ceramic? You should be able to get an extra low price on your order then.

M: Perfect!

W: Also, all of our floor tiles are very sturdy. They don't crack easily, so they look good for a long time. (67)

Macmore's Flooring
Special Discount Event!
(Offer Valid Until June 30)

Ceramic Tile (66) Installation: 40% off
Porcelain Tile Installation: 30% off
Stone Tile Installation: 20% off
Marble Tile Installation: 10% off

65-67번은 다음 대화와 광고에 관한 문제입니다.

여: Macmore Flooring에 전화 주셨습니다. 저는 Katie입니다.

남: 안녕하세요, 저희 집 거실에 바닥 타일을 새로 깔고 싶은데요. 지금 있는 건 이곳으로 이사 오고 나서 바꾼 적이 없어요, 그게 40년 전이네요. (65)

여: 연락 잘 주셨습니다. 그리고 참고로 말씀 드리면, 현재 저희 제품들에 대한 할인을 제공하고 있습니다. 가격은 어떤 종류의 바닥 타일을 원하시는 지에 따라 다릅니다.

남: 음... 지금 있는 것은 석재라서요, 이번에는 세라믹 타일로 하고 싶어요. (66)

여: 세라믹이요? 그러시다면 더 낮은 가격으로 주문하실 수 있을 겁니다.

남: 너무 좋네요!

여: 게다가 저희 바닥 타일은 모두 매우 튼튼합니다. 쉽게 깨지지도 않아 외관도 오랫동안 좋게 유지됩니다. (67)

```
┌─────────────────────────────┐
│      Macmore Flooring       │
│         특별 할인 행사!        │
│       (6월 30일까지 할인)      │
│  ┌───────────────────────┐  │
│  │ 세라믹 타일(66) 설치: 40 퍼센트 할인 │  │
│  │ 도자기 타일 설치: 30 퍼센트 할인   │  │
│  │ 석재 타일 설치: 20 퍼센트 할인    │  │
│  │ 대리석 타일 설치: 10 퍼센트 할인   │  │
│  └───────────────────────┘  │
└─────────────────────────────┘
```

어휘 just so you know 참고로 말씀 드리는데 vary v. 서로 다르다 depending on ~에 따라 sturdy adj. 튼튼한, 견고한 crack v. 깨지다, 부서지다 offer n. (보통 짧은 기간 동안의) 할인 off prep. 할인하여 porcelain tile 도자기 타일 marble n. 대리석 accommodate v. (살거나 지낼) 공간을 제공하다 floor space (건물의) 바닥 면적

65 세부정보   난이도 중

해석 남자는 왜 새 바닥 타일을 설치하고 싶어 하는가?
(A) 오래된 바닥재를 교체하기 위해
(B) 거실 벽지와 어울리게 하기 위해
(C) 더 많은 바닥 면적을 제공하기 위해
(D) 집을 팔기 위해

해설 남자가 I want to install new floor tiles in my living room. I haven't changed the current ones since I moved in here, which was 40 years ago. (저희 집 바닥 타일을 새로 깔고 싶은데요. 지금 있는 건 이곳으로 이사 오고 나서 바꾼 적이 없어요, 그게 40년 전이네요.)라고 말했으므로 (A)가 정답

Paraphrasing changed ➡ replace, 40 years ago ➡ old

66 시각 정보 연계   난이도 중

해석 시각 자료를 보시오. 남자의 주문금액에서 얼만큼 할인되겠는가?
(A) 10 퍼센트
(B) 20 퍼센트
(C) 30 퍼센트
(D) 40 퍼센트

해설 남자가 I'd like to go with ceramic tiles. (세라믹 타일로 하고 싶어요.)라고 말했고, 시각 자료에서 Ceramic Tile Installation: 40 퍼센트 off (세라믹 타일 설치: 40 퍼센트 할인)임을 확인할 수 있으므로 (D)가 정답

67 세부정보   난이도 중

해석 여자는 바닥 타일에 관하여 무엇을 강조하는가?
(A) 가볍다.
(B) 내구성이 있다.
(C) 환경 친화적이다.
(D) 저렴하다.

해설 여자가 all of our floor tiles are very sturdy. They don't crack easily, and they look good for a long time. (저희 바닥 타일은 모두 매우 튼튼합니다. 쉽게 깨지지도 않아 외관도 오랫동안 좋게 유지됩니다.)라고 말했으므로 (B)가 정답

Paraphrasing sturdy ➡ durable

미국 ⇄ 미국

Questions 68-70 refer to the following conversation and poster.

W: Hey, Jerome. Are you looking forward to the cooking contest?
M: I am! I heard all the contestants are famous local chefs.
W: **How about riding to the fair together?**[68] John from Purchasing has a van, and he says he's got room for a couple more people.
M: Ah, I have some errands to run early afternoon. **But I should arrive in time to watch my favorite cuisine being prepared at 3 o'clock.**[69] I'll see you all in front of Elk Arena.
W: Alright. Also, **remember to wear a thick jacket.**[70] It's going to be cloudy and chilly all day.

Mayertown Cooking Contest	
May 25 Schedule	
Time/Location	Cuisine
2:00 P.M./Elk Arena	Chinese
3:00 P.M.[69]/Elk Arena	Italian
4:00 P.M./Remo Arena	Mexican
5:00 P.M./Remo Arena	Greek

68-70번은 다음 대화와 포스터에 관한 문제입니다.

여: Jerome. 요리 경연대회를 기대하고 있나요?
남: 네! 모든 경연자들이 지역에서 유명한 요리사들이라고 들었어요.
여: **행사장까지 함께 차를 타고 가시는 건 어떠세요?**[68] 구매부의 John에게 밴이 있는데, 몇 사람 더 탈 자리가 있다고 하네요.
남: 아, 제가 오후 일찍 급히 해야 할 일이 좀 있어서요. **하지만 3시에 하는, 제가 가장 좋아하는 요리를 보러 시간에 맞춰 갈 수 있을 거예요.**[69] 여러분 모두 Elk 아레나 앞에서 뵐게요.
여: 알겠어요. 그리고, **잊지 말고 두꺼운 재킷을 입고 오세요.**[70] 하루 종일 흐리고 쌀쌀할 거라고 하네요.

Mayertown 요리 경연대회	
5월 25일 일정	
시간/장소	요리
오후 2시/Elk 아레나	중식
오후 3시[69]/Elk 아레나	이탈리아식
오후 4시/Remo 아레나	멕시코식
오후 5시/Remo 아레나	그리스식

어휘 look forward to ~하기를 고대하다 contestant n. 경연자, 참가자 errand n. 일, 심부름 in time 제 때에, 시간 맞춰 cuisine n. 요리 cloudy adj. 구름 낀, 흐린 chilly adj. 쌀쌀한, 추운

| 68 | 요청/제의/제안 | 난이도 중 |

해석 여자는 무엇을 하자고 제안하는가?
(A) 자리를 바꾸자고
(B) 일찍 만나자고
(C) 차를 같이 타고 가자고
(D) 음식을 주문하자고

해설 여자가 How about riding to the fair together? (행사장까지 함께 차를 타고 가시는 건 어떠세요?)라고 말했으므로 (C)가 정답

Paraphrasing riding together ➡ sharing a ride

| 69 | 시각 정보 연계 | 난이도 중 |

해석 시각 자료를 보시오. 남자가 가장 좋아하는 음식은 무엇인가?
(A) 중식
(B) 이탈리아식
(C) 멕시코식
(D) 그리스식

해설 남자가 But I should arrive in time to watch my favorite cuisine being prepared at 3 o'clock. (하지만 3시에 하는 있는, 제가 가장 좋아하는 요리를 보러 시간에 맞춰 갈 순 있을 거예요.)라고 말했고, 시각 자료에서 3:00 P.M./Elk Arena - Italian (오후 3시/Elk 아레나 - 이탈리아식)를 확인할 수 있으므로 (B)가 정답

| 70 | 세부정보 | 난이도 중 |

해석 여자는 남자에게 무엇을 하라고 다시 알려주고 있는가?
(A) 테이블을 예약하라고
(B) 따뜻한 옷을 입으라고
(C) 서식을 제출하라고
(D) 우산을 가져오라고

해설 여자가 remember to wear a thick jacket (잊지 말고 두꺼운 재킷을 입고 오세요.)라고 말했으므로 (B)가 정답

Paraphrasing thick jacket ➡ warm clothing

PART 4 P. 25

[영국]

Questions 71-73 refer to the following advertisement.

W: Are you looking to give your business a new look? If so, Olympus Interior is your answer. Our team of specialists will design your store to make it more appealing to customers.(71) The biggest advantage of hiring us is that we're willing to work around your schedule, even if it means coming on the weekend.(72) That way, you don't have to worry about us interrupting your daily operations. Go to our Web site to see some projects we've done in the past.(73) Give us a call anytime to schedule a consultation.

71-73번은 다음 광고에 관한 문제입니다.
여: 당신의 사업체를 새롭게 단장하고 싶으신가요? 그러시다면 Olympus 인테리어가 답입니다. 전문가로 이루어진 저희 팀이 귀하의 매장을 고객에 더 매력적으로 보일 수 있도록 디자인해 드립니다.(71) 저희에게 맡겨주실 경우 가장 큰 장점은 저희가 주말에 작업하는 일이 있더라도 기꺼이 귀하의 일정에 맞춰 드린다는 것입니다.(72) 그러면 정상영업에 지장이 있진 않을지 염려하실 일이 없을 겁니다. 저희 웹 사이트를 방문하셔서 저희가 이전에 한 작업들을 살펴봐 주시기 바랍니다.(73) 상담 일정을 잡으시려면 언제든지 전화주세요.

어휘 **look** n. 외관, 모양 **appealing** adj. 매력적인, 흥미로운 **advantage** n. 이점, 장점 **hire** v. 고용하다 **be willing to do** 기꺼이 ~하다 **interrupt** v. 방해하다 **operation** n. 사업, 영업 **consultation** n. 상담

| 71 | 주제/목적 | 난이도 하 |

해석 어떤 서비스가 광고되고 있는가?
(A) 행사 기획
(B) 인테리어 디자인
(C) 디지털 마케팅
(D) 제품 포장

해설 화자가 Are you looking to give your business a new look? If so, Olympus Interior is your answer. Our team of specialists will design your store to make it more appealing to customers. (당신의 사업체를 새롭게 단장하고 싶으신가요? 그러시다면 Olympus 인테리어가 답입니다. 전문가로 이루어진 저희 팀이 귀하의 매장을 고객에 더 매력적으로 보일 수 있도록 디자인해 드립니다.)라고 말했으므로 (B)가 정답

| 72 | 세부정보 | 난이도 중 |

해석 광고는 어떤 장점을 언급하는가?
(A) 빠른 배송
(B) 고품질 상품
(C) 저렴한 가격
(D) 탄력적인 영업시간

해설 화자가 The biggest advantage of hiring us is that we're willing to work around your schedule, even if it means coming on the weekend. (저희에게 맡겨주실 경우 가장 큰 장점은 저희가 주말에 작업하는 일이 있더라도 기꺼이 귀하의 일정에 맞춰 드린다는 것입니다.)라고 말했으므로 (D)가 정답

Paraphrasing work around your schedule ➡ flexible hours

| 73 | 세부정보 | 난이도 하 |

해석 청자들은 왜 웹 사이트를 확인해야 하는가?
(A) 직원에게 연락하기 위해
(B) 이전 작업들을 살펴보기 위해
(C) 프로그램을 다운로드하기 위해
(D) 등록 양식을 작성하기 위해

해설 화자가 Go to our Web site to see some projects we've done in the past. (저희 웹 사이트를 방문하셔서 저희가 이전에 한 작업들을 살펴봐 주시기 바랍니다.)라고 말했으므로 (B)가 정답

Paraphrasing go to our Web site to see ➡ check a Web site, see some projects we've done in the past ➡ view previous projects

호주

Questions 74-76 refer to the following telephone message.

M: Hi, it's Victor O'Brien at Riptide Publishing. **I appreciate you sending over the cover design of Mr. Wong's novel.**(74) My manager, Ms. Yoon, was impressed with how quick you were. She has looked over the details and really liked the font and colors you have chosen. **However, she is worried about the total cost you quoted for creating all of the illustrations.** (75) **Do you mind emailing me a detailed pricing chart? Ms. Yoon needs to review it by the end of the day.**(76) Let me know if you have any other inquiries.

74-76번은 다음 전화 메시지에 관한 문제입니다.

남: 안녕하세요, Riptide 출판사의 Victor O'Brien입니다. Mr. Wong의 소설 표지 디자인을 보내주셔서 감사합니다.(74) 빨리 해 주셔서 저희 Ms. Yoon 부장님이 감명하셨어요. 세부 사항들을 살펴보시고선 골라 주신 색상과 서체를 정말 마음에 들어 하셨어요. 그런데 뽑아 주신 전체 삽화 견적에 대해서는 염려하고 계십니다.(75) 상세 가격표를 이메일로 보내주시겠어요? Ms. Yoon이 오늘 퇴근 전까지 검토하셔야 되거든요.(76) 다른 문의사항 있으시면 연락주세요.

어휘 appreciate v. 고마워하다 be impressed with ~에 감명을 받다 look over ~을 살펴보다 detail n. 세부 사항 font n. 서체 quote v. 견적을 내다 illustration n. 삽화 detailed adj. 상세한 pricing n. 가격 책정 review v. 재검토하다 inquiry n. 문의

74 장소/근무지 난이도 중

해석 청자는 어디에서 근무하겠는가?
(A) 소프트웨어 개발업체
(B) 서점
(C) 출판사
(D) 그래픽 디자인 대행사

해설 화자가 I appreciate you sending over the cover design of Mr. Wong's novel. (Mr. Wong의 소설 표지 디자인을 보내주셔서 감사합니다.)라고 말했으므로 (D)가 정답

Paraphrasing cover design ➡ graphic design

75 세부정보 난이도 중

해석 화자의 상사는 무엇에 대하여 염려하는가?
(A) 출간 마감일
(B) 배송 날짜
(C) 현지 법규
(D) 가격 견적

해설 화자가 However, she is worried about the total cost you quoted for creating all of the illustrations. (그런데 뽑아 주신 전체 삽화 견적에 대해서는 염려하고 계십니다.)라고 말했으므로 (D)가 정답

Paraphrasing the total cost you quoted ➡ a price estimate

76 화자 의도 파악 난이도 중

해설 화자가 "Ms. Yoon이 오늘 퇴근 전까지 검토하셔야 되거든요"라고 말할 때, 그가 내비친 것은?

(A) 문서에 몇 가지 오류가 있다.
(B) 상사가 휴가를 갈 것이다.
(C) 혼자서는 업무를 완료할 수 없다.
(D) 요청 사항이 빨리 처리되어야 한다.

해설 화자가 Do you mind emailing me a detailed pricing chart? (상세 가격표를 이메일로 보내주시겠어요?)라고 하면서, Ms. Yoon needs to review it by the end of the day (Ms. Yoon이 오늘 퇴근 전까지 검토하셔야 되거든요.)라고 말했으므로 (D)가 정답

영국

Questions 77-79 refer to the following telephone message.

W: Good morning. My name is Yuka Matsumoto. **I was shopping at your store last night, checking out some sofas,**(77) and... **I believe I left my scarf there.**(78) It's made of silk with a green and red pattern on it. I last remember having it when I was sitting on one of the brown leather couches. **I'm planning to come by after work tonight to have a look.** (79) But if you find it before then, please give me a call. My number is 555-4598. Thank you.

77-79번은 다음 전화 메시지에 관한 문제입니다.

여: 안녕하세요. 제 이름은 Yuka Matsumoto입니다. 제가 어제 저녁에 그쪽 매장에서 소파들을 좀 보면서 쇼핑을 했어요.(77) 그런데... 스카프를 두고 온 것 같아요.(78) 실크재질이고, 녹색과 빨간색 무늬가 있습니다. 제가 마지막으로 기억하는 건 갈색 가죽 소파 중 하나에 앉아 있었을 때 가지고 있었다는 거예요. 오늘 저녁 퇴근 후에 들러서 살펴 보려고 합니다.(79) 하지만 그 전에 찾게 되신다면 전화 좀 부탁 드립니다. 제 번호는 555-4598입니다. 고맙습니다.

어휘 check out 확인하다 last adv. 마지막으로, 가장 최근에 leather n. 가죽 couch n. 긴 의자, 소파 plan v. 계획하다 come by 잠깐 들르다 have a look 보다 give a call 전화하다

77 장소/근무지 난이도 하

해석 여자는 어느 업체에 전화했겠는가?
(A) 가구 매장
(B) 카페
(C) 페인트 시공업체
(D) 도서관

해설 화자가 I was shopping at your store last night, checking out some sofas. (제가 어제 저녁에 그쪽 매장에서 소파들을 좀 보면서 쇼핑을 했는데요)라고 말했으므로 (A)가 정답

78 주제/목적 난이도 중

해석 여자는 왜 전화했는가?
(A) 분실된 물건에 관하여 문의하기 위해
(B) 영업시간을 알아보기 위해
(C) 할인을 요청하기 위해
(D) 예약을 다시 잡기 위해

해설 화자가 I believe I left my scarf there. (스카프를 두고 온 것 같아요.)라고 말했으므로 (A)가 정답

79 다음 행동/계획 난이도 중

해석 여자는 오늘 저녁에 무엇을 할 것이라고 말하는가?
(A) 고객을 데리러 갈 것이다
(B) 다른 지점에 전화할 것이다
(C) 초과근무를 할 것이다
(D) 사업장을 살펴볼 것이다

해설 화자가 I'm planning to come by after work tonight to have a look. (오늘 저녁퇴근 후에 들러서 살펴 보려고 합니다.)라고 말했으므로 (D)가 정답

Paraphrasing have a look ➡ check out

[미국]

Questions 80-82 refer to the following broadcast.

W: In local news, Everson High School's history teacher, Mr. Matthew Barnes,(80) will be starting up his annual summer project again. Mr. Barnes will be recruiting local students to intern at the Gelson Museum during the summer. (81) This will give them a chance to work in an academic environment. Participating students will be given $3,000 in cash at the end of August.(82) More details can be found on the Gelson Museum Web site.

80-82번은 다음 방송에 관한 문제입니다.

여: 지역 소식입니다. Everson 고등학교의 역사 교사인 Mt. Matthew Barnes(80)가 또 한 번 연례 프로젝트를 시작합니다. Mr. Barnes는 여름 방학 동안 Gelson 박물관에서 인턴으로 근무할 지역 학생들을 모집할 예정입니다.(81) 이는 학생들이 학적 환경에서 일하는 기회가 될 것입니다. 참가 학생들에게는 8월 말에 현금 3,000달러가 현금으로 지급됩니다.(82) 더 자세한 사항은 Gelson 박물관 웹 사이트에서 보실 수 있습니다.

어휘 start up ~을 시작하다 annual adj. 연례의 recruit v. 모집하다 intern v. 인턴으로 근무하다 academic adj. 학구적인, 학문의 participating a. 참가하는 in cash 현금으로

80 정체/신분 난이도 하

해석 Mr. Barnes는 누구인가?
(A) 교사
(B) 언론인
(C) 공무원
(D) 미술가

해설 화자가 Everson High School's history teacher, Mr. Matthew Barnes (Everson 고등학교의 역사 교사인 Mr. Matthew Barnes)라고 말했으므로 (A)가 정답

81 세부정보 난이도 중

해석 여름에 무슨 일이 있을 것인가?
(A) 박물관이 개조된다.
(B) 인턴십 프로그램이 열린다.
(C) 지역 공무원이 선출된다.
(D) 수상자가 발표된다.

해설 화자가 Mr. Barnes will be recruiting local students to intern at the Gelson Museum during the summer. (Mr. Barnes는 여름 방학 동안 Gelson 박물관에서 인턴으로 근무할 지역 학생들을 모집할 예정입니다.)라고 말했으므로 (B)가 정답

82 세부정보 난이도 중

해석 화자에 따르면, 8월에 무엇이 주어질 것인가?
(A) 설문조사 양식
(B) 주차권
(C) 콘서트 티켓
(D) 현금

해설 화자가 Participating students will be given $3,000 in cash at the end of August. (참가 학생들에게는 8월 말에 현금 3,000달러가 현금으로 지급됩니다.) 라고 말했으므로 (D)가 정답

Paraphrasing given ➡ distributed

[호주]

Questions 83-85 refer to the following advertisement.

M: Do you feel that too few people know about your company? If that's the case, you should attend the Welmont Global Marketing Conference, where you will learn how to build brand awareness.(83) Small conferences usually feature the same group of speakers from the local area. However, we invite experts from across the world.(84) And as an added incentive for your participation, we're giving businesses who register a month in advance a 15 percent discount.(85) Head over to our Web site to register now!

83-85번은 다음 광고에 관한 문제입니다.

남: 귀사를 아는 사람이 너무 적다고 생각하세요? 그러시다면, Welmont 세계 마케팅 콘퍼런스에 참석하세요. 그곳에서 브랜드 인지도 구축 방법을 배울 수 있습니다.(83) 보통 소규모 콘퍼런스에서는 해당 지역 출신의 동일한 강사들이 나와 강연합니다. 하지만 저희는 전 세계에서 전문가를 초청합니다.(84) 그리고 참가자 우대 추가 특전으로, 한 달 전에 등록하는 사업체에 15퍼센트 할인을 제공합니다.(85) 저희 웹 사이트에서 지금 바로 등록하세요!

어휘 the case 실정, 사실 attend v. 참석하다 conference n. 콘퍼런스, 학회 brand awareness 브랜드 인지도 feature v. 특별히 포함하다 expert n. 전문가 added adj. 추가된 incentive n. 장려[우대]책 participation n. 참여 register v. 등록하다 in advance 미리, 앞서 head over to (특정 방향으로) 향하다

83 세부정보 난이도 중

해석 학회의 주제는 무엇인가?
(A) 자격을 갖춘 직원 채용
(B) 더 좋은 제품의 개발
(C) 운영 비용 삭감
(D) 브랜드 인지도 구축

해설 화자가 you should attend the Welmont Global Marketing Conference, where you will learn how to build brand awareness. (Welmont 세계 마케팅 콘퍼런스에 참석하세요. 그곳에서 브랜드 인지도 구축방법을 배울 수 있습니다.)라고 말했으므로 (D)가 정답

84 화자 의도 파악 난이도 중

해석 화자가 "저희는 전 세계에서 전문가들을 초청하죠"라고 말할 때, 그가 내비친 것은?
(A) 청자들이 다양한 연사들에게 배우게 된다.
(B) 청자들이 올해 더 많은 요금을 내야 한다.
(C) 컨벤션 입장권이 빠르게 매진될 것이라고 생각한다.
(D) 행사에 더 많은 통역사가 필요하다고 생각한다.

해설 화자가 Small conferences usually feature the same group of speakers from the local area. (보통 소규모 콘퍼런스에서는 해당 지역 출신의 동일한 강사들이 나와 강연합니다.)라고 하면서, However, we invite experts from across the world. (하지만 저희는 전 세계에서 전문가를 초청합니다.)라고 말했으므로 (A)가 정답

85 세부정보 난이도 중

해석 청자들은 어떻게 할인 받을 수 있는가?
(A) 발표자를 추천해서
(B) 단체 패키지 상품을 준비해서
(C) 주최자에게 연락해서
(D) 일찍 등록해서

해설 화자가 And as an added incentive for your participation, we're giving businesses who register a month in advance a 15 percent discount. (그리고 참가자 우대 추가 특전으로, 한 달 전에 등록하는 사업체에 15퍼센트 할인을 제공합니다.)라고 말했으므로 (D)가 정답

Paraphrasing a month in advance ➡ early

호주

Questions 86-88 refer to the following excerpt from a meeting.

M: Thank you all for attending this morning's HR meeting. **Today, we'll be preparing a new evaluation form that we'll send out to all department managers.**(86) The executives decided that we will now be holding quarterly employee reviews rather than biannual ones. Remember, **our major objective this year is to increase staff productivity,**(87) and we believe keeping track of employees' performance more often will help with that. Now, for the next 20 minutes, I'd like you all to come up with some ideas for the format of the evaluation form. **So please get into groups of three and start brainstorming some ideas.**(88) Thanks.

86-88번은 다음 회의 발췌록에 관한 문제입니다.

남: 오늘 오전 인사부 회의에 참석해 주신 여러분께 감사 드립니다. 오늘 우리는 모든 부서장에게 발송할 새 평가 양식을 준비할 예정입니다.(86) 경영진에서 이제부터 직원 평가를 연 2회가 아니라 분기별로 진행하기로 결정했습니다. 기억하세요. 올해 주요 목표는 직원 생산성을 향상하는 것이며,(87) 직원들의 성과를 더 자주 파악해 두는 것이 이에 도움이 될 것이라고 믿습니다. 자, 이제 20분 동안 평가양식의 형식에 대해 아이디어를 구상해 주셨으면 합니다. 3명씩 그룹 지어서 떠오르는 아이디어를 나눠 보세요.(88) 감사합니다.

어휘 attend v. 참석하다 HR(=human resources) 인사부 evaluation n. 평가, 사정 send out to ~로 발송하다 executive n. 경영[운영] 간부 biannual adj. 연 2회의 major adj. 주요한 objective n. 목적, 목표 productivity n. 생산성 keep track of ~에 대해 계속 파악하고 있다 performance n. 실적, 성과 come up with (해답 등을) 내놓다 format n. 형식 brainstorm v. 여러 사람들이 동시에 자유롭게 자기 생각을 제시하다

86 주제/목적 난이도 중

해석 회의의 목적은 무엇인가?
(A) 입사 지원자를 평가하는 것
(B) 행사를 준비하는 것
(C) 평가 양식을 개발하는 것
(D) 직원들을 소개하는 것

해설 화자가 Today, we'll be preparing a new evaluation form that we'll send out to all department managers. (오늘 우리는 모든 부서장에게 발송할 새 평가양식을 준비할 예정입니다.)라고 말했으므로 (C)가 정답

87 세부정보 난이도 중

해석 화자에 따르면, 올해 목표는 무엇인가?
(A) 사업을 확장하는 것
(B) 생산성을 향상시키는 것
(C) 부서를 합치는 것
(D) 운영비를 절감하는 것

해설 화자가 our major objective this year is to increase staff productivity (올해 주요 목표는 직원 생산성을 향상하는 것이며)라고 말했으므로 (B)가 정답

Paraphrasing increase ➡ improve

88 요청/제의/제안 난이도 중

해석 화자는 청자들에게 무엇을 하라고 지시하는가?
(A) 다른 방으로 이동하라고
(B) 노트북 컴퓨터를 켜라고
(C) 그룹 토론을 하라고
(D) 몇 가지 서류에 서명하라고

해설 화자가 So please get into groups of three and start brainstorming some ideas. (3명씩 그룹 지어서 떠오르는 아이디어를 나눠 보세요.)라고 말했으므로 (C)가 정답

호주

Questions 89-91 refer to the following recorded message.

M: You have reached the Quigley Recreation Center. **For the next two months of spring, our building will be inaccessible due to some reconstruction. In the meantime, we have rented a space on the other side of town at 748 Yosemite Road.**(89) **For directions on how to get there, please check our Web site.**(90) Because this rental property isn't as big as our facility, it does not have a fitness center. **You will, however, be able to check out various sports equipment. In order to do so, please hand over your recreation center ID card at the front desk.**(91)

89-91번은 다음 녹음 메시지에 관한 문제입니다.

M: Quigley 레크리에이션 센터입니다. 봄 시즌인 다음 두 달 동안, 복원 공사로 인해 저희 건물을 이용하실 수 없습니다. 그 동안, 저희가 시 맞은 편, Yosemite 로 748번지에 있는 장소를 하나 임차했습니다.(89) 찾아보시는 법은 저희 웹 사이트를 확인해 주세요.(90) 이 임차 건물이 저희 시설만큼 크지 않아서, 피트니스 센터는 없습니다. 하지만, 다양한 운동 기구를 대여하실 수 있습니다. 그렇게 하시려면, 안내 데스크에서 고객님의 레크리에이션 센터 ID 카드를 건네주세요.(91)

어휘 inaccessible adj. 접근할 수 없는 reconstruction n. 복원공사, 재건축 in the meantime 그 동안, 그 사이에 rent v. 임차하다, 빌리다 directions n. 길 안내 property n. 부지, 건물 check out 대여하다, 대출하다 various adj. 다양한 hand over 건네주다, 넘겨주다

89 주제/목적   난이도 중

해석 메시지는 주로 무엇에 관한 것인가?
(A) 봄철 프로그램
(B) 도로변 공사
(C) 스포츠 경기
(D) 장소 변경

해설 화자가 For the next two months of spring, our building will be inaccessible due to some reconstruction. In the meantime, we have rented a space on the other side of town at 748 Yosemite Road. (봄 시즌인 다음 두 달 동안, 복원 공사로 인해 저희 건물을 이용하실 수 없습니다. 그 동안, 저희가 시 맞은 편, Yosemite 로 748번지에 있는 장소를 하나 임차했습니다.)라고 말했으므로 (D)가 정답

90 세부정보   난이도 하

해석 화자에 따르면, 웹 사이트에서 무엇을 이용할 수 있는가?
(A) 길 안내
(B) 사진
(C) 신청서
(D) 행사 일정표

해설 화자가 For directions on how to get there, please check our Web site. (찾아보시는 법은 저희 웹 사이트를 확인해 주세요.)라고 말했으므로 (A)가 정답

91 세부정보   난이도 하

해석 청자들은 스포츠 용품을 어떻게 빌릴 수 있는가?
(A) ID 카드를 제출해서
(B) 신청서를 작성해서
(C) 요금을 지불해서
(D) 온라인으로 예약해서

해설 화자가 You will, however, be able to check out various sports equipment. In order to do so, please hand over your recreation center ID card at the front desk. (하지만, 다양한 운동 기구를 대여하실 수 있습니다. 그렇게 하시려면, 안내 데스크에서 고객님의 레크리에이션 센터 ID 카드를 건네주세요.)라고 말했으므로 (A)가 정답

Paraphrasing hand over ➡ submit

[호주]

Questions 92-94 refer to the following telephone message.

M: Good morning. I represent Covington's Tools and Supplies. We will be setting up a kiosk at an upcoming expo this fall and would like an eye-catching banner for our stand.(92) I was browsing through some of your creations on your online catalog, and it's completely different from what I've seen in the past! I knew that we had to go with you.(93) Our designated area isn't that big, but I don't think it will be much of an issue. I'll email you the dimensions of our kiosk. Would it be possible to get a price quote by the end of the week?(94)

92-94번은 다음 전화메시지에 관한 문제입니다.

남: 안녕하세요. 저는 Covington's Tools and Supplies를 대표하고 있습니다. 저희가 올 가을에 있을 박람회에 키오스크를 설치할 예정이어서 저희 가판대를 위해 눈길을 끄는 현수막을 원합니다.(92) 당신의 온라인 카탈로그에 있는 제작물들 몇 개를 훑어 봤는데, 제가 이전에 봤던 거랑은 완전히 다르더라고요! 저는 우리가 당신과 함께 해야 한다는 것을 알았어요.(93) 우리의 지정 구역이 그렇게 크지는 않지만, 크게 문제가 되진 않을 거라고 봐요. 제가 저희 키오스크의 치수를 이메일로 보내 드릴게요. 가격 견적을 이번 주까지 받아볼 수 있을까요?(94)

어휘 represent v. 대표하다, 대신하다 set up 설치하다 kiosk n. 키오스크 (물건 등을 판매하는 매점) upcoming adj. 다가오는, 곧 있을 expo n. 박람회(=exposition) eye-catching adj. 눈길을 끄는 banner n. 현수막, 배너 browse through ~을 훑어보다 designated adj. 지정된 dimension n. 크기, 치수 quote n. 견적(액)

92 세부정보   난이도 중

해석 화자의 회사는 올 가을에 무엇을 할 계획인가?
(A) 박람회에 참석한다
(B) 세미나를 진행한다
(C) 인턴을 고용한다
(D) 웹 사이트를 출시한다

해설 화자가 We will be setting up a kiosk at an upcoming expo this fall and would like an eye-catching banner for our stand. (저희가 올 가을에 있을 박람회에 키오스크를 설치할 예정이어서 저희 가판대를 위해 눈길을 끄는 현수막을 원합니다.)라고 말했으므로 (A)가 정답

93 화자 의도 파악   난이도 상

해석 화자가 "제가 이전에 봤던 거랑은 완전히 다르더라고요"라고 말할 때 그가 의미한 것은?
(A) 결과에 기분이 상했다.
(B) 디자인에 만족해 한다.
(C) 공구와 물건들을 옮기는 데 도움이 필요하다.
(D) 제안을 따르는 것에 대해 확신이 없다.

해설 화자가 I was browsing through some of your creations on your online catalog, and it's completely different from what I've seen in the past! (당신의 온라인 카탈로그에 있는 제작물들 몇 개를 훑어 봤는데, 제가 이전에 봤던 거랑은 완전히 다르더라고요!)라면서, I knew that we had to go with you. (저는 우리가 당신과 함께 해야 한다는 것을 알았어요.)라고 말했으므로 (B)가 정답

| 94 | 요청/제의/제안 | 난이도 중 |

해석   화자는 무엇을 요청하는가?
(A) 비용 견적
(B) 전화 번호
(C) 크기 측정
(D) 샘플 카탈로그

해설   화자가 Would it be possible to get a price quote by the end of the week? (가격 견적을 이번 주까지 받아볼 수 있을까요?)라고 말했으므로 (A)가 정답

Paraphrasing   price quote ➡ cost estimate

미국

Questions 95-97 refer to the following instructions and map.

M: It's great to see all of you here at our city's yearly half-marathon race.(95) I'd like to wish each of you a safe and successful event. To get started, participants should make their way to the welcome desk by 10 A.M. There, you'll complete your registration and pick up a complimentary towel to use during the event.(96) Keep in mind that you need to stay on the running course as it is marked. Once you get to the finish line, please cross Dover Avenue to participate in a group photo.(97) It shouldn't take too long.

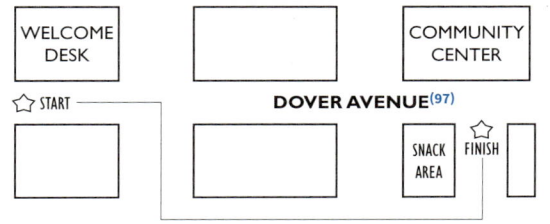

95-97번은 다음 지시문과 지도에 관한 문제입니다.

남: 시 연례 하프 마라톤 경기에서 여러분 모두를 보게 되어 기쁩니다.(95) 여러분 모두에게 안전하고 성공적인 행사가 되시길 바랍니다. 우선, 참가자분들은 오전 10시까지 환영 데스크로 가셔야 합니다. 그곳에서 신청서를 작성하시고 행사에서 사용할 무료 타월을 받으세요.(96) 표시되어 있는대로 경주 코스를 지켜야 한다는 점을 명심하세요. 결승전에 도착하시면, Dover 대로를 건너서 단체 사진 촬영에 참여해 주세요.(97) 아주 오래 걸리진 않을 것입니다.

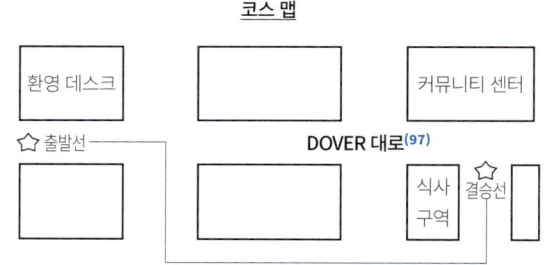

어휘   yearly adj. 매년 있는   race n. 경주, 경기   participant n. 참가자   make one's way 나아가다   complete v. 작성하다   pick up 얻다; 가져오다   complimentary adj. 무료의   keep in mind 명심하다   mark v. 표시하다   finish line 결승선   cross v. 건너다

| 95 | 세부정보 | 난이도 중 |

해석   청자들은 어느 행사에 참석하고 있겠는가?
(A) 가이드 투어
(B) 청소 계획
(C) 육상 대회
(D) 거리 행진

해설   화자가 It's great to see all of you here at our city's yearly half-marathon race. (시 연례 하프 마라톤 경기에서 여러분 모두를 보게 되어 기쁩니다.)라고 말했으므로 (C)가 정답

Paraphrasing   half-marathon race ➡ athletic contest

| 96 | 세부정보 | 난이도 하 |

해석   화자에 따르면, 청자들은 무엇을 받아야 하는가?
(A) 허가증
(B) 음료
(C) 타월
(D) 모자

해설   화자가 There, you'll complete your registration and pick up a complimentary towel to use during the event. (그곳에서 신청서를 작성하시고 행사에서 사용할 무료 타월을 받으세요.)라고 말했으므로 (C)가 정답

| 97 | 시각 정보 연계 | 난이도 상 |

해석   시각 자료를 보시오. 청자들은 단체 사진을 어디에서 찍을 것인가?
(A) 환영 데스크에서
(B) 출발선에서
(C) 식사 구역에서
(D) 커뮤니티 센터에서

해설   화자가 Once you get to the finish line, please cross Dover Avenue to participate in a group photo. (결승전에 도착하시면, Dover 대로를 건너서 단체 사진 촬영에 참여해 주세요.)라고 말했고, 시각 자료에서 결승선 건너편에 있는 건물은 Community Center(커뮤니티 센터)이므로 (D)가 정답

미국

Questions 98-100 refer to the following telephone message and recipe card.

W: Hello, Oscar. This is Whitney. I really appreciate you giving me a hand in coordinating the celebration of our company's fifth year in business last Monday.(98) I think everyone enjoyed it. Now, I forgot to mention this earlier, but for the chili recipe I gave you, I only put in three red peppers, and it's just right for me. But if you like spicy foods, you can put in the full amount as the recipe card states.(99) I just didn't want you to be surprised if it tastes different than what you had at the party. **A friend of mine gave me that recipe a little while back,**⁽¹⁰⁰⁾ and I didn't get around to changing it. Call me if you run into any problems!

Five-Alarm Chili Recipe

2 onions
5 red peppers⁽⁹⁹⁾
6 tomatoes
7 cloves of garlic
1 cup of shredded cheese
1 can of beans
500g beef

98-100번은 다음 전화 메시지와 조리법 카드에 관한 문제입니다.

여: 안녕하세요, Oscar. Whitney예요. 지난주 월요일 회사 창립 5주년 기념행사 진행을 도와줘서 정말 고마워요.⁽⁹⁸⁾ 모두 즐거운 시간을 보낸 것 같아요. 저, 미리 얘기한다는 걸 깜빡 했거든요, 제가 드린 칠리 조리법 말이에요. 저는 고추를 세 개만 넣는데, 그게 저한테는 딱 맞거든요. 그런데 매운 음식을 좋아하신다면 조리법 카드에 나와 있는 양대로 다 넣으셔도 돼요.⁽⁹⁹⁾ 파티에서 드셨던 거랑 맛이 달라서 놀라실까 봐요. 제 친구가 오래 전에 그 조리법을 줬는데,⁽¹⁰⁰⁾ 미처 고쳐놓질 못 했네요. 문제 있으면 전화 주세요!

매운 칠리 조리법

양파 2개
고추 5개⁽⁹⁹⁾
토마토 6개
마늘 7쪽
슈레드 치즈 1컵
콩 1캔
소고기 500g

어휘 appreciate v. 고마워하다 give a hand 거들어 주다 coordinate v. 조직화[편성]하다 celebration n. 기념행사 in business 사업을 하는 mention v. 언급하다 chili n. 칠리 red pepper 고추 spicy adj. 양념 맛이 강한, 매콤한 state v. 명시하다 a while back 예전에 get around to ~을 할 시간[짬]을 내다 run into (곤경 등을) 겪다 clove n. 마늘 한 쪽 shred v. 채를 썰다

98 세부정보 | 난이도 중

해석 화자는 지난주 월요일에 어떤 행사에 참석했는가?
(A) 요리 대회
(B) 회사 기념일 파티
(C) 신입사원 오찬
(D) 매장 개업식

해설 화자가 I really appreciate you giving me a hand in coordinating the celebration of our company's fifth year in business last Monday. (지난주 월요일 회사 창립 5주년 기념행사 진행을 도와줘서 정말 고마워요.)라고 말했으므로 (B)가 정답

Paraphrasing the celebration of our company's fifth year in business ➡ a corporate anniversary party

99 시각 정보 연계 | 난이도 상

해석 시각 정보를 보시오. 화자는 어떤 양을 바꾸라고 제안하는가?
(A) 2
(B) 5
(C) 6
(D) 7

해설 화자가 for the chili recipe I gave you, I only put in three red peppers, and it's just right for me. But if you like spicy foods, you can put in the full amount as the recipe card states. (제가 드린 칠리 요리 조리법 말이에요. 저는 고추를 세 개만 넣는데, 그게 저한테는 딱 맞거든요. 그런데 매운 음식을 좋아하신다면 조리법 카드에 나와 있는 양대로 다 넣으셔도 돼요.)라고 말했고, 시각자료에서 red peppers (고추)가 5임을 확인할 수 있으므로 (B)가 정답

100 세부정보 | 난이도 중

해석 화자는 어디에서 조리법을 구했는가?
(A) 기사
(B) 친구
(C) TV 프로그램
(D) 요리책

해설 화자가 A friend of mine gave me that recipe a little while back (제 친구가 오래 전에 그 조리법을 줬는데)라고 말했으므로 (B)가 정답

PART 5

101 어휘 • 명사 | 난이도 중

해석 Ms. Park의 영화가 끝난 후, 관객들은 짧은 토론을 위해 남아있도록 권장된다.

해설 빈칸은 전치사 for의 목적어자리. 문맥상 '영화가 끝난 후, 토론을 위해 남아 있도록 권장된다'는 의미가 되어야 자연스러우므로 (B)가 정답

Key word
After Ms. Park's film, viewers are encouraged to **stay** for a short **discussion**.

오답보기 확인
(A) participation 참가, 참여
(C) attendance 참석, 참석율, 참가자 수
(D) concurrence 동의, 의견 일치

어휘 viewer n. 보는 사람, 시청자 encourage v. 권장하다, 격려하다 stay v. 머무르다, 남다 discussion n. 토론, 논의, 상의

102 구조/문법 • 동사의 수/태일치 | 난이도 하

해석 Ms. Guelph는 최신 마케팅 설문조사 결과로 세미나를 마칠 것이다.

해설 이 문장에는 동사가 없으므로 빈칸은 동사자리. 동사가 아닌 (A) 탈락, 주어가 3인칭 단수명사이므로 (D)는 수일치 탈락, 빈칸 뒤에 목적어가 있으므로 (C)는 태일치에서 탈락, 주어의 수와 상관없이 쓸 수 있는 조동사 will이 있는 능동형의 (B)가 정답

어휘 result n. 결과 latest adj. 최근[최신]의 customer n. 고객 survey n. 설문조사

| 103 | 구조/문법 • 형용사 | 난이도 중 |

해석 Takagawa사는 아름다운 야외 식사 공간을 만들어서 건물을 개조했다.

해설 빈칸은 관사와 명사구 사이의 자리. 문맥상 '아름다운 야외 식사 공간'이라는 의미가 되어야 자연스러우므로 명사구를 수식하는 형용사 (B)가 정답

Key point
부사는 형용사를, 형용사는 명사(구)를 수식할 수 있다. 이 문제에서는 빈칸이 outside라는 형용사 앞에 위치하여, 자칫하면 부사를 고를 수 있는데, '아름답게 외부의'는 말이 되지 않는다. '아름다운 야외 식사 공간'으로, 바로 뒤의 outside를 수식하는 게 아니라 outside dining area을 하나의 명사구로 간주하여 수식하는 자리이므로 형용사를 골라야 한다.

어휘 construct v. 구성하다, 건설하다 outside adj. 외부의 dining area 식사 공간

| 104 | 구조/문법+어휘 • 부사 | 난이도 중 |

해석 어제 5,000명 이상의 사람들이 Kowloon 금융의 웹 사이트를 방문했다.

해설 빈칸은 수를 나타내는 표현 5,000을 수식하는 부사 자리이므로 (A)가 정답. 참고로, over는 '~동안, ~위에' 등의 전치사로도 쓰이지만 숫자 앞에서 '~이상'이라는 의미로, 수 강조 부사로도 사용된다.

Key point
수를 나타내는 표현과 주로 함께 사용되는 부사는 다음과 같다: about, around, approximately(대략), nearly(거의), more than / over(~이상), at least(적어도) 등

어휘 visit v. 방문하다 finance n. 금융

| 105 | 어휘 • 동사 | 난이도 중 |

해석 국립 전시 센터에서 열리는 널리 광고된 기술 컨벤션은 많은 관중을 끌어 모을 것이다.

해설 빈칸은 주어와 목적어 사이 현재진행형 구문을 완성하는 동사자리. 문맥상 '관객을 끌어 모을 것이다'라는 의미가 되어야 자연스러우므로 (D)가 정답

Key word
The broadly advertised technology **convention** at the National Exhibition Center **is attracting** a large audience.

오답보기 확인
(A) call 부르다, 전화하다
(B) suggest 제안하다
(C) happen 일어나다, 발생하다

어휘 broadly adv. 널리 advertised adj. 광고된 technology n. 기술 attract v. (어디로) 끌어들이다; (마음을) 끌다 audience n. 관중

| 106 | 어휘 • 형용사 | 난이도 중 |

해석 Dr. Muniz는 목요일 오후 5시 15분에 환자를 진찰할 수 있다.

해설 빈칸은 be동사 뒤 보어자리. 문맥상 '목요일 오후 5시 15분에 진료를 할 수 있다'는 의미가 되어야 자연스러우므로 (C)가 정답. possible이 오답 보기로 제시되었는데, 이 문장에서 가능한 것은 Mr. Muniz가 아니라, 환자를 진찰하는 것이므로 possible이 답이 되기 위해서는 to see 이하가 주어가 되어야 한다.

Key point
형용사 available vs. possible: available은 사람을 주어로, possible은 사물 또는 가주어 it을 주어로 취할 수 있다.

오답보기 확인
(A) comfortable 편안한
(B) probable 사실일 것 같은
(D) possible 가능한

어휘 available adj. (사람이) 시간이 되는, (사물이) 이용 가능한 be available to do ~할 수 있다 patient n. 환자

| 107 | 구조/문법 • 부사 | 난이도 하 |

해석 GHM사의 규정에 따라, 모든 직원들은 출장 2개월 이내에 정식으로 환급을 신청해야 한다.

해설 빈칸은 조동사와 동사원형 사이에서 동사를 수식하는 부사 자리이므로 (B)가 정답

Key point
동사를 수식할 수 있는 품사는 부사이다.

어휘 regulation n. 규정 reimbursement n. 환급 business trip 출장

| 108 | 어휘 • 전치사 | 난이도 중 |

해석 오늘 오전 부서 회의 동안 Mr. Insel은 국제적인 사업 관행에 관한 추가 조사의 필요성을 인정했다.

해설 빈칸은 team meeting을 목적어로 하는 전치사 자리. 주절의 내용을 고려할 때, '부서 회의를 하는 동안 추가 조사의 필요성을 인정했다'는 의미가 되어야 자연스러우므로 기간 전치사 (D)가 정답

Key word
During this morning's team **meeting**, Mr. Insel acknowledged the need for further research regarding environmentally friendly business practices.

오답보기 확인
(A) upon ~하자마자
(B) across ~건너편에, ~전체에 걸쳐
(C) with ~와 함께

어휘 acknowledge v. 인정하다 further adj. 추가의 research n. 조사 environmentally friendly 친환경적인 business practice 사업 관행

| 109 | 구조/문법 • 형용사 | 난이도 중 |

해석 서빙 직원들을 즉시 알아볼 수 있도록, 레스토랑 체인은 멋진 직원 유니폼 제작을 위한 유명한 패션 디자이너를 고용했다.

해설 빈칸은 동사 make의 목적격 보어 자리이자, 부사 instantly의 수식을 받는 형용사 자리. 문맥상 '서빙 직원들이 즉시 눈에 띄게 하기 위해, 유니폼 제작을 위한 디자이너를 고용했다'는 의미가 되어야 자연스러우므로 형용사 (C)가 정답

Key point
① 동사 make는 5형식 문장에서 [make+목적어+목적격보어(~가 ...하게 하다, ~를 ...상태로 만들다)]의 구조를 취하며, 보어 자리에는 일반적으로 형용사(목적어의 상태) 또는 명사(목적어와 동격)가 올 수 있다.
② 형용사를 목적격 보어로 취하는 빈출 5형식 동사를 꼭 외워 둔다.
[make (~상태로 만들다), consider (~라고 여기다), find (~라고 생각하다), keep (~상태로 유지하다)+목적어+형용사]

| 어휘 | server n. 서빙하는 사람 instantly adv. 즉각, 즉시 chain n. (식당 등의) 체인 hire v. 고용하다 well-known adj. 잘 알려진 stylish adj. 멋진, 유행을 따른 uniform n. 유니폼 |

110 어휘 • 부사   난이도 중

| 해석 | Mountaindell 민박집의 주인은 방문객들이 인터넷에 올리는 모든 후기에 직접 답한다. |
| 해설 | 빈칸은 주어와 동사 사이 부사자리. 문맥상 '주인이 후기에 직접 답한다'는 의미가 되어야 자연스러우므로 (B)가 정답 |

Key word
The **owner** of the Mountaindell Bed and Breakfast **personally** **responds to** all **reviews** that visitors post on the Internet.

오답보기 확인
(A) slightly 약간
(C) approximately 대략, 거의(수 강조)
(D) recklessly 무모하게

| 어휘 | Bed and Breakfast 아침식사를 제공하는 숙박시설, 민박집 (B&B) personally adj. 개인적으로, 직접 review n. 논평, 비평 post v. (정보 등을) 올리다 |

111 어휘 • 동사   난이도 중

| 해석 | 의사들의 80%는 General Department의 항균 손세정 비누가 경쟁업체들의 것보다 더 좋다는 점에 동의한다. |
| 해설 | 빈칸은 주어와 목적어인 that 명사절 사이 동사자리. 문맥상 '의사들이 ~인 것에 동의한다'는 의미가 되어야 자연스러우므로 (D)가 정답. assure도 의미가 통하기는 하지만, that절을 바로 취할 수 없고, <assure+목적어+that절: ~에게 that 이하를 보장하다>의 패턴을 갖는다는 점에서 답이 될 수 없다. |

Key word
Eighty percent of **doctors** **agree that** General Department's antibacterial hand wash is better than the competitions'.

오답보기 확인
(A) favor 호의를 보이다
(B) assure 확언하다
(C) confess 자백하다

| 어휘 | agree v. 동의하다 antibacterial adj. 항균성의 hand wash 손세정 비누 competitor n. 경쟁 상대 |

112 구조/문법+어휘 • 종속접속사 - 부사절   난이도 중

| 해석 | 연례 점검이 완료되었으므로, 창고 작업반은 추가 선반의 설치를 시작할 수 있다. |
| 해설 | 빈칸은 두 개의 문장을 연결하는 접속사자리. 문맥상 '점검이 완료되었으므로, 선반 설치를 시작할 수 있다'는 의미의 인과관계로 연결되어야 자연스러우므로 (D)가 정답 |

Key word
Now that the annual **inspection** has **been completed**, the warehouse **crew can begin installing** the additional shelving units.

오답보기 확인
(A) With that 그것과 함께, 그러고는 바로
(B) In order that ~하도록
(C) In that ~라는 점에서

| 어휘 | now that conj. ~이므로, ~이기 때문에 inspection n. 점검 complete v. 완료하다 warehouse n. 창고 crew n. (함께 일을 하는) 팀, 조 install v. 설치하다 shelving unit 선반 |

113 문법/구조 • 부정대명사   난이도 중

| 해석 | Mr. Griffon은 한정된 예산으로 재설계 프로젝트를 맡을 누군가를 찾기 위해 지원서들을 검토했다. |
| 해설 | 빈칸은 전치사 for의 목적어이자, 주격 관계사 who의 선행사자리. 문맥상 '한정된 예산으로 프로젝트를 맡을 누군가'라는 의미가 되어야 자연스러우므로, 불특정 대상을 가리키는 부정대명사 (D)가 정답 |

Key point
'anyone who ~(~하는 사람은 누구든지)', 'those who ~(~하는 사람들)'은 불특정 대상을 지칭할 때 사용된다.

| 어휘 | examine v. 검토하다 application n. 지원(서) handle v. 다루다, 처리하다 redesign n. 재설계 budget n. 예산 |

114 문법/구조+어휘 • 명사   난이도 중

| 해석 | 실험실 관리자는 모든 화학약품의 올바른 보관을 확실히 해야 한다. |
| 해설 | 빈칸은 동사 ensure의 목적어 자리로, 빈칸 앞 부분에 관사가 없음을 고려할 때 명사의 복수형 또는 불가산명사자리. 문맥상 '화학약품의 올바른 보관'이라는 의미가 되어야 자연스러우므로 불가산명사 (D)가 정답 |

Key point
명사 store vs. storage: 가산명사 store는 '상점', 불가산명사 storage는 '보관(공간)'을 의미한다.

| 어휘 | ensure v. 확실히 하다, 보장하다 chemicals n. 화학약품 |

115 어휘 • 형용사   난이도 중

| 해석 | 현재 귀하의 임차료 지불 기한이 2주 지났다는 점에서, 계약서에 명시된 바와 같이 추가 연체료를 지불하셔야 합니다. |
| 해설 | 빈칸은 since 종속절 내 be동사 뒤 주격보어자리. 기간을 나타내는 표현 two weeks가 빈칸 앞에 있음을 고려할 때, 문맥상 '임차료 지불 기한이 2주 지난 점에서'라는 의미가 되어야 자연스러우므로 (C)가 정답 |

Key word
Seeing that your **rent** is now **two weeks** **overdue**, you **must pay** an additional **late fee** as stated in the contract.

오답보기 확인
(A) valuable 소중한, 귀중한
(B) remaining 남아 있는
(D) owed 빚진

| 어휘 | seeing that ~인 것으로 보아 overdue a. (지불, 반납 등의) 기한이 지난 rent n. 임차료 pay v. 지불하다 additional adj. 추가의 late fee 연체료 as stated 명시된 바와 같이 contract n. 계약서 |

116 문법/구조 • 동사 - 3인칭 단수 현재시제   난이도 중

| 해석 | Ms. Pangchorn는 수요일에 출장에서 돌아와서 이메일에 답장할 것이다. |
| 해설 | 빈칸은 when 종속절 내 주어 she의 동사자리. (A)는 수일치에서 탈락. 주절의 시제가 미래(will answer)이므로 현재시제 (C)가 정답 |

Key point
시간·조건의 접속사(when, after, before, until, if, unless, once, as

TEST 01   25

soon as 등)가 이끄는 부사절에서는 현재(완료)시제가 미래시제를 대신한다.

어휘 answer v. 회신하다 return v. 돌아오다; 반납하다, 반품하다

117 어휘 • 전치사   난이도 하

해석 Sultan 금융 그룹의 웹 사이트는 오전 2시에서 4시 사이에는 접속할 수 없습니다.

해설 빈칸은 시간표현을 목적어로 하는 전치사자리. 빈칸 뒤쪽에 and가 있음을 고려할 때, 'between A and B(A와 B 사이에)'라는 구조를 완성하는 전치사 (D)가 정답

Key word
The Sultan Financial Group's Web site will be inaccessible **between** the hours of 2 A.M. and 4 A.M.

어휘 financial adj. 금융의 inaccessible adj. 접근할 수 없는

118 어휘 • 명사   난이도 중

해석 Ms. O'Driscoll은 10월 13일 금요일에 연설 일정이 있다.

해설 빈칸은 speaking과 복합명사를 이루는 목적어 자리. 문맥상 '연설을 해야 하는 (약속으로) 일정이 잡혀있다'는 의미가 되어야 자연스러우므로 (D)가 정답

Key word
Ms. O'Driscoll **has a speaking engagement** on Friday, October 13.

오답보기 확인
(A) recruitment 채용
(B) term 임기, 기간
(C) topic 주제

어휘 engagement 약속, 업무

119 문법/구조 • 부사   난이도 중

해석 판매에 포함된 가전제품들은 여러 공장들에서 조립되었기 때문에 따로따로 도착했다.

해설 빈칸은 동사 arrive를 수식하는 부사자리이므로 (A)가 정답

Key point
동사 arrive는 보어나 목적어를 필요로 하지 않는 1형식 자동사이다.

어휘 appliances n. 가전제품 assemble v. 조립하다

120 구조/문법 • 명사   난이도 중

해석 모든 고객 문의들은, 아무리 사소할지라도, 항상 신속하고 정중하게 답변되어야 한다.

해설 빈칸은 명사 customer와 함께 복합명사를 이루는 문장의 주어자리. 부정 형용사 all 뒤에는 가산 복수명사와 불가산 명사가 올 수 있는데 inquiry(문의사항)는 가산 명사이므로 복수형태가 와야 한다.

Key point
① 복합명사는 두 개 이상의 명사가 [명사+명사]의 형태로 하나의 단어처럼 쓰이며, 마지막 명사를 기준으로 복합명사의 성격(가산/불가산, 단/복수 등)이 결정된다.
② 부정형용사 all은 뒤에 가산명사 복수 또는 불가산 명사가 온다.

어휘 minor adj. 작은, 사소한 answer v. 대답하다 promptly adv. 즉시, 신속하게 politely adv. 정중히

121 구조/문법+어휘 • 전치사   난이도 상

해석 그 회사의 생산라인 위생 관리 기준은 대부분의 다른 회사들의 것을 뛰어넘는다.

해설 빈칸은 동사와 명사구 사이의 자리. 문맥상 '위생 기준이 다른 회사들의 위생기준을 뛰어넘는다'라는 의미가 되어야 자연스러우므로, 'extend beyond(~를 넘어서다, 뛰어넘다)'의 관용표현을 완성하는 전치사 (D)가 정답

Key point
지시대명사 those는 앞에서 언급된 명사가 반복될 때 사용되며 전치사구의 수식을 받는다: those = sanitation standards.

어휘 sanitation n. 위생 시설[관리] extend v. 연장하다, 늘리다, 포괄하다

122 구조/문법+어휘 • 등위접속사   난이도 중

해석 BMV 컨버터블 자동차의 법적 보증기간은 5년 또는 30만 킬로미터인데, 어느 쪽이든 먼저 발생하는 것으로 한다.

해설 빈칸은 be동사 뒤 주격보어자리의 두 명사구를 연결하는 접속사자리. 문맥상 '5년 또는 30만 킬로미터 중 먼저 발생하는 것'이라는 의미가 되어야 자연스러우므로 (B)가 정답

Key point
등위접속사(and, but, or 등)는 같은 위치에 있는 단어, 구, 절 등을 대등하게 연결해준다.

어휘 legal adj. 법적인 guarantee n. 보증 period n. 기간 convertible n. 컨버터블 자동차 take place 일어나다, 발생하다 first adv. 우선, 먼저

123 어휘 • 부사   난이도 중

해석 시간 부족으로 인해, 회사 프로그래머들이 최근에 모바일 애플리케이션을 업데이트하지 못했다.

해설 빈칸은 문장 끝 동사를 수식하는 부사자리. 문맥상 '시간부족으로 인해, 최근에 앱을 업데이트하지 못했다'는 의미가 되어야 자연스러우므로 (D)가 정답

Key word
Due to a lack of time, the company's programmers **have not updated** the mobile application **recently**.

Key point
shortly는 미래시제와 같이 쓰이는 부사이고 recently는 과거나 현재완료와 같이 쓰이는 시제를 나타내는 부사이다.

오답보기 확인
(A) continually 계속해서
(B) shortly 곧
(C) firmly 단호히

어휘 lack n. 부족 mobile n. 핸드폰 application n. 응용 프로그램, 앱(약어:app) recently adj. 최근에

124 어휘 • 전치사   난이도 중

해석 더 엄격해진 정부 규정의 결과로 많은 제조업체들이 에너지 효율이 좋은 에어컨을 더 많이 생산하고 있다.

해설 빈칸은 명사구를 목적어로 취하는 전치사 자리. 문맥상 '더 엄격해진 규정의 결과로 에너지 효율이 좋은 에어컨을 더 많이 생산하고 있다'는 의미가 되어야 자연스러우므로, 인과관계로 연결해주는 구전치사 (C)가 정답. (B)는 접속사이므로 뒤에 절을 연결되어야 한다.

오답보기 확인
(A) prior to ~전에
(B) inasmuch as ~인 점을 고려하면, ~이므로
(D) further from 전혀 ~이 아닌

어휘 energy-efficient adj. 에너지 효율적인 air conditioner 에어컨 as a result of prep. ~의 결과로 strict adj. 엄격한 government n. 정부 regulation n. 규정

125 구조/문법+어휘·형용사   난이도 중

해석 Randit사의 30년에 걸친 신뢰할만한 서비스 역사는 업계에서 유일무이하다.

해설 빈칸은 명사 service를 수식하는 자리. 문맥상 '30년에 걸친 신뢰할만한 서비스'라는 의미가 되어야 자연스러우므로 (A)가 정답
Key point
명사 앞 자리에는 형용사, 분사, 명사가 올 수 있으므로, 문맥을 통해 파악한다. 일반적으로[한정사+형용사+명사]의 자리가 출제된다.

어휘 unique adj. 유일한 industry n. 업계

126 구조/문법·동사의 수/태일치   난이도 중

해석 직원 인센티브에 영향을 주는 예산 변경 안은 즉시 CEO에게 제출되어야 한다.

해설 빈칸은 주어 Budget changes에 대한 동사자리. 주어가 복수이므로 (D)는 수일치에서 탈락. 동사 submit은 목적어를 취하는 타동사인데 빈칸 뒤 목적어가 없으므로 태일치에서 (B), (C) 탈락.

어휘 budget n. 예산 impact v. 영향[충격]을 주다 incentive n. 인센티브, 장려금 right away 즉시, 곧바로

127 어휘·명사   난이도 중

해석 Morrison시는 시 창립 100주년을 기념하는 새로운 기념 명판을 세우려는 계획에 대해 대중의 의견을 묻고 있다.

해설 빈칸은 형용사 public의 수식을 받는 문장의 목적어자리. 문맥상 '명판을 세우는 계획에 대한 시민의 의견을 묻고 있다'는 의미가 되어야 자연스러우므로 (C)가 정답
Key word
The city of Morrison is inviting public comment on its plan to put up a commemorative plaque celebrating the city's centennial.
오답보기 확인
(A) arrangement 준비, 마련, 주선
(B) interest 관심, 흥미
(D) order 주문

어휘 invite v. 요청하다 public adj. 대중의 comment n. 의견, 논평, 언급 commemorative adj. 기념하는 plaque n. 명판 centennial n. 100주년

128 구조/문법·관계대명사 - 주격   난이도 중

해석 출장 중인 Mr. Ponchartrain은 Ms. Hyun이 계속 Carter사 계정을 담당하게 했다.

해설 Mr. Ponchartrain을 선행사로 하는 관계절이 문장 내 콤마(,) 사이에 삽입된 구조. 선행사가 사람이고 빈칸 뒤 동사가 있으므로 주격 관계대명사 (D)가 정답

Key point
관계대명사 that은 콤마(,)로 연결된 계속적 용법의 관계절에는 올 수 없다.

어휘 away adj. 부재의 on business 업무상 leave v. (어떤 상태 등에 계속) 있게 만들다 in charge of ~을 담당하여 account n. 계좌, 계정, 고객

129 어휘·동사   난이도 상

해석 안전상의 이유로, Militech 공장의 방문객은 현장에 있는 동안 에스코트 받아야 한다.

해설 빈칸은 must be와 함께 수동태 동사구문을 완성하는 과거분사자리. 문맥상 '안전상의 이유로, 방문객은 현장에서 에스코트 받아야 한다'는 의미가 되어야 자연스러우므로, '에스코트하다, (무사하도록) 호위하다'를 의미하는 (B)가 정답
Key word
For safety reasons, visitors to the Militech plant must be escorted while on site.
오답보기 확인
(A) consult 상담하다
(C) present 제시하다, 보여주다
(D) support 지지하다, 지원하다

어휘 safety n. 안전 escort v. 호위하다, 에스코트하다 on site 현장의

130 어휘·형용사   난이도 중

해석 Duchene 투자회사는 경험이 부족한 사업주들이 대출 신청하는 것을 돕기 위해 무료 상담을 제공한다.

해설 빈칸은 business owners를 수식하는 형용사 자리. 문맥상 '경험이 부족한 사업주들을 돕기 위해 무료 상담을 제공한다'는 내용이 되어야 자연스러우므로 (A)가 정답
Key word
Duchene Investment Firm provides free consultations to help inexperienced business owners apply for loans.
오답보기 확인
(B) indisputable 반론의 여지가 없는
(C) unwilling 꺼리는
(D) unfomiliar 익숙지 않은

어휘 investment n. 투자 firm n. 회사 consultation n. 상담 inexperienced adj. 경험이 부족한, 미숙한 owner n. 주인 apply for 신청하다 loan n. 대출(금)

PART 6   P. 31

131-134번은 다음 광고에 관한 문제입니다.

> 최신 패션을 찾고 계신가요?
>
> 당신의 선택이 환경에 미치는 영향이 신경 쓰이시나요?
>
> 그러시다면, Eka 양품점을 방문하세요. **131. 저희는 환경을 파괴하지 않는 직물로 만들어진 드레스와 재킷 및 기타 유행 아이템을 취급합니다.** 여기에는 재활용된 면, 모, 그리고 3가지 종류의 실크가 포함됩니다. 보시면 마음에 드실 거예요!

저희 Eka 양품점은 언제나 제품의 원산지에 **132. 관심을 가집니다.** 이것이 저희가 검증된 제조시설에서 만들어진 의류만을 제공**133.하는 이유입니다**. 더 자세한 내용을 알아보시고 **134. 전체** 카탈로그를 보시려면, 저희 웹사이트 www.ekasboutique.co.uk를 방문해 주세요.

어휘 care about ~에 마음을 쓰다, ~에 관심을 가지다 impact n. 영향, 충격 boutique n. 양품점 recycle v. 재활용하다 cotton n. 면직물 wool n. 모직 guarantee v. 보장하다 source n. 근원, 원천 verified adj. 검증된 manufacturing n. 제조업 facility n. 시설

131 문맥이해 • 문장삽입   난이도 중

해석 (A) 저희 양품점은 최근 지역의 방직공장과 계약을 체결했습니다.
(B) 저희는 환경을 파괴하지 않는 직물로 만들어진 드레스와 재킷 및 기타 유행 아이템을 취급합니다.
(C) 저희 양품점은 Fashion Valley에 편리하게 위치해 있습니다.
(D) 저희는 오전 10시부터 오후 8시까지, 주 7일 영업합니다.

해설 빈칸 뒤 문장의 '재활용된 면, 모, 실크가 여기에 포함된다'는 내용을 고려할 때, 환경친화적 직물로 제품을 만든다는 내용이 앞에 나와야 자연스러우므로 (B)가 정답

Key word
We have dresses, jackets, and other fashionable items made from sustainable fabrics. This includes recycled cotton, wool, and three types of silk.

132 어휘 • 전치사   난이도 중

해설 빈칸은 our products' sources를 목적어로 하는 전치사 자리. 빈칸 앞 동사와 함께 'care about(~에 관심을 가지다, 신경 쓰다)'의 표현을 완성하는 (D)가 정답

Key word
We at Eka's Boutique always **care about** our products' sources.

133 어휘 + 문맥이해 • 의문 부사   난이도 중

해설 빈칸은 주어 this에 대한 보어 자리. 빈칸 뒤 완전한 문장이 이어지므로, 문장을 주격 보어인 명사절로 만들어줄 의문 부사 자리. 빈칸 앞 문장에서 this가 가리키는 내용을 알 수 있으므로, 문맥상 '이것(원산지에 관심을 갖는 것)이 저희가 검증된 제조시설에서 만든 의류만을 취급하는 이유'라는 의미가 되어야 자연스러우므로 (A)가 정답

Key word
We at Eka's Boutique always care about our products' sources. This is **why** we only offer clothing made in verified manufacturing facilities.

134 구조 / 문법 • 형용사   난이도 중

해설 빈칸은 명사 catalogue를 수식하는 자리. 문맥상 '전체 카탈로그를 보시려면, 웹 사이트를 방문하라'는 의미가 되어야 자연스러우므로 '완전한, 전체의'라는 의미의 형용사 (B)가 정답

Key point
completed는 '(일이) 완료된, (문서가) 작성된'이라는 뜻으로 의미상 맞지 않다.

Key word
To learn more and view our **complete** catalogue, please go to our Web site, www.ekasboutique.co.uk.

135-138번은 다음 기사에 관한 문제입니다.

<안전 장치 및 예방 조치>

국립 조각 갤러리(NSG)는 전시 환경을 세심히 **135. 모니터링**하여 전시 중인 귀중한 작품을 보호하기 위해 최선을 다하고 있습니다. 나무로 만들어진 작품들은 덥고 건조한 환경에 취약합니다. **136. 따라서**, 갤러리에서는 햇빛 또는 다른 훼손 가능성이 있는 조명이 있는 공간에 작품을 보관하지 않습니다. 또한, 우기로 인한 **137. 습도**로 인해 여름에는 외부에 작품을 전시하지 않습니다. **138. 또한, 전시 중인 작품을 만지지 마십시오.** 저희는 귀중한 소장품을 지키려 이러한 노력을 함으로써, 역사와 국가의 유산을 먼 미래까지 보존하길 바랍니다.

어휘 safeguard n. 보호[안전] 장치 precaution n. 예방조치 sculpture n. 조각 protect v. 보호하다 priceless adj. 매우 귀중한 on display 전시[진열] 중인 exhibit n. 전시품, 전시회 vulnerable to ~에 취약한, 연약한 strictly adv. 엄격히, 절대적으로 control v. 통제[제어]하다 temperature n. 온도 area n. 구역, 지역 display v. 전시하다 piece n. 작품 cause v. 야기하다 guard v. 지키다, 보호하다 collection n. 소장품, 수집품 preserve v. 지키다, 보존하다 genius n. 천재(성), 특별한 재능

135 어휘 • 동사   난이도 중

해설 빈칸은 전치사 by의 목적어인 동명사자리. 주절의 내용을 고려할 때, 문맥상 '전시 환경을 세심히 모니터링함으로써, 전시 중인 작품 보호를 위해 노력한다'는 의미가 되어야 자연스러우므로 (D)가 정답

Key word
The National Sculpture Gallery (NSG) **makes every effort to protect the priceless work on display by** carefully **monitoring** the environment of the exhibits.

136 어휘 + 문맥이해 • 연결어 - 접속부사   난이도 중

해설 빈칸 앞 문장의 '나무로 만들어진 작품들은 덥고 건조한 환경에 취약하다'는 내용과 빈칸 뒷 부분의 '갤러리에서는 모든 구역의 온도를 엄격히 통제한다'는 내용을 고려할 때, 두 문장이 인과관계로 연결되어야 자연스러우므로 '그런 이유로, 따라서'를 의미하는 (A)가 정답

Key word
Works made of wood **are vulnerable to hot and dry conditions. Accordingly,** the gallery **strictly controls the temperature of all areas.**

137 구조 / 문법 • 명사   난이도 하

해설 빈칸은 관사 뒤 명사 자리이므로 (A)가 정답

Key point
관사(a/the) 뒤에 올 수 있는 품사는 명사이다.

138 문맥이해 • 문장삽입   난이도 중

해석 (A) 또한, 전시 중인 작품을 만지지 마십시오.
(B) 이것들은 올 가을에 갤러리로 돌아오면 다시 전시될 것입니다.
(C) 아쉽게도, 일부 조각품은 응급 수리를 위해 치워졌습니다.
(D) 일부 미술품은 300년이 넘었습니다.

해설 빈칸 앞 문장의 '습도 때문에 여름에는 외부 작품 전시를 하지 않는다'는 내용과 빈칸 뒷 문장의 '귀중한 소장품을 지키기 위해 노력한다'는

내용을 고려할 때, 문맥상 박물관의 작품 보호와 관련된 내용이 들어가야 자연스러우므로 (A)가 정답

Key word
Nor will the museum display pieces outside during the summer months due to the humidity caused by the rainy season. Additionally, please refrain from touching any of the pieces on display. By making this effort to guard our priceless collection, we hope to preserve the history and genius of our nation far into the future.

139-142번은 다음 공지에 관한 문제입니다.

Auto-Smart 고객 여러분께 알려드립니다:

자동차 창문을 교체하실 때, 교체되는 창문(혹은 전면유리) 한 장당 10달러의 추가 요금이 발생합니다. 이 요금은 자동차 유리 처리 비용을 부담하기 위한 것입니다. 달리 명시 **139.** 하지 않으면, 이대로 창문 작업을 진행해 드리겠습니다.

자동차 창문에서의 유리와 플라스틱의 조합은 다루기가 까다로우며, 부적절한 처리는 심각한 환경 피해를 유발합니다. 희소식은 창문이 제대로 **140.** 재활용되기만 한다면, 이 자재가 카펫 뒤판과 단열 처리용으로 안성맞춤이라는 것입니다. 단 10달러로 이렇게 중요한 과정을 처리할 수 있습니다.

이 비용의 지불은 **141.** 자율입니다. 폐창문을 가져가셔서 모든 것을 직접 처리하셔도 되며, 이 경우 저희는 비용을 청구하지 않습니다. **142.** 환경친화적인 방식으로 처리하는 것만 기억해주십시오.

어휘 notice n. 공고 v. (보거나 들어서) 알다 auto n. 자동차 replace v. 대신하다, 교체하다 windshield n. (자동차 등의) 앞[전면]유리 fee n. 요금 cover v. (무엇을 하기에 충분한 돈을[이]) 대다 disposal n. 처리, 처분 indicate v. 나타내다, 시사하다 otherwise adv. 달리, 그 외에는 take care of ~을 처리하다 combination n. 조합, 결합 tricky adj. 힘든[까다로운] improper adj. 부적절한 cause v. 야기하다 significant adj. 중요한, 의미 있는 backing n. (물건의) 뒤를 받치는 재료, 뒤판 insulation n. 절연[단열/방음] 처리[처리용 자재] payment n. 지불(금), 지급 charge v. (요금·값을) 청구하다

139 어휘 · 접속사   난이도 중

해설 빈칸은 두 개의 절을 연결하는 접속사 자리. 주절의 '창문 교체작업을 진행해드리겠다' 내용을 고려할 때, 문맥상 '달리 명시하지 않으면'이라는 의미가 되어야 자연스러우므로 (C)가 정답

Key point
분사구문 관용표현 [unless otherwise p.p. (달리 ~되지 않으면)]: [분사구문] unless otherwise indicated (달리 명시되어 있지 않으면) = [부사절] unless you indicate otherwise (당신이 달리 명시하지 않으면)

140 구조/문법 · 과거분사   난이도 중

해설 빈칸은 주어 the windows와 be동사 뒤 자리. 접속사 as long as로 연결된 주절과 종속절의 관계를 고려할 때, '창문이 제대로 재활용되기만 한다면, 이 자재는 카펫 뒤판과 단열 처리용으로 안성맞춤'이라는 내용이 되어야 자연스러우므로 수동태 문장을 완성하는 과거분사 (B)가 정답

Key point
be동사 뒤에는 주어를 보충 설명하는 주격 보어에 해당하는 명사/형용사, 'be+p.p.'의 수동태 구조를 완성하는 과거분사가 올 수 있다. 이 문제에서는 be 동사 뒤에 명사 recycling, 형용사 recyclable, p.p.의 recycled가 올 수 있지만, recycling은 명사로 부사 뒤에 올 수 없고 are recycling의 진행형으로 보더라도 뒤에 목적어가 없어서 안 된다. recyclable은 "재활용 가능한"이라는 의미인데 이 문장에서는 의미상 맞지 않다.

141 어휘+문맥이해 · 형용사   난이도 중

해설 빈칸은 주어 This payment의 보어 자리. 빈칸 앞 단락의 '교체 창문 한 개당 10달러의 추가요금이 발생한다'는 내용과 빈칸 뒤 문장의 '폐창문을 가져가도 되며, 이 경우 비용을 청구하지 않는다'는 내용을 고려할 때, 문맥상 '(창문 처리를 위해 부과되는) 10달러의 요금 지불은 자율적'이라는 내용이 되어야 자연스러우므로 (D)가 정답

Key word
When you have car windows replaced, **you will notice an extra fee of $10 per window** (or windshield) replaced. This fee is to cover the cost of auto glass disposal.
This payment is voluntary. You are free to take the old windows with you and handle everything yourself, **in which case, we will not charge you.**

142 문맥이해 · 문장삽입   난이도 중

해석 (A) 새 창문이 매우 마음에 드실 거라고 확신합니다.
(B) 환경친화적인 방식으로 처리하는 것만 기억해주십시오.
(C) 균열이나 기타 손상을 발견하시는 경우, 즉시 고객 서비스 부서로 연락하셔야 합니다.
(D) 연례 점검이 필수는 아니지만, 매우 권장됩니다.

해설 빈칸 앞 문장의 '폐창문을 가져가서 직접 처리해도 된다'는 내용을 고려할 때, 문맥상 '(창문을 직접 처리할 때에는) 환경친화적인 방식으로 처리해야 한다'는 당부의 메시지로 이어져야 자연스러우므로 (B)가 정답

Key word
You are free to take the old windows with you and handle everything yourself, in which case, we will not charge you. Just remember to deal with the process in an eco-friendly way.

143-146번은 다음 편지에 관한 문제입니다.

1월 5일

Dana Wilkinson
Salmon River로, 12654번지
San Diego, CA 92129

Ms. Wilkinson께,

귀하의 Golf and Tennis 클럽(GTC) 회원권이 지난달에 만료되었음을 다시 알려드립니다. 회원권을 지속하지 않을 계획이시라면, **143.** 저희에게 알려주셔서 저희 쪽 기록을 갱신할 수 있게 해주시기 바랍니다. 그러나, 연장을 원하신다면, 현재 회원권 갱신에 대해 30% 할인을 제공하고 있다는 사실을 알려드리고자 합니다. 이는 단 2,000달러로 GTC 수영장 **144.** 이용을 포함하는 정회원 자격을 1년 더 유지하게 됨을 의미합니다. **145.** 이 혜택을 받으시려면 1월 10일까지 답장해주시기 바랍니다. 회원권을 갱신하시려면, **146.** 단지 동봉해드린 신청서를 제출해 주시면 됩니다.

저희 GTC의 소중한 고객으로 계속 남아주시기를 기대합니다.

진심을 담아,

Kelso Montburg
회원서비스 담당

동봉물재중

어휘 expire v. 만기가 되다 extend v. 연장하다 currently adv. 현재 renewal n. 갱신 full membership 정회원 자격 submit v. 제출하다 application n. 신청서

143 어휘 • 인칭대명사   난이도 중

해설 빈칸은 동사 let의 목적어자리. 접속사 so that으로 연결된 문장 뒷부분의 내용을 고려할 때, '저희가 기록을 갱신할 수 있도록 저희에게 알려주세요'라는 의미가 되어야 자연스러우므로 (D)가 정답

Key word
If you do not plan to continue your membership, please let <u>us</u> know so that we may update our records.

144 구조/문법 • 명사   난이도 중

해설 빈칸은 전치사 including의 목적어이자, of 전치사구의 수식을 받는 명사자리. 문맥상 '수영장 사용을 포함한 정회원권'이라는 의미가 되어야 자연스러우므로 '사용(권)'을 뜻하는 (A)가 정답이며, 이 의미로 쓰일 때 use는 불가산 명사이므로 (B)는 답이 될 수 없다.

Key point
명사 use vs. uses: 불가산명사 use는 '사용(권), 사용허가'를, 가산명사 a use/uses는 '용도, 쓰임새'를 의미한다.

145 문맥이해 • 문장삽입   난이도 중

해석 (A) 이 혜택을 받으시려면 1월 10일까지 답장해주시기 바랍니다.
(B) 이미 청구대금을 지불하셨다면 이 편지는 무시하셔도 좋습니다.
(C) 주 2회 개인 교육을 제공합니다.
(D) 회원권 취소에 관한 확인 이메일이 곧 발송될 것입니다.

해설 빈칸 앞 부분에서는 회원권 갱신 할인 혜택을, 빈칸 뒤 문장에서는 갱신방법을 언급하고 있음을 고려할 때, 문맥상 할인 혜택 기한을 알려주는 내용이 들어가야 자연스러우므로 (A)가 정답

Key word
However, if you would like to extend, I should mention that <u>we are currently offering a 30 percent discount on membership renewals</u>. This means that for just $2,000, you would have one more year of full membership including use of GTC's swimming pool. <u>Please reply by January 10 to take advantage of this deal.</u> To renew your membership, 146. -------- submit the application form enclosed here.

146 어휘 • 부사   난이도 중

해설 빈칸은 동사를 수식하는 부사자리. 문맥상 '갱신하려면, 단지 양식을 제출하기만 하면 된다'는 의미가 되어야 자연스러우므로 (B)가 정답

Key word
To renew your membership, <u>simply</u> submit the application form enclosed here.

PART 7   P. 35

147-148번은 다음 초대장에 관한 문제입니다.

올해의 David Conrad 기념 마케팅 세미나에
귀하를 초대하게 되어 영광입니다.

Toronto 중소기업센터(TSBC)의 기업고문이자 Alpine Grill의 사장인
James Nakamoto가 진행합니다.

주제: 디지털 마케팅
일시: 6월 28일 오후 1~3시
장소: 그랜드 호텔 콘퍼런스룸

이 세미나는 Toronto 지역의 모든 사업가들에게 열려있습니다.[147] 참석하시는 모든 분들은 등록하실 때 사업자등록증 사본을 제출해야 합니다.[148] 더 자세한 정보를 알아보시려면 TSBC로 전화 주십시오.

어휘 honor v. 명예를 주다, 존중하다 memorial adj. 기념하기 위한, 추모의 n. 기념비 host v. 주최하다, 진행하다 advisor n. 고문, 자문 available adj. 이용할 수 있는 entrepreneur n. 사업가, 기업가 attendee n. 참석자 present v. 제출하다, 보여주다 business registration certificate 사업자등록증 sign up 등록하다

147 암시/추론   난이도 중

해석 초대장은 누구를 대상으로 하겠는가?
(A) 마케팅 전문가
(B) 자영업자
(C) 재정 고문
(D) 호텔 매니저

해설 네 번째 단락에서 This seminar is available to all entrepreneurs in the Toronto area.(이 세미나는 Toronto 지역의 모든 사업가들에게 열려있습니다.)라고 했으므로 (B)가 정답

Paraphrasing entrepreneurs ➡ business owners

148 상세정보   난이도 중

해석 관심 있는 사람들은 무엇을 하라고 요청 받는가?
(A) 증명서를 제공하라고
(B) 세미나실을 준비하라고
(C) Mr. Nakamoto의 레스토랑으로 전화하라고
(D) 행사 일정을 살펴보라고

해설 네 번째 단락에서 All attendees must present a copy of their business registration certificate when signing up.(참석하시는 모든 분들은 등록하실 때 사업자등록증 사본을 제출해야 합니다.)라고 했으므로 (A)가 정답

Paraphrasing present ➡ provide

149-150번은 다음 양식에 관한 문제입니다.

RK사

고객: Top Ten 전자
주소: Cleveland로 446번지
수신: Angela Martin

거래해 주셔서 다시 한번 감사 드립니다. 아래는 10월 30일에 이용하신 서비스에 대한 청구서입니다. **문제가 있으시면, 언제든지 Gerry Martin에게 (555) 212-9891로 전화하시기 바랍니다.**[150A]

서비스/제품[149]	수량[149]	개당 가격	가격
부속품	수도꼭지 (황동) x20	20달러	400달러
파이프 설치	L자관(구리) x10	25달러	250달러
설비 교체	개수대 (도자기) x4	40달러	160달러
공임	35시간[150D]	25달러/시간	875달러
		총	1,685달러

어휘 attn ~앞 (for the attention of의 약어) fittings n. 부속품 faucet n. 수도꼭지 brass n. 황동 pipe n. 관, 파이프 installation n. 설치 piping n. 관 copper n. 구리 fixture n. (붙박이) 설비, 시설 replacement n. 교체 porcelain n. 도자기 labor n. 노동, 수고

149 암시/추론   난이도 중

해석 RK사는 무엇이겠는가?
(A) 전기회사
(B) 배관업체
(C) 철물점
(D) 금속 제조업체

해설 표에서 Service/Product(서비스/제품)과 Amount(수량)의 항목명이 Fittings(부속품) - x20 Faucets (Brass)(수도꼭지(황동)x20), Pipe Installation(파이프 설치) - x10 Type L Piping (Copper)(L자관(구리) x10), Fixture Replacement(설비 교체) - x4 Sinks (Porcelain)(개수대 (세라믹) x4)인 걸로 미루어, 배관 서비스를 제공하는 업체임을 알 수 있으므로 (B)가 정답

150 사실확인   난이도 중

해석 어떤 정보가 포함되지 않았는가?
(A) RK사 담당직원
(B) 관여 직원의 수
(C) 구매된 파이프의 종류
(D) 프로젝트 기간

해설 지문의 단서와 보기를 매칭시키면, If you have any issues, don't hesitate to call Gerry Martin at (555) 212-9891.(문제가 있으시면, 언제든지 Gerry Martin에게 (555) 212-9891로 전화하시기 바랍니다.) → (A) The contact representative of RK Co./x10 Type L Piping (Copper)(L자관(구리)x10) → (C) The kind of pipes that were purchased/35 hours (35시간) → (D) The length of a project와 일치하지만, 관여 직원의 수는 언급된 바 없으므로 (B)가 정답

151-152번은 다음 이메일에 관한 문제입니다.

발신: jingram@hae.com
수신: ugrant@baltor.com
날짜: 9월 5일
제목: Milton 호텔 숙박시설

무역 박람회 참여업체께,

무엇보다 먼저, **저희 가전제품 박람회(HAE)팀**[151]은 올해 귀하의 참가에 감사 드리고 싶습니다. 저희는 인근 Milton 호텔과 협의하여 모든 판매업체에 숙박요금 할인혜택을 드리게 되었음을 알려드리게 되어 기쁩니다. 모든 HAE 판매업체는 Milton에서 투숙하시는 동안 20 퍼센트 할인을 받게 됩니다. HAE 판매업체 공식 확인서에 귀사의 고유 식별번호가 있습니다. 할인을 적용하시려면, 호텔 웹 사이트로 객실을 예약하실 때 판촉 코드 란에 이 번호를 입력하시면 됩니다.[152] 이 호텔은 만실이 될 것이 확실하므로 조속히 이 혜택을 이용하시길 권장 드립니다.

Janette Ingram[151]

어휘 accommodation n. 숙박시설 trade show 무역 박람회 vendor n. 판매업체 first and foremost 다른 무엇보다도 exposition n. 전시회, 박람회 participation n. 참가, 참여 inform v. 알리다 negotiate v. 협상하다 nearby adj. 인근의 discounted adj. 할인된 rate n. 요금 stay n. 숙박 official adj. 공식적인 confirmation n. 확인 unique adj. 고유의, 특유의 apply v. 적용하다 promo code 판촉코드 reserve v. 예약하다 encourage v. 권장하다 take advantage of ~을 이용하다 deal n. 혜택 run out of ~을 다 써버리다

151 암시/추론   난이도 중

해석 Janette Ingram은 누구겠는가?
(A) 호텔 지배인
(B) 여행사 직원
(C) 행사 진행자
(D) 사업체 소유주

해설 Janette Ingram이 보낸 이메일, 첫 번째 줄에서 the team here at the Household Appliances Exposition (HAE)(저희 가전제품 박람회(HAE)팀)이라고 하여 박람회팀 소속임을 알 수 있으므로 (C)가 정답

152 상세정보   난이도 중

해석 식별번호는 어떻게 사용될 수 있는가?
(A) 시설에 입장하기 위해
(B) 가격 할인을 받기 위해
(C) 기기를 구매하기 위해
(D) 회원 계정에 접속하기 위해

해설 In your official HAE vendor confirmation letter, you will see a unique ID number for your company. To apply the discount, enter this number in the promo code box when reserving your room through the hotel's Web site.(HAE 판매업체 공식 확인서에 귀사의 고유 식별번호가 있습니다. 할인을 적용하시려면, 호텔 웹 사이트로 객실을 예약하실 때 판촉 코드 란에 이 번호를 입력하시면 됩니다.)라고 했으므로 (B)가 정답

Paraphrasing apply the discount ➡ receive a price reduction

153-154번은 다음 문자 메시지 대화에 관한 문제입니다.

Barret Hansen (오후 2시 26분)
저기, Melissa. David Butler가 내일 하려고 했던 Westford 센터 투어를 취소했어요.

Melissa Cloud (오후 2시 29분)
아쉽네요. 그분 회사 기념 행사 장소로 완벽한 것 같은데 말이죠.(153) 새로 약속을 잡았나요?(154)

Barret Hansen (오후 2시 30분)
네. 다음 주 월요일이에요, Grocer사 시상식 연회 일정에 관한 전화회의 이후로요.(153)/(154) 회의가 3시니까, 준비하고 합류하시는 데 시간이 충분할 거예요.

Melissa Cloud (오후 2시 31분)
좋아요.(154) 오늘 Grocer사에 전화해서 다시 안내 좀 해주겠어요?

Barret Hansen (오후 2시 31분)
알았어요.

어휘 That's a shame. 아쉽다 venue n. 장소 conference call 전화회의 regarding prep. ~에 관하여

155-157번은 다음 안내문에 관한 문제입니다.

산호를 구해주세요

호주 환경 에너지청(ADEE)이 Great Barrier Reef를 구하기 위한 글로벌 기금 마련 행사를 진행하고 있습니다. —[1]—. 월말까지 1,000만 호주 달러라는 목표가 설정되었으며, 전 세계의 친구 여러분이 세계의 위대한 자연계 불가사의 중 하나의 보존을 돕는데 기여해주시기 바랍니다.(155) —[2]—. 모금액은 상승하는 해수 온도나 증가한 악천후의 빈도와 같은 위협으로부터 산호를 더 잘 보호할 방법에 대한 연구에 사용될 것입니다.(156)/(157) —[3]—.

산호를 구하기 위해 할 수 있는 일에 관해 더 자세히 알아보시려면, www.environment.gov.au/savethereef/info를 방문해주세요. —[4]—.

오늘 여러분의 도움을 보여 주세요!

어휘 Great Barrier Reef 대보초(호주 해안에 있는 큰 산호초) environment n. 환경 fundraiser n. 모금행사 AUD 호주달러 (Australian dollar의 약어) set v. 정하다 contribute v. 기여하다 preserve v. 보존[관리]하다 wonder n. 경이(로운 것), 불가사의 raise v. (자금·사람 등을) 모으다 apply v. 쓰다, 적용하다 threat n. 협박, 위협 temperature n. 온도 frequency n. 빈도 severe weather 악천후, 험한 날씨

---

153 암시/추론 난이도 중

해석 Ms. Cloud의 직업은 무엇이겠는가?
(A) 시설 관리 근로자
(B) 식당 지배인
(C) 행사 기획자
(D) 인사 담당자

해설 오후 2시 29분 ~ 2시 30분 대화에서 Melissa Cloud가 I think it's the perfect venue for his company's anniversary.(그분 회사 기념 행사 장소로 완벽한 것 같은데 말이죠.)라고 하자, Barret Hansen이 It'll be next Monday, following your conference call regarding the schedule for Grocer, Inc.'s awards banquet.(다음 주 월요일이에요, Grocer사 시상식 연회 일정에 관한 전화회의 이후로요.)라고 한 것이므로 (C)가 정답

---

154 화자 의도 파악 난이도 중

해석 오후 2시 31분에, Ms. Cloud가 "좋아요"라고 할 때 무엇을 의미하겠는가?
(A) 시설을 방문하고 싶다.
(B) Mr. Butler와 통화하는 것이 기대된다.
(C) 프로젝트의 진행이 만족스럽다.
(D) Mr. Hansen의 일처리에 만족한다.

해설 오후 2시 29분 ~ 2시 31분 대화에서 Melissa cloud가 Did you make another appointment with him?(새로 약속을 잡았나요?)라고 한 말에 Barret Hansen이 It'll be next Monday, following your conference call regarding the schedule for Grocer, Inc.'s awards banquet.(다음 주 월요일이에요, Grocer사 시상식 연회 일정에 관한 전화회의 이후로요.)라고 대답했고, 이에 Melissa Cloud가 Nice.(좋아요.)라고 말한 것이므로 (D)가 정답

---

155 주제/목적/대상 난이도 중

해석 안내문은 왜 작성되었는가?
(A) 새로운 에너지 계획을 설명하기 위해
(B) 월간 혜택을 알리기 위해
(C) 기부를 요청하기 위해
(D) 새로운 연구 결과를 보고하기 위해

해설 첫 번째 단락에서 A goal of $10 million (AUD) by the end of the month has been set, and friends from all over the world are encouraged to contribute to help preserve one of the great natural wonders of the world.(월말까지 1,000만 호주 달러라는 목표가 설정되었으며 전 세계의 친구 여러분이 세계의 위대한 자연계 불가사의 중 하나의 보존을 돕는 데 기여해주시기 바랍니다.)라고 했으므로 (C)가 정답

---

156 암시/추론 난이도 중

해석 Great Barrier Reef에 관하여 알 수 있는 것은?
(A) 다양한 해양 생물들의 서식지이다.
(B) 기후 변화의 영향을 받고 있다.
(C) 호주 최대의 관광 명소이다.
(D) 일반 대중에게 공개되지 않는다.

해설 첫 번째 단락에서 Money raised will be applied towards research on how to better protect the Reef from threats such as rising sea temperatures and the increased frequency of severe weather events.(모금액은 상승하는 해수 온도나 증가한 악천후의 빈도와 같은 위협으로부터 산호를 더 잘 보호할 방법에 대한 연구에 사용될 것입니다.)라고 했으므로 (B)가 정답

Paraphrasing rising sea temperatures and the increased frequency of severe weather events ➡ climate change

157 문장 삽입   난이도 중

해석 [1], [2], [3], [4]로 표시된 곳 중, 다음 문장이 들어갈 위치로 가장 적절한 것은?

"또한 일부는 주변 지역의 수질을 개선하는 데 사용될 것입니다."

(A) [1]
(B) [2]
(C) [3]
(D) [4]

해설 첫 번째 단락에서 Money raised will be applied towards research on how to better protect the Reef from threats such as rising sea temperatures and the increased frequency of severe weather events.(모금액은 상승하는 해수 온도나 증가한 악천후의 빈도와 같은 위협으로부터 산호를 더 잘 보호할 방법에 대한 연구에 사용될 것입니다.)라고 하여, 모금액의 또 다른 사용처를 추가로 언급하는 주어진 문장이 이어지기에 자연스러우므로 (C)가 정답

158-160번은 다음 회람에 관한 문제입니다.

수신: Camcom 전직원
발신: Katie Comstock 부사장
제목: Rhonda Hanna
날짜: 9월 1일

Rhonda Hanna가 영업 이사직을 맡게 되었음을 모두에게 알리게 되어 기쁩니다.(158) Ms. Hanna는 Pennsylvania 주립 대학교 졸업생이며, Boston의 Ernst and Sawyer에서 6년 동안 근무한 후 우리 회사에 입사했습니다.

지난 여름, Ms. Hanna는 외부 영업팀에 합류했습니다. 그녀는 판매 수치를 거의 두 배로 만들면서 바로 영향을 주었는데, 이전까지는 수치가 저조했습니다. 그녀의 리더십으로 저희는 GloboTech와의 계약을 수주할 수 있었고, 그녀의 부서는 사내 최고 매출 부서 중 한 곳이 되었습니다.(159)

Ms. Hanna의 새 직위는 월요일에 공식 발표될 것입니다. 그리고 승진을 축하하기 위해,(158) 저는 이번 주 목요일 Dorsia에 연회장을 예약했습니다. 많은 분들께 그 식당의 유명한 랍스터 스튜에 대해 듣고 나니, 어서 먹어보고 싶네요. 자리가 한정되어 있으므로, 오실 계획이라면 꼭 오늘 오후까지 Terry Wright에게 이메일을 보내주시기 바랍니다.(160)

어휘 take on (일 등을) 맡다 graduate n. 졸업자 make an impact 영향을 주다 nearly adv. 거의 double v. 두 배로 만들다 previously adv. 이전에 flat adj. (매출 등이) 저조한 earn v. (수익을) 올리다 officially adv. 공식적으로 promotion n. 승진 book v. 예약하다 banquet n. 연회[만찬] stew n. 스튜 seating n. 좌석, 자리

---

158 주제/목적/대상   난이도 중

해석 회람은 왜 게시되었는가?
(A) 계약 체결을 알리려고
(B) 구인광고를 하려고
(C) 새로운 동료를 소개하려고
(D) 직원의 승진을 알리려고

해설 첫 번째 단락에서 I am happy to tell everyone that Rhonda Hanna will be taking on the role of Director of Sales.(Rhonda Hanna가 영업이사직을 맡게 되었음을 모두에게 알리게 되어 기쁩니다.)라고 했고, 세 번째 단락에서 Ms. Hanna's new position will be officially announced on Monday. And to celebrate her promotion,(Ms. Hanna의 새 직위는 월요일에 공식 발표될 것입니다. 그리고 승진을 축하하기 위해,)라고 했으므로 (D)가 정답

---

159 사실확인   난이도 중

해석 외부 영업팀에 관하여 언급된 것은?
(A) 팀원들에게 급여를 인상해주었다.
(B) 직원들이 정기적으로 교육에 참석할 것이다.
(C) 수익이 상당히 증가했다.
(D) Boston 지점으로 이전할 것이다.

해설 두 번째 단락에서 Last summer, Ms. Hanna joined the Outside Sales Department. She immediately made an impact, nearly doubling sales numbers, which had previously been flat. Her leadership helped us win the GloboTech contract and made her team one of the highest earning departments in the company.(지난 여름, Ms. Hanna는 외부 영업팀에 합류했습니다. 그녀는 판매 수치를 거의 두 배로 만들면서 바로 영향을 주었는데, 이전까지는 수치가 저조했습니다. 그녀의 리더십으로 저희는 GloboTech와의 계약을 수주할 수 있었고, 그녀의 부서는 사내 최고 매출 부서 중 한 곳이 되었습니다.)라고 했으므로 (C)가 정답

Paraphrasing nearly doubling sales numbers ➡ revenue has increased significantly

---

160 암시/추론   난이도 중

해석 Dorsia에 관하여 알 수 있는 것은?
(A) Camcom 직원들 사이에서 인기 있다.
(B) 영업시간이 매우 한정되어 있다.
(C) 전용 좌석은 없다.
(D) 해산물만을 제공한다.

해설 세 번째 단락에서 I've booked the private banquet room at Dorsia this Thursday. I've heard from many of you about their famous lobster stew, so I can't wait to try it.(저는 이번 주 목요일 Dorsia에 연회장을 예약했습니다. 많은 분들께 그 식당의 유명한 랍스터 스튜에 대해 듣고 나니, 어서 먹어보고 싶네요.)라고 하여 Dorsia의 랍스터 스튜가 직원들에게 인기 있음을 알 수 있으므로 (A)가 정답

Paraphrasing famous ➡ popular

161-164번은 다음 이메일에 관한 문제입니다.

수신: Alexa Ramirez<ramrez@gibbs.com>
발신: Jesse Auerbach<auerbach@gibbs.com>
제목: 도움 요청
참조: Beth Park<part@gibbs.com>
날짜: 7월 8일

Ms. Ramirez께,

중요한 프로젝트에 당신의 도움이 필요합니다. ―[1]―. 저희 팀은 Colbert Medical이 환자 기록 추적에 사용할 신규 시스템 개발을 담당하고 있습니다.(161) 업무를 수행할 수 있는 경험 많은 직원이 부족해, 예정보다 진행이 늦어지고 있습니다. ―[2]―. 일이 원활히 진행되도록, 당분간 당신이 데이터 이동용 소프트웨어를 맡아주셨으면 합니다.(161)

당신의 부서장 Beth Park에게 저희 상황에 관해 얘기했더니, 몇 주 동안은 당신의 도움을 받아도 된다고 하더군요.(162)/(164) —[3]—.

이 업무를 하는 동안 민감한 정보를 많이 접할 것이라서, 저와 함께 비공개 서약서를 검토하셔야 합니다. 오늘 오후에 40층에 있는 제 사무실에 들러 주실래요?(163) —[4]—. 그리고 팀원들에게 당신을 소개할 수 있게 다음 주 월요일 저희 회의에도 와주셨으면 좋겠습니다.

Best,
Jesse Auerbach

어휘 assistance n. 도움, 지원 track v. 추적하다 patient n. 환자 record n. 기록 lack n. 부족 on hand (특히 도움을) 구할 수 있는 behind schedule 예정보다 늦은 run v. 진행되다 take charge of ~을 책임지다, 떠맡다 migration n. (컴퓨터 시스템의) 이송, 이동 for now 우선, 당분간은 head n. (조직의) 책임자 encounter v. 맞닥뜨리다, 접하다 sensitive adj. 민감한, 예민한 non-disclosure adj. 비공개

161 암시/추론 난이도 중

해석 Ms. Ramirez의 직업은 무엇이겠는가?
(A) 공사 감독자
(B) 의사
(C) 채용 담당자
(D) 컴퓨터 프로그래머

해설 첫 번째 단락에서 My team is responsible for developing the new system Colbert Medical will be using to track patient records.(저희 팀은 Colbert Medical이 환자 기록 추적에 사용할 신규 시스템 개발을 담당하고 있습니다.)라고 하며, I need you to take charge of our migration software for now.(당분간 당신이 데이터 이동용 소프트웨어를 맡아주셨으면 합니다.)라고 했으므로 (D)가 정답

162 상세정보 난이도 중

해석 Mr. Auerbach는 무엇을 요청했는가?
(A) 프로젝트를 위한 추가 자금
(B) 환자기록 모음
(C) 직원의 일시적인 도움
(D) 빈 사무실의 평면도

해설 두 번째 단락에서 I told your department head, Beth Park, about my situation, and told me I could use you for a few weeks.(당신의 부서장 Beth Park에게 저희 상황에 관해 얘기했더니, 몇 주 동안은 당신의 도움을 받아도 된다고 하더군요.)라고 했으므로 (C)가 정답

163 상세정보 난이도 중

해석 Mr. Auerbach는 왜 Ms. Ramirez와 만나고 싶어 하는가?
(A) 교육을 제공하려고
(B) 양식을 논의하려고
(C) 신제품을 소개하려고
(D) 평가회를 열려고

해설 세 번째 단락에서 I'll need to go over some non-disclosure forms with you. Why don't you come by my office on the 40th floor this afternoon?(저와 함께 비공개 서약서를 검토하셔야 합니다. 오늘 오후에 40층에 있는 제 사무실에 들러 주실래요?)라고 했으므로 (B)가 정답

Paraphrasing go over → discuss

164 문장 삽입 난이도 중

해석 [1], [2], [3], [4]로 표시된 곳 중, 다음 문장이 들어갈 위치로 가장 적절한 것은?
"그녀가 이번 달에는 부서에 당신이 없어도 괜찮을 거라고 했습니다."
(A) [1]
(B) [2]
(C) [3]
(D) [4]

해설 두 번째 단락에서 I told your department head, Beth Park, about my situation, and told me I could use you for a few weeks.(당신의 부서장 Beth Park에게 저희 상황에 관해 얘기했더니, 몇 주 동안은 당신의 도움을 받아도 된다고 하더군요.)라고 하여 주어진 문장이 이어지기에 자연스러우므로 (C)가 정답

165-168번은 다음 온라인 채팅 대화문에 관한 문제입니다.

Mayumi Ohta [오전 10시 15분]
Mr. Young, Ms. Olson, 잠깐 알려드릴 게 있어요. 두 회사에서 더 RFT 기술 박람회 참가신청을 했어요.(165) 이제 참가 업체수가 충분할 겁니다.

Eric Young [오전 10시 16분]
좋은 소식이네요. 어느 회사들인가요?

Mayumi Ohta [오전 10시 18분]
Natural Power는 그들의 최신 태양 전지판의 효율성에 대한 시연회를 할 예정이고, Aperture사는 초보자용 최신 카메라 제품군을 선보일 거예요.(166)

Ingrid Olson [오전 10시 19분]
기대되는데요. 실은 제가 사진을 시작하려고 생각 중이었거든요.(166)

Mayumi Ohta [오전 10시 21분]
저도요. 그래서, Natural Power는 6월 5일로 확정지었고, Aperture사는 곧 선호하는 날짜를 저에게 알려줄 거예요. 제가 지금 비품을 가지러 매장에 가는 길인데, 정오까지는 돌아올 거예요.(167) 소식 들으면 알려드릴게요.

Ingrid Olson [오전 10시 23분]
알았어요. 확정되면, 박람회 전체 일정을 수신자 명단에 있는 모든 사람에게 이메일로 보낼게요.

Mayumi Ohta [오전 10시 24분]
행사장으로 가는 길 안내를 포함하는 걸 잊지 마세요.

Ingrid Olson [오전 10시 25분]
그럴게요. 다시 알려줘서 고마워요!

Eric Young [오전 10시 26분]
저기, Ms. Olson, 이메일을 보내기 전에 잠깐 기다려주세요.(168) 소식지를 신청한 사람들이 더 있어서, 명단에 주소를 추가해야 해요.

Ingrid Olson [오전 10시 27분]
알았어요!

Mayumi Ohta [오전 10시 29분]
잠깐 운전 좀 할게요. 잠시 후에 다시 이야기해요, 여러분.

| 어휘 | participate v. 참여하다 vendor n. 판매업체 demonstrate v. 시연하다 efficiency n. 효율성 solar panel 태양 전지판 line n. 제품군 promising adj. 전망이 좋은, 기대되는 photography n. 사진술 mean v. 작정하다, 의도하다 confirm v. 확인해 주다 preferred adj. 선호하는, 원하는 on one's way to ~로 가는 길[도중]인 supplies n. 용품, 비품 complete adj. 완전한, 완벽한 directions n. 길 안내 venue n. 장소 reminder n. 상기시키는 것 hang on 기다리다 |

165 주제/목적/대상   난이도 중

해석 Ms. Ohta는 왜 동료들에게 연락했는가?
(A) 최근의 등록 사항을 알려주려고
(B) 전시 부스 배치를 설명하려고
(C) 곧 구매할 물품의 최신 정보를 알려주려고
(D) 행사장의 위치에 대해 문의하려고

해설 오전 10시 15분, Mayumi Ohta의 메시지에서 Two more companies have signed up to participate in the RFT Technology Convention.(두 회사에서 더 RFT 기술 박람회 참가신청을 했어요.)라고 말했으므로 (A)가 정답

166 화자 의도 파악   난이도 중

해석 오전 10시 19분에, Ms. Olson이 "기대되는데요"라고 할 때 무엇을 의미하겠는가?
(A) 많은 사람들이 태양 전지판을 원한다고 생각한다.
(B) 유명 사진작가를 만나게 되어 신난다.
(C) 얼마 전에 새 카메라를 구매했다.
(D) 프레젠테이션이 기대된다.

해설 오전 10시 18분 ~ 10시 19분 대화에서 Mayumi Ohta가 Aperture, Inc. will introduce their newest line of cameras for beginners. (Aperture사는 초보자용 최신 카메라 제품군을 선보일 거예요.)라고 말하자, Ingrid Olson이 That sounds promising. I've actually been meaning to get into photography.(기대되는데요. 실은 제가 사진을 시작하려고 생각 중이었거든요.)라고 말한 것이므로 (D)가 정답

167 암시/추론   난이도 중

해석 Ms. Ohta는 오후에 어디에 있겠는가?
(A) 병원
(B) 컨벤션 센터
(C) 카메라 매장
(D) 자신의 사무실

해설 오전 10시 21분, Mayumi Ohta의 메시지에서 I'm on my way to the store to pick up some supplies, but I should return by noon.(제가 지금 비품을 가지러 매장에 가는 길인데, 정오까지는 돌아올 거예요.)라고 하여 오후에는 사무실에 있을 것임을 알 수 있으므로 (D)가 정답

168 상세정보   난이도 중

해석 Mr. Young은 Ms. Olson에게 무엇을 하라고 지시하는가?
(A) 이메일 발송을 미루라고
(B) 회의실을 예약하라고
(C) 목록에 몇 개의 주소를 포함하라고
(D) 지역 납품 업체에 연락하라고

해설 오전 10시 26분, Eric Young의 메시지에서 Actually, Ms. Olson, hang on a moment before you email that out.(저기, Ms. Olson, 이메일을 보내기 전에 잠깐 기다려주세요.)라고 했으므로 (A)가 정답

169-171번은 다음 설명서에 관한 문제입니다.

Sparkle Again

우선, 쏟은 액체의 넘치는 잔여물을 종이 수건으로 흡수시켜 닦아내세요. 그 다음에, 소량의 용액을 직물에 발라주세요. Sparkle Again 용액을 원을 그리며 부드럽게 문질러줍니다. 얼룩이 옅어지면서 사라지기 시작할 것입니다. 여전히 얼룩이 보인다면 덧발라주세요.(169)

Sparkle Again은 천연 원료만을 사용하여 옷이 변색되지 않습니다. 최상의 효과를 위해서는, 쏟은 직후에 도포해주세요. Sparkle Again은 세심한 취급을 요하는 재료로 만들어진 옷을 손상시킬 수 있기 때문에 그렇지 않은 직물에만 도포하실 것을 강력히 권장합니다.(170)

추가정보를 얻거나 Sparkle Again 사용법에 관한 동영상을 보시려면, 웹 사이트 www.sparkleagain.com/howto를 방문해 주세요.(171) 저희 친절한 고객 서비스 상담원과 직접 대화하고 싶으시면, +(41) 555-8274로 전화하시거나 cs@sparkleagain.com으로 이메일을 보내주세요.

| 어휘 | sparkle v. 반짝이다 absorb v. 흡수하다 wipe v. 닦다 excess adj. 과도한 residue n. 잔여물 spill n. 유출[물]; 흘린 액체 apply v. (크림 등을) 바르다 solution n. 용액 fabric n. 직물, 천 gently adv. 부드럽게 rub v. 문지르다[비비다] in a circular motion 원을 그리며 stain n. 얼룩 lighten v. 밝아지다 reapply v. 다시 바르다 visible adj. (눈에) 보이는 discoloring n. 변색 non-delicate adj. 세심한 주의가 필요하지 않은 ruin v. 망치다 |

169 상세정보   난이도 중

해석 Sparkle Again의 용도는 무엇인가?
(A) 표면에 광을 내는 것
(B) 색상을 밝게 하는 것
(C) 얼룩을 제거하는 것
(D) 악취를 방지하는 것

해설 첫 번째 단락에서 Gently rub the Sparkle Again solution in a circular motion. The stain will begin to lighten and disappear. Reapply if the stain is still visible.(Sparkle Again 용액을 원을 그리며 부드럽게 문질러줍니다. 얼룩이 옅어지면서 사라지기 시작할 것입니다. 여전히 얼룩이 보인다면 덧발라주세요.)라고 했으므로 (C)가 정답

170 상세정보   난이도 중

해석 설명서에 따르면, 제품 사용시 무엇을 하는 것이 중요한가?
(A) 세심한 주의가 필요한 직물에 사용을 피하는 것
(B) 여러 번 바르는 것을 피하는 것
(C) 옷에 바른 후 말리는 것
(D) 액체를 모두 흡수시키는 것

해설 두 번째 단락에서 It is highly recommended that you only apply Sparkle Again to non-delicate fabrics, as it may ruin clothes made from other materials.(Sparkle Again은 세심한 취급을 요하는 재료로 만들어진 옷을 손상시킬 수 있기 때문에 그렇지 않은 직물에만 도포하실 것을 강력히 권장합니다.)라고 했으므로 (A)가 정답

TEST 01 35

Paraphrasing only a apply Sparkle Again to non-delicate fabrics ➡ avoid using it on delicate fabrics

171 사실확인 난이도 중

해석 Sparkle Again에 관하여 알 수 있는 것은?
(A) 제품이 합성 원료를 함유하고 있다.
(B) 회사 웹 사이트에서 사용 지침서를 제공한다.
(C) 제품을 온라인이나 매장에서 구매할 수 있다.
(D) 손상된 옷에 대해서는 고객에게 변상해준다.

해설 세 번째 단락에서 To get more information and for videos on how to use Sparkle Again, visit our Web site at www.sparkleagain.com/howto.(추가정보를 얻거나 Sparkle Again 사용법에 관한 동영상을 보시려면 웹 사이트 www.sparkleagain.com/howto를 방문하시기 바랍니다.)라고 했으므로 (B)가 정답

Paraphrasing videos on how to use ➡ tutorials

172-175번은 다음 웹 페이지에 관한 문제입니다.

Screech.com/il/italian

Italia Soleggiata
509 E Main
Libertyville, IL 60049
219-999-2218
영업시간: 매일 오후 12시 – 11시 (일부 공휴일 제외)

추천 86%

테이블을 예약하시려면, 식당 웹 사이트(www.italiasoleggiata/reservations)를 방문하십시오. 특별 행사나 준비가 필요하시면, 정규 영업 시간에 전화해 주세요. **대규모 인원(최대 30명)의 경우, East 다이닝 룸을 예약할 수 있지만, 보증금을 지불하셔야 합니다.**(173)

평가	메뉴	지도에서 찾기

Barry Evans 추천
이 식당에 관해 많이 들었는데, 정말 기대했던 대로였습니다. 긴 테이블 대기 시간을 제외하면, 정말 좋은 식사 경험이었습니다. **뭘 주문할지 고민했는데, 담당 웨이터가 매우 사려 깊었고 도움이 되는 추천을 해줬습니다.**(172) 그리스식 샐러드는 최고였고,(175) 식사와 함께 올리브 한 접시가 무료로 나왔습니다. 정말 따뜻한 곳입니다!

Kim Gordon 추천
음식이 맛있었고,(175) 의외로 채식주의 메뉴가 많았습니다. 하지만 실내 장식은 정말 좀 바꿔야겠어요. 너무 구식입니다.

Sheila Rajneesh Jr. 비추천
음식의 품질이 훌륭(175)했지만 사람들이 말하는 것처럼 특별하지는 않았습니다. 위치가 시내에서 멀고, 대부분 메뉴는 독창적이지 않습니다. 멀리까지 간 보람도 없고, 물론 돈을 쓴 보람도 없었습니다.

Dave Lynch 강력 추천
최고 수준의 식당입니다. 싸지는 않지만, **제 생일파티를 하기에 완벽한 곳이었어요. 모두 East 다이닝 룸이 얼마나 아름다운지를 보고 감동하였습니다.**(173) 무엇을 주문하든 후회하지 않을 겁니다. 메뉴 전체가 환상적입니다.(175)

Paul Mulhouse 추천
멋진 식사였어요. 이 식당에서 사무실 크리스마스 파티 음식을 공급받았습니다. 직원들이 여기 와 있는 동안 정말 많이 신경 써주어서,(174) 빠르게 모두에게 서비스해 주었고 이 지역 최고의 이탈리아 요리(175)도 먹을 수 있었습니다.

어휘 arrangement n. 준비, 계획 deposit n. 보증금 live up to expectations 기대에 부응하다 aside from ~외에는 thoughtful adj. 배려심 있는, 친절한 complimentary adj. 무료의 plate n. 접시, 그릇 welcoming adj. (방문객에게) 따뜻한 old-fashioned adj. 구식의 top-notch adj. 최고의, 아주 뛰어난 terrific adj. 아주 좋은, 멋진 cuisine n. 요리

172 상세정보 난이도 중

해석 Barry Evans는 Italia Soleggiata의 무엇을 가장 좋아했는가?
(A) 식당의 인테리어
(B) 채식주의 옵션의 다양함
(C) 훌륭한 고객 서비스
(D) 할인쿠폰

해설 Barry Evans의 평가에서 I wasn't sure what to order, but our waiter was very thoughtful and made helpful recommendations.(뭘 주문할지 고민했는데 담당 웨이터가 매우 사려 깊었고 도움이 되는 추천을 해줬습니다.)라고 했으므로 (C)가 정답

173 암시/추론 난이도 중

해석 Dave Lynch가 한 예약에 관하여 무엇이 사실이겠는가?
(A) 보증금이 필요했다.
(B) 웹 사이트에서 이루어졌다.
(C) 밤 11시 이후에 이루어졌다.
(D) 할인을 받을 수 있었다.

해설 첫 번째 단락에서 For big parties(up to 30 guests), you can reserve the East Dining Room, but you must pay a security deposit.(대규모 인원(최대 30명)의 경우, East 다이닝 룸을 예약할 수 있지만, 보증금을 지불하셔야 합니다.)라고 했는데, Reviews(평가) 표의 네 번째 단락에서 Dave Lynch이 but it was a perfect location for my birthday party. Everyone was impressed with how beautiful the East Dining Room was.(제 생일파티를 하기에 완벽한 곳이었어요. 모두 East 다이닝 룸이 얼마나 아름다운지를 보고 감동하였습니다.)라고 하여 보증금이 필요한 East 다이닝 룸을 예약했음을 알 수 있으므로 (A)가 정답

174 사실확인 난이도 상

해석 Italia Soleggiata에 관하여 언급된 것은?
(A) 출장 뷔페 서비스를 제공한다.
(B) 시내 지점을 개장할 것이다.
(C) 연중 무휴로 운영된다.
(D) 이탈리아 음식만 제공한다.

해설 Reviews(평가) 표, 다섯 번째 단락에서 Paul Mulhouse가 The restaurant provided food to our office Christmas event. And while they were here, the staff really took care of us,(이 식당에서 사무실 크리스마스 파티 음식을 공급받았습니다. 직원들이 여기 와 있는 동안 정말 많이 신경 써주어서,)라고 하여 Italia Soleggiata에서 출장뷔페 서비스를 제공함을 알 수 있으므로 (A)가 정답

175 상세정보 　　　　　　　　　　　　난이도 중

해석 모든 평가자들은 식당의 어떤 면에 동의하는가?
(A) 요리의 맛
(B) 장식의 수준
(C) 널찍한 주차장
(D) 저렴한 메뉴

해설 Reviews(평가) 표에서 Barry Evans는 The Greek salad was superb(그리스식 샐러드는 최고였고), Kim Gordon은 The food was delicious,(음식이 맛있었고), Sheila Rajneesh는 Great quality food(음식의 품질이 훌륭), Dave Lynch는 Whatever you order, you won't regret it—the entire menu is fantastic.(무엇을 주문하든 후회하지 않을 겁니다. 메뉴 전체가 환상적입니다.), Paul Mulhouse는 some of the best Italian cuisine in the area.(이 지역 최고의 이탈리아 요리)라고 하여 모든 평가자들이 요리가 맛있다고 평가했음을 알 수 있으므로 (A)가 정답

176-180번은 다음 웹 페이지와 이메일에 관한 문제입니다.

---

www.alphalumenstar.co.uk/review/LU-X/ad52d

Huntsdale 식물원 안내서

방문해주셔서 감사 드립니다! **Grand 중앙과 도시 내 가장 유명한 호텔 및 레스토랑에서 도보 거리에 위치한**[176] Huntsdale 식물원은 방문객들에게 도시를 떠나지 않고도 휴식을 취하고 자연의 아름다움을 경험할 수 있는 훌륭한 방법을 선사합니다. 식물원 방문을 최대한 활용하고 싶은 분들은 투어 또한 이용할 수 있습니다. 자동차 및 자전거 주차공간이 충분히 마련되어 있습니다. 저희 식물원 부페 샐러드 바에서의 점심식사는 어떠신가요?

요금표:

입장단계	금액	입장 권한
General	5달러	주 식물원과 온실
Deluxe	10달러	General 입장 구역+일본 정원 투어
Executive	15달러	Deluxe 입장 구역+유기농 농장 투어
VIP[179]	25달러	Executive 입장 구역+**야생동물 쇼**[179]

야생동물 쇼:[180]
치타를 만나요: 대도시의 큰 고양이과 동물들 (1월-3월)
아름다운 코요테: 코요테, 여우 및 늑대 (4월-6월)
대탈출: 고릴라, 침팬지와 Orlando 오랑우탄 (7월-9월)
어둠이 내린 공원: 야행성 사막 동물들 (10월-12월)[180]

어휘 botanical garden 식물원 popular adj. 인기 있는 offer v. 제공하다 relax v. 휴식을 취하다 explore v. 탐험하다 nature n. 자연 leave v. 떠나다 tour n. 투어, 견학 available adj. 이용 가능한 plenty n. 풍부한 양 on-site adj. 현지의, 현장의 stay v. 머무르다 admission n. 입장(권) access n. 입장, 접근 greenhouse n. 온실 organic adj. 유기농의 wildlife adj. 야생의 coyote n. 코요테 escape n. 탈출, 도피 gorilla n. 고릴라 chimpanzee n. 침팬지 orangutan n. 오랑우탄 nocturnal adj. 야행성의 desert n. 사막

수신: HPers@huntsdalegarden.org
발신: Damian@indioschools.edu
날짜: 11월 6일
제목: 예정된 방문

Mr. Pers께,

저는 Indio 중학교 자연 클럽(IMSNC)의 설립자인 Leticia Damian입니다. 이름에서 짐작하시겠지만, 저희 클럽은 자연계 및 그것이 직면한 생태 문제들에 대한 어린 학생들의 인식 증대를 추구합니다.[178]

저희는 11월 22일 식물원을 방문할 계획입니다.[180] 현재, 최소 20명의 회원이 참석할 예정이고, 참석자들은 일본정원과 현지 유기농 농장 견학에 관심을 보였습니다.[177]

저는 저희가 계획한 투어의 일부로 이 장소들에 입장할 수 있는지를 확인 받고 싶었습니다.[177] 또한 쇼가 예정되어 있다면, 저희는 현재 진행 중인 야생동물 쇼를 관람하고 싶습니다.[179]/[180] 이 조건들을 충족하려면 저희가 어떤 종류의 티켓을 구입해야 할지 알려주세요.[177]

Best Regards,

Leticia Damian
멘토 교수, IMSNC

어휘 plan v. 계획하다 organizer n. 조직자, 설립자 seek v. 찾다, 추구하다 awareness n. 인식 natural adj. 자연의, 타고난 ecological adj. 생태계의 issue n. 문제, 쟁점, 사안 face v. 마주보다, 직면하다 attend v. 참석하다 individual n. 개인 express v. 표현하다 interest n. 흥미 tour v. 견학하다 confirm v. 확인해주다, 확정하다 access n. 입장, 접근 arrange v. 마련하다, 준비하다 current adj. 현재의 schedule v. 일정을 잡다 n. 일정 advise v. 조언하다 ensure v. 반드시~하게 하다 condition n. 조건 faculty n. 교수단

---

176 암시/추론 　　　　　　　　　　　　난이도 중

해석 Huntsdale 식물원에 관하여 알 수 있는 것은?
(A) 최근 식당을 오픈했다.
(B) 단체에 할인을 제공한다.
(C) 편리한 장소에 위치한다.
(D) 자전거 투어를 허용한다.

해설 첫 번째 지문[웹 페이지], 첫 번째 단락에서 Just a short walk from Grand Central Station and our city's most popular hotels and restaurants(Grand 중앙역과 도시 내 가장 유명한 호텔 및 레스토랑에서 도보 거리에 위치한)라고 했으므로 (C)가 정답

---

177 주제/목적/대상 　　　　　　　　　　난이도 중

해석 이메일의 목적은 무엇인가?
(A) 투어 선택사항에 대해 문의하려고
(B) 클럽 창단을 발표하려고
(C) 방문 일정을 변경하려고
(D) 멘토 교수로서 Ms. Damian의 역할을 설명하려고

해설 두 번째 지문[이메일], 두 번째 단락에서 We plan to visit your botanical garden on November 22. At this time, we know that at least 20 members plan to attend, and those individuals have expressed interest in touring the Japanese Garden and the on-site Organic Farm.(저희는 11월 22일 식물원을 방문할 계획입니다. 현재, 최소 20명의 회원이 참석할 예정이고, 참석자들은 일본 정원과 현지 유기농 농장 견학에 관심을 보였습니다.)라고 했고, 세 번째 단락에서 I wanted to confirm that we would have access to these areas as part of the tour we arrange.(저는 저희가 계획한 투어의 일부로 이 장소들에 입장할 수 있는지를 확인 받고 싶었습니다.)라고 했으므로 (A)가 정답

178 상세정보 난이도 중

해석 Ms. Damian에 따르면, IMSNC는 무엇인가?
(A) 오락 프로그램
(B) 정부 부처
(C) 교환학생 대행업체
(D) 환경 교육 단체

해설 두 번째 지문[Ms. Damian이 보낸 이메일], 첫 번째 단락에서 I am Leticia Damian, organizer of the Indio Middle School Nature Club (IMSNC). As you might guess from the name, our club seeks to increase young students' awareness of the natural world and ecological issues that face it.(저는 Indio 중학교 자연 클럽(IMSNC)의 창시자인 Leticia Damian입니다. 이름에서 짐작하시겠지만, 저희 클럽은 자연계 및 그것이 마주하는 생태 문제들에 대한 어린 학생들의 인식 증대를 추구합니다.)라고 했으므로 (D)가 정답

179 암시/추론 [연계문제] 난이도 중

해석 IMSNC는 어떤 종류의 입장권을 선택하겠는가?
(A) General
(B) Deluxe
(C) Executive
(D) VIP

해설 두 번째 지문[이메일], 세 번째 단락에서 We also hope to see the current wildlife show(저희는 현재 진행중인 야생동물 쇼를 관람하고 싶습니다.)라고 했는데, 첫 번째 지문[웹 페이지], Prices(요금표)에서 Wildlife Show(야생동물 쇼)가 포함된 입장권이 VIP임을 알 수 있으므로 (D)가 정답

180 암시/추론 [연계문제] 난이도 중

해석 IMSNC 회원들은 어떤 공연을 보겠는가?
(A) 치타를 만나요
(B) 아름다운 코요테
(C) 대탈출
(D) 어둠이 내린 공원

해설 두 번째 지문[이메일], 두 번째 단락에서 We plan to visit your botanical garden on November 22.(저희는 11월 22일 식물원을 방문할 계획입니다.)라고 했는데, 첫 번째 지문[웹 페이지], Wildlife Shows(야생동물 쇼)에서 The Park After Dark: Nocturnal Animals of the Desert (October-December)(The Park After Dark(어둠이 내린 공원): 야행성 사막 동물들(10월-12월))라고 하여 11월에 진행하는 쇼가 The Park After Dark(어둠이 내린 공원)이라는 것을 알 수 있으므로 (D)가 정답

181-185번은 다음 보도자료와 이메일에 관한 문제입니다.

보도자료
연락처: media@ropavieja.com

Phoenix, 3월 15일 – Ropavieja Retailers는 6월 1일까지 80개 지점에 700명의 신입직원을 배치하기를 희망하며 다음 주에 춘계 신입 채용을 시작한다고 밝혔다.(181) Ropavieja는 전 지점에 판매사원과 계산직원을 증원하려고 한다. 이 소매 체인은 교육비 지원이나 어린이집 같은 복리후생과 더불어 보수가 좋기로 유명하다.

일부 도시의 Ropavieja 지점에서는 4월 매주 수요일 저녁 지역 관리자들이 진행하는 설명회도 개최할 것이다.(183)/(185) 참석자들은 개별 인터뷰를 통해 회사에 관해 질문하고 채용 기회에 대해 이야기할 기회를 얻게 된다. 설명회 자리를 예약하려면, 3월 22일까지 recruit@ropavieja.com으로 이메일을 보내야 한다.(183) 전체 구인 목록을 보려면, www.ropavieja.com을 방문하면 된다.

Ropavieja는 20년 전 Tucson 시내의 작은 상점으로 시작했다. 현재는 북미 전역에 지점이 있으며 앞으로 몇 주 이내 캘리포니아 El Centro에 하나를 더 오픈할 예정이다.(182)

어휘 press release 보도자료 launch v. 시작[개시]하다 recruitment drive 신입사원 모집 in hopes of ~를 희망하여 place v. 배치하다, 놓다 branch n. 지점 retail n. 소매 compensation n. 보수, 보상(금) tuition n. 수업(료) assistance n. 지원 daycare n. 보육 select adj. 엄선된 regional adj. 지역의, 지방의 spot n. 장소, 자리 job opening (직장의) 빈 자리, 구인 start out (사업을) 시작하다 be set to do ~할 예정이다

수신: Steve Henry <shenry@bkmail.com>
발신: Brad Narukawa <narukawa@ropavieja.com>
제목: 세부사항
날짜: 4월 10일

Mr. Henry께,

지난주 수요일 저녁에 만나서 반가웠습니다.(185) 그날의 만남을 토대로, 다시 만나서 남부 캘리포니아에서 영업 부장으로 일할 가능성에 관해 논의하고 싶습니다. 저희 영업 담당 이사인 Letty Cantu도 면접에 참석하실 겁니다.

4월 12일 오후에 시간 괜찮으신가요?(184) (505) 555-1212로 저에게 전화 주셔서 확인해 주세요.

Best regards,

Brad Narukawa(185)

어휘 based on ~을 토대로, ~에 근거하여 opportunity n. 기회 free adj. 다른 계획[약속]이 없는 confirm v. 확인해주다

181 상세정보 난이도 중

해석 보도자료에 따르면, Ropavieja Retailers는 곧 무엇을 시작할 것인가?
(A) 신제품 홍보
(B) 대규모 채용 활동
(C) 회사 합병
(D) 이사회 선거

| 해설 | 첫 번째 지문[보도자료], 첫 번째 단락에서 Ropavieja Retailers announced that next week, they will launch a spring recruitment drive in hopes of placing 700 new employees in its 80 branches by June 1.(Ropavieja Retailers는 6월 1일까지 80개의 지점에 700명의 신입직원을 배치하기를 희망하며 다음 주에 춘계 신입 채용을 시작한다고 밝혔다.)라고 했으므로 (B)가 정답 |

Paraphrasing launch ➡ begin,
           recruitment drive ➡ hiring campaign

182 암시/추론 난이도 중

해설 Ropavieja Retailers에 관하여 알 수 있는 것은?
(A) 회장이 사임할 것이다.
(B) 예산이 삭감될 것이다.
(C) 최초 매장이 캘리포니아에 있다.
(D) 사업이 성장하고 있다.

해설 첫 번째 지문[보도자료], 세 번째 단락에서 These days, it has branches all over North America, and is set to open one more in El Centro, California, in the coming weeks.(현재는 북미 전역에 지점이 있으며 앞으로 몇 주 이내 캘리포니아 El Centro에 하나를 더 오픈할 예정이다.)라고 했으므로 (D)가 정답

183 상세정보 난이도 중

해설 수요일 저녁 행사에 관심 있는 사람들은 무엇을 해야 하는가?
(A) 예약을 해야 한다
(B) 양식을 다운로드해야 한다
(C) 회사 본사를 방문해야 한다
(D) 교육에 관한 정보를 조사해야 한다

해설 첫 번째 지문[보도자료], 두 번째 단락에서 Ropavieja branches in select cities will also hold information sessions, led by regional managers, on every Wednesday evening of April.(일부 도시의 Ropavieja 지점에서는 4월 매주 수요일 저녁 지역 관리자들이 진행하는 설명회도 개최할 것이다.)라고 하면서 To reserve a spot for a session, send an e-mail to recruit@ropavieja.com by March 22.(설명회 자리를 예약하려면, 3월 22일까지 recruit@ropavieja.com으로 이메일을 보내야 한다.)라고 했으므로 (A)가 정답

184 주제/목적/대상 난이도 중

해설 이메일의 목적은 무엇인가?
(A) 신규 서비스를 홍보하는 것
(B) 프로젝트 일정을 논의하는 것
(C) 곧 있을 할인 행사를 알리는 것
(D) 시간 약속을 잡는 것

해설 두 번째 지문[이메일], 두 번째 단락에서 Are you free on April 12 in the afternoon?(4월 12일 오후에 시간 괜찮으신가요?)라고 했으므로 (D)가 정답

185 암시/추론 [연계문제] 난이도 상

해설 Brad Narukawa에 관하여 알 수 있는 것은?
(A) El Centro에서 태어났다.
(B) 최근에 Ropavieja Retailers에 채용되었다.
(C) 지역 관리자이다.
(D) 신규 지점으로 옮겨갈 것이다.

| 해설 | 첫 번째 지문[보도자료], 두 번째 단락에서 Ropavieja branches in select cities will also hold information sessions, led by regional managers, on every Wednesday evening of April.(일부 도시의 Ropavieja 지점에서는 4월 매주 수요일 저녁 지역 관리자들이 진행하는 설명회도 개최할 것이다.)라고 했는데, 두 번째 지문[Brad Narukawa가 보낸 이메일], 첫 번째 단락에서 It was nice meeting you last Wednesday night.(지난 주 수요일 저녁에 만나서 반가웠습니다.)라고 하여 그가 수요일 저녁 설명회를 진행한 지사장임을 알 수 있으므로 (C)가 정답 |

186-190번은 다음 공지, 기사, 이메일에 관한 문제입니다.

Bradbury 미술관 관람객 여러분께:

Pioneer시에서 41번가에 보수작업을 하는 동안 때때로 미술관 출입구가 폐쇄됩니다. 안타깝게도, 이는 미술관이 가끔 문을 닫아야 함을 의미합니다.(186) 이 일정에 관한 가장 최신 정보를 보시려면 미술관 웹 사이트를 방문해 주세요.

시내에는 현대사 박물관이나 우표 박물관 같은 다른 박물관들이 있음을 기억해주시기 바랍니다. 보수작업은 7월 31일까지 완료될 예정입니다.(187) 이 일로 인해 발생할 혼란에 대해 사과 드립니다.

어휘 patron n. 고객 from time to time 가끔, 때때로 entrance n. 출입구 block v. 막다 up-to-date adj. 최신의 disruption n. 혼란, 중단 cause v. 야기하다

Pioneer시 Observer

(9월 2일)— 8월말까지 이어진 거의 두 달에 걸친 보수작업 끝에, 41번가 공사가 드디어 완료되었다.(187) Bradbury 미술관은 이 기간 동안 방문객 수의 상당한 감소를 겪었기에, 마침내 한숨 돌릴 수 있게 되었다. 미술관은 정상 일정을 재개하는 것 외에, 새로 추가된 시설도 곧 공개할 것이다. 시의회의 자금 지원 덕분에, 미술관은 마침내 라이브 콘서트 및 공연용 무대를 갖춘, 경치가 좋은 안뜰을 제작하는 자체 건설 프로젝트를 마무리 지을 수 있었다.(188)

Bradbury 미술관은 축하행사로 10월 20일에 새 뜰에서 무료 음악 축제를 주최한다. 출연이 예정된 공연그룹에는 Charles Liou의 재즈 메신저와 색소폰 연주자 Ann Sandman이 포함된다. 모든 참석자는 경품추첨 행사에 응모된다.(189)

날씨가 좋지 않을 경우, 행사는 10월 22일로 옮겨질 수 있다.(190) 추가 세부사항은 www.bradburymuseum.org/events에서 확인할 수 있다.

어휘 carry over 이어지다 breathe easy 안심하다 significantly adv. 상당히 resume v. 재개하다 unveil v. 공개하다 funding n. 자금(지원) scenic adj. 경치가 좋은 courtyard n. 뜰[마당] reserve v. (자리 등을) 따로 잡아두다, 예약하다 host v. 주최하다 act n. 공연자[그룹] raffle n. (경품) 추첨 inclement adj. (날씨가) 궂은

발신: terrygreen@bradburymuseum.org
수신: charlesliou@messengers.net
제목: 축하합니다.
날짜: 10월 23일(190)

Mr. Liou께,

어제 오후의 공연에 대해 감사 드리고 싶었어요.⁽¹⁹⁰⁾ 날씨가 개어서 시민들이 당신 밴드의 훌륭한 공연을 들을 수 있어 다행입니다. 그렇게 열광적인 관객들을 볼 수 있어 너무 좋았습니다. 제가 아는 사람들은 모두 아직도 그 공연 얘기를 하고 있어요!

곧 Pioneer시에 다시 와주세요.

Best,

Terry Green

어휘 clear up 날씨가 개다 performance n. 공연 enthusiastic adj. 열광적인 crowd n. 군중, 무리

---

186 주제/목적/대상 　　　　　　　　　　난이도 **중**

해석 공지는 주로 무엇에 관한 것인가?
(A) 곧 있을 건물 폐쇄
(B) 인상된 회비
(C) 박물관 일자리
(D) 고객 서비스 정책

해설 첫 번째 지문[공지], 첫 번째 단락에서 From time to time, during Pioneer City's upcoming renovations on 41st Street, the museum's entrance will be blocked. Unfortunately, this means that the museum will sometimes have to close.(Pioneer시에서 41번가에 보수작업을 하는 동안 때때로 미술관 출입구가 폐쇄됩니다. 안타깝게도, 이는 미술관이 가끔 문을 닫아야 함을 의미합니다.)라고 했으므로 (A)가 정답

---

187 암시/추론 [연계문제] 　　　　　　　난이도 **상**

해석 도로 보수 프로젝트에 관하여 알 수 있는 것은?
(A) 8월에 시작되었다.
(B) 추가 자금이 필요했다.
(C) Mr. Green이 감독했다.
(D) 예상보다 오래 걸렸다.

해설 첫 번째 지문[공지], 두 번째 단락에서 The renovations are expected to be completed by July 31.(보수작업은 7월 31일까지 완료될 예정입니다.)라고 했는데, 두 번째 지문[기사], 첫 번째 단락에서 After nearly two months of renovations that carried over until late August, work on 41st Street has finally finished.(8월말까지 이어진 거의 두 달에 걸친 보수작업 끝에, 41번가 공사가 드디어 완료되었다.)라고 하여 공사가 예정보다 한 달 더 걸렸음을 알 수 있으므로 (D)가 정답

---

188 상세정보 　　　　　　　　　　　　난이도 **중**

해석 기사에 따르면, 박물관에 무엇이 건설되었는가?
(A) 주차장
(B) 오락 공간
(C) 기념품점
(D) 실내 극장

해설 두 번째 지문[기사], 첫 번째 단락에서 the museum was finally able to finish its own construction project of a scenic court that has a stage reserved for live concerts and shows.(미술관은 마침내 라이브 콘서트 및 공연용 무대를 갖춘, 경치가 좋은 안뜰을 제작하는 자체 건설 프로젝트를 마무리 지을 수 있었다.)라고 했으므로 (B)가 정답

---

189 상세정보 　　　　　　　　　　　　난이도 **중**

해석 기사에서 축제의 특징으로 무엇이 언급하는가?
(A) 시식 행사
(B) 신규 미술 전시회
(C) 경품 추첨
(D) 경매

해설 두 번째 지문[기사], 두 번째 단락에서 All attendees will be entered into a raffle for gifts.(모든 참석자는 경품 추첨 행사에 응모된다.)라고 했으므로 (C)가 정답

Paraphrasing a raffle for gifts ➡ a prize drawing

---

190 암시/추론 [연계문제] 　　　　　　　난이도 **상**

해석 축제에 관하여 알 수 있는 것은?
(A) 연기되었다.
(B) 지역 주민들에게만 개방되었다.
(C) 매년 열릴 것이다.
(D) 많은 참석자들을 유치하지 못했다.

해설 두 번째 지문[기사], 세 번째 단락에서 In the event of inclement weather, the event may be rescheduled for October 22.(날씨가 좋지 않을 경우, 행사는 10월 22일로 옮겨질 수 있다.)라고 했는데, 세 번째 지문[10월 23일에 발송된 이메일], 첫 번째 단락에서 I just wanted to thank you for your performance yesterday afternoon.(어제 오후의 공연에 대해 감사 드리고 싶었어요.)라고 하여 10월 22일로 행사가 연기되었음을 알 수 있으므로 (A)가 정답

Paraphrasing rescheduled ➡ postponed

191-195번은 다음 기사, 이메일, 온라인 후기에 관한 문제입니다.

Sherbrooke 신문

3월 9일 – Rue Papineau와 Rue Eymard 사이 Sherbrooke 시내에 새로운 아이스링크장이 건립 중이다.⁽¹⁹¹⁾ Leopold 경기장 건설은 6개월 전에 시작되었다. 프랑스 회사 Ayoub의 Quebec 지사에서 근무하는 Steven Fontaine이 경기장의 독특한 설계의 지휘자이다.

Ayoub는 북미와 서유럽에서 스포츠 복합단지를 만들어왔다. **Ayoub의 CEO인 Jean-Baptiste Charpentier는 링크장 공사가 지연될 수 있다는 우려 때문에, Leopold 경기장이 Bantam Sherbrooke 국제 하키 대회를 주최할 수 있게 제때에 완공되면,⁽¹⁹⁴⁾ 모든 캐나다 직원들에게 현금 인센티브를 준다고 제안했다.⁽¹⁹³⁾** 대회는 내년 1월 말로 예정되어 있다.

새로운 경기장의 건립을 지지하는 사람들은 그것이 지역 경제에 매우 필요한 부양책이 될 것이라고 믿는다.⁽¹⁹²⁾ Ayoub는 시설 건립을 돕기 위해 100명이 넘는 Sherbrooke 주민을 고용하고 있다. 또한 시의원 Yvette Sevigny는 아이스하키가 장기적인 수입원이 될 것이라고 언급한다. 티켓 판매뿐만 아니라, 팬들이 Sherbrooke에서 음식과 숙박, 기념품 등을 구매할 때 지역 사업체들도 분명 이득을 볼 것이다.

어휘 gazette n. 관보 mastermind n. 지휘[조종]하는 사람 sports complex 체육관, 종합운동장 run into (곤경 등을) 만나다, 겪다 tournament n. 시합, 대회 back v. 지지[후원]하다 creation n. 창조, 창작(품) area n. 지역, 구역 boost n. 부양책, 격려 employ v. 고용하다 facility n. 시설 councilor n. (시의회 등의) 의원 point out 언급하다, 지적하다 long-term adj. 장기적인 revenue source 수입원 benefit v. 득을 보다 lodging n. 임시 숙소, 하숙 souvenir n. 기념품

수신: Steven Fontaine <fontaine@ayoub.ca>
발신: David Harrachi <harrachi@ayoub.fr>
날짜: 1월 12일
제목: 새로운 소식

안녕하세요, Steven.

큰 대회에 맞춰 Leopold 경기장을 준비하신 것에 축하의 말씀 짧게 드립니다. 모든 캐나다 직원들도 Mr. Charpentier만큼 기뻐할 것이라 확신합니다.**(193)/(194)** 그는 당신이 다음 번 회사 본사를 방문할 때 다시 만나기를 기대하고 있습니다.

Sincerely,

David Harrachi
비서실장

어휘 note n. 편지, 쪽지 delighted adj. 아주 기쁜 corporate adj. 기업의 headquarters n. 본사

---

www.quebecstays.ca/reviews_hotels_sherbrooke

후기 → Sherbrooke의 호텔들

Caméléon 호텔
2월 19일, Armand Boucher 작성**(194)**

제가 가장 좋아하는 하키팀이 Bantam Sherbrooke 국제 대회에서 결승에 진출해서, 저는 당연히 이곳에 와서 응원해야 했습니다.**(194)** 정말 흥미진진한 시간이었습니다!

Caméléon 호텔은 경기를 보러 지역에 온 모든 하키팬들을 따뜻하게 맞아주었으며, 나중에 축하자리도 훌륭했습니다. 특히 호텔 식당에서 대회 마지막 날 저녁에 마련해준 특별 '승리 만찬'에 감명받았습니다.**(195)** 저희는 하키 시합을 보러 온 것이었지만, 솔직히 그 음식만 다시 먹기 위해서라도 Sherbrooke은 다시 올 만한 가치가 있습니다. 붐비는 쇼핑 및 유흥가 바로 옆에 위치해서, 약간 시끄럽기는 합니다. 그러나 전체적으로 Caméléon 호텔은 투숙하기 매우 좋은 곳이었기에, 저는 강력히 추천합니다.

어휘 make it to ~에 이르다 final n. 결승전 cheer on ~을 응원하다 welcoming adj. (방문객에게) 따뜻한 afterwards adv. 나중에 impressed with ~에 감명받은 honestly adv. 솔직히 locate v. (특정 위치에) 두다 entertainment n. 오락 district n. 지역, 구역 overall adv. 전반적으로

---

191 주제/목적/대상   난이도 중

해석 기사는 왜 작성되었는가?
(A) 건설 회사들을 비교하기 위해
(B) 관광객 수의 감소를 논하기 위해
(C) 건축 프로젝트를 소개하기 위해
(D) 임대용 부동산을 광고하기 위해

해설 첫 번째 지문[기사], 첫 번째 단락에서 A new skating rink is being created in downtown Sherbrooke between Rue Papineau and Rue Eymard.(Rue Papineau와 Rue Eymard 사이 Sherbrooke 시내에 새로운 아이스링크장이 건립 중이다.)고 했으므로 (C)가 정답

192 동의어   난이도 중

해석 기사에서 세 번째 단락, 첫 번째 줄의 단어 "back"과 의미상 가장 가까운 것은?
(A) 뒤집다
(B) 지지하다
(C) 돕다
(D) 돌리다

해설 첫 번째 지문[기사], 세 번째 단락의 People who back the creation of the new arena believe that it will give the area's economy a much-needed boost.(신규 경기장의 건립을 지지하는 사람들은 그것이 지역 경제에 매우 필요한 부양책을 가져다 줄 것이라고 믿는다.)에서 'back'은 '지지하다'라는 의미로 쓰였으므로 보기 중 같은 의미를 갖는 (B)가 정답

193 암시/추론 [연계문제]   난이도 상

해석 이메일에서 알 수 있는 것은?
(A) 캐나다에 있는 직원들이 보너스를 받을 것이다.
(B) Mr. Charpentier가 Quebec 지역을 방문할 것이다.
(C) Ayoub가 몇몇 하키 선수들을 후원할 것이다.
(D) Mr. Fontaine이 승진을 제안 받을 것이다.

해설 첫 번째 지문[기사], 두 번째 단락에서 Because of concerns that construction of the rink would run into delays, Ayoub CEO Jean-Baptiste Charpentier has offered a cash incentive to all Canadian staff if Leopold Arena is finished in time to host the Bantam Sherbrooke International Hockey Tournament.(Ayoub의 CEO인 Jean-Baptiste Charpentier는 링크장 공사가 지연될 수 있다는 우려때문에, Leopold 경기장이 Bantam Sherbrooke 국제 하키 대회를 주최할 수 있게 제때에 완공되면, 모든 캐나다 직원들에게 현금 인센티브를 준다고 제안했다.)라고 했는데, 두 번째 지문[이메일], 첫 번째 단락에서 Just a quick note to congratulate you on having Leopold Arena ready for the big tournament. I'm sure all the Canadian staff are delighted.(큰 대회에 맞춰 Leopold 경기장을 준비하신 것에 축하의 말씀 짧게 드립니다. 모든 캐나다 직원들도 Mr. Charpentier만큼 기뻐할 것이라 확신합니다.)라고 하여 캐나다 직원들이 현금 인센티브를 받을 것임을 알 수 있으므로 (A)가 정답

Paraphrasing a cash incentive ➡ a bonus

TEST 01

| 194 | 암시/추론 [연계문제] | 난이도 상 |

해석 Armand Boucher에 관하여 무엇이 사실이겠는가?
(A) Mr. Charpentier를 안다.
(B) Sherbrooke 인근에서 근무한다.
(C) **Leopold 경기장을 방문했다.**
(D) 프로 운동선수였다.

해설 세 번째 지문[Armand Boucher가 작성한 온라인 후기], 첫 번째 단락에서 My favorite hockey team made it to the finals at the Bantam Sherbrooke International Tournament, so of course, I had to come here and cheer them on.(제가 가장 좋아하는 하키팀이 Bantam Sherbrooke 국제대회에서 결승에 진출해서, 저는 당연히 이곳에 와서 응원해야 했습니다.)라고 했는데, 첫 번째 지문[기사], 두 번째 단락에서 if Leopold Arena is finished in time to host the Bantam Sherbrooke International Hockey Tournament(Leopold 경기장이 Bantam Sherbrooke 국제하키대회를 주최할 수 있게 제때에 완공될 경우)라고 했고, 두 번째 지문[이메일]에서 Just a quick note to congratulate you on having Leopold Arena ready for the big tournament.(큰 대회에 맞춰 Leopold 경기장을 준비하신 것에 축하의 말씀 짧게 드립니다.)라고 하여 그가 Bantam Sherbrooke 국제 대회가 열린 Leopold 경기장을 방문했음을 알 수 있으므로 (C)가 정답

| 195 | 상세정보 | 난이도 중 |

해석 Mr. Boucher는 Caméléon 호텔의 무엇을 특히 마음에 들어 했는가?
(A) 운동 시설
(B) 널찍한 방
(C) 기념품 가게
(D) **저녁 식사**

해설 세 번째 지문[Armand Boucher가 작성한 온라인 후기], 두 번째 단락에서 I was especially impressed with the special "victory dinner" that the hotel's restaurant prepared on the last night of the tournament.(특히 호텔 식당에서 대회 마지막 날 저녁에 마련해준 특별 '승리 만찬'에 감명받았습니다.)라고 했으므로 (D)가 정답

Paraphrasing dinner ➡ evening meal

196-200번은 다음 이메일, 전단지, 일정표에 관한 문제입니다.

날짜: 4월 30일(197)
발신: Julian Kojima <julian@maddux.com>
수신: Christine Walters<christine@maddux.com>
제목: 팀워크 행사

Christine께,

잘하고 계시리라 믿습니다. 처음에는 모든걸 다 따라가는 게 다소 힘들 수 있지만, 곧 익숙해지실 거라 믿습니다. 매년 이맘 때 저희 관리팀 직원이 전사 차원의 행사를 준비합니다.(196) 2월 면접 때 이 이야기를 나눈 걸로 알고 있어요.(196)/(197) 지난 몇 년간, 저희는 축구경기를 보러 갔었고, 국립 공원에서 등산을 한 적도 있어요. 업무 외적으로 서로를 알게 되는 좋은 기회입니다.

올해는 콘서트에 가면 좋을 것 같아요. 많은 직원들이 음악 광팬이고 Leeper Pavilion에서 열리는 야외 콘서트 시리즈에 관해 이야기해 왔어요. 평일에 하는 콘서트여야 할 거고, 재즈 공연이어야 해요.(200) 우리는 올해 예산으로 400달러가 있어요. 그리고 가격을 훑어보니, 전 직원에게 티켓을 제공하기에 충분할 거 같아요.(199)

도움이 필요하면, Scott이 당신을 도와줄 수 있어요. 그가 예전에 행사 준비하는 걸 도왔었거든요.(196)

Regards,

Julian Kojima
Maddux Industries 사장

어휘 rather adv. 상당히, 다소 challenging adj. 힘든, 도전적인 keep track of ~를 계속 파악하고 있다 get the hang of it 요령을 알다, 익숙해지다 administrative adj. 관리의, 행정의 coordinator n. 진행자 organize v. 조직하다, 준비하다 company-wide adj. 회사 전반의 hike n. 하이킹, 도보여행 outdoor adj. 야외의 pavilion n. 공연장 weekday n. 평일 budget v. 예산을 세우다 pricing n. 가격 책정 sufficient adj. 충분한

<Leeper Pavilion에서 기억에 남을 저녁시간을 함께 하세요>

단체의 경우 콘서트 티켓을 할인가에 구입할 수 있습니다. 12장 이상 구입 시 할인이 시작되고, 많으면 많을수록 좋습니다!(198) 보너스로, 귀하의 단체에게는 조기입장과 무료 다과가 제공되며, 무대 뒤에서 연주자들을 만날 수 있는 VIP 입장권을 받을 수 있는 콘테스트에 응모됩니다.

단체 요금
- 12매 240달러
- 25매 375달러(199)
- 50매 650달러
- 100매 1,200달러

문의사항이 있으시면, 219-555-5040으로 전화나 문자주세요.

어휘 available adj. 구할 수 있는 reduced adj. 할인한 rate n. 요금 saving n. 절약 merry adj. 즐거운 admit v. 입장을 허락하다 venue n. 장소 complimentary adj. 무료의 refreshment n. 다과 access n. 입장 backstage adj. 무대 뒤의

Leeper Pavilion의 봄
5월 콘서트 일정표

연주자	날짜	요일	장르	시간
Merrion-Clark 앙상블	5월 11일	토요일	재즈	오후 4시 30분
Hill Street Seven	5월 16일(200)	목요일(200)	재즈(200)	오후 7시
Marcia Barton 5중주	5월 26일	일요일	클래식	오후 2시
Elkhart 교향악단	5월 29일	수요일	클래식	오후 8시

티켓은 현재 www.leeperpavilion.gov/concertseries에서 구입할 수 있습니다.

어휘 springtime n. 봄철 performer n. 연주자 ensemble n. 합주단, 앙상블 quintet n. 5중 주단 philharmonic n. 교향악단 on sale 판매 중인

196 주제/목적/대상   난이도 중

해석 Ms. Walters에게 이메일을 보낸 주된 이유는 무엇인가?
(A) 그녀를 팀워크 하이킹에 초대하려고
(B) 새로운 파일링 프로토콜을 소개하려고
(C) 그녀에게 행사 준비를 지시하려고
(D) 그녀에게 곧 있을 휴가를 알려주려고

해설 첫 번째 지문[이메일], 첫 번째 단락에서 Every year, around this time, our administrative coordinator organizes a company-wide event. I believe we discussed it when you interviewed in February.(매년 이맘때 저희 관리팀 직원이 전사 차원의 행사를 준비합니다. 2월 면접 때 이 이야기를 나눴던 걸로 알고 있어요.)라고 하며, 세 번째 단락에서 If you need any help, Scott can help you with this. He has helped organize the event in the past.(도움이 필요하면, Scott이 당신을 도와줄 수 있어요. 그가 예전에 행사 준비하는 걸 도왔었거든요.)라고 했으므로 (C)가 정답

Paraphrasing organize a event ➡ arrange an outing

197 암시/추론   난이도 중

해석 이메일은 Ms. Walters에 관하여 무엇을 암시하는가?
(A) Maddux에 최근 고용되었다.
(B) 신규 프로젝트 착수를 위해 이전할 것이다.
(C) Leeper Pavilion에서 하는 공연을 본 적이 있다.
(D) 재즈 음악팬이다.

해설 첫 번째 지문[Ms. Walters에게 보낸 이메일], 첫 번째 단락에서 I believe we discussed it when you interviewed in February.(2월 면접 때 이 이야기를 나눴던 걸로 알고 있어요.)라고 했는데, 이메일 발송 날짜가 4월 30일인 걸로 미루어 Ms. Walters가 최근 입사했다는 것을 알 수 있으므로 (A)가 정답

198 상세정보   난이도 중

해석 전단지에 따르면, 티켓 대량 구입의 장점은 무엇인가?
(A) 더 낮은 티켓 가격
(B) VIP석
(C) 매점 할인
(D) 선물 가방

해설 두 번째 지문[전단지], 첫 번째 단락에서 Concert tickets are available at reduced rates for large groups. Savings start when you buy 12 or more, and the more, the merrier!(단체의 경우 콘서트 티켓을 할인가에 구입할 수 있습니다. 12장 이상 구입 시 할인이 시작되고, 많으면 많을수록 좋습니다!)라고 했으므로 (A)가 정답

Paraphrasing reduced rates ➡ lower prices

199 암시/추론 [연계문제]   난이도 중

해석 Maddux Industries의 직원 수는 몇 명이겠는가?
(A) 12
(B) 25
(C) 50
(D) 100

해설 첫 번째 지문[이메일], 두 번째 단락에서 We have $400 budgeted for this year. And, after a quick look at the pricing, it looks like that will be sufficient to get every employee a ticket.(우리는 올해 예산으로 400달러가 있어요. 그리고 가격을 훑어보니, 전 직원에게 티켓을 제공하기에 충분할 것 같아요.)라고 했는데, 두 번째 지문[전단지], 두 번째 단락[Group Rates(단체요금)]에서 25 tickets for $375(25매 375달러)라고 하여 Maddux Industries의 직원 수가 25명임을 알 수 있으므로 (B)가 정답

200 상세정보 [연계문제]   난이도 중

해석 Maddux Industries은 몇 일에 행사를 개최할 것인가?
(A) 5월 11일
(B) 5월 16일
(C) 5월 26일
(D) 5월 29일

해설 첫 번째 지문[이메일], 두 번째 단락에서 It would need to be a concert on a weekday, and it should be a jazz show.(평일에 하는 콘서트여야 할 거고, 재즈공연이어야 해요.)라고 했는데, 세 번째 지문[일정표]에서 평일에 하는 재즈공연이 May 16(5월 16일) 공연임을 알 수 있으므로 (B)가 정답

TEST 02

PART 1 — P. 60
1 (A) 2 (D) 3 (A) 4 (B) 5 (D) 6 (C)

PART 2 — P. 64
7 (A) 8 (A) 9 (C) 10 (B) 11 (B) 12 (A)
13 (C) 14 (B) 15 (A) 16 (A) 17 (A) 18 (A)
19 (A) 20 (C) 21 (A) 22 (C) 23 (C) 24 (B)
25 (B) 26 (B) 27 (C) 28 (B) 29 (B) 30 (C)
31 (A)

PART 3 — P. 65
32 (A) 33 (B) 34 (B) 35 (A) 36 (D) 37 (C)
38 (D) 39 (B) 40 (A) 41 (C) 42 (A) 43 (C)
44 (D) 45 (B) 46 (A) 47 (A) 48 (A) 49 (D)
50 (D) 51 (D) 52 (B) 53 (C) 54 (D) 55 (D)
56 (A) 57 (D) 58 (A) 59 (B) 60 (A) 61 (D)
62 (C) 63 (A) 64 (B) 65 (C) 66 (C) 67 (C)
68 (B) 69 (A) 70 (D)

PART 4 — P. 69
71 (B) 72 (D) 73 (B) 74 (B) 75 (D) 76 (C)
77 (B) 78 (A) 79 (C) 80 (B) 81 (B) 82 (D)
83 (B) 84 (D) 85 (A) 86 (A) 87 (B) 88 (B)
89 (B) 90 (B) 91 (A) 92 (A) 93 (B) 94 (C)
95 (A) 96 (B) 97 (D) 98 (D) 99 (C) 100 (C)

PART 5 — P. 72
101 (B) 102 (B) 103 (C) 104 (D) 105 (C) 106 (C)
107 (B) 108 (C) 109 (C) 110 (A) 111 (D) 112 (A)
113 (B) 114 (A) 115 (C) 116 (A) 117 (D) 118 (C)
119 (D) 120 (B) 121 (D) 122 (C) 123 (C) 124 (B)
125 (B) 126 (C) 127 (C) 128 (B) 129 (C) 130 (D)

PART 6 — P. 75
131 (A) 132 (C) 133 (C) 134 (D) 135 (B) 136 (A)
137 (D) 138 (D) 139 (A) 140 (B) 141 (D) 142 (D)
143 (D) 144 (A) 145 (B) 146 (B)

PART 7 — P. 79
147 (A) 148 (D) 149 (A) 150 (B) 151 (A) 152 (D)
153 (C) 154 (A) 155 (C) 156 (D) 157 (A) 158 (C)
159 (B) 160 (D) 161 (C) 162 (B) 163 (A) 164 (C)
165 (A) 166 (B) 167 (C) 168 (B) 169 (B) 170 (B)
171 (C) 172 (D) 173 (D) 174 (A) 175 (C) 176 (D)
177 (A) 178 (B) 179 (C) 180 (A) 181 (D) 182 (C)
183 (D) 184 (A) 185 (D) 186 (A) 187 (D) 188 (C)
189 (D) 190 (C) 191 (B) 192 (C) 193 (C) 194 (D)
195 (D) 196 (B) 197 (D) 198 (D) 199 (B) 200 (C)

PART 1 — P. 60

1 1인 중심 난이도 하

미국

(A) A man is looking at a file.
(B) A man is shutting a cabinet drawer.
(C) A man is pointing at a picture frame.
(D) A man is turning on a desk lamp.

(A) 남자가 파일을 보고 있다.
(B) 남자가 캐비닛 서랍을 닫고 있다.
(C) 남자가 액자를 가리키고 있다.
(D) 남자가 탁상용 스탠드를 켜고 있다.

해설 (A) ⭕ 남자가 파일을 보고 있는 모습을 적절히 묘사했으므로 정답
(B) ✖ 동작 묘사 오류 (is shutting)
(C) ✖ 동작 묘사 오류 (is pointing at)
(D) ✖ 동작 묘사 오류 (is turning on)

Possible Answer
A file is being examined. 파일이 검토되고 있다.

어휘 shut v. 닫다 picture frame 액자 turn on (전기 등을) 켜다 examine v. 검토하다

2 2인 이상 난이도 중

영국

(A) A woman is repairing a wheel.
(B) A man is unzipping his backpack.
(C) They are locking up their bicycles.
(D) They are wearing helmets.

(A) 여자가 바퀴를 수리하고 있다.
(B) 남자가 배낭의 지퍼를 열고 있다.
(C) 사람들이 자전거에 자물쇠를 채우고 있다.
(D) 사람들이 헬멧을 쓰고 있다.

해설 (A) ✖ 동작 묘사 오류 (is repairing)
(B) ✖ 동작 묘사 오류 (is unzipping)
(C) ✖ 동작 묘사 오류 (are locking up)
(D) ⭕ 사람들이 헬멧을 착용한 모습을 적절히 묘사했으므로 정답

Possible Answer
They are cycling on a path. 사람들이 길에서 자전거를 타고 있다.

어휘 unzip v. 지퍼를 열다 lock up 자물쇠를 채우다 wear v. 입고 있다, 착용하고 있다

3   1인 중심   난이도 중

미국

(A) Some supplies have been left on a kitchen floor.
(B) Some rags are being washed in a sink.
(C) A man is adjusting the temperature of an oven.
(D) Some cupboard doors are being opened.

(A) 몇몇 물건들이 주방 바닥에 놓여져 있다.
(B) 싱크대에서 행주가 빨리고 있다.
(C) 남자가 오븐의 온도를 조절하고 있다.
(D) 몇몇 찬장 문들이 열리고 있다.

해설 (A) ⭕ 주방 바닥에 청소용 도구들이 놓여 있는 모습을 적절히 묘사했으므로 정답
(B) ❌ 동작 묘사 오류 (are being washed), 사진에 없는 사물 (sink)
(C) ❌ 동작 묘사 오류 (is adjusting)
(D) ❌ 동작 묘사 오류 (are being opened)

Possible Answer
A kitchen appliance is being polished. 주방 기구가 닦이고 있다.

어휘 supplies n. 물품, 비품 be left 남겨져 있다 rag n. 걸레, 행주 adjust v. 조절하다 temperature n. 온도 cupboard n. 찬장

4   1인 중심   난이도 중

호주

(A) A woman is reaching into her bag.
(B) A woman is holding onto a railing.
(C) The walkway is closed for maintenance.
(D) The staircase is being constructed.

(A) 여자가 가방 안에 손을 넣고 있다.
(B) 여자가 난간을 꼭 잡고 있다.
(C) 보도가 보수공사로 폐쇄되어 있다.
(D) 계단이 지어지고 있다.

해설 (A) ❌ 동작 묘사 오류 (is reaching into)
(B) ⭕ 여자가 난간을 잡고 있는 모습을 적절히 묘사했으므로 정답
(C) ❌ 사진에 없는 사물 (the walkway)
(D) ❌ 상태 묘사 오류 (is being constructed)

Possible Answer
A woman is climbing up some stairs. 여자가 계단을 오르고 있다.

어휘 reach into ~안에 손을 넣다 hold onto ~를 꼭 잡다 walkway n. 보도 maintenance n. 보수 관리 staircase n. 계단 construct v. 건설하다

5   1인 중심   난이도 중

미국

(A) A man is writing on a clipboard with a pen.
(B) A man is pushing a cart in a factory.
(C) A man is placing an item on a display shelf.
(D) A man is pressing a button on a panel.

(A) 남자가 펜으로 클립보드에 쓰고 있다.
(B) 남자가 공장에서 카트를 밀고 있다.
(C) 남자가 진열칸에 물건을 놓고 있다.
(D) 남자가 패널에 있는 버튼을 누르고 있다.

해설 (A) ❌ 동작 묘사 오류 (is writing)
(B) ❌ 사진에 없는 사물 (cart)
(C) ❌ 동작 묘사 오류 (is placing), 사진에 없는 사물 (display shelf)
(D) ⭕ 남자가 버튼을 누르고 있는 모습을 적절히 묘사했으므로 정답

Possible Answer
He's operating a control panel. 남자가 제어판을 조작하고 있다.

어휘 clipboard n. 클립보드 (종이를 끼울 수 있는 집게가 달린 판) cart n. 수레 panel n. (계기)판

6   사물/풍경   난이도 상

영국

(A) Some lights have been hung across a bridge.
(B) Some smoke is rising from the buildings.
(C) Some umbrellas have been set up at tables.
(D) Some boats are floating in a harbor.

(A) 몇몇 전등들이 다리를 가로질러 걸려 있다.
(B) 건물들에서 연기가 피어 오르고 있다.
(C) 몇몇 파라솔들이 테이블에 설치되어 있다.
(D) 항구에 몇몇 보트들이 떠 있다.

해설 (A) ❌ 위치 묘사 오류 (across a bridge)
(B) ❌ 사진에 없는 사물 (smoke)
(C) ⭕ 테이블들에 파라솔이 설치되어 있는 모습을 적절히 묘사했으므로 정답
(D) ❌ 사진에 없는 사물 (boats)

Possible Answer
A bridge extends over a waterway. 수로 위로 다리가 나 있다.

어휘 light n. 등, 전등 smoke n. 연기 rise v. 오르다 umbrella n. 파라솔; 우산 set up 설치하다 float v. 뜨다, 떠 있다 harbor n. 항구

PART 2

P. 64

7 What 의문문   난이도 하

미국↑↓영국

What brand of snacks should I get?
(A) You should get Hunter's Cookies.
(B) I don't remember getting it.
(C) No, that won't be necessary.

어느 브랜드의 스낵을 살까요?
(A) Hunter's Cookies를 한번 사 보세요.
(B) 그걸 산 기억이 없는데요.
(C) 아니요, 그러실 필요 없어요.

해설 (A) ◯ Hunter's Cookies를 사보라며 브랜드 종류로 말했으므로 정답
(B) ✗ 동어 반복 함정 (get – getting)
(C) ✗ 의문사 의문문 Yes/No 응답 불가
Possible Answer
The one with the best value. 가성비가 가장 좋은 거요.

어휘 remember v. 기억하다 value n. 가치

8 Where 의문문   난이도 하

미국↑↓호주

Where is the nearest public library?
(A) On Queens Road.
(B) I have to return a book.
(C) About once a week.

가장 가까운 공립 도서관이 어디에 있나요?
(A) Queens Road에요.
(B) 제가 책을 반납해야 해요.
(C) 일주일에 한 번 정도요.

해설 (A) ◯ Queens Road라며 장소로 말했으므로 정답
(B) ✗ 연상 어휘 함정 (library – book)
(C) ✗ How often에 어울리는 대답
Possible Answer
It's right around the corner. 모퉁이를 돌면 바로예요.

어휘 nearest adj. 가장 가까운 public library 공립 도서관 return v. 반납하다

9 제안/요청   난이도 중

호주↑↓미국

Please notify your team members about the anniversary dinner on Friday.
(A) For 35 years.
(B) The department head.
(C) I've already let them know.

팀원들에게 금요일에 있을 기념일 만찬에 대해 알려주세요.
(A) 35년 동안이요.
(B) 부서장이요.
(C) 제가 이미 알려줬어요.

해설 (A) ✗ 연상 어휘 함정 (anniversary – 35 years)
(B) ✗ 연상 어휘 함정 (team – department)
(C) ◯ 이미 알렸다며 질문에 적절히 말했으므로 정답
Possible Answer
Human Resources already sent out an e-mail. 인사부에서 이미 이메일을 보냈어요.

어휘 notify v. 알리다, 통지하다 anniversary dinner 기념일 만찬 department head 부서장

10 Who 의문문   난이도 중

영국↑↓미국

Who's going to drop Maria off at the train station?
(A) At platform 5.
(B) I'm planning to take her at 1 P.M.
(C) They're at a training session.

누가 Maria를 기차역에 내려줄 건가요?
(A) 5번 승강장에요.
(B) 제가 오후 1시에 그녀를 데려다 주려고 해요.
(C) 그들은 연수 중이에요.

해설 (A) ✗ 연상 어휘 함정 (train station – platform)
(B) ◯ 본인이 데려다 주려고 한다며 질문에 적절히 말했으므로 정답
(C) ✗ 유사 발음 함정 (train station – training session)
Possible Answer
She's taking a taxi. 그녀는 택시를 탈 거예요.

어휘 drop ~ off ~를 내려주다 platform n. 승강장 training session 연수

11 평서문   난이도 중

미국↑↓영국

You should take woodworking classes after work.
(A) Sorry, our classes are full.
(B) Yes, I'd love to pick up a new hobby.
(C) Well, I enjoy walking to the office.

퇴근 후에 목공 수업을 들어보세요.
(A) 죄송해요, 저희 수업이 마감됐네요.
(B) 네, 정말 새 취미를 만들고 싶어요.
(C) 음, 저는 사무실까지 걸어가는 걸 좋아해요.

해설 (A) ✗ 동어 반복 함정 (classes – classes)
(B) ◯ 'Yes'로 대답하고, 새로운 취미를 만들고 싶다며 질문에 적절하게 덧붙여 말했으므로 정답
(C) ✗ 유사 발음 함정 (woodworking – walking)
Possible Answer
Do you know where I can sign up? 제가 어디서 신청할 수 있는지 아세요?

어휘 woodworking n. 목공 pick up (재주를) 익히다 hobby n. 취미 sign up 등록하다

12 When 의문문   난이도 하

미국↑↓호주

When will we leave from the convention center?
(A) In an hour.
(B) We'll be at the arrival hall.
(C) The lectures were very informative.

컨벤션 센터에서 언제 출발하나요?
(A) 한 시간 뒤에요.
(B) 입국장에 있을게요.
(C) 강연은 아주 유익했어요.

해설 (A) ◯ 한 시간 뒤라며 시점으로 말했으므로 정답
(B) ✗ 연상 어휘 함정 (leave – arrival)
(C) ✗ 연상 어휘 함정 (convention – lectures)
Possible Answer
After Sandy Hall's lecture. Sandy Hall 강연이 끝나고요.

어휘 arrival hall 입국장 informative adj. 유익한

13 부가 의문문 난이도 중

We haven't sent out the attendance list yet, have we?
(A) For the awards ceremony.
(B) A list of corporate sponsors.
(C) Yes, we did.

우리가 아직 참석자 명단을 발송하지 않았죠, 그렇죠?
(A) 시상식용이요.
(B) 후원 업체 명단이요.
(C) 네, 이미 했어요.

해설 (A) ✗ 연상 어휘 함정 (attendance list – awards ceremony)
(B) ✗ 동어 반복 함정 (list – list)
(C) ○ 'Yes'라고 대답하고, 이미 했다며 적절히 덧붙여 말했으므로 정답

Possible Answer
Daniel's still working on it. Daniel이 아직 작업 중이에요.

어휘 send out ~을 보내다, 발송하다 attendance list 참석자 명단 awards ceremony 시상식 corporate adj. 기업의

14 How 의문문 난이도 중

How do you like your new apartment?
(A) Last Saturday.
(B) It has a nice view.
(C) The department office is downstairs.

새 아파트는 어떠세요?
(A) 지난 토요일이요.
(B) 전망이 좋아요.
(C) 부서 사무실은 아래층에 있어요.

해설 (A) ✗ When에 어울리는 대답
(B) ○ 전망이 좋다며 질문에 적절히 말했으므로 정답
(C) ✗ 유사 발음 함정 (apartment – department)

Possible Answer
I won't be moving in until next week. 다음 주나 되야 입주할 거에요.

Key point
How do you like ~? (의견: ~는 어때요?), How did ~ go? (상태: ~는 어땠어요?)와 같은 빈출 관용 표현을 익혀둬야 해석이 빨리 될 수 있다.
How did you like the play? 그 연극 어땠어요?
How did the product demonstration go last week? 지난 주 제품 시연회는 어땠어요?

어휘 view n. 전망 department n. 부서 downstairs adv. 아래층에서

15 Who 의문문 난이도 중

Who will be leading the marketing seminar?
(A) It hasn't been decided yet.
(B) In conference room B.
(C) Yes, I'll be reading it.

누가 마케팅 세미나를 진행하나요?
(A) 아직 결정되지 않았어요.
(B) B 회의실에서요.
(C) 네, 제가 읽을 거에요.

해설 (A) ○ 아직 결정되지 않았다며 질문에 적절하게 말했으므로 정답
(B) ✗ Where에 어울리는 대답, 연상 어휘 함정 (seminar – conference)
(C) ✗ 의문사 의문문 Yes/No 응답 불가, 유사 발음 함정 (leading – reading)

Possible Answer
Linda told me she will. Linda가 할 거라고 했어요.

Key point
아직 결정되지 않았다는 대답은 잘 모르겠다는 대답과 함께 거의 대부분 정답이 되는 표현이다. 질문을 잘 못 들었거나, 답이 뭔지 모를 때는 아래와 같은 대답을 정답으로 고르면 맞힐 확률이 높다.

> It hasn't been decided. 아직 결정되지 않았어요.
> We haven't decided yet. 아직 결정하지 않았어요.
> We're still deciding. 아직도 결정 중이에요.
> We haven't made a decision. 아직 결정하지 못했어요.
> We've not made up our mind. 아직 마음을 정하지 못했어요.
> It hasn't been discussed yet. 아직 논의되지 않았어요.
> It hasn't been confirmed. 아직 확정되지 않았어요.
> He'll let me know this afternoon. 오후에 알려줄 겁니다.
> We'll find out in today's meeting. 오늘 회의 때 알게 될 거예요.
> It's too soon to tell. 아직 말하긴 일러요.

어휘 lead v. ~을 지휘하다, 이끌다 decide v. 결정하다 conference room 회의실

16 일반 의문문 난이도 하

Do you want me to make the dinner reservation?
(A) No, I'll take care of it.
(B) I made a mistake.
(C) For the client dinner.

제가 저녁 식사 예약을 할까요?
(A) 아니에요. 제가 할게요.
(B) 제가 실수했어요.
(C) 고객 저녁 식사를 위해서요.

해설 (A) ○ 'No'로 대답하고, 본인이 처리하겠다며 적절히 덧붙여 말했으므로 정답
(B) ✗ 유사 발음 함정 (make – made)
(C) ✗ 동어반복 함정 (dinner – dinner)

Possible Answer
Yes, if you don't mind. 네, 괜찮으시다면요.

어휘 reservation n. 예약 take care of ~을 처리하다

17 Where 의문문 난이도 하

Where's the bus terminal?
(A) Across the street from the hospital.
(B) A short-term lease.
(C) No, I usually take the subway.

버스 터미널이 어디에 있나요?
(A) 병원 길 건너예요.
(B) 단기 임대요.
(C) 아니요, 저는 주로 지하철을 이용해요.

해설 (A) ○ 병원 길 건너라며 위치로 말했으므로 정답
(B) ✗ 유사 발음 함정 (terminal – term)
(C) ✗ 의문사 의문문 Yes/No 응답 불가, 연상 어휘 함정 (bus – subway)

Possible Answer
It's pretty far from here. 여기에서 꽤 멀어요.

어휘 across prep. 건너편에 short-term adj. 단기의 lease n. 임대차 계약

18 부가 의문문 　　　　　　　　　　난이도 중

영국↔미국

This printer is on sale, right?
(A) No, but that one is.
(B) Yes, I repaired it yesterday.
(C) I'll print more labels.

이 프린터가 세일 중이죠, 그렇죠?
(A) 아니요, 하지만 저게 하고 있어요.
(B) 네, 제가 어제 수리했어요.
(C) 제가 라벨을 더 출력할게요.

해설 (A) ◎ 'No'로 대답하고, 다른 상품은 세일하고 있다며 적절히 덧붙여 말했으므로 정답
(B) ✘ 연상 어휘 함정 (printer – repaired)
(C) ✘ 유사 발음 함정 (printer – print)
Possible Answer
Yes, and it's our best-selling model. 네, 그리고 이게 제일 잘 팔리는 모델이에요.

어휘 **repair** v. 수리하다 **label** n. 표, 라벨, 상표

19 제안/요청 　　　　　　　　　　난이도 중

미국↔영국

Could you help me find the mail room?
(A) Of course. Come with me.
(B) I already emailed it to you.
(C) That was very helpful. Thanks.

우편실 찾는 걸 도와주실 수 있나요?
(A) 그럼요. 절 따라오세요.
(B) 제가 이미 이메일 드렸어요.
(C) 매우 도움이 되었어요. 감사해요.

해설 (A) ◎ 'Of course'로 대답하고, 따라오라며 적절히 덧붙여 말했으므로 정답
(B) ✘ 유사 발음 함정 (mail – emailed)
(C) ✘ 유사 발음 함정 (help – helpful)
Possible Answer
I'm not sure where that is. 그곳이 어딘지 잘 모르겠어요.

어휘 **mail room** 우편실 **helpful** adj. 도움이 되는

20 What 의문문 　　　　　　　　　　난이도 중

미국↔호주

What is this tea made of?
(A) That T-shirt looks great on you.
(B) At a nearby café.
(C) Why don't you check the packaging?

이 차는 무엇으로 만들어졌나요?
(A) 그 티셔츠가 잘 어울리시네요.
(B) 근처 카페에서요.
(C) 포장을 확인해보는 건 어때요?

해설 (A) ✘ 유사 발음 함정 (tea – T-shirt)
(B) ✘ 연상 어휘 함정 (tea – café)
(C) ◎ 포장을 확인해보라고 반문하며 질문에 적절하게 말했으므로 정답
Possible Answer
Let's ask the server. 종업원에게 물어봅시다.

어휘 **nearby** adj. 인근의, 가까운 곳의 **packaging** n. 포장

21 일반 의문문 　　　　　　　　　　난이도 상

호주↔미국

Will the office move take place before next month?
(A) The memo was just sent.
(B) I'll order more supplies this week.
(C) No, the Maintenance Department.

다음 달 전에 사무실 이전이 진행되나요?
(A) 메모가 방금 발송됐어요.
(B) 이번 주에 물품을 더 주문할게요.
(C) 아니요, 유지보수부서요.

해설 (A) ◎ 메모가 방금 발송됐다며 질문에 적절하게 말했으므로 정답
(B) ✘ 연상 어휘 함정 (office – supplies), (next month – this week)
(C) ✘ 연상 어휘 함정 (office – department)
Possible Answer
It has been rescheduled to next year. 내년으로 일정이 변경되었어요.

Key point
직접적인 대답 대신에 다른 곳을 확인해보라는 대답도 정답이 될 확률이 아주 높은 대답이다. 아래 대답들을 숙지해 놓으면 쉽게 답을 고를 수 있다.

> Check the bulletin board. 게시판을 확인해 보세요.
> It's listed in the itinerary. 일정표에 나와 있어요.
> We emailed it to everyone. 모든 사람에게 이메일을 보냈어요.
> You can find it on our Web site. 웹 사이트에 있어요.

어휘 **move** n. 이사 **supply** n. 물품 **maintenance** n. 유지보수

22 선택 의문문 　　　　　　　　　　난이도 하

영국↔미국

Which laptop do you prefer, the silver one or the white one?
(A) I contacted the IT Department.
(B) It comes with a wireless mouse.
(C) The silver one looks better.

어떤 노트북 컴퓨터를 선호하세요, 은색인가요 아니면 흰색인가요?
(A) 제가 IT 부서에 연락했어요.
(B) 무선 마우스도 딸려 있어요.
(C) 은색이 더 좋아 보여요.

해설 (A) ✘ 연상 어휘 함정 (laptop – IT Department)
(B) ✘ 연상 어휘 함정 (laptop – wireless mouse)
(C) ◎ 은색이 더 좋아 보인다며 선택하여 말했으므로 정답
Possible Answer
The one with the larger screen. 화면이 더 큰 거요.

어휘 **laptop** n. 노트북 컴퓨터 **prefer** v. 선호하다 **come with** ~이 딸려 있다 **wireless** adj. 무선의

23 Why 의문문 　　　　　　　　　　난이도 중

미국↔영국

Why was the meeting postponed today?
(A) To tomorrow morning.
(B) I already went to the post office.
(C) Because the rooms are fully booked.

오늘 회의가 왜 연기되었나요?
(A) 내일 아침으로요.
(B) 제가 이미 우체국에 다녀왔어요.
(C) 방들이 모두 예약됐기 때문이에요.

해설 (A) ✗ 연상 어휘 함정 (today – tomorrow morning)
(B) ✗ 유사 발음 함정 (postponed – post office)
(C) ○ 방들이 모두 예약됐기 때문이라며 이유를 들어 말했으므로 정답

Possible Answer
Mr. Collins isn't here yet. Mr. Collins가 아직 안 왔어요.

어휘 **postpone** v. 연기하다 **post office** 우체국 **book** v. 예약하다

24 부가 의문문 난이도 상

미국 ↕ 호주
This magazine cover looks nice, doesn't it?
(A) Yes, it was a great article.
(B) I think you should try a different font.
(C) At the newspaper stand down the street.

잡지 표지가 좋아 보여요, 그렇지 않아요?
(A) 네, 좋은 기사였어요.
(B) 다른 폰트를 사용해보셔야 할 것 같아요.
(C) 길 아래에 있는 신문 가판대예요.

해설 (A) ✗ 연상 어휘 함정 (magazine – article)
(B) ○ 다른 폰트를 사용해봐야 할 것 같다며 질문에 동의하지 않음을 우회적으로 말했으므로 정답
(C) ✗ 연상 어휘 함정 (magazine – newspaper)

Possible Answer
Don't you think it's too dark? 너무 어두운 것 같지 않으세요?

어휘 **cover** n. 표지 **article** n. 기사 **newspaper stand** 신문 가판대

25 제안/요청 난이도 중

호주 ↕ 미국
How would you like to pay for your clothes?
(A) In a medium size, please.
(B) Do you accept credit cards?
(C) We're having a sale.

옷 결제를 어떻게 하시겠어요?
(A) 미디엄 사이즈로 주세요.
(B) 신용 카드도 되나요?
(C) 저희가 지금 세일 중이에요.

해설 (A) ✗ 연상 어휘 함정 (clothes – medium size)
(B) ○ 신용 카드로 결제하고 싶다는 의사를 우회적으로 말했으므로 정답
(C) ✗ 연상 어휘 함정 (pay, clothes – sale)

Possible Answer
With cash, thanks. 현금으로요, 고마워요.

어휘 **accept** v. 받아주다, 수락하다 **credit card** 신용카드 **have a sale** 할인 판매하다

26 When 의문문 난이도 상

영국 ↕ 미국
When are you going on your holidays?
(A) We'll be taking a direct flight.
(B) I haven't received approval from my manager yet.
(C) There's a travel agency at the airport.

언제 휴가 가세요?
(A) 저희는 직항편을 탈 거에요.
(B) 아직 관리자 승인을 받지 못했어요.
(C) 공항 근처에 여행사가 있어요.

해설 (A) ✗ 연상 어휘 함정 (holidays – flight)
(B) ○ 아직 관리자의 승인을 받지 못했다며 질문에 적절히 말했으므로 정답
(C) ✗ 연상 어휘 함정 (holidays – travel agency, airport)

Possible Answer
After the product launch. 제품 출시 이후예요.

어휘 **direct flight** 직항편 **approval** n. 승인 **travel agency** 여행사

27 평서문 난이도 중

미국 ↕ 영국
The jazz performance was entertaining.
(A) No, I can't play any instruments.
(B) It was at Lee Theater.
(C) Yes, the songs were very enjoyable.

재즈 공연이 재미있었어요.
(A) 아니요, 저는 악기를 전혀 다룰 줄 몰라요.
(B) Lee 극장에서 있었어요.
(C) 맞아요, 곡들이 매우 즐거웠어요.

해설 (A) ✗ 연상 어휘 함정 (jazz performance – instruments)
(B) ✗ 연상 어휘 함정 (performance – theater)
(C) ○ 'Yes'로 대답하고, 곡들이 매우 즐거웠다며 적절히 덧붙여 말했으므로 정답

Possible Answer
I thought so, too. 저도 그렇게 생각했어요.

어휘 **performance** n. 공연 **entertaining** adj. 재미있는 **instrument** n. 악기 **theater** n. 극장 **enjoyable** adj. 즐거운

28 How 의문문 난이도 상

미국 ↕ 호주
How long do you plan to stay with our company?
(A) I'll contact the HR Department.
(B) I don't have any immediate plans to move.
(C) At a hotel downtown.

우리 회사에서 얼마 동안 근무할 계획이신가요?
(A) 제가 인사과에 연락할게요.
(B) 당장은 옮길 계획이 없습니다.
(C) 시내 호텔에서요.

해설 (A) ✗ 연상 어휘 함정 (company – HR Department)
(B) ○ 당장은 옮길 계획이 없다며 질문에 적절하게 말했으므로 정답
(C) ✗ 연상 어휘 함정 (stay – hotel)

Possible Answer
My plan is to stay long term. 제 계획은 오랫동안 있는 겁니다.

어휘 **HR(Human Resources) Department** 인사과 **downtown** adv. 시내에

29 부정 의문문 난이도 상

호주 ↕ 미국
Don't you provide a special discount for gym members?
(A) I left it in my locker.
(B) That offer ended last month.
(C) Yes, a membership fee.

체육관 회원에게 특별 할인을 제공하지 않나요?
(A) 제 사물함에 두었어요.
(B) 그 할인은 지난 달에 종료됐어요.
(C) 네, 회원가입비요.

해설 (A) ✗ 연상 어휘 함정 (gym – locker)
(B) ○ 지난달에 할인이 종료되었다며 질문에 적절히 말했으므로 정답
(C) ✗ 유사 발음 함정 (members – membership)

Possible Answer
Yes, 20 percent off. 네, 20퍼센트 할인해 드려요.

어휘 **provide** v. 제공하다 **discount** n. 할인 **gym** n. 체육관 **locker** n. 사물함 **offer** n. 할인 **membership fee** 회원가입비

---

30 Where 의문문   난이도 하

영국↔미국

Where should I go when I finish filling out these forms?
(A) By Friday morning.
(B) Thank you. I'm feeling much better.
(C) To the registration office.

이 서류를 작성하면 어디로 가야 하나요?
(A) 금요일 아침까지요.
(B) 감사합니다. 훨씬 나아졌어요.
(C) 등록 사무소요.

해설 (A) ✗ When 의문문에 어울리는 대답
(B) ✗ 유사 발음 함정 (filling – feeling)
(C) ○ 등록 사무소라며 장소로 말했으므로 정답

Possible Answer
Please wait in the lobby. 로비에서 기다려주세요.

어휘 **fill out** ~을 작성하다 **form** n. 서식 **feel better** 기분이 나아지다, 몸이 회복하다 **registration office** 등록 사무소

---

31 일반 의문문   난이도 상

영국↔호주

Has anyone made copies of the meeting agenda?
(A) The meeting has been canceled.
(B) We'll be presenting the new product.
(C) Did you use the coffee maker?

누가 회의 안건을 복사했나요?
(A) 회의가 취소되었어요.
(B) 저희가 신제품을 발표할 거예요.
(C) 커피 메이커를 사용하셨나요?

해설 (A) ○ 회의가 취소되었다며 안건을 복사하지 않았음을 우회적으로 말했으므로 정답
(B) ✗ 연상 어휘 함정 (meeting – presenting)
(C) ✗ 유사 발음 함정 (copies – coffee)

Possible Answer
Piper was in charge of that. 그건 Piper가 담당이었어요.

어휘 **make a copy** 복사하다 **agenda** n. 안건 **present** v. 발표하다 **product** n. 제품

PART 3

P. 65

미국 ⇄ 미국

Questions 32-34 refer to the following conversation.

W: Jordan, **ever since we began expanding our clothing store, I've noticed we haven't been getting many customers.**(32) Let's discuss some ways we can increase our sales.

M: You know, construction workers are always going in and out of the building. So it might look like our store is closed. **We should put a big sign out front**(33) to show that we're open.

W: That's a great idea. We should make sure the text on the sign stands out so that it catches the customers' attention right away.

M: Alright. **Let's get Kay to make it. She's skilled in graphic design.**(34) She's the one who created the store's logo.

32-34번은 다음 대화에 관한 문제입니다.

여: Jordan, 제가 보니까 우리가 옷가게를 확장한 이후로 손님이 많지 않네요.(32) 판매량을 늘릴 방법을 의논해 봐요.

남: 아시다시피, 공사 인부들이 항상 건물을 드나들고 있잖아요. 그래서 우리 가게가 문을 닫은 것처럼 보일 수 있어요. 우리가 영업 중이라는 걸 보여줄 수 있게 입구 쪽에 큰 표지판을 내걸어야겠어요.(33)

여: 정말 좋은 생각이에요. 고객들의 시선을 바로 사로잡을 수 있게 표지판의 문구는 반드시 눈에 잘 띄게 해야 해요.

남: 알겠어요. Kay가 만들게 하죠. 그래픽 디자인을 잘 하거든요.(34) 그 친구가 바로 매장 로고를 만든 사람이에요.

어휘 **out front** (건물의) 입구 쪽에 **stand out** 쉽게 눈에 띄다 **skilled** adj. 숙련된, 노련한

---

32 장소/근무지   난이도 하

해설 화자들은 어떤 종류의 사업체에서 근무하는가?
(A) 의류 소매업체
(B) 광고 대행사
(C) 건설회사
(D) 식료품점

해설 여자가 ever since we began expanding our clothing store, I've noticed we haven't been getting many customers. (제가 보니까 우리가 옷가게를 확장한 이후로 손님이 많지 않네요.)라고 말했으므로 (A)가 정답

Paraphrasing store ➡ retailer

---

33 요청/제의/제안   난이도 중

해설 남자는 무엇을 권장하는가?
(A) 할인을 제공하는 것
(B) 표지판을 거는 것
(C) 회사를 고용하는 것
(D) 예산을 조정하는 것

해설 남자가 We should put a big sign out front (입구 쪽에 큰 표지판을 내걸어야겠어요)라고 말했으므로 (B)가 정답

Paraphrasing put ➡ displaying

---

34 세부정보   난이도 하

해설 남자는 Kay가 무엇에 능숙하다고 말하는가?
(A) 상품을 판매하는 것
(B) 그래픽을 디자인하는 것

(C) 웹 사이트를 제작하는 것
(D) 신규 입사자를 교육하는 것

해설 남자가 Let's get Kay to make it. She's skilled in graphic design. (Kay가 만들게 하죠. 그래픽 디자인을 잘 하거든요.)라고 말했으므로 (B)가 정답

미국 ⇄ 영국

Questions 35-37 refer to the following conversation.

M: Ms. Fieldman, the representatives from CTM, Inc. just called to cancel. I rescheduled them for tomorrow afternoon.(35)

W: OK. That'll actually give me more time to prepare for that meeting. Anyway, since no more clients are coming in, I'll let the staff leave an hour early today.(36)

M: Oh, I'm sure everyone will be happy to hear that! By the way, some workers are coming by this evening to begin renovations on the dining lounge.(37) They'll be here every day until Friday.

35-37번은 다음 대화에 관한 문제입니다.

남: Ms. Fieldman, CTM 사 직원들이 방금 전화해서 취소했어요. 내일 오후로 일정을 다시 잡았습니다.(35)

여: 알겠어요. 사실 그게 회의를 준비할 시간을 더 벌어주겠네요. 그러면, 더 올 고객이 없으니, 오늘은 직원들을 한 시간 일찍 퇴근시켜야겠어요.(36)

남: 오, 그 얘기 들으면 모두 기뻐할 거예요! 그런데, 인부들 몇 명이 오늘 저녁에 식당 구역에 개조 작업을 시작하러 잠깐 들를 거예요.(37) 금요일까지 매일 올 거예요.

어휘 representative n. 대표(자) come by 잠깐 들르다 dining lounge 휴게 식당 supplies n. 용품, 비품 catering n. 출장 연회업

35 세부정보   난이도 중

해석 남자는 자신이 무엇을 했다고 말하는가?
(A) 회의 시간을 옮겼다고
(B) 고객 사무실을 방문했다고
(C) 배송을 처리했다고
(D) 프레젠테이션을 수정했다고

해설 남자가 the representatives from CTM, Inc. just called to cancel. I rescheduled them for tomorrow afternoon. (CTM사 직원들이 방금 전화해서 취소했어요. 내일 오후로 일정을 다시 잡았습니다.)라고 말했으므로 (A)가 정답

Paraphrasing rescheduled ➡ moved a meeting time

36 세부정보   난이도 중

해석 여자는 무엇을 하기로 결정하는가?
(A) 출장을 가기로
(B) 휴게실 비품을 더 주문하기로
(C) 출장연회 메뉴를 변경하기로
(D) 직원들을 일찍 퇴근하게 하기로

해설 여자가 I'll let the staff leave an hour early today.(오늘은 직원들을 한 시간 일찍 퇴근시켜야겠어요.)라고 말했으므로 (D)가 정답

Paraphrasing let the staff leave ➡ allow employees to leave

37 세부정보   난이도 중

해석 남자에 따르면, 저녁에 무슨 일이 있을 것인가?
(A) 주차장이 폐쇄될 것이다.
(B) 기계가 수리될 것이다.
(C) 어떤 구역이 개조될 것이다.
(D) 시스템이 다시 시작될 것이다.

해설 남자가 some workers are coming by this evening to begin renovations on the dining lounge.(인부들 몇 명이 오늘 저녁에 식당 구역에 개조 작업을 시작하러 잠깐 들를 거예요.)라고 말했으므로 (C)가 정답

Paraphrasing the dining lounge ➡ an area

호주 ⇄ 미국

Questions 38-40 refer to the following conversation.

M: You've reached Lastow Home Improvement. This is Martin speaking.

W: Hello, I just received the four cans of blue paint I purchased from your online store three days ago.(38) However, I noticed that one of the cans was opened, and some of the paint spilled. It wasn't sealed properly.(39)

M: I'm so sorry about that.

W: I can get this exchanged for another one, right?

M: Definitely. We'll send you a new one at no cost. Please give me your name and phone number, so I can look up your order.(40)

38-40번은 다음 대화에 관한 문제입니다.

남: Lastow 주거용품점입니다. 저는 Martin입니다.

여: 안녕하세요, 제가 3일 전에 그곳 온라인 상점에서 구입한 파란색 페인트 4통을 방금 받았는데요.(38) 그런데, 보니까 통 하나가 개봉된 상태고 페인트도 좀 쏟아졌네요. 밀봉이 제대로 안 돼 있더라고요.(39)

남: 정말 죄송합니다.

여: 이거 다른 걸로 교환받을 수 있는 거죠?

남: 물론입니다. 새 제품을 무료로 보내드리겠습니다. 주문 정보를 찾을 수 있도록 성함과 전화 번호를 알려주세요.(40)

어휘 reach v. (전화로) 연락하다 improvement n. 개조, 개선 purchase v. 구입하다 notice v. 인지하다 spill v. 쏟아지다 seal v. 밀봉하다 properly adv. 제대로, 적절히 exchange v. 교환하다 definitely adv. 분명히, 틀림없이 look up 찾아보다

38 세부정보   난이도 중

해석 여자는 최근에 무엇을 했는가?
(A) 소포를 배달했다.
(B) 상사와 만났다.
(C) 새 집으로 이사했다.
(D) 비품을 샀다.

해설 여자가 I just received the four cans of blue paint I purchased from your online store three days ago. (제가 3일 전에 그곳 온라인 상점에서 구입한 파란색 페인트 4통을 방금 받았는데요.)라고 말했으므로 (D)가 정답

Paraphrasing the four cans of blue paint ➡ some supplies,
purchased ➡ bought,
three days ago ➡ recently

39 주제/목적 난이도 상

해석 여자가 전화를 건 이유는 무엇인가?
(A) 대금을 납입하기 위해
(B) 불만을 제기하기 위해
(C) 추가 물품을 구매하기 위해
(D) 상담 일정을 잡기 위해

해설 여자가 I noticed that one of the cans was opened, and some of the paint spilled. It wasn't sealed properly. (보니까 통 하나가 개봉된 상태고 페인트도 좀 쏟아졌네요. 밀봉이 제대로 안 돼 있더라고요.)라고 말했으므로 (B)가 정답

40 요청/제의/제안 난이도 하

해석 남자는 무엇을 요청하는가?
(A) 개인정보
(B) 쿠폰 번호
(C) 매장 안내도
(D) 제품 견본

해설 남자가 Please give me your name and phone number, so I can look up your order. (주문 정보를 찾을 수 있도록 성함과 전화 번호를 알려주세요.)라고 말했으므로 (A)가 정답

Paraphrasing name and phone number ➡ some personal information

---

호주 ⇄ 영국 ⇄ 미국

Questions 41-43 refer to the following conversation with three speakers.

M: Hi, June, my name's Alex. I'm glad you've decided to join us here at Ottimo Accounting. **I'll be in charge of your training as the office administrator.**(41)

W1: It's great to meet you, Alex!

M: This is Tanya. Tanya, meet June, our new office administrator.

W2: Welcome, June. I look forward to working with you.

M: This is June's orientation manual. **Tanya, could you help her work through the first training assignment?**(42)

W2: I'd be glad to help.

M: OK. Once she's finished with that, bring her up to my office, and I'll show her how to use the AccountMaster 2000 software.

W1: **Oh, I also used AccountMaster 2000 at the office where I did my internship.**(43)

41-43번은 다음 세 화자에 관한 문제입니다.

남: 안녕하세요, June, 제 이름은 Alex입니다. 이곳 Ottimo Accounting에서 저희와 함께 하기로 하셔서 기쁩니다. **제가 당신의 사무 관리자 교육을 담당할 거에요.**(41)

여1: 만나서 반갑습니다, Alex!

남: 이 분은 Tanya예요. Tanya, 새로 오신 저희 사무 관리자이신 June이세요.

여2: 환영해요, June. 당신과 함께 일하기를 고대하고 있어요.

남: 이건 June의 오리엔테이션 설명서예요. **Tanya, 첫 번째 교육 과제를 하는 동안 그녀가 하는 일을 도와주시겠어요?**(42)

여2: 기꺼이 도울게요.

남: 좋아요. 그녀가 그 일을 마치는 대로, 제 사무실로 데려와 주시면, 제가 그녀에게 AccountMaster 2000 소프트웨어 사용법을 알려 드릴게요.

여1: **아, 저도 제가 인턴으로 일했던 회사에서 AccountMaster 2000을 사용했어요.**(43)

어휘 in charge of ~을 담당하는 look forward to ~하기를 고대하다
manual n. 설명서 assignment n. 과제 internship n. 인턴십

41 정체/신분 난이도 하

해석 June의 직업은 무엇인가?
(A) 컴퓨터 프로그래머
(B) 회계 직원
(C) 사무 관리자
(D) 재무 책임자

해설 남자가 I'll be in charge of your training as the office administrator. (제가 당신의 사무 관리자 교육을 담당할 거에요.)라고 말했으므로 (C)가 정답

42 다음 행동/계획 난이도 상

해석 June은 다음에 무엇을 하겠는가?
(A) 과제를 완료할 것이다
(B) 관리자를 만날 것이다
(C) 기사를 읽을 것이다
(D) 웹 사이트를 방문할 것이다

해설 남자가 Tanya, could you help her work through the first training assignment? (Tanya, 첫 번째 교육 과제를 하는 동안 그녀가 하는 일을 도와주시겠어요?)라고 말했으므로 (A)가 정답

43 세부정보 난이도 상

해석 소프트웨어에 관하여 June이 말한 것은?
(A) 업계에서 널리 쓰인다.
(B) 자신의 컴퓨터에 다운로드했다.
(C) 이미 그것에 익숙하다.
(D) 다른 나라에서 온 것이다.

해설 여자1이 Oh, I also used AccountMaster 2000 at the office where I did my internship. (아, 저도 제가 인턴으로 일했던 회사에서 AccountMaster 2000을 사용했어요.)라고 말했으므로 (C)가 정답

영국 ⇌ 호주

Questions 44-46 refer to the following conversation.

W: Hi, Aaron. Did you enjoy the staff appreciation dinner yesterday?

M: I did. **I received a reward for acquiring the most client accounts**(44) this quarter.

W: That's great news. Congratulations! You are always very good at securing new clients. What's the reward?

M: Two front-row seats to next Friday's performance of the world-famous Newmore Orchestra.

W: Oh, that's nice!

M: Yeah, but unfortunately, **I'll be out of town all next week visiting my parents,**(45) so I can't go.

W: Ah, I see. **What will you do with the tickets then?**(46)

M: **I'll probably offer them to someone in my department.**(46)

44-46번은 다음 대화에 관한 문제입니다.

여: 안녕하세요, Aaron. 어제 직원 감사 만찬이 즐거우셨나요?

남: 네, 그랬어요. 저는 이번 분기 **최다 고객 유치로 상품을 받았어요.**(44)

여: 정말 좋은 소식이네요. 축하드려요! 신규고객 유치를 항상 잘하시니까요. 상품이 뭔가요?

남: 다음 주 금요일 세계적인 Newmore 오케스트라의 공연에 앞자리 좌석 티켓 두 장이요.

여: 오, 좋네요!

남: 네, 그런데 안타깝게도, **다음 주 내내 부모님댁에 가 있을거라,**(45) 못 가요.

여: 아, 그렇군요. **그럼 티켓을 어떻게 하실 거예요?**(46)

남: **우리 부서에 있는 분에게 드릴까 해요.**(46)

어휘 appreciation n. 감사 receive v. 받다 reward n. 보상 acquire v. 얻다, 획득하다 account n. 고객 quarter n. 분기 secure v. 얻어내다, 확보하다 world-famous adj. 세계적으로 유명한 unfortunately adv. 유감스럽게도 out of town 도시를 떠나서 offer v. (이용할 수 있도록) 내놓다

44 세부정보   난이도 중

해석 남자는 무엇에 대한 상품을 받았는가?
(A) 성공적인 제품을 디자인한 것
(B) 운영비를 절감한 것
(C) 해외 프로젝트를 감독한 것
(D) 많은 고객을 유치한 것

해설 남자가 I received a reward for acquiring the most client accounts (최다 고객유치로 상품을 받았어요)라고 말했으므로 (D)가 정답

Paraphrasing acquiring ➡ attracting, client ➡ customer

45 다음 행동/계획   난이도 하

해석 남자는 다음 주에 무엇을 할 계획인가?
(A) 스포츠 대회에 참가할 것이다
(B) 가족을 만날 것이다
(C) 공연에 참석한다
(D) 회사 연회를 주최할 것이다

해설 남자가 I'll be out of town all next week visiting my parents (다음 주 내내 부모님댁에 가 있을거라)라고 말했으므로 (B)가 정답

Paraphrasing visit ➡ meet, parents ➡ family members

46 세부정보   난이도 중

해석 남자는 상품을 어떻게 하겠다고 하는가?
(A) 동료에게 주겠다고
(B) 온라인에서 판매하겠다고
(C) 나중에 사용하겠다고
(D) 액자에 넣겠다고

해설 여자가 What will you do with the tickets then? (그럼 티켓을 어떻게 하실 거예요?)라고 하자, 남자가 I'll probably offer them to someone in my department. (우리 부서에 있는 분에게 드릴까 해요.)라고 말한 것이므로 (A)가 정답

Paraphrasing offer ➡ give,
someone in my department ➡ colleague

미국 ⇌ 미국

Questions 47-49 refer to the following conversation.

W: Sorry for calling you over here on such short notice, David. **There is an issue with the air conditioning unit your technician installed in our conference room this morning. No cold air is coming out.**(47)

M: We're the ones who need to apologize! You've been a loyal client for many years, and we'd like to keep it that way. Alright, let me turn the unit on.

W: As you can see, the air isn't cool. **I tried setting the unit to the lowest temperature, but nothing happened. We use this room frequently for meetings.**(48)

M: I'm so sorry about that. We'll take care of it right away. **I'll call the shop right now**(49) and have someone deliver a new unit within the hour.

47-49번은 다음 대화에 관한 문제입니다.

여: 이렇게 갑자기 오시라고 연락 드려서 죄송해요, David. **오늘 아침에 기사분께서 저희 회의실에 설치해주신 에어컨에 문제가 있어서요. 찬 바람이 나오지 않아요.**(47)

남: 사과는 저희가 드려야죠! 여러 해 동안 단골 고객이셨는데, 계속 이렇게 유지되었으면 좋겠습니다. 그럼, 제가 장치를 켜볼게요.

여: 보시다시피 바람이 차갑지가 않아요. **장치를 최저 온도로 설정해 보기도 했는데, 아무 변화도 없었어요. 저희가 회의할 때 이 방을 자주 사용하거든요.**(48)

남: 정말 죄송합니다. 즉시 처리해드리겠습니다. **지금 바로 매장에 전화해서**(49) 한 시간 내에 새 기계를 배송해 드리겠습니다.

어휘 on short notice 갑자기, 충분한 예고 없이 loyal adj. 충실한, 충성스러운 that way 그와 같이

| 47 | 주제/목적 | 난이도 중 |

해석 화자들은 주로 무엇을 논하고 있는가?
(A) 오작동하는 기계
(B) 다가오는 회의
(C) 방 예약
(D) 배송요금

해설 여자가 There is an issue with the air conditioning unit your technician installed in our conference room this morning. No cold air is coming out. (오늘 아침에 기사분께서 저희 회의실에 설치해주신 에어컨에 문제가 있어서요. 찬바람이 나오지 않아요.)라고 말했으므로 (A)가 정답

Paraphrasing air conditioning unit ➡ machine,
No cold air is coming out. ➡ malfunctioning

| 48 | 화자 의도 파악 | 난이도 상 |

해석 여자는 왜 "저희가 회의할 때 이 방을 자주 사용하거든요"라고 말하는가?
(A) 요청이 중요한 이유를 설명하기 위해
(B) 회의 장소를 변경하기 위해
(C) 추가 가구 구매를 권장하기 위해
(D) 장소가 너무 좁다는 것을 나타내기 위해

해설 여자가 I tried setting the unit to the lowest temperature, but nothing happened. (장치를 최저 온도로 설정해 보기도 했는데, 아무 변화도 없었어요.)라고 하면서, We use this room frequently for meetings. (저희가 회의할 때 이 방을 자주 사용하거든요.)라고 말한 것이므로 (A)가 정답

| 49 | 다음 행동/계획 | 난이도 중 |

해석 남자는 이후에 무엇을 할 것인가?
(A) 절차를 설명할 것이다
(B) 환불을 해줄 것이다
(C) 계약서를 수정할 것이다
(D) 매장에 연락할 것이다

해설 남자가 I'll call the shop right now (지금 바로 매장에 전화해서)라고 말했으므로 (D)가 정답

Paraphrasing call the shop ➡ contact a store

영국 ⇄ 호주 ⇄ 미국

Questions 50-52 refer to the following conversation with three speakers.

W1: Welcome to Maxwell Laundry Cleaners.(50) How may I assist you?

M: Hi. **I dropped off a suit here yesterday for dry cleaning. I was told that it would be done today by 2 P.M.**(51) My name is Roman Park.

W1: OK, give me a moment to see if it's done. Corinna, did you take care of Mr. Park's request?

W2: Yes. Your suit is ready to go, Mr. Park.

M: Thanks for the speedy service!

W2: No problem. I'll grab it for you now.

W1: While she's doing that, I can process your payment. Also, if you have some time, **do you mind filling out a comment card?**(52) It'll help us improve our services.

M: Sure, I don't mind.(52)

50-52번은 다음 세 화자의 대화에 관한 문제입니다.

여1: Maxwell 세탁소에 오신 것을 환영합니다.(50) 어떻게 도와드릴까요?

남: 안녕하세요. 제가 어제 여기에 정장을 드라이클리닝 맡겼어요. 오늘 오후 2시까지 될 거라고 들었습니다.(51) 제 이름은 Roman Park이에요.

여1: 알겠습니다, 다 됐는지 알아볼 테니 잠깐만 기다려주세요. Corinna, Mr. Park께서 맡기신 것 처리했나요?

여2: 네. 정장 완료됐습니다, Mr. Park.

남: 빠른 서비스 고맙습니다!

여2: 별 말씀을요. 지금 가져다 드릴게요.

여1: 가져다 드리는 동안, 결제 도와드리겠습니다. 그리고 시간이 좀 있으시면, 의견 카드를 작성해주실 수 있으신가요?(52) 저희 서비스를 개선하는 데 도움이 될 겁니다.

남: 그럼요, 해드릴게요.(52)

어휘 drop off (어떤 장소에 물건을) 가져다 주다, 맡기다 grab v. 붙잡다, 움켜잡다 process v. 처리하다 fill out 작성하다 comment n. 논평, 의견

| 50 | 장소/근무지 | 난이도 하 |

해석 여자들은 어디서 근무하는가?
(A) 정장 의류 소매점
(B) 직물 공장
(C) 패션 잡지 출판사
(D) 세탁 업체

해설 여자가 Welcome to Maxwell Laundry Cleaners. (Maxwell 세탁소에 오신 것을 환영합니다.)라고 말했으므로 (D)가 정답

| 51 | 주제/목적 | 난이도 하 |

해석 남자는 왜 사업체를 방문하고 있는가?
(A) 계약서에 서명하기 위해
(B) 환불을 받기 위해
(C) 일자리에 지원하기 위해
(D) 물건을 찾기 위해

해설 남자가 I dropped off a suit here yesterday for dry cleaning. I was told that it would be done today by 2 P.M. (제가 어제 여기에 정장을 드라이클리닝 맡겼어요. 오늘 오후 2시까지 될 거라고 들었습니다.)라고 말했으므로 (D)가 정답

| 52 | 세부정보 | 난이도 중 |

해석 남자는 무엇을 하는 데 동의하는가?
(A) 다음에 다시 오는 것에
(B) 의견을 제공하는 것에
(C) 특별 방문을 하는 것에
(D) 현금으로 지불하는 것에

해설 여자가 do you mind filling out a comment card? (의견 카드를 작성해주실 수 있으신가요?)라고 하자, 남자가 Sure, I don't mind. (그럼요, 해드릴게요.) 라고 말했으므로 (B)가 정답

Paraphrasing fill out a comment card ➡ provide some comments

미국 ⇄ 영국

Questions 53-55 refer to the following conversation.

M: Hey, Rosie. **You're covering the story on the IT Trade Show**(53) next week, right?

W: Yeah, I am. Why?

M: **One of my old colleagues develops his own mobile applications, and he's going to be revealing a new kind of camera app at the convention.**(54) I know you were looking to interview exhibitors, and I think he'd be a perfect candidate.

W: Ah, that sounds good. I'm actually meeting with the lead event planner tomorrow, so I'll try to arrange an interview with your colleague sometime after that.

M: OK, **let me give you his e-mail address.**(55) I'll tell him to expect your message.

53-55번은 다음 대화에 관한 문제입니다.

남: 저기, Rosie. 다음 주 있는 **IT 무역 박람회에 대한 취재하시죠?**(53)

여: 네, 맞아요. 왜요?

남: 제 예전 동료 중 한 명이 직접 모바일 앱을 개발하는데, 박람회에서 새로운 종류의 카메라 앱을 공개할 거예요.(54) 당신이 출품자들을 인터뷰하려고 한 걸로 알고 있는데, 제 생각에 그라면 아주 훌륭한 후보자가 될 것 같아요.

여: 아, 그거 좋죠. 실은 내일 행사 총 기획자와 만나기로 했는데, 그 후에 당신 동료와 인터뷰 자리를 마련해볼게요.

남: 알았어요, **그 친구 이메일 주소를 알려드릴게요.**(55) 그 친구에게는 당신이 메시지를 보낼거라고 말해둘게요.

어휘 **cover** v. 취재하다 **colleague** n. 동료 **application** n. 응용 프로그램, 애플리케이션 **reveal** v. 드러내다, 밝히다 **convention** n. 박람회 **look to do** ~하기를 기대하다 **exhibitor** n. (전시회) 출품자 **arrange** v. 마련하다

---

53 정체/신분   난이도 중

해설 여자는 누구겠는가?
(A) 행사 준비위원
(B) 전문 사진작가
(C) 뉴스 기자
(D) 컴퓨터 기술자

해설 남자가 You're covering the story on the IT Trade Show (IT 무역 박람회에 대한 취재하시죠?)라고 말했으므로 (C)가 정답

---

54 세부정보   난이도 중

해설 남자의 친구는 무엇을 만드는가?
(A) 스피커
(B) 노트북 컴퓨터
(C) 디지털 카메라
(D) 모바일 프로그램

해설 남자가 One of my old colleagues develops his own mobile applications, and he's going to be revealing a new kind of camera app at the convention. (제 예전 동료 중 한 명이 직접 모바일 앱을 개발하는데, 박람회에서 새로운 종류의 카메라 앱을 공개할 거예요.)라고 말했으므로 (D)가 정답

Paraphrasing develop ➡ make, applications ➡ programs

---

55 세부정보   난이도 하

해설 남자는 여자에게 무엇을 주는가?
(A) 콘퍼런스 일정표
(B) 방문자 출입증
(C) 신청서
(D) 연락처

해설 남자가 let me give you his e-mail address. (그 친구 이메일 주소를 알려드릴게요.)라고 말했으므로 (D)가 정답

Paraphrasing e-mail address ➡ contact information

미국 ⇄ 호주

Questions 56-58 refer to the following conversation.

W: Darren, before your team gets started, **I'd like to discuss what renovation work you'll be doing on the backyard this afternoon.**(56) Please follow me.

M: Oh, **check out these fountains. They've got to be at least 50 years old!**(57) I don't think they'll suit the new backyard design.

W: The patio isn't great, either. Everything there needs to be removed and replaced. So the first thing you'll do today is install floor tiles and put in new furniture in that area.

M: Hmm... **This patio area is larger than I thought. Do we also have to finish planting all the flowers today?**(58)

W: No. When I saw how big the patio was, I decided to put that work off until tomorrow.

56-58번은 다음 대화에 관한 문제입니다.

여: Darren, 당신 팀이 일을 시작하기 전에 **오늘 오후에 뒤뜰에서 어떤 개조 작업을 하실 건지 의논했으면 좋겠어요.**(56) 저를 따라오세요.

남: 오, **이 분수대 좀 보세요. 최소 50년은 되었을 거예요!**(57) 새 뒤뜰 디자인에 어울릴 것 같지는 않군요.

여: 테라스도 그리 좋지는 않아요. 거기 있는 걸 전부다 제거하고 교체해야 해요. 그래서 여러분이 오늘 할 첫 작업은 그 구역에 바닥 타일을 깔고 새 가구를 넣는 거예요.

남: 음... **이 테라스는 제가 생각했던 것보다 넓네요. 꽃 심는 것도 전부 오늘 다 끝내야 하나요?**(58)

여: 아니요, 테라스가 너무 커서 그 작업은 내일로 미루기로 했어요.

어휘 **check out** (흥미로운 것을) 보다 **fountain** n. 분수 **suit** v. 어울리다 **patio** n. 테라스 **supplies** n. 용품, 비품

56 주제/목적　　　　　　　　　　　　　　　　　난이도 상

해석　대화의 주제는 무엇인가?
(A) 조경 프로젝트
(B) 가격 견적
(C) 비어 있는 부동산
(D) 원예 도구

해설　여자가 I'd like to discuss what renovation work you'll be doing on the backyard this afternoon. (오늘 오후에 뒤뜰에서 어떤 개조 작업을 하실 건지 의논했으면 좋겠어요.)라고 말했으므로 (A)가 정답

57 세부정보　　　　　　　　　　　　　　　　　난이도 중

해석　남자는 분수대에 관하여 뭐라고 말하는가?
(A) 제대로 작동하지 않는다.
(B) 내일 설치될 것이다.
(C) 너무 무겁다.
(D) 구식으로 보인다.

해설　남자가 check out these fountains. They've got to be at least 50 years old! (이 분수대 좀 보세요. 최소 50년은 되었을 거예요.)라고 말했으므로 (D)가 정답

58 화자 의도 파악　　　　　　　　　　　　　　난이도 상

해석　남자가 "이 테라스는 제가 생각했던 것보다 넓네요"라고 말할 때, 그가 내비친 것은?
(A) 업무를 끝내는 데 시간이 좀 걸릴 것이다.
(B) 매니저의 승인이 필요하다.
(C) 추가 용품을 주문해야 한다.
(D) 인부들을 더 요청하고자 한다.

해설　남자가 This patio area is larger than I thought. (이 테라스는 제가 생각했던 것보다 넓네요.)라고 하면서, Do we also have to finish planting all the flowers today? (꽃 심는 것도 전부 오늘 다 끝내야 하나요?) 라고 말한 것이므로 (A)가 정답

호주 ⇄ 미국

Questions 59-61 refer to the following conversation.

M: Janice, **I wanted to talk to you about our café's produce supplier.**(59)

W: Sure. What is it?

M: **They just started charging 10 percent more for their strawberries.**(60) This means that we'll have to charge more for our strawberry-based items.

W: Hmm... I wonder if this will lead to lower sales.

M: I don't think so. Our strawberry drinks and desserts sell pretty well, and we still have a variety of other items that won't be affected by this change.

W: Alright. **I'll get everyone together for a brief meeting tomorrow morning, and I'll explain what's going on.**(61)

59-61번은 다음 대화에 관한 문제입니다.

남: Janice, 우리 카페의 농산물 납품 업체에 관해 말씀 드리고 싶었어요.(59)

여: 그래요. 무슨 얘기인가요?

남: 그쪽에서 최근에 딸기 가격에 10퍼센트를 더 청구하기 시작했어요.(60) 이건 우리가 딸기를 원료로 한 제품의 가격을 올려야 한다는 걸 의미해요.

여: 음… 이게 판매량 하락으로 이어질지 궁금하군요.

남: 그렇지는 않을 거예요. 딸기 음료와 디저트는 꽤 잘 팔리고 있고, 이런 변화에 영향을 받지 않을 다른 다양한 제품들도 있으니까요.

여: 알았어요. 제가 내일 오전에 모두 모아 간단한 회의를 열고, 상황을 설명할게요.(61)

어휘　produce n. 농산물　charge v. (요금·값을) 청구하다　lead to ~로 이어지다　affect v. 영향을 미치다　get ~ together ~을 모으다　brief adj. 짧은, 잠시 동안의

59 장소/근무지　　　　　　　　　　　　　　　　난이도 하

해석　화자들은 어디서 근무하는가?
(A) 슈퍼마켓에서
(B) 카페에서
(C) 농장에서
(D) 병 음료 공장에서

해설　남자가 I wanted to talk to you about our café's produce supplier. (우리 카페의 농산물 납품업체에 말씀 드리고 싶었어요.)라고 말했으므로 (B)가 정답

60 세부정보　　　　　　　　　　　　　　　　　난이도 중

해석　남자에 따르면, 최근에 무슨 일이 있었는가?
(A) 제품 가격이 인상되었다.
(B) 계약이 종료되었다.
(C) 사업주가 변경되었다.
(D) 할인 행사가 열렸다.

해설　남자가 They just started charging 10 percent more for their strawberries. (그쪽에서 최근에 딸기 가격에 10퍼센트를 더 청구하기 시작했어요.)라고 말했으므로 (A)가 정답

Paraphrasing　just ➡ recently

61 다음 행동/계획　　　　　　　　　　　　　　　난이도 하

해석　여자는 내일 무엇을 하겠다고 말하는가?
(A) 새 납품업체에 전화하겠다고
(B) 지원자 면접을 보겠다고
(C) 설문조사를 실시하겠다고
(D) 회의를 열겠다고

해설　여자가 I'll get everyone together for a brief meeting tomorrow morning, and I'll explain what's going on. (제가 내일 오전에 모두 모아 간단한 회의를 열고, 상황을 설명할게요.)라고 말했으므로 (D)가 정답

영국 ⇄ 미국

Questions 62-64 refer to the following conversation and map.

W: Hello. **I signed up to hand out water to the participants in today's 16-mile mini-marathon race.**(62) An event staff member said that I should talk to you about what I need to do.

M: Ah, OK. Thank you for volunteering. Take this map of the mini-marathon route. **You'll be stationed at the 4-mile mark to give water to the runners.**(63)

W: Sounds good. I'll go over there right now and get ready for the event.

M: Alright. Also, **once the race ends, please help clean up any trash around your station.**(64)

16-MILE MINI-MARATHON MAP

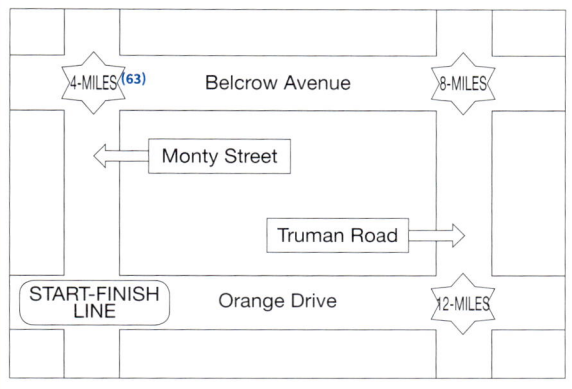

62-64번은 다음 대화와 지도에 관한 문제입니다.

여: 안녕하세요. 저는 오늘 16 마일 미니 마라톤 경주에서 참가자들에게 물을 나누어 주는 일에 신청했는데요.(62) 행사 직원이 제가 해야 할 일에 관해서 당신과 이야기하라고 알려줬어요.

남: 아, 그러시군요. 자원해주셔서 고맙습니다. 이 미니 마라톤 경로 지도를 받으세요. 4 마일 지점에서 선수들에게 물을 주시면 됩니다.(63)

여: 네. 바로 거기로 가서 행사를 준비할게요.

남: 좋습니다. 그리고 경주가 끝나면, 자리 주변의 쓰레기 치우는 일을 좀 도와주세요.(64)

16 마일 미니 마라톤 지도

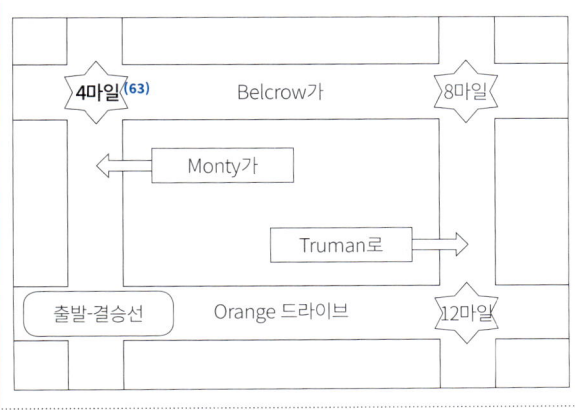

어휘 sign up 신청하다 hand out 나누어 주다 participant n. 참가자 volunteer v. 자원하다 station v. 배치하다 n. (업무 대기·감시 등을 위한) 위치 mark n. 표시

62 세부정보   난이도 중

해석 여자는 마라톤 대회에서 무엇을 할 것인가?
(A) 사진을 촬영할 것이다
(B) 교통정리를 할 것이다
(C) 음료를 제공할 것이다
(D) 참가자들을 인터뷰할 것이다

해설 여자가 I signed up to hand out water to the participants in today's 16-mile mini-marathon race. (저는 오늘 16 마일 미니 마라톤 경주에서 참가자들에게 물을 나누어 주는 일에 신청했는데요.)라고 말했으므로 (C)가 정답

Paraphrasing hand out water ➡ provide some beverages

63 시각 정보 연계   난이도 중

해석 시각 자료를 보시오. 여자는 어느 교차로로 갈 것인가?
(A) Monty가와 Belcrow가
(B) Belcrow가와 Truman로
(C) Truman로와 Orange드라이브
(D) Orange드라이브와 Monty가

해설 남자가 You'll be stationed at the 4-mile mark to give water to the runners. (4 마일 지점에서 선수들에게 물을 주시면 됩니다.)라고 말했고, 시각 자료에서 4 MILES (4 마일)은 Monty Street(Monty가)와 Belcrow Avenue(Belcrow가) 교차로에 있음을 확인할 수 있으므로 (A)가 정답

64 요청/제의/제안   난이도 중

해석 여자는 마라톤이 끝난 후 무엇을 하라고 지시 받는가?
(A) 구역을 청소하라고
(B) 상을 나누어 주라고
(C) 설문지를 작성하라고
(D) 사진을 공유하라고

해설 남자가 once the race ends, please help clean up any trash around your station. (경주가 끝나면, 자리 주변의 쓰레기 치우는 일을 좀 도와주세요.)라고 말했으므로 (A)가 정답

Paraphrasing once the race ends ➡ after the marathon,
              around your station ➡ an area

미국 ⇄ 영국

Questions 65-67 refer to the following conversation and event calendar.

M: OK, this is your gym membership ID and a list of our spring seminars.(65)

W: Great!

M: Since you're a member, you can participate in any seminar, free of charge.(65) But they fill up quickly, so register in advance!

W: In that case, can I sign up for the yoga seminar on March 29?

M: Ah, unfortunately, that session is already full. But we still have a few spaces available at the one on a jogging program, if you're interested.⁽⁶⁶⁾

W: Sure, I'd like to check that out.⁽⁶⁶⁾

M: OK, I've signed you up. And if you want, you can join tonight's special group fitness class. It's being led by Brianne Pyle, a local trainer. She's going to be introducing a special workout routine using a variety of gymnastics moves.⁽⁶⁷⁾

Upcoming Spring Seminars	
March 12	Eating for Energy
March 29	Starting Yoga
April 3	Creating a Jogging Program⁽⁶⁶⁾
April 16	Keeping a Training Journal

65-67번은 다음 대화와 행사 일정표에 관한 문제입니다.

남: 자, 여기 체육관 회원증과 봄 세미나 목록입니다.⁽⁶⁵⁾

여: 네!

남: 회원이시니까, 어떤 세미나든 무료로 참석하실 수 있습니다.⁽⁶⁵⁾ 하지만 자리가 빨리 차니 미리 등록하셔야 돼요.

여: 그럼 3월 29일 요가 세미나에 등록할 수 있나요?

남: 아, 죄송하지만, 그 수업은 이미 다 찼어요. 하지만, 조깅 프로그램 수업은 아직 빈 자리가 몇 개 있어요, 혹시 관심 있으시면요.⁽⁶⁶⁾

여: 네, 한번 참여해 보고 싶네요.⁽⁶⁶⁾

남: 좋습니다, 등록해 드렸고요. 원하실 경우, 오늘 밤 그룹 피트니스 특별 수업에 참여하실 수 있어요. 이 지역 트레이너 Brianne Pyle이 진행하고요. 다양한 체조 동작을 활용한 특별한 운동법을 소개해 드릴 거예요.⁽⁶⁷⁾

다가올 봄 세미나	
3월 12일	에너지를 위한 식사
3월 29일	요가 입문
4월 3일	조깅 프로그램 짜기⁽⁶⁶⁾
4월 16일	훈련 일지 기록하기

어휘   since conj. ~이므로   participate in ~에 참가하다   free of charge 무료로   fill up 가득 차다   register v. 등록하다   in advance 사전에   sign up for ~을 신청[가입]하다   session n. (특정한 활동을 위한) 시간[기간]   full adj. 만원의   space n. (빈) 자리   available adj. 구할[이용할] 수 있는   check out 살펴보다   lead v. 지휘[인솔]하다   workout n. 운동   routine n. 차례, 기계적 절차   a variety of 다양한   gymnastics n. 체조   move n. 동작, 운동   keep a journal 일기를 쓰다

65 세부정보 난이도 중

해석   여자는 왜 무료 세미나에 참석할 수 있는가?
(A) 지역 주민이다.
(B) 헬스 트레이너이다.
(C) 회원권을 구매했다.
(D) 조기 등록을 완료했다.

해설   남자가 OK, this is your gym membership ID and a list of our spring seminars. (자, 여기 회원증과 봄 세미나 목록입니다.), Since you're a member, you can participate in any seminar, free of charge. (회원이시니까 어떤 세미나든 무료로 참석하실 수 있습니다.)라고 말했으므로 (C)가 정답

66 시각 정보 연계 난이도 상

해석   시각 자료를 보시오. 여자는 어느 날짜에 행사에 참가할 것인가?
(A) 3월 12일
(B) 3월 29일
(C) 4월 3일
(D) 4월 16일

해설   남자가 But we still have a few spaces available at the one on a jogging program, if you're interested. (하지만, 조깅 프로그램 수업은 아직 빈 자리가 몇 개 있어요, 혹시 관심 있으시면요.)라고 하자, 여자가 Sure, I'd like to check that out. (네, 한번 참여해 보고 싶네요.)라고 말했고, 시각 자료에서 Creating a Jogging Program (조깅 프로그램 짜기)가 April 3 (4월 3일)임을 확인할 수 있으므로 (C)가 정답

67 다음 행동/계획 난이도 중

해석   Brianne Pyle은 무엇을 소개할 것인가?
(A) 영양가 있는 식단 계획
(B) 운동 기계
(C) 운동법
(D) 건강 관련 도서

해설   남자가 It's being led by Brianne Pyle, a local trainer. She's going to be introducing a special workout routine using a variety of gymnastics moves. (이 지역 트레이너 Brianne Pyle이 진행하고요. 다양한 체조 동작을 활용한 특별한 운동법을 소개해 드릴 거예요.)라고 말했으므로 (C)가 정답

Paraphrasing   workout ➡ exercise

미국 ⇄ 호주

Questions 68-70 refer to the following conversation and sketch.

W: Thank you for calling Golden Horn Carpeting. This is Denise.

M: Hi, Denise. I spoke to you in the store yesterday about some carpeting for my coffee shop.⁽⁶⁸⁾

W: Ah, yes. Mr. Jenkins, right? How did your business partner like the design?

M: She loved it.

W: So would you like us to make your carpeting based on yesterday's drawing?

M: Well, yes, but **please make it wider** so that it will cover the entire interior of the shop. **We'd like it to be 4.3 meters wide, if possible.**(69)

W: Let's see. I think we can do that. But **let me just email the new measurements to our factory to confirm.**(70)

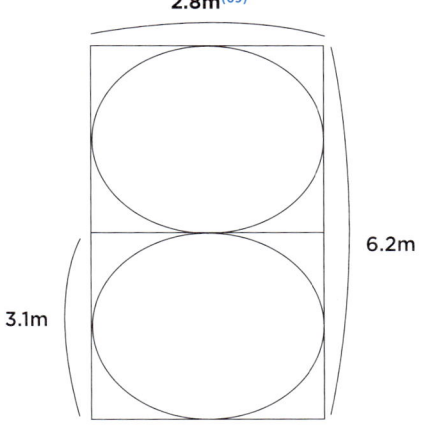

68-70번은 다음 대화와 스케치에 관한 문제입니다.

여: Golden Horn Carpeting에 전화 주셔서 감사합니다. 저는 Denise라고 합니다.

남: 안녕하세요, Denise. 제가 어제 매장에서 제 커피숍 카펫 작업에 관해서 상담 받았었는데요.(68)

여: 아, 네. Mr. Jenkins 맞으시죠? 동업자분은 디자인을 좋아하셨나요?

남: 아주 좋아했어요.

여: 그럼 어제 그린 것을 기준으로 해서 카펫을 제작해 드릴까요?

남: 음, 네, 그런데 폭을 더 넓게 만들어주세요. 가게 실내 전체를 커버할 수 있게요. 가능하다면, 폭이 4.3미터가 되면 좋겠어요.(69)

여: 어디 봅시다. 가능할 것 같아요. 하지만 새 치수를 저희 공장에 이메일로 보내서 확실히 하겠습니다.(70)

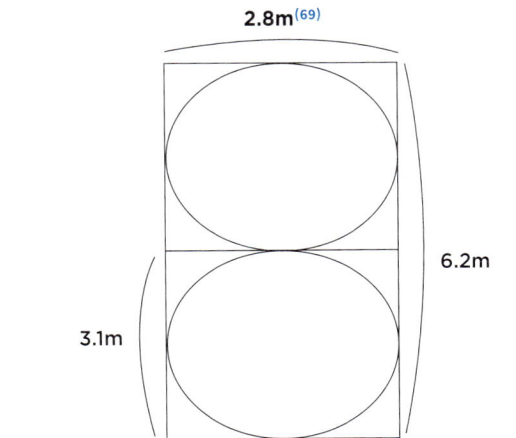

어휘 based on ~에 기초하여 entire adj. 전체의 wide adj. 폭이 ~인 measurement n. 치수, 크기

68 세부정보 난이도 중

해석 남자는 어떤 사업체를 소유하는가?
(A) 저장 시설
(B) 커피숍
(C) 직업 소개소
(D) 미술관

해설 남자가 Hi, Denise. I spoke to you in the store yesterday about some carpeting for my coffee shop. (안녕하세요, Denise. 제가 어제 매장에서 제 커피숍 카펫작업에 관해서 상담 받았었는데요.)라고 말했으므로 (B)가 정답

69 시각 정보 연계 난이도 상

해석 시각 자료를 보시오. 남자는 어느 치수를 변경하고 싶어하는가?
(A) 2.8미터
(B) 3.1미터
(C) 4.3미터
(D) 6.2미터

해설 남자가 please make it wider (폭을 더 넓게 만들어주세요)라고 하면서, We'd like it to be 4.3 meters wide, if possible. (가능하다면, 폭이 4.3미터가 되면 좋겠어요.)라고 말했고, 시각 자료에서 폭이 2.8m임을 확인할 수 있으므로 (A)가 정답

70 다음 행동/계획 난이도 중

해석 여자는 다음에 무엇을 하겠는가?
(A) 가격을 계산할 것이다
(B) 재료를 측정할 것이다
(C) 샘플을 제공할 것이다
(D) 제조업체에 연락할 것이다

해설 여자가 But let me just email the new measurements to our factory to confirm. (하지만 새 치수를 저희 공장에 이메일로 보내서 확실히 하겠습니다.)라고 말했으므로 (D)가 정답

Paraphrasing email ➡ contact, factory ➡ manufacturer

PART 4

미국

Questions 71-73 refer to the following excerpt from a meeting.

W: I want to thank the district managers for attending today's meeting to talk about a new approach our restaurant will be taking.(71) In the coming weeks, our entire menu will be available for delivery.(72) The purpose is to be more accessible for our customers. Some people may want to eat our food for lunch but can't because of their short lunch hours. By offering delivery, these customers can place their order beforehand, so their food can arrive in time for lunch. José Alvarez, the Director of Operations, is in charge of this task. **José, what will the restaurants need to plan in order to properly execute this arrangement?**(73)

71-73번은 다음 회의 발췌록에 관한 문제입니다.

여: 우리 식당이 도입할 새로운 접근법에 관해 논의하려고 마련한 오늘 회의에 참석해 주신 지역 매니저들께 감사의 말씀을 드립니다.(71) 다음 몇 주 동안, 전체 메뉴가 배달 가능합니다.(72) 목적은 우리 고객들이 더 쉽게 이용할 수 있게 하는 것입니다. 어떤 분들은 점심으로 우리의 음식을 먹고 싶어할 수 있는데, 점심 시간이 짧아 그럴 수가 없습니다. 배달을 제공함으로써, 이러한 고객들이 미리 주문을 할 수 있게 되어서 음식이 점심시간에 맞춰 도착할 수 있습니다. 운영 책임자인 José Alvarez가 이 업무를 담당하고 있습니다. **José, 이 일을 제대로 실행하려면, 식당에서는 무슨 계획을 세워야 할까요?**(73)

어휘 district n. 지역, 구역 approach n. 접근법 entire adj. 전체의 accessible adj. 이용 가능한, 접근 가능한 beforehand adv. 사전에, 미리 in time for ~할 시간에 맞춰 in charge of ~을 담당하는 task n. 업무 in order to do ~하기 위하여 properly adv. 제대로, 적절히 execute v. 실행하다 arrangement n. 준비, 마련

71 세부정보   난이도 하

해석 회사는 어떤 종류의 사업체를 소유하는가?
(A) 문구점
(B) 음식 서비스
(C) 도매 시장
(D) 자동차 대여

해설 화자가 I want to thank the district managers for attending today's meeting to talk about a new approach our restaurant will be taking. (우리 식당이 도입할 새로운 접근법에 관해 논의하려고 마련한 오늘 회의에 참석해 주신 지역 매니저들께 감사의 말씀을 드립니다.)라고 말했으므로 (B)가 정답

72 세부정보   난이도 중

해석 업체들은 무엇을 하기 시작할 것인가?
(A) 자동 결제 준비
(B) 시간대별 할인 제공
(C) 영업 시간 연장
(D) 물품 배송 제공

해설 화자가 In the coming weeks, our entire menu will be available for delivery. (다음 몇 주 동안, 전체 메뉴의 배달이 가능해질 것입니다.)라고 말했으므로 (D)가 정답

73 요청/제의/제안   난이도 중

해석 화자는 José Alvarez에게 무엇을 하라고 요청하는가?
(A) 이메일을 발송하라고
(B) 실행 계획을 설명하라고
(C) 일정표를 나눠주라고
(D) 음식 공급 업체에 전화하라고

해설 화자가 José, what will the restaurants need to plan in order to properly execute this arrangement? (José, 이 일을 제대로 실행하려면, 식당에서는 무슨 계획을 세워야 할까요?)라고 말했으므로 (3)가 정답

호주

Questions 74-76 refer to the following announcement.

M: May I have your attention, please? **I've just received notice that there is some road construction ahead that is causing delays on the highway.**(74)/(75) As a result, we will be arriving at the terminal about an hour later than originally scheduled. We'll be pulling into a rest area shortly to fill up on gas. You may use this time to purchase snacks and use the restroom. **Please make sure to take your belongings with you when you get off the bus.**(76) We are not responsible for any lost items. We apologize for the inconvenience.

74-76번은 다음 안내 방송에 관한 문제입니다.

남: 승객 여러분께 안내말씀 드립니다. 방금 전방에 고속도로 정체를 유발하고 있는 도로공사가 있다는 통보를 받았습니다.(74)(75) 따라서 터미널에는 원래 예정보다 한 시간 늦게 도착할 것입니다. 곧 주유를 위해 휴게소에 도착합니다. 이 시간을 이용하여 간식을 구매하시거나 화장실을 이용하실 수 있습니다. **버스에서 내리실 때는 반드시 소지품을 챙기시기 바랍니다.**(76) 당사는 분실물에 대한 책임을 지지 않습니다. 불편을 끼쳐드리는 점 사과 드립니다.

어휘 pull into ~에 도착하다 shortly adv. 곧 fill up on ~을 가득 채우다

74 장소/근무지   난이도 중

해석 안내방송이 어디서 나오겠는가?
(A) 기차 안에서
(B) 버스 안에서
(C) 비행기 안에서
(D) 페리 안에서

해설 화자가 I've just received notice that there is some road construction ahead that is causing delays on the highway. (방금 전방에 고속도로 정체를 유발하고 있는 도로 공사가 있다는 통보를 받았습니다.)라고 말했으므로 (B)가 정답

75 세부정보   난이도 중

해석 화자는 어떤 문제점을 언급하는가?
(A) 궂은 날씨
(B) 인력 부족
(C) 시스템 결함
(D) 도로 공사

해설 화자가 I've just received notice that there is some road construction ahead that is causing delays on the highway. (방금 전방에 고속도로 정체를 유발하고 있는 도로 공사가 있다는 통보를 받았습니다.)라고 말했으므로 (D)가 정답

Paraphrasing road construction ➡ Road work

76 요청/제의/제안   난이도 하

해석 청자들은 무엇을 하라고 안내 받는가?
(A) 자리에 계속 앉아있으라고
(B) 할인 쿠폰을 가져가라고
(C) 소지품을 챙기라고
(D) 가족들에게 연락하라고

해설 화자가 Please make sure to take your belongings with you when you get off the bus. (버스에서 내리실 때는 반드시 소지품을 챙기시기 바랍니다.)라고 말했으므로 (C)가 정답

[미국]

Questions 77-79 refer to the following advertisement.

W: Have you been wanting to remodel the rooms in your house, but thought it was too expensive? Michelle's Design is your solution.(77) Working with our creative team, you'll be able to create a modern design for any space, from your kitchen to your bathroom. Stop by our office for a consultation and mention this advertisement, and we'll give you a complimentary picture frame.(78) This beautiful frame is available in several colors to match any casual space you have in your home. Give your house the makeover it deserves. Give us a call at 555-3426 to set up an appointment today.(79)

77-79번은 다음 광고에 관한 문제입니다.

여: 집의 방들을 리모델링하고 싶었는데 너무 비싸다고 생각하셨나요?(77) Michelle 디자인이 해결책입니다.(77) 저희 창의적인 팀과 함께하시면 주방부터 욕실까지 어떤 공간에든 현대적인 디자인을 만들어내실 수 있을 겁니다. 저희 사무실에 들러서 상담을 받으시고 이 광고를 보고 오셨다고 말씀하시면 무료 액자를 드립니다.(78) 이 아름다운 액자는 여러 가지 색상이 있어서 가정의 모든 편한 공간에 잘 어울립니다. 당신의 집에 마땅히 해야 할 단장을 해주세요. 오늘 555-3426으로 전화 주셔서 예약하시기 바랍니다.(79)

어휘 complimentary adj. 무료의 picture frame 사진틀, 액자 makeover n. (사람·장소의 모습을 개선하기 위한) 단장 deserve v. ~을 받을 만하다

---

77 주제/목적   난이도 중

해설 어떤 종류의 업체가 광고되고 있는가?
(A) 가정 조경 회사
(B) 인테리어 디자인 서비스 업체
(C) 사진 스튜디오
(D) 미술관

해설 화자가 Have you been wanting to remodel the rooms in your house, but thought it was too expensive? Michelle's Design is your solution.(집의 방들을 리모델링하고 싶으셨는데 너무 비싸다고 생각하셨나요? Michelle 디자인이 해결책입니다.)라고 말했으므로 (B)가 정답

78 세부정보   난이도 중

해설 청자들은 어떻게 무료 선물을 받을 수 있는가?
(A) 광고를 언급함으로써
(B) 후기를 게재함으로써
(C) 사진을 제출함으로써
(D) 설문조사를 작성함으로써

해설 화자가 Stop by our office for a consultation and mention this advertisement, and we'll give you a complimentary picture frame. (저희 사무실에 들러서 상담을 받으시고 이 광고를 보고 오셨다고 말씀하시면 무료 액자를 드립니다.)라고 말했으므로 (A)가 정답

Paraphrasing advertisement ➡ announcement

79 세부정보   난이도 중

해설 화자는 청자들이 전화 통화로 무엇을 할 수 있다고 말하는가?
(A) 액자를 주문할 수 있다고
(B) 길안내를 받을 수 있다고
(C) 시간 약속을 잡을 수 있다고
(D) 조언을 받을 수 있다고

해설 화자가 Give us a call at 555-3426 to set up an appointment today. (오늘 555-3426으로 전화 주셔서 예약하시기 바랍니다.)라고 말했으므로 (C)가 정답

Paraphrasing set up ➡ schedule

[호주]

Questions 80-82 refer to the following introduction.

M: Thank you all for joining us for the 15th Annual World Convention on Wildlife and Ecology.(80) I am excited to introduce our keynote speaker for today, Benedict Freeman from the Endangered Animals Association. Mr. Freeman is recognized as one of the leading activists involved in protecting endangered species.(81) For the past decade, he has gone on countless tours across the world advocating the preservation of wildlife habitats. But before we bring Mr. Freeman to the stage, I'd like to urge each of you to consider donating to the association.(82) Anything you can give will be a big help.

80-82번은 다음 소개말에 관한 문제입니다.

남: 제15회 연례 세계 야생 동물 및 생태계 박람회에 와주신 모든 분께 감사의 말씀 드립니다.(80) 오늘의 기조연설자이신 멸종 위기 동물협회의 Benedict Freeman을 소개해드리게 되어 정말 기쁩니다. Mr. Freeman은 멸종 위기종 보호에 관여하는 주요 활동가 중 한 분으로 인정받고 있습니다.(81) 그는 지난 10년 동안 전 세계를 수없이 다니시며 야생 동물 서식지의 보존을 주장해오셨습니다. Mr. Freeman을 무대로 모시기 전에, 협회에 대한 기부를 고려해주실 것을 여러분 모두에게 강력히 권장 드립니다.(82) 얼마를 기부하시든 큰 도움이 될 것입니다.

어휘 convention n. 박람회 wildlife n. 야생 동물 ecology n. 생태(계) keynote speaker 기조 연설자 endangered adj. (동식물이) 멸종될 위기에 이른 association n. 협회 be recognize as (~으로) 인정받다 activist n. (정치·사회운동) 운동가, 활동가 species n. 종 countless adj. 무수한, 셀 수 없이 많은 advocate v. 주장하다 preservation n. 보존 habitat n. 서식지 urge v. 강력히 권고하다

---

80 장소/근무지   난이도 하

해설 소개는 어디에서 이루어지고 있는가?
(A) 시상식
(B) 국제 박람회
(C) 기념일 파티
(D) 직원 오찬

해설 화자가 Thank you all for joining us for the 15th Annual World Convention on Wildlife and Ecology. (제15회 연례 세계 야생 동물

및 생태계 박람회에 와주신 모든 분께 감사의 말씀 드립니다.)라고 말했으므로 (B)가 정답

81 세부정보   난이도 중

해석 화자는 Benedict Freeman이 무엇으로 유명하다고 말하는가?
(A) 여행 서적
(B) 멸종 위기종을 위한 일
(C) 문제 해결 기술
(D) 식물 도감

해설 화자가 Mr. Freeman is recognized as one of the leading activists involved in protecting endangered species. (Mr. Freeman은 멸종 위기 종 보호에 관여하는 주요 활동가 중 한 분으로 인정받고 있습니다.)라고 말했으므로 (B)가 정답

Paraphrasing   recognized as ➡ known for

82 요청/제의/제공   난이도 중

해석 청자들은 무엇을 하도록 권장받는가?
(A) 초청 연사를 환영해달라고
(B) 설문지를 작성하라고
(C) 여행을 가라고
(D) 기부를 하라고

해설 화자가 But before we bring Mr. Freeman to the stage, I'd like to urge each of you to consider donating to the association. (Mr. Freeman을 무대로 모시기 전에, 협회에 대한 기부를 고려해주실 것을 여러분 모두에게 강력히 권장 드립니다.)라고 말했으므로 (D)가 정답

Paraphrasing   urge ➡ encourage, donate ➡ make a donation

[미국]

Questions 83-85 refer to the following announcement.

M: Hello, everybody. Good to see you all. **I know that we've got quite a few vehicles to fix today,**(83) so I'll make this quick. Before we start work for the day, I want to inform you about the new process for handling staff complaints and concerns. Employee feedback is very important to us, but it has been difficult getting your opinions on certain issues. **We realize that it's not always easy to speak up at work,**(84) even when you think something needs our attention. Now, we've added a section on our Web site, and every Monday morning, I will make a compilation of all the feedback provided in that section so that it can be reviewed by the supervisors.(84)/(85)

83-85번은 다음 공지에 관한 문제입니다.

남: 안녕하세요, 여러분. 모두 뵙게 되어 좋군요. **오늘 상당히 많은 차량을 수리해야 한다는 것을 알기에,**(83) 빨리 하도록 하겠습니다. 오늘 근무를 시작하기 전에, 새로운 직원 불만 및 고충처리 절차에 대해 알려드리고자 합니다. 직원 의견은 우리에게 매우 중요하지만, 특정 사안에 대한 의견을 듣는 건 어려웠습니다. 주목해야 할 부분이 있다고 생각하더라도, **직장에서 목소리를 내는 게 늘 쉽지만은 않다는 것을 알고 있습니다.**(84) 이제, 웹 사이트에 게시판을 하나 추가했습니다. 그리고 제가 매주 월요일 아침에 그 게시판에 올라온 의견을 모두 취합해서 관리자들이 검토할 수 있도록 할 것입니다.(84)(85)

어휘   quite a few 상당한 수   vehicle n. 차량   inform v. 알리다   process n. 절차   handle v. 처리하다   complaint n. 불만   concern n. 우려   opinion n. 의견   speak up 거리낌 없이 말하다   attention n. 주의, 주목, 관심   section n. 부문   compilation n. 모음집   review v. 검토하다   supervisor n. 관리자

83 장소/근무지   난이도 상

해석 청자들은 어떤 업체에서 일하겠는가?
(A) 채용 업체
(B) 자동차 정비소
(C) 전자제품 매장
(D) 마케팅 회사

해설 화자가 I know that we've got quite a few vehicles to fix today (오늘 상당히 많은 차량을 수리해야 한다는 것을 알기에)라고 말했으므로 (B)가 정답

Paraphrasing   vehicles ➡ auto, fix ➡ repair

84 화자 의도 파악   난이도 중

해석 화자가 "이제, 웹 사이트에 게시판을 하나 추가했습니다"라고 말할 때, 그가 의미한 것은?
(A) 신제품이 소개될 것이다.
(B) 직원 한 명이 채용되었다.
(C) 배치가 변경될 것이다.
(D) 문제가 해결되었다.

해설 화자가 We realize that it's not always easy to speak up at work (직장에서 목소리를 내는 게 늘 쉽지만은 않다는 것을 알고 있습니다.)라면서, Now, we've added a section on our Web site, and every Monday morning, I will make a compilation of all the feedback provided in that section so that it can be reviewed by the supervisors. (이제, 웹 사이트에 게시판을 하나 추가했습니다. 그리고 제가 매주 월요일 아침에 그 게시판에 올라온 의견을 모두 취합해서 관리자들이 검토할 수 있도록 할 것입니다.)라고 말했으므로 (D)가 정답

85 세부정보   난이도 중

해석 화자는 월요일마다 무엇을 할 계획인가?
(A) 의견을 취합한다
(B) 고객과 대화한다
(C) 재고를 점검한다
(D) 상품을 발송한다

해설 화자가 every Monday morning, I will make a compilation of all the feedback provided in that section (제가 매주 월요일 아침에 그 게시판에 올라온 의견을 모두 취합해서 관리자들이 검토할 수 있도록 할 것입니다)라고 말했으므로 (A)가 정답

Paraphrasing   make a compilation ➡ compile, feedback ➡ comments

영국

Questions 86-88 refer to the following telephone message.

W: Good afternoon, Mr. Herzog. When we spoke on the phone yesterday, **I asked you to come by our office to give us your bank account details to ensure that your wages get deposited correctly.**(86) **But I just realized that we already have your information from the last job you did for us.**(87) Your payment will be sent to that account on the tenth of next month. Additionally, **I suggest that you contact Human Resources and arrange to collect the official papers you'll need when filing your taxes. I'd do that sooner rather than later.**(88)

86-88번은 다음 전화 메시지에 관한 문제입니다.

여: 안녕하세요, Mr. Herzog. 어제 통화할 때, 임금이 제대로 입금되는지 확인할 수 있게 저희 사무실에 들러서 은행계좌 정보를 알려달라고 요청 드렸습니다.(86) 그런데 지난 번에 해주셔서 정보를 이미 가지고 있다는 걸 방금 알았어요.(87) 다음 달 10일에 그 계좌로 입금될 거예요. 그리고 세금을 신고하실 때 필요한 공식 서류를 받아가실 수 있도록 인사팀에 연락하시기를 권해드립니다. 빨리 하시는 게 나을 거예요.(88)

어휘 deposit v. 입금하다 arrange v. 예정을 세우다, 마련하다 file a tax 세금을 신고하다

---

86 장소/근무지   난이도 중

해석 화자는 어느 부서에서 근무하겠는가?
(A) 급여 관리
(B) 정보 기술
(C) 영업
(D) 연구 개발

해설 화자가 I asked you to come by our office to give us your bank account details to ensure that your wages get deposited correctly. (임금이 제대로 입금되는지 확인할 수 있게 사무실에 들러서 은행계좌 정보를 알려달라고 요청 드렸습니다.)라고 말했으므로 (A)가 정답

---

87 화자 의도 파악   난이도 상

해석 화자는 "지난번에 해주셔서 정보를 이미 가지고 있다"라고 말할 때 무엇을 의미하는가?
(A) 청자가 파일을 복구할 수 있었다.
(B) 청자가 방문할 필요가 없다.
(C) 화자에게 다른 업무가 있다.
(D) 화자에게 전화번호가 없다.

해설 화자가 I asked you to come by our office to give us your bank account details to ensure that your wages get deposited correctly. (임금이 제대로 입금되는지 확인할 수 있게 저희 사무실에 들러서 은행계좌 정보를 알려달라고 요청 드렸습니다.)라고 하면서, But I just realized that we already have your information from the last job you did for us. (그런데 지난 번에 해주셔서 정보를 이미 가지고 있다는 걸 방금 알았어요.)라고 말했으므로 (B)가 정답

---

88 요청/제의/제안   난이도 중

해석 화자는 청자에게 무엇을 얼른 하라고 권장하는가?
(A) 신규 계좌를 개설하라고
(B) 문서를 찾아가라고
(C) 다른 일자리에 대해 문의하라고
(D) 이력서를 이메일로 보내라고

해설 화자가 I suggest that you contact Human Resources and arrange to collect the official papers you'll need when filing your taxes. I'd do that sooner rather than later. (세금을 신고하실 때 필요한 공식 서류를 받아가실 수 있도록 인사팀에 연락하시기를 권해드립니다. 빨리 하시는 게 나을 거예요.)라고 말했으므로 (B)가 정답

Paraphrasing collect the official papers ➡ retrieve some documents

---

영국

Questions 89-91 refer to the following excerpt from a meeting.

W: Let's begin by taking a look at last month's production numbers. As you can see, we saw a seven percent decline in output, which means we'll need to raise our manufacturing rate in the factory. **We, as managers,**(89) are aware that a few of our packaging machines on the production line have been malfunctioning and that it is the cause of the decline. **So we've decided to install new ones this Friday.**(90) These machines function a lot quicker and won't require frequent repairs. **We have scheduled several training workshops next week, so please sign up for one as soon as possible.**(91) A list will be posted in the staff room.

89-91번은 다음 회의 발췌록에 관한 문제입니다.

여: 지난달 생산 수치를 보면서 시작합시다. 보시다시피 생산량이 7퍼센트 감소했는데, 이는 공장 생산률을 높여야 한다는 것을 의미합니다. 저희 관리자들은(89) 생산 라인의 포장기계 몇 대가 오작동을 일으키고 있으며 이것이 감소의 원인이라는 걸 알고 있는 바입니다. 따라서 이번 주 금요일에 새 기계를 설치하기로 했습니다.(90) 이 기계는 훨씬 더 빠르게 가동되며 잦은 수리도 필요하지 않을 것입니다. 다음 주에 교육 워크숍 일정을 잡아 놓았으니 되도록 빨리 신청하시기 바랍니다.(91) 목록은 직원 사무실에 게시하겠습니다.

어휘 production n. 생산 decline n. 감소 output n. 생산량, 산출량 raise v. (양·수준 등을) 올리다 manufacturing adj. 제조(업)의 rate n. 비율 aware adj. (~을) 알고 있는 packaging n. 포장 production line (일관 작업의) 제조[생산] 라인 malfunction v. 제대로 작동하지 않다 cause n. 원인 install v. 설치하다 function v. 기능하다 frequent adj. 잦은, 빈번한 repair n. 수리 schedule v. 일정을 잡다 sign up for ~을 신청[가입]하다 post v. 게시하다 staff room 직원 사무실

---

89 정체/신분   난이도 중

해석 화자는 누구겠는가?
(A) 수리 기사
(B) 공장 감독관

TEST 02 63

(C) 프로그램 개발자
(D) 자동차 판매사원

해설 화자가 which means we'll need to raise our manufacturing rate in the factory. We, as managers (이는 공장 생산률을 높여야 한다는 것을 의미합니다. 저희 관리자들은)라고 말했으므로 (B)가 정답

Paraphrasing factory ➡ plant, manager ➡ supervisor

90 세부정보   난이도 중

해석 화자에 따르면, 이번 주에 무엇이 교체될 것인가?
(A) 소프트웨어
(B) 기계
(C) 이름표
(D) 보관시설

해설 화자가 are aware that a few of our packaging machines on the production line have been malfunctioning, and that it is the cause of the decline. So we've decided to install new ones this Friday. (생산 라인의 포장기계 몇 대가 오작동을 일으키고 있으며 이것이 감소의 원인이라는 걸 알고 있는 바입니다. 따라서 이번 주 금요일에 새 기계를 설치하기로 했습니다.)라고 말했으므로 (B)가 정답

Paraphrasing packaging machines ➡ some machinery, install new ones ➡ replace

91 요청/제의/제안   난이도 중

해석 청자들은 무엇을 하라고 요청 받는가?
(A) 교육에 등록하라고
(B) 안전 장비를 착용하라고
(C) 다가오는 검사에 대비하라고
(D) 아이디어를 제안하라고

해설 화자가 We have scheduled several training workshops next week, so please sign up for one as soon as possible. (다음 주에 교육 워크숍 일정을 잡아 놓았으니 되도록 빨리 신청하시기 바랍니다.) 라고 말했으므로 (A)가 정답

Paraphrasing training workshops ➡ training session, sign up ➡ register

[미국]

Questions 92-94 refer to the following announcement.

W: As you may have heard, Greg Velasquez, who has always handled our Web site, will be retiring next month. Here at Diamante Dairy, we fully understand the importance of the Web site for our Sales Department, which processes online orders from supermarkets and eateries all over the state for our farm's products.(92) We've interviewed a few candidates but finally chose to work with an outside firm, Web Maestros, instead of hiring somebody to do Greg's job in-house. This is a well-respected company that Greg himself thought would do a great job.(93) Now, I know it's been great having Greg right here to help us, but keep in mind, Web Maestros will designate a qualified technician to us.(94)

92-94번 문제는 다음 공지에 관한 문제입니다.

여: 아마 들으셨겠지만, 항상 우리 웹 사이트를 관리해주셨던 Greg Velasquez께서 다음 달에 은퇴하십니다. Diamante Dairy는 우리 영업부에게 주 전역의 슈퍼마켓과 식당에서 들어오는 우리 농장 제품의 온라인 주문을 처리하는 웹 사이트가 얼마나 중요한지 잘 알고 있습니다.(92) 몇 명의 지원자들을 인터뷰했지만, Greg의 업무를 맡을 직원을 채용하는 대신, 외부 업체 Web Maestros와 함께 하기로 최종 선택했습니다. 이 회사는 높이 평가되며, Greg 본인이 생각하기에도 업무 수행을 잘 할거라네요.(93) 자, Greg가 여기 계시면서 저희에게 도움을 주셔서 정말 좋았지만, Web Maestros도 우리에게 능력 있는 전문가를 지정해줄 거라는 걸 기억해 주세요.(94)

어휘 dairy n. 유제품 회사 process v. 처리하다 eatery n. 음식점, 식당 in-house adv. 사내에서 well-respected adj. 높이 평가되는 keep in mind 명심하다 designate v. 지명하다

92 장소/근무지   난이도 중

해석 청자들은 어디에서 근무하는가?
(A) 낙농장에서
(B) 식료품점에서
(C) 제과점에서
(D) 식당에서

해설 화자가 Here at Diamante Dairy, we fully understand the importance of the Web site for our Sales Department, which processes online orders from supermarkets and eateries all over the state for our farm's products. (Diamante Dairy는 우리 영업부에게 주 전역의 슈퍼마켓과 식당에서 들어오는 우리 농장제품의 온라인 주문을 처리하는 웹 사이트가 얼마나 중요한지 잘 알고 있습니다.) 라고 말했으므로 (A)가 정답

93 세부정보   난이도 상

해석 회사는 Web Maestros에 관하여 어떻게 알게 되었는가?
(A) TV 광고를 통해
(B) 현 직원을 통해
(C) 전 고객을 통해
(D) 신문 광고를 통해

해설 화자가 This is a well-respected company that Greg himself thought would do a great job. (이 회사는 높이 평가되며, Greg 본인이 생각하기에도 업무 수행을 잘 할거라네요.)라고 말했으므로 (B)가 정답

94 화자 의도 파악   난이도 상

해석 화자는 왜 "Web Maestros도 우리에게 능력있는 전문가를 지정해줄 것입니다"라고 말하는가?
(A) 프로젝트가 지연될 것이다.
(B) 계약이 검토되어야 한다.
(C) 청자들은 걱정할 필요가 없다.
(D) 청자들이 입사 지원자 면접을 진행해야 한다.

해설 화자가 Now, I know it's been great having Greg right here to help us,(자, Greg가 여기 계시면서 저희에게 도움을 주셔서 정말 좋았지만,)라고 하면서, but keep in mind Web Maestros will designate a qualified technician to us.(Web Maestros도 우리에게 능력 있는 전문가를 지정해줄 거라는 걸 기억해 주세요.)라고 말했으므로 (C)가 정답

[호주]

Questions 95-97 refer to the following announcement and schedule.

M: I am excited to announce that our company will soon begin its month-long Productivity Challenge. As you can see by this schedule, for each week in March, we'll hold daily sessions on one aspect of becoming a more effective employee. **Teams with 100-percent participation will be rewarded with generous prize money.**(95) In addition, the company will be holding a health seminar at the local recreation center. This event will be held at the end of the week that is dedicated to physical activity.(96) This will give you a chance to learn how to eat right and adopt a healthy lifestyle. For those of you who'd like to participate in the special seminar, complete a registration form online.(97)

Productivity Challenge	
WEEK 1	Organize your life and your work
WEEK 2	Energize with physical activity(96)
WEEK 3	Update your technical skills
WEEK 4	Improve your public speaking

95-97번은 다음 공지와 일정표에 관한 문제입니다.

남: 우리 회사가 한 달간 생산성 증진 프로그램을 시작할 예정임을 알려드리게 되어 기쁩니다. 이 일정표에서 보실 수 있는 것처럼, 3월 한 달간 매주 더욱 유능한 직원이 되는 한 가지 방법에 관해 매일 교육을 진행할 예정입니다. **참석률이 100퍼센트인 팀은 후한 상금을 포상으로 받게 됩니다.**(95) 뿐만 아니라 우리 회사는 이 지역 레크리에이션 센터에서 건강 세미나를 주최합니다. 이 행사는 주로 운동을 많이 하는 주말에 열릴 예정입니다.(96) 이 세미나를 통해 여러분은 올바른 식습관을 갖고 건강한 생활방식으로 바꿀 수 있는 기회를 얻게 될 것입니다. 특별 세미나에 참석하시고 싶은 분들은 온라인 등록양식을 작성하시기 바랍니다.(97)

생산성 증진 프로그램	
1주차	삶과 일을 정리하라
2주차	신체 활동으로 활기를 얻어라(96)
3주차	기술 역량을 개발하라
4주차	발표력을 향상시켜라

어휘 productivity n. 생산성 challenge n. (해볼 만한) 과제 session n. (특정한 활동을 위한) 시간[기간] aspect n. 측면 effective adj. 효과적인 be rewarded with ~로 포상[보상]받다 generous adj. 후한 in addition 게다가 hold 개최하다 be dedicated to ~에 바치다 adopt v. (특정한 방식이나 자세를) 쓰다[취하다] participate in ~에 참가하다 complete v. 작성하다 registration n. 등록 organize v. 정리하다 energize v. 활기[기운]를 북돋우다 improve v. 개선하다 public speaking 연설

95 세부정보 난이도 중

해석 일부 직원들은 어떤 보상을 받을 것인가?
(A) 상금
(B) 1일 휴가
(C) 할인 쿠폰
(D) 무료 식사

해설 화자가 Teams with 100-percent participation will be rewarded with generous prize money. (참석률이 100퍼센트인 팀은 후한 상금을 포상으로 받게 됩니다.) 라고 말했으므로 (A)가 정답

Paraphrasing prize money ➡ cash prize

96 시각 정보 연계 난이도 상

해석 시각 정보를 보시오. 세미나는 언제 있을 것인가?
(A) 1주차
(B) 2주차
(C) 3주차
(D) 4주차

해설 화자가 In addition, the company will be holding a health seminar at the local recreation center. This event will be held at the end of the week that is dedicated to physical activity. (뿐만 아니라 저희는 이 지역 레크리에이션 센터에서 건강 세미나를 주최합니다. 이 행사는 주로 운동을 많이 하는 주말에 열릴 예정입니다.)라고 말했고, 시각 자료에서 Energize with physical activity (신체 활동으로 활기를 얻어라)가 WEEK 2 (2주차)임을 확인할 수 있으므로 (B)가 정답

97 세부정보 난이도 중

해석 세미나에 참석하고 싶은 청자들은 어떻게 해야 하는가?
(A) 행사 주최측에 연락해야 한다
(B) 설명회에 가야 한다
(C) 보증금을 지불해야 한다
(D) 신청서를 작성해야 한다

해설 화자가 For those of you who'd like to participate in the special seminar, complete a registration form online. (특별 세미나에 참석하시고 싶은 분들은 온라인 등록양식을 작성하시기 바랍니다.) 라고 말했으므로 (D)가 정답

Paraphrasing want to attend ➡ would like to participate, complete ➡ fill out

[영국]

Questions 98-100 refer to the following excerpt from a conference and diagram.

W: So far, we've discussed identifying your target market, researching the competition, and determining the prices of your services and products. As you know, finding success in any industry is difficult, so **as new entrepreneurs in the tourism sector,**(98) you must find ways to differentiate and make your business stand out. Before we move on to discuss launching your business, there is an important stage that we need to cover. **We have a guest speaker today, a renowned Web designer, who will talk about building your Web site and the essential elements it should contain.**(99) Before we invite our guest speaker to the stage, I'd like to remind everyone that there is a site builder program that you can try out in the computer lab on the first floor, so please check it out at the end of the conference.(100)

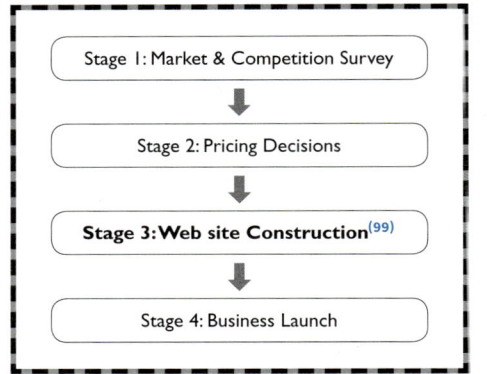

98-100번은 다음 회의 발췌록과 도표에 관한 문제입니다.

여: 지금까지 우리는 목표 시장 확인하기, 경쟁업체 조사하는 것, 그리고 서비스와 제품의 가격 결정하는 것에 대해 논했습니다. 아시다시피, 어떤 업계에서든 성공하기란 어렵습니다. 따라서 **관광업 분야의 새내기 사업자로서,** ⁽⁹⁸⁾ 여러분은 자신의 사업체를 차별화하고 눈에 띄게 할 방법을 찾아내야 합니다. 이어서 사업체 설립을 논하기 전에 다루어야 할 중요한 단계가 하나 있습니다. **오늘 유명 웹 디자이너를 연사로 모셨는데, 웹 사이트 제작 및 필수 포함 요소에 대해 알려주실 거예요.**⁽⁹⁹⁾ 연사분을 강당으로 모시기 전에 다시 한번 알려드리면, **1층 컴퓨터실에 사용해보실 수 있는 사이트 제작 프로그램이 있으니 학회가 끝나면 가서 확인해 보시기 바랍니다.**⁽¹⁰⁰⁾

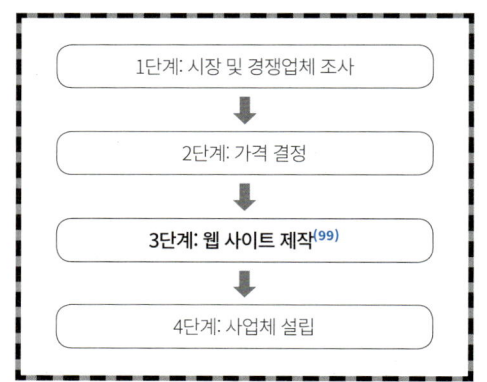

어휘 so far 지금까지 identify v. 확인하다, 알아보다 entrepreneur n. 사업가, 기업가 differentiate v. ~을 차별화시키다 stand out 눈에 띄다, 두드러지다 launch v. 시작하다, 착수하다 cover v. 다루다 renowned adj. 유명한, 명성 있는 element n. 요소 try out 시험 적으로 사용해보다 lab n. 실습실

98 장소/근무지   난이도 중

해석 청자들은 어떤 업계에 종사하는가?
(A) 정보 기술
(B) 식품 산업
(C) 건강 관리
(D) 관광업

해설 화자가 as new entrepreneurs in the tourism sector, (관광업 분야의 새내기 사업자로서,)라고 말했으므로 (D)가 정답

99 시각 정보 연계   난이도 상

해석 시각 자료를 보시오. 연사는 어느 단계에 대해 논할 것인가?
(A) 1단계
(B) 2단계
(C) 3단계
(D) 4단계

해설 화자가 We have a guest speaker today, a renowned Web designer, who will talk about building your Web site and the essential elements it should contain. (오늘 유명 웹 디자이너를 연사로 모셨는데, 웹 사이트 제작 및 필수 포함 요소에 대해 알려주실 거예요.)라고 말했고, 시각 자료에서 Stage 3: Web site construction (3단계: 웹 사이트 제작)을 확인할 수 있으므로 (C)가 정답

Paraphrasing building your Web site ➡ Web site construction

100 세부정보   난이도 중

해석 화자에 따르면, 청자들은 1층에서 무엇을 할 수 있는가?
(A) 다른 세미나에 참석할 수 있다
(B) 우려를 표할 수 있다
(C) 컴퓨터 프로그램을 이용할 수 있다
(D) 지도를 확인할 수 있다

해설 화자가 I'd like to remind everyone that there is a site builder program that you can try out in the computer lab on the first floor, so please check it out at the end of the conference. (1층 컴퓨터실에 사용해보실 수 있는 사이트 제작 프로그램이 있으니 학회가 끝나면 가서 확인해 보시기 바랍니다.)라고 말했으므로 (C)가 정답

Paraphrasing try out ➡ access

PART 5

101 어휘 • 명사   난이도 중

해석 Meilee Zhang은 계약 협상가로서 행한 수많은 기여로 승진 대상자로 지명되었다.

해설 빈칸은 전치사 for의 목적어인 명사자리. 문맥상 '협상가로서 많은 기여를 하여 승진 대상자로 지명되었다'는 의미가 되어야 자연스러우므로 (B)가 정답

Key word
Meilee Zhang was **nominated for a promotion for** her many **contributions** as contract negotiator.

오답보기 확인
(A) competitor 경쟁자
(C) computation 계산
(D) consideration 고려사항

어휘 nominate v. (후보자로) 지명하다 promotion n. 승진 contribution n. 기여, 공헌; 기부(금) contract n. 계약 negotiator n. 협상가

102 어휘 • 부사   난이도 중

해석 콘서트 주최자들은 원래 Dartmoor 대학에서 행사를 주최하려고 계획했지만, 그곳은 너무 외진 곳으로 여겨졌다.

해설 빈칸은 주어와 동사 사이 부사 자리. 접속사 but으로 연결된 두 문장 관계를 고려할 때, 문맥상 '원래 Dartmoor 대학에서의 행사를 계획했지만, 너무 외지다고 여겨졌다'는 내용으로 이어져야 자연스러우므로 (B)가 정답

Key word
The concert organizers **originally** planned to hold the event at Dartmoor College, **but** it was deemed too remote.

오답보기 확인
(A) evenly 균등하게
(C) relatively 비교적
(D) excellently 훌륭하게

어휘 organizer n. 주최자, 조직자 originally 원래 plan v. 계획하다 hold v. 개최하다 deem v. ~로 여기다 remote adj. 외진

103 어휘 • 형용사　　　난이도 중

해석 매달 20일 이후 청구된 금액은 그 다음 달 명세서에 반영될 것입니다.

해설 빈칸은 명사 month를 수식하는 형용사 자리. 문맥상 '20일 이후 청구 금액은 그 다음 달 명세서에 반영된다'는 의미가 되어야 자연스러우므로 (C)가 정답

Key word
Amount charged after the 20th of every month will be reflected on the **following** month's statement.

오답보기 확인
(A) developing 발전하는
(B) incoming 들어오는
(D) accompanying 수반하는

어휘 amount n. 액수, 양 charge v. 청구하다 reflect v. 반영하다 following 그 다음의 statement n. 명세서

104 구조/문법 • 소유대명사　　　난이도 중

해석 인사팀원들은 그들의 것이 수리되는 동안 마케팅 부서의 복사기를 사용할 수 있다.

해설 빈칸은 while 종속절 내 주어 자리. 빈칸 뒤 단수동사(is)가 있으므로 they는 올 수 없고, 문맥상 '인사팀의 복사기가 수리되는 동안'이라는 의미가 되어야 자연스러우므로 '인사팀의 것'을 지칭하는 소유대명사 (D)가 정답

Key point
주격 인칭대명사와 소유대명사 모두 주어 자리에 올 수 있으므로, 주어-동사 간 수일치 및 문맥 등을 통해 대명사가 가리키는 대상을 파악한다.

어휘 photocopier n. 복사기 repair v. 수리하다

105 구조/문법 • 부사　　　난이도 중

해석 가상 사설 통신망을 사용하지 않으신다면, 비밀번호를 정기적으로 변경하는 것이 권장됩니다.

해설 빈칸은 주어인 동명사를 수식하는 자리이므로 부사 (C)가 정답

Key point
동명사는 부사의 수식을 받는다.

어휘 virtual private network 가상 사설 통신망 advise v. 권고하다

106 구조/문법 • 관계부사　　　난이도 상

해석 올 봄 저희 West 음악 축제로 초대합니다, 거기에서 저희 신곡이 처음으로 연주될 것입니다.

해설 빈칸은 콤마로 연결된 완전한 두 문장을 연결하는 자리이므로 접속사 where만 가능하다. (A) thus, (B) together, (D) resulting은 접속사가 아니므로 답이 될 수 없다. 문맥상으로도 '음악 축제에 오세요, 그리고 거기에서(음악 축제에서) 저희 신곡이 최초로 연주됩니다'라는 의미로 이어져야 자연스러우므로 관계부사 (C)가 정답

Key point
관계부사 where는 '접속사+시간부사(구)' 역할을 하며, 문장에서 수식어 역할을 하는 부사구를 대신하기에 관계부사 뒤에는 완전한 문장이 온다.

어휘 catch v. 잡다, ~를 듣다[보다] perform v. 연주[공연]하다 for the first time 처음으로

107 구조/문법 • 형용사　　　난이도 중

해석 Min-hee Park는 신체 운동의 긍정적인 효과에 대한 자신의 연구를 인기 논픽션 영화로 만들었다.

해설 빈칸은 명사 effects를 수식하는 형용사 자리. 문맥상 '신체운동의 긍정적인 효과에 대한 연구'라는 의미가 되어야 자연스러우므로 형용사 (B)가 정답

Key point
형용사 자리인데 보기에 일반적인 형용사와 분사가 같이 나와 있으면 일부 특별한 경우 외에는 일반 형용사의 정답 확률이 높다. ~ing와 -ed만 붙인다고 다 형용사가 되는 건 아니기 때문이다. 일반 형용사와 같이 있을 때 답이 될 수 있는 분사형 형용사는 pleased, delighted, extended, respected 정도만 기억하면 된다.

어휘 transform v. 변형시키다 effect n. 영향, 효과 favorable adj. 유리한, 좋은 physical exercise 신체운동 popular adj. 인기 있는 nonfiction n. 논픽션

108 구조/문법 • 과거분사　　　난이도 중

해석 도착시간은 교통상황에 따라 달라질 수 있기에, 표에 나온 일정은 예상치일 뿐입니다.

해설 빈칸은 주절의 주어 The schedule과 동사 is 사이 주어를 수식하는 자리. 문맥상 '차트에 보이는 일정'이라는 수동의 의미가 되어야 자연스러우므로 과거분사 (C)가 정답

Key point
분사를 푸는 방법은 의외로 간단하다.
(1) 보기에 동사와 분사가 나와 있으므로 빈칸이 동사 자리인지 분사 자리인지부터 파악한다. 이 문장에는 이미 is라는 동사가 있으므로, 빈칸에는 동사가 들어갈 수 없다. 따라서 (A), (D) 탈락
(2) 이제 현재분사와 과거분사 중 고르는 문제이므로 빈칸 뒤에 목적어의 유무를 따져 목적어가 있으면 현재분사를, 없으면 과거분사를 고른다. 뒤에 목적어가 없으므로 (B) 탈락
의미상으로도 과거분사는 수식하는 대상과 의미상 수동 관계(~한 상태를 당한), 현재분사는 수식하는 대상과 의미상 능동 관계(~한 상태를 유발시키는)를 갖는다.

어휘 chart n. 도표, 차트 estimate n. 추정치 depending on ~에 따라 traffic conditions 교통 상황

109 구조/문법+어휘•접속사 난이도 중

해석 창고 관리자는 작업자들에게 더 많은 직원들이 이전할 때까지 그들이 추가 근무를 해야 할거라고 말했다.

해설 빈칸은 that 명사절 내 주절과 종속절을 연결하는 접속사 자리. 문맥상 '더 많은 직원들이 이전할 때까지 추가근무를 해야 할 것'이라는 의미가 되어야 자연스러우므로 (C)가 정답

> **Key word**
> The warehouse manager told the order fillers that **until more employees relocated**, they would have to work additional hours.

어휘 warehouse n. 창고 order filler 주문 이행자 relocate v. 이전하다 additional adj. 추가의

110 구조/문법•동사 – 수동태 난이도 중

해석 Mr. Watson은 정규 영업 시간이 끝난 후 배송되는 모든 농산물과 육류 수송품을 받는 것을 담당한다.

해설 빈칸은 when 종속절 내 주어 뒤 동사자리. 뒤에 목적어가 없으므로 수동태 (A)가 정답. 의미상으로도 they가 가리키는 대상이 'all produce or meat shipment'이므로, '모든 농산물 및 육류 수송품이 배송될 때'라는 의미를 완성하는 수동태 동사구문 (A)가 정답

> **Key point**
> 대명사를 주어로 하는 동사문제에서는 대명사가 지칭하는 대상이 무엇인지를 먼저 문맥을 통해 파악한 후, 그 대상과 수/태/시제가 일치하는 동사를 찾는다.

어휘 accept v. 받아주다 produce n. 농산물 meat n. 고기 shipment n. 수송(품) business hours 영업시간

111 어휘•부사 난이도 중

해석 우리 지역 공급업체는 우리가 현지에서 필요로 하는 원료를 가지고 있지 않기 때문에, 우리는 대신 더 규모가 큰 공급업체에서 그것들을 주문했다.

해설 빈칸은 문장 끝에서 동사구를 수식하는 부사 자리. 접속사 as로 연결된 두 문장 관계를 고려할 때, 문맥상 '우리가 거래하는 업체에 필요한 원료가 없어서, 대신 더 큰 제조사에서 주문했다'는 의미로 이어져야 자연스러우므로 (D)가 정답

> **Key word**
> As our local supplier **did not have** the raw **materials we required** on site, **we ordered them from a larger provider instead**.

> **오답보기 확인**
> (A) alike 마찬가지로
> (B) rather 상당히, 오히려
> (C) though 그렇지만

어휘 local adj. 지역의 supplier n. 공급업체 raw materials 원자재 require v. 필요로 하다 on site 현장의 provider n. 공급업체 instead adj. 대신에

112 문법/구조+어휘•명사 난이도 중

해석 Marie Speer의 훌륭한 리더십의 결과, 스마트폰 부서는 빠른 성장을 이루었다.

해설 빈칸은 형용사 rapid의 수식을 받는 명사자리. rapid 앞에 관사가 없으므로 가산단수명사인 grower는 답이 될 수 없고, 문맥상으로도 '빠른 성장을 이루었다'는 의미가 되어야 자연스러우므로 불가산명사 (A)가 정답

> **Key point**
> ① 명사 growth vs. grower: 불가산명사 growth는 '성장'을, 가산명사 grower는 '재배자'를 의미한다.
> ② 가산명사는 반드시 관사와 함께, 또는 복수형으로 사용한다.

어휘 able adj. 재간 있는, 훌륭한 achieve v. 이루다, 성취하다 rapid adj. 빠른

113 어휘•형용사 난이도 중

해석 새로운 시각을 얻기 위해, Ellerton Security에서는 새로운 인사 분야 임원을 외부에서 찾고 있다.

해설 빈칸은 명사 search를 수식하는 형용사 자리. 문두의 to부정사구를 고려할 때, 문맥상 '새로운 시각을 얻기 위해 새로운 인사 분야 임원을 외부에서 찾고 있다'는 의미가 되어야 자연스러우므로 (B)가 정답

> **Key word**
> **To gain a new perspective**, Ellerton Security is **conducting an external search for a new director** of human resources.

> **오답보기 확인**
> (A) available 이용 가능한
> (C) alternating 교차의
> (D) organized 조직적인, 체계적인

어휘 gain v. 얻다 perspective n. 관점, 시각 security n. 보안 conduct v. (특정 활동을) 하다 external adj. 외부의 search n. 탐색 human resources 인사

114 구조/문법•접속사 난이도 상

해석 건축업자들은 건설현장에 있는 동안 항상 안전모를 착용해야 한다.

해설 의미상 '건설현장에 있는 동안에는 항상 안전모를 써야 한다'는 의미가 되어야 자연스러우므로 (A) while이 정답이 되고, 이는 while they are on the construction site에서 they are가 생략되어 접속사 뒤에 전치사구만 남아 있는 형태이다. 문장구조상 부사들도 들어갈 수는 있지만 의미상 맞지 않다.

> **Key point**
> 접속사 while의 특징: 'while+(주어+be동사)+전치사구'의 구조에서 종속절과 주절의 주어가 동일한 경우, '주어+be동사'는 함께 생략할 수 있다.

어휘 builder n. 건축업자 wear v. 입다 hard hat 안전모 at all times 항상 construction n. 건설 site n. 현장, 장소

115 어휘•부사 난이도 상

해석 Top Post 문구는 사려 깊게 만들어진 다양한 축하카드 및 선물들을 판매한다.

해설 빈칸은 형용사 자리의 과거분사를 수식하는 부사 자리. 문맥상 '사려깊게 제작된 다양한 축하카드들'이라는 의미가 되어야 자연스러우므로 (C)가 정답

> **Key word**
> Top Post Stationery offers a range of **thoughtfully created** greeting cards and gifts.

> **오답보기 확인**
> (A) tremendously 엄청나게
> (B) neglectfully 무관심하게
> (D) considerably 상당히

어휘	stationery n. 문구류 offer v. 제공하다 a range of 다양한 thoughtfully adv. 사려 깊게 greeting card 축하카드

116 구조/문법 • 동사 – 능동태, 수일치 　난이도 중

해석 누락된 허가증 때문에, Ms. Cheung은 그 부지에 새로운 건물을 지으려는 신청이 기각되었다.

해설 빈칸은 주어와 목적어 사이 동사 자리. 주어가 단수이므로 수일치에서 (B) 탈락, 빈칸 뒤에 목적어가 있으므로 빈칸에는 능동태 동사가 와야 한다는 점에서 수동태인 (C), (D) 탈락

Key point
동사 문제는 '주어의 단/복수에 따른 수일치 확인 → 빈칸 뒤 목적어 유무에 따른 태일치 확인 → 시간 부사구를 찾아 시제 일치 확인'순으로 푼다.

어휘 missing adj. 빠진, 없어진 permit n. 허가증 application n. 신청서 construct v. 건설하다 property n. 부동산, 재산

117 어휘 • 전치사 　난이도 중

해석 증가하는 석유 비용을 고려하여, 상품 판매 부서는 무료 배송의 이용 가능성을 줄이라고 권고 받고 있다.

해설 빈칸은 명사구를 목적어로 하는 전치사 자리. 주절과 명사구의 의미관계를 고려할 때, 문맥상 '증가하는 석유비용을 고려하여, 무료 배송의 이용 가능성을 줄이라고 권고 받고 있다'는 내용으로 이어져야 자연스러우므로 (D)가 정답

Key word
<u>Given</u> the rising cost of petroleum, the merchandising team is being advised to decrease the availability of free shipping.

어휘 given prep. ~을 고려해서, ~를 고려해 볼 때 rising adj. 증가하는 cost n. 비용 petroleum n. 석유 merchandising n. 판매, 판촉 decrease v. 감소하다 availability n. 이용 가능성

118 구조/문법 • 형용사 　난이도 중

해석 Mr. Briggs의 프로그램 설명서는 새로운 소프트웨어에 익숙하지 않은 고객들에게 유익하다고 판명되어야 한다.

해설 빈칸은 동사 prove 뒤 주격 보어 자리. 문맥상 '설명서는 유익하다고 판명되어야 한다'는 의미가 되어야 자연스러우므로 형용사 (C)가 정답

Key point
주격보어를 필요로 하는 대표적인 2형식 동사는 be(~이다), become(~하게 되다), remain(여전히 ~이다), seem(~인 것 같다), appear(~인 것 같다) 등이며, 주격 보어 자리에는 주어와 의미상 동격을 이루는 명사 또는 주어를 설명하는 형용사가 올 수 있는데, 토익 시험에서는 주격 보어 자리에 거의 형용사가 답이 되는 문제가 출제되고 있다.

어휘 manual n. 설명서 prove v. 증명하다 customer n. 고객 unfamiliar adj. 익숙하지 않은

119 어휘 • 동사 　난이도 중

해석 Hancock 금융 서비스는 계정 소유자의 허가 없이 절대 고객 정보를 다른 당사자들에게 공개하지 않습니다.

해설 빈칸은 주어와 목적어 사이 동사 자리. 문맥상 '고객정보를 다른 당사자들에게 절대 공개하지 않는다'는 의미가 되어야 자연스러우므로 (D)가 정답

Key word
Hancock Financial Services never <u>discloses</u> client information to other parties without the account holder's authorization.

오답보기 확인
(A) locate (특정 위치에) 두다
(B) manage 운영하다
(C) collect 수집하다

어휘 disclose v. 노출하다, 공개하다 client n. 고객 party n. 당사자 account holder 계좌 소유자 authorization n. 허가(증)

120 어휘 • 전치사구 　난이도 상

해석 모든 서류가 유효하다면, 임시 취업 비자를 발급하는 데 일주일도 걸리지 않을 것이다.

해설 빈칸은 if 종속절 내 be동사 뒤 보어자리. 주절과의 관계를 고려할 때, 문맥상 '모든 서류가 유효하다면, 비자 발급에 일주일도 걸리지 않을 것'이라는 의미가 되어야 자연스러우므로 (B)가 정답

Key word
If all of your paperwork is <u>in order</u>, the temporary working visa should take less than a week to issue.

오답보기 확인
(A) on call 대기 중인
(C) on duty 근무 중인
(D) in advance 사전에, 미리

어휘 paperwork n. 서류 (작업) in order 유효한, 적법한 temporary adj. 임시의 working visa 취업비자 issue v. 발부하다

121 어휘 • 명사 　난이도 중

해석 Belknap 협회의 회원 자격은 전문 과학자들뿐만 아니라 아마추어에게도 열려 있다.

해설 빈칸은 문장의 주어 자리. 문맥상 '협회 회원 자격은 전문 과학자뿐만 아니라 아마추어에게도 열려 있다'는 의미가 되어야 자연스러우므로 (D)가 정답

Key word
<u>Membership</u> in the Belknap Association is open to amateur as well as professional scientists.

오답보기 확인
(A) allowance 허용량
(B) endorsement (공개적인) 지지
(C) certification 증명

어휘 membership n. 회원, 회원자격 amateur adj. 아마추어의 as well as 뿐만 아니라 professional adj. 전문적인

122 어휘 • 부사 　난이도 중

해석 예전에 우리 법무 부장이었던 Mr. Belfort가 방금 법무 임원으로 임명되었다.

해설 빈칸은 바로 뒤 Mr. Belfort의 보어에 해당하는 명사구(our deportment manager)를 수식하는 부사 자리. 문맥상 '예전에 법무 부장이었던 Mr. Belfort가 법무 임원으로 임명되었다'는 의미가 되어야 자연스러우므로 (C)가 정답

Key word
<u>Formerly</u> our Legal Department manager, Mr. Belfort has just been appointed Director of Legal Affairs.

오답보기 확인
(A) exclusively 오로지, 독점적으로
(B) candidly 솔직히
(D) exactly 정확히

어휘 formerly adj. 예전에 legal department 법무부 appoint v. 임명하다 legal affairs 법무

123 구조/문법+어휘 • 전치사 　난이도 중

해석 Ms. Romanov는 유통망을 늘림으로써 Robertson사에서 소중한 재원이 되었다.

해설 빈칸은 동명사구를 목적어로 하는 전치사 자리. 문맥상 '유통망을 늘림으로써, 회사의 인재가 되었다'는 의미가 되어야 자연스러우므로 전치사 (C)가 정답

Key word
전치사 by는 'by ~ing'의 형태로 쓰여 '~함으로써'라는 '수단, 방법'을 의미한다.

어휘 valued adj. 소중한 resource n. 자원 distribution network 유통망

124 어휘 • 동사 　난이도 상

해석 감정사가 예술 작품의 가격을 50,000달러로 평가하기는 했지만, 당신이 온라인으로 송금할 수 있다면 소유주가 기꺼이 협상해 줄 수도 있다.

해설 빈칸은 the owner를 주어로 하는 주절의 동사 자리. 문장 앞, 뒤의 while 및 if 종속절의 내용을 고려할 때, 문맥상 '감정가는 5만 달러이지만, 온라인으로 송금할 경우, 소유주가 협상해 줄 수도 있다'는 의미가 되어야 자연스러우므로 (B)가 정답

Key word
While the auditor has valued the artwork at $50,000, the owner may be willing to negotiate if you can pay by wire transfer.

오답보기 확인
(A) diminish 줄어들다, 약해지다
(C) include 포함하다
(D) contradict 반박하다, 모순되다

어휘 auditor n. 감정사 value v. (가치, 가격을) 평가하다 negotiate v. 협상하다 wire transfer 온라인 송금

125 구조/문법 • 형용사 - 최상급 　난이도 중

해석 Toronto에 있는 제조공장은 9월 마지막 주에 생산량이 사상 최고치에 도달했다고 발표했다.

해설 빈칸은 명사 rate을 수식하는 형용사 자리. 빈칸 뒤 부사 ever가 있음을 고려할 때, '생산량이 9월 마지막 주에 사상 최고치에 도달했다'는 의미가 되어야 자연스러우므로 최상급 형용사 (B)가 정답

Key point
최상급 강조부사 ever: '이제까지 중 가장 ~한'이라는 최상급의 의미를 더욱 강조해 주는 역할을 한다.

어휘 manufacturing plant 제조공장 report v. 알리다, 발표하다 production n. 생산 figure n. 수치 reach v. 도달하다 rate n. 속도, 비율

126 구조/문법 • 명사 　난이도 중

해석 교육 감독관들은 공식 승인을 위해 최근 채용된 인턴들에 대한 최종 평가를 제출했다.

해설 빈칸은 명사 training과 복합명사를 이루는 문장의 주어자리. 빈칸 뒤 복수동사 have가 있으며, 문맥상 '교육 감독관들이 평가를 제출했다'는 의미가 되어야 자연스러우므로 복수 사람명사 (C)가 정답

Key point
명사 supervision vs. supervisor: 'supervision'은 '감독, 관리'를, supervisor는 '감독관'을 의미한다.

어휘 turn in 제출하다 final adj. 최종의 evaluation n. 평가 official adj. 공식적인 approval n. 승인

127 어휘 • 형용사 　난이도 상

해석 많은 사람들이 정기 검진을 위해 치과 의사를 기다리는 시간을 거의 참을 수 없어한다.

해설 빈칸은 동사 find의 목적격 보어인 형용사 자리. 문맥상 '치과 검진 전 대기하는 것을 참을 수 없어 한다'는 의미가 되어야 자연스러우므로 (A)가 정답

Key word
Many people find the wait before seeing the dentist for their routine checkup almost unbearable.

오답보기 확인
(B) irresistible 거부할 수 없는, 불가항력의
(C) inexplicable 설명할 수 없는, 이해하기 힘든
(D) unbeatable 타의 추종을 불허하는, 무적의

어휘 wait n. 기다림, 기다리는 시간 dentist n. 치과의사 routine checkup 정기검진 unbearable adj. 참을 수 없는

128 어휘 • 동사 　난이도 상

해석 Cornwall Barriers는 안전 점검을 받을 수 있도록 생산 시설의 일주일간 폐쇄를 시행할 것이다.

해설 빈칸은 주어와 목적어 사이 문장의 동사 자리. so that으로 연결될 두 절의 관계를 고려할 때, 문맥상 '안전 점검을 위해 시설 폐쇄를 실시할 것'이라는 의미가 되어야 자연스러우므로 (B)가 정답

Key word
Cornwall Barriers is implementing a week long shutdown of its production facilities so that they may be inspected for safety.

오답보기 확인
(A) generate 발생시키다
(C) induce 설득하다
(D) arbitrate 중재하다

어휘 implement v. 시행하다 week-long adj. 일주일간의 shutdown n. 폐쇄 facility n. 시설 inspect v. 점검하다 safety n. 안전

129 구조/문법+어휘 • 접속사 　난이도 중

해석 고대 이집트 예술에 관한 세미나 시리즈에 대한 관심이 기대에 미치지 못했기 때문에, 바로 취소되었다.

해설 빈칸은 두 개의 문장을 연결하는 접속사 자리. 문맥상 '세미나 시리즈에 대한 관심이 기대에 미치지 못했기 때문에 취소되었다'는 내용이 되어야 자연스러우므로 이유를 나타내는 접속사 (C)가 정답

Key point
'------ 문장1, 문장2'의 구조에서 빈칸은 부사절 접속사 자리이다. due to도 '~때문에'라는 의미이지만 전치사이기 때문에 절을 이끌 수 없다.

어휘 interest n. 관심, 흥미 ancient adj. 고대의 Egyptian adj. 이집트의 fail v. 실패하다 meet expectations 기대에 미치다 cancel v. 취소하다

130 어휘 • 명사   난이도 중

해석 동남 아시아 교육 계획은 교육자와 가족들 간 지속적인 공동 작업이 매우 중요하다고 믿는다.

해설 빈칸은 문장의 목적어인 that 명사절 내 주어 자리. 빈칸을 후치수식하는 between 전치사구를 고려할 때, 문맥상 '교육자와 가족들 간 지속적인 공동 작업이 매우 중요하다'는 내용이 되어야 자연스러우므로 (D)가 정답

Key word
The Southeast Asian Education Initiative believes that continued **collaboration** between educators and families is critical.

오답보기 확인
(A) competence 능력, 능숙함
(B) assistance 도움, 지원
(C) compliance 준수

어휘 initiative n. 계획 continued adj. 지속적인 collaboration 공동작업, 공동연구 educator n. 교육자 critical adj. 중대한

PART 6   P. 75

131-134번은 다음 공지에 관한 문제입니다.

> Wyandotte 카운티 주민 여러분께 알려드립니다.
>
> Wyandotte 카운티 공공사업부(WCPW)가 연간 보수작업 일정에 따라 5월 한 달 내내 카운티 내 주요 도로와 고속도로의 재포장작업을 진행한다는 점에 유의하시기 바랍니다. 도로재포장은 이달 매주 월요일 새벽 3시부터 오전 5시 사이로 계획되어 있습니다. **131.** 운전자 여러분은 이 시간대에 도로 사용이 금지됩니다. 또한 재포장작업 완료 후 며칠 동안은 노면이 무른 상태이기 때문에, 속도를 더 줄여서 운전하실 것을 권장합니다. 이것은 **132.** 일시적이지만 피할 수는 없는 일입니다. 카운티 주민 여러분은 약 6주 동안은 통근 시간을 더 길게 **133.** 잡으셔야 합니다. WCPW는 다음 연례 보수작업 기간 **134.** 전에 이와 유사한 공지문을 발송할 것인데, 이는 보통 늦봄경입니다. 문의사항이나 기타 의견이 있으시면, WCPW에 555-1212로 연락 주시기 바랍니다.

어휘 resident n. 주민 resurface v. (도로 등에) 표면 처리를 다시 하다 throughout prep. ~동안 죽, 내내 in accordance with ~에 부합되게, (규칙·지시 등에) 따라 maintenance n. 유지보수 completion n. 완료, 완성 pavement n. 노면 temporary adj. 임시의, 일시적인 commute n. 통근 announcement n. 공지, 발표 period n. 시기, 기간 normally adv. 보통 occur v. 일어나다, 발생하다

131 문맥이해 • 문장삽입   난이도 중

해석 (A) 운전자 여러분은 이 시간대에 도로 사용이 금지됩니다.
(B) 되도록 신속히 수정된 일정표를 게재하겠습니다.
(C) 대안으로, 카운티 공무원들은 버스 노선에 자금 지원하는 것을 선택할 수 있습니다.

(D) 자정에서 오전 6시 사이에는 대부분의 사업체들이 문을 닫습니다.

해설 빈칸 앞 문장의 '도로재포장 작업이 새벽 3시에서 5시 사이로 계획되어 있다'는 내용을 고려할 때, 문맥상 '이 시간대에 도로 사용이 금지된다'는 내용으로 이어져야 자연스러우므로 (A)가 정답

Key word
Road resurfacing is planned for every Monday of this month between 3 A.M. and 5 A.M. During these times, motorists are prohibited from accessing these roads.

132 어휘+문맥이해 • 형용사   난이도 중

해설 빈칸은 주어 this에 대한 보어자리. 빈칸 앞 문장의 '재포장 작업 완료 후 며칠 간, 속도를 더 줄여서 운전할 것이 권장된다'는 내용을 고려할 때, '며칠 간'이라는 한정된 기간 동안이라는 표현이 있으므로 문맥상 '이는 일시적이나, 피할 수 없다'는 내용으로 이어져야 자연스러우므로 (C)가 정답

오답보기 확인
(A) ideal 이상적인
(B) complete 완전한; 완료된
(D) cautious 조심스러운, 신중한

Key word
Also, in the days following the completion of resurfacing, the pavement will be soft, so slower driving speeds are recommended. This is **temporary** but cannot be avoided.

133 구조/문법+문맥이해 • 동사   난이도 중

해설 빈칸은 주어와 목적어 사이 동사자리. 주어가 복수명사이며, 빈칸 앞 부분의 '당분간 천천히 운전할 것을 권장한다'는 내용을 고려할 때, '주민들은 통근시간이 더 길어질 것을 예상해야 한다'는 내용이 되어야 자연스러우므로 (C)가 정답

Key word
Also, in the days following the completion of resurfacing, the pavement will be soft, so slower driving speeds are recommended. This is temporary but cannot be avoided. County residents **should expect** longer commute times for about two weeks.

134 구조/문법+어휘 • 전치사   난이도 중

해설 빈칸은 명사구를 목적어로 하는 전치사 자리. 시점을 나타내는 표현이 목적어자리에 있으므로, 주절과의 관계를 고려할 때 문맥상 '다음 보수작업 시기(가 오기) 전에 공지를 발송할 것'이라는 의미가 되어야 자연스러우므로 (D)가 정답

Key word
WCPW will send out a similar announcement **before** the next yearly maintenance period, which normally occurs in late spring.

135-138번은 다음 이메일에 관한 문제입니다.

> 수신: Vasquez@watertown.gov
> 발신: SHenderson@bryantconsulting.com
> 제목: 웹 사이트 피드백
> 날짜: 12월 3일
> 첨부: 분석 자료

Ms. Vasquez께,

아래에 귀하의 도시의 시립 웹 사이트에 대한 제 동료들의 의견을 요약해 드립니다.

전반적으로, 그들은 그것이 예상만큼 **135.** **효과적이지 않다고** 생각했습니다. 사용 편의를 위해 디자인을 간소화하여, 외관을 단순화하는 것이 도움이 될 것입니다. 또한 그들은 사이트 **136.** **전체에** 버그가 지속적으로 나타나, 페이지가 아주 느리게 로딩되는 것을 발견했습니다.

그들은 또한 첫 페이지에 사용된 사진을 보완할 것을 권장했습니다. **137.** **이미지만으로 사용자의 주의를 끄는 것은 어렵습니다.** 이에, 사용자에게 웹 사이트 사용법을 안내하는 간략하면서도, 전문가수준의 비디오를 올리는 것은 자원의 좋은 활용이 될 것입니다. **138.** **또한**, 사용자들이 실시간으로 도움을 요청할 수 있는 라이브 채팅 기능을 추가할 것을 권장했습니다.

문의사항이 있으시면, 저에게 알려주세요.

Sincerely,

Spencer Henderson

어휘 analysis n. 분석 compile v. (자료를) 엮다, 편집하다 colleague n. 동료 municipal adj. 시립의 space n. 공간 overall adv. 전반적으로, 대체로 streamline v. 간소화하다, 효율화하다 simplify v. 단순화하다 appearance n. 외형, 외모 ease of use 사용 용이성 notice v. 의식하다, 알아차리다 bug n. (프로그램의) 오류, 벌레 appear v. 나타나다, 발생하다 persistently adv. 끈질기게, 지속적으로 cause v. 야기하다 load v. (프로그램이) 로딩되다 supplement v. 보충하다, 추가하다 accordingly adv. 그래서, 그런 이유로 resource n. 자원 post v. 게시하다, 올리다 professional-looking adj. 전문적인 형태의, 전문가 수준의 guide v. 인도하다 feature n. 특성, 기능 allow v. 허용하다

135 구조/문법 • 형용사   난이도 중

해설 빈칸은 as ~ as 원급 비교구문을 완성하는 자리. 빈칸 앞, 뒤에 있는 as를 제외하면, 빈칸은 주어와 be동사 뒤 주격보어자리. 문맥상 '웹 사이트가 예상만큼 효과적이지 않았다'는 의미가 되어야 자연스러우므로 형용사 (B)가 정답

Key point
① 원급비교 구문은 'A as 형용사/부사 as B(A는 B만큼 ~하다)'의 형태를 취한다. as 원급비교 구문 내 품사문제는 as를 제외한 후 문장구조를 파악하여 결정한다.
② 주격보어자리에는 주어와 의미상 동격을 이루는 명사 또는 주어의 상태를 서술하는 형용사가 올 수 있다.

136 구조/문법 + 어휘 • 전치사   난이도 중

해설 빈칸은 the site를 목적어로 하는 전치사자리. 문맥상 '사이트 전체에서 지속적으로 나타나는 버그'라는 내용이 되어야 자연스러우므로 (A)가 정답

Key word
They also noticed some **bugs appearing persistently throughout the site**, causing pages to load very slowly.

137 문맥이해 • 문장삽입   난이도 중

해석 (A) 이 사진들은 더 높은 해상도로 게시되어야 합니다.
(B) 제대로 된 파일 명명 프로토콜이 없으면 이미지 파일들은 엉망이 됩니다.
(C) 사진은 전문 사진작가가 찍은 것처럼 보이지 않습니다.
(D) 이미지만으로 사용자의 주의를 끄는 것은 어렵습니다.

해설 빈칸 앞 문장의 '첫 페이지에 사용된 사진을 보완할 것을 권장했다'는 내용과 빈칸 뒤 문장의 '이에, 사용자에게 웹 사이트 사용법을 안내하는 비디오를 올리면 좋을 것'이라는 내용이 접속부사 accordingly로 시작하고 있음을 고려할 때, 이미지만을 이용한 안내는 부족하다는 내용이 들어가야 자연스러우므로 (D)가 정답

Key word
It is difficult to keep users engaged with images alone. Accordingly, it would be a good use of resources to post some brief, professional-looking **videos that guide users** on how to use the Web site.

138 어휘 + 문맥이해 • 연결어   난이도 중

해설 빈칸 앞 문장의 '사용자들에게 웹 사이트 사용법을 안내하는 비디오를 올리는 것은 자원의 좋은 활용이 될 것'이라는 내용과 빈칸 뒤 부분의 '사용자들이 실시간으로 도움을 요청할 수 있는 라이브 채팅 기능을 추가할 것을 권장했다'는 내용을 고려할 때, 동영상과 함께 사용자들에게 유용할만한 기능을 추가적으로 제안하고 있으므로 (D)가 정답

오답보기 확인
(A) To be clear 명확히 하기 위해서
(B) As a result 그 결과
(C) Nonetheless 그렇더라도

Key word
Accordingly, it would be **a good use of resources to post** some brief, professional-looking **videos that guide users on how to use the Web site. In addition**, they have recommended adding a live chat feature which allows users to ask for help in real time.

139-142번은 다음 상품 설명에 관한 문제입니다.

DB Mallex의 새로 나온 "Anywhere" 와이셔츠는 가볍고 냄새를 흡수하는 유기농 면으로 만들어져 어느 곳을 가든 적합합니다. **139.** **이 첨단 직물은 구김이 가지 않아 다림질이 필요 없습니다. 140.** **소매**의 특수한 세트인 디자인은 뛰어난 이동성과 편안함을 제공해줍니다. 세련된 핏과 통기성이 결합되어 회의에서도, 등산로에서도 안성맞춤입니다. 이 셔츠에는 광범위한 활용도를 제공하 **141.** **는**, 양면으로 사용 가능한 칼라 플랩이 있습니다. 모든 구매는 Wharton의 본사에서 **142.** **발송되며** 국내 어디든 주문 후 48시간 내 배송을 보장합니다.

어휘 dress shirt n. 와이셔츠 lightweight adj. 가벼운 odor-absorbing adj. 냄새를 흡수하는 organic adj. 유기농의 set-in adj. 세트인의, 꿰매어 넣는(소매를 의복의 몸통 부분에 붙인) sleeve n. 소매 allow for ~을 감안[고려]하다 mobility n. 이동성, 기동성 comfort n. 편안, 안락 combination n. 결합, 조합 fit n. ~하게 맞는 옷 breathability n. (옷감의) 통기[통풍]성 hiking trail 등산로, 하이킹 코스 come with ~이 딸려 있다 reversible adj. (의류가) 양면을 다 이용할 수 있는 collar n. (옷의) 칼라 flap n. 덮개 degree n. 정도 versatility n. 다재다능, 융통성 purchase n. 구매 headquarters n. 본사 guarantee v. 보장하다

139 문맥이해 • 문장삽입 　　　　　난이도 중

해석 (A) 이 첨단 직물은 구김이 가지 않아 다림질이 필요 없습니다.
(B) 숨겨진 주머니는 중요한 물품을 보관하기에 적합합니다.
(C) 가벼운 면 베개커버는 밤새 시원하게 유지됩니다.
(D) 세련된 디자인은 어떤 스타일의 셔츠와도 잘 어울립니다.

해설 빈칸 앞 문장의 '새로 나온 와이셔츠는 가볍고 냄새를 흡수하는 유기농 면으로 만들어져 어느 곳을 가든 적합하다'는 내용을 고려할 때, 문맥상 옷의 소재와 관련된 내용이 이어져야 자연스러우므로 (A)가 정답

Key word
DB Mallex's **new "Anywhere" dress shirt** is **made of lightweight, odor-absorbing organic cotton perfect for traveling** wherever you need to go. **This high-tech fabric stays wrinkle-free and never needs ironing.**

140 어휘 • 명사 　　　　　난이도 중

해설 빈칸은 전치사 on의 목적어 자리. 빈칸 앞 문장들에서 새로운 와이셔츠를 소개하고 있으며, on 전치사구가 명사 design을 수식하고 있음을 고려할 때, 문맥상 '소매의 특수한 세트인 디자인'이라는 의미가 되어야 자연스러우므로 (B)가 정답

오답보기 확인
(A) button 단추
(C) brim (모자의) 챙
(D) packaging 포장재

Key word
DB Mallex's **new "Anywhere" dress shirt** is made of lightweight, odor-absorbing organic cotton perfect for traveling wherever you need to go. This high-tech fabric stays wrinkle-free and never needs ironing. Our special **set-in design on** the **sleeves** allows for greater mobility and comfort.

141 구조/문법 • 관계대명사 　　　　　난이도 중

해설 빈칸은 완전한 문장과 주어가 빠진 불완전한 문장 사이의 자리이므로 주격 관계대명사 (D)가 정답

Key point
주격 관계대명사 앞에는 명사(선행사), 뒤에는 동사가 온다.

142 구조/문법 • 동사 　　　　　난이도 중

해설 빈칸은 주어와 전치사구 사이 동사자리. 주어가 단수 사물명사이므로 문맥상 '모든 주문은 본사에서 배송될 것'이라는 의미의 수동태 문장이 자연스러우며, 주어-동사 간 수 일치가 되어야 하므로 미래시제 수동태 (D)가 정답

Key point
한정사 every는 단수명사 및 단수동사와 함께 쓰인다.

143-146번은 다음 기사에 관한 문제입니다.

Escondido (10월 5일) - Sleek Mobile (SM)과 Bexmont Cellular Services (BCS)가 하나의 조직으로 **143.** 합병될 것이다. 기업합병은 12월 1일에 마무리될 예정이다. 새롭게 **144.** 형성되는 기업은 West Coast Telecommunications라는 이름으로 알려지게 될 것이다. SM은 캘리포니아에 150개가 넘는 지점을 가지고 있고, BCS는 Washington과 Oregon 전역에 100개의 지점이 있다. **145.** 정확한 조건은 이번 주 있을 주주총회 후 발표될 것이다. 합동 기자회견에서 SM의 CEO인 Sheena Kim과 BCS의 회장 Timothy Rogers는 현재 제공하는 서비스에서 변하는 것은 없을 것이라고 언급했다. **146.** 그들은 또한 모든 직원들이 직장을 계속 다닐 수 있을 것임을 시사했다.

어휘 organization n. 조직 merger n. 합병 v. 합병하다 expect v. 예상하다 complete v. 마무리하다, 완성하다 form v. 구성하다, 형성시키다 firm n. 회사 location n. 지점, 위치 spread v. 펼치다, 펴다 across prep. ~전체에 걸쳐, 가로질러 joint adj. 합동의, 공동의 press conference 기자회견 state v. 언급하다 indicate v. 가리키다, 시사하다

143 구조/문법 + 문맥이해 • 동사 　　　　　난이도 중

해설 빈칸은 주어 다음 동사자리. 기사 작성일이 10월 5일이고, 빈칸 뒷 문장의 '합병이 12월 1일까지 완료될 것'이라는 내용을 고려할 때 '두 기업이 하나로 합병될 것'이라는 미래시제를 완성하는 (D)가 정답

Key word
Escondido (**October 5**) – Sleek Mobile (SM) and Bexmont Cellular Services (BCS) **will be merging** into one organization. The business **merger** is **expected to be completed by December 1.**

144 어휘 + 문맥이해 • 분사 　　　　　난이도 중

해설 빈칸은 주어인 명사 firm을 수식하는 자리. 빈칸 앞 문장의 '기업 합병이 12월 1일까지 완료될 것'이라는 내용을 고려할 때, '새로 형성된 기업'이라는 의미가 되어야 자연스러우므로 (A)가 정답

오답보기 확인
(B) acquire 인수하다, 획득하다
(C) admit 인정하다
(D) remedy 바로 잡다

Key word
The business merger is expected to be completed by December 1. The newly **formed firm** will be known as West Coast Telecommunications.

145 문맥이해 • 문장삽입 　　　　　난이도 중

해석 (A) 양사는 각각 업계에서 리더로 알려져 있다.
(B) 정확한 조건은 이번 주 있을 주주총회 후 발표될 것이다.
(C) 통신분야는 West Coast 경제에서 매우 중요하다.
(D) 양사는 다른 국가들로의 확장을 계획하고 있다.

해설 빈칸 앞 부분에서 곧 있을 두 기업의 합병소식을 전하며, 각 회사의 규모를 지점수로 간략히 소개하고 있음을 고려할 때, 합병 조건과 관련된 내용으로 이어져야 자연스러우므로 (B)가 정답

Key word
The business merger is expected to be completed by December 1. The newly formed firm will be known as West Coast Telecommunications. **SM has over 150 locations in California, and BCS has** 100 locations spread across Washington and Oregon. **The exact terms will be announced after this week's shareholder meeting.**

146 문맥이해 • 인칭대명사   난이도 중

해설 빈칸은 문장의 주어자리. 빈칸 앞 문장의 '각 회사의 대표 Sheena Kim과 Timothy Rogers가 ~를 언급했다'는 내용과 빈칸 뒤 부사 also가 있음을 고려할 때, '그들은 또한 ~을 시사했다'는 내용으로 이어져야 자연스러우므로 복수의 대상을 가리키는 대명사 (B)가 정답

Key word
During a joint press conference, **Sheena Kim**, CEO of SM, **and Timothy Rogers**, President of BCS, stated that there will not be any changes to their current services. **They also indicated** that all staff members will be able to keep their jobs.

PART 7   P. 79

147-148번은 다음 양식에 관한 문제입니다.

Kurtz BBQ and Wings

Kurtz BBQ and Wings에 들러주셔서 감사합니다. 잠시 시간을 내어 아래 설문지를 작성해 주시면 감사하겠습니다.

	그렇다	보통	그렇지 않다
음식이 아주 좋아 보였고 맛있었다.		X	
음식 가격은 적당했다.(147)	X		
오래 기다릴 필요가 없었다.		X	
서비스는 친절했고 도움이 되었다.	X		
식당은 아주 깔끔했다.		X	
조명과 음악이 적당한 수준이었다.			X

이름 및 연락처:
Gerald Brunswick
555 032-4592

의견:
식당엔 사람이 꽉 차 있었지만, 저는 서비스에 감명받았습니다. 직원 수가 적었음에도, 저희 음식이 모두 빨리 나왔고, 제대로 준비되었습니다. **식당이 너무 어둡지 않았더라면 더 좋았을 거예요. 천장 조명이 몇 개 있다면 장소를 밝게 하는데 매우 도움이 될 거예요.**(148)

어휘 stop by 들르다 appreciate v. 고마워하다 fill out 작성하다 neutral adj. 중립의, 중간의 disagree v. 동의하지 않다 reasonably adv. 합리적으로 priced adj. 가격이 매겨진 friendly adj. 친절한 helpful adj. 도움이 되는 exceptionally adv. 특별히, 유난히 lighting n. 조명 proper adj. 제대로 된, 적절한 level n. 수준, 정도 packed adj. (사람들이) 꽉 들어찬 impressed adj. 감명을 받은 quickly adv. 빨리 prepare v. 준비하다 properly adv. 제대로, 적절히 dim adj. 어둑한 overhead adj. 머리 위의 fixture n. 내부 시설 brighten up 밝히다

---

147 사실확인   난이도 중

해석 Mr. Brunswick은 자신의 식사 경험에 관하여 무엇을 언급하는가?
(A) 메뉴 항목들은 값어치가 있었다.
(B) 주문이 몇 분 지연되었다.
(C) 일부 음식이 식어서 나왔다.
(D) 음식 양이 많았다.

해설 표의 두 번째 항목 The food was reasonably priced.(음식 가격은 적당했다.)에 대해 agree(그렇다)라고 답했으므로 (A)가 정답

Paraphrasing reasonably priced ➡ a good value for the price

---

148 상세정보   난이도 중

해석 Mr. Brunswick은 어떤 개선을 제안하는가?
(A) 추가 직원이 고용되어야 한다.
(B) 고객 카드가 제공되어야 한다.
(C) 메뉴 항목들이 더 잘 보여져야 한다.
(D) 더 많은 조명이 설치되어야 한다.

해설 Comments(의견)에서 It would have been better if the restaurant wasn't so dim—some overhead fixtures would really help brighten up the place.(식당이 너무 어둡지 않았더라면 더 좋았을 거예요. 천장 조명이 몇 개 있다면 장소를 밝게 하는데 매우 도움이 될 거예요.)라고 했으므로 (D)가 정답

149-150번은 다음 안내문에 관한 문제입니다.

Remington Lawn Masters:
잔디 깎기 및 정원관리 필수품

Lawn Master MM2500d를 구매해주셔서 감사 드립니다. 다음 정보를 유념하시면, 당신의 기계는 오랫동안 잘 작동할 것입니다.

잔디 깎기 기간이 끝나면 반드시 휘발유 탱크를 비워주세요.(150A) 오래된 연료는 긴 겨울이 지난 후 엔진 시동을 어렵게 할 수 있습니다.

이물질이 쌓이는 것을 방지하기 위해 정기적으로 기계 바닥을 청소해주세요. 시간이 지나면서 칼날에 풀이나 먼지가 쌓여, 오작동을 유발할 수 있습니다.(149)

매년 점화 플러그를 교체해주세요.(150C) 저렴하고 교체가 용이한 이 부품을 바꾸는 것으로, 더 큰 비용이 드는 수리를 예방할 수 있습니다.

주기적으로 점검을 받으세요. 기계의 수명을 보장하는 좋은 방법은 정기적으로 수리점에 가져가서 전문가의 점검을 받는 것입니다.(150D)

어휘 lawn n. 잔디 mowing n. 풀베기 gardening n. 원예, 정원 가꾸기 keep in mind 명심하다 drain v. 액체를 빼내다 mower n. 잔디 깎는 기계 buildup n. 축적 blade n. (칼·도구의) 날 be filled with ~로 가득 차다 malfunction n. 오작동 sparkplug n. 점화플러그 inexpensive adj. 비싸지 않은 component n. (구성)요소, 부품 periodic adj. 주기적인 tune-up n. 튠업 (엔진 등의 철저한 조정) last v. 지속되다 professional n. 전문가 inspect v. 점검하다

---

149 사실확인   난이도 중

해석 Lawn Master MM2500d의 칼날에 관하여 언급된 것은?
(A) 막힐 수 있다.
(B) 교체비용이 많이 든다.
(C) Remington에서만 구할 수 있다.
(D) 어떤 종류의 잔디라도 깎을 수 있다.

해설 세 번째 단락에서 Clean the bottom of the mower regularly to prevent buildup. The blades can be filled with grass and dirt over time, causing malfunction.(이물질이 쌓이는 것을 방지하기 위해 정기적으로 기계 바닥을 청소해주세요. 시간이 지나면 칼날에 풀이나 먼지가 쌓여 오작동을 유발할 수 있습니다.)라고 했으므로 (A)가 정답

150 사실확인 난이도 중

해석 잔디 깎는 기계 관리의 팁으로 언급되지 않은 것은?
(A) 연료탱크를 비우는 것
(B) 특정 청소제품을 사용하는 것
(C) 매년 새 부품을 구매하는 것
(D) 전문가를 찾아가는 것

해설 지문의 단서와 보기를 매칭시키면, 두 번째 단락의 Make sure to drain the tank of gasoline at the end of the mowing season.(잔디 깎기 기간이 끝나면 반드시 휘발유 탱크를 비워주세요.) → (A) Emptying the gas tank/네 번째 단락의 Replace the sparkplug every year.(매년 점화 플러그를 교체해주세요.) → (C) Buying a new part annually/다섯 번째 단락의 A good way to ensure your machine lasts a long time is to take it into a repair shop regularly so that a professional can inspect it.(기계의 수명을 보장하는 좋은 방법은 정기적으로 수리점에 가져가서 전문가의 점검을 받는 것입니다.) → (D) Visiting a specialist와 일치하지만, 특정 청소제품을 사용하라는 내용은 언급된 바 없으므로 (B)가 정답

151-152번은 다음 공지에 관한 문제입니다.

> **Haynes 의류 재개장**
>
> 동부 고속도로 2117번지에 있는 저희의 아름다운 현대적인 시설 공사가 완료되었습니다. 따라서 2개월 동안 여러분의 곁을 떠나 있던 저희 Haynes 의류는 4월 1일에 Tri-state 지역으로 이전하게 됨을 기쁘게 알려 드립니다.
>
> 동부 고속도로 지점은 시내 중심부에 위치하게 됩니다. 이는 도시 전역에 있는 고객이 매장을 이용하기 더 쉬워진다는 것을 의미합니다.⁽¹⁵¹⁾
>
> Haynes 의류 재개장을 기념하기 위해, 저희는 4월 1일에 특별행사를 개최합니다. 오전 10시 개장 시간에 입장하는 고객 선착순 50명은 경품 추첨행사에 응모됩니다. 500달러 상품권을 받게 될 행운의 주인공 2명을 추첨합니다.⁽¹⁵²⁾ 오세요! 이 행사를 놓치지 마세요!
>
> 그리고 저희 온라인 상점 www.haynesapparel.com을 둘러보시는 것도 잊지 마세요.

어휘 apparel n. 의류 absence n. 부재, 없음 announce v. 알리다, 발표하다 relocate v. 이전하다 in the heart of ~의 중심부에 accessible adj. 접근[이용] 가능한 throughout prep. 도처에 metro region 도시지역 raffle n. 경품추첨 draw v. 추첨하다 reward v. 보상하다

---

151 상세정보 난이도 중

해석 공지에 따르면, Haynes 의류는 왜 이전하는가?
(A) 더 편리한 장소에 위치하기 위해
(B) 다른 고객층을 유치하기 위해
(C) 더욱 다양한 의류를 제공하기 위해
(D) 더 빠른 배송서비스를 제공하기 위해

해설 두 번째 단락에서 The East Highway location will be in the heart of downtown. This will mean that the store will be more accessible to customers throughout the metro region.(동부 고속도로 지점은 시내 중심부에 위치하게 됩니다. 이는 도시 전역에 있는 고객이 매장을 이용하기 더 쉬워진다는 것을 의미합니다.)라고 했으므로 (A)가 정답

Paraphrasing accessible → convenient

---

152 상세정보 난이도 중

해석 Haynes 의류는 4월 1일에 어떻게 재개장을 기념할 것인가?
(A) 온라인 할인을 제공해서
(B) 평소보다 일찍 문을 열어서
(C) 신상품을 공개해서
(D) 경품을 나눠줘서

해설 세 번째 단락에서 To celebrate Haynes Apparel's re-opening, we will be holding a special event on the first of April. The first 50 customers to arrive when the store opens at 10:00 A.M. will be entered in a raffle. We will draw the names of two lucky winners who will be rewarded with $500 gift cards.(Haynes 의류 재개장을 기념하기 위해, 저희는 4월 1일에 특별행사를 개최합니다. 오전 10시 개장 시간에 입장하는 고객 선착순 50명은 경품 추첨행사에 응모됩니다. 500달러 상품권을 받게 될 행운의 주인공 2명을 추첨합니다.)라고 했으므로 (D)가 정답

Paraphrasing reward with $500 gift cards → distribute some prizes

---

153-154번은 다음 문자메시지 대화에 관한 문제입니다.

> **Michelle Ingles (오전 8시 05분)**
> 안녕하세요, 저는 Ingles and Company의 Michelle입니다. 저희에게 오전 8시 Belmont와 1번가에 있는 귀하의 신규 점포에 싱크대 수리를 예약해 주셨는데요.⁽¹⁵³⁾ 저희에게 알려주신 사무실 번호로 전화 드리고 문을 두드렸는데, 아무런 대답이 없습니다.⁽¹⁵⁴⁾
>
> **Monte Derwin (오전 8시 07분)**
> 죄송해요!⁽¹⁵⁴⁾ 제가 방금 도착한 재고를 확인하느라 창고에 있어서요, 그리고 내일은 지나야 초인종이 설치될 거에요. 제가 가려면 10분 정도 더 걸리겠지만, 저희 직원에게 문을 열어드리라고 할게요.
>
> **Michelle Ingles (오전 8시 08분)**
> 알겠습니다.
>
> **Monte Derwin (오전 8시 10분)**
> 기다리시게 해서 죄송합니다. 다음 번에는 비밀번호 '56813'를 이용해서, 필요하실 때 출입하세요.

어휘 arrange v. 마련하다, 주선하다 fix v. 수리하다 sink n. 싱크대 knock v. (문을) 두드리다 response n. 반응, 대답 storage n. 창고 track v. 추적하다 inventory n. 물품, 목록 doorbell n. 초인종 install v. 설치하다 security n. 보안

---

153 상세정보 난이도 중

해석 오전 8시에 무엇이 예정되어 있었는가?
(A) 재고 회의
(B) 초인종 설치
(C) 배관 수리
(D) 상품 배달

해설 오전 8시 05분, Michelle Ingles의 메시지에서 You had arranged with us to fix a sink at your new store on 1st and Belmont at 8:00 A.M.(저희에게 오전 8시 Belmont와 1번가에 있는 귀하의 신규

점포에 싱크대 수리를 예약해 주셨는데요.)라고 했으므로 (C)가 정답

Paraphrasing arrange ➡ schedule,
to fix a sink ➡ plumbing repair

154 화자 의도 파악 　　　　　　　　　난이도 중

해석 오전 8시 07분에, Mr. Derwin은 왜 "죄송해요!"라고 하는가?
(A) 그는 점포에 들어올 수 없다는 것을 깜빡했다.
(B) 그는 Ms. Ingles를 언제 도울 수 있는지 불확실하다.
(C) 그는 Ms. Ingles가 다음 날 올 거라고 생각했다.
(D) 그는 직원이 비밀번호를 공유할 거라고 예상했다.

해설 오전 8시 05분 ~ 8시 07분 대화에서 Michelle Ingles가 We tried calling the office number you left us and knocked the door, but we got no response.(저희에게 알려주신 사무실 번호로 전화 드리고 문을 두드렸는데, 아무런 대답이 없습니다.)라고 한 말에, Monte Derwin이 My apologies!(죄송해요!)라고 한 것이므로 (A)가 정답

155-157번은 다음 이메일에 관한 문제입니다.

수신: Jane Shepheard <jshepheard@bibbomail.com>
발신: Tad Maynor <tad83@destinationstore.com>
제목: 인사
날짜: 1월 2일
첨부문서: j_shepheard

Ms. Shepheard께,

같은 팀에서 일하게 되어 반갑습니다. **만나서 이야기 나눈 것처럼, 당신은 Barksdale로 1774번지에 있는 Oaklands 공원 지점에서 부점장직을 맡게 됩니다. 교육은 1월 22일에 시작할 예정입니다. 그날 오전 8시에 본사 21층으로 가시기 바랍니다.**(155) 그곳에서 일주일간 새로운 동료 몇 명과 함께 Destination 매장 필수 교육을 받게 됩니다. 이 수업으로 회사 제품군 및 핵심 철학을 익히게 됩니다. 이 기간 동안 당신의 근무시간은 오전 9시부터 오후 6시까지입니다. 오리엔테이션이 끝난 후에는 매장 정규 교대 근무조로 배정되고, 퇴직연금을 비롯한 회사 복리후생을 신청할 수 있습니다.(156)

우선, 첨부해드린 서류를 작성해 주세요. 거기에 작성 및 서명하시면, 새로운 직위 및 업무를 이해하고 수락함을 인정하게 됩니다.(157) 문의사항이 있으시면, 저에게 바로 이메일을 보내주세요.

Best of Luck,

Tad Maynor
인사부장

어휘 greetings n. 인사(말) **in person** 직접 assume v. (권력·책임을) 맡다 **as far as ~ go** ~에 관한 한 headquarters n. 본사 undergo v. 겪다 mandatory adj. 의무적인 destination store 대형 종합 할인매장 colleague n. 동료 familiarize v. 익숙하게 하다 product range 제품 범위 core adj. 핵심적인, 가장 중요한 philosophy n. 철학 conclude v. 끝나다 assign v. (일·책임 등을) 맡기다, 배정하다 shift n. 교대 근무조 company benefit 회사 복리후생 retirement plan 퇴직자 연금제도 fill in (서식을) 작성하다 complete v. 완료하다, (서식을) 작성하다 acknowledge v. (사실로) 인정하다

155 주제/목적/대상 　　　　　　　　　난이도 중

해석 Mr. Maynor는 왜 이메일을 썼는가?
(A) 매장 홍보계획을 의논하려고
(B) 퇴직 정책을 설명하려고
(C) 직위에 대한 세부사항을 알려주려고
(D) 회의 일정을 다시 잡으려고

해설 첫 번째 단락에서 As we discussed in person, you will be assuming the role of assistant manager at our Oaklands Park location, 1774 Barksdale Road. As far as training goes, you are scheduled to begin on 22 January. Please go to the 21st floor of our headquarters that morning at 8:00 A.M.(만나서 이야기 나눈 것처럼, 당신은 Barksdale로 1774번지에 있는 Oaklands 공원 지점에서 부점장직을 맡게 됩니다. 교육은 1월 22일에 시작할 예정입니다. 그날 오전 8시에 본사 21층으로 가시기 바랍니다.)라고 했으므로 (C)가 정답

156 암시/추론 　　　　　　　　　난이도 상

해석 Mr. Maynor에 따르면, 일주일 후에 무슨 일이 있겠는가?
(A) Ms. Shepheard가 기념행사에 참석할 것이다.
(B) Ms. Shepheard의 임금이 인상될 것이다.
(C) Ms. Shepheard가 다른 도시로 이주할 것이다.
(D) Ms. Shepheard의 근무시간이 조정될 것이다.

해설 첫 번째 단락에서 There, you'll be undergoing the mandatory Destination Store training with several new colleagues for one week. The course will familiarize you with the company's product range and our core philosophy. During this time, your work schedule will be from 9 A.M. to 6 P.M. After the orientation concludes, you'll be assigned your regular shift at the store and will be able to sign up for company benefits, including the retirement plan.(그곳에서 일주일간 새로운 동료 몇 명과 함께 Destination 매장 필수 교육을 받게 됩니다. 이 수업으로 회사 제품군 및 핵심 철학을 익히게 됩니다. 이 기간 동안 당신의 근무시간은 오전 9시부터 오후 6시까지입니다. 오리엔테이션이 끝난 후에는 매장 정규 교대근무조로 배정되고, 퇴직연금을 비롯한 회사 복리후생을 신청할 수 있습니다.)라고 하여 Ms. Shepheard의 근무시간이 바뀔 것임을 알 수 있으므로 (D)가 정답

157 상세정보 　　　　　　　　　난이도 중

해석 Mr. Maynor는 이메일에 무엇을 포함했는가?
(A) 계약서 양식
(B) 보험 안내서
(C) 오리엔테이션 일정표
(D) 제품 카탈로그

해설 두 번째 단락에서 For now, we need you to fill in the attached document. By completing and signing it, you acknowledge that you understand and accept your new role and responsibilities.(우선, 첨부해드린 서류를 작성해 주세요. 거기에 작성 및 서명하시면, 새로운 직위 및 업무를 이해하고 수락함을 인정하게 됩니다.)라고 했으므로 (A)가 정답

Paraphrasing attach ➡ include

158-160번은 다음 광고에 관한 문제입니다.

> **Auckland 요리학교 학생들의 연습용 식당에서
> 저녁식사를 하실 수 있습니다.**
>
> 금액부담 없이 미식을 경험해보고 싶으신가요? ―[1]―.
>
> Auckland 요리학교에서 단 10달러에 저녁식사를 만들어드립니다. 매월 첫째 주 내내 저희 학생들이 일반인들에게 음식을 요리해드립니다. 연습용 식당의 운영 경험은 저희 학생들에게 해당 분야에서의 소중한 경험을 제공해 줍니다. ―[2]―. 식사시간이 저희의 높은 기준에 부합될 수 있도록, 저희 최고 강사진 중 한 명이 식당에서 서비스를 감독할 것입니다.[158]
>
> 연습용 식당은 매월 마지막 주에 예약 가능하나, 일찍 하시기 바랍니다. 저희 매장에는 테이블이 8개밖에 없습니다.[159C] ―[3]―. Fork and Knife 앱을 이용해 마감되기 전에 예약하실 수 있습니다.[159A]
>
> 학생이 요리를 제대로 준비하는 데 시간이 조금 더 걸릴 수 있다는 점을 유의해 주시기 바랍니다.[159D] 또한 학생들은 연습용 식당의 조리법을 준수해야 하기에, 대체식단이나 특별 요청은 받을 수 없다는 점도 양해해주시기 바랍니다.[160] ―[4]―.

어휘 culinary adj. 요리의 gourmet n. 미식가 price tag 가격표 general adj. 일반적인 run v. 운영하다 valuable adj. 귀중한 field n. 분야 up to (특정한 기준·수준)만큼 standard n. 기준 instructor n. 강사 oversee v. 감독하다 run out (공급품이) 다 떨어지다 aware adj. 알고 있는, 의식하고 있는 dish n. 요리 note v. 주의하다, 주목하다 recipe n. 조리법 substitution n. 대체(품) request n. 요청

158 사실확인 <난이도 중>

해석 Auckland 요리학교 강사들에 관하여 언급된 것은?
(A) 한 달에 일주일 근무한다.
(B) 어느 학생이 요리할지 결정한다.
(C) 연습용 식당에서 서비스를 감독한다.
(D) 학생들에게 안전교육을 해준다.

해설 두 번째 단락에서 To make sure your dining experience is up to our high standards, one of our top instructors will be in the kitchen to oversee the service.(식사시간이 저희의 높은 기준에 부합될 수 있도록, 저희 최고 강사진 중 한 명이 식당에서 서비스를 감독할 것입니다.)라고 했으므로 (C)가 정답

Paraphrasing supervise ➡ oversee

159 사실확인 <난이도 중>

해석 연습용 식당에 관하여 언급되지 <u>않은</u> 것은?
(A) 앱으로 예약할 수 있다.
(B) 야외 식사공간이 있다.
(C) 고객들이 앉을 공간이 많지 않다.
(D) 요리가 나오는 데 시간이 걸릴 수 있다.

해설 지문의 단서와 보기를 매칭시키면, 세 번째 단락의 You can use the Fork and Knife app to get a table before they run out.(Fork and Knife 앱을 이용해 마감되기 전에 예약하실 수 있습니다.) ➡ (A) It can be reserved through an application./ 세 번째 단락의 Reservations for the Test Kitchen can be made in the last week of each month, but book quickly. Our location only has eight tables.(연습용 식당은 매월 마지막 주에 예약 가능하나, 일찍 하시기 바랍니다. 저희 매장에는 테이블이 8개밖에 없습니다.) ➡ (C) It does not have much space for customers./네 번째 단락의 Be aware that the student may require a little longer to get your dish exactly right.(학생이 요리를 제대로 준비하는 데 시간이 조금 더 걸릴 수 있다는 점을 유의해 주시기 바랍니다.) ➡ (D) It might take some time to serve dishes.와 일치하지만, 야외 식사공간에 대한 내용은 언급된 바 없으므로 (B)가 정답

Paraphrasing app ➡ application, get a table ➡ reserve, one full week ➡ seven days

160 문장삽입 <난이도 중>

해석 [1], [2], [3], [4]로 표시된 곳 중, 다음 문장이 들어갈 위치로 가장 적절한 것은?

"이러한 이유로, 식단 제한사항이 있으시면 반드시 메뉴를 주의 깊게 확인하시기 바랍니다."

(A) [1]
(B) [2]
(C) [3]
(D) [4]

해설 네 번째 단락에서 It should also be noted that the students are required to follow Test Kitchen recipes, so no substitutions or special requests will be taken.(또한 학생들은 연습용 식당의 조리법을 준수해야 하기에, 대체식단이나 특별 요청은 받을 수 없다는 점도 양해해주시기 바랍니다.)라고 하여 주어진 문장이 이어지기에 자연스러우므로 (D)가 정답

161-163번은 다음 초대장에 관한 문제입니다.

> **4월 10일 일요일, 정오부터 오후 4시까지**
>
> **시립 문화유산 박물관에 오셔서 Chesterton의 200주년을 기념해 주세요!**
>
> 올해는 우리 도시가 200주년이 되는 해입니다. 200년의 역사를 기리기 위해, 박물관에서 수년간 보존해온 우리 지역 사회의 독특한 문화 및 유산을 기념하는 행사를 개최합니다.[162] 시립 문화유산 박물관을 후원해 주신 모든 기부자 여러분을 영화 및 고급 식사, 그리고 저희 최신 전시의 최초 관람을 즐기실 수 있는 오후로 초대합니다.[161] Chesterton대학교 Chloe Emmerich 교수의 기조연설과 함께, 저명한 학자들이 참여하는 프레젠테이션과 패널 토론을 즐기십시오. 그리고 Geoffrey Maxwell 감독의 다큐멘터리 영화 <From Frontier to Front Yard>의 상영을 놓치지 마세요. 점심과 음료는 Twin Rivers Pub에서 공급합니다. 모든 티켓 및 음식 판매 수익은 시의 <미래 영화제작자> 프로젝트에 사용됩니다.
>
> 티켓을 예약하시려면, www.chestertonCHM.com/bookings를 방문해주세요. 최소 48시간 전에 미리 구입하셔야 하고 수량이 한정되어 있다는 것을 명심하시기 바랍니다.[163]

어휘 commemorate v. 기념하다 civic adj. 도시의, 시민의 heritage n. 유산 bicentennial adj. 200년마다의 honor v. 영예를 주다, 존경하다 present v. 주다, 제시하다 commemorative adj. 기념하는 celebrate v. 축하하다 unique adj. 유일한 culture n. 문화 donor n. 기부자 support v. 지원하다, 지지하다 fine adj. 좋은, 고급의 dining n. 식사 exhibit n. 전시 presentation n. 발표, 프레젠테이션 panel discussion 패널 토론 feature v. ~를 특징으로 하다 noted adj. 유명한 scholar n. 학자 keynote speech 기조연설 screening n. 상영 acclaimed adj. 호평 받는 director n. 감독 beverage n. 음료 pub n. 술집, 펍 profit n. 수익, 이익 filmmaker n. 영화 제작자

161 암시/추론 난이도 중

해석 초대장은 누구를 대상으로 하겠는가?
(A) 역사 교수들
(B) Chesterton 시 공무원들
(C) 과거 기부자들
(D) 영화를 공부하는 학생들

해설 첫 번째 단락에서 All donors who have supported the Civic Heritage Museum are invited to come for an afternoon of film, fine dining, and a first look at our newest exhibit.(시립 문화유산 박물관을 후원해 주신 모든 기부자 여러분을 영화 및 고급 식사, 그리고 저희 최신 전시의 최초 관람을 즐길 수 있는 오후로 초대합니다.)라고 하여 박물관 기부자들을 초대함을 알 수 있으므로 (C)가 정답

Paraphrasing donors ➡ contributors

162 동의어 난이도 중

해석 첫 번째 단락, 세 번째 줄의 단어 "over"와 의미상 가장 가까운 것은?
(A) ~보다 위에
(B) 더 많은
(C) ~를 너머
(D) ~내내

해설 첫 번째 단락의 To honor 200 years of history, the museum is presenting a commemorative event that celebrates the unique culture and heritage of our community over the years.(200년의 역사를 기리기 위해, 박물관에서 수년간 보존해온 우리 지역 사회의 독특한 문화 및 유산을 기념하는 행사를 개최합니다.)에서 'over'는 '~동안'라는 의미로 쓰였으므로 보기 중 '~내내'를 뜻하는 (D)가 정답

163 사실확인 난이도 상

해석 행사에 관하여 사실인 것은?
(A) 일정한 수의 티켓 만을 판매할 것이다.
(B) 무료 점심을 제공한다.
(C) 영화사에 관한 연설이 있을 것이다.
(D) 매년 개최된다.

해설 두 번째 단락에서 To reserve a ticket, visit www.chestertonCHM.com/bookings. Keep in mind that they must be purchased at least 48 hours in advance, and only a limited number are available.(티켓을 예약하시려면, www.chestertonCHM.com/bookings를 방문해 주세요. 최소 48시간 전에 미리 구입하셔야 하고 수량이 한정되어 있다는 것을 명심하시기 바랍니다.)라고 했으므로 (A)가 정답

Paraphrasing a limited number ➡ a certain number

164-167번은 다음 온라인 채팅 대화문에 관한 문제입니다.

Tony Gandolfini [오후 7시 45분]
모두 안녕하세요. 제가 이 동네에 새로 이사 왔는데요, 여기가 질문을 하기에 좋은 곳이라고 들었습니다.(164) 창문을 직접 설치해보신 분 계신가요?

Sam Rockwell [오후 7시 47분]
Glenview 동네 채팅방에 오신 걸 환영해요, Tony.(164) 작업을 직접 하실 계획인가요? 제가 작년에 다락에 창문을 새로 달았어요. 하지만 그런 일을 다시 할지는 잘 모르겠어요.(165)

Tony Gandolfini [오후 7시 48분]
제가 알아본 바로는, 직접 하면 돈을 많이 절약할 수 있는 것 같아서요. 하지만 솔직히 제가 이런 일을 해본 적이 없어요.

Deidre Stapleton [오후 7시 52분]
이런 종류의 작업을 잘 하신다면, 다른 사람이 하는 걸 몇 번 본 후에 창문을 설치하는 게 가능해요. 하지만 매우 정확하게 해야 해요. 실수하면 창문 일부를 망가뜨리기 쉽거든요.

Sam Rockwell [오후 7시 53분]
저는 할 때 먼저 www.yourhouseproj.com에서 온라인 자료들을 많이 읽어보고 안내 동영상도 봤어요. 하지만 전 다음 번에는 전문가를 고용할 것 같아요.(165)

Sam Rockwell [오후 7시 54분]
Deidre, 이런 프로젝트를 많이 맡아봤나요? Tony가 혼자 작업을 할 수 있게 조언 좀 해주시겠어요?

Tony Gandolfini [오후 7시 54분]
그건 매우 도움이 됩니다. 조언 감사 드려요.

Deidre Stapleton [오후 7시 55분]
제가 창문과 외장재 사업을 하거든요.(166) 그 작업을 권할지 여부는 몇 가지에 달려 있어요. Tony, 새 창문을 설치하시나요, 아니면 쓰던 걸 제거하셔야 하나요? 그리고 알맞은 연장을 확실히 모두 가지고 계신가요?

Tony Gandolfini [오후 7시 55분]
창문 하나만 교체하려고 했는데, 새내기 집주인이 하기에는 고생스러운 일 같네요. Deidre, 당신 회사 전화번호를 알려주시겠어요?(167)

Deidre Stapleton [오후 7시 57분]
저희가 기꺼이 도와드릴게요. 제 사무실 번호는 555-4220이에요. 저와 얘기 했다고만 말씀하시면 돼요.

어휘 neighborhood n. 지역 install v. 설치하다 attic n. 다락 admit v. 인정[시인]하다 precise adj. 정확한 resource n. 재료, 자료 how-to video 사용 안내 비디오 grateful adj. 고마워하는, 감사하는 input n. 조언, 입력 operate v. 운영하다, 경영하다 siding n. (건물) 외장용 자재 fit v. 설치하다 remove v. 제거하다

164 주제/목적/대상 난이도 중

해석 채팅방은 누구를 대상으로 하는가?
(A) 함께 휴가 가는 사람들
(B) 같은 사무실에서 근무하는 사람들
(C) 같은 수업을 듣는 사람들
(D) 같은 지역에 사는 사람들

해설 오후 7시 45분 ~ 7시 47분 대화에서 Tony Gandolfini가 I'm new to the neighborhood, and I heard this was a good place to ask questions.(제가 이 동네에 새로 이사 왔는데요 여기가 질문을 하기에 좋은 곳이라고 들었습니다.)라고 한 말에, Sam Rockwell이 Welcome to the Glenview neighborhood chat, Tony.(Glenview 동네 채팅방에 오신 걸 환영해요, Tony.)라고 했으므로 (D)가 정답

Paraphrasing neighborhood ➡ area

165 화자 의도 파악　　　　　　　　　난이도 중

해석　오후 7시 47분에, Mr. Rockwell이 "하지만 그런 일을 다시 할지는 잘 모르겠어요"라고 할 때 무엇을 의미하겠는가?
(A) 전문가를 고용하지 않은 것을 후회한다.
(B) 프로젝트에 너무 많은 비용이 들었다고 생각했다.
(C) 신뢰할 수 없는 자재를 구매했다.
(D) 집을 다시 꾸며야 한다.

해설　오후 7시 47분, Sam Rockwell의 메시지에서 I put in new windows in my attic last year. I'm not sure I would do it again, though. (제가 작년에 다락에 창문을 새로 달았어요. 하지만 그런 일을 다시 할지는 잘 모르겠어요.)라고 했고, 오후 7시 53분에 그가 다시 But I will probably hire a professional next time.(하지만 전 다음 번에는 전문가를 고용할 것 같아요.)라고 했으므로 (A)가 정답

166 암시/추론　　　　　　　　　난이도 중

해석　Ms. Stapleton에 관하여 무엇이 사실이겠는가?
(A) Mr. Gandolfini와 함께 근무한다.
(B) 창문 설치 경험이 있다.
(C) 정기적으로 www.yourhouseproj.com에 동영상을 업로드한다.
(D) 새로 집을 장만했다.

해설　오후 7시 55분, Deidre Stapleton의 메시지에서 I operate a windows and siding business.(제가 창문과 외장재 사업을 하거든요.)라고 하여 그녀가 창문 설치 경험이 있음을 알 수 있으므로 (B)가 정답

167 암시/추론　　　　　　　　　난이도 중

해석　Mr. Gandolfini는 이후에 무엇을 하겠는가?
(A) 파손된 창문을 교체할 것이다.
(B) 교육용 동영상을 시청할 것이다.
(C) 사업체에 전화할 것이다.
(D) 가격견적을 검토할 것이다.

해설　오후 7시 55분, Tony Gandolfini의 메시지에서 I was thinking of replacing just one window, but it sounds like something a new homeowner would have trouble doing. Deidre, can I get your company's phone number?(창문 하나만 교체하려고 했는데, 새내기 집주인이 하기에는 고생스러운 일 같네요. Deidre, 당신 회사 전화번호를 알려주시겠어요?)라고 하여 그녀의 회사로 전화할 것임을 알 수 있으므로 (C)가 정답

Paraphrasing　company ➡ business

168-171번은 다음 이메일에 관한 문제입니다.

제목: 회신: 설계도
날짜: 5월 29일
발신: sandra.lukacs@renosmith.com
수신: b.obafemi@lwmail.com

Ms. Obafemi께,

설계도와 관련해 빠른 답변 주셔서 감사 드립니다. 저는 우리가 지난 금요일에 만났을 때 많은 진전이 있었다고 생각합니다. 당신의 주거용품점은 곧 현실이 될 것입니다.

제안된 상점의 규격과 저희가 논의한 사양에 따라, 저희가 이제 일을 진행하는데 어떤 움직임을 취해야 하는 지가 더 명확해지고 있습니다.[168] 말씀하셨던 자금 문제에 주목했습니다. 하지만 저는 적당히 비용 효율적인 부품들로 화강암 외관과 타일 작업을 하기에 충분하다고 생각합니다.[169] 제가 다음주 화요일까지 전체 항목별 견적서를 보내드리겠습니다. 한 줄 한 줄 검토해 보신 후 저에게 알려주세요. 그리고 나서 저희는 회의를 잡아서 필요한 수정사항들을 반영할 수 있고, 당신은 전체 내용에 대해 승인해 주시면 됩니다.[170]

그리고 제가 굴착 중장비[171]를 7월 1일부터 7일까지 대여하기로 일정을 잡았습니다. 제가 사전에 작업 허가증을 받아야 해서 이 날짜들이 곤란하시면 저에게 바로 연락주세요. 시 규정 때문에, 주거지역에서 그렇게 소음이 큰 기계를 가동하려면 특별 허가를 받아야 할거에요.[171]

함께 일하게 되어 기쁘고, 이렇게 중요한 프로젝트에 Reno-Smith를 파트너로 선택해 주셔서 다시 한번 감사드립니다.

Sincerely,
Sandra Lukacs

어휘　response n. 답장, 회신　blueprint n. 계획, 청사진　progress n. 진척, 진행　home improvement 주택개조　reality n. 현실　proposed adj. 제안된　dimension n. (공간의) 크기, 치수　specification n. 사양　move n. 조치, 행동　go forward (일이) 진척되다　note v. 주의[주목]하다　funding n. 자금(제공)　issue n. 문제, 사안　mention v. 언급하다　granite n. 화강암　exterior n. 외부　tile v. 타일을 붙이다　cost-effective adj. 비용 효율적인　component n. 요소, 부품　itemize v. 항목별로 적다　estimate n. 견적서　assess v. 평가하다, 사정하다　line by line 한줄 한줄　revision n. 수정, 변경　sign off on ~에 대해 승인하다　tentative adj. 잠정적인　rent v. 대여하다　excavation n. 발굴　equipment n. 기기, 장비　right away 곧바로　obtain v. 얻다　permit n. 허가증　beforehand adv. 사전에, 미리　regulation n. 규정　authorization n. 허가(증)　operate v. 가동하다　machinery n. 기계(류)　otherwise adv. 그 외에는, 그렇지 않으면　residential adj. 주택지의　pleasure n. 기쁨, 즐거움　choose v. 선택하다

168 주제/목적/대상　　　　　　　　　난이도 중

해석　이메일의 목적은 무엇인가?
(A) 문서의 승인을 요청하려고
(B) 프로젝트의 다음 단계를 상세히 설명하려고
(C) 계획에 추가된 내용을 설명하려고
(D) 프로젝트의 총 비용을 설명하려고

해설　두 번째 단락에서 it's getting clearer what moves we now need to make going forward.(저희가 이제 일을 진행하는데 어떤 움직임을 취해야 하는 지가 더 명확해지고 있습니다.)라고 했으므로 (B)가 정답

169 암시/추론 　　　　　　　　　난이도 중

해석 Ms. Obafemi에 관하여 알 수 있는 것은?
(A) 성공적인 점포를 소유하고 있다.
(B) 한정된 예산을 가지고 있다.
(C) 허가증을 신청해야 한다.
(D) 자신의 사업체를 이전하고 싶어한다.

해설 두 번째 단락에서 I've noted the funding issues you mentioned. Still, I think we have enough for the granite exterior and tiling with the right cost-effective components.(말씀하신 자금 문제에 주목했습니다. 하지만 저는 적당히 비용 효율적인 부품들로 화강암 외관과 타일 작업을 하기에 충분하다고 생각합니다.)라고 하여 Ms. Obafemi의 예산이 한정되어 있음을 알 수 있으므로 (B)가 정답

Paraphrasing funding ➡ budget

170 상세정보 　　　　　　　　　난이도 중

해석 이메일에 따르면, Ms. Obafemi는 다음 회의를 위해 무엇을 준비해야 하는가?
(A) 설계도를 만들어야 한다
(B) 일부 수치를 검토해야 한다
(C) 일부 자재를 구입해야 한다
(D) 계약서에 서명해야 한다

해설 두 번째 단락에서 I'll send over the full itemized estimate by next Tuesday. Let me know after you've had a chance to assess it line by line. We can then schedule a meeting to make any necessary revisions, and you can sign off on everything.(제가 다음주 화요일까지 전체 항목별 견적서를 보내드리겠습니다. 한 줄 한 줄 검토해 보신 후 저에게 알려주세요. 그리고 나서 저희는 회의를 잡아서 필요한 수정사항들을 반영할 수 있고, 당신은 전체 내용에 대해 승인해 주시면 됩니다.)라고 했으므로 (B)가 정답

Paraphrasing assess ➡ review

171 상세정보 　　　　　　　　　난이도 중

해석 Ms. Lukacs는 왜 중장비를 언급하는가?
(A) 요청 날짜에 이용 가능함을 확인하려고
(B) 그녀에게 충분히 대규모의 건설 작업반이 있음을 확실히 하려고
(C) 규정이 준수되고 있는지 확실히 하려고
(D) 그것이 건물 규격에 맞을 지 확인하려고

해설 세 번째 단락에서 heavy excavation equipment(굴착 중장비)라고 하며 Due to city regulations, I will need to get special authorization to operate such noisy machinery in an otherwise residential area.(시 규정 때문에, 주거지역에서 그렇게 소음이 큰 기계를 가동하려면 특별 허가를 받아야 할거에요.)라고 했으므로 (C)가 정답

172-175번은 다음 기사에 관한 문제입니다.

무제한 휴가?
Greg Waiters, 전속작가

근로자들은 종종 업무 스트레스로부터 벗어나 휴가를 떠나는 것을 꿈꾼다. 아쉽게도, 한정된 휴가 일수는 직원들에게 필요한 만큼의 휴식과 여가를 허용하지 않을 지도 모른다. —[1]—. 하지만 일부 회사에서 직원들에게 무제한 유급 휴가를 제공하기 시작했다. 이 제도가 회사에 불리하게 작용

할 것처럼 보일 수 있지만, 긍정적인 영향을 주는 것으로 드러났다. 회사는 직원들이 더 열심히 근무한다는 것과, (173C)핵심 인재를 채용 및 유지할 수 있다는 점, (173A)그리고 사용해야 하는, 정해진 휴가일수가 없으므로, 미사용 휴가에 대해 비용을 지급할 필요가 없다는 점에 주목했다.(173B)

이러한 정책을 실행하기 전, 고용주들은 반드시 이 제도가 모두의 이해를 기반으로 하고 있으며, 기대치가 현실적인 지를 확실히 해야 한다.(172) —[2]—. 이는 무제한 휴가가 각자의 업무 할당량에 대한 책임 축소를 의미하지 않음을 강조하는 것과 더불어, 자사 직원들에게 이 제도가 전반적으로 회사에 어떠한 이득을 가져다 줄 것인지에 대해 교육하는 것을 포함한다. 직원들은 휴가를 사용하는 올바른 절차에 대해서도 명확히 인지해야 한다.(175) —[3]—. 고용주들은 이 부분에 대해 문제가 없도록 정기적으로 확인해야 한다.(174) —[4]—.

어휘 unlimited adj. 무제한의 vacation n. 휴가 dream v. 꿈을 꾸다 stress n. 스트레스, 압박 v. 강조하다 unfortunately adv. 유감스럽게도, 안타깝게도 allow v. 허용하다 employee n. 직원 rest n. 휴식 relaxation n. 휴식 offer v. 제공하다 paid leave 유급휴가 policy n. 정책, 제도 disadvantage n. 불리한 점, 약점 impact n. 영향, 효과 notice v. 주목하다, 의식하다 recruit v. 채용하다 retain v. 유지하다, 보유하다 talent n. 재능 pay out (돈을) 치르다, 지불하다 implement v. 실행하다 measure n. 조치, 정책 ensure v. 보장하다 expectation n. 기대 realistic adj. 현실적인 benefit v. 유익하다 overall adv. 전부, 대체로 emphasize v. 강조하다 translate v. 의미하다 reduction n. 감소 responsibility n. 책임 proper adj. 올바른, 적절한 procedure n. 절차 regularly adv. 정기적으로 issue n. 쟁점, 문제

172 주제/목적/대상 　　　　　　　　　난이도 상

해석 기사는 주로 누구를 대상으로 하는가?
(A) 잡지 작가
(B) 법률 전문가
(C) 여행사 직원
(D) 회사 임원진

해설 두 번째 단락에서 Before implementing such measures, employers must ensure that the policy is well-understood and that expectations are realistic.(이러한 정책을 실행하기 전, 고용주들은 반드시 이 제도가 모두의 이해를 기반으로 하고 있으며, 기대치가 현실적인 지를 확실히 해야 한다.)라고 하여 무제한 휴가 정책을 실행하기 전 고려해야 할 점들을 알려주어 정책 결정권자를 대상으로 한 기사임을 알 수 있으므로 (D)가 정답

173 사실확인 　　　　　　　　　난이도 중

해석 무제한 휴가의 이점으로 언급되지 않은 것은?
(A) 회사로 하여금 직원을 잃지 않게 해준다.
(B) 회사가 비용을 절약할 수 있다.
(C) 생산성을 증가시킨다.
(D) 직원들에게 재택근무 옵션을 제공한다.

해설 지문의 단서와 보기를 매칭시키면, 첫 번째 단락에서 Companies have noticed that their employees work harder(직원들이 더 열심히 근무한다는 것) → (C) It increases productivity levels./ they are able to recruit and retain top talent(핵심 인재를 채용 및 유지할 수 있다는 점) → (A) It keeps a company from losing employees./they don't need to pay out unused vacation time, since there is no fixed number of days to be taken.(사

용해야 하는, 정해진 휴가일수가 없으므로, 미사용 휴가에 대해 비용을 지급할 필요가 없다는 점) → (B) It allows a company to save money.와 일치하지만, 재택근무에 대한 내용은 언급된 바 없으므로 (D)가 정답

174 상세정보 _{난이도 중}

해석 기사에 따르면, 주기적으로 무엇이 이루어져야 하는가?
(A) 절차에 대한 검토
(B) 관리방식의 변경
(C) 교육 세미나
(D) 업무에 대한 논의

해설 두 번째 단락에서 Employees should also be clear on the proper procedure for taking days off of work. –[3]–. Employers should check on this regularly to make sure there are no issues.(직원들은 휴가를 사용하는 올바른 절차에 대해서도 명확히 인지해야 한다. –[3]–. 고용주들은 이 부분에 대해 문제가 없도록 정기적으로 확인해야 한다.)라고 했으므로 (A)가 정답

Paraphrasing regularly ➡ periodically

175 문장 삽입 _{난이도 중}

해석 [1], [2], [3], [4]로 표시된 곳 중, 다음 문장이 들어갈 위치로 가장 적절한 것은?
"예를 들면, 직원들은 장기휴가 사용 시, 미리 휴가를 신청해야 할 지도 모른다."
(A) [1]
(B) [2]
(C) [3]
(D) [4]

해설 두 번째 단락에서 Employees should also be clear on the proper procedure for taking days off of work.(직원들은 휴가를 사용하는 올바른 절차에 대해서도 명확히 인지해야 한다.)라며 휴가 사용 절차에 대해 언급하고 있어, 주어진 문장이 이어지기에 자연스러우므로 (C)가 정답

176-180번은 다음 전단지와 편지에 관한 문제입니다.

18세에서 42세 사이시며 Chicago 지역에 거주하고, 약간의 여유 돈이 필요하신가요? 그렇다면 Mercer 리서치에 연락하세요!

Mercer 리서치에서는 고객사를 위한 소중한 의견을 얻기 위해 유급 포커스그룹 세션에 참여하실 분들을 찾고 있습니다.^{(176)/(178)} 아래 목록에서 관심 있는 것이 있으시면, www.mercerresearch.com/focusgroups에서 신청해 주세요. 당신이 적합한 지원자인지 확인하기 위한 설문지를 작성하셔야 합니다.

G918 – 지역 밴드의 신규 앨범에 대해 의견을 주실 음악 애호가를 찾습니다. 참가자들은 90분 동안 청취하시고 75달러를 받게 됩니다.

G929 – 2시간 동안 태블릿 PC 신제품을 테스트 및 리뷰해주실 전자제품 애호가를 찾습니다. 참가자들은 간단한 설문을 작성한 후, 내주신 시간에 대한 보상으로 125달러를 받게 됩니다.

G951 – 5세 이하의 자녀를 둔 부모님들을 이틀간 진행되는 장난감 주제의 포커스 그룹에 초대합니다. 모임은 하루 3시간 동안 진행되며, 참가자들은 내주신 시간에 대한 보상으로 300달러를 받게 됩니다.

G996 – 지역 프로야구팀에 의견을 주실 스포츠 팬을 모십니다. 새로운 팬과 오랜 팬 모두 2회로 진행되는 1시간분량의 토론회에 참석을 신청 하실 수 있습니다. 참가자들은 보상으로 50달러와 다음 홈경기 입장권 2매를 받게 됩니다.⁽¹⁷⁷⁾

어휘 focus group 포커스그룹(시장조사나 여론조사를 위해 각 계층을 대표하도록 뽑은 소수의 사람들로 이뤄진 그룹) obtain v. 얻다, 구하다 input n. 조언 sign up 등록하다 complete v. 작성하다 questionnaire n. 설문지 confirm v. 확인해 주다 suitable adj. 적합한, 알맞은 earn v. 벌다, 얻다 electronics n. 전자제품 enthusiast n. 열광적인 팬 brand-new adj. 아주 새로운 attendee n. 참석자 take part in 참여하다 last v. 지속하다 attend v. 참석하다 in return 보답으로

10월 3일

Jacob Tambor
1912 Farland Way
Chicago, IL 60606

Mr. Tambor께,

귀하는 G996 모임의 참가자로 선정되셨습니다. 웹 페이지에 나와 있는 대로, 8월 18일 오후 12시와 8월 20일 오후 1시로 예정된 1시간 동안의 모임에 2회 참석하셔야 합니다.⁽¹⁷⁷⁾ 모임은 모두 제가 주재합니다.⁽¹⁷⁸⁾ 시간이 한정되어 있으므로, 모임에 참석하시기 전에 짧은 동영상을 보시고 설문지 작성을 요청 드립니다. 이는 더 생산적인 토론을 가능하게 해줄 것입니다.

저희 건물에 현재 보수작업이 진행 중이라서, 본사에서 모이지 않을 것입니다. 대신, 시 중심부에 있는 작업공간을 하나 예약했습니다(약도는 웹 사이트에서 확인하실 수 있습니다). 또한, 그 건물 주차장에 출입하실 수 있는 주차권을 동봉해드렸습니다.⁽¹⁷⁹⁾

신청하신 모임에 참석하실 수 없는 경우, 되도록 빨리 저희에게 알려주시는 것이 중요합니다. 그래야 저희도 대체 지원자에게 통보할 수 있습니다.⁽¹⁸⁰⁾

시간 내어 도와주셔서 감사드립니다.

Nathaniel Olsen
Nathaniel Olsen
Mercer 연구소

동봉물 재중

어휘 set v. [장소·일시를] 정하다 lead v. 이끌다 fill out 작성하다 productive adj. 생산적인 currently adv. 현재, 지금 undergo v. (변화 등을) 겪다 workspace n. 작업[업무] 공간 directions n. 길 안내 enclosed adj. 동봉된 access n. 입장[접근] parking garage 주차장 notify v. 알리다 alternative adj. 대체 가능한, 대안이 되는

176 주제/목적/대상 _{난이도 상}

해석 전단지의 목적은 무엇인가?
(A) 자격을 갖춘 보조 연구원을 채용하는 것

(B) 새 마케팅 회사를 홍보하는 것
(C) 곧 있을 운동경기들을 나열하는 것
(D) 토론 기회를 광고하는 것

해설 첫 번째 지문[전단지], 첫 번째 단락에서 We at Mercer Research are looking for people to participate in paid focus group sessions, so we can obtain valuable input for our clients.(Mercer 리서치에서는 고객사를 위한 소중한 의견을 얻기 위해 유급 포커스그룹 세션에 참여하실 분들을 찾고 있습니다.)라고 했으므로 (D)가 정답

177 암시/추론 [연계문제] 난이도 중

해석 Mercer 리서치는 Mr. Tambor에게 얼마를 지불하겠는가?
(A) 50달러
(B) 75달러
(C) 125달러
(D) 300달러

해설 두 번째 지문[Mr. Tambor에게 보낸 편지], 첫 번째 단락에서 You have been accepted to participate in session #G996. As our Web page states, you will be asked to attend two one-hour meetings set for August 18 at 12 P.M. and August 20 at 1 P.M.(귀하는 G996 모임의 참가자로 선정되셨습니다. 웹 페이지에 나와 있는 대로 8월 18일 오후 12시와 8월 20일 오후 1시로 예정된 한 시간 동안의 모임에 2회 참석하셔야 합니다.)라고 했는데, 첫 번째 지문[전단지], 두 번째 단락에서 #G996 – Sports fans are needed to give their opinions on the local professional baseball team. Both new and old fans are encouraged to sign up to attend a pair of one-hour discussions. In return, participants will receive $50 and two tickets to the next home game.(G996 – 지역 프로야구 팀에 의견을 주실 스포츠 팬을 모십니다. 새로운 팬과 오랜 팬 모두 2회로 진행되는 1시간분량의 토론회에 참석을 신청 하실 수 있습니다. 참가자들은 보상으로 50달러와 다음 홈경기 입장권 2매를 받게 됩니다.)라고 했으므로 (A)가 정답

178 암시/추론 [연계문제] 난이도 중

해석 Mr. Olsen에 관하여 알 수 있는 것은?
(A) 태블릿 PC를 구입해야 한다.
(B) 포커스그룹을 조직한다.
(C) 파트타임으로 일한다.
(D) 스포츠 경기장에서 근무한다.

해설 첫 번째 지문[전단지], 첫 번째 단락에서 We at Mercer Research are looking for people to participate in paid focus group sessions, so we can obtain valuable input for our clients.(Mercer 리서치에서는 고객사를 위한 소중한 의견을 얻기 위해 유급 포커스그룹 세션에 참여하실 분들을 찾고 있습니다.)라고 했고, 두 번째 지문[편지], 첫 번째 단락에서 I will lead both of the sessions.(모임은 모두 제가 주재합니다.)라고 하여 그가 Mercer 리서치에서 모임을 주관하고 있음을 알 수 있으므로 (B)가 정답

179 상세정보 난이도 중

해석 편지에 무엇이 포함되어 있는가?
(A) 건물 안내도
(B) 신청서
(C) 주차권
(D) 식권

해설 두 번째 지문[편지], 두 번째 단락에서 Also, enclosed, you'll find a pass that will give you access to the building's parking garage.(또한, 그 건물 주차장에 출입하실 수 있는 주차권을 동봉해드렸습니다.)라고 했으므로 (C)가 정답

Paraphrasing enclosed ➡ included,
a pass that will give you access to the building's parking garage ➡ a parking pass

180 상세정보 난이도 중

해석 Mr. Tambor가 약속을 취소하면 Mercer 리서치는 무엇을 할 것인가?
(A) 다른 지원자에게 연락할 것이다
(B) 자료집을 발송할 것이다
(C) 회의 일정을 다시 잡을 것이다
(D) 전액 환불해줄 것이다

해설 두 번째 지문[편지], 세 번째 단락에서 In the event that you are unable to attend your session, it is important that you let us know as quickly as you can. This will allow us to notify an alternative candidate.(신청하신 모임에 참석하실 수 없는 경우, 되도록 빨리 저희에게 알려주시는 것이 중요합니다. 그래야 저희도 대체 지원자에게 통보할 수 있습니다.)라고 했으므로 (A)가 정답

Paraphrasing notify an alternative candidate ➡ contact another applicant

181-185번은 다음 웹 페이지와 이메일에 관한 문제입니다.

www.adventureexcursions.com/self-drivingtours

어드벤처 여행: 남미
자주 묻는 질문: 자가운전 투어

비자가 필요한가요?
유럽연합 시민의 경우, 여권이 유효한 한 특별 비자 없이 자유롭게 여행할 수 있습니다. 기타 국가 시민의 경우, 관련 정부당국에 최신 입국 요건을 확인하십시오.(182) **모든 여행자는 투어 첫 날 복사를 위해 여권을 제시할 준비가 되어 있어야 합니다.** 이후, 국경 보안을 통과할 때마다 보여주도록 소지해야 함을 기억하시기 바랍니다.(181) 국제 운전면허증과 자동차 보험증서 또한 필요합니다.

차량을 어디서 픽업하고, 어디에 반납하나요?
도착하실 때 저희가 운전기사를 공항으로 보내드립니다. 거기서부터 직접 운전하시거나 지원차량에서 휴식을 취할 수 있습니다. **출국하실 때는, 공항에서 저희에게 차량을 주시기만 하면 됩니다. 바로 비행기를 타는 게 아니라면, 공항으로 가는 교통수단을 직접 마련하셔야 합니다.**(183)

어떤 정보를 알고 있어야 하나요?
각 여행에는 험난한 지형을 통과할 수 있는 튼튼한 사륜구동 차량이 제공됩니다. **여행 30일 전, 저희는** 예상 이동시간 및 도로 상태, 예정 숙소가 포함된 **최종 여행일정과 함께 정확한 제조사 및 모델에 관한 정보를 이메일로 보내드립니다.**(184)

무엇을 싸가야 하나요?
다용도로 활용할 수 있는 옷을 가져오는 게 중요합니다. 해수면 근처의 습한 정글과 높은 고도의 눈 덮인 산꼭대기를 모두 경험하시게 됩니다. 그에 맞게 짐을 싸주세요.

어휘 adventure n. 모험 excursion n. 여행, 소풍 EU 유럽연합 (European Union의 약어) citizen n. 시민 freely adv. 자유롭게 as long as ~하는 한 current adj. 현재의, 통용되는 confirm v. 확인해주다 latest adj. 최근의 entry n. 입장 requirement n. 요건 relevant adj. 관련 있는 government authorities 정부당국 present v. 제시하다 passport n. 여권 photocopy n. 복사 subsequently adv. 그 뒤에, 나중에 on hand 구할 수 있는 pass through ~를 통과하다 border n. 국경 security n. 보안, 경비 insurance n. 보험 vehicle n. 차량 drop off 맡기다 fly out 비행기로 출발하다 organize v. 준비하다 means n. 수단, 방법 transport n. 차량, 이동 be aware of ~를 알다 equipped with ~를 갖춘 heavy-duty adj. 튼튼한 4-wheel-drive adj. 4륜 구동 capable of ~를 할 수 있는 pass v. 통과하다, 지나다 rough adj. 거친 terrain n. 지형 make n. 제조사 along with ~과 함께 itinerary n. 여행일정 pack v. 짐을 싸다 versatile adj. 다용도의, 다재 다능한 experience v. 경험하다 humid adj. 습한 jungle n. 정글, 밀림 sea level 해수면 snow-capped adj. 눈 덮인 peak n. 꼭대기, 정상 altitude n. 고도 accordingly adv. 그에 맞춰, 그런 이유로

날짜: 4월 22일
수신: jorge_montero@adventureexcursions.com
발신: moira_oriordan@iemail.com
제목: 자가운전 투어

저는 지난주 자가운전 여행을 예약했는데, 8월 7일부터 8월 19일까지 진행될 예정입니다.[184] 저는 알래스카의 꽤 외진 지역들은 탐험했지만, 남미에는 가본 적이 없습니다. 장거리 비행을 하기 때문에, 여행이 끝난 후에 몇몇 장소들을 더 보고 싶습니다. 가능하다면, **Huascaran 국립공원 근처에서 제 투어를 마무리하고, 그 근방으로 루트를 조정하고 싶습니다.**[183] 그리고, 거기서 배낭여행 계획하는 걸 도와주실 수 있으신가요? 저는 며칠 간 추가 장비를 대여해야 할지도 몰라요. 저는 Cordillera Blanca 산이 꽤 아름다운 걸로 알고 있습니다. 저는 제안을 환영하지만, 제가 그곳에 가기 전에 계획을 세우고 싶습니다.[185]

Best Regards,

Moira O'Riordan

어휘 book v. 예약하다 due adj. ~하기로 예정된 run v. (일정 기간 동안) 계속되다, 유효하다 explore v. 탐험하다, 답사하다 pretty adv. 꽤 remote adj. 외진, 먼 flight n. 비행 additional adj. 추가적인 site n. 장소 end v. 끝나다 adjust v. 조정하다 route n. 길, 경로 backpacking trip 배낭여행 rent v. 빌리다 extra adj. 추가의 suggestion n. 제안 figure out 알아내다, 이해하다

181 암시/추론 난이도 중

해석 <어드벤쳐 여행: 남미의 자가운전 투어>에 관하여 알 수 있는 것은?
(A) 방문객들이 전통적인 관광보다 더 많은 장소들을 볼 수 있게 해준다.
(B) 대규모로 여행하는 사람들을 위한 것이다.
(C) 주로 날씨가 서늘한 장소들을 지난다.
(D) 여러 국가로의 여행을 포함한다.

해설 첫 번째 지문[웹 페이지], 첫 번째 단락에서 Every traveler should be ready to present their passport on the first day of the tour for a photocopy. Subsequently, remember to keep it on hand to display whenever we pass through border security.(모든 여행자는 투어 첫 날 복사를 위해 여권을 제시할 준비가 되어 있어야 합니다. 이후, 국경 보안을 통과할 때마다 보여주도록 소지해야 함을 기억하시기 바랍니다.)라고 하여 여러 국가를 여행한다는 것을 알 수 있으므로 (D)가 정답

182 상세정보 난이도 중

해석 웹 페이지에 따르면, 여행자들은 투어 전에 무엇을 해야 하는가?
(A) 투어사무실로 가는 교통편을 준비해야 한다
(B) 국제운전면허증 사본을 팩스로 보내야 한다
(C) 비자가 필요한 지 알아내야 한다
(D) 특정 여행 백신을 맞아야 한다

해설 첫 번째 지문[웹 페이지], 첫 번째 단락에서 For EU citizens, you will be able to travel freely without a special visa, as long as your passport is current. For citizens of other countries, please confirm the latest entry requirements with the relevant government authorities.(유럽연합 시민의 경우, 여권이 유효한 한 특별 비자 없이 자유롭게 여행할 수 있습니다. 기타 국가 시민의 경우, 관련 정부당국에 최신 입국 요건을 확인하십시오.)라고 했으므로 (C)가 정답

183 상세정보 [연계문제] 난이도 중

해석 이메일에 설명된 대로 여행 계획을 변경한다면 Ms. O'Riordan는 무엇을 해야 하는가?
(A) 비행시간을 조정해야 한다
(B) 다른 모델을 대여해야 한다
(C) 추가 서비스요금을 지불해야 한다
(D) 공항으로 가는 방법을 마련해야 한다

해설 첫 번째 지문[웹 페이지], 두 번째 단락에서 On your way out of the country, you can simply leave the vehicle with this us at the airport. If you are not flying out immediately, you will need to organize your own means of transport to the airport.(출국하실 때는, 공항에서 저희에게 차량을 주시기만 하면 됩니다. 바로 비행기를 타는 게 아니라면, 공항으로 가는 교통수단을 직접 마련하셔야 합니다.)라고 했는데, 두 번째 지문[이메일]에서 I'd love to end my tour near Huascaran National park and adjust the route around that.(Huascaran 국립공원 근처에서 제 투어를 마무리하고, 그 근방으로 루트를 조정하고 싶습니다.)라고 하여 바로 비행기를 타고 출국하지 않을 것임을 알 수 있으므로 (D)가 정답

Paraphrasing organize your own means of transport to the airport
➡ arrange a trip to the airport

184 암시/추론 [연계문제] 난이도 상

해석 7월에 무슨 일이 있겠는가?
(A) Ms. O'Riordan이 상세한 투어정보를 받을 것이다.
(B) Mr. Montero가 Cordillera Blanca 산 투어를 이끌 것이다.
(C) Mr. Montero가 몇 가지 여행 서류를 복사할 것이다.
(D) Ms. O'Riordan이 알래스카에서 차를 빌릴 것이다.

해설 첫 번째 지문[웹 페이지], 두 번째 단락에서 Thirty days prior to your excursion, we will send an e-mail information on the exact make and model, along with a final itinerary(여행 30일 전, 저희는 최종 여행일정과 함께 정확한 제조사 및 모델에 관한 정보를 이메일로 보내드립니다.)라고 했는데, 두 번째 지문[이메일]에서 I booked

TEST 02 83

a self-driving trip last week, which is due to run from August 7 to August 19.(저는 지난주 자가운전 여행을 예약했는데, 8월 7일부터 8월 19일까지 진행될 예정입니다.)라고 하여 Ms. O'Riordan이 여행 한달 전인 7월에 여행 정보 이메일을 받을 것임을 알 수 있으므로 (A)가 정답

185 동의어   난이도 중

해석   이메일에서 여덟 번째 줄의 구 "figure out"과 의미상 가장 가까운 것은?
(A) 추론하다
(B) 평가하다
(C) 받아들이다
(D) 명확하게 하다

해설   두 번째 지문[이메일]의 but I'd like to figure out the plan before I get there.(제가 그곳에 가기 전에 계획을 세우고 싶습니다.)에서 'figure out'은 '알아내다, 이해하다'라는 의미로 쓰였으므로 보기 중 '명확하게 하다'를 뜻하는 (D)가 정답

186-190번은 다음 이메일, 양식, 기사에 관한 문제입니다.

날짜: 2월 13일
제목: 신흥 지도자 계획
수신: 전원
발신: 인사팀
첨부: 신청서

JTB Motors에서 근무한지 2년 미만인 직원은 새로운 리더십 계획에 신청하실 수 있는데,⁽¹⁸⁸⁾ 이는 선발된 20명의 주니어 직원들을 사내 가장 경력 있는 직원과 짝을 맞춰 줍니다.⁽¹⁸⁶⁾ 프로그램은 주니어 직원들에게 다양한 능력을 가다듬고 네트워크를 만들 기회를 제공하는 것을 목표로 하는데, 이는 그들이 경력상 다음 단계로 나아갈 수 있도록 준비시켜 줍니다. 참여자들은 오로지 전문분야와 업무를 기반으로 멘토들과 매칭됩니다.⁽¹⁸⁹⁾ 4월부터 각 팀은 매주 최소 1시간 동안 정기적으로 만나게 됩니다

이 프로그램에 선발되려면, 첨부 문서를 작성하셔서 <신흥 지도자 계획> 담당자 Daria Donnelly에게 2월 25일까지 이메일을 보내주세요. 선발된 지원자는 3월 3일에 Ms. Donnelly에게 수락 이메일을 받게 됩니다.⁽¹⁸⁷⁾

어휘   emerging adj. 신흥의, 새로 생겨난 leader n. 지도자 initiative n. (특정 목적 달성을 위한 새로운) 계획 invite v. 초대하다 sign up 등록하다 pair v. 짝을 짓다 select adj. 엄선된 experienced adj. 경력이 있는 aim v. 목표하다 opportunity n. 기회 refine v. 개선하다 skill set 다양한 능력[재주] build v. 짓다, 만들다 network n. 네트워크 prepare v. 준비하다 career n. 경력 participant n. 참가자 match v. 연결시키다 mentor n. 멘토 solely adv. 오로지, 단독으로 based on ~에 근거하여 area of expertise 전문분야 professional adj. 전문적인 responsibility n. 책임 meet up 만나다 regularly adv. 정기적으로 attachment n. 첨부 coordinator n. 진행자, 코디네이터 selected adj. 선택된 applicant n. 지원자 acceptance n. 수락

신흥 지도자
신청서

이름: Ned Griffin⁽¹⁸⁸⁾
부서: 상품개발

직원 ID: N_Griffin

커리어 목표 및 직업적 포커스
저는 국제시장에 국한된 상품을 디자인하는 과정과 그러한 아이디어를 보다 설득력 있는 방식으로 상사에게 더 잘 제시하는 방법에 대해 더 배우고 싶습니다.⁽¹⁸⁹⁾ 모든 커리어 관련 조언을 환영합니다.

가능 시간
수요일에서 금요일 오후

어휘   goal n. 목표 design v. 설계하다 localize v. 현지화하다 present v. 제시하다 appealing adj. 매력적인, 흥미로운

JTB Motors Quarterly

<신흥 지도자 계획, 결실을 맺다>

베테랑 크리에이티브 디렉터 Phillip Jackson은 지난 봄 인사팀에서 연락해 그가 사내 젊은 직원들 중 한 명을 멘토링해줄 수 있는지 물었을 때 어떨지 궁금했다. 그는 희망적이긴 했지만, 이렇게 보람 있을 거라고는 예상하지 못했다. "Mr. Griffin과 함께 일한 후로,⁽¹⁸⁹⁾ 저는 제가 유망한 직원에게 도움이 되고 있다고 느끼게 되어 매일 출근하는 게 더 즐겁습니다.⁽¹⁹⁰⁾ 다만 아쉬운 점은 제가 오래 전에 여기서 근무를 시작했을 당시 저에게는 조언을 해준 사람이 없었다는 점이에요"라고 Jackson은 말했다.⁽¹⁸⁹⁾

Mr. Griffin은 자신의 입장에 대해, "저는 제 디자인 아이디어를 설득하는 법을 저에게 알려줄 사람을 찾고 있었어요,"라고 말한다. 프로그램에 참여한 후로, 그는 전기 엔진의 필수적 부분을 포함해서, 자신의 디자인 몇 개가 사용되었다고 말한다. 그는 보다 자신감이 생겼고, 이제는 JTB Motors에서 성공하는데 필요한 것이 무엇인지 안다. "저는 이보다 더 명확한 목표를 가진 적도, 직장에서 이보다 더 성취감을 느낀 적도 없었어요, 그리고 이건 모두 Mr. Jackson 덕분입니다."⁽¹⁹⁰⁾

프로그램은 확대될 예정이다. 참여하고 싶으면, 인사팀의 Daria Donnelly에게 연락하면 된다.

어휘   bear fruit 결실을 맺다 veteran n. 전문가, 베테랑 happen v. 일어나다 reach out to 연락을 취하다 rewarding adj. 보람 있는 up-and-coming adj. 전도유망한 regret n. 후회 pitch v. 홍보하다, 설득하다 put to use 이용하다 integral adj. 필수적인 electric adj. 전기의 engine n. 엔진 confident adj. 자신감 있는 rise v. 오르다 rank n. 지위, 등급, 계급 fulfilled adj. 성취감을 느끼는 expand v. 확대되다

186 암시/추론   난이도 중

해석   이메일에서는 계획에 관해 무엇을 암시하는가?
(A) 참가자 수가 한정될 것이다.
(B) 제품 개발 직원들을 위한 것이다.
(C) 회사의 신입직원들이 요청했다.
(D) 참가자들은 친목교류 행사에 참석해야 할 것이다.

해설   첫 번째 지문[이메일], 첫 번째 단락에서 a new leadership initiative, which will pair a select group of 20 junior workers(이는 선발된 20명의 주니어 직원들을 사내 가장 경력 있는 직원과 짝을 맞춰 줍니다)라고 하여 한정된 수의 직원들만 참여한다는 것을 알 수 있으므로 (A)가 정답

Paraphrasing a select group of ➡ a limited number of

187 암시/추론   난이도 중

해석 주니어 직원들은 어떻게 선발되겠는가?
(A) 상사들의 추천을 받을 것이다.
(B) 잠재 멘토들과 면접을 볼 것이다.
(C) 학력에 기반하여 선발될 것이다.
(D) Ms. Donnelly의 평가를 받을 것이다.

해설 첫 번째 지문[이메일], 두 번째 단락에서 To be selected for this program, fill out the attachment and email it to the Emerging Leaders Initiative coordinator, Daria Donnelly by 25 February. Selected applicants will receive an acceptance e-mail from Ms. Donnelly on 3 March.(이 프로그램에 선발되려면, 첨부 문서를 작성하셔서 <신흥 지도자 계획> 담당자 Daria Donnelly에게 2월 25일까지 이메일을 보내주세요. 선발된 지원자는 3월 3일에 Ms. Donnelly에게 수락 이메일을 받게 됩니다.)라고 하여 Ms. Donnelly가 지원자들의 신청서를 검토한다는 것을 알 수 있으므로 (D)가 정답

188 암시/추론 [연계문제]   난이도 상

해석 Mr. Griffin에 관하여 알 수 있는 것은?
(A) Mr. Jackson의 부서로 이동했다.
(B) 해외 고객들에게 디자인 제안서를 제출했다.
(C) JTB Motors에서 근무한 지 3년 미만이다.
(D) 최근 승진을 했다.

해설 첫 번째 지문[이메일], 첫 번째 단락에서 Any staff member who has been with JTB Motors for less than two years is invited to sign up(JTB Motors에서 근무한 지 2년 미만인 직원들은 신흥 지도자 계획에 신청하실 수 있는,)라고 했는데, 두 번째 지문[양식]에서 Emerging Leaders Application Form(신흥 지도자 신청서)의 신청자 이름에 Ned Griffin이 있으므로 Mr. Griffin이 JTB Motors에 입사한 지 2년 미만인 신입사원임을 알 수 있으므로 (C)가 정답

Paraphrasing has been with ➡ has worked at

189 암시/추론 [연계문제]   난이도 상

해석 Mr. Jackson에 관하여 무엇이 사실이겠는가?
(A) 여러 직원들의 멘토였다.
(B) 인사팀에서 근무한다.
(C) 회사의 최장 근속 직원 중 한 명이다.
(D) 국제 상품 개발 경험이 있다.

해설 첫 번째 지문[이메일], 첫 번째 단락에서 Participants will be matched with mentors solely based on their area of expertise and professional responsibilities.(참여자들은 오로지 전문분야와 업무를 기반으로 멘토들과 매칭됩니다.)라고 했는데, 두 번째 지문[Mr. Griffin이 제출한 신청서], 두 번째 단락에서 I want to learn more about the process of designing products localized for emerging international markets and how to better present those ideas to my managers in an appealing way.(저는 신흥 국제시장에 국한된 상품을 디자인하는 과정과 그러한 아이디어를 보다 설득력 있는 방식으로 상사에게 더 잘 제시하는 방법에 대해 더 배우고 싶습니다.)라고 했고, 세 번째 지문[기사], 첫 번째 단락에서 After working with Mr. Griffin, said Jackson.("Mr. Griffin과 함께 일한 후로"라고 Mr. Jackson이 말했다)하는 것으로 보아 그가 국제시장에서 상품을 디자인한 경험이 있음을 알 수 있으므로 (D)가 정답

Paraphrasing designing products ➡ product development

190 상세정보   난이도 중

해석 Mr. Griffin과 Mr. Jackson 둘 다 계획으로부터 어떻게 이익을 얻었는가?
(A) 보다 명확한 목표
(B) 급여 인상
(C) 향상된 직무 성취감
(D) 더 나은 고용 안정

해설 세 번째 지문[기사], 첫 번째 단락에서 After working with Mr. Griffin, I feel happier coming into work every day knowing that I am helping an up-and-coming employee.(Mr. Griffin과 함께 일한 후로, 저는 제가 유망한 직원에게 도움이 되고 있다고 느끼게 되서 매일 출근하는 게 더 즐겁습니다.)라고 했고, 두 번째 단락에서 I have never had clearer goals, nor have I been more fulfilled in the office—and it is all thanks to Mr. Jackson.(저는 이보다 더 명확한 목표를 가진 적도, 직장에서 이보다 더 성취감을 느낀 적도 없었어요. 그리고 이건 모두 Mr. Jackson 덕분입니다.)라고 했으므로 (C)가 정답

191-195번은 다음 광고, 이메일, 그리고 정보지에 관한 문제입니다.

MeiHua Bamboo

MeiHua Bamboo는 25년 간 최고 품질의 대나무 제품들을 중국과 전 세계에 공급해 온 것을 축하하게 되어 영광입니다!

대나무로 제작한 집과 가구는 그 아름다움과 내구성으로 인해 수천 년간 아시아에서 사랑받아 왔습니다. 건축 자재로서 대나무는 많은 주목할만한 특성을 갖고 있습니다.

1. **가벼움**: 대나무는 그 어떤 건축 자재보다 훨씬 가볍습니다. 이는 대부분의 대나무 제품들을 옮기고, 보관하고, 설치하는 데 힘이 덜 든다는 것을 의미합니다.
2. **견고함**: 대나무는 목재보다 훨씬 더 강합니다. 사실, 콘크리트보다 더 강한 압력을 견딜 수 있으며, 거의 강철만큼의 장력을 갖고 있습니다.
3. **쉬운 관리**: 대나무는 상당히 내구성이 좋고, 대부분의 목재보다 수분에 강합니다. 따라서 대나무를 청소하는 것은 어렵지 않습니다. 예를 들어, 대나무 바닥에 무언가를 흘리면, 마른 걸레로 닦아주기만 하면 됩니다.
4. **활용성**: 대나무는 그 견고함에도 불구하고 쉽게 절단할 수 있고, 다양한 형태로 변형될 수 있습니다. 이는 바닥재부터 캐비닛, 심지어 커튼에 이르기까지 여러분의 자택과 사업장에 추가하고 싶은 제품은 무엇이든지 저희가 주문 제작해드릴 수 있음을 의미합니다!^{(191)/(193)}
5. **친환경**: 대나무는 완벽히 재사용이 가능하며, 무공해 자원입니다. 남은 자재들은 쉽게 재활용되거나 안전하게 폐기될 수 있습니다.

어휘 bamboo n. 대나무 celebrate v. 축하하다, 기념하다 top-quality adj. 고품질의 furniture n. 가구 durability n. 내구성 material n. 재료, 자재 notable adj. 주목할만한, 중요한 feature n. 특징, 특성 lightweight adj. 가벼운 light adj. 가벼운 require v. 요구하다 labor n. 노동 transport v. 옮기다, 이동하다 store v. 저장하다, 보관하다 install v. 설치하다 strength n. 힘, 견고함, 내구력 far adv. 훨씬 더 wood n. 목재, 나무 withstand v. 견디다 pressure n. 압력 concrete n. 콘크리트 tension n. 긴장, 장력 steel n. 강철 maintenance n. 유지 보수 quite adv. 꽤, 상당히 durable adj. 내구성이 있는 water-resistant adj. 물이 잘 스며들지 않는, 방수의 spill v. 흘리다, 쏟다 versatility n. 다재다능함 custom-design

v. 주문 제작하다 **eco-friendly** adj. 친환경의 **completely** adv. 완전히 **renewable** adj. 재생 가능한 **non-polluting** adj. 무공해의 **resource** n. 자원, 재원 **leftover** adj. (쓰고) 남은 **recycle** v. 재활용하다 **discard** v. 버리다

수신: Giuseppine Nieddu
발신: Earl Doherty
제목: 대나무 조리대
날짜: 6월 27일

Ms. Nieddu께,

저와의 만남에 시간을 내주시고, 주문제작 대나무 조리대의 설계 제안서를 보여주셔서 감사 드립니다.(193) 조리대는 이제까지 제가 본 것들과 다르고, 저는 그 조리대가 캐나다 내 신규 DDD 도넛 및 커피 체인점에 아주 잘 어울릴 거라고 생각합니다.

저희 회사 경영진도 같은 의견입니다만, 한가지 문의사항이 있습니다. 저희는 이 조리대 위에서 음식 및 음료를 준비하고 제공할 거라서요. **표면을 보호할만한 적당한 화학 용액을 제안해주실 수 있으신가요?**(192) 당연히, 저희는 오랜 시간 동안 조리대를 깨끗하고 보기 좋게 유지해주되, 무엇보다 중요한 것은 음식 준비 및 섭취에 가장 안전한 환경을 제공할 용액을 써야 합니다.(195)

미리 감사의 말씀 드립니다.

Earl Doherty
Doherty's Donut Domain (DDD)사

어휘 **countertop** n. 조리대, 작업대 **proposal** n. 제안 **custom** adj. 주문제작의 **addition** n. 추가(된 것) **chain** n. 체인(점) **management** n. 경영, 운영 **opinion** n. 의견 **prepare** v. 준비하다 **serve** v. (음식을) 제공하다, 내다 **beverage** n. 음료 **suggest** v. 제안하다 **proper** adj. 올바른, 적절한 **chemical** adj. 화학의 **solution** n. 용액 **protect** v. 보호하다 **surface** n. 표면 **naturally** adv. 당연히, 자연스럽게 **apply** v. (크림 등을) 바르다 **attractive** adj. 매력적인 **environment** n. 환경 **preparation** n. 준비 **consumption** n. 소비

대나무 제품용 마감 옵션

마감은 대나무 용품 제작의 마지막 단계입니다. **마감은 아주 소량의 물, 먼지, 오일입자만을 흡수하는 화학 용액으로 제품의 표면을 덧바르는 것입니다.**(194) 용액이 건조되면서, 사용 중에 생긴 습기나 박테리아로부터 원래의 표면을 보호해줍니다. 제품이 어떻게, 어디서 사용될 지에 따라, 다음의 마감 제품들 중 하나를 선택하시면 됩니다.

재료	내구성(195)	식품 안전?(195)
천연 왁스	약함	항상
수성 광택제	우수	보통
유성 광택제	매우 좋음	해당 없음
미네랄 오일(195)	**매우 좋음**(195)	**항상**(195)

어휘 **finish** v. 마감질하다 **manufacture** n. 제조 **involve** v. 포함하다 **cover** v. 덮다 **dirt** n. 먼지 **particle** n. 입자, 조각 **dry** v. 마르다 adj. 건조한 **protect** v. 보호하다 **original** adj. 원래의 **moisture** n. 수분, 습기 **bacteria** n. 박테리아 **depend** v. 의존하다 **choose** v. 고르다, 선택하다 **varnish** n. 광택제

---

191 사실확인   난이도 중

해석 MeiHua에 관하여 언급된 것은?
(A) 캐나다에 본사를 두고 있다.
(B) 주문제작 상품을 만들 수 있다.
(C) 올해 오픈할 것이다.
(D) 가구 세척 제품을 만든다.

해설 첫 번째 지문[광고], 두 번째 단락의 4. Versatility(활용성)에서 Despite its strength, bamboo is easy to cut and form into various shapes. That means we can work with you to custom-design just about anything you'd like to add to your home or business, from floors, to cabinets, and even curtains!(대나무는 그 견고함에도 불구하고 쉽게 절단할 수 있고, 다양한 형태로 변형될 수 있습니다. 이는 바닥재부터 캐비닛, 심지어 커튼에 이르기까지 여러분의 자택과 사업장에 추가하고 싶은 제품은 무엇이든지 저희가 주문 제작해드릴 수 있음을 의미합니다!)라고 했으므로 (B)가 정답

Paraphrasing custom-design ➡ customize

192 주제/목적/대상   난이도 중

해석 Ms. Doherty는 왜 이메일을 썼는가?
(A) 배송을 미루기 위해
(B) 회의 일정을 잡기 위해
(C) 추천을 요청하기 위해
(D) 주문을 수정하기 위해

해설 두 번째 지문[Earl Doherty가 보낸 이메일], 두 번째 단락에서 Can you suggest a proper chemical solution to protect the surfaces?(표면을 보호할만한 적당한 화학 용액을 제안해주실 수 있으신가요?)라고 했으므로 (C)가 정답

193 상세정보 [연계문제]   난이도 상

해석 Ms. Nieddu와 Mr. Doherty는 MeiHua 대나무 건축자재의 어떤 특성에 대해 논의했는가?
(A) 특성 2
(B) 특성 3
(C) 특성 4
(D) 특성 5

해설 두 번째 지문[Mr. Doherty가 Ms. Nieddu에게 보낸 이메일], 첫 번째 단락에서 Thank you for meeting with me and showing me your design proposal for custom bamboo countertops.(저와의 만남에 시간을 내주시고, 주문제작 대나무 조리대의 설계 제안서를 보여주셔서 감사드립니다.)라고 했는데, 첫 번째 지문[광고], 두 번째 단락의 4. Versatility(활용성)에서 Despite its strength, bamboo is easy to cut and form into various shapes. That means we can work with you to custom-design just about anything you'd like to add to your home or business, from floors, to cabinets, and even curtains!(대나무는 그 견고함에도 불구하고 쉽게 절단할 수 있고, 다양한 형태로 변형될 수 있습니다. 이는 바닥재부터 캐비닛, 심지어 커튼에 이르기까지 여러분의 자택과 사업장에 추가하고 싶은 제품은 무엇이든지 저희가 주문 제작해드릴 수 있음을 의미합니다!)라고 하여 4번 특성에 대해 논의했음을 알 수 있으므로 (C)가 정답

194 상세정보 　　　　　　　　　　　난이도 중

해석 정보지에 따르면, 마감에 필요한 것은?
(A) 매끈한 표면
(B) 특수 직물로 만들어진 천
(C) 시원한 환경
(D) 흡수율이 낮은 용액

해설 세 번째 지문[정보지]에서 Finishing simply involves covering the surface of the item with a chemical solution that absorbs only a small amount of water, dirt, and oil particles.(마감은 아주 소량의 물, 먼지, 오일입자만을 흡수하는 화학 용액으로 제품의 표면을 덧바르는 것입니다.)라고 했으므로 (D)가 정답

195 암시/추론 [연계문제] 　　　　　　　난이도 상

해석 DDD사는 어떤 마감제품을 선택하겠는가?
(A) 천연왁스
(B) 수성 광택제
(C) 유성 광택제
(D) 미네랄 오일

해설 두 번째 지문[이메일], 두 번째 단락에서 Naturally, we need to apply a solution that will keep the counters clean and attractive for a long time, but most importantly provide the safest possible environment for food preparation and consumption.(당연히, 저희는 오랜 시간 동안 조리대를 깨끗하고 보기 좋게 유지해주되, 무엇보다 중요한 것은 음식 준비 및 섭취에 가장 안전한 환경을 제공할 용액을 써야 합니다.)라고 했는데, 세 번째 지문[정보지], 표에서 Durability(내구성)이 Very good(매우 좋음)이면서 Food-Safe?(식품 안전?)이 Always(항상)인 물질이 Mineral oil(미네랄 오일)임을 알 수 있으므로 (D)가 정답

어휘 estimate n. 견적서 FAQ 자주 묻는 질문(frequently asked questions) fit v. (모양·크기가 어떤 사람·사물에) 맞다 consultation n. 상담 plan n. 요금제 transportation n. 운송, 수송 secure adj. 안전한 storage n. 보관(소) facility n. 시설 be subject to ~의 대상이다 fully equipped adj. (시설이나 장비가) 완비된 plus prep. ~뿐만 아니라 object n. 물건 scale up (규모를) 확대하다 operation n. 작업, 사업(체) full-sized adj. 대형의 transition n. 이동 executive adj. 고급의 monitor v. 추적관찰하다

196-200번은 다음 웹 페이지와 이메일들에 관한 문제입니다.

http://www.bunncorp.com/movingservices

| 이사 패키지 | 견적 요청 | 보험 정보 | 자주 묻는 질문 |

귀사의 필요에 맞는 이사 패키지를 선택하신 후, '견적 요청' 페이지로 가셔서 상담을 예약하세요. 각 요금제에는 인건비와 운송비가 포함되며, 안전 보관시설 서비스(SSFS) 신청은 선택사항입니다. SSFS 요금은 9월 30일에 변경될 수 있습니다.

기본형: 운송 트럭과 가구 및 장비, 파일을 해체 및 운송, 설치하는 4인으로 구성된 장비를 갖춘 팀을 포함. 중소 규모 사무실에 안성맞춤. **SSFS 요금: 99달러/월**(196)

특별형: 기본형 패키지의 모든 내용을 포함하면서, 무겁거나 옮기기 힘든 물건 운송을 위한 추가 장비 포함. **SSFS 요금: 199-300달러/월**(196)

기업형: 특별형 패키지의 모든 내용을 포함하면서, 더 규모가 큰 작업에 맞춰 확대. 대형 세미트레일러와 최대 20명으로 구성된 운송팀이 필요하신 곳으로 모셔다 드립니다. **SSFS 요금: 월 1,500달러부터**(196)

고급형: 기업형 패키지의 모든 내용을 포함하면서, **민감한 장비나 데이터의 안전보장을 위한 보안 카메라 감시 시스템과 경보기 포함.**(198) **SSFS 요금: 월 4,000달러부터**(196)

수신　BMoore@kraussfinancial.com
발신　BBunn@bunncorp.com
날짜　7월 2일
제목　이전 첫 단계: 완료

Mr. Moore께,

저희 직원들이 귀사의 모든 장비를 Huxley가 2000번지에 있는 저희 대형 보관창고로 성공적으로 옮겼음을 알려드립니다. 지난 주 회의에서의 합의사항과 귀사의 SSFS에 따라, 물품은 7월 31일까지 그곳에 보관됩니다. 그 날 오전 10시경에 Brookhurst가 19724번지, Crytech 빌딩에 있는 귀사의 새 사무실로 물품을 옮겨드리겠습니다.(197)

7월 31일 이후에도 SSFS를 이용하셔야 한다면, 저희에게 최소 5일 전 사전통지를 해주셔야 합니다. 또한, 물건이 창고에 있는 동안 매월 요금이 부과될 것입니다. 요금은 매월 1일에 청구서에 반영됩니다.(200)

Sincerely,
Bradley Bunn
Bunn사

어휘 phase n. 단계, 시기 relocation n. 이전, 이동 in accordance with ~에 따라 store v. 보관하다 transport v. 수송하다 prior notice 사전통보 assess v. [세금·회비 등을]부과하다 reflect v. 반영하다

수신　BBunn@bunncorp.com
발신　BMoore@kraussfinancial.com
날짜　7월 3일
제목　회신: 이전 첫 단계 완료

Mr. Bunn께,

이사를 하는 동안 귀사 직원들이 보여준 효율성과 노련함에 감사 드립니다. 특히 운송 중 경보기와 카메라 시스템을 통해 저희 물품을 관찰 및 감시할 수 있다는 점이 만족스러웠습니다.(198)

그러나 긴급한 업무로 인해, 저희는 이사 들어가는 날짜를 변경해야 했습니다. 그래서, 이제 저희 장비를 8월 29일 화요일에 Brookhurst가 19724번지로 옮겨주실 것을 요청 드립니다.(200)

그리고 보관창고에 온도 조절장치가 있나요? 여름 장마철 열기와 습기로 저희 소파나 테이블이 손상될까 봐 약간 염려됩니다.(199)

다시 한번 고맙습니다.
Barney Moore
Krauss 금융

어휘	efficient adj. 효율적인　skilled adj. 숙련된, 노련한　in transit 수송 중인　urgent adj. 긴급한　revise v. 변경[수정]하다　move-in n. 전입　temperature n. 온도　control n. 조절　humidity n. 습도　couch n. 소파　deteriorate v. 악화되다

196 사실확인　난이도 중

해석　Bunn사 웹 페이지에 따르면, 안전 보관시설 서비스에 관하여 사실인 것은?
(A) 현재 할인 중이다.
(B) 이사 패키지에 따라 가격이 다르다.
(C) 사전에 비용을 지불해야 한다.
(D) 요금이 6개월마다 업데이트된다.

해설　첫 번째 지문[웹 페이지]에서 요금제별 금액을 살펴보면, Basic(기본형): SSFS fee: $99/month(SSFS 요금: 99달러/월) Special(특별형): SSFS fee: $199-$300/month(SSFS 요금: 199-300달러/월) Corporate(기업형): SSFS fee from $1,500/month(SSFS 요금: 월 1,500달러부터) Executive(고급형): SSFS fee from $4,000/month(SSFS 요금: 월 4,000달러부터)라고 했으므로 (B)가 정답

Paraphrasing　fee ➡ price

197 주제/목적/대상　난이도 중

해석　첫 번째 이메일의 목적은 무엇인가?
(A) 청구서상의 실수를 이야기하는 것
(B) 고객의 문의사항에 응답하는 것
(C) 보증금을 요청하는 것
(D) 프로젝트에 대한 최신정보를 제공하는 것

해설　두 번째 지문[첫 번째 이메일], 첫 번째 단락에서 This is to confirm that our workers have successfully moved all of your company's equipment into our large storage warehouse on 200 0 Huxley Drive. As agreed upon during our meeting last week and in accordance with your SSFS, the items will be stored there until July 31. And at approximately 10 A.M. on that day, we will transport them into your new office in the Crytech Building on 19724 Brookhurst Street.(저희 직원들이 귀사의 모든 장비를 Huxley가 2000번지에 있는 저희 대형 보관창고로 성공적으로 옮겼음을 알려드립니다. 지난 주 회의에서의 합의사항과 귀사의 SSFS에 따라, 물품은 7월 31일까지 그곳에 보관됩니다. 그 날 오전 10시경에 Brookhurst가 19724번지, Crytech 빌딩에 있는 귀사의 새 사무실로 물품을 옮겨드리겠습니다.)라고 했으므로 (D)가 정답

198 암시/추론 [연계문제]　난이도 중

해석　Mr. Moore는 어떤 이사 패키지를 선택했겠는가?
(A) 기본형
(B) 특별형
(C) 기업형
(D) 고급형

해설　첫 번째 지문[웹 페이지], 다섯 번째 단락에서 Executive: monitored security camera systems and alarms to ensure the safety of sensitive equipment or data.(고급형: 민감한 장비나 데이터의 안전을 보장하기 위한 보안 카메라 감시 시스템과 경보기 포함.)이라고 했는데, 세 번째 지문[두 번째 이메일], 첫 번째 단락에서 We were especially happy to be able to observe and monitor our items when they were in transit through the alarm and camera system.(특히 운송 중 경보기와 카메라 시스템을 통해 저희 물품을 관찰 및 감시할 수 있다는 점이 만족스러웠습니다.)라고 했으므로 (D)가 정답

199 상세정보　난이도 중

해석　두 번째 이메일에 따르면, Mr. Moore는 무엇에 관하여 걱정하는가?
(A) 개정된 계약 조건
(B) 일부 가구의 손상
(C) 증가된 연료비
(D) 건물에의 출입

해설　세 번째 지문[두 번째 이메일], 세 번째 단락에서 I am a bit concerned that the heat and humidity from summer rains may cause some of our couches and tables to deteriorate.(여름 장마철 습기로 저희 소파나 테이블을 손상될까 봐 약간 염려됩니다.)라고 했으므로 (B)가 정답

Paraphrasing　concerned ➡ worried,
　　　　　　　couches and tables ➡ furniture

200 암시/추론 [연계문제]　난이도 상

해석　Bunn사에 관하여 알 수 있는 것은?
(A) 본사가 Crytech 빌딩으로 이전할 것이다.
(B) 추가 장비를 옮기지 못할 것이다.
(C) 8월 1일에 Krauss 금융에 추가 비용을 청구할 것이다.
(D) 직원들이 업무에 대해 상을 받았다.

해설　첫 번째 지문[첫 번째 이메일], 두 번째 단락에서 Should you need to use the SSFS beyond July 31, you will have to give us prior notice at least five days before. Furthermore, you will be assessed a fee for every month that your items remain in our warehouse. The charge will be reflected in your bill on the first date of each month.(7월 31일 이후에도 SSFS를 이용하셔야 한다면 저희에게 최소 5일 전 사전통지를 해주셔야 합니다. 또한, 물건이 창고에 있는 동안 매월 요금이 부과될 것입니다. 요금은 매월 1일에 청구서에 반영됩니다.)라고 했는데, 세 번째 지문[두 번째 이메일], 두 번째 단락에서 Therefore, we now request that our equipment be transported to 19724 Brookhurst Street on Tuesday, August 29.(그래서, 이제 저희 장비를 8월 29일 화요일에 Brookhurst가 19724번지로 옮겨주실 것을 요청 드립니다.)라고 하여 Krauss Financial(Krauss 금융)에서 연장한 보관기간만큼 추가 요금이 8월 1일에 청구될 것임을 알 수 있으므로 (C)가 정답

TEST 03

PART 1   P. 104
1 (D)   2 (A)   3 (D)   4 (C)   5 (A)   6 (C)

PART 2   P. 108
7 (C)   8 (C)   9 (C)   10 (B)   11 (B)   12 (B)
13 (C)   14 (B)   15 (C)   16 (B)   17 (C)   18 (B)
19 (C)   20 (A)   21 (C)   22 (A)   23 (B)   24 (A)
25 (A)   26 (B)   27 (A)   28 (C)   29 (A)   30 (B)
31 (A)

PART 3   P. 109
32 (D)   33 (C)   34 (A)   35 (B)   36 (D)   37 (D)
38 (C)   39 (D)   40 (B)   41 (A)   42 (C)   43 (D)
44 (A)   45 (C)   46 (C)   47 (B)   48 (A)   49 (D)
50 (B)   51 (C)   52 (A)   53 (C)   54 (B)   55 (D)
56 (D)   57 (A)   58 (C)   59 (D)   60 (C)   61 (D)
62 (A)   63 (C)   64 (D)   65 (C)   66 (A)   67 (A)
68 (C)   69 (B)   70 (A)

PART 4   P. 113
71 (A)   72 (D)   73 (C)   74 (B)   75 (A)   76 (B)
77 (B)   78 (D)   79 (B)   80 (B)   81 (C)   82 (A)
83 (D)   84 (A)   85 (B)   86 (C)   87 (A)   88 (A)
89 (D)   90 (C)   91 (B)   92 (C)   93 (B)   94 (D)
95 (A)   96 (D)   97 (D)   98 (A)   99 (A)   100 (A)

PART 5   P. 116
101 (B)   102 (C)   103 (C)   104 (C)   105 (D)   106 (D)
107 (D)   108 (B)   109 (D)   110 (C)   111 (D)   112 (D)
113 (C)   114 (C)   115 (C)   116 (B)   117 (A)   118 (B)
119 (C)   120 (D)   121 (A)   122 (C)   123 (C)   124 (C)
125 (B)   126 (C)   127 (B)   128 (D)   129 (A)   130 (B)

PART 6   P. 121
131 (B)   132 (A)   133 (D)   134 (B)   135 (D)   136 (C)
137 (B)   138 (C)   139 (B)   140 (D)   141 (A)   142 (C)
143 (A)   144 (B)   145 (D)   146 (B)

PART 7   P. 123
147 (C)   148 (D)   149 (C)   150 (D)   151 (A)   152 (B)
153 (C)   154 (B)   155 (B)   156 (D)   157 (C)   158 (D)
159 (D)   160 (A)   161 (C)   162 (B)   163 (C)   164 (C)
165 (D)   166 (D)   167 (D)   168 (B)   169 (C)   170 (B)
171 (A)   172 (A)   173 (C)   174 (D)   175 (A)   176 (C)
177 (C)   178 (A)   179 (C)   180 (B)   181 (C)   182 (A)
183 (D)   184 (B)   185 (C)   186 (D)   187 (A)   188 (A)
189 (B)   190 (A)   191 (C)   192 (D)   193 (B)   194 (A)
195 (C)   196 (B)   197 (B)   198 (C)   199 (A)   200 (D)

PART 1   P. 104

1   2인 이상   난이도 중

미국

(A) She's holding a dish.
(B) She's setting the table for a meal.
(C) He's sipping from a mug.
(D) He's speaking to a server.

(A) 여자가 접시를 들고 있다.
(B) 여자가 식사를 위해 식탁을 차리고 있다.
(C) 남자가 머그잔으로 조금씩 마시고 있다.
(D) 남자가 종업원과 대화하고 있다.

해설   (A) ✗ 사진에 없는 사물 (a dish)
      (B) ✗ 동작 묘사 오류 (is setting the table)
      (C) ✗ 동작 묘사 오류 (is sipping)
      (D) ○ 남자가 종업원과 대화하고 있는 모습을 적절히 묘사했으므로 정답

Possible Answer
A customer is placing an order. 고객이 주문을 하고 있다.

어휘   plate n. 접시   set a table 식탁을 차리다   meal n. 식사   sip v. 조금씩 마시다   mug n. 머그잔   server n. 종업원

2   1인 중심   난이도 상

영국

(A) She's loading some items into an automobile.
(B) She's inserting a coin into a shopping cart.
(C) She's handing some bags to a customer.
(D) She's parking a vehicle near a supermarket.

(A) 여자가 자동차에 물품들을 싣고 있다.
(B) 여자가 쇼핑 카트에 동전을 넣고 있다.
(C) 여자가 고객에게 가방들을 건네주고 있다.
(D) 여자가 슈퍼마켓 근처에 차를 주차하고 있다.

해설   (A) ○ 여자가 자동차에 물품들을 싣고 있는 모습을 적절히 묘사했으므로 정답

(B) ❌ 동작 묘사 오류 (is inserting a coin)
(C) ❌ 사진에 없는 사람 (a customer)
(D) ❌ 동작 묘사 오류 (is parking)

Possible Answer
A shopping cart is next to a car. 쇼핑 카트가 자동차 옆에 있다.

Key point
토익에서 '자동차'는 car 뿐만 아니라 automobile, auto, vehicle 등 다양하게 표현된다. 마찬가지로, '운전자'를 나타내는 표현으로 driver 뿐만 아니라 motorist도 알아 두어야 한다.

어휘 **load** v. (짐 등을) 싣다 **automobile** n. 자동차 **insert** v. 넣다, 삽입하다 **hand** v. 건네주다, 넘겨주다 **vehicle** n. 차량

3 1인 중심   난이도 하

호주

(A) A man is raking the lawn.
(B) A man is repairing a fence.
(C) A man is trimming some bushes.
(D) A man is working on some equipment.

(A) 남자가 잔디에 갈퀴질을 하고 있다.
(B) 남자가 울타리를 고치고 있다.
(C) 남자가 관목을 다듬고 있다.
(D) 남자가 장비를 살피고 있다.

해설 (A) ❌ 동작 묘사 오류 (is raking)
(B) ❌ 사진에 없는 사물 (a fence)
(C) ❌ 동작 묘사 오류 (is trimming)
(D) ⭕ 남자가 장비를 살피고 있는 모습을 적절히 묘사했으므로 정답

Possible Answer
A man is examining a machine. 남자가 기계를 점검하고 있다.

Key point 청소와 관련된 동사를 알아둔다.
be washing (창문 등을) 닦고 있다, 씻고 있다
be mopping (대걸레로) 닦고 있다
be wiping (행주 등으로) 닦고 있다
be sweeping (빗자루로) 쓸고 있다
be vacuuming 진공청소기로 청소하고 있다
be raking (낙엽 등을) 갈퀴로 긁어 모으고 있다
be polishing (윤이 나도록) 닦고 있다
be mowing 잔디를 깎고 있다
be operating 작동하고 있다
be maneuvering 조종하고 있다

어휘 **rake** v. 갈퀴질을 하다 **lawn** n. 잔디 **repair** v. 고치다 **fence** n. 울타리 **trim** v. 손질하다 **bush** n. 관목 **equipment** n. 장비

4 사물/풍경   난이도 상

영국

(A) A pot has been put in an oven.
(B) Utensils have been hung from hooks.
(C) Some food has been prepared.
(D) Some plates are beside a sink.

(A) 오븐에 냄비가 놓여있다.
(B) 주방 기구들이 고리에 걸려있다.
(C) 음식이 준비되어 있다.
(D) 접시들이 싱크대 옆에 있다.

해설 (A) ❌ 사진에 없는 사물 (an oven)
(B) ❌ 상태 묘사 오류 (have been hung)
(C) ⭕ 음식이 준비된 상태를 적절히 묘사했으므로 정답
(D) ❌ 사진에 없는 사물 (a sink)

Possible Answer
A selection of dishes is on display. 엄선된 요리들이 진열되어 있다.

어휘 **pot** n. 냄비 **put** v. (특정한 장소·위치에) 놓다 **utensil** n. (가정에서 사용하는) 기구 **hang** v. 걸다, 매달다 **hook** n. 고리, 걸이 **plate** n. 접시, 그릇

5 2인 이상   난이도 중

미국

(A) Some people are seated in front of a window.
(B) Some people are gathered around a table.
(C) One of the men is looking down at a clipboard.
(D) One of the women is adjusting a chair.

(A) 몇몇 사람들이 창문 앞에 앉아 있다.
(B) 몇몇 사람들이 테이블 주위에 모여 있다.
(C) 남자들 중 한 명이 클립보드를 내려다 보고 있다.
(D) 여자들 중 한 명이 의자를 조절하고 있다.

해설 (A) ⭕ 몇몇 사람들이 창문 앞에 앉아있는 모습을 적절히 묘사했으므로 정답
(B) ❌ 사진에 없는 사물 (a table)
(C) ❌ 동작의 대상 오류 (a clipboard)
(D) ❌ 동작 묘사 오류 (is adjusting)

Possible Answer
The people are sitting side by side. 사람들이 나란히 앉아 있다.

어휘 **be seated** 앉아 있다 **gather** v. 모으다 **adjust** v. 조정[조절]하다 **side by side** 나란히

6 1인 중심   난이도 상

미국

(A) A woman is buttoning up a safety vest.
(B) A woman is stacking some packages by a wall.
(C) A woman is taping a box in a warehouse.
(D) A woman is moving some cartons with a forklift.

(A) 여자가 안전 조끼의 단추를 잠그고 있다.
(B) 여자가 벽 옆에 상자들을 쌓고 있다.
(C) 여자가 창고에서 상자에 테이프를 붙이고 있다.

(D) 여자가 지게차로 상자들을 옮기고 있다.

해설 (A) ✗ 동작 묘사 오류 (is buttoning up)
(B) ✗ 동작 묘사 오류 (is unloading)
(C) O 여자가 창고에서 상자에 테이프를 붙이고 있는 모습을 적절히 묘사했으므로 정답
(D) ✗ 동작 묘사 오류 (is moving)

Possible Answer
A worker is wearing a helmet. 작업자가 헬멧을 쓰고 있다.

어휘 **button up** ~을 단추로 잠그다 **safety vest** 안전조끼 **stack** v. 쌓다 **package** n. 상자, 소포, 작은 짐 **tape** v. 테이프로 붙이다 **warehouse** n. 창고 **carton** n. 판지상자 **forklift** n. 지게차 **wear** v. 입고 있다

PART 2

P. 108

7 Who 의문문 난이도 중

Who can drive Ms. Edwards to the bus terminal?
(A) To see a live performance.
(B) A three hour ride.
(C) I don't have a license.

누가 Ms. Edwards를 버스 터미널까지 태워 주실 수 있으세요?
(A) 라이브 공연을 보려고요.
(B) 세 시간 거리예요.
(C) 저는 면허가 없어요.

해설 (A) ✗ 유사 발음 함정 (drive - live)
(B) ✗ 연상 어휘 함정 (drive, bus - ride)
(C) O 자신은 면허가 없다며 운전해서 데려다 줄 수 없음을 우회적으로 말했으므로 정답

Possible Answer
Hector is free. Hector가 시간이 돼요.

어휘 **performance** n. 공연 **ride** n. 길, 여정 **license** n. 면허증

8 Which 의문문 난이도 중

Which beverage would you prefer?
(A) Sure. With extra ice, please.
(B) At the diner.
(C) I'll have some tea. Thanks.

어떤 음료를 드시겠어요?
(A) 네, 얼음을 추가해 주세요.
(B) 작은 식당에서요.
(C) 저는 차 마실게요. 감사해요.

해설 (A) ✗ 연상 어휘 함정 (beverage – ice)
(B) ✗ 연상 어휘 함정 (beverage – diner)
(C) O 차를 마시겠다며 선택하여 말했으므로 정답

Possible Answer
May I get some water? 물을 좀 마실 수 있을까요?

어휘 **beverage** n. 음료 **prefer** v. 선호하다 **diner** n. 작은 식당

9 부정 의문문 난이도 중

Aren't you managing the Parker account?
(A) Before 11 A.M.
(B) At the management office.
(C) Yes, Ashley and I are.

Parker 거래처를 관리하고 계시지 않으세요?
(A) 오전 11시 전에요.
(B) 관리 사무소에서요.
(C) 네, Ashley와 제가 하고 있어요.

해설 (A) ✗ When 의문문에 어울리는 대답
(B) ✗ 유사 발음 함정 (managing - management)
(C) O 'Yes'로 대답하고, Ashley와 내가 하고 있다며 적절히 덧붙여 말했으므로 정답

Possible Answer
Pauline is in charge of it. Pauline이 맡고 있어요.

어휘 **manage** v. 관리하다 **account** n. 거래처; 단골 고객

10 Where 의문문 난이도 중

Where can I get the tourist visa application form?
(A) For Shanghai and Beijing.
(B) At the information desk.
(C) A travel schedule.

관광비자 신청서는 어디서 받을 수 있나요?
(A) Shanghai와 Beijing행이요.
(B) 안내 데스크에서요.
(C) 여행일정표요.

해설 (A) ✗ 연상 어휘 함정 (tourist visa – Shanghai and Beijing)
(B) O 안내데스크라며 위치로 말했으므로 정답
(C) ✗ 연상 어휘 함정 (tourist visa – travel schedule)

Possible Answer
You can get it on our Web site. 저희 웹 사이트에서 받으실 수 있습니다.

어휘 **tourist visa** 관광비자 **application form** 신청서

11 평서문 난이도 상

Let's stay longer to finish this budget report.
(A) Yes, a financial report.
(B) But I've already made plans.
(C) No, Sue no longer works here.

예산 보고서를 마무리하게 조금만 더 있읍시다.
(A) 네, 재무보고서요.
(B) 근데 저는 선약이 있어요.
(C) 아니요, Sue는 이제 여기서 근무하지 않아요.

해설 (A) ✗ 동어 반복 함정 (report – report)
(B) O 약속이 있다며 우회적으로 거절한 대답이므로 정답
(C) ✗ 동어 반복 함정 (longer – longer)

Possible Answer
Sure. It won't take long anyway. 그래요. 오래 걸리지 않을 테니까요.

어휘 **budget report** 예산보고서 **financial report** 재무보고서 **plan** n. 계획 **no longer** 더 이상 ~하지 않는

12 When 의문문 난이도 중

When is the due date for the registration fee?
(A) From the Operations Department.
(B) You should call Eugene.
(C) Yes, on your desk.

등록비 납기일은 언제인가요?
(A) 운영 부서에서요.
(B) Eugene에게 전화해보세요.
(C) 네, 당신 책상 위에요.

해설 (A) ✗ 연상 어휘 함정 (registration fee - Operations Department)
(B) ○ (자신은 모르니) Eugene에게 전화해 보라고 우회적으로 말했으므로 정답
(C) ✗ 의문사 의문문 Yes/No 응답 불가

Possible Answer
This Friday, I believe. 이번 주 금요일일 거예요.

어휘 **due date** 기한, 마감일 **registration fee** 등록비

13 Why 의문문 난이도 중

Why is this file cabinet here?
(A) From the furniture catalog.
(B) The official documents.
(C) I'll move it to the storage room.

이 파일 캐비닛이 왜 여기에 있죠?
(A) 가구 카탈로그에서요.
(B) 공식 서류요.
(C) 제가 그걸 창고로 옮겨 놓을게요.

해설 (A) ✗ 연상 어휘 함정 (file cabinet - furniture catalog)
(B) ✗ 연상 어휘 함정 (file - documents)
(C) ○ 창고로 옮기겠다며 질문에 적절하게 반응했으므로 정답

Possible Answer
Accounting needed a new one. 회계부서에서 새 것을 원했어요.

어휘 **official** adj. 공식적인 **storage room** 창고

14 부가 의문문 난이도 중

You've attended the annual marketing convention, haven't you?
(A) Yes, a new marketing strategy.
(B) There were some great sessions.
(C) Is that why we haven't?

연례 마케팅 총회에 참석하셨죠, 그렇지 않나요?
(A) 네, 새로운 마케팅 전략이요.
(B) 훌륭한 세션들이 좀 있었어요.
(C) 그래서 우리가 안 하지 않았나요?

해설 (A) ✗ 동어 반복 함정 (marketing – marketing)
(B) ○ 훌륭한 세션들이 있었다며 참석했음을 우회적으로 말했으므로 정답
(C) ✗ 동어 반복 함정 (haven't – haven't)

Possible Answer
No, Calvin went instead. 아니요, Calvin이 대신 갔어요.

어휘 **annual** adj. 연례의 **convention** n. 총회, 컨벤션 **marketing strategy** 마케팅 전략 **session** n. 세션, (특정 모임) 시간

15 제안/요청 난이도 중

Would you like to have dinner with us after work?
(A) Let me take you to your table.
(B) The supermarket should have them in stock.
(C) I have to go to the airport early tomorrow morning.

퇴근하고 저희랑 저녁 식사 같이 하시겠어요?
(A) 앉으실 테이블로 안내해 드릴게요.
(B) 그 슈퍼마켓에 재고가 있을 거예요.
(C) 제가 내일 아침 일찍 공항에 가야 해요.

해설 (A) ✗ 연상 어휘 함정 (dinner - table)
(B) ✗ 질문과 무관한 대답
(C) ○ 같이 저녁 식사하자는 제의에 우회적으로 거절했으므로 정답

Possible Answer
Sure, where are we going? 좋아요, 어디로 가세요?

어휘 **in stock** 재고에 있는

16 When 의문문 난이도 중

When can I make a dental appointment with Dr. Price?
(A) For about half an hour.
(B) She's fully booked until next Thursday.
(C) Yes, I read about it this afternoon.

Dr. Price의 치과진료 예약을 언제로 할 수 있나요?
(A) 약 30분 동안이요.
(B) 다음 주 목요일까지 예약이 다 찼어요.
(C) 네, 오늘 오후에 그걸 봤어요.

해설 (A) ✗ How long 의문문에 어울리는 대답
(B) ○ 다음주 목요일까지는 예약이 꽉 찼다며 그 이후에나 가능함을 우회적으로 말했으므로 정답
(C) ✗ 의문사 의문문 Yes/No 응답 불가

Possible Answer
Would Wednesday at 3 P.M. work for you? 수요일 오후 3시 괜찮으세요?

어휘 **make an appointment** 예약하다 **book** v. 예약하다

17 일반 의문문 난이도 중

Did you see the advertisement for the new movie at Jameson Theater?
(A) I already met with him.
(B) Many moviegoers.
(C) Yes, and it looks like it'll be a lot of fun.

Jameson 극장에서 하는 새 영화 광고를 보셨나요?
(A) 이미 그를 만났어요.
(B) 많은 영화 애호가들이요.
(C) 네, 정말 재미있을 것 같아요.

해설 (A) ✗ 연상 어휘 함정 (Jameson – him)
(B) ✗ 유사 발음 함정 (movie –moviegoers), 연상 어휘 함정 (theater – moviegoers)
(C) ○ 'Yes'로 대답하고, 정말 재미있을 것 같다며 적절하게 덧붙여 말했으므로 정답

Possible Answer
I stayed in all weekend. 저는 주말 내내 집에만 있었어요.

어휘 **advertisement** n. 광고 **moviegoer** n. 영화 보러 극장에 자주 가는 사람 **stay in** (밖으로) 나가지 않다, 집에 있다

18 How 난이도 상

호주↔미국

How long does it take to become a pharmacist?
(A) A new medicine for colds.
(B) Do you want to pursue a career in that field?
(C) Since the hospital was founded.

약사가 되는데 시간이 얼마나 걸리나요?
(A) 감기 신약이요.
(B) 그 분야에서 경력을 쌓고 싶으세요?
(C) 병원이 설립된 후부터요.

해설 (A) ✗ 연상 어휘 함정 (pharmacist – medicine, colds)
(B) ○ 그 분야의 직업이 갖고 싶은지 반문하며 질문에 적절하게 말했으므로 정답
(C) ✗ 연상 어휘 함정 (how long – since), (pharmacist – hospital)

Possible Answer
You should ask Dr. Chang. Dr. Chang에게 여쭤보세요.

어휘 pharmacist n. 약사 medicine n. 약 cold n. 감기 pursue v. 추구하다 field n. 분야 hospital n. 병원 found v. 설립하다

19 Why 의문문 난이도 중

미국↔미국

Why hasn't the company profile been updated on the Web site?
(A) A photograph of the employees.
(B) Amelia will set the date.
(C) We're having technical difficulties.

회사 프로필이 왜 웹 사이트에 업데이트되지 않았죠?
(A) 직원들 사진이요.
(B) Amelia가 날짜를 정할 거예요.
(C) 기술적인 문제가 있어서요.

해설 (A) ✗ 연상 어휘 함정 (company profile – photograph, employees)
(B) ✗ 유사 발음 함정 (updated – date)
(C) ○ 기술적인 문제가 있어서라며 이유를 들며 말했으므로 정답

Possible Answer
The Internet's been down all day. 인터넷이 하루종일 먹통이에요.

20 부가 의문문 난이도 상

미국↔영국

Our manager printed the agenda for us, right?
(A) No, he had Ms. Long do it.
(B) Thanks, I just printed one.
(C) We'll be discussing the new project.

저희 매니저가 안건을 출력했죠, 그렇죠?
(A) 아니요, Ms. Long에게 시켰어요.
(B) 고마워요, 제가 방금 하나 출력했어요.
(C) 새 프로젝트를 논의하게 될 거예요.

해설 (A) ○ 'No'로 대답하고, Ms. Long에게 시켰다며 적절히 덧붙여 말했으므로 정답
(B) ✗ 동어 반복 함정 (printed – printed)
(C) ✗ 연상 어휘 함정 (agenda – discussing, new project)

Possible Answer
Yes, it's on your desk. 네, 그건 당신 책상 위에 있어요.

어휘 agenda n. 의제, 안건

21 제안/요청 난이도 중

영국↔호주

Do you mind if I take the afternoon off?
(A) Sorry, I had to take yours.
(B) Try turning it on instead.
(C) Have you completed your article?

제가 오후에 휴가를 내도 될까요?
(A) 죄송해요, 제가 당신 걸 가져가야 했어요.
(B) 대신 그걸 켜 보세요.
(C) 기사 작성은 다 하셨어요?

해설 (A) ✗ 동어 반복 함정 (take – take)
(B) ✗ 연상 어휘 함정 (off – on)
(C) ○ 휴가를 쓰기 전에 업무를 완료해야 함을 우회적으로 말했으므로 정답

Possible Answer
Check with Ms. Powell. Ms. Powell에게 문의하세요.

어휘 take ~ off ~동안 쉬다 instead adv. 그 대신

22 What 의문문 난이도 중

호주↔미국

What did you think of the training seminar?
(A) I thought it was very beneficial.
(B) During the orientation.
(C) Yes, it stopped raining.

교육 세미나는 어떠셨어요?
(A) 매우 유익했던 것 같아요.
(B) 오리엔테이션 기간 동안이요.
(C) 네, 비가 그쳤어요.

해설 (A) ○ 매우 유익했다는 생각을 들어 말했으므로 정답
(B) ✗ When 의문문에 어울리는 대답, 연상 어휘 함정 (training seminar – orientation)
(C) ✗ 의문사 의문문 Yes/No 응답 불가

Possible Answer
I was on vacation. 저는 휴가 중이었어요.

어휘 beneficial adj. 유익한, 이로운

23 일반의문문 난이도 상

미국↔미국

Has anyone reserved the conference room for today's team meeting?
(A) The main course will be served now.
(B) We're meeting tomorrow.
(C) Did you see the patient in the waiting room?

오늘 팀 회의를 위해 누가 회의실을 예약 했나요?
(A) 주요리가 지금 나올 거예요.
(B) 저희 회의는 내일이에요.
(C) 대기실에 있는 환자 분 보셨어요?

해설 (A) ✗ 유사 발음 함정 (reserved – served)
(B) ○ 회의는 내일 있다며 아직 예약할 필요가 없음을 우회적으로 말했으므로 정답
(C) ✗ 동어 반복 함정 (room – room)

Possible Answer
Jonathan took care of it. Jonathan이 했어요.

24 평서문   난이도 중

Ms. Rosa's presentation has been postponed to this afternoon.
(A) I see. I'll let everyone know.
(B) Please refer to the poster.
(C) Yes, the director is present.

Ms. Rosa의 프레젠테이션이 오늘 오후로 연기되었어요.
(A) 알겠어요. 제가 모두에게 알릴게요.
(B) 포스터를 참조해 주세요.
(C) 네, 이사님께서 참석하세요.

해설 (A) O 'I see'로 대답하고, 모두에게 알리겠다며 적절히 덧붙여 말했으므로 정답
(B) X 유사 발음 함정 (postponed – poster)
(C) X 유사 발음 함정 (presentation – present)

Possible Answer
I wonder why. 이유가 궁금하네요.

어휘 **postpone** v. 연기하다 **refer to** ~을 참조하다 **director** n. 임원, 이사 **present** adj. 참석[출석]한

25 How 의문문   난이도 상

How are we advertising our new laptop to young consumers?
(A) Claudia's responsible for that project.
(B) The warranty has expired.
(C) I'd like to get my computer repaired.

젊은 소비자들에게 우리 신상 노트북을 어떻게 광고하나요?
(A) Claudia가 그 프로젝트를 담당하고 있어요.
(B) 보증서가 만료되었어요.
(C) 제 컴퓨터를 수리 받고 싶어요.

해설 (A) O Claudia가 프로젝트 담당자라 자신은 잘 모르고 있음을 우회적으로 말했으므로 정답
(B) X 연상 어휘 함정 (laptop – warranty)
(C) X 연상 어휘 함정 (laptop – computer)

Possible Answer
We'll offer special discounts to college students. 대학생들에게 특별할인을 제공할 거예요.

어휘 **advertise** v. 광고하다 **consumer** n. 소비자 **be responsible for** ~를 책임지고 있다 **warranty** n. 보증 **expire** v. 만료되다 **repair** v. 수리하다

26 부정 의문문   난이도 상

Weren't the department heads supposed to give us feedback on our proposal?
(A) It was supposed to be open.
(B) They're still at the CEO briefing.
(C) She's working at the cash register.

부서장 분들이 우리 제안서에 대한 피드백을 주시기로 하지 않았었나요?
(A) 그건 개봉되었어야 했어요.
(B) 그분들이 아직 CEO 브리핑 중이세요.
(C) 그녀는 계산대에서 일하고 있어요.

해설 (A) X 동어 반복 함정 (supposed to – supposed to)
(B) O 아직 CEO 브리핑 중이라며 피드백을 주지 못하고 있는 이유를 들어 말했으므로 정답
(C) X 질문과 무관한 대답

Possible Answer
They postponed it to tomorrow afternoon. 그분들이 그걸 내일 오후로 연기했어요.

어휘 **department head** 부서장 **be supposed to do** ~하기로 되어 있다 **proposal** n. 제안(서) **cash register** 계산대; 금전 등록기

27 일반 의문문   난이도 상

Do you want to hold the banquet at Gold Coast Hotel?
(A) Do they have any openings?
(B) My supervisor and his colleagues.
(C) No, on November 21.

Gold Coast 호텔에서 연회를 열고 싶으세요?
(A) 그곳에 빈자리가 있나요?
(B) 제 상사와 그 분 동료들이요.
(C) 아니요, 11월 21일이에요.

해설 (A) O 그 호텔에 빈자리가 있냐며, 그곳에서 연회를 열고 싶다는 의사를 우회적으로 말했으므로 정답
(B) X 질문과 무관한 대답
(C) X 질문과 무관한 대답

Possible Answer
How many people are we inviting? 몇 명이나 초대할 건가요?

어휘 **hold** v. 열다, 개최하다 **banquet** n. 연회 **opening** n. 빈자리 **supervisor** n. 감독관, 관리자 **colleague** n. 동료

28 제안/요청   난이도 중

Why don't you make photocopies of the report so we can go over it?
(A) A decision has been made.
(B) You should go sit over there.
(C) I've already done that.

검토할 수 있게 보고서를 복사하시는 게 어때요?
(A) 결정이 내려졌어요.
(B) 저쪽 가서 앉아 계세요.
(C) 제가 이미 했어요.

해설 (A) X 유사 발음 함정 (make – made), 연상 어휘 함정 (go over – decision)
(B) X 동어 반복 함정 (go over – go, over)
(C) O 복사해두라는 제안에 이미 했다며 적절하게 대답했으므로 정답

Possible Answer
The machine is broken. 기계가 고장났어요.

어휘 **make photocopies** 복사하다 **go over** 검토하다

29 부가의문문   난이도 중

We should buy some decorations for Melissa's birthday party, shouldn't we?
(A) Yes, I'll do that right away.
(B) By Saturday morning at 11.
(C) It's not a good location.

우리가 Melissa의 생일 파티용 장식용품을 좀 사야 해요, 그렇죠?
(A) 네, 제가 지금 바로 할게요.
(B) 토요일 오전 11시까지요.

(C) 좋은 장소는 아니네요.

| 해설 | (A) ⭕ 'Yes'로 대답하고, 지금 바로 하겠다며 적절히 덧붙여 말했으므로 정답
(B) ❌ when 의문문에 어울리는 대답
(C) ❌ 유사 발음 함정 (decorations – location) |

Possible Answer
Nicole brought some already. Nicole이 벌써 좀 가져왔어요.

| 어휘 | decoration n. 장식품 |

30 일반 의문문　　난이도 상

호주 ⇄ 미국

Does the subway go to your office?
(A) Did you check the schedule?
(B) Actually, I'll be taking a cab.
(C) The records are on my desk.

지하철이 당신 사무실쪽으로 가나요?
(A) 일정표를 확인하셨나요?
(B) 실은, 저는 택시를 탈 거예요.
(C) 그 기록들은 제 책상에 있어요.

| 해설 | (A) ❌ 연상 어휘 함정 (subway – schedule)
(B) ⭕ 택시를 탈 거라며 지하철로 가지 않을 것임을 우회적으로 말했으므로 정답
(C) ❌ 연상 어휘 함정 (office – desk) |

Possible Answer
No, I'll have to take a bus. 아니요, 버스를 타야 할거예요.

| 어휘 | subway n. 지하철　schedule n. 일정표　cab n. 택시　record n. 기록 |

31 선택 의문문　　난이도 상

미국 ⇄ 미국

Do we have to finish the promotional video by this week, or is next week OK?
(A) Sonya was set on the deadline.
(B) It still needs to be edited.
(C) He just got promoted last week.

홍보 영상을 이번 주에 완료해야 할까요, 아니면 다음주도 괜찮은가요?
(A) Sonya는 마감일에 대해 의지가 확고했어요.
(B) 그건 아직 편집이 필요해요.
(C) 그는 지난주에 승진했어요.

| 해설 | (A) ⭕ Sonya가 마감일에 대해 확고하다며 전자를 우회적으로 선택한 것이므로 정답
(B) ❌ 연상 어휘 함정 (video – edited)
(C) ❌ 유사 발음 함정 (promotional – promoted), 연상 어휘 함정 (this week, next week – last week) |

Possible Answer
You can take your time. 천천히 하셔도 돼요.

| 어휘 | promotional adj. 홍보의　set v. (마음을) 정하다, 굳히다　edit v. 편집하다　get promoted 승진하다 |

PART 3　　P. 109

미국 ⇄ 영국

Questions 32-34 refer to the following conversation.

M: Hello, you've reached the Johnson County Museum of History. This is Larry.

W: Hi, Larry. This is Anita from the Blue Valley Sun Times. **I'm writing an article in our newspaper about an old trolley line, and I'd like to use one of the pictures from your exhibit.** (32)/(33)

M: That should be fine. **Could you tell me the exact title of the picture you want to use?** (34) I'll get approval and then email you a digital copy.

32-34번은 다음 대화에 관한 문제입니다.

남: 안녕하세요, Johnson 카운티 역사 박물관입니다. 저는 Larry라고 합니다.

여: 안녕하세요, Larry. 저는 <Blue Valley Sun Times>의 Anita입니다. 제가 저희 신문에 실을 옛 시가전차 노선에 관한 기사를 쓰고 있는데, 이곳에 전시된 사진 중 한 장을 사용하고 싶어요. (32)/(33)

남: 괜찮을 겁니다. 제게 사용하고 싶으신 사진의 정확한 제목을 알려 주시겠어요? (34) 제가 승인을 받고 나서 디지털 파일을 이메일로 보내 드리겠습니다.

| 어휘 | reach v. (전화로) 연락하다　trolley line 시가전차 노선　exhibit n. 전시품　exact adj. 정확한　approval n. 승인 |

32 장소/근무지　　난이도 하

| 해석 | 여자는 어디서 일하는가?
(A) 공립대학교
(B) 여행사
(C) 미술관
(D) 신문사 |

| 해설 | 여자가 I'm writing an article in our newspaper about an old trolley line, and I'd like to use one of the pictures from your exhibit. (제가 저희 신문에 실을 옛 시가 전차 노선에 관한 기사를 쓰고 있는데, 이곳에 전시된 사진들 중 한 장을 사용하고 싶어요.)라고 말했으므로 (D)가 정답 |

33 세부정보　　난이도 중

| 해석 | 여자가 전화한 이유는 무엇인가?
(A) 장비 이용을 요청하려고
(B) 구매에 관한 불만을 제기하려고
(C) 사진 이용에 대한 관심을 표현하려고
(D) 출간물 몇 부를 주문하려고 |

| 해설 | 여자가 I'm writing an article in our newspaper about an old trolley line, and I'd like to use one of the pictures from your exhibit. (제가 저희 신문에 실을 옛 시가 전차 노선에 관한 기사를 쓰고 있는데, 이곳에 전시된 사진들 중 한 장을 사용하고 싶어요.)라고 말했으므로 (C)가 정답 |

34 요청/제의/제안　난이도 중

해석 남자가 여자에게 요청한 것은?
(A) 물건 이름
(B) 이메일 주소
(C) 신분 증명서
(D) 제품 코드

해설 남자가 Could you tell me the exact title of the picture you want to use? (사용하고 싶으신 사진의 정확한 제목을 알려 주시겠어요?)라고 말했으므로 (A)가 정답

Paraphrasing title of the picture ➡ name of an item

영국 ⇄ 미국

Questions 35-37 refer to the following conversation.

W: Nice to meet you, Mr. Gao. The first question I would like to ask today is this: **why do you want to work here at Percell Publishing?**(35)

M: Well, **my sister, Sharon Gao, used to work here. She was in the graphic design team and told me that I would really enjoy the work.**(36)

W: Ah, yes. I remember Sharon. Anyway, why do you want to leave your current company? It looks like you've been there for four years.

M: Well, all my work there involves creating logos and banners for various clients. **But my real interest is Web design. I want to concentrate on that more.**(37)

35-37번은 다음 대화에 관한 문제입니다.

여: 만나서 반갑습니다, Mr. Gao. 제가 오늘 첫 번째로 물어보고 싶은 질문은요, 왜 이 곳 Percell 출판사에서 일하고 싶으신가요?(35)

남: 음, 제 여동생 Sharon Gao가 여기서 일했었어요. 그래픽 디자인팀에 있었는데, 제가 일을 아주 즐기게 될 거라고 이야기해줬어요.(36)

여: 아, 네. Sharon 기억나네요. 그러면, 왜 현재 회사를 떠나고 싶으신가요? 그곳에 4년 동안 계셨던 것 같은데요.

남: 음, 거기서 제 업무는 다양한 고객들을 위한 로고와 배너 제작과 관련되어 있습니다. 하지만 저의 진짜 관심사는 웹 디자인이에요. 거기에 더 집중하고 싶습니다.(37)

어휘 leave v. 떠나다　current adj. 현재의　involve v. 관련되다, 수반하다　banner n. 배너, 현수막　various adj. 다양한　concentrate on ~에 집중하다

35 주제/목적　난이도 중

해석 남자는 왜 여자와 만나고 있는가?
(A) 이용 가능한 사무실 공간을 확인하기 위해
(B) 취업 면접에 참여하기 위해
(C) 서비스에 관해 문의하기 위해
(D) 계약을 타결하기 위해

해설 여자가 why do you want to work here at Percell Publishing? (왜 이 곳 Percell 출판사에서 일하고 싶으신가요?)라고 말했으므로 (B)가 정답

36 세부정보　난이도 중

해석 남자는 왜 자신의 여동생을 언급하는가?
(A) 잘 알려진 작가에 관해 논하기 위해
(B) 자신이 기술을 배운 곳을 설명하기 위해
(C) 특별 금액을 요청하기 위해
(D) 회사에 관해 어떻게 알게 되었는지 설명하기 위해

해설 남자가 my sister, Sharon Gao, used to work here. She was in the graphic design team and told me that I would really enjoy the work. (제 여동생 Sharon Gao가 여기서 일했었어요. 그래픽 디자인팀에 있었는데, 제가 일을 아주 즐기게 될 거라고 이야기해줬어요.)라고 말했으므로 (D)가 정답

37 세부정보　난이도 하

해석 남자는 어느 분야에 집중하고 싶어하는가?
(A) 소프트웨어 프로그래밍
(B) 도서 편집
(C) 고객 관리
(D) 웹 디자인

해설 남자가 But my real interest is Web design. I want to concentrate on that more. (하지만 저의 진짜 관심사는 웹 디자인이에요. 그것에 더 집중하고 싶습니다.)라고 말했으므로 (D)가 정답

미국 ⇄ 미국

Questions 38-40 refer to the following conversation.

M: Hi, my name is Shawn Lamar, and **I made a reservation for a deluxe suite. I'm here to check in.**(38)

W: Of course. Welcome to Granier Hotel. You'll need to complete this short form before I can give you your room key.

M: Alright. Ahm... **It says here that I have to provide my confirmation code, but unfortunately, I don't have it with me.**(39)

W: That's OK. **I can just search for it in our system.**(40) Can you give me your phone number?

38-40번은 다음 대화에 관한 문제입니다.

남: 안녕하세요, 제 이름은 Shawn Lamar이고, 디럭스 스위트룸을 예약했어요. 체크인하려구요.(38)

여: 네. Granier 호텔에 오신 것을 환영합니다. 제가 방 열쇠를 드리기 전에 이 간단한 서식을 작성해주셔야 해요.

남: 알겠습니다. 음... 여기 보니 확인코드를 적으라고 되어 있는데, 유감스럽게도 제가 지금 몰라요.(39)

여: 괜찮습니다. 제가 시스템에서 검색할 수 있어요.(40) 전화번호를 알려주시겠어요?

어휘 reservation n. 예약　suite n. 스위트룸　complete v. 작성하다　form n. 서식　confirmation n. 확인　unfortunately adv. 유감스럽게　search v. 검색하다

38 세부정보　난이도 하

해석 남자는 무엇을 하려고 하는가?
(A) 테이블 예약하려고
(B) 기차표를 예매하려고
(C) 방에 체크인하려고
(D) 자기소개서를 제출하려고

해설 남자가 I made a reservation for a deluxe suite. I'm here to check in. (디럭스 스위트룸을 예약했어요. 체크인하려구요.)라고 말했으므로 (C)가 정답

Paraphrasing suite ➡ room

39 세부정보　난이도 중

해석 남자는 무엇을 빠트렸는가?
(A) 사진이 부착된 신분증
(B) 할인권
(C) 휴대폰
(D) 확인 코드

해설 남자가 It says here that I have to provide my confirmation code, but unfortunately, I don't have it with me. (여기 보니 확인코드를 적으라고 되어 있는데, 유감스럽게도 제가 지금 몰라요.)라고 말했으므로 (D)가 정답

Paraphrasing not have ➡ missing

40 요청/제의/제안　난이도 중

해석 여자가 무엇을 하겠다고 제안하는가?
(A) 동료에게 전화하겠다고
(B) 시스템을 검색하겠다고
(C) 작업요청서를 전송하겠다고
(D) 청구서를 검토하겠다고

해설 여자가 I can just search for it in our system. (제가 시스템에서 검색할 수 있어요.)라고 말했으므로 (B)가 정답

Paraphrasing search ➡ browse

[미국 ⇄ 미국]

Questions 41-43 refer to the following conversation

M: Hi, Irina. I just found out that our CEO rescheduled his travel plans. He'll be here this Thursday, rather than the next.(41)

W: Then we should finish our sales report quickly.(42) It's not even half done!

M: I don't think it will be too difficult, but you're right. We need to get it done. Let me just finish looking over these customer feedback surveys.

W: Isn't the assistant manager coming in at 1 o'clock? Why don't you have her review them?(43) That way, we can get started right away.

M: That's a great idea.

41-43번은 다음 대화에 관한 문제입니다.

남: 안녕하세요, Irina. 저희 CEO가 출장 계획을 변경했다는 사실을 방금 알게 됐어요. 그 분이 다음주 목요일이 아니고 이번 주 목요일에 이곳에 오실 거예요.(41)

여: 그러면 영업 보고서를 빨리 끝내야겠네요.(42) 아직 반도 못 끝냈거든요!

남: 그렇게 어려운 것은 아니지만, 당신 말이 맞아요. 그걸 마무리 해야 해요. 제가 일단 이 고객 피드백 설문 검토부터 끝낼게요.

여: 1시에 부매니저가 오지 않아요? 그녀에게 검토를 맡기는 건 어때요?(43) 그렇게 하면, 우리가 바로 시작할 수 있잖아요.

남: 좋은 생각이에요.

어휘 find out 알게 되다, 알아내다　reschedule v. 일정을 재조정하다　rather than ~보다는　look over 훑어 보다, 살펴보다　review v. 검토하다

41 세부정보　난이도 중

해석 남자는 최근에 무엇을 알게 됐나?
(A) CEO의 방문 날짜가 변경됐다.
(B) 새 직원이 고용되었다.
(C) 미팅 장소가 옮겨졌다.
(D) 잡지사가 그 회사에 대해 보도할 것이다.

해설 남자가 Hi, Irina. I just found out that our CEO rescheduled his travel plans. He'll be here this Thursday, rather than the next. (안녕하세요, Irina. 저희 CEO가 여행 계획을 변경했다는 사실을 방금 알게 됐어요. 그 분이 다음주 목요일이 아니고 이번 주 목요일에 이곳에 오실 거예요.)라고 말했으므로 (A)가 정답

Paraphrasing our CEO rescheduled his travel plans ➡ The date of a CEO's visit has changed.

42 세부정보　난이도 중

해석 화자들은 무엇을 해야 하는가?
(A) 소프트웨어를 업데이트해야 한다
(B) 후보자들을 만나야 한다
(C) 보고서를 끝내야 한다
(D) 고객에게 답장해야 한다

해설 여자가 Then we should finish our sales report quickly. (그러면 영업 보고서를 빨리 끝내야겠네요.)라고 말했으므로 (C)가 정답

43 요청/제의/제안　난이도 중

해석 여자는 남자에게 무엇을 제안하는가?
(A) 영업 보고서를 수정할 것
(B) 점심 시간을 가질 것
(C) 전화 회의에 참가할 것
(D) 동료에게 업무를 처리하게 할 것

해설 여자가 Why don't you have her review them? (그녀에게 검토를 맡기는 건 어때요?)라고 말했으므로 (D)가 정답

Paraphrasing have ➡ let

영국 ⇄ 미국 ⇄ 호주

Questions 44-46 refer to the following conversation with three speakers.

W: I hope your stay at our inn was pleasant. Did you enjoy your time here?(44)

M1: We did. This place made us really comfortable during our business trip. But the fitness room seemed a bit outdated. Have you considered replacing the old exercise machines with new ones?(45)

M2: Yeah, I imagine other guests have complained that the machines are too old.(45)

W: We've actually been meaning to renovate that facility, but I'm not sure when that will be. My manager might be able to give you a better answer.(46)

M2: Ah, yes. I'd like to know about that before we leave today.

W: OK, I'll give her a call and see if she can come down now to talk to you.(46)

M1: Thank you.

44-46번은 다음 세 화자의 대화에 관한 문제입니다.

여: 저희 호텔 투숙이 즐거우셨기를 바랍니다. 이곳에서 좋은 시간 보내셨나요?(44)

남1: 네. 이곳은 출장 기간 동안 저희를 정말 편안하게 해줬어요. 그런데 헬스장은 약간 구식인 것 같았어요. 오래된 운동기구들을 새 걸로 교체하는 걸 고려해보셨나요?(45)

남2: 네. 다른 투숙객들도 장비가 너무 낡았다고 불평했을 것 같아요.(45)

여: 안 그래도 그 시설을 개조하려고 하는데, 그게 언제가 될지는 모르겠습니다. 저희 지배인이 더 나은 답변을 드릴 수 있을지도 모르겠네요.(46)

남2: 아, 그렇군요-오늘 떠나기 전에 알고 싶네요.

여: 알겠습니다. 지금 내려와서 손님과 이야기 나눌 수 있는지 전화해 보겠습니다.(46)

남1: 고맙습니다.

어휘 **inn** n. 여관, (작은) 호텔 **outdated** adj. 구식인 **mean to do** ~할 셈이다

---

44 정체/신분   난이도 중

해석 여자는 누구겠는가?
(A) 호텔 직원
(B) 비행기 승무원
(C) 여행사 직원
(D) 헬스 트레이너

해설 여자가 I hope your stay at our inn was pleasant. Did you enjoy your time here? (저희 호텔 투숙이 즐거우셨기를 바랍니다. 이곳에서 좋은 시간 보내셨나요?)라고 말했으므로 (A)가 정답

Paraphrasing inn ➡ hotel

---

45 세부정보   난이도 중

해석 남자들은 무엇에 관하여 문의하는가?

(A) 항공권 구매
(B) 수업 등록
(C) 장비 개선
(D) 시설 견학

해설 남자1이 Have you considered replacing the old exercise machines with new ones? (오래된 운동기구들을 새 걸로 교체하는 걸 고려해보셨나요?)라고 하자, 남자2가 Yeah, I imagine other guests have complained that the machines are too old. (맞아요. 다른 투숙객들도 장비가 너무 낡았다고 불평했을 것 같아요.)라고 말했으므로 (C)가 정답

Paraphrasing replacing the old exercise machines with new ones ➡ upgrading some equipment

---

46 요청/제의/제안   난이도 중

해석 여자는 무엇을 하겠다고 제안하는가?
(A) 가격을 할인해 주겠다고
(B) 송장을 인쇄해 주겠다고
(C) 상사에게 연락해 주겠다고
(D) 지도를 제공해 주겠다고

해설 여자가 My manager might be able to give you a better answer. (저희 지배인이 더 나은 답변을 드릴 수 있을지도 모르겠네요.), I'll give her a call and see if she can come down now to talk to you. (지금 내려와서 손님과 이야기 나눌 수 있는지 전화해보겠습니다.)라고 말했으므로 (C)가 정답

Paraphrasing manager ➡ supervisor, give a call ➡ contact

미국 ⇄ 영국

Questions 47-49 refer to the following conversation.

M: Hi, could you show me where the children's clothing section is? I've looked all over this department store.(47)

W: I can help you with that. We just renovated, and the facilities are a lot nicer now.(48) But everything is in different places. Children's clothing has been relocated to the third floor. Is there anything else you're looking for?

M: Just one thing. Do you still have El Gato Footwear?

W: I'll check. I know we adjusted some of the brands that we carry.(49)

47-49번은 다음 대화에 관한 문제입니다.

남: 안녕하세요, 아동복 코너가 어디에 있는지 알려주시겠어요? 제가 이 백화점을 다 살펴봤거든요.(47)

여: 제가 도와드리겠습니다. 저희가 수리한지 얼마 안 돼서, 이제 시설이 훨씬 더 좋아졌어요.(48) 그런데 모두 장소가 바뀌었어요. 아동복은 3층으로 옮겨졌어요. 찾으시는 게 또 있으신가요?

남: 하나만 더요. 아직 El Gato Footwear가 있나요?(49)

여: 확인하겠습니다. 저희가 취급하는 브랜드 중 일부가 조정된 걸로 알고 있어요.

어휘 **look ~ over** ~을 살펴보다 **department store** 백화점 **renovate** v. 개조하다, 수리하다 **facility** n. 시설(물) **relocate to** ~로 이전하다 **look for** ~을 찾다 **footwear** n. 신발(류) **adjust** v. 조정하다 **carry** v. 취급하다

| 47 | 장소/근무지 | 난이도 하 |

해석 화자들은 어디에 있는가?
(A) 의류 소매점
(B) 백화점
(C) 건설 회사
(D) 초등학교

해설 남자가 I've looked all over this department store. (제가 이 백화점을 다 살펴봤거든요.)라고 말했으므로 (B)가 정답

| 48 | 세부정보 | 난이도 중 |

해석 여자는 무슨 일이 있었다고 말하는가?
(A) 건물이 리모델링되었다.
(B) 마케팅 캠페인이 시작되었다.
(C) 새로운 근로자들이 고용되었다.
(D) 새로운 정책들이 채택되었다.

해설 여자가 We just renovated, and the facilities are a lot nicer now. (저희가 수리한지 얼마 안 돼서, 이제 시설이 훨씬 더 좋아졌어요.)라고 말했으므로 (A)가 정답

Paraphrasing renovated ➡ remodeled, facilities ➡ building

| 49 | 화자 의도 파악 | 난이도 상 |

해석 여자가 "저희가 취급하는 브랜드 중 일부가 조정된 걸로 알고 있어요"라고 말할 때, 그녀가 내비친 것은?
(A) 남자가 어떤 상품을 좋아할 것이다.
(B) 남자가 부서장과 얘기해봐야 한다.
(C) 남자가 다른 건물로 걸어가야 한다.
(D) 남자가 찾고 있는 것을 못 찾을 수도 있다.

해설 남자가 Do you still have El Gato Footwear? (아직 El Gato Footwear가 있나요?)라고 하자, 여자가 I'll check. I know we adjusted some of the brands that we carry. (확인하겠습니다. 저희가 취급하는 브랜드 중 일부가 조정된 걸로 알고 있어요.)라고 말한 것이므로 (D)가 정답

미국 ⇄ 영국

Questions 50-52 refer to the following conversation.

M: Good morning. **I want to reserve a seat on a bus for Gwangju this Saturday.**(50) I prefer to get on the one that departs at 1 P.M.

W: Hmm… **Unfortunately, all the bus tickets to Gwangju that day are sold out.**(51) Because of the special promotion we held this week, many people purchased tickets early. If you want, there are some open seats for Sunday.

M: That'll be too late. Maybe I should just take a train to Gwangju.

W: You can do that too. **I recommend getting the train booking app. It's free and easy to use.**(52)

50-52번은 다음 대화에 관한 문제입니다.

남: 안녕하세요. **이번 주 토요일 광주행 버스 좌석을 예약하고 싶은데요.**(50) 오후 1시에 출발하는 버스를 탈 수 있으면 좋겠어요.

여: 음… **죄송하지만, 그날 광주행 버스표는 전석 매진이에요.**(51) 이번 주에 연 특별 판촉행사 때문에, 많은 분이 표를 일찍 구입하셨거든요. 원하신다면 일요일에 빈 좌석이 몇 개 있긴 합니다.

남: 그건 너무 늦어서요. 그냥 광주행 기차를 타야겠어요.

여: 그렇게 하셔도 되고요. **열차예매 앱 이용을 추천 드려요. 무료인데다 사용하기도 쉽거든요.**(52)

어휘 reserve v. 예약하다 depart v. 출발하다 sell out 매진되다 promotion n. 홍보[판촉] (활동) purchase v. 구입하다 open adj. (~가) 이용[사용]할 수 있는 booking n. 예약

| 50 | 장소/근무지 | 난이도 하 |

해석 대화는 어디에서 일어나고 있는가?
(A) 기차역에서
(B) 버스 터미널에서
(C) 공항 게이트에서
(D) 연락선 부두에서

해설 남자가 I want to reserve a seat on a bus for Gwangju this Saturday. (이번 주 토요일 광주행 버스 좌석을 예약하고 싶은데요.)라고 말했으므로 (B)가 정답

| 51 | 세부정보 | 난이도 중 |

해석 여자는 어떤 문제점을 언급하는가?
(A) 결제를 처리할 수 없다.
(B) 컴퓨터가 작동하지 않는다.
(C) 좌석을 이용할 수 없다.
(D) 문서가 분실되었다.

해설 여자가 Unfortunately, all the bus tickets to Gwangju that day are sold out. (죄송하지만, 그날 광주행 버스표는 전석 매진이에요.)라고 말했으므로 (C)가 정답

Paraphrasing sold out ➡ unavailable

| 52 | 요청/제의/제안 | 난이도 하 |

해석 여자는 남자에게 무엇을 하라고 제안하는가?
(A) 애플리케이션을 다운받으라고
(B) 회원권을 구매하라고
(C) 식당에 가라고
(D) 쿠폰을 인쇄하라고

해설 여자가 I recommend getting the train booking app. It's free and easy to use. (열차예매 앱 이용을 권해드리고 싶군요. 무료인데다 사용하기도 쉽거든요.)라고 말했으므로 (A)가 정답

Paraphrasing get the train booking app ➡ download an application, recommed ➡ suggest

영국 ⇄ 미국

Questions 53-55 refer to the following conversation

W: Hey, Matt. I just spoke with the director of all Techno Tree Computer Education Centers in the Chicago area. **It looks like all the equipment in our branch will be replaced on the first week of August,**(53) so we'll be closed for seven days.

M: Oh. Our students need to know about that right away, so they can go to another center.

W: Right. **The director also mentioned that the students should receive 25 percent of their tuition back for this month to make up for any inconvenience.**(54)

M: That's good. **I'll start calling our students now to let them know.**(55)

53-55번은 다음 대화에 관한 문제입니다.

여: Matt. 제가 방금 Chicago지역의 Techno Tree 컴퓨터 교육센터 총괄이사님과 얘기를 나눴는데요. **저희 지점에 있는 전체 장비가 8월 첫 번째 주에 교체될 것 같아서,**(53) 7일 간 문을 닫을 거예요.

남: 오. 그럼 저희 학생들이 다른 센터로 갈 수 있게, 지금 바로 알려야겠네요.

여: 네. 그리고 이사님이 학생들이 겪을 불편함을 만회할 수 있게 이번 달 수업료의 25퍼센트를 돌려 받아야 한다고 말씀하셨어요.(54)

남: 좋네요. 제가 지금부터 저희 학생들에게 전화해서 알려 줄게요.(55)

어휘   **director** n. 이사, 책임자   **branch** n. 지점, 지사   **replace** v. 교체하다   **mention** v. 언급하다   **tuition** n. 수업료   **make up for** 벌충하다, 만회하다   **inconvenience** n. 불편(함)

---

53   세부정보   난이도 중

해설   8월 첫째 주에 무슨 일이 있을 것인가?
(A) 새 강사들이 채용될 것이다.
(B) 시상식이 열릴 것이다.
(C) 기계가 교체될 것이다.
(D) 이사가 Chicago 지역을 방문할 것이다.

해설   여자가 It looks like all the equipment in our branch will be replaced on the first week of August (저희 지점에 있는 전체 장비가 8월 첫 번째 주에 교체될 것 같아서)라고 말했으므로 (C)가 정답

---

54   세부정보   난이도 중

해설   학생들에게 무엇이 제공될 것인가?
(A) 무료 기기
(B) 환불
(C) 할인
(D) 온라인 상담

해설   여자가 The director also mentioned that the students should receive 25 percent of their tuition back for this month to make up for any inconvenience. (그리고 이사님이 학생들이 겪을 불편함을 만회할 수 있게 이번 달 수업료의 25퍼센트를 돌려 받아야 한다고 말씀하셨어요.)라고 말했으므로 (B)가 정답

Paraphrasing   25 percent of their tuition back ➡ refund

---

55   다음 행동/계획   난이도 중

해설   남자는 다음에 무엇을 하겠는가?
(A) 컴퓨터를 점검할 것이다
(B) 수업을 할 것이다
(C) 웹 사이트를 디자인할 것이다
(D) 학생들과 이야기 할 것이다

해설   남자가 I'll start calling our students now to let them know. (제가 지금부터 저희 학생들에게 전화해서 알려 줄게요.)라고 말했으므로 (D)가 정답

Paraphrasing   call ➡ contact

호주 ⇄ 미국 ⇄ 영국

Questions 56-58 refer to the following conversation with three speakers.

M: **Tricia, are the arrangements for Anthony's retirement party going alright?**(56) I know you haven't planned something like this before.

W1: It's going great. I've already got a venue reserved.

M: Oh, good. And you've ordered food?

W1: Well, Chelsea's actually taking care of that. Let's check. Hey, Chelsea, have we ordered food for the retirement party yet?

W2: **Actually, I'm still waiting for a list of foods that people prefer.**(57)

M: Hmm. We need to make sure there is a catering service available to make enough food for us that night. **I really think you should order something right away.**(58) We can change the menu later if it's necessary.

56-58번은 다음 세 화자의 대화에 관한 문제입니다.

남: **Tricia, Anthony의 은퇴식 준비는 잘 돼가고 있어요?**(56) 전에 이런 일을 계획해보지 않은 걸로 알고 있어서요.

여1: 잘 돼가고 있어요. 이미 장소도 예약했고요.

남: 오, 좋아요. 음식은 주문하셨어요?

여1: 어, 그건 Chelsea가 할 거예요. 확인해보죠. Chelsea, 은퇴식을 위해 음식을 주문했어요?

여2: **실은, 사람들이 선호하는 음식 명단을 아직 기다리고 있어요.**(57)

남: 흠. 그날 저녁에 우리에게 충분한 음식을 제공할 수 있는 케이터링 서비스가 있는지 확실히 알아봐야 해요. **지금 바로 주문을 하셔야 할 것 같아요.**(58) 메뉴는 필요하면 나중에 바꿀 수 있어요.

어휘   **retirement** n. 은퇴   **venue** n. 장소   **reserve** v. 예약하다   **take care of** ~을 다루다   **catering service** 출장연회 서비스

---

56   주제/목적   난이도 하

해설   화자들은 무엇에 관해 논의하고 있는가?
(A) 재무 계획을 짜는 일
(B) 회사 합병을 완료하는 일
(C) 음악 공연에 참석하는 일
(D) 은퇴식을 준비하는 일

해설   남자가 Tricia, are the arrangements for Anthony's retirement party going alright? (Tricia, Anthony의 은퇴식 준비는 잘 돼가고 있어요?)라고 말했으므로 (D)가 정답

---

57   세부정보   난이도 중

해설   Chelsea는 어떤 정보를 필요로 하는가?
(A) 음식 선호 명단

(B) 예산안 승인
(C) 공급업체 연락처
(D) 발표 안건

해설 여자가 Actually, I'm still waiting for a list of foods that people prefer. (실은, 사람들이 선호하는 음식 명단을 아직 기다리고 있어요.)라고 말했으므로 (A)가 정답

어휘 landscaping n. 조경 currently adv. 현재, 지금 complimentary adj. 무료의 consultation n. 상담 lawn n. 잔디 set up v. 정하다 come by 들르다 문제는 work overtime 야근하다 make the time 시간을 내다 flexible adj. 유연한, 융통성 있는 accommodate v. 수용하다 detail n. 세부사항

---

58 요청/제의/제안 — 난이도 중

해석 남자는 가급적 빨리 무엇을 하라고 제안하는가?
(A) 예약을 변경하라고
(B) 응답을 확인하라고
(C) 주문을 하라고
(D) 대금을 보내라고

해설 남자가 I really think you should order something right away. (지금 바로 주문을 하셔야 할 것 같아요.)라고 말했으므로 (C)가 정답

Paraphrasing order ➡ place an order

---

59 장소/근무지 — 난이도 하

해석 화자들은 어디에 있는가?
(A) 스키 리조트
(B) 철물점
(C) 제조 공장
(D) 조경 회사

해설 여자가 Welcome to Rosaline's Garden Care. We offer customers a variety of landscaping services. (Rosaline's Garden Care에 오신 것을 환영합니다. 저희는 고객들에게 다양한 조경서비스를 제공합니다.)라고 말했으므로 (D)가 정답

---

60 화자 의도 파악 — 난이도 상

해석 남자는 왜 "곧 겨울이 올 거예요"라고 말하는가?
(A) 다가오는 마감기한을 지적하기 위해
(B) 여행으로 들떠 있음을 나타내기 위해
(C) 서비스에 관심이 있음을 보이기 위해
(D) 새 제품을 주문하기 위해

해설 여자가 a specialist will come by your home to check out the lawn. (전문가가 귀하의 댁에 들러 잔디를 점검해드립니다.)라고 하자, 남자가 it's going to be winter soon. (곧 겨울이 올 거예요.)라고 말한 것이므로 (C)가 정답

---

61 세부정보 — 난이도 하

해석 여자가 남자에게 무엇을 주는가?
(A) 프로젝트 포트폴리오
(B) 작업 일정
(C) 샘플 계약서
(D) 정보 팸플릿

해설 여자가 Here's a pamphlet with complete details about our business. (이건 저희 업체에 관한 전체 내용이 들어있는 팸플릿입니다.)라고 말했으므로 (D)가 정답

Paraphrasing a pamphlet with complete details ➡ an information pamphlet

---

미국 ⇄ 호주

Questions 59-61 refer to the following conversation.

W: Welcome to Rosaline's Garden Care. We offer customers a variety of landscaping services.**(59)** We're currently providing complimentary consultations on how to prepare your lawn for the cold weather.

M: Oh, can you give me more details?

W: Sure. Once you set up a time and date, **a specialist will come by your home to check out the lawn.(60)**

M: Well, **it's going to be winter soon.(60)** But the thing is, I'm going to be working overtime this entire month, so I don't know if I can make the time.

W: That's OK. We have flexible hours to accommodate our customers.

M: Hmm... I'll get back to you on this.

W: Alright. **Here's a pamphlet with complete details about our business.(61)**

59-61번은 다음 대화에 관한 문제입니다.

여: Rosaline 정원 관리에 오신 것을 환영합니다. 저희는 고객 여러분께 다양한 조경서비스를 제공합니다.**(59)** 저희가 현재 추운 날씨에 여러분의 잔디를 어떻게 대비해야 하는지에 관한 무료 상담을 제공하고 있습니다.

남: 아, 더 자세히 말씀해 주시겠어요?

여: 그럼요. 일단 시간과 날짜를 정하시면, **전문가가 귀하의 댁에 방문해 잔디를 점검해드립니다.(60)**

남: 음, **곧 겨울이 올 거예요.(60)** 그런데 문제는 제가 이번 달 내내 야근을 할 거라서, 시간을 낼 수 있을지 모르겠다는 거예요.

여: 괜찮습니다. 저희는 고객님들의 시간에 맞춰 유연하게 운영합니다.

남: 음... 이 문제에 대해 다시 연락 드릴게요.

여: 알겠습니다. **이건 저희 업체에 관한 전체 내용이 들어있는 팸플릿입니다.(61)**

미국 ⇄ 미국

Questions 62-64 refer to the following conversation and schedule.

M: Good morning, Kotono. Are you available this week to go over the design plan? The client made some additional requests.

W: Hi, Leon. I'm free to meet this week. The thing is, **I'll be going out of town on vacation this Thursday.(62)** So we'll have to meet before then.

M: Alright. Does Wednesday work for you, then? I have client meetings all afternoon, but I can make some time in the morning.

W: OK, let's set something up for the morning.(63)

M: I need to participate in a videoconference, so why don't we meet right after that?(63)

W: Sounds good.

M: OK. I'll book the small conference room for that time right now.(64)

Leon's Wednesday Schedule	
8:00 A.M.	Department Meeting
9:00 A.M.	
10:00 A.M.	**Videoconference Session**(63)
11:00 A.M.	
12:00 P.M.	Team Luncheon
1:00 P.M.	
2:00 – 5:00 P.M.	Client Meetings

62-64번은 다음 대화와 일정표에 관한 문제입니다.

남: 안녕하세요, Kotono. 이번 주에 디자인 계획을 검토할 시간이 있으세요? 고객이 몇 가지를 추가로 요청했어요.

여: 안녕하세요, Leon. 저는 이번 주에 시간 됩니다. 그런데 문제는 **제가 이번 주 목요일에 휴가를 가거든요.**(62) 그래서 그 전에 만나야 해요.

남: 알았어요. 그럼 수요일 괜찮으세요? 제가 오후 내내 고객 회의가 있지만, 오전에는 시간을 좀 낼 수 있거든요.

여: 알겠어요, 오전으로 시간을 잡읍시다.(63)

남: 제가 화상회의에 참석해야 하는데, 그 직후에 만나는 건 어떠세요?(63)

여: 좋아요.

남: 좋습니다. 제가 지금 소회의실을 그 시간으로 예약할게요.(64)

Leon의 수요일 일정	
오전 8시	부서 회의
오전 9시	
오전 10시	화상회의 시간(63)
오전 11시	
오후 12시	부서 점심회식
오후 1시	
오후 2시 – 5시	고객 회의

어휘 **available** adj. (사람들을 만날) 시간이 있는 **go over** ~을 검토하다 **the thing is** 실은, 문제는 **work** v. (계획 등이) 잘 되어 가다 **set up** v. (어떤 일이 있도록) 마련하다 **videoconference** n. 화상 회의 **conference room** 회의실

62 세부정보 난이도 중

해석 여자에 따르면, 목요일에 무슨 일이 있을 것인가?
(A) 그녀가 휴가를 떠날 것이다.
(B) 고객들이 사무실을 방문할 것이다.
(C) 그녀가 동영상을 촬영할 것이다.
(D) 소프트웨어가 설치될 것이다.

해설 여자가 I'll be going out of town on vacation this Thursday. (제가 이번 주 목요일에 휴가를 가거든요.)라고 말했으므로 (A)가 정답

Paraphrasing go out of town on vacation ➡ leave for vacation

63 시각 정보 연계 난이도 상

해석 시각 자료를 보시오. 화자들은 몇 시에 만나겠는가?
(A) 오전 8시
(B) 오전 10시
(C) 오전 11시
(D) 오후 1시

해설 여자가 let's set something up for the morning.(오전으로 시간을 잡읍시다.)라고 하자, 남자가 I need to participate in a videoconference, so why don't we meet right after that? (제가 화상회의에 참석해야 하는데, 그 직후에 만나는 건 어떠세요?)라고 말했고, 시각 자료에서 Videoconference Session (화상회의 시간)후는 오전 11시임을 확인할 수 있으므로 (C)가 정답

64 다음 행동/계획 난이도 중

해석 남자는 이후에 무엇을 하겠다고 말하는가?
(A) 시스템을 업데이트하겠다고
(B) 문서를 편집하겠다고
(C) 동료에게 이메일을 보내겠다고
(D) 방을 예약하겠다고

해설 여자가 I'll book the small conference room for that time right now. (제가 지금 소회의실을 그 시간으로 예약할게요.)라고 말했으므로 (D)가 정답

Paraphrasing book ➡ reserve

영국 ⇄ 호주

Questions 65-67 refer to the following conversation and graph.

W: Can you take a look at this monthly sales report for our X5 Slim Laptop?(65) I'd like to get your thoughts.

M: Let's see... I figured that sales for this product would be high for February. But, I didn't expect that they'd drop so much in the following month.(66)

W: Yeah, but we did have that month-long special deal in February. And there haven't been any promotions since that month.

M: I think we should set up a meeting with Catherine Burke, the new head of marketing.(67) She has overseen some successful ad campaigns.

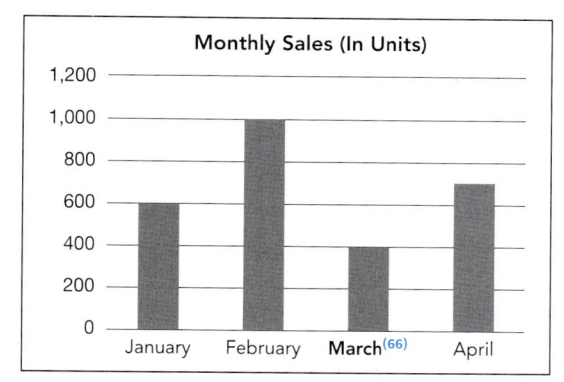

65-67번은 다음 대화와 그래프에 관한 문제입니다.

여: 저희 X5 슬림 랩톱의 이번 월간 매출 보고서를 봐주시겠어요?(65) 당신의 생각을 듣고 싶어요.

남: 봅시다... 이 제품의 매출이 2월에는 높았던 걸로 보이네요. 그런데, 그 다음 달에 그렇게 많이 떨어질 거라고는 예상하지 못했어요.(66)

여: 네, 그런데 저희가 2월 내내 특별 할인을 했거든요. 그리고 그 달 이후로는 아무런 프로모션도 하지 않았고요.

남: 새 마케팅 책임자인 Catherine Burke와 회의를 잡아야 할 것 같은데요.(67) 그 분이 여러 광고 캠페인을 성공적으로 감독한 경험이 있거든요.

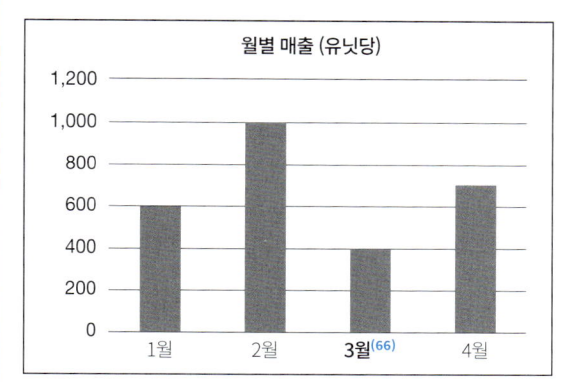

어휘 figure v. 판단하다, 생각하다 drop v. 떨어지다 following adj. 다음의 oversee v. 감독하다

65 장소/근무지 난이도 중

해석 화자들은 어느 업종에서 일하겠는가?
(A) 사무용품점
(B) 자동차 영업소
(C) 전자제품 제조사
(D) 스포츠용품 소매점

해설 여자가 Can you take a look at this monthly sales report for our X5 Slim Laptop? (저희 X5 슬림 랩톱의 이번 월간 매출 보고서를 봐주시겠어요?)라고 말했으므로 (C)가 정답

Paraphrasing laptop ➡ electronics

66 시각 정보 연계 난이도 상

해석 시각 자료를 보시오. 남자는 어떤 매출액에 놀랐는가?
(A) 600
(B) 1,000
(C) 400
(D) 500

해설 남자가 I figured that sales for this product would be high for February. But, I didn't expect that they'd drop so much in the following month. (이 제품의 매출이 2월에는 높았던 걸로 보이네요. 그런데, 그 다음 달에 그렇게 많이 떨어질 거라고는 예상하지 못했어요.)라고 말했고, 시각 자료에서 매출이 급락한 March(3월) - 400을 확인할 수 있으므로 (C)가 정답

67 정체/신분 난이도 중

해석 Catherine Burke는 누구인가?
(A) 마케팅 전문가
(B) 금융 컨설턴트
(C) IT 관리자
(D) 인사 채용 담당자

해설 남자가 I think we should set up a meeting with Catherine Burke, the new head of marketing. (새 마케팅 책임자인 Catherine Burke 씨와 회의를 잡아야 할 것 같은데요.)라고 말했으므로 (A)가 정답

Paraphrasing head of marketing ➡ a marketing specialist

미국 ⇄ 미국

Questions 68-70 refer to the following conversation and sign.

W: Hello. I forgot to sign up in advance for today's convention. Is it still possible to participate?

M: That's fine. You can sign up right now.

W: Thanks. I was worried that you wouldn't accept last-minute registrations.(68) I'm here because I heard Baymox, Inc. is giving a product demonstration on their newest tablet device.(69) That's still happening, right?

M: Yes. They will be doing that during the last morning session, following Professor Salinsky's presentation on the future of the Internet.(69)

W: Alright. Where is it being held?

M: You'll find a guide in this registration packet. Also, it looks like we're all out of free convention pens. I'm sorry.(70) We brought just enough pens for all the participants who registered ahead of time.

W: That's OK.

Statesville Technology Convention [Morning Sessions]				
	Diamond Hall	Star Room	Emerald Lounge	Crystal Auditorium
7:30 – 9:30 A.M.	Using Social Media	Future of Internet(69)		
9:40 – 11:40 A.M.		Tablets and Smartphones		Online Payment Platforms

68-70번은 다음 대화와 표지판에 관한 문제입니다.

여: 안녕하세요. 제가 오늘 컨벤션에 사전 등록하는 것을 깜박했는데요. 아직 참가하는 것이 가능한가요?

남: 괜찮습니다. 지금 바로 등록하실 수 있어요.

여: 고맙습니다. **막판 등록을 안 받아주실까봐 걱정했어요.**(68) 저는 **Baymox사가 자사 최신 태블릿 기기의 시연을 한다고**(69) 들어서 여기 왔어요. 그대로 하는 거 맞죠?

남: 맞아요. **Salinsky 교수의 인터넷의 미래에 관한 프레젠테이션에 뒤이어, 오전 마지막 세션에서 할 거에요.**(69)

여: 알겠습니다. 어디서 하나요?

남: 이 등록자료집에 안내서가 있습니다. 그리고, **저희 무료 컨벤션 펜이 다 떨어진 것 같네요. 죄송합니다.**(70) 저희가 미리 등록한 전체 참가자 수에 딱 맞게 펜을 가져왔거든요.

여: 괜찮아요.

Statesville 기술 컨벤션 [오전 세션]				
	Diamond 홀	Star 룸	Emerald 라운지	Crystal 강당
오전 7시 30분 – 오전 9시 30분	소셜 미디어 사용하기	인터넷의 미래(69)		
오전 9시 40분 – 오전 11시 40분		태블릿과 스마트폰		온라인 결자 플랫폼

어휘 sign up 등록하다 in advance 미리, 사전에 convention n. 총회 participate v. 참가하다 last-minute adj. 막판의 demonstration n. 시연 following prep. ~에 뒤이어 packet n. 자료집 ahead of time 미리

68 세부정보 난이도 중

해석 여자는 무엇에 관하여 우려했는가?
(A) 신분증을 가져오지 않은 것
(B) 중요한 자료집을 잃어버린 것
(C) 등록할 수 없는 것
(D) 잘못된 장소로 가는 것

해설 여자가 I was worried that you wouldn't accept last-minute registrations. (막판 등록을 안 받아주실까봐 걱정했어요.)라고 말했으므로 (C)가 정답

69 시각 정보 연계 난이도 상

해석 시각 자료를 보시오. Baymox사는 어디서 제품 시연을 할 것인가?
(A) Diamond 홀에서
(B) Star 룸에서
(D) Emerald 라운지에서
(D) Crystal 강당에서

해설 여자가 Baymox, Inc. is giving a product demonstration on their newest tablet device. (Baymox사가 그들의 최신 태블릿 장치의 시연을 한다)라고 하자, 남자가 They will be doing that during the last morning session, following Professor Salinsky's presentation on the future of the Internet. (Salinsky 교수의 인터넷의 미래에 관한 프레젠테이션에 뒤이어, 오전 마지막 세션에서 할 거에요.)라고 말했고, 시각 자료에서 Star Room (Star 룸)에서 Future of Internet (인터넷의 미래)와 Tablets and Smartphones (태블릿과 스마트폰)을 진행함을 알 수 있으므로 (B)가 정답

70 세부정보 난이도 중

해석 남자는 왜 사과하는가?
(A) 더 이상 무료 펜이 없다.
(B) 가이드에 있는 일부 정보가 잘못 됐다.
(C) 프레젠테이션이 지연되었다.
(D) 여자의 신용카드가 처리될 수 없다.

해설 남자가 it looks like we're all out of free convention pens. I'm sorry. (저희 무료 컨벤션 펜이 다 떨어진 것 같네요. 죄송합니다.) 라고 말했으므로 (A)가 정답

Paraphrasing out of free pens ➡ no more complimentary pens

PART 4

P. 113

[영국]

Questions 71-73 refer to the following excerpt from a meeting.

W: I've called this emergency meeting to discuss one of our T-shirt orders.(71) Initially, we were asked by BTA Marketing Co. to prepare 300 custom T-shirts for their sports festival on April 25. However, I just received a call from them saying that they'll now be having the event on April 15.(72) I know that leaves us with less time, but I think we can still get it done. I'll be requesting that everyone put in some extra hours over the next two weeks.(73) Of course, you'll be compensated for your time.

71-73번은 다음 회의 발췌록에 관한 문제입니다.

여: 저희 티셔츠 주문 건에 대해 논의 드리려고 이 긴급회의를 소집했습니다.(71) 처음에 BTA 마케팅사로부터 4월 25일에 있을 체육대회용 주문제작 티셔츠 300장을 준비해달라고 의뢰 받았는데, 방금 행사를 4월 15일에 할 거라는 전화를 받았습니다.(72) 우리에게 시간이 얼마 없다는 건 알지만, 그래도 해낼 수 있다고 생각합니다. 여러분께 앞으로 2주간 몇 시간 정도 추가 근무를 해주기를 요청 드립니다.(73) 물론 근무 시간에 대한 보상은 받으실 겁니다.

어휘 call v. 소집하다 initially adv. 처음에 prepare v. 준비하다 sports festival 체육대회 request v. 요청하다 compensate v. 보상하다

71 장소/근무지 난이도 중

해석 화자는 어디에서 일하겠는가?
(A) 의류 제조업체
(B) 스포츠 경기장
(C) 마케팅 회사
(D) 회계 법인

| 해설 | 화자가 I've called this emergency meeting to discuss one of our T-shirt orders. (저희 티셔츠 주문 건에 대해 논의 드리려고 이 긴급회의를 소집했습니다.)라고 말했으므로 (A)가 정답

Paraphrasing T-shirt ➡ clothing

72 주제/목적   난이도 중

| 해석 | 화자는 주로 무엇을 논하고 있는가?
(A) 서비스 요금
(B) 새로운 회사 방침
(C) 행사 장소
(D) 일정 변동

| 해설 | 화자가 Initially, we were asked by BTA Marketing Co. to prepare 300 custom T-shirts for their sports festival on April 25. However, I just received a call from them saying that they'll now be having the event on April 15. (처음에 BTA 마케팅사로부터 4월 25일에 있을 체육대회용 주문제작 티셔츠 300장을 준비해달라고 의뢰 받았는데, 방금 행사를 4월 15일에 할 거라는 전화를 받았습니다.)라고 말했으므로 (D)가 정답

73 요청/제의/제안   난이도 중

| 해석 | 화자는 청자들이 무엇을 하길 요청하는가?
(A) 배송을 준비하라고
(B) 보고서를 제출하라고
(C) 추가 근무를 하라고
(D) 고객에게 연락하라고

| 해설 | 화자가 I'll be requesting that everyone put in some extra hours over the next two weeks. (여러분께 앞으로 2주간 몇 시간 정도 추가 근무를 해주기를 요청 드립니다.)라고 말했으므로 (C)가 정답

Paraphrasing extra ➡ additional

[미국]

Questions 74-76 refer to the following telephone message.

W: Hi. This message is for the property manager of Begamot Plaza. I'm the owner of Leah's Gift Shop at the plaza, and **I'm calling regarding an issue I have with the store next door, CS Diner.**(74) As you know, there are garbage bins for each store at the back of the building. But the diner has been leaving their trash outside. Our customers have been complaining about the smell, and **I've already spoken to the restaurant owner,**(75) but the issue has not been resolved. **I'm going to take pictures of the trash left outside and send them to you today**(76) so that you can see for yourself. Please call me back when you get this message. Thank you.

74-76번은 다음 전화 메시지에 관한 문제입니다.

여: 안녕하세요. Begamot Plaza 건물 관리자님께 메시지 드립니다. 저는 플라자에 있는 Leah's 선물 가게의 주인이며, **저희 옆 가게인 CS 식당과 문제가 있어 이에 관하여 전화 드립니다.**(74) 아시다시피, 건물 뒤에 각 상점의 쓰레기통이 있습니다. 하지만 그 식당은 쓰레기를 밖에 버리고 있어요. 저희 손님들이 냄새 때문에 불만을 제기해서, **제가 이미 식당 주인과도 이야기해봤지만,**(75) 이 문제가 해결되지 않았습니다. 직접 보실 수 있도록, **오늘 밖에 버려진 쓰레기 사진들을 찍어서 보내드리겠습니다.**(76) 이 메시지를 받으시면 제게 전화해주세요. 감사합니다.

| 어휘 | property n. 부동산 issue n. 문제 diner n. 식당 garbage bin n. 쓰레기통 trash n. 쓰레기 complain v. 항의하다 resolve v. 해결하다

74 주제/목적   난이도 하

| 해석 | 화자는 왜 메시지를 남겼나?
(A) 일정을 설명하려고
(B) 문제를 알리려고
(C) 회의를 잡으려고
(D) 실수를 사과하려고

| 해설 | 화자가 I'm calling regarding an issue I have with the store next door, CS Diner. (저희 옆 가게인 CS 식당과 문제가 있어 이에 관하여 전화 드립니다.)라고 말했으므로 (B)가 정답

Paraphrasing issue ➡ problem

75 세부정보   난이도 중

| 해석 | 화자가 이미 무엇을 했는가?
(A) 사업주와 이야기를 했다
(B) 서비스 비용을 지불했다
(C) 테이블을 예약했다
(D) 장비를 확인했다

| 해설 | 화자가 I've already spoken to the restaurant owner (제가 이미 식당 주인과도 이야기해봤지만)라고 말했으므로 (A)가 정답

Paraphrasing spoken ➡ talked, restaurant ➡ business

76 다음 행동/계획   난이도 중

| 해석 | 화자는 오늘 무엇을 하겠다고 하는가?
(A) 점검을 진행하겠다고
(B) 사진을 보내겠다고
(C) 상점을 개조하겠다고
(D) 사무실을 방문하겠다고

| 해설 | 화자가 I'm going to take pictures of the trash left outside and send them to you today (오늘 밖에 버려진 쓰레기 사진들을 찍어서 보내드리겠습니다)라고 말했으므로 (B)가 정답

Paraphrasing pictures ➡ photos

[호주]

Questions 77-79 refer to the following broadcast.

M: Good evening and thanks for tuning in to KS Radio's business report. **In a press statement today, WIE Motors, one of the top manufacturers of auto parts in the country, announced its long-awaited merger with JD Incorporated,**(77) who will start selling WIE Motors' car parts on their popular online shopping site. Also, during the press statement, **Terry Logan, the CEO of WIE Motors, said that the company plans to construct a new plant next year to make its renowned products.**(78)/(79) Mr. Logan added that the plant will create hundreds of new jobs in the community.

77-79번은 다음 방송에 관한 문제입니다.

남: 안녕하십니까, KS 라디오의 비즈니스 리포트를 청취해주셔서 감사합니다. 국내 최고 자동차 부품 제조업체 중 하나인 WIE 자동차가 오늘 언론 발표를 통해 오래 기다려온 JD 주식회사와의 합병을 발표했는데요.(77) JD 주식회사는 인기 있는 자사 온라인 쇼핑 사이트에서 WIE 자동차의 차량 부품 판매를 시작할 것입니다. 또한, 언론 발표에서, **WIE 자동차 CEO인 Terry Logan이 자사 유명 제품을 만들기 위해 내년에 새로운 공장을 설립할 계획이라고 밝혔습니다.**(78)/(79) Mr. Logan은 공장이 지역 사회에 수백 개의 새로운 일자리를 창출할 것이라고 덧붙였습니다.

어휘 tune in 청취하다 press statement 언론 발표 manufacturer n. 제조사 auto part 자동차 부품 announce v. 발표하다 long-awaited adj. 대망의, 기다린 지 오랜 merger n. 합병 incorporated adj. 주식회사 construct v. 건설하다 plant n. 공장 renowned adj. 유명한 community n. 지역사회

77 주제/목적 난이도 중

해석 방송의 주제는 무엇인가?
(A) 자동차 콘퍼런스
(B) 법인 합병
(C) 최신 쇼핑 동향
(D) 개정된 채용 과정

해설 화자가 In a press statement today, WIE Motors, one of the top manufacturers of auto parts in the country, announced its long-awaited merger with JD Incorporated (국내 최고 자동차 부품 제조업체 중 하나인 WIE 자동차가 오늘 언론 발표를 통해 오래 기다려온 JD 주식회사와의 합병을 발표했는데요)라고 말했으므로 (B)가 정답

78 정체/신분 난이도 하

해석 화자에 따르면, Terry Logan은 누구인가?
(A) 웹 디자이너
(B) 뉴스 기자
(C) 공사 감독관
(D) 임원

해설 화자가 Terry Logan, the CEO of WIE Motors, said that the company plans to construct a new plant next year to make its renowned products. (WIE 자동차 CEO인 Terry Logan이 자사 유명 제품을 만들기 위해 내년에 새로운 공장을 설립할 계획이라고 밝혔습니다)라고 말했으므로 (D)가 정답

79 다음 행동/계획 난이도 중

해석 화자에 따르면, WIE 자동차는 내년에 무엇을 할 것인가?
(A) 본사로 이전할 것이다
(B) 제조 시설을 지을 것이다
(C) 신제품을 출시할 것이다
(D) 재정 기부를 할 것이다

해설 화자가 Terry Logan, the CEO of WIE Motors, said that the company plans to construct a new plant next year to make its renowned products. (WIE 자동차 CEO인 Terry Logan이 자사 유명 제품을 만들기 위해 내년에 새로운 공장을 설립할 계획이라고 밝혔습니다)라고 말했으므로 (B)가 정답

Paraphrasing construct ➡ build, plant ➡ manufacturing facility

[미국]

Questions 80-82 refer to the following talk.

M: My name is Min-ho, and during today's demonstration, **I'll be introducing you all to the DX Portable Wireless Speaker.** (80) Available at the end of this month, this speaker provides amazing sound quality in a lightweight and compact size. **The feature that really makes this audio equipment unique, however, is that it is waterproof.**(81) That means you can play your favorite music at the beach or the pool without any worries. The speaker will most likely sell out quickly, so I recommend that you reserve one in advance on the DX Electronics' Web site.(82) This will ensure that you receive it in a timely manner.

80-82번은 다음 담화에 관한 문제입니다.

남: 제 이름은 Min-ho이며, 저는 오늘 시연회에서 **DX 휴대용 무선 스피커를 여러분께 소개해 드리겠습니다.**(80) 이달 말부터 구입하실 수 있는 이 스피커는 가볍고 작은 크기로 놀라운 음질을 제공합니다. **그러나 이 오디오 장비를 정말 독특하게 만들어주는 특징은 방수 제품이라는 점입니다.**(81) 여러분이 가장 좋아하는 음악을 아무 걱정 없이 해변이나 수영장에서 틀 수 있다는 걸 의미합니다. 이 스피커는 금세 매진될 가능성이 크므로 DX 전자 웹 사이트에서 사전 예약하실 것을 권장드립니다.(82) 이렇게 하면, 물건을 빠른 시일 내 받아보실 수 있을 거예요.

어휘 portable adj. 휴대용 lightweight adj. 가벼운 compact adj. 소형의 waterproof adj. 방수(防水)의 sell out 매진되다 in advance 미리, 사전에 in a timely manner 적시에, 빠른 시일 내에

80 주제/목적 난이도 하

해석 무엇이 논의되고 있는가?
(A) 최첨단 스포츠 시계
(B) 무선 오디오 장치
(C) 디지털 카메라
(D) 휴대용 히터

해설 화자가 I'll be introducing you all to the DX Portable Wireless Speaker. (DX 휴대용 무선 스피커를 여러분께 소개해드리겠습니다.)라고 말했으므로 (B)가 정답

Paraphrasing speaker ➡ audio device

81 세부정보 난이도 중

해석 화자에 따르면, 제품에 관하여 무엇이 특별한가?
(A) 에너지 효율성이 높다.
(B) 착용하기 편하다.
(C) 방수가 된다.
(D) 비싸지 않다.

해설 화자가 The feature that really makes this audio equipment unique, however, is that it is waterproof. (그러나 이 오디오 장비를 정말 독특하게 만들어주는 특징은 방수 제품이라는 점입니다.)라고 말했으므로 (C)가 정답

Paraphrasing unique ➡ special, waterproof ➡ wate-resistant

82 요청/제의/제안 난이도 중

해석 화자는 무엇을 하라고 권장하는가?
(A) 온라인으로 제품 예약하라고
(B) 사용안내 프로그램을 시청하라고
(C) 연장된 품질보증을 구입하라고
(D) 제품을 직접 찾아 가라고

해설 화자가 The speaker will most likely sell out quickly, so I recommend that you reserve one in advance on the DX Electronics' Web site. (이 스피커는 금세 매진될 가능성이 크므로 DX전자 웹 사이트에서 사전 예약하실 것을 권장드립니다.)라고 말했으므로 (A)가 정답

Paraphrasing on the DX Electronics' Web site ➡ online

미국

Questions 83-85 refer to the following telephone message.

M: Hi, Erica. This is Daniel. **I just got off the phone with a client who's using the payroll program that our IT Department is in charge of.**(83) It looks like there are a few issues regarding the way overtime is being calculated. **Tony referred me to you since you have extensive experience with this kind of application and would probably know how to deal with this problem.**(84) **This needs to get fixed by next week, and... Most of my teammates are at a seminar until Friday.**(85) Let's talk when you have a moment. Thanks in advance!

83-85번은 다음 전화 메시지에 관한 문제입니다.

남: 안녕하세요, Erica. Daniel이에요. 방금 우리 IT 부서가 담당하는 급여관리 프로그램을 사용하고 있는 고객과의 통화했는데요.(83) 초과근무가 계산되는 방식에 관련해서 몇 가지 문제가 있는 것 같아요. Tony가 당신이 이런 종류의 응용 프로그램에 대한 경험이 풍부하고 이런 문제를 처리하는 방법을 아마 알 거라고 당신과 얘기해보라고 하더군요.(84) 이게 다음 주까지는 해결되어야 하거든요, 그런데... 우리 팀원들 대부분이 금요일까지 세미나에 참석해요.(85) 당신이 시간이 있을 때 이야기 나눠요. 미리 고마워요!

어휘 get off the phone 전화를 끊다 payroll n. (한 기업의) 급여 대상자 명단 be in charge of ~을 담당하다 regarding prep. ~에 관하여 overtime n. 초과근무 refer A to B (도움·조언 등을 받을 수 있도록) A를 B에게 보내다 application n. 응용 프로그램 in advance 미리

83 장소/근무지 난이도 중

해석 화자의 부서는 무슨 작업을 맡고 있는가?
(A) 고객 설문조사 응답
(B) 고객 서비스 절차
(C) 신규 핸드폰
(D) 컴퓨터 소프트웨어

해설 화자가 I just got off the phone with a client who's using the payroll program that our IT Department is in charge of. (방금 우리 IT 부서가 담당하는 급여관리 프로그램을 사용하고 있는 고객과의 통화했는데요.)라고 말했으므로 (D)가 정답

Paraphrasing in charge of ➡ work on,
payroll program ➡ computer software

84 세부정보 난이도 상

해석 Tony는 왜 청자를 추천했는가?
(A) 그녀에게 기술 지식이 있어서
(B) 그녀가 전에 회사와 일해본 적이 있어서
(C) 그녀가 교육 워크숍을 맡을 수 있어서
(D) 그녀가 외부 업체를 추천할 수 있어서

해설 화자가 Tony referred me to you since you have extensive experience with this kind of application and would probably know how to deal with this problem. (Tony가 당신이 이런 종류의 응용 프로그램에 대한 경험이 풍부하고 이런 문제를 처리하는 방법을 아마 알 거라고 당신과 얘기해보라고 하더군요.)라고 말했으므로 (A)가 정답

Paraphrasing refer to ➡ recommend, experience with this kind of application ➡ technical knowledge

85 화자 의도 파악 난이도 중

해석 화자는 왜 "우리 팀원들 대부분은 금요일까지 세미나에 참석해요"라고 말하는가?
(A) 행사를 연기해달라고 요청하기 위해
(B) 도움을 요청하는 이유를 설명하기 위해
(C) 마감기한 연장을 제안하기 위해
(D) 물품을 더 주문하기 위해

해설 화자가 This needs to get fixed by next week (이게 다음 주까지는 해결되어야 하거든요)라고 하면서, and… Most of my teammates are at a seminar until Friday. (그런데... 우리 팀원들 대부분이 금요일까지 세미나에 참석해요.)라고 말했으므로 (B)가 정답

영국

Questions 86-88 refer to the following announcement.

W: Good morning. **I have a quick announcement regarding the color copier our office just received today.**(86) I understand that you all wanted new laptops instead, but it just wasn't in the company's budget this year. Anyway, **the new photocopier is very simple to use.**(87) If you need to make a copy, just place the document in the tray and follow the instructions on the display screen. If an error message shows up, you can contact the Maintenance Department. But keep in mind that they're pretty busy this time of year. **It may take a few hours for them to respond to your request.**(88)

86-88번은 다음 공지에 관한 문제입니다.

여: 좋은 아침입니다. 오늘 사무실에 도착한 컬러복사기에 관련해 간단히 알려드립니다.(86) 여러분 모두가 대신에 새 노트북 컴퓨터를 원하셨던 걸 알지만, 올해 회사 예산에 포함되지 않았습니다. 아무튼, 새 복사기는 사용이 아주 간단합니다.(87) 복사하시려고, 트레이에 문서를 올려놓고 표시 화면에 적힌 설명만 따라 하시면 됩니다. 오류 메시지가 뜨면, 유지보수부서에 연락하시면 됩니다. 하지만, 매년 이맘때에 그 부서가 아주 바쁘다는 걸 명심하세요. 그쪽에서 요청에 응답하는 데 몇 시간이 걸릴 수도 있습니다.(88)

어휘 quick adj. 빠른, 신속한 announcement n. 소식 regarding prep. ~에 관하여 budget n. 예산 place v. 놓다 maintenance n. 유지보수 respond v. 응답하다 request n. 요청

TEST 03 107

86 세부정보 난이도 하

해석 화자에 따르면, 오늘 무엇이 도착했는가?
(A) 에어컨
(B) 노트북 컴퓨터
(C) 복사기
(D) 라벨기

해설 화자가 I have a quick announcement regarding the color copier our office just received today. (오늘 사무실에 도착한 컬러 복사기에 관련해 간단히 알려드립니다.)라고 말했으므로 (C)가 정답

Paraphrasing color copier ➡ photocopier

87 세부정보 난이도 중

해석 화자는 제품의 무엇을 강조하는가?
(A) 사용하기 쉽다.
(B) 가장 잘 팔리는 모델이다.
(C) 오래 지속된다.
(D) 환경친화적이다.

해설 화자가 the new photocopier is very simple to use (새 복사기는 사용이 아주 간단합니다)라고 말했으므로 (A)가 정답

Paraphrasing photocopier ➡ product, simple ➡ easy

88 화자 의도 파악 난이도 상

해석 화자는 왜 "하지만, 매년 이맘때에 그 부서가 아주 바쁘다는 걸 명심해두세요"라고 하는가?
(A) 청자에게 인내심을 가져달라고 요청하기 위해
(B) 직원을 더 채용해달라고 요청하기 위해
(C) 무리한 프로젝트 일정을 지적하기 위해
(D) 제조사에 연락하는걸 추천하기 위해

해설 화자가 If an error message shows up, you can contact the Maintenance Department. (오류 메시지가 뜨면, 유지보수부서에 연락하시면 됩니다.)라고 하면서, But keep in mind that they're pretty busy this time of year. It may take a few hours for them to respond to your request. (하지만, 매년 이맘때에 그 부서가 아주 바쁘다는 걸 명심하세요. 그쪽에서 요청에 응답하는 데 몇 시간이 걸릴 수도 있습니다.)라고 말한 것이므로 (A)가 정답

[미국]

Questions 89-91 refer to the following excerpt from a meeting.

W: As many of you know, **we included a questionnaire in the last issue of our magazine.**(89)/(90) **We asked subscribers to rate our articles according to how much they enjoyed reading them and to write down any suggestions they have.**(90) It's only been two weeks since our last issue went out, but we've already received over a thousand responses. This is quite an accomplishment. **I am not surprised, however, because we did offer discount vouchers to those who filled out the questionnaire.**(91) This was a great idea by our market research team, and something we should remember if we ever need to collect information about our consumers again.

89-91번은 다음 회의 발췌록에 관한 문제입니다.

여: 많은 분들이 아시다시피, **우리 잡지의 지난 호에 설문지를 포함했었습니다.**(89)/(90) 구독자에게 기사를 얼마나 즐겁게 읽었는지 평점을 매기고 의견이 있으면 적어달라고 요청했습니다.(90) 지난 호가 나간 지 2주밖에 안 됐지만, 이미 천 개가 넘는 회신을 받았습니다. 이건 꽤 큰 성과입니다. **하지만 설문지를 작성해주신 분들께 할인권을 제공했기에 놀랍지는 않습니다.**(91) 이건 우리 시장 조사팀의 좋은 아이디어였고, 우리가 소비자들에 대한 정보를 다시 취합해야 할 때 이를 기억하는 게 좋겠습니다.

어휘 include v. 포함하다 questionnaire n. 설문지 subscriber n. 구독자 rate v. 평가하다 according to ~에 따라 suggestion n. 의견 response n. 회신 accomplishment n. 업적

89 장소/근무지 난이도 중

해석 청자들은 어디에서 근무하겠는가?
(A) 방송국
(B) 도서관
(C) 서점
(D) 출판사

해설 화자가 we included a questionnaire in the last issue of our magazine (우리 잡지 지난 호에 설문지를 포함했었습니다)라고 말했으므로 (D)가 정답

90 세부정보 난이도 상

해석 설문지는 무엇에 대해 알아보려고 고안되었는가?
(A) 보안 정책
(B) 새로 출시된 제품
(C) 독자 만족도
(D) 구독료

해설 화자가 we included a questionnaire in the last issue of our magazine. We asked subscribers to rate our articles according to how much they enjoyed reading them and to write down any suggestions they have. (우리 잡지의 지난 호에 설문지를 포함했었습니다. 구독자에게 기사를 얼마나 즐겁게 읽었는지 평점을 매기고 의견이 있으면 적어달라고 요청했습니다.)라고 말했으므로 (C)가 정답

Paraphrasing subscriber ➡ reader

91 세부정보 난이도 상

해석 설문지 작성을 장려하기 위해 무엇이 제공됐는가?
(A) 서비스 업그레이드
(B) 할인권
(C) 무료 가방
(D) 상금

해설 화자가 I am not surprised, however, because we did offer discount vouchers to those who filled out the questionnaire. (하지만 설문지를 작성해주신 분들께 할인권을 제공했기에 놀랍지는 않습니다)라고 말했으므로 (B)가 정답

Paraphrasing fill out ➡ complete

Questions 92-94 refer to the following broadcast.

W: Thanks for tuning in to the local evening news. **Tonight, we're going to take a look at Kensington's new subway line,**(92) **which was constructed in just under one year. Having lived in this town for over 30 years, I know that this kind of thing takes a lot of time.**(93) Quite a few people are already using the new line, and the reviews have been very positive. **With me tonight is Mr. Rodney Rames, Kensington's Transportation Director. He will go over some helpful tips on how you can use this line to travel efficiently throughout the town.**(94)

92-94번은 다음 방송에 관한 문제입니다.

여: 저녁 지역뉴스를 청취해주셔서 감사드립니다. 오늘은 Kensington의 지하철 신규 노선에 대해 알아보겠습니다.(92) 짓는데 일년도 안 걸렸는데요. 저는 이 도시에서 30년 넘게 살면서 이런 일은 긴 시간이 걸린다고 알고 있습니다.(93) 이미 꽤 많은 사람들이 새 노선을 이용하고 있으며 평가도 매우 긍정적입니다. 오늘 제 옆에는 Kensington 교통 국장이신 Mr. Rodney Rames가 나와 계십니다. 이 노선을 이용하여 도시 이곳저곳을 효율적으로 이동하는 방법에 관한 몇 가지 유용한 팁을 알려주실겁니다.(94)

어휘 tune in to (라디오 다이얼, TV 채널을) ~에 맞추다 quite a few 상당수의 go over ~을 점검[검토]하다

92 주제/목적 난이도 중

해석 프로그램의 주제는 무엇인가?
(A) 시내 퍼레이드
(B) 도로공사 프로젝트
(C) 대중교통 서비스
(D) 취업 기회

해설 화자가 Tonight, we're going to take a look at Kensington's new subway line, (오늘은 Kensington의 지하철 신규 노선에 대해 알아보겠습니다.) 라고 말했으므로 (A)가 정답

Paraphrasing subway line ➡ public transit service

93 화자 의도 파악 난이도 상

해석 화자는 "이러한 종류의 일은 많은 시간이 걸립니다"라고 말할 때 무엇을 의미하는가?
(A) 마감기한을 지키기 어렵다.
(B) 프로젝트의 결과가 인상적이다.
(C) 예산이 증액되어야 한다.
(D) 업무를 위해 자원 봉사자들이 더필요하다.

해설 화자가 Tonight, we're going to take a look at Kensington's new subway line, which was constructed in just under one year. Having lived in this town for over 30 years (짓는데 일년도 안 걸렸는데요. 저는 이 도시에서 30년 넘게 살면서)라고 하면서, I know that this kind of thing takes a lot of time. (이런 일은 긴 시간이 걸린다고 알고 있습니다.)라고 말했으므로 (B)가 정답

94 세부정보 난이도 상

해석 화자에 따르면, Mr. Rames는 무엇을 할 것인가?
(A) 후기를 읽을 것이다
(B) 주민을 인터뷰할 것이다
(C) 책임자를 소개할 것이다
(D) 조언을 해줄 것이다

해설 화자가 With me tonight is Mr. Rodney Rames, Kensington's Transportation Director. He will go over some helpful tips on how you can use this line to travel efficiently throughout the town. (제 옆에는 Kensington 교통 국장이신 Mr. Rodney Rames가 나와 계십니다. 이 노선을 이용하여 도시 이곳저곳을 효율적으로 이동하는 방법에 관한 몇 가지 유용한 팁을 알려 주실겁니다.)라고 말했으므로 (D)가 정답

Paraphrasing tips ➡ advice

Questions 95-97 refer to the following telephone message and floor plan.

M: **It's Jordan Coppard, the head organizer for the food and beverage convention.**(95) I emailed you a revised floor plan of your booth area. In addition to providing you with display shelves, **we'll set up one special display case so that your newest line of pasta sauces can be displayed in the front.**(96) Also, **we acted on your suggestion that we add a section towards the back for customers to taste some samples. It'll be separated by a partition.**(97) Please let me know if you have any other requests. Thank you.

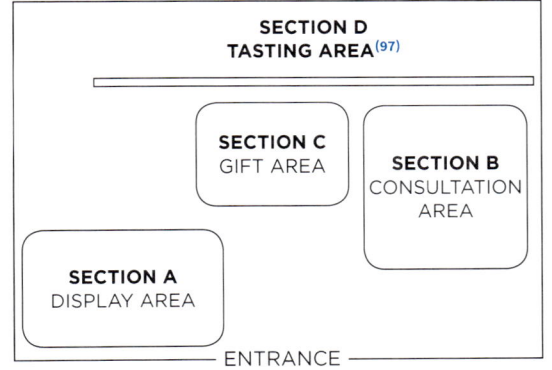

95-97번은 다음 전화 메시지와 평면도에 관한 문제입니다.

남: 저는 식음료 컨벤션 책임기획자 Jordan Coppard입니다.(95) 수정된 부스구역 평면도를 이메일로 보내드렸습니다. 진열대를 제공해 드릴 뿐 아니라, 최신 파스타 소스 제품군을 앞에 전시하실 수 있도록 특별 진열장 하나를 설치하도록 하겠습니다.(96) 또한, 뒤쪽에 고객 시식 구역을 추가해달라고 제안하셨던 대로 해드렸습니다. 그곳은 칸막이로 분리될 것입니다.(97) 다른 요청사항이 있으시다면 알려주세요. 감사합니다.

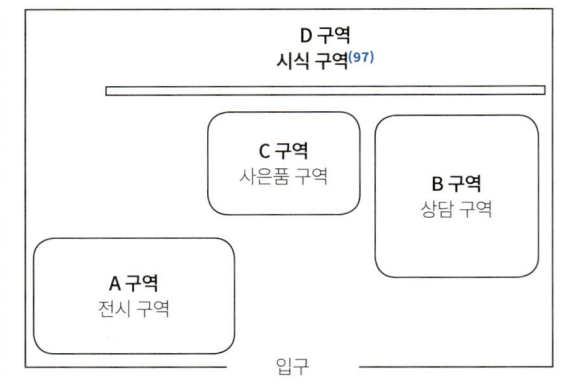

| 어휘 | floor plan 평면도 head n. 책임 organizer n. 기획자 food and beverage 식음료 revised adj. 수정된 in addition to ~뿐 아니라 provide v. 제공하다 display shelf 진열대 display case 진열장 display v. 진열하다 act on ~에 따라 행동하다 separate v. 분리하다 partition n. 칸막이 consultation n. 상담 entrance n. 입구 |

95 신분/정체   난이도 하

해석   화자의 직업은 무엇이겠는가?
(A) 이벤트 기획자
(B) 수석 주방장
(C) 인테리어 디자이너
(D) 컴퓨터 기술자

해설   화자가 It's Jordan Coppard, the head organizer for the food and beverage convention. (저는 식음료 컨벤션 책임 기획자 Jordan Coppard 입니다.)라고 말했으므로 (A)가 정답

Paraphrasing   organizer ➡ planner, convention ➡ event

96 세부정보   난이도 중

해석   화자는 파스타 소스에 관하여 뭐라고 말하는가?
(A) 서늘한 곳에 보관해야 한다.
(B) 할인가에 판매될 수 있다.
(C) 사은품으로 배포될 것이다.
(D) 앞쪽에 위치할 것이다.

해설   화자가 we'll set up one special display case so that your newest line of pasta sauces can be displayed in the front. (최신 파스타 소스 제품군을 앞에 전시하실 수 있도록 특별 진열장 하나를 설치하도록 하겠습니다.)라고 말했으므로 (D)가 정답

Parahrasing   displayed ➡ located

97 시각 정보 연계   난이도 상

해석   시각 자료를 보시오. 어느 구역이 추가되었는가?
(A) A구역
(B) B구역
(C) C구역
(D) D구역

해설   화자가 we acted on your suggestion that we add a section towards the back for customers to taste some samples. It'll be separated by a partition. (뒤쪽에 고객 시식 구역을 추가해달라고 제안하셨던 대로 해드렸습니다. 그곳은 칸막이로 분리될 것입니다.)라고 말했고, 시각 자료에서 'SECTION D - TASTING AREA(D 구역 - 시식 구역)'를 확인할 수 있으므로 (D)가 정답

영국

Questions 98-100 refer to the following excerpt from a meeting and form.

W: Thank you all for attending the Langston Community Center staff meeting.(98) If you don't know me, I'm Paula Wong, the director here. As you know, **our annual membership registration initiative is this weekend, and I wanted to give my appreciation to all of our employees who volunteered to help.**(99) Our center relies heavily on the financial support of its members. Therefore, we'll be going around our neighborhood asking people to register for a membership. For those that do agree to join, we have this application form. There are four types of membership. **If you are familiar with our pricing, you'll notice that the fee for students has decreased this year.**(100)

```
            Membership Application
Name: _____           Date: _____
Address: _____

Adult $50  ___           (99)Youth $25 ___
Senior $30 ___           Family $90 ___
```

98-100번은 다음 회의 발췌록과 서식에 관한 문제입니다.

여: Langston 시민문화회관 직원회의에 참석해주신 분들께 모두 감사드립니다.(98) 저를 모르신다면, 제 이름은 Paula Wong이고 이곳의 책임자입니다. 아시다시피, 이번 주말에 저희 연간 회원등록이 시작되어, 자원해주신 모든 직원분들께 감사의 말씀을 전하고 싶었습니다.(99) 우리 회관은 회원분들의 금전적인 지원에 많이 의존하고 있습니다. 그래서 저희는 동네를 돌며 회원 가입을 요청할 겁니다. 가입에 동의하시는 분들을 위해 이 신청서를 준비했습니다. 회원권에는 4가지 종류가 있습니다. 금액을 잘 아시는 분들은 올해 학생 가입비가 낮아졌다는 걸 보실 수 있을 겁니다.(100)

```
            회원 신청서
이름: _____           날짜: _____
주소: _____

성인 50달러   ___        (99)청년 25달러 ___
고령자 30달러 ___        가족 90달러   ___
```

| 어휘 | attend v. 참석하다 community center 시민문화회관 director n. 책임자, 이사 annual adj. 연례의 registration n. 가입, 등록 appreciation n. 감사 volunteer v. 자원하다 financial support 재정적 원조 rely v. 의존하다 heavily adv. 심하게, 많이 application form 신청서 familiar with ~에 익숙하다 pricing n. 가격책정 decrease v. 감소하다 |

98 장소/근무지 난이도 하

해석 회의는 어디에 하고 있겠는가?
(A) 시민문화회관에서
(B) 놀이공원에서
(C) 백화점에서
(D) 헬스클럽에서

해설 화자가 Thank you all for attending the Langston Community Center staff meeting. (Langston 시민 문화 회관 직원회의에 참석해주신 분들께 모두 감사드립니다.)라고 말했으므로 (A)가 정답

99 세부정보 난이도 상

해석 화자는 왜 청자에게 고마워하는가?
(A) 업무에 도움을 주어서
(B) 잡지를 구독해서
(C) 오리엔테이션에 참석해서
(D) 회원권을 구입해서

해설 화자가 our annual membership registration initiative is this weekend, and I wanted to give my appreciation to all of our employees who volunteered to help. (이번 주말에 저희 연간 회원등록이 시작되어, 자원해주신 모든 직원분들께 감사의 말씀을 전하고 싶었습니다)라고 말했으므로 (A)가 정답

Paraphrasing give ~ appreciation ➡ thank, help ➡ assist

100 시각 정보 연계 난이도 상

해석 시각 자료를 보시오. 어떤 금액이 변경되었는가?
(A) 25달러
(B) 30달러
(C) 50달러
(D) 90달러

해설 화자가 If you are familiar with our pricing, you'll notice that the fee for students has decreased this year. (금액을 잘 아시는 분들은 올해 학생 가입비가 낮아졌다는 걸 보실 수 있을 겁니다.)라고 말했고, 시각 자료에서 'Youth $25(청년 25달러)'를 확인할 수 있으므로 (A)가 정답

Paraphrasing fee ➡ amount, students ➡ youth

PART 5 P. 116

101 어휘・부사 난이도 중

해석 사무실 인터넷 연결이 충분히 빠르지 않아서, 직원들은 CEO 연설의 생중계 영상 피드를 시청할 수 없었다.

해설 빈칸은 because 종속절 내 보어자리의 형용사 fast를 수식하는 자리. 문맥상 '인터넷이 충분히 빠르지 않아서, 생중계 연설을 볼 수 없었다'는 내용으로 연결되어야 자연스러우므로 (B)가 정답

Key point
부사 enough는 형용사/부사를 뒤에서 수식한다.

오답보기 확인
(A) either 둘 중 하나
(C) around 약
(D) almost 거의

어휘 connection n. 연결 enough adj. 충분한 adv. 충분히 feed n. 피드, 텔레비전 방송 프로그램

102 어휘・명사 난이도 중

해석 Ali 갤러리는 주로 후원자들의 기부로 전시 작품을 결정한다.

해설 빈칸 앞, 뒤 각각 by, of의 전치사가 있음을 고려할 때, 'by means of(~를 써서, ~의 도움으로)'라는 관용표현을 완성하는 (C)가 정답

Key word
Ali Gallery determines artwork for exhibition mainly by means of patron donations.

오답보기 확인
(A) petition 탄원(서)
(B) expense 비용
(D) regard 고려, 관심

어휘 determine v. 결정하다 artwork n. 미술품 exhibition n. 전시 mainly adv. 주로 by means of ~의 도움으로, ~을 써서 patron n. 후원자 donation n. 기부

103 어휘・형용사 난이도 중

해석 SKG 회계에서의 10년의 경력 덕분에, Mrs. Ho는 기업 세무 컨설팅에 대한 완벽한 지식을 갖고 있다.

해설 빈칸은 명사 understanding을 수식하는 자리. Thanks to 전치사구와 주절과의 관계를 고려할 때, 문맥상 '10년의 경력 덕분에, 완벽하게 알게 되었다'는 내용이 되어야 자연스러우므로 (C)가 정답

Key word
Thanks to her 10-year experience at SKG Accounting, Mrs. Ho has a thorough understanding of business tax consulting.

오답보기 확인
(A) prospective 장래의
(B) preliminary 예비의
(D) misleading 오해의 소지가 있는

어휘 experience n. 경험 thorough a. 완전한, 철저한 understanding n. 이해 tax n. 세금 consulting n. 자문, 컨설팅

104 구조/문법・부정대명사 난이도 중

해석 음식공급업체들은 모든 농산물 공급업자들의 호가를 평가하고 자신들의 메뉴에 맞는 것을 선택할 것이다.

해설 빈칸은 동사 select의 목적어자리. 빈칸을 수식하는 that 주격 관계절 내 동사가 단수동사 suits이므로 복수인 few와 several은 탈락. 문맥상 '공급업자들의 호가들을 살펴보고 그 중에서 자신들의 메뉴에 맞는 것을 선택할 것'이라는 의미가 되어야 자연스러우므로 단수형 부정대명사 (C)가 정답

Key point
부정대명사 one은 문장 내 '앞서 언급된 명사와 같은 종류/성격의 것'을 가리킨다.

어휘 caterer n. 음식공급자 evaluate v. 평가하다, 감정하다 produce n. 농산물 supplier n. 공급사 bid n. 호가, 응찰 select v. 선택하다 suit v. ~에 맞다, 어울리다

105 구조/문법 • 동사 - 미래시제 난이도 중

해석 Whole Grains 식료품점은 다음주 금요일까지 계산원 자리에 대한 이력서 및 자기소개서를 받을 것이다.

해설 빈칸은 주어와 목적어 사이 동사자리. 문장 끝에 미래시점을 나타내는 표현 next Friday가 있으므로 미래시제 동사 (D)가 정답

> **Key point**
> 시간 부사구와 시제 간 일치: next, soon, shortly 등 미래 시점을 나타내는 시간 부사구는 미래시제와 함께 쓰인다.

어휘 grocery store 식료품점 cover letter 자기소개서 cashier n. 계산원 position n. 일자리

106 어휘 • 동사 난이도 중

해석 Rocket Bikes의 사장은 공장직원들에게 빠른 생산 가동에 대해 칭찬하는 이메일을 발송했다.

해설 빈칸은 목적어인 an e-mail을 수식하는 현재분사자리. 빈칸 뒤 전치사 for가 있으며, 문맥상 '빠른 생산 가동에 대해 칭찬하는 이메일을 발송했다'는 의미가 되어야 자연스러우므로 (D)가 정답

> **Key word**
> The president of Rocket Bikes **sent an e-mail** to his factory workers **complimenting** them for the rapid production run.

> **오답보기 확인**
> (A) advance 증진시키다
> (B) substitute 교체하다
> (C) distribute 분배하다

어휘 factory n. 공장 rapid adj. 빠른 compliment v. 칭찬하다 production n. 생산 run n. 운행

107 구조/문법 • 부사 난이도 하

해석 Pyreen 주방용품점은 어떤 요리를 제공하든 당신의 레스토랑이 원활하게 영업하도록 도와줄 것입니다.

해설 빈칸은 동사 run과 수식어구 사이의 자리. 문맥상 '레스토랑이 원활히 운영되다'라는 의미가 되어야 자연스러우며, 이 때 동사 run은 목적어를 필요로 하지 않는 자동사이므로 수식어 역할을 하는 부사 (D)가 정답

> **Key point**
> ① 동사 help는 목적격보어 자리에 to부정사 또는 동사원형을 취할 수 있다.
> ② 동사를 수식할 수 있는 품사는 부사이다.

어휘 kitchen appliances 주방용품 operate v. 영업하다 cuisine n. 요리 serve v. (음식을) 제공하다

108 어휘 • 명사 난이도 중

해석 새로운 보건시설의 완공이 가까워지면서, Fitness First는 자격을 갖춘 개인 트레이너 채용으로 초점을 옮기고 있다.

해설 빈칸은 현재분사 nearing의 목적어자리. 문맥상 '신규 보건시설이 완공에 가까워지면서'라는 의미가 되어야 자연스러우므로, 'near completion(거의 끝나가다, 완료되다)'의 표현을 완성하는 (B)가 정답

> **Key word**
> With its new health **facilities nearing completion**, Fitness First is **changing its focus to hiring** qualified personal trainers.

> **오답보기 확인**
> (A) conception 구상
> (C) compilation 편집
> (D) competition 경쟁

어휘 health facility 보건시설 near v. 가까워지다 focus n. 초점, 중심 qualified adj. 자격이 있는 personal trainer 개인 트레이너

109 구조/문법+어휘 • 종속접속사 – 부사절 난이도 중

해석 바람이 예상보다 빨리 바뀌지 않으면, Ms. Salina의 항공편은 제시간에 도착하지 않을지도 모른다.

어휘 flight n. 항공편, 비행 on time 제시간에 shift v. 바뀌다 predict v. 예측하다

해설 빈칸은 두 개의 완전한 문장을 연결하는 접속사자리. 문맥상 '바람이 더 빨리 바뀌지 않는다면, 비행기가 정시에 도착하지 않을 수도 있다'는 내용이 되어야 자연스러우므로 (D)가 정답

> **Key word**
> Ms. Salina's **flight may not arrive on** time unless the **wind shifts** sooner than predicted.

110 구조/문법 • 부사 난이도 중

해석 Mr. Davidson과의 대화는 단연 Biznet 잡지의 올해 인터뷰 중 최고였다.

해설 빈칸은 be동사와 보어인 명사구 사이의 자리이므로 동사구 전체를 강조하는 부사 (C)가 정답

> **Key point**
> 부사 easily는 문장에서 최상급 비교표현과 함께 쓰여 '분명히, 의심할 여지 없이' 등을 의미하며 최상급을 강조하는 역할을 한다.

어휘 conversation n. 대화 magazine n. 잡지

111 어휘 • 형용사 난이도 중

해석 Canberra 사진작가 협회는 매우 뛰어난 구성원들로 이루어진 저명한 단체입니다.

해설 빈칸은 명사 members를 수식하는 자리. 문맥상 '뛰어난 구성원들로 이루어진 저명한 단체'라는 의미가 자연스러우므로 (D)가 정답

> **Key word**
> The Canberra Photographers Association is a **prominent group with very accomplished** members.

> **오답보기 확인**
> (A) lenient 관대한
> (B) anonymous 익명인
> (C) fundamental 근본적인, 핵심적인

어휘 association n. 협회 prominent adj. 유명한, 중요한 accomplished adj. 기량이 뛰어난, 재주가 많은

112 어휘 • 형용사 난이도 중

해석 상환 신청을 할 때, 직원들은 이 양식을 작성하고 열거된 구매내역에 대한 영수증을 제공해야 한다.

해설 빈칸은 명사 purchase를 수식하는 자리. When 종속절과 주절의 관계를 고려할 때, 문맥상 '상환신청을 할 때, 양식을 작성하고 (양식에) 열거된 구매내역들에 대한 영수증을 제공해야 한다'는 내용이 되어야 자연스러우므로 (D)가 정답

Key word
When requesting a reimbursement, employees must fill out this form and provide receipts for the listed purchases.

오답보기 확인
(A) exposed 노출된
(B) forwarded 전달된, 보내진
(C) gained 얻은, 쌓인

어휘 request v. 요청하다 reimbursement n. 상환 fill out 작성하다 form n. 양식 listed adj. 열거된, 표에 실린 purchase n. 구매

113 구조/문법+어휘 • 전치사   난이도 상

해석 Papillion사는 일단 문서의 세부 내용들 일부를 재조정한 후 Lunae기업과 기업 계약에 들어갈 것이다.

해설 빈칸은 동사 enter와 목적어에 해당하는 명사구 a business contract 사이의 자리. 문맥상 '계약에 들어갈 것'이라는 의미가 되어야 자연스러우므로, 'enter into((논의 등)에 들어가다, ~를 시작하다)'라는 표현을 완성하는 전치사 (C)가 정답

어휘 enter into ~에 들어가다, ~을 시작하다 contract n. 계약 renegotiate v. (계약 등을) 재조정하다 fine adj. 미세한 document n. 문서

114 구조/문법+어휘 • 부사   난이도 중

해석 Jun Lin은 전세계를 여행하는 것을 좋아했지만 본인 소유의 국제 리조트 체인을 설립하리라고는 상상도 못했다.

해설 빈칸은 접속사와 동사 사이의 자리. 동일한 주어(Jun Lin)의 두 문장이 접속사 but으로 연결된 구조로, '전세계를 여행하는 걸 좋아하지만, 국제 리조트 체인을 세우리라고는 상상도 못했다'는 내용으로 이어져야 문맥상 자연스러우므로 동사를 수식하는 부사 (C)가 정답

Key word
Jun Lin loved to travel around the world but never imagined he would found his own international resort chain.

어휘 imagine v. 상상하다 found v. 설립하다 resort chain 리조트 체인

115 어휘 • 명사   난이도 중

해석 Builders Safety Group은 설계도를 검토하여 건축가들에게 피드백을 제공할 것이다.

해설 빈칸은 동사 provide의 목적어자리. 접속사 and로 연결된 두 문장관계를 고려할 때, 문맥상 '설계도를 검토해 건축가들에게 피드백을 제공할 것'이라는 의미가 되어야 자연스러우므로 'provide feedback to(~에게 피드백을 제공하다)'라는 관용표현을 완성하는 명사 (C)가 정답

Key word
The Builders Safety Group will examine the blueprints and provide feedback to the architects.

오답보기 확인
(A) opinion 의견
(B) reaction 반응
(D) knowledge 지식

어휘 builder n. 건축가 safety n. 안전 examine v. 검토하다 blueprint n. 설계도 architect n. 건축가

116 어휘 • 형용사   난이도 중

해석 갑작스러운 배관 파열로 인해, 반경 200미터 이내 사업체들은 미처리 하수가 거리로 흘러 들어왔을 때 문을 닫아야만 했다.

해설 빈칸은 명사구 pipe burst를 수식하는 형용사자리. 주절과의 내용관계를 고려할 때, 문맥상 '갑작스런 배관 폭발로 인해, 반경 200미터 내의 사업체들이 문을 닫아야만 했다'는 의미가 되어야 자연스러우므로 (B)가 정답

Key word
Due to the sudden pipe burst, businesses within 200 meter radius were forced to close when raw sewage flowed into the streets.

오답보기 확인
(A) appropriate 적절한
(C) impending 임박한
(D) immediate 즉각적인

어휘 pipe n. 배관 burst n. 파열 business n. 사업체 radius n. 반경 force v. 강요하다 close v. (상점 등이) 문을 닫다 raw sewage 미처리 하수 flow v. 흐르다

117 문법/구조+어휘 • 종속접속사 – 부사절   난이도 중

해석 마케팅 담당자 직무의 최종 후보자 5명은 선발되자마자 연락을 받을 것이다.

해설 빈칸은 두 개의 완전한 문장을 연결하는 부사절 접속사자리. 보기 중에 부사절 접속사는 (A) as soon as 밖에 없으며 문맥상 '후보자들은 선발되자마자 연락을 받을 것이다'라는 의미가 되어야 자연스러우므로 (A)가 정답

오답보기 확인
(B) along with ~와 함께
(C) rather than ~보다는, ~대신에
(D) on behalf of ~를 대신해서

어휘 candidate n. 지원자, 후보자 officer n. 담당자 contact v. 연락하다 as soon as ~하자마자

118 구조/문법+어휘 • 과거분사구   난이도 중

해석 Costa Sol 농산물 회사는 대단히 습한 봄과 여름으로 인한 사상 최고의 아보카도 수확량을 발표했다.

해설 빈칸은 문장과 명사구 사이를 연결하는 자리. 문맥상 '습한 봄, 여름으로 인한 사상 최고의 아보카도 수확량'이라는 의미가 되어야 자연스러우므로 명사를 후치수식하는 과거분사를 완성해주는 (B)가 정답

Key word
The Costa Sol Produce Company announced a record-high crop yield of avocadoes caused by an unusually wet spring and summer.

오답보기 확인
(A) apart from ~외에도
(C) depending on ~에 따라
(D) exempt from ~에서 면제된

어휘 announce v. 발표하다 record-high adj. 사상 최고의 crop n. 농작물 yield n. 수확량 avocado n. 아보카도 unusually adv. 대단히, 보기 드문

119 어휘 • 부사   난이도 중

해석 Mr. Zhukov는 차량 리모콘이 제대로 작동하지 않아서 교체했다.

해설 빈칸은 동사 work를 수식하는 부사자리. 문맥상 '리모콘이 제대로 작동하지 않아서'라는 의미가 되어야 자연스러우므로 (C)가 정답

Key word
Mr. Zhukov **replaced** his car **remote since** it had **not** been working **properly**.

오답보기 확인
(A) deliberately 고의로
(B) actively 활발히
(D) moderately 적당히

어휘 replace v. 교체하다 remote n. 리모컨 properly adv. 제대로, 올바로

120 구조/문법+어휘 • 명사   난이도 중

해석 초반의 비난에도 불구하고, Covington 시 축제는 인기 있는 행사였다.

해설 빈칸은 전치사의 목적어인 명사자리. 주절과의 의미관계를 고려할 때, 문맥상 '초기의 비난에도 불구하고, 축제는 인기 있는 행사였다'는 내용이 되어야 자연스러우므로 명사 (D)가 정답

Key point
명사 critic vs. criticism: critic은 '비평가'를, criticism은 '비판, 비난'을 의미한다.

어휘 notwithstanding prep. ~에도 불구하고 initial adj. 초기의

121 어휘 • 동사   난이도 중

해석 의류 디자인에의 몇 가지 변경으로 제조사는 수천 유로를 절약할 수 있었다.

해설 빈칸은 주어 뒤 문장의 동사자리. 빈칸 뒤 목적어에 해당하는 명사구가 2개 있으며, 문맥상 '의류 디자인 변경이 제조사에게 수천 유로를 절약하도록 해주었다'는 의미가 되어야 자연스러우므로 (A)가 정답

Key point
4형식 동사는 목적어를 2개 필요로 하며(~에게 ...을), 대표적인 동사들은 다음과 같다: award, give, offer, save, show 등

Key word
A few **alterations** in the garment's design **saved** the manufacturer thousands of euros.

오답보기 확인
(B) examine 검토하다
(C) intend 의도하다
(D) prevent 예방하다

어휘 alteration n. 개조, 변화 save v. 절약하다, 구하다 garment n. 의복 manufacturer n. 제조업자

122 구조/문법+어휘 • 분사   난이도 중

해석 Arcadia 국립은행의 복원작업은 3개월 안에 재개될 것으로 예상된다.

해설 빈칸은 be동사와 to부정사 사이의 자리. 문맥상 '복원작업이 3개월 내 재개될 것으로 예상되다'라는 의미가 되어야 자연스러우므로, 'be expected to do(~할 것으로 기대되다, 예상되다)'라는 표현을 완성하는 과거분사 (C)가 정답

Key point
to부정사를 목적격 보어로 취하는 동사들의 수동태 표현이 시험에 자주 출제된다.

be required to do ~하도록 요구되다
be asked to do ~하도록 요구되다
be requested to do ~하도록 요청 받다
be instructed to do ~하도록 지시 받다
be expected to do ~할 것으로 예상되다
be encouraged to do ~하도록 권장되다
be allowed to do ~하도록 허용되다
be enabled to do ~하도록 가능하게 되다
be reminded to do ~하도록 알림을 받다

Key word
The Arcadia National Bank **restorations are expected** to within the next three months.

오답보기 확인
(A) yet 아직 → be yet to do '아직 ~하지 않고 있다'
(B) almost 거의
(D) relevant 관련 있는

어휘 restoration n. 복원, 복구 be expected to do ~할 것으로 예상(기대)되다 resume v. 재개하다, 재개되다

123 구조/문법+어휘 • 형용사   난이도 상

해석 표본 그룹이 Route 1 Shoes의 현재 광고를 기억에 남지 않는다고 묘사한 후, 회사는 새로운 버전을 촬영하기로 결정했다.

해설 빈칸은 전치사 as의 목적어자리. 'describe ~ as ...(~를 ...라고 묘사하다)'의 구조이므로, 문맥상 '표본그룹이 현재 광고를 기억에 남지 않는다고 묘사한 후, 회사는 새로운 버전을 촬영하기로 했다'는 내용이 자연스러우므로 (C)가 정답

Key point
형용사 forgetful vs. forgettable: forgetful은 '잘 잊어 버리는'을, forgettable는 '쉽게 잊혀질'을 의미한다.

어휘 current adj. 현재의 commercial n. 광고 film v. 촬영하다 version n. 버전, 형태

124 구조/문법 • 복합관계대명사   난이도 상

해석 Ms. Chun은 그녀가 가장 좋은 보안회사라고 판단한 어느 회사든지 고르라고 지시 받았다.

해설 빈칸은 뒤에 이어지는 문장을 to부정사 pick의 목적어로 만들어주는 명사절 접속사자리. 빈칸 뒤 동사가 2개 나온다는 점을 고려할 때, 빈칸은 she concluded를 명사절의 주어자리에 올 또 다른 명사절로 묶어주면서 두 번째 동사 was를 to부정사 pick의 목적어인 명사절 내 동사로 만들어주는 복합관계대명사 (C)가 정답

Key point
anything과 whichever가 의미는 같지만 anything은 부정대명사이기 때문에 절을 이끌 수 없다. 뒤에 있는 절을 이끌 수 있는 것은 접속사 whichever이다. 복합관계대명사 whichever가 문장에서 명사절 접속사로 역할 할 때, 'anything that'으로 바꿔 쓸 수 있다.

어휘 instruct v. 지시 하다, 가르치다 conclude v. 결론을 내리다 security n. 보안 firm n. 회사

125 구조/문법 • 동사   난이도 상

해석 Ms. Orrin는 완전한 매출보고서를 보지 못했지만, 그래도 최근 온라인 홍보 결과에 만족해 했다.

해설 빈칸은 although 종속절 내 동사자리. 빈칸은 목적어를 취하는 능동

태 동사자리이고 주절의 시제가 과거(was satisfied)이므로 종속절의 시제는 과거나 과거완료를 써야 한다. 따라서 과거완료시제 (B)가 정답

Key point
종속절의 시제는 주절의 시제보다 미래가 될 수 없다.

어휘 complete adj. 완전한 satisfy v. 만족시키다 result n. 결과 recent adj. 최근의 promotion n. 홍보활동

126 어휘 • 명사 난이도 상

해석 우리의 새로운 노트북을 위해 ABM Computers를 선택한 것에는 신뢰도와 단가가 동등하게 고려되었다.

해설 빈칸은 unit price와 함께 문장의 주어를 구성하는 명사자리. 문맥상 'ABM Computers의 노트북을 선택한 것에는 (회사, 제품 등에 대한) 신뢰도와 제품의 가격이 동등하게 고려되었다'는 의미가 되어야 자연스러우므로 (C)가 정답

Key word
Reliability and unit price were factored equally in selecting ABM Computers for our new notebooks.

오답보기 확인
(A) accommodation 시설
(B) estimation 평가
(D) dependency 의존

어휘 reliability 신뢰도 unit n. 단위 factor ~ in ~를 고려하다 equally adv. 똑같이, 동등하게 select v. 선택하다

127 구조/문법 • 부사 난이도 중

해석 Shackleton사의 어느 누구도 회사 주차장 건설 문제에 대해 Garrett Nguyen보다 더 열심히 로비를 하지 않았다.

해설 빈칸은 자동사 뒤에서 동사를 수식하는 부사자리. 문장 뒷 부분에 비교급 표현 than이 있음을 고려할 때, 비교급 구문의 문장을 완성하는 비교급 부사 (B)가 정답

Key point
비교급 구문을 활용한 최상급 관용표현 <No one[부정주어] ~ more … than N>은 'N보다 더 … 한 사람은 없다'를 의미한다.

어휘 lobby v. 로비를 하다, 영향력을 행사하다 construction n. 건설

128 구조/문법 • 재귀대명사 난이도 중

해석 Mr. Ramirez는 임원들에게 정오까지 그가 직접 문서를 수정하겠다고 장담했다.

해설 이 문장은 필수 구성요소를 모두 갖추고 있으므로 빈칸은 부사역할을 하는 강조용법의 재귀대명사 자리이고, 재귀대명사는 주어가 다시 나올 때 쓰는 대명사이므로 주어가 Mr. Ramirez임을 고려할 때 (D)가 정답

Key point
재귀대명사의 강조용법: 주어나 목적어를 강조할 때, 강조하는 말 바로 뒤나 문장 끝에 자리하며, 수식어 역할을 하므로 생략 가능하다.

어휘 assure v. 장담하다, 확약하다 revise v. 수정하다

129 구조/문법 • 종속접속사 - 부사절 난이도 중

해석 도로 확장이 완료되지 않은 경우에는, 뒷문을 이용해 주시기 바랍니다.

해설 빈칸은 완전한 두 문장을 연결하는 부사절 접속사 자리인데 보기 중에 접속사는 (A) in the event that 밖에 없다.

Key point
'------ 문장1, 문장2'의 구조에서 빈칸은 부사절 접속사 자리이다.

오답보기 확인
(B) Overall 종합적인, 전체의; 전반적으로
(C) In response to ~에 응하여
(D) Nevertheless 그럼에도 불구하고

어휘 expansion n. 확장 complete adj. 완료된 rear entrance 뒷문

130 어휘 • 동사 난이도 중

해석 Barrow Road사는 자사 히터가 업계 내 가장 에너지효율이 좋다고 주장한다.

해설 빈칸은 주어와 목적어인 that 명사절 사이 동사자리. 문맥상 '자사 히터가 업계에서 에너지효율이 가장 좋다고 주장한다'는 내용이 되어야 자연스러우므로 (B)가 정답

Key word
Barrow Road Inc. claims that its heaters are the most energy efficient in the industry.

오답보기 확인
(A) compare 비교하다
(C) feature 특징으로 삼다
(D) inquire 문의하다

어휘 claim v. 주장하다 heater n. 히터, 난방기 energy-efficient adj. 에너지 효율적인 industry n. 산업

PART 6

131-134번은 다음 기사에 관한 문제입니다.

TRA사, 신규 임원 선임

Tokyo (3월 10일) – 오늘 오전 기자회견에서, TRA의 관계자는 Hiro Musashi가 고객관리 담당 임원직을 맡게 될 것이라고 발표했다. Mr. Musashi는 국내의 기업들과 사업 관계를 **131. 구축하는** 부서를 관리하게 될 것이다.

TRA 회장 Aiko Ogawa는 "저희는 Mr. Musashi와 함께 일하게 되어 기대되며, 그는 저희가 다른 지역들에 진출하여 새로운 협력관계를 구축 **132. 할 수 있게 할 것**이라 생각합니다."라고 말했다. **133. Mr. Musashi는 거의 20년의 업계 경력을 갖고 TRA에 합류하게 된다.** 그는 Wango Solutions에서 기업 관계 책임자로 있을 때, 매년 연간 매출을 평균 5퍼센트씩 증가시키는 데 도움을 주었다.

TRA는 일본 전역의 주요 도시들에서 상업용 컴퓨터 네트워크에 대한 **134. 지원**을 제공한다. 아시아와 유럽의 다른 지역에도 서비스를 제공하고 있다.

어휘 appoint v. 임명[지명]하다 director n. 임원[중역/이사] press conference 기자회견 representative n. 대표자, 대리인 take over 인계받다 manage v. 운영하다, 관리하다 domestic adj. 국내의 state v. 말하다 expand v. 확장되[시키]다 region n. 지역 partnership n. 동반자관계 annual adj. 연간의 service v. 서비스를 제공하다

131 구조/문법 • 주격 관계대명사 + 동사   난이도 중

해설   빈칸은 문장과 명사구를 연결하는 자리. 빈칸 앞 문장이 주어, 동사, 목적어를 갖춘 완전한 구조임을 고려할 때, 보기 중 빈칸 앞 문장의 목적어 a department를 선행사로, 빈칸 뒤 명사 business relationships를 관계절 내 목적어로 만들어 주는 주격 관계절 구조 '관계대명사+동사'를 완성하는 (B)가 정답

> **Key word**
> Mr. Musashi will manage **a department that develops business relationships** with domestic and international companies.

132 구조/문법 • 동사   난이도 중

해설   빈칸은 주어 he에 대한 동사자리. 빈칸 뒤 목적어 us 및 목적격 보어 to부정사구가 있으므로 to부정사를 목적격 보어로 취할 수 있는 동사 (A)가 정답

> **Key point**
> 목적격 보어자리에 to부정사를 취하는 대표적인 5형식 동사들은 다음과 같다: advise, allow, cause, enable, encourage, remind, require 등

133 문맥이해 • 문장삽입   난이도 중

해석   (A) Mr. Musashi는 Tokyo에 있는 본사로 전근 갈 것이다.
(B) Mr. Musashi는 Wango Solutions의 전 회장이었다.
(C) Mr. Musashi를 환영하는 회사 파티가 있을 것이다.
(D) Mr. Musashi는 거의 20년의 업계 경력을 갖고 TRA에 입사하게 된다.

해설   빈칸 뒷 문장에서 신규 임원의 과거 업적을 구체적으로 설명하고 있음을 고려할 때, 그의 업계 경력을 소개하는 문장이 앞에 나오는 것이 자연스러우므로 (D)가 정답

> **Key word**
> **Mr. Musashi joins TRA with nearly 20 years of industry experience.** When he was the business relations manager at Wango Solutions, he helped increase annual sales by an average of 5 percent every year.

134 어휘 + 문맥이해 • 명사   난이도 중

해설   빈칸은 동사 offer의 목적어자리. 빈칸 뒤 for 전치사구와 이어지는 문장의 내용을 고려할 때, '일본 주요 도시에 상업용 컴퓨터 네트워크에 대한 지원을 제공하며, 다른 지역에도 서비스를 제공한다'는 의미가 되어야 자연스러우므로 (B)가 정답

> **Key word**
> TRA **offers support** for commercial computer networks in major cities across Japan. **It also services other areas** in Asia and Europe.

135-138번은 다음 이메일에 관한 문제입니다.

수신: Eric Bollman <ebollman@leihouma.com>
발신: Nancy Jensen <njensen@leihouma.com>
제목: 수도 문제
날짜: 9월 10일 월요일

Leihouma 샌프란시스코 지점에 오신 것을 환영합니다. 저는 당신이 새로운 이곳 지점에 잘 적응하시도록 책임지고 있습니다.

135. 배관공을 부르셔야 한다는 메시지를 받았습니다. 욕실 개수대가 작동하지 않고 있다니 유감입니다. 수리기사가 내일 오전 7시에 댁에 들르도록 일정을 잡아 놓았습니다만, 만약 **136. 그** 전에 문제가 해결된다면 취소될 수 있습니다. 이런 경우에는, 알려주시기 바랍니다. 그리고, 기사가 댁에 방문하면, 반드시 **137. 사원증을** 보여주시기 바랍니다.

사후 조치로 모든 것이 제대로 진행되고 있는지 확인하기 위해 내일 오전에 다시 **138. 이메일로 연락 드리겠습니다.**

Best Regards,

Nancy Jensen
인사담당자

어휘   branch n. 지점   in charge of ~을 담당하여, 맡아서   ensure v. 보장하다   adjust to ~에 적응하다   arrange v. 마련하다, (일을) 처리[주선]하다   technician n. 기술자   resolve v. 해결하다   advise v. 알리다   present v. 제시[제출]하다   follow up 후속조치를 취하다   properly adv. 제대로, 적절히

135 문맥이해 • 문장삽입   난이도 중

해석   (A) Ichiro 배관사 직원이 다음 주 금요일 오후 3시에 당신과 만날 수 있습니다.
(B) 이 물 배송 서비스는 첫 달 동안은 무료입니다.
(C) 식수의 품질은 크게 향상되었습니다.
(D) 배관공을 부르셔야 한다는 메시지를 받았습니다.

해설   빈칸 뒷 문장의 '욕실 개수대가 작동하지 않고 있다'는 내용을 고려할 때, '배관공을 불러야 한다는 메시지를 받았다'는 내용이 앞에 들어가야 자연스러우므로 (D)가 정답

> **Key word**
> **I got your message that you need to call for a plumber.** I am sorry that **your bathroom sink is not working**.

136 어휘 + 문맥이해 • 부사   난이도 하

해설   빈칸은 시점을 나타내는 전치사 before의 목적어자리. 접속사 but으로 연결된 앞 문장의 내용을 고려할 때, '내일 오전 7시에 기사가 방문 예정이지만, 그 (시간) 전에 문제가 해결되면 취소될 수 있다'는 의미가 되어야 자연스러우므로 (C)가 정답

> **Key word**
> I have arranged for **a technician to come by your place tomorrow at 7 A.M., but this can be canceled if the issue is resolved before then**.

137 어휘 • 명사   난이도 중

해설   빈칸은 명사 company와 함께 복합명사를 완성하는 명사자리. When 종속절의 내용을 고려할 때, '기사가 댁에 방문하면, 사원증을 보여주라'는 의미가 되어야 자연스러우므로 (B)가 정답

> **Key word**
> please be sure to **present your company identification when the technician visits your home**.

138 구조/문법・동사   난이도 하

해설 빈칸은 주어와 목적어 사이 동사자리. 문장 내 미래시점을 나타내는 표현이 있으므로 미래시제 (C)가 정답

Key word
I **will email** you again to follow up and make sure that everything is working properly **tomorrow morning**.

139-142번은 다음 공지에 관한 문제입니다.

실험실 장비: 유리 비커 프로토콜

뛰어난 재사용성으로 인해, 저희 실험실 장비 대부분은 플라스틱 보다는 유리로 만들어집니다. **139.** 반면, 플라스틱과 달리, 유리는 깨지기 쉽습니다. 그 결과, 유리로 된 도구를 사용하여 실험을 할 때는 특별한 주의가 필요합니다. 특히, 유리용기를 원심분리기에 싣거나 내릴 때는 용기에 이가 나가거나 긁히거나, 아니면 손상되지 않았는지 간단히 점검해 주세요. **140.** 시작하기 전, 안전 지침을 먼저 읽어주시기 바랍니다. 저희가 소다 석회 유리로 **141.** 만들어진 플라스크를 포함해 최고 내성 기준에 미치지 않는 모든 장비를 없애고 있지만, 일부는 남아서 쓰이고 있습니다. 혹시 발견하시게 되면, 사용하지 마시기 바랍니다. 제대로 측정되지 않을 수 있습니다. 종이에 잘 싸서 일반 **142.** 쓰레기통 대신, 초록색 재활용 통에 넣어 주시는 것만 기억하시면 됩니다.

어휘 lab n. 실험실 equipment n. 장비 glass beaker 유리 비커 protocol n. 프로토콜, 규약, 규칙 superior adj. 우수한 reusability n. 재사용가능성 dissimilar to ~과 다른 fragile adj. 깨지기[손상되기] 쉬운 precaution n. 예방책 perform v. 행하다, 실시하다 experiment n. 실험 composed of ~로 구성된 in particular 특히 load v. (짐을) 싣다 unload v. (짐을) 내리다 centrifuge n. 원심분리기 ensure v. 보장하다 chip v. 이가 빠지다 scratch v. 긁다 compromise v. ~를 위태롭게 하다 be in the process of ~ing ~하는 과정이다 remove v. 없애다, 제거하다 meet v. (필요, 요구 등을) 충족시키다 tolerance n. 내성, 저항력 standard n. 기준 flask n. (실험용) 병, 플라스크 soda lime glass 소다석회 유리 in circulation 현재 쓰이고 있는, 유통되고 있는 come across 우연히 발견하다 attempt v. 시도하다 unlikely adj. 있을 것 같지 않은, 예상 밖의 properly adv. 제대로, 적절히 calibrate v. 측정하다, 눈금을 맞추다 wrap v. 싸다, 포장하다 place v. 놓다, 두다 receptacle n. 용기, 통

139 어휘+문맥이해・접속부사   난이도 중

해설 빈칸 앞 문장의 '실험실 장비는 플라스틱보다는 유리로 만들어진다'는 내용과 빈칸 뒷 부분의 '플라스틱과 달리 유리는 깨지기 쉽다'는 내용을 고려할 때, 문맥상 내용이 서로 상반되므로 (B)가 정답

Key word
Due to its superior reusability, most of our lab equipment is made out of glass rather than plastic. **On the other hand**, dissimilar to plastic, glass is quite fragile.

140 문맥이해・문장삽입   난이도 중

해석 (A) 이것은 플라스틱 용기가 유리보다 우수한 한가지 장점이다.
(B) 유리 비커는 사용 전 완전히 말려야 한다.
(C) 그것들은 앞으로 따로 보관되어야 한다.
(D) 시작하기 전, 안전 지침을 먼저 읽어주시기 바랍니다.

해설 빈칸 앞 문장의 '유리용기가 손상되지 않도록 특별히 신경 써 달라'는 내용을 고려할 때, 문맥상 '사용 전 안전지침을 먼저 읽으라'는 내용으로 이어져야 자연스러우므로 (D)가 정답

Key word
In particular, when loading and unloading glass containers from the centrifuge, perform a brief check to ensure they are not chipped, scratched, or otherwise compromised. **Before doing so, read all of the safety guidelines first**.

141 구조/문법・과거분사   난이도 중

해설 빈칸은 명사 flask를 후치수식하는 분사자리. 빈칸 뒤 전치사 of가 있음을 고려할 때, 'made of(~로 만들어진)'의 형태를 완성하는 과거분사 (A)가 정답

Key point
과거분사는 수식하는 대상과 의미상 수동 관계를, 현재분사는 수식하는 대상과 의미상 능동 관계를 갖는다.

142 어휘+문맥이해・명사   난이도 중

해설 빈칸은 형용사 normal의 수식을 받는 명사자리. rather than으로 연결된 구조를 고려할 때, 문맥상 '일반 쓰레기통이 아니라 초록색 재활용통에 넣어달라'는 내용이 되어야 자연스러우므로 (C)가 정답

Key word
Just remember to carefully wrap it in paper, and **place it in the green recycling box, rather than the receptacle for normal waste**.

143-146번은 다음 웹 페이지에 관한 문제입니다.

Kansas 주 Lawrence 시청 옆에 편리한 곳에 위치한 Coscia 국제 교육원(CFSI)은 모든 연령과 국적의 학습자들에게 개인 및 단체 수업을 제공합니다. **143.** 저희 강사진은 당신이 최고의 교육을 받도록 보장해 드립니다.

현재, CFSI는 다양한 **144.** 언어의 개인 수업을 제공하고 있습니다. 선택하실 수 있는 과목은 스페인어, 프랑스어, 독일어, 아랍어, 중국어입니다. **145.** 저희는 듣기와 쓰기, 읽기는 물론, 말하기까지 아우르는 종합 언어능력에 필요한 모든 기술을 알려드립니다. 전수해드립니다. 이달의 특별행사와 시설견학에 대해 알아보시려면, 785-555-1212로 전화하시기 바랍니다. 그리고 강사 페이지 www.cosciafsi.edu/biographies를 확인하셔서 저희 강사진**146.**에 대해 알아보는 것도 잊지 마세요.

어휘 conveniently adv. 편리하게 locate v. (특정한 위치에) 두다 institute n. (특히 교육·전문 직종과 관련된) 기관[협회] nationality n. 국적 at present 현재는, 지금은 competency n. 능숙함, 능숙도 facility n. 시설, 기관 instructor n. 강사

143 문맥이해・문장삽입   난이도 중

해석 (A) 저희 강사들은 반드시 당신이 가능한 최고의 교육을 받도록 해줄 것입니다.
(B) 교육원의 교무처는 금요일에는 일찍 문을 닫습니다.
(C) 등록하신 모든 수업이 청구서에 나와 있습니다.
(D) 시설은 다음 달 수리에 들어갑니다.

해설 빈칸 앞 문장의 '국제교육원은 학습자에게 수업을 제공한다'는 내용을 고려할 때, 문맥상 기관을 소개 및 홍보하는 내용이 이어져야 자연스러우므로 강사진을 소개하는 문장 (A)가 정답

TEST 03

Key word
Conveniently located next to City Hall in Lawrence, Kansas, the Coscia Foreign Studies Institute (CFSI) **offers** individual and group **lessons to learners** of all ages and nationalities. **Our instructors will ensure you receive the best education possible**.

144 어휘+문맥이해・명사　　　난이도 중

해설 빈칸 뒷 문장에서 선택할 수 있는 언어의 종류를 소개하고 있음을 고려할 때, '다양한 종류의 언어수업을 제공한다'는 의미가 되어야 자연스러우므로 (B)가 정답

Key word
At present, CFSI offers individual **classes in** a variety of **languages**. You'll **have a choice of Spanish, French, German, Arabic, and Chinese**.

145 문맥이해・인칭대명사　　　난이도 중

해설 빈칸은 문장의 주어자리. 글을 읽는 대상을 you로 지칭하고 있음을 고려할 때, 교육을 제공하는 기관을 '우리'로 일컫는 것이 문맥상 자연스러우므로 (D)가 정답

Key word
You'll have a choice of Spanish, French, German, Arabic, and Chinese. **We teach** every skill for total competency, including listening, writing, reading, and of course, speaking.

146 어휘・전치사　　　난이도 중

해설 빈칸은 our teachers를 목적어로 하는 전치사자리. 빈칸 앞 동사 learn과 함께 'learn about(~에 대해 알아보다)'라는 표현을 완성하는 (B)가 정답

Key word
And remember to check out our instructor section, www.cosciafsi.edu/biographies, to **learn about our teachers**.

PART 7　　　P. 123

147-148번은 다음 온라인 기사에 관한 문제입니다.

http://www.yeoviltribune.co.uk/local

우승자 선발을 도와주세요:
연례 Yeovil 최우수업체 여론조사

3년 연속, 저희는 주민 여러분께 지역 내 최우수 업체 선정을 도와주시길 부탁 드리는 바입니다. 올해에는 구독자뿐만 아니라, 모든 Yeovil 시민들이 참여할 수 있습니다.

저희 직원들이 최우수 소매점, 카페, 식당, 및 숙박업소에 대한 후보목록을 만들었습니다. 고객만족도 설문조사를 근거로, 부문별 6개의 우수업체가 후보로 선정되었습니다. 설문조사 결과를 보시려면, 여기를 클릭해 주세요.

가장 좋아하는 후보를 우승자로 만들어주시려면, 이번 달에 참가업체들 중 한 곳을 방문하셔서 투표용지를 작성해주세요.(147)/(148) 참여하시면, 우리 지역을 특별하게 만들어주는 기관들의 홍보를 돕게 됩니다. 너무 오래 지체하지 마세요. 투표는 5월 9일 오전 11시에 종료됩니다.

어휘　crown v. 영예를 주다　poll n. 여론조사　running adj. ('수사+year・day・time 등의 명사' 뒤에서) ~연속의　local n. 현지인　region n. 지역　resident n. 주민　take part 참여하다　subscriber n. 구독자　put together (모아) 만들다　nominee n. 지명자, 후보자　retail shop 소매상점　inn n. 여관　based on ~에 근거하여　candidate n. 후보자　fill out 작성하다　ballot n. 투표용지　establishment n. 기관, 시설　voting n. 투표, 선거

147 주제/목적/대상　　　난이도 중

해석 이 기사의 주요 목적은 무엇인가?
(A) 업체들에게 돈을 기부해달라고 요청하는 것
(B) 독자들에게 선택을 하도록 독려하는 것
(C) 신규 잡지구독을 홍보하는 것
(D) 대회 우승자를 거론하는 것

해설 세 번째 단락에서 To make your favorite candidate a winner, visit one of our many participating businesses this month and fill out a ballot.(가장 좋아하는 후보를 우승자로 만들어주시려면, 이번 달에 참가업체들 중 한 곳을 방문하셔서 투표용지를 작성해주세요.)라고 했으므로 (B)가 정답

148 사실확인　　　난이도 중

해석 Yeovil 최우수업체 여론조사에 관하여 알 수 있는 것은?
(A) 온라인으로 할 수 있다.
(B) 참가자들에게 현금 인센티브를 제공한다.
(C) 6개 부문이 있다.
(D) 여러 장소에서 실시된다.

해설 세 번째 단락에서 To make your favorite candidate a winner, visit one of our many participating businesses this month and fill out a ballot.(가장 좋아하는 후보를 우승자로 만들어주시려면, 이번 달에 참가업체들 중 한 곳을 방문하셔서 투표용지를 작성해주세요.)라고 하여 여러 장소에서 실시된다는 것을 알 수 있으므로 (D)가 정답

149-150번은 다음 문자메시지 대화에 관한 문제입니다.

Andre Wiseau (16:58) 저기, Dana. 오늘 피자가 충분하지 않은 것 같아요. 8상자를 주문했는데, 7상자밖에 없네요.

Dana Blanc (16:59) 그러면 안 되는데... 주문을 확인하지 않아서 죄송해요. 지금 피자가게에 연락해볼게요.

Andre Wiseau (17:16) 한국에서 오는 관광단체가 곧 도착해요. 지금 돌아오는 길이세요?

Dana Blanc (17:18) 10분 후에 도착해요. **피자는 새로 만들어야 하는 것 같아요. 바로 시작했어요.**(150)

Andre Wiseau (17:19) 알겠어요, 방금 Will에게 서관도 들르라고 했어요. 그들에게 고대, 중국 유물들을 짧게 견학시켜줄 거예요.(149)

Dana Blanc (17:28) 다행이에요. 여기는 지연된 것 때문에 음료를 무료로 주신대요.

Andre Wiseau (17:28) 네. 계속 상황을 알려주세요.

어휘 confirm v. 확인해 주다 on one's way back 돌아오는 길에 stop by 잠시 들르다 wing n. 부속건물 brief adj. (시간이) 짧은 ancient adj. 고대의 artifact n. 공예품 relief n. 안도, 안심 beverage n. 음료 delay n. 연기, 지연

어휘 multi adj. 다수의 tool n. 공구 needle-nose plier 바늘코 플라이어, 펜치 reach into ~에 이르다 compact adj. (공간이) 작은 object n. 물건, 물체 strip v. 벗기다 coating n. 피막, 코팅 wire n. 전선 high-carbon stainless steel 고탄소 스테인리스강 tough adj. 단단한 scissors n. 가위 assist v. 돕다 strain n. 부담 canned goods 통조림 제품 screwdriver n. 드라이버 loosen v. 느슨하게 하다, 풀다 tighten v. 조이다 flathead screw (머리가 납작한) 접지 나사

149 암시/추론 난이도 중

해석 Mr. Wiseau에 관하여 무엇이 사실이겠는가?
(A) 관광단체를 인솔하고 있다.
(B) 피자 만드는 것에 능숙하다.
(C) 역사 박물관에서 근무한다.
(D) 음료수를 구입할 것이다.

해설 17시 19분, Andre Wiseau의 메시지에서 He's going to be giving them a brief tour of the ancient and Chinese artifacts.(그들에게 고대, 중국 유물들을 짧게 견학시켜줄 거예요.)라고 하여 그가 역사 박물관에서 근무함을 알 수 있으므로 (C)가 정답

150 화자 의도 파악 난이도 중

해석 17시 18분에, Ms. Blanc이 "바로 시작했어요."라고 할 때 무엇을 의미하는가?
(A) 음료수가 다시 채워지고 있다.
(B) 새로운 관광단체가 방금 도착했다.
(C) 몇몇 손님들이 식사를 하기 시작했다.
(D) 주문이 빠르게 처리되고 있다.

해설 17시 18분, Dana Blanc의 메시지에서 It looks like they'll need to make a new pizza. They got started right away.(피자는 새로 만들어야 하는 것 같아요. 바로 시작했어요.)라고 말한 것으로, 주문접수 후 바로 피자를 만들기 시작했다는 의미임을 알 수 있으므로 (D)가 정답

151-152번은 다음 광고에 관한 문제입니다.

Supreme 만능공구 – 필요한 모든 것을 주머니 속에
50달러

공구

바늘코 펜치 – 좁은 공간에 넣거나 작은 물체를 잡기에 알맞음[151]

와이어 스트리퍼 – 모든 유형의 전선 둘레의 플라스틱 피복을 안전하게 벗겨냄

나이프 – 단단한 재료를 자를 수 있는 고탄소 스테인리스강으로 제작

스프링 가위 – 스프링이 자르는 동작을 도와 손의 부담을 덜어줌

캔 및 병따개 – 통조림 제품과 병 음료를 쉽게 열어줌

중간크기 드라이버 – 어떤 접지 나사든 풀거나 조여줌

쉽게 주머니에 넣고 다닐 수 있게 해주는 가죽 케이스 포함[152]

151 사실확인 난이도 중

해석 바늘코 펜치에 관하여 언급된 것은?
(A) 좁은 공간에서 사용할 수 있다.
(B) 다양한 종류의 재료를 자른다.
(C) 헐거워진 나사를 조인다.
(D) 금속용기를 연다.

해설 첫 번째 단락, Needle-nose Pliers(바늘코 펜치)에서 Great for reaching into compact spaces and holding small objects(좁은 공간에 넣거나 작은 물체를 잡기에 알맞음)이라고 했으므로 (A)가 정답

Paraphrasing compact spaces ➡ tight areas

152 사실확인 난이도 중

해석 Supreme 만능도구에 관하여 언급된 것은?
(A) 여러 색상으로 출시된다.
(B) 부대용품이 딸려 온다.
(C) 평생 품질보증을 받는다.
(D) 읽기 쉬운 설명서가 들어있다.

해설 일곱 번째 단락에서 Includes a leather case for easy carrying in your pocket(쉽게 주머니에 넣고 다닐 수 있게 해주는 가죽케이스 포함)라고 했으므로 (B)가 정답

Paraphrasing include ➡ come with

153-154번은 다음 이메일에 관한 문제입니다.

발신: Thomas Satoransky
수신: Antonia Montoya
제목: Satoransky 대리점[153]
날짜: 6월 2일

Ms. Montoya께,

일전에 당신의 매장에서 제 클래식 스포츠카 문제에 관해 대화하려고 Ronnie를 만났습니다. 요즘에도 크롬 범퍼 같은 옛날 부품을 구할 수 있는 사람이 있을 거라고, 생각도 못해서 감명받았습니다. Ronnie 말로는, **다음 주에 캘리포니아에서 후드 장식품 고정용 플라스틱 부속품이 입고된다고 하는데요.**[154] 그게 장착되면, 이 차는 완전히 복원됩니다.

전에도 말씀 드렸다시피, 차는 6월 10일까지 가져다 주셔야 합니다. 6월 11일에 저희 대리점에서 20주년 기념행사를 열거든요. **이 스포츠카는 저희 매장의 주요 명물입니다. 저희 로고와 기타 모든 홍보자료에 들어가 있어요.**[153] 후드 장식품은 차를 운전하는 데 필요하지는 않지만, 확실히 차가 더 멋져 보이게 해줄 겁니다.[154]

Best,
Thomas

어휘 dealership n. 자동차 대리점 the other day 일전에, 지난번에 vintage adj. 클래식[빈티지] 카의 impressed adj. 감명을 받은 chrome n. 크롬 bumper n. 범퍼 attachment n. 부속품 hold v. (특정 위치에) 유지하다, 고정하다 hood ornament (자동차) 후드 장식물 vehicle n. 자동차 fully adv. 완전히 restore v. 복원하다 automobile n. 자동차 drop off 전달하다 dealership n. 대리점 attraction n. (사람을 끄는) 명소[명물] feature v. 특징으로 하다 promotional adj. 홍보의 definitely adv. 확실히, 틀림없이

153 사실확인 난이도 중

해석 스포츠카에 관하여 언급된 것은?
(A) 엔진이 안정적이지 않다.
(B) 20년 전에 만들어졌다.
(C) Santoransky의 대리점을 상징한다.
(D) Thomas Santoransky가 만들었다.

해설 두 번째 단락에서 This sports car is my business' main attraction. It's featured in our logo and all other promotional materials.(이 스포츠카는 저희 매장의 주요 명물입니다. 저희 로고와 기타 모든 홍보자료에 들어가 있어요.)라고 하여 Satoransky 대리점을 상징함을 알 수 있으므로 (C)가 정답

154 암시/추론 난이도 중

해석 플라스틱 부속품에 관하여 알 수 있는 것은?
(A) 수리될 수 없다.
(B) 차량을 가동하는 데 필요하지 않다.
(C) 캘리포니아에서 더 이상 생산되지 않는다.
(D) 품질보증에 의해 보장된다.

해설 첫 번째 단락에서 a plastic attachment to hold the hood ornament is coming in from California next week.(다음 주에 캘리포니아에서 후드 장식품 고정용 플라스틱 부속품이 입고된다고 하는데요.)라고 했고, 두 번째 단락에서 The hood ornament is not needed to drive the car, but it would definitely make the vehicle look nicer.(후드 장식품은 차를 운전하는 데 필요하지는 않지만, 확실히 차가 더 멋져 보이게 해줄 겁니다.)라고 했으므로 (B)가 정답

Paraphrasing not needed to drive the car ➡ not required to operate a vehicle

155-157번은 다음 청구서에 관한 문제입니다.

DeLaurentis 보안 시스템

청구번호: AHD84-1113
예약일: 3월 25일
의뢰인: Antonia Brown (3월 31일까지 지불)

현장 상담 (2시간, 35달러/시간당)	70.00달러
지역 외 서비스 요청	50.00달러(155)
소계	120.00달러
추천 코드(25 퍼센트 할인)(156)	24.00달러
총 주문액	96.00달러

예약에 관한 귀하의 의견을 저희에게 알려주세요! 오늘 저희 모바일 앱 DL Secure으로 Sonya Young의 서비스에 대한 피드백을 저희에게 보내주세요.(157) 청구절차와 관련하여 우려사항이 있으시거나 더 많은 정보가 필요하시면, Thomas Nwamba에게 tnwamba@delaurentissecuritysys.com으로 연락 주십시오.

어휘 security n. 보안 bill v. 청구서를 보내다 appointment n. 약속, 예약 due adj. 돈을 지불해야 하는 on-site adj. 현장의 consultation n. 상담 out-of-area adj. 지역 외의 request n. 요청 subtotal n. 소계 referral n. 추천 total adj. 총 amount n. 양, 금액 via prep. ~를 통해 concern n. 우려, 걱정 regarding prep. ~에 관하여 procedure n. 절차, 과정

155 사실확인 난이도 중

해석 청구서에서 언급된 것은?
(A) 3월 31일에 발행되었다.
(B) 현장 서비스 요금이 부과되었다.
(C) 상담료가 최근 인상되었다.
(D) 민간기업에게 제공되었다.

해설 두 번째 단락, 표에서 Out-of-Area service request(지역 외 서비스 요청) 항목에 대해 $50.00(50달러)가 부과되어 현장서비스를 요청한 것에 대한 요금이 부과되었음을 알 수 있으므로 (B)가 정답

156 암시/추론 난이도 중

해석 Ms. Brown은 왜 할인을 받았겠는가?
(A) 전에 회사에서 제품을 구입한 적이 있다.
(B) 주문이 3월 프로모션 기간에 이루어졌다.
(C) 상담은 3시간을 넘지 않았다.
(D) 이전 고객이 그녀에게 서비스를 추천했다.

해설 두 번째 단락, 표에서 Referral Code(25% off)(추천 코드(25 퍼센트 할인))라고 하여 추천 할인을 받았음을 알 수 있으므로 (D)가 정답

157 암시/추론 난이도 중

해석 누가 상담을 제공했겠는가?
(A) Ms. Brown
(B) Mr. DeLaurentis
(C) Ms. Young
(D) Mr. Nwamba

해설 세 번째 단락에서 Let us know what you thought about your appointment! Send us feedback on Sonya Young's service via our mobile app, DL Secure, today.(예약에 관한 귀하의 의견을 저희에게 알려주세요! 오늘 저희 모바일 앱 DL Secure으로 Sonya Young의 서비스에 대한 피드백을 저희에게 보내주세요.)라고 하여 Sonya Young이 상담서비스를 제공했음을 알 수 있으므로 (C)가 정답

158-160번은 다음 안내문에 관한 문제입니다.

Douglas EasyBooks

Douglas EasyBooks 회계 프로그램 구매를 축하 드립니다.(159) 저희 응용 프로그램은 귀하의 시간을 절약해주어, 귀하의 사업체가 최고가 되는 데 집중할 수 있게 해줄 것입니다.(160)

이번 구매로, **귀하의 사업체는 무료로 교육 세미나를 받으실 수 있습니다.**[(158)] 3회로 구성된 이 온라인 교육 시리즈는 소프트웨어를 효과적으로 사용하는 방법에 관해 직원들을 교육할 수 있는 아주 좋은 방법입니다.

짧지만 유익한 이 세미나는 자신들의 회사에서 업무를 간소화하는데 저희 제품을 활용한 강사들에 의해 실시됩니다.[(159)] 교육 세미나를 예약하시려면, 오늘 Douglaseasybooks.com/training에 로그인해 주세요.

| 어휘 | **accounting** n. 회계 (업무) **application** n. 응용 프로그램 **eligible** adj. ~를 할 수 있는 **free of charge** 무료로 **brief** adj. 짧은 **session** n. (특정한 활동을 위한) 시간 **utilize** v. 활용하다 **simplify** v. 간소화하다 **practice** n. (의사·변호사 등 전문직 종사자의) 업무 **firm** n. 회사 |

---

158 주제/목적/대상   난이도 중

해석   안내문의 목적은 무엇인가?
(A) 강사들을 모집하는 것
(B) 신간도서를 광고하는 것
(C) 요금에 대하여 설명하는 것
(D) 서비스에 대하여 설명하는 것

해설   두 번째 단락에서 your business is eligible for a training seminar, free of charge.(당신의 사업체는 무료로 교육 세미나를 받을 수 있습니다.)라고 했으므로 (D)가 정답

Paraphrasing a training seminar ➡ a service

---

159 상세정보   난이도 중

해석   안내문에 따르면, 강사들은 어떤 자격을 갖추고 있는가?
(A) 경제학 석사학위가 있다.
(B) Douglas' EasyBooks에서 장기간 근무해왔다.
(C) 회계 프로그램 개발을 도왔다.
(D) 회계 프로그램을 사용해본 경험이 있다.

해설   첫 번째 단락에서 Congratulations on purchasing the Douglas' EasyBooks accounting program.(Douglas' EasyBooks 회계 프로그램 구매를 축하드립니다.)라고 했고, 세 번째 단락에서 These brief but helpful sessions are conducted by trainers who have utilized our product to simplify practices in their own firms.(짧지만 유익한 이 세미나는 자신들의 회사에서 업무를 간소화하는데 저희 제품을 활용한 강사들에 의해 실시됩니다.)라고 했으므로 (D)가 정답

Paraphrasing utilize ➡ use

---

160 동의어   난이도 중

해석   첫 번째 단락, 두 번째 줄의 단어 "focus"와 의미상 가장 가까운 것은?
(A) 집중하다
(B) 지시하다
(C) 조정하다
(D) 채택하다

해설   첫 번째 단락의 Our application will save you time, allowing you to focus on being the best business you can be.(저희 응용 프로그램은 귀하의 시간을 절약해주어, 귀하의 사업체가 최고가 되는 데 집중하게 해줄 것입니다.)에서 'focus'는 '목표에 집중하다'라는 의미로 쓰였으므로, 보기 중 '집중하다'를 뜻하는 (A)가 정답

161-163번은 다음 이메일에 관한 문제입니다.

발신: Alan Chang
수신: 마케팅팀 전원
제목: 최신정보
날짜: 1월 12일

모두 안녕하세요.

몇 가지 매우 좋은 소식이 있습니다. Dunkirk 항공의 취항지들을 홍보하는 우리 캠페인이 큰 성공을 거뒀습니다. ―[1]―. Dunkirk사의 웹 사이트는 최근 Christchurch와 Napier시로 가는 여행을 예약하려는 수많은 방문객으로 인해 높은 접속량을 경험하고 있습니다.[(161)] ―[2]―.

하지만 이제, 우리는 Morton & Alonzo 프로젝트에 집중해야 합니다. 우리의 과제는 그들의 새 스포츠음료가 젊은 운동선수들에게 안성맞춤인 음료라는 걸 보여주는 것입니다. ―[3]―. 그러나, 우리가 회사 외부 사람들을 만나기 전에,[(163)] TV 광고 아이디어 회의를 했으면 합니다. 오늘 퇴근 전에, 목요일 오전과 오후 중 언제 모이는 게 좋을지 단체 채팅방으로 메시지를 보내주세요.[(162)] ―[4]―. 전원 참석하여 아이디어를 제시해주시기 바랍니다. 지난번처럼 잘 협력한다면, 이번 캠페인이 Dunkirk 프로젝트보다 훨씬 더 큰 성공을 거둘 수 있을 거라 믿습니다.

Best regards,

Alan Chang
마케팅담당 이사

| 어휘 | **promote** v. 홍보하다 **destination** n. 목적지 **athlete** n. 운동선수 **commercial** n. 광고 (방송) **indicate** v. 나타내다, 보여 주다 **effort** n. 활동 |

---

161 사실확인   난이도 중

해석   Dunkirk 항공 캠페인이 성공적이었다는 증거로 무엇이 언급되는가?
(A) 회원 가입의 증가
(B) 긍정적인 고객 후기의 수
(C) 휴가 예약의 양
(D) 항공요금 인하

해설   첫 번째 단락에서 I have some great news. Our campaign to promote Dunkirk Airlines flight destinations has proven to be a major success. ―[1]―. Dunkirk's Web site has been experiencing a lot of Web traffic recently from numerous visitors booking trips to the cities of Christchurch and Napier.(몇 가지 매우 좋은 소식이 있습니다. Dunkirk 항공의 취항지들을 홍보하는 우리 캠페인이 큰 성공을 거둔 것으로 판명되었습니다. Dunkirk사의 웹 사이트는 최근 Christchurch와 Napier시로 가는 여행을 예약하려는 수많은 방문객으로 인해 높은 접속량을 경험하고 있습니다.)라고 했으므로 (C)가 정답

---

162 상세정보   난이도 중

해석   Mr. Chang은 마케팅 직원들에게 무엇을 하라고 요청하는가?
(A) 설문조사를 만들라고
(B) 참석 가능 시간을 확인해 달라고
(C) 여행사에 연락하라고
(D) 소비자 보고서를 읽으라고

해설   두 번째 단락에서 Before the end of the day, please send a

message on our group chat indicating whether you'd rather meet in the morning or the afternoon on Thursday.(오늘 퇴근 전에, 목요일 오전과 오후 중 언제 모이는 게 좋을지 단체 채팅방으로 메시지를 보내주세요.)라고 했으므로 (B)가 정답

163 문장 삽입 난이도 중

해석 [1], [2], [3], [4]로 표시된 곳 중, 다음 문장이 들어갈 위치로 가장 적절한 것은?

"이를 위해, 운동선수들과 영양 상담가들을 모두 인터뷰할 계획입니다."

(A) [1]
(B) [2]
(C) [3]
(D) [4]

해설 두 번째 단락에서 Before we meet with people outside the company, however,(그러나, 우리가 회사 외부 사람들을 만나기 전에)라고 하여 주어진 문장이 앞에 들어가야 자연스러우므로 (C)가 정답

164-167번은 다음 온라인 채팅 대화문에 관한 문제입니다.

Edith Crawley (오후 12시 38분)
안녕하세요, Joan, Dave. 여러분 중에 저희가 곧 출시할 FPX-2220 에어컨에 대한 최신 자료를 보신 분 있나요?

Joan Mitchell (오후 12시 39분)
방금 전에 봤어요. 저는 그게 에너지 효율이 더 좋은데, 더 빠르게 냉각될 수 있다는 점에 놀랐어요.

Dave Edison (오후 12시 40분)
맞아요! 제가 Baez Systems와 회의할 때 그 점을 보여줄 수 없다는 게 아쉬워요.(165)

Joan Mitchell (오후 12시 40분)
제가 사본을 부서원 전체에게 이메일로 보냈어요.

Edith Crawley (오후 12시 42분)
그런데 그건 3시 30분으로 예정되어 있잖아요.(165) 가장 적당한 그래프를 골라서 슬라이드쇼에 넣을 시간이 충분할 거예요.

Dave Edison (오후 12시 44분)
문제는 제가 1시에 교육 세미나를 하고, 끝나면 바로 Baez 본사로 운전해서 가야 하거든요. 그곳이 이제 거의 30마일 떨어진 거리에 있어요.(166)

Edith Crawley (오후 12시 45분)
제가 대신 처리해 드릴 텐데, 전 이미 공항으로 가는 길이에요.

Joan Mitchell (오후 12시 46분)
제가 할게요. 제가 제일 좋은 표로 파일을 만들어서 플래시 드라이브에 넣어 놓을게요.(167) 가시기 전에 제 자리에서 꼭 챙겨가세요.

Edith Crawley (오후 12시 48분)
회의가 성공길 바래요. Baez가 주 구매자가 되면, 분명 축하할 일이 될 거예요.(164)

Dave Edison (오후 12시 51분)
응원 감사해요!

어휘 air conditioner 에어컨 release v. 출시하다 cool v. 식다, 차가워지다 energy-efficient adj. 에너지 효율적인 email v. 이메일을 보내다 copy n. 복사본 department n. 부서 schedule v. 일정을 잡다 pick out ~를 고르다 pertinent adj. 적절한, 관련 있는 slideshow n. 슬라이드 쇼 chart n. 도표 flash drive 컴퓨터의 휴대용 저장장치 agree v. 동의하다, 찬성하다 purchase n. 구매자 worth ~ing ~할 가치가 있는 celebrate v. 축하하다 support n. 지지, 지원

164 암시/추론 난이도 중

해석 Mr. Edison의 직업은 무엇이겠는가?
(A) 컴퓨터 프로그래머
(B) 프로젝트 매니저
(C) 판매 대리인
(D) 수리공

해설 오후 12시 48분, Edith Crawley의 메시지에서 I hope the meeting is a success. If Baez agrees to a major purchase, it will definitely be worth celebrating.(회의가 성공하길 바랍니다. Baez가 주 구매자가 되면, 분명 축하할 일이 될 거예요.)라고 하여 그가 업무를 한다는 것을 알 수 있으므로 (C)가 정답

165 상세정보 난이도 중

해석 오후 3시 30분에 무슨 일이 일어나는가?
(A) 비행기가 이륙할 것이다.
(B) 지원서가 제출될 것이다.
(C) 회의가 열릴 것이다.
(D) 상이 수여될 것이다.

해설 오후 12시 40분 ~ 12시 42분 대화에서 Dave Edison이 It's a shame I won't be able to show it at my meeting with Baez Systems.(제가 Baez Systems와 회의할 때 그 점을 보여줄 수 없다는 게 아쉬워요.)라고 한 말에 Edith Crawley가 That's scheduled for 3:30, though.(그런데 그건 3시 30분으로 예정되어 있잖아요.)라고 했으므로 (C)가 정답

166 암시/추론 난이도 상

해석 Baez Systems에 관하여 알 수 있는 것은?
(A) 곧 신상품을 출시할 것이다.
(B) Ms. Crawley는 그곳에 고객이 많다.
(C) Mr. Edison은 한때 거기서 근무했었다.
(D) 본사가 최근 이전했다.

해설 오후 12시 44분, Dave Edison의 메시지에서 The problem is I'm giving a training seminar at 1:00, and I'll have to drive out to the Baez main office immediately after. It's almost 30 miles away now.(제가 1시에 교육 세미나를 하고, 끝나면 바로 Baez 본사로 운전해서 가야 하거든요. 그곳이 이제 거의 30마일 떨어진 거리에 있어요.)라고 하여 Baez 본사 사무실이 더 먼 곳으로 이전했음을 알 수 있으므로 (D)가 정답

Paraphrasing main office ➡ headquarters

167 화자 의도 파악 난이도 중

해석 오후 12시 46분에, Ms. Mitchell이 "제가 할게요."라고 할 때 무엇을 의미하겠는가?
(A) 그녀가 교육을 실시할 것이다.
(B) 그녀가 이메일을 보낼 것이다.
(C) 그녀가 자료를 모을 것이다.
(D) 그녀가 시각자료를 만들 것이다.

해설 오후 12시 46분, Joan Mitchell의 메시지에서 I'm on it. I'll make a file with the best charts and put it in a flash drive. Just make sure to pick it up from my desk before you go.(제가 할게요. 제가 제일 좋은 표로 파일을 만들어서 플래시 드라이브에 넣어 놓을게요.)라고 했으므로 (D)가 정답

Paraphrasing make a file with the best charts ➡ create some visual aids

---

168-171번은 다음 기사에 관한 문제입니다.

> **Cheesman 공원에서 접시 채우기**
>
> Eldorado, 7월 7일 – Hayward's가 지난 주 금요일 Cheesman 공원에서 열린 뒤뜰 요리대회에서 최고 요리상을 차지했다.(168)/(169) 11개의 참가업체들 중 1위를 차지했다.
>
> 뒤뜰 요리대회는 인기 있는 행사로, Eldorado 지역 전역에서 참가식당과 관람객을 끌어 모으고 있다.(168) 행사 진행자 Malcolm Jones의 간단한 소개말에 이어, 모든 식당에서 온 요리사들이 공원 이곳 저곳에서 고기를 훈제하고 굽기 시작했다. 참석자들은 각 식당이 내놓은 다양한 종류의 바비큐를 맛볼 기회를 얻었다. 그리고 나서 맛본 음식을 평가해달라고 요청받았다. 그날 밤, 평가가 전부 검토된 후, 시상식을 위해 모두 한자리에 모였다.(169)
>
> Hayward's는 올해 행사에서도 성공을 이어갔다. 작년에는 훈제 풀드 포크로 2위를 차지했고, 그 전 해에는 매운 치킨으로 3위에 올랐다.(170) 이 식당을 방문한다면 반드시 두 요리를 모두 먹어봐야 한다.
>
> Hayward's는 최근 Eldorado에서 10주년 기념행사를 가졌다. 영업 첫 해에 Hayward's는 동네 슈퍼마켓 바깥에 놓은 바비큐 훈제통 하나와 피크닉 테이블 몇 개가 전부였다. 이제는 최대 40가구를 수용할 수 있는 공간에서 영업한다.
>
> Hayward's가 수상하기 전에, 2위와 3위 입상자들이 발표되었다. Rattlesnake Barbecue가 후자의 영예를 가져갔으며, Joe's Smokehouse가 양지머리요리로 2위를 차지했다.(171)

어휘 fill up ~을 가득 채우다 take home the award 수상하다 cook-off 요리경연대회 win first place 1등을 하다 contestant n. (대회·시합 등의) 참가자 draw v. 끌어모으다 spectator n. 구경꾼, 관람객 organizer n. 주최자 cook n. 요리사 establishment n. 기관, 시설 smoke v. 훈제하다 grill v. 그릴[석쇠]에 굽다 meat n. 고기 attendee n. 참석자 sample v. 시식하다 rate v. 평가하다 rating n. 평점 gather v. 모이다 presentation n. 수여 string n. 일련, 연속 smoky adj. 훈제한 pulled pork 풀드 포크(연해질 때까지 장시간 구운 돼지고기) operate v. 영업[작업]하다 fit v. (크기가 어떤 사람·사물에) 맞다 latter adj. 후자의 honor n. 명예(가 되는 것) brisket n. 양지머리

---

168 사실확인 난이도 중

해석 기사에 어떤 종류의 행사가 언급되는가?
(A) Eldorado 남부의 새 지점 개장
(B) 자선기금 모금을 위한 식품 판매
(C) 새로 선출된 정부 관료를 위한 축하행사
(D) 지역 업체들이 참가하는 요리대회

해설 첫 번째 단락에서 Hayward's took home the award for Best Tasting Food at the Backyard Cook-off at Cheesman Park last Friday.(Hayward's가 지난 주 금요일 Cheesman 공원에서 열린 뒤뜰 요리대회에서 최고 요리상을 차지했다.)라고 했는데, 두 번째 단락에서 The Backyard Cook-off is a popular event, drawing participating restaurants and spectators from all over the greater Eldorado area.(뒤뜰 요리대회는 인기 있는 행사로, Eldorado 지역 전역에서 참가식당과 관람객을 끌어 모으고 있다.)라고 했으므로 (D)가 정답

Paraphrasing cook-off ➡ cooking competition, restaurant ➡ business

---

169 암시/추론 난이도 중

해석 기사에 따르면, 금요일 밤에는 무슨 일이 있었겠는가?
(A) Rattlesnake Barbecue가 새로운 장소로 이전했다.
(B) Joe's Smokehouse에서 새 그릴을 구입했다.
(C) Hayward's가 상을 받았다.
(D) Cheesman 공원이 일찍 폐장했다.

해설 첫 번째 단락에서 Hayward's took home the award for Best Tasting Food at the Backyard Cook-off at Cheesman Park last Friday.(Hayward's가 지난 주 금요일 Cheesman 공원에서 열린 뒤뜰 요리대회에서 최고 요리상을 차지했다.)라고 했는데, 두 번째 단락에서 Later that night, after all the ratings were reviewed, everyone gathered for the awards presentation.(그날 밤, 평가가 전부 검토된 후, 시상식을 위해 모두 한자리에 모였다.)라고 하여 Hayward's가 금요일 밤 시상식에서 상을 받았음을 알 수 있으므로 (C)가 정답

Paraphrasing took home ➡ was given

---

170 사실확인 난이도 중

해석 Hayward's에 관하여 사실인 것은?
(A) 직접 닭을 사육한다.
(B) 이전 두 번의 뒤뜰 요리대회에서 상을 받았다.
(C) Eldorado 지역의 슈퍼마켓들에게 상품을 판매한다.
(D) Malcolm Jones가 소유하고 있다.

해설 세 번째 단락에서 Last year, their smoky pulled pork came in second, and the year before, their spicy chicken took third place.(작년에는 훈제 풀드 포크로 2위를 차지했고, 그 전 해에는 매운 치킨으로 3위에 올랐다.)라고 했으므로 (B)가 정답

---

171 암시/추론 난이도 상

해석 Rattlesnake Barbecue에 관하여 알 수 있는 것은?
(A) Joe's Smokehouse보다 낮은 평점을 받았다.
(B) 이전에 Hayward's에서 근무했던 요리사에 의해 시작되었다.
(C) 가족이 운영하는 사업체이다.
(D) 양지머리요리로 유명하다.

해설 다섯 번째 단락에서 Before Hayward's received their prize, the winners for second place and third place were announced. Rattlesnake Barbecue took home the latter honor, while Joe's Smokehouse won second for their brisket.(Hayward's가 수상하기 전에, 2위와 3위 입상자들이 발표되었다. Rattlesnake Barbecue가 후자의 영예를 가져갔으며, Joe's Smokehouse가 양지머리요리로 2위를 차지했다.)라고 하여 Joe's Smokehouse가 2위, Rattlesnake Barbecue가 3위임을 알 수 있으므로 (A)가 정답

172-175번은 다음 웹 페이지에 관한 문제입니다.

www.lsw.net

| 잡지 | 팁 | 연락처 | 기회 |

<Logan Square Weekly>는 이곳 Logan Square와 Palmer Square, Humboldt Park 지역 주민들에 의해 제작됩니다. 매주 화요일 저녁에 온라인으로 게재됩니다.(172) 여름 슬램 뮤직 페스티벌을 위한 <최고의 LSW 수집가 에디션>도 인쇄판으로 출간됩니다.(175) —[1]—.

<Logan Square Weekly>는 지역 관점의 뉴스와 지역 내 최고 상점 정보, 다가오는 지역 행사 정보를 알려줍니다.(172) —[2]—. Peter Moorman이나 Anna Kim과 같은 유능한 칼럼니스트들이 식당 추천부터 부동산 정보까지 모든 걸 알려줍니다.

올 가을, <Logan Square Weekly>에서 지역 상인을 표창하는 기획을 시작합니다.(173) 이를 위해, 독자 여러분께 지역사회에 상당한 기여를 한 우수 자영업자 추천을 요청드립니다. —[3]—. 후보를 추천하려면, RyanS@LSW.net으로 이메일을 보내주시기 바랍니다. 여러분의 선택을 검토한 후, 올해의 최우수 상인 2명을 선발할 것입니다. 수상자들은 10월 15일 지역 공로자 연회에서 상을 수여 받게 됩니다.(174) —[4]—. 또한 둘 다 <LSW> 10월 12일호 첫 페이지에 프로필이 실리게 됩니다.

어휘 **square** n. 광장 **weekly** n. 주간지 **resident** n. 주민 **neighborhood** n. 지역, 지방 **post** v. (정보 등을) 게시하다 **print** v. (책·신문 등을) 찍다, 발행하다 **throughout** prep. ~동안 죽, 내내 **present** v. 주다, 수여하다 **perspective** n. 관점, 시각 **real estate** n. 부동산 **initiative** n. (특정한 문제 해결·목적 달성을 위한 새로운) 계획 **honor** v. (공적을 기려 훈장 등을) 수여하다 **to this end** 이것을 위하여 **nomination** n. 지명, 추천 **outstanding** adj. 우수한 **significant** adj. 중요한, 의미 있는 **contribution** n. 기여 **nominate** v. 추천하다 **look over** 살펴보다 **selection** n. 선택, 선발 **recipient** n. 받는 사람 **recognize** v. (공로를) 인정하다 **property** n. 부동산

172 주제/목적/대상 난이도 중

해석 웹 페이지의 목적은 무엇인가?
(A) 지역 출판물을 광고하는 것
(B) 식당 개업을 보도하는 것
(C) 지역 선거에 관해 설명하는 것
(D) 콘서트 일정을 발표하는 것

해설 첫 번째 단락에서 We post it online every Tuesday evening.(매주 화요일 저녁에 온라인으로 게재됩니다.)라고 했고, 두 번째 단락에서 Logan Square Weekly presents news from a local perspective, information on the best stores in the area, and details on upcoming events in the area.(<Logan Square Weekly>는 지역 관점의 뉴스와 지역 내 최고 상점 정보, 다가오는 지역 행사 정보를 알려줍니다.)라고 했으므로(A)가 정답

---

173 상세정보 난이도 상

해석 어떤 새로운 특징이 발표되고 있는가?
(A) 재무 조언을 위한 신규 칼럼
(B) 웹 채팅 서비스
(C) 상인들을 표창하려는 계획
(D) 부동산 목록 페이지

해설 세 번째 단락에서 This fall, Logan Square Weekly will start an initiative to honor shop owners in our area.(올 가을, <Logan Square Weekly>는 지역 상인을 표창하는 기획을 시작합니다.)라고 했으므로 (C)가 정답

Paraphrasing initiative ➡ plan, honor ➡ recognize, shop owners ➡ store owners

---

174 상세정보 난이도 중

해석 10월 15일에는 어떤 일이 있을 것인가?
(A) 출판물에 기사가 실릴 것이다.
(B) 시공무원들이 임명될 것이다.
(C) 새 상점이 문을 열 것이다.
(D) 상이 수여될 것이다.

해설 세 번째 단락에서 On October 15, those recipients will be presented with prizes at the Community Excellence Banquet.(이 수상자들은 10월 15일 지역 공로자 연회에서 상을 수여 받게 됩니다.)라고 했으므로 (D)가 정답

Paraphrasing presented ➡ distributed

---

175 문장 삽입 난이도 중

해석 [1], [2], [3], [4]로 표시된 곳 중, 다음 문장이 들어갈 위치로 가장 적절한 것은?
"늘 그렇듯, 행사기간 내내 1달러에 구매하실 수 있습니다."
(A) [1]
(B) [2]
(C) [3]
(D) [4]

해설 첫 번째 단락에서 We also print a Best of LSW Collector's Edition for the Summer Slam Music Festival.(여름 슬램 뮤직 페스티벌을 위한 <최고의 LSW 수집가 에디션>도 인쇄판으로 출간됩니다.)라고 하여 주어진 문장이 이어지기에 자연스러우므로 (A)가 정답

176-180번은 다음 광고와 이메일에 관한 문제입니다.

Chanthavong 무에타이 아카데미
12856 Salmon River Road
San Diego, CA 92129
858-555-1212

Chanthavong 무에타이 아카데미에 관심을 가져주셔서 감사 드립니다. 저희는 현재 내년도 학생을 모집 중입니다. 회원권은 1월 1일부터 12월 31일까지 유효합니다.

수업 단계:
- **기초 수업(JFK):** JFK 학생들은 수요일과 금요일 저녁 7시부터 8시까지 킥복싱 훈련에 입문하게 됩니다.(179) 이 수업은 적응훈련과 예절을 강조합니다. 학생들은 3가지 기본 주먹기술과 2가지 기본 발차기도 배웁니다.

- 초급 수업(HBC): HBC 학생들은 월요일과 수요일 저녁 7시 30분부터 8시 30분까지 무에타이 공부를 계속 합니다. 주로 펀치백(샌드백)으로 연습하며, 다양한 주먹기술과 발차기의 조합을 배우기 시작합니다.

- 중급 수업(IBT): IBT 학생들은 파트너와 함께 하는 훈련에 주로 집중합니다. 스파링이 권장되지만 의무는 아닙니다. 수업은 화요일과 목요일 저녁 6시부터 7시까지입니다.

- 낙무에타이(NMT): NMT 학생들은 아카데미의 대회 준비반입니다. 아카데미의 동계 및 하계 대회 참가가 필수이며,(180) 주 5회의 연습에도 출석해야 합니다. 월요일부터 목요일까지는 오후 8시부터 9시까지, 토요일은 오후 4시부터 6시까지입니다.(179)

일요일에는 수업이 없지만, 개별 연습을 위해 오전 9시부터 오후 7시까지 아카데미를 개방합니다.(177)

모든 회원들은 아카데미 티셔츠와(176A) 연 2회 있는 대회의 무료 티켓,(176B) 글러브 및 기타 훈련용품에 대한 20 퍼센트 할인을 받게 됩니다.(176D)

어휘 Thai boxing 무에타이 effective adj. 시행[발효]되는 conditioning n. 적응훈련 etiquette n. 에티켓 punch n. 주먹으로 한 대 침, 펀치 kick n. 발길질 heavy bag (권투 연습용) 펀치백 focus on ~에 중점을 두다 heavily adv. 아주 많이 sparring n. (권투) 스파링 mandatory adj. 의무적인 attendance n. 출석 independent adj. 별개의, 독립적인 semi-annual adj. 한 해에 두 번의 supplies n. 용품, 비품

수신: Diana Langley <dlangley@ujjp.com>
발신: Sakda Khongsawatwaja <s.khongsawatwaja@ctba.com>
날짜: 12월 12일
제목: 내년도 회원권
첨부파일 양식.doc

Ms. Langley께,

다가오는 해에 아드님 Tony와 따님 Josephine을 학생으로 맞게 되어 매우 기쁩니다. Tony는 기초 수업(JFK)으로 시작시키겠습니다. 분명 좋아하고 금방 발전할 것입니다!(178)/(179)

반면, Josephine은 대회 준비반에 들어갈 자격이 됩니다.(178)/(179)/(180) 이 수업은 힘든 훈련과 실전 스파링을 수반하기 때문에, 참가자 부모님의 특별 동의서가 필요합니다. 첨부해드린 양식에 서명하셔서 12월 20일에 있는 학부모 설명회 때 주시기 바랍니다.

Best Regards,

Sakda Khongsawatwaja
수석 사범
Chanthavong 무에타이 아카데미

어휘 advance v. (기술 등이) 진전을 보다 qualify for ~의 자격을 얻다 involve v. 포함하다, 수반하다 consent n. 동의 participant n. 참가자 information session 설명회 head n. (조직의) 책임자 instructor n. 강사

---

176 사실확인 난이도 중

해석 Chanthavong 무에타이 아카데미 회원의 혜택으로 언급되지 않은 것은?
(A) 무료 의상
(B) 무료 대회 입장
(C) 개인 교습비 할인
(D) 훈련장비 할인

해설 지문의 단서와 보기를 매칭시키면, 첫 번째 지문[광고], 일곱 번째 단락에서 All members get an academy T-shirt, free tickets to the semi-annual tournaments, and a 20 percent discount on gloves and other training supplies. (모든 회원들은 아카데미 티셔츠와 연 2회 있는 대회의 무료 티켓, 글러브 및 기타 훈련용품에 대한 20 퍼센트 할인을 받게 됩니다.)와 (A) 무료 의상 (B) 무료 대회 입장 (D) 훈련장비 할인과 일치하지만, 개인 교습비를 할인해준다는 내용은 언급된 바 없으므로 (C)가 정답

Paraphrasing an academy T-shirt ➡ clothing item,
free tickets ➡ complimentary admission,
gloves and other training supplies ➡ training equipment

177 사실확인 난이도 중

해석 Chanthavong 무에타이 아카데미에 관하여 언급된 것은?
(A) 오전 수업이 있다.
(B) 강사들이 프로선수 출신이다.
(C) 매주 연습기회를 제공한다.
(D) 시설이 최근 확장되었다.

해설 첫 번째 지문[광고], 여섯 번째 단락에서 No classes are held on Sundays, but the Academy is open from 9:00 A.M. to 7:00 P.M. for independent practice.(일요일에는 수업이 없지만, 개별 연습을 위해 오전 9시부터 오후 7시까지 아카데미를 개방합니다.)라고 했으므로 (C)가 정답

178 주제/목적/대상 난이도 중

해석 Mr. Khongsawatwaja는 왜 Ms. Langley에게 편지를 썼는가?
(A) 자녀들의 반배치를 알려주려고
(B) 자녀들의 회비 납입을 요청하려고
(C) 아카데미의 신규 상품을 광고하려고
(D) 새로운 등록절차를 설명하려고

해설 두 번째 지문[이메일], 첫 번째 단락에서 We are very glad to have your son, Tony, and your daughter, Josephine, as students this coming year. We will start Tony out in the Just for Kicks (JFK) class—we're sure he'll love it and advance quickly! (다가오는 해에 아드님 Tony와 따님 Josephine을 학생으로 맞게 되어 매우 기쁩니다. Tony는 기초 수업(JFK) 수업으로 시작시키겠습니다. 분명 좋아하고 금방 발전할 것입니다!)라고 하며, 이어 두 번째 단락에서 Josephine, on the other hand, is qualified for our competition team.(반면, Josephine은 대회 준비반에 들어갈 자격이 됩니다.)라고 했으므로 (A)가 정답

179 암시/추론 [연계문제] 난이도 상

해석 어느 요일에 Ms. Langley의 자녀들이 모두 아카데미에 있겠는가?
(A) 월요일
(B) 화요일

(C) 수요일
(D) 목요일

해설 두 번째 지문[이메일], 첫 번째 및 두 번째 단락에서 We are very glad to have your son, Tony, and your daughter, Josephine, as students this coming year. We will start Tony out in the Just for Kicks (JFK) class—we're sure he'll love it and advance quickly! Josephine, on the other hand, is qualified for our competition team.(다가오는 해에 아드님 Tony와 따님 Josephine을 학생으로 맞게 되어 매우 기쁩니다. Tony는 기초 수업(JFK)으로 시작시키겠습니다. 분명 좋아하고 금방 발전할 것입니다! 반면 Josephine은 대회 준비반에 들어갈 자격이 됩니다.)라고 했는데, 첫 번째 지문[광고], 두 번째 단락에서 Just for Kicks (JFK): JFK students will get an introduction to kickboxing training Wednesday and Friday nights from 7:00 to 8:00 P.M.(기초 수업(JFK): JFK 학생들은 수요일과 금요일 저녁 7시부터 8시까지 킥복싱 훈련에 입문하게 됩니다.)라고 하였고, 다섯 번째 단락에서 Nak Muay Thai (NMT): Participation in the Academy's Winter Tournament and Summer Tournament is required, as is attendance at five weekly practices: Monday through Thursday from 8:00 P.M. to 9:00 P.M., and Saturdays from 4:00 P.M. to 6:00 P.M.(낙무에타이)NMT): 아카데미의 동계 및 하계 대회 참가가 필수이며, 주 5회의 연습에도 출석해야 합니다.(월요일부터 목요일까지는 오후 8시부터 9시까지, 토요일은 오후 4시부터 6시까지입니다)라고 하여, 기초 수업과 대회 준비반 수업이 모두 있는 요일이 수요일임을 알 수 있으므로 (C)가 정답

180 암시 / 추론 [연계문제]   난이도 ❶

해석 Josephine은 내년에 무엇을 하겠는가?
(A) 스포츠 경기장에서 시간제로 근무 할 것이다
(B) 두 개의 대회에 참가할 것이다
(C) 설명회에 참석할 것이다
(D) 초급 수업으로 올라갈 것이다

해설 첫 번째 지문[광고], 다섯 번째 단락에서 Participation in the Academy's Winter Tournament and Summer Tournament is required, (아카데미의 동계 및 하계 대회 참가가 필수이며)라고 했는데, 두 번째 지문[이메일], 두 번째 단락에서 Josephine, on the other hand, is qualified for our competition team.(반면, Josephine은 대회 준비반에 들어갈 자격이 됩니다.)라고 하여 Josephine이 두 개의 대회에 참가할 것임을 알 수 있으므로 (B)가 정답

Paraphrasing tournament ➡ competition

181-185번은 다음 웹 페이지와 이메일에 관한 문제입니다.

https://www.looper.com/packages

| 왜 Looper인가? | **패키지** | 이용약관 | 연락처 |

Looper는 신생기업과 대기업 모두에게 안성맞춤인 온라인 플랫폼입니다. **저희 프로젝트 관리 소프트웨어는 직원들이 서로 교류하고 사내 일상 업무에 대한 알림을 받을 수 있게 해줘서 귀사의 효율성과 생산성을 극대화 해줄 것입니다.**(181)

신생기업 패키지
직원 수 100명 이하인 신생기업에 적합합니다. 메시지 발송과 파일 공유 기능 및 단체 일정표, 팀원 당 10GB의 클라우드 저장공간을 제공하는 모바일 및 데스크톱 버전을 이용해보세요.

프리미엄 패키지
직원 수 500명 이하의 사업체에 추천합니다. 신생기업 패키지의 모든 기능에 추가도, 토론 게시판과 포트폴리오 관리, 프로젝트 진행상태 추적, 팀원 당 20GB의 클라우드 저장공간을 이용하실 수 있습니다.

기업 패키지
직원 수 800명까지의 기업에 안성맞춤입니다. 프리미엄 패키지의 기능 외에도 각 팀원 당 35GB의 클라우드 저장공간과 더불어 활동 피드와 설문조사 및 피드백 발송 기능, 일대일 화상 회의를 즐겨 보세요.

다국적 패키지
직원 수 1,000명 이상인 기업을 위한 것입니다. 기업 패키지의 모든 기능 외에도, 양방향 화면공유 기능으로 최대 20명까지 참여할 수 있는 음성 및 화상 회의와 연중무휴 고객지원, 동기화된 문서 편집, 직원당 50GB의 저장공간을 이용하실 수 있습니다.(184)

한 달 무료체험을 신청하세요. **무료체험이 끝날 때쯤에는 왜 세계에서 가장 크고 성공한 기업들이 경쟁업체가 아닌 저희 소프트웨어를 선택하는지 알게 되실 겁니다.**(182) 귀사에 어느 패키지가 적합한지 더 알아보시려면, '연락처' 탭을 클릭하셔서 영업사원과 상담하시기 바랍니다.

어휘 terms n. (합의·계약 등의) 조건 platform n. 플랫폼(사용 기반이 되는 컴퓨터 소프트웨어) startup n. 신생기업, 스타트업 corporation n. 기업 maximize v. 극대화하다 efficiency n. 효율성 productivity n. 생산성 connected adj. 연속된, 일관된 informed adj. 잘 아는 ideal adj. 이상적인 built-in adj. 내장된 function n. 기능 storage n. 저장공간 feature n. 기능, 특성 access n. 접근, 이용 status n. 상황, 상태 track v. 추적하다 on top of ~외에 feed n. 피드 one-on-one adj. 일대일의 video conferencing 화상 회의 시스템 plan n. 요금제 interactive adj. 상호적인, 상호작용을 하는 24/7 adj. 연중 무휴의 synchronize v. 동기화하다 trial n. 시도, 시험 competition n. 경쟁상대 sales associate 영업 사원

발신: p.malkin@capsun.ca
수신: a.crosby@looper.com
날짜: 5월 19일
제목: Looper 패키지

Ms. Crosby께,

제 이름은 Paul Malkin이고, 저는 Capsun산업의 최고 전략책임자입니다. 저희는 지난 5년 동안 Looper를 사용해왔으며, 저희의 성장에 있어 귀사의 소프트웨어가 얼마나 중요했는지는 아무리 강조해도 지나치지 않습니다.(185) 저희는 최근 확장 계획을 완료하여, 조만간 캐나다 전역에 1,300명 이상의 직원을 보유할 것입니다. 귀사에서 제공하는 클라우드 저장공간을 잘 활용해왔습니다만, 이제는 업무 진행상황을 추적할 더 좋은 방법 뿐만 아니라, 직원당 35GB 이상이 필요할 것입니다.(184) 여기에 맞는 것이 있으신가요?(183)

답장 기다리겠습니다.

Paul Malkin
최고 전략책임자
Capsun 산업

어휘 **chief strategy officer** 최고 전략책임자 **stress** v. 강조하다 **growth** n. 성장 **finalize** v. 마무리 짓다 **expand** v. 확장하다 **make use of** ~을 이용[활용]하다 **track** v. 추적하다 **progress** n. 진행상황 **tailored** adj. 맞춤의

181 암시/추론 난이도 중

해석 Looper 소프트웨어는 어떻게 사용되겠는가?
(A) 신입사원 모집을 위해
(B) 온라인 상품 광고를 위해
(C) 고객지원 제공을 위해
(D) 직원생산성 향상을 위해

해설 첫 번째 지문[웹 페이지], 첫 번째 단락에서 Our project management software will maximize your company's efficiency and productivity by keeping your employees connected and informed on your company's daily activities.(저희 프로젝트 관리 소프트웨어는 직원들이 서로 교류하고 사내 일상업무에 대한 알림을 받을 수 있게 해줘서 귀사의 효율성과 생산성을 극대화 해줄 것입니다.)라고 했으므로 (D)가 정답

Paraphrasing maximize → improve

182 사실확인 난이도 중

해석 Looper사에 관하여 사실인 것은?
(A) 제품들이 주요 기업들에 의해 사용된다.
(B) Capsun산업과 합병했다.
(C) 첫 소프트웨어 제품군이 5년 전에 출시되었다.
(D) 200명 이상의 직원이 있다.

해설 첫 번째 지문[웹 페이지], 여섯 번째 단락에서 By the end of your trial, you'll see why some of the largest and most successful companies in the world choose our software over the competition's.(무료체험이 끝날 때쯤에는 왜 세계에서 가장 크고 가장 성공한 기업들이 경쟁업체가 아닌 저희 소프트웨어를 선택하는지 알게 되실 겁니다.)라고 했으므로 (A)가 정답

Paraphrasing some of the largest and most successful companies in the world → major companies

183 주제/목적/대상 난이도 중

해석 이메일의 목적은 무엇인가?
(A) 제품 구매를 확정하는 것
(B) 제품 선택에 대한 조언을 구하는 것
(C) 프로그램 문제에 대해 불만을 제기하는 것
(D) 최신 사용자 매뉴얼을 요청하는 것

해설 두 번째 지문[이메일], 여섯 번째 줄에서 We've recently finalized plans to expand, and we will soon have over 1,300 staff members across Canada. We've made good use of the cloud storage that your company offers, but we're going to be needing more than 35 GB per employee now, as well as a better way to track work progress. Do you have anything that is tailored to this?(저희는 최근 확장 계획을 완료하여, 조만간 캐나다 전역에 1,300명 이상의 직원을 보유할 것입니다. 귀사에서 제공하는 클라우드 저장공간을 잘 활용해왔습니다만, 이제는 업무 진행상황을 추적할 더 좋은 방법 뿐만 아니라, 직원당 35GB 이상이 필요할 것입니다. 여기에 맞는 것이 있으신가요?)라고 했으므로 (B)가 정답

184 암시/추론 [연계문제] 난이도 중

해석 Ms. Crosby는 어느 제품을 추천하겠는가?
(A) 신생기업 패키지
(B) 프리미엄 패키지
(C) 기업 패키지
(D) 다국적 패키지

해설 두 번째 지문[이메일], 다섯 번째 줄에서 We've recently finalized plans to expand, and we will soon have over 1,300 staff members across Canada. We've made good use of the cloud storage that your company offers, but we're going to be needing more than 35 GB per employee now, as well as a better way to track work progress.(저희는 최근 확장 계획을 완료하여, 조만간 캐나다 전역에 1,300명 이상의 직원을 보유할 것입니다. 귀사에서 제공하는 클라우드 저장공간을 잘 활용해왔습니다만, 이제는 업무 진행상황을 추적할 더 좋은 방법 뿐만 아니라, 직원당 35GB 이상이 필요할 것입니다.)라고 했는데, 첫 번째 지문[웹 페이지], 다섯 번째 단락에서 MULTINATIONAL PACKAGE This plan is for companies with over 1,000 employees. In addition to all of the features from the Corporate Package, enjoy audio and video conferencing with up to 20 participants with interactive screen sharing, 24/7 customer support help, synchronized editing for documents, and 50 GB of storage for each employee.(직원 수 1,000명 이상인 기업을 위한 것입니다. 기업 패키지의 모든 기능 외에도, 양방향 화면공유 기능으로 최대 20명까지 참여할 수 있는 음성 및 화상 회의와 연중무휴 고객지원, 동기화된 문서 편집, 직원당 50GB의 저장공간을 이용하실 수 있습니다.)라고 했으므로 (D)가 정답

185 동의어 난이도 중

해석 이메일에서 첫 번째 단락, 두 번째 줄의 단어 "stress"와 의미상 가장 가까운 것은?
(A) 예상하다
(B) 걱정하다
(C) 강조하다
(D) 압력을 가하다

해설 두 번째 지문[이메일], 두 번째 줄의 I can't stress enough how important your software has been to our growth.(저희의 성장에 있어 귀사의 소프트웨어가 얼마나 중요했는지는 아무리 강조해도 지나치지 않습니다.)에서 'stress'는 '강조하다'라는 의미로 쓰였으므로 보기 중 같은 의미를 갖는 (C)가 정답

186-190번은 다음 이메일들과 요금표에 관한 문제입니다.

발신: Maggie Jones<maggiejones@albanytours.ca> [186]
수신: David Davis<daviddavis@orourkeschools.edu>
제목: 4월 대회 견적
날짜: 3월 6일
첨부: ORourke_4월.pdf; 오락옵션.pdf

안녕하세요, David.

지난 12월 수학여행 준비도 정말 즐겁게 해드렸는데, 이번 달 Edmonton Bears의 주 하키 플레이오프를 준비해드릴 기회도 주셔서 고맙습니다.[186]/[190] 제가 이해하기로 팀의 투숙 기간이 대회 진출 단계에 따라 결정될 것이라 무기한 예약이 필요한데, 저희가 대회 장소 인근에서 이러한 요청을 수용해줄 수 있는 호텔을 찾았습니다.[190]

아래에 요금을 상세히 설명해놓은 첨부문서가 있습니다. **그리고 지역 관광명소와 추천 액티비티를 설명하는 팸플릿도 몇 개 넣어드렸습니다.**[189]

계속 거래해주셔서 감사 드립니다.

Best,
Maggie B. Jones

어휘 **estimate** n. 견적서 **put together** (이것저것을 모아) 만들다, 준비하다 **make arrangements for** ~을 준비하다 **playoff** n. 우승결정전, 플레이오프 **venue** n. 장소 **meet** v. 충족시키다 **request** n. 요청 **open-ended** adj. (기간·수량 따위에) 제한이 없는 **reservation** n. 예약 **duration** n. 기간 **stay** n. 숙박 **determine** v. 결정하다 **reach** v. 이르다, 도달하다 **competition** n. 대회, 시합 **detail** v. 상세히 열거하다 **rate** n. 요금 **pamphlet** n. 팸플릿 **tourist attraction** 관광명소

Richview시 Alpine 호텔

체크인 날짜: 4월 21일[190]
투숙객: Edmonton Bears (학생 선수들, 팀 매니저들 및 코치들)
담당자: David Davis (818) 555-3143

대회 라운드	총 투숙기간	라운드별 총 객실요금
1라운드	5박	10,000달러
2라운드	4박	8,000달러
3라운드[190]	3박[190]	6,000달러[190]
결승	2박	4,000달러

요금은 매 경기가 끝날 때 지급하시기 바랍니다. **일일 단체요금은 1박에 2,000달러입니다.**[187]

어휘 **inn** n. 여관, 숙소 **athlete** n. 운동선수 **round** n. (스포츠 대회에서) 회전, 라운드 **charge** n. 요금 **due** adj. (돈을) 지불해야 하는

발신: David Davis<daviddavis@orourkeschools.edu>
수신: Maggie Jones<maggiejones@albanytours.ca>
날짜: 4월 27일[190]
제목: 4월 행사

Maggie께,

팀 여행의 최신 항목별 청구서를 보내주셔서 감사합니다. **제 비서가 오늘 오후에 당신의 사무실을 방문해서 합의한대로 6,000달러 수표를 전해드렸습니다.**[188]/[190] 여행과 관련해서 감사의 말씀을 드리고 싶습니다. 숙박과 식사, 교통의 모든 면이 매우 원활하게 진행되었고, 특히 **제안해주신 승마 투어가 정말 좋았습니다. 끝나고 팀원들이 동물과 사진을 찍으면서 아주 즐거운 시간을 보냈습니다.**[189]

다음 여행에 관해 곧 알려드리겠습니다. 10월이 될 것 같지만, 자세한 내용이 들어오면 알려드리겠습니다.

David Davis

어휘 **itemize** v. 항목별로 적다 **assistant** n. 비서 **drop off** 전달하다 **smoothly** adv. 순조롭게 **lodging** n. 숙박 **transportation** n. 교통 **afterwards** adv. 나중에, 후에 **fill ~ in** ~에게 지금까지 있은 일을 들려주다

---

186 암시/추론 난이도 중

해석 Ms. Jones는 누구겠는가?
(A) 하키 코치
(B) 호텔 직원
(C) 교직원
(D) 여행사 직원

해설 첫 번째 지문[Maggie Jones가 보낸 이메일], 첫 번째 단락에서 We really enjoyed putting together the school trip this past December, and we appreciate the opportunity to make arrangements for the Edmonton Bears for this month's Provincial Hockey Playoffs.(지난 12월 수학여행 준비도 정말 즐겁게 해드렸는데, 이번 달 Edmonton Bears의 주 하키 플레이오프를 준비해드릴 기회도 주셔서 고맙습니다.)라고 했으므로 (D)가 정답

187 사실확인 난이도 상

해석 Mr. Davis에게 발송된 객실 요금에 관하여 사실인 것은?
(A) 투숙기간에 따라 변경되지 않는다.
(B) 무료 아침식사를 포함한다.
(C) 스포츠팀에게만 제공된다.
(D) 최근에 인상되었다.

해설 두 번째 지문[요금표], 표에서 Your daily group rate is $2,000 per night.(일일 단체요금은 1박에 2,000달러입니다.)라고 하여 투숙기간에 상관없이 요금이 하루 2,000달러임을 알 수 있으므로 (A)가 정답

188 사실확인 난이도 중

해석 두 번째 이메일에 따르면, Mr. Davis의 지불에 관하여 언급된 것은?
(A) 만나서 지불되었다.
(B) 할부로 이루어졌다.
(C) 예상보다 높았다.
(D) 10월 여행 대금이었다.

해설 세 번째 지문[David Davis가 보낸 이메일], 첫 번째 단락에서 My assistant visited your office earlier in the afternoon and dropped off a check for $6,000 as agreed.(제 비서가 오늘 오후에 당신의 사무실을 방문해서 합의한대로 6,000달러 수표를 전해드렸습니다.)라고 했으므로 (A)가 정답

189 암시/추론 [연계문제] 난이도 상

해석 Mr. Davis는 Ms. Jones가 보낸 팸플릿으로 무엇을 했겠는가?
(A) 정보를 갱신했다.
(B) Edmonton Bears에 배포했다.
(C) 더 제작해줄 것을 요청했다.
(D) 동료에게 이메일로 보냈다.

해설 첫 번째 지문[Maggie Jones가 보낸 이메일], 두 번째 단락에서 I've also included some pamphlets describing local tourist attractions and recommended activities.(그리고 지역 관광명소와 추천 액티비티를 설명하는 팸플릿도 몇 개 넣어드렸습니다)라고 했는데, 세 번째 지문[David Davis가 보낸 이메일], 첫 번째 단락에서 and we especially loved the horse-riding tour you suggested. The team had so much fun taking photos with the animals afterwards.(특히 제안해주신 승마 투어가 정말 좋았습니다. 끝나고 팀원들이 동물과 사진을 찍으면서 아주 즐거운 시간을 보냈습니다.)라고 하여 Ms. Jones가 보내준 팸플릿을 Mr. Davis가 Edmonton Bears 팀원들에게 보여줬다는 것을 알 수 있으므로 (B)가 정답

190 상세정보 [연계문제] 난이도 상

해석 Edmonton Bears가 참가한 대회의 마지막 라운드는 무엇인가?
(A) 1라운드
(B) 2라운드
(C) 3라운드
(D) 결승

해설 세 번째 지문[David Davis가 보낸 이메일], 첫 번째 단락에서 My assistant visited your office earlier in the afternoon and dropped off a check for $6,000 as agreed.(제 비서가 오늘 오후에 당신의 사무실을 방문해서 합의한대로 6,000달러 수표를 전해드렸습니다.)라고 했는데, 두 번째 지문[요금표], 표에서 6,000달러의 객실요금에 해당하는 대회 라운드가 3라운드임을 알 수 있으므로 (C)가 정답

191-195번은 다음 기사, 웹 페이지, 온라인 주문서에 관한 문제입니다.

BROOKLYN (9월 25일) – 최근 출시된 앱이 Williamsburg 지역에서 사람들의 식습관을 변화시키고 있다. Thrive Fresh은 현지인 Jason Vernon이 시작한 음식 배달 앱이다. 앱은 사용자에게 다양한 현지 식당의 수백 가지 메뉴에 대한 영양 및 원산지 정보를 상세히 제공한다. 월 요금으로, 사용자의 주문내역을 추적할 수도 있고 필요 및 선호사항을 기반으로 식단 추천 또한 해준다.

Mr. Vernon은 전통적인 배달 음식이 얼마나 기름기가 많은 지 알아차렸을 때 이런 생각을 하게 되었다.(191) 제가 예전 직장동료들과 꽤 자주 야근을 했는데, 그때마다 음식을 주문하곤 했는데, 신선한 재료는 거의 없었어요. 저희 대부분은 먹는 것에 신경쓰려고 노력했지만 배달음식에 관해서라면 저희는 음지에 있었죠."

이에 대응하여 Mr. Vernon은 투명성과 건강을 촉진하는 시스템을 개발했다. Thrive Fresh는 유기농 음식만을 판매하는 현지 식품 제공업체들과 협력한다.(194) 매우 다양한 건강 옵션들과 저렴한 가격 덕분에 이 서비스는 거대한 단골 고객층을 구축할 수 있었다.(192) 앱은 아직 Williamsburg 지역 내 이용자들에게만 배달해 주지만 12월에는 New York시의 나머지 지역으로 확대될 것이다.(195)

어휘 recently adv. 최근에 launch v. 출시하다 app n. 앱 (application의 약어) way n. 방식, 방법 delivery n. 배달 local n. 현지인 access n. 입장 detailed adj. 상세한 nutritional adj. 영양상의 source v. (특정한 곳에서 무엇을) 얻다 diverse adj. 다양한 a range of 다양한 monthly adv. 매월 track v. 추적하다 order n. 주문 dietary adj. 식이요법의 recommendation n. 추천, 권고 need n. 필요, 요구 preference n. 선호 notice v. 알아차리다 greasy adj. 기름진 traditional adj. 전통의 tend v. 경향이 있다 former adj. 이전의 coworker n. 동료 stay v. 머무르다 hardly ever 거의 ~ 않는 fresh adj. 신선한 ingredient n. 재료 in response 이에 대응하여 develop v. 개발하다 promote v. 촉진하다, 고취하다 transparency n. 투명성, 명료성 wellness n. 건강(함) provider n. 제공자 exclusively adv. 독점적으로 sell v. 팔다 organic adj. 유기농의 dish n. 요리 a wide variety of 매우 다양한 healthy adj. 건강한 option n. 옵션, 선택권 affordable adj. (가격이) 알맞은 base n. 기초, 토대, 바탕 deliver v. 배달하다 expand v. 확장되다, 확대되다 rest n. 나머지

---

http://www.squawk.com/chakra

| 소개 | 후기 | 연락 | 예약 |

Chakra Indian Cuisine이 Thrive Fresh와 제휴한 새로운 서비스를 자랑스럽게 알려드립니다.(193)/(194) 거의 20년 간, 최첨단과 전통 조리법 모두를 활용한 고급 요리를 제공해 드리는 것이 저희의 사명이었습니다. 저희는 Thrive Fresh를 통해 더 많은 사람들에게 저희의 요리를 제공해 드리게 되어 기쁩니다.

물론, Broadway와 Leonard 근처에 위치한 Chakra Indian Cuisine의 새로 개조된 공간은 변함없이 매일 오전 11시부터 오후 9시까지 영업합니다. 그리고 언제나처럼, 저희 시그니처 맛을 내주는 허브와 향신료를 판매하는 Chakra 수입마켓은 화요일부터 토요일까지 옆 건물에서 영업할 것입니다.

어휘 proud adj. 자랑스러운 announce v. 알리다, 발표하다 in association with ~과 공동으로 mission n. 임무 finest adj. 질 높은 cuisine n. 요리(법) recipe n. 조리법 cutting edge adj. 최첨단의 traditional adj. 전통의 cooking n. 요리 sell v. 팔다 signature adj. 특징의 flavor n. 맛 remain v. 계속 ~이다 next door adv. 옆 집[건물]에

Thrive Fresh 주문 확인서

주문:

Manpasand 퀴노아 샐러드	7.00달러
시금치 코프타 카레	12.00달러
달 마카니	13.00달러
음식	32.00달러
회원 할인	-3.20달러
세금	1.06달러
총액	30.05달러

(신용카드로 문 앞 결제)

이름: Jill Klein(195)
주소: 169 Lynch St., Apartment 3B
전화번호: 718-555-9922
배달시간: 9월 29일, 14:35-14:50 사이(195)

어휘 confirmation n. 확인 quinoa n. 퀴노아 spinach n. 시금치 kofta n. 코프타(고기, 생선, 치즈로 만든 남아시아 지역 음식) curry n. 카레 Dal Makhani 달 마카니(렌즈콩, 버터, 크림 등으로 만든 인도요리) membership n. 회원 자격 discount n. 할인 payment n. 지불

---

191 주제/목적/대상 난이도 중

해석 기사는 주로 무엇에 관한 것인가?
(A) 어떤 식단이 독자들로 하여금 건강한 생활방식을 갖도록 도와줄 것인지
(B) 어디서 저렴한 가격대의 식료품을 살 수 있는 지
(C) 식사 서비스 앱이 어떻게 생겨났는지
(D) 식당이 왜 성공했는지

해설 첫 번째 지문[기사], 두 번째 단락에서 Mr. Vernon got the idea when he noticed how greasy the food from traditional delivery services tended to be(Mr. Vernon은 전통적인 배달 음식이 얼마나 기름기가 많은 지 알아차렸을 때 이런 생각을 하게 되었다.)라고 했으므로 (C)가 정답

192 상세정보 난이도 중

해석 기사에 따르면, Thrive Fresh가 인기 있는 이유는 무엇인가?
(A) 빠른 배송 시간
(B) 고품질 사용자 인터페이스
(C) 24시간 이용가능
(D) 합리적인 가격

해설 첫 번째 지문[기사], 세 번째 단락에서 Its wide variety of healthy options and affordable prices have helped the service build a large and loyal customer base.(매우 다양한 건강 옵션들과 저렴한 가격이 이 서비스가 거대한 단골 고객층을 가질 수 있게 해주었다.)라고 했으므로 (D)가 정답

Paraphrasing affordable prices ➡ reasonable prices

193 상세정보 난이도 중

해석 Chakra Indian Cuisine 홈페이지에 무엇이 발표되는가?
(A) 신규 지점
(B) 사업 제휴
(C) 구인 공고
(D) 곧 있을 보수작업

해설 두 번째 지문[웹 페이지], 첫 번째 단락에서 Chakra Indian Cuisine is proud to announce a new service in association with Thrive Fresh.(Chakra Indian Cuisine이 Thrive Fresh와 제휴한 새로운 서비스를 자랑스럽게 알려드립니다.)라고 했으므로 (B)가 정답

Paraphrasing association ➡ partnership

194 암시/추론 [연계 문제] 난이도 상

해석 Chakra Indian Cuisine에 관하여 무엇이 사실이겠는가?
(A) 유기농 음식만 판매한다.
(B) Thrive Fresh를 통해서만 이용할 수 있다.
(C) 20년 동안 영업해왔다.
(D) 여러 지점이 있다.

해설 첫 번째 지문[기사], 세 번째 단락에서 Thrive Fresh works with local food providers that exclusively sell organic dishes.(Thrive Fresh는 유기농 음식만 판매하는 현지 식품 제공업체들과 협력한다.)라고 했는데, 두 번째 지문[웹 페이지], 첫 번째 단락에서 Chakra Indian Cuisine is proud to announce a new service in association with Thrive Fresh. (Chakra Indian Cuisine이 Thrive Fresh와 제휴한 새로운 서비스를 자랑스럽게 알려드립니다.)라고 했으므로 (A)가 정답

195 암시/추론 [연계 문제] 난이도 중

해석 Ms. Klein에 관하여 알 수 있는 것은?
(A) 엄격한 영양 식단을 따른다.
(B) Mr. Vernon의 동료이다.
(C) Williamsburg에 산다.
(D) 9월 29일에 행사를 열 것이다.

해설 첫 번째 지문[기사], 세 번째 단락에서 The app still only delivers to users in the Williamsburg area but will expand to the rest of the New York area in December.(앱은 아직 Williamsburg 지역 내 이용자들에게만 배달해 주지만 12월에는 New York의 나머지 지역으로 확대될 것이다.)라고 했고, 세 번째 지문[Jill Klein의 온라인 주문확인서]에서 Delivery Time(배달시간)이 Between 14:35-14:50, September 29(9월 29일, 14:35-14:50 사이)로 되어 있어 Ms. Klein이 Williamsburg에 산다는 것을 알 수 있으므로 (C)가 정답

196-200번은 다음 온라인 양식, 이메일, 웹 페이지에 관한 문제입니다.

www.nguyensportswear.vn/service

다음 정보를 작성해주신 후에, 자세한 의견을 적어주세요. 저희가 더 나은 서비스를 제공해 드릴 수 있게 해주셔서 감사 드립니다.

이름: Hassina Boulmerka
이메일: hassina.b@elwatan.vn
전화번호: 514-555-1212

의견:
Ho chi Minh City에 첫 오프라인 매장이 생겼을 때부터 Nguyen Sportswear에서 물건을 구매해왔고, 항상 만족했습니다. 이런 이유로, 가장 최근에 주문한 물건에 놀라고 실망했습니다. 운동복 상의가 도착했을 때, 딱 봐도 전보다 더 저렴하고 덜 편안한 재질로 만들어졌다는 게 분명했습니다. 설상가상으로, 겨우 몇 번 입고 나니 팔꿈치 쪽 소매 천이 닳아서 터져버렸습니다!(196)

어휘 fill out 작성하다 detailed adj. 자세한, 상세한 serve v. (손님의 구매에) 도움을 주다 purchase v. 구매하다 disappointed adj. 실망한 sweatshirt n. 운동복 상의, 스웻셔츠 clear adj. 분명한, 명백한 right away 곧바로 comfortable adj. 편안한 wear v. (옷을) 입다 sleeve n. 소매 elbow n. 팔꿈치 wear down 마모되다 tear v. 찢어지다

수신: hassina.b@elwatan.vn
발신: ggruber@nguyensportswear.vn
날짜: 5월 23일
제목: 고객님의 의견

Ms. Boulmerka께,

귀하의 가장 최근의 경험이 긍정적이지 못했다는 것을 알게 되어 유감입니다. 훨씬 더 낮은 가격에 고객들이 요구하는 품질을 제공하려는 바람으로, 저희는 최근 일부 제조 공정을 다른 회사에 위탁했습니다.(197) 저희의 기준이 충족되지 않아, 저희는 현재의 방식을 재평가하는 중입니다.

초기 구매하신 물품가격에 해당하는 상품권을 보내드리며, 사과와 감사의 표시로 저희 인기상품 중 하나인 495-Z 운동복 상의도 무료로 드리고자 합니다.(200) 내구성이 강한 특별 직물로 만들어진 이 제품은(198) 극한의 환경을 견딜 수 있고 오래 사용하실 수 있음을 보장합니다. 이 이메일에 답장으로 원하시는 사이즈와 색상을 알려주세요.(199)

앞으로도 계속 저희와 거래해주시기 바랍니다.

Best Regards,

Glenn Gruber
고객서비스 직원

어휘 outsource v. 외부에 위탁하다 arrangement n. (처리) 방식 voucher n. 할인권, 쿠폰 equal to ~과 동일한 free of charge 무료로 apology n. 사과 token n. 표시, 징표 appreciation n. 감사

durable adj. 내구성 있는 guarantee v. 보장하다 endure v. 견디다 extreme adj. 극도의, 극단적인 last v. 지속되다 reply v. 답장을 보내다 desired adj. 바랐던, 희망했던 do business with ~와 거래하다

www.nguyensportswear.vn/products/Z

Z 시리즈는 운동 또는 야외활동에 완벽한 의복입니다. 이 멋진 운동복 상의는 다음 종류 중에 주문하실 수 있습니다.

제품 번호	스타일	가격
225-Z	크루넥	33.00달러
315-Z	브이넥	33.00달러
405-Z	버튼다운	41.00달러
495-Z(200)	후드(200)	44.00달러

어휘 attire n. 의복, 복장 outdoor adj. 야외의 variation n. 변화, 차이 crew-neck adj. 크루넥의(옷의 목 주변이 둥근) v-neck adj. 브이넥의 button-down adj. 단추로 채우게 되어 있는 hooded adj. 모자가 달린

196 상세정보   난이도 중

해석 Ms. Boulmerka의 주요 문제는 무엇인가?
(A) 가격이 인상되었다.
(B) 제품의 품질이 저하되었다.
(C) 주문품이 늦게 배송되었다.
(D) 웹 사이트가 작동하지 않았다.

해설 '첫 번째 지문[온라인 양식], Feedback(의견)에서 Once the sweatshirt arrived, it was clear right away that it was made from a cheaper—and less comfortable—material than before. (운동복 상의가 도착했을 때, 딱 봐도 전보다 더 저렴하고 덜 편안한 재질로 만들어졌다는 게 분명했습니다.)라고 했으므로 (B)가 정답

197 암시/추론   난이도 중

해석 Nguyen Sportswear의 일부 상품에 관하여 알 수 있는 것은?
(A) 다른 제품군보다 더 낮은 가격에 판매되었다.
(B) 다른 회사에서 생산했다.
(C) 선수용으로 디자인되지 않았다.
(D) 현재 재고가 없다.

해설 두 번째 지문[이메일], 첫 번째 단락에서 In hopes of providing the quality our clients require at even lower prices, we recently outsourced some of our manufacturing operations to another firm.(훨씬 더 낮은 가격에 고객들이 요구하는 품질을 제공하려는 바람으로, 저희는 최근 일부 제조 운영을 다른 회사에 위탁했습니다.)라고 하여 일부 상품을 다른 회사에서 생산했음을 알 수 있으므로 (B)가 정답

Paraphrasing firm ➡ company

198 사실확인   난이도 상

해석 Z 시리즈에 관하여 언급된 것은?
(A) 다른 제품들보다 더 빨리 닳는다.
(B) Ho chi Minh City에서 제조되었다.
(C) 독특한 재료로 만들어진다.
(D) 최근에 새로운 옵션을 추가했다.

해설 두 번째 지문[이메일], 두 번째 단락에서 we would also like to offer you one of our popular 495-Z sweatshirts, free of charge, as an apology and a token of our appreciation. This item, created from our special durable fabric,(사과와 감사의 표시로 저희 인기 상품 중 하나인 495-Z 운동복 상의도 무료로 드리고자 합니다. 내구성이 강한 특별 직물로 만들어진 이 제품은)이라고 했으므로 (C)가 정답

Paraphrasing created from ➡ made of,
                 special fabric ➡ unique material

199 상세정보   난이도 중

해석 Ms. Boulmerka는 무엇을 하라고 요청 받는가?
(A) 주문 선호 사항을 알려달라고
(B) 매장에 들르라고
(C) 다른 신용카드를 사용하라고
(D) 의류제품을 반품하라고

해설 두 번째 지문[이메일], 두 번째 단락에서 Simply reply to this e-mail with your desired size and color.(이 이메일에 답장으로 원하시는 사이즈와 색상을 알려주세요.)라고 했으므로 (A)가 정답

Paraphrasing desired size and color ➡ order preferences

200 상세정보 [연계문제]   난이도 중

해석 Mr. Gruber는 Ms. Boulmerka에게 어떤 종류의 운동복 상의를 제공하는가?
(A) 크루넥
(B) 브이넥
(C) 버튼다운
(D) 후드

해설 두 번째 지문[이메일], 두 번째 단락에서 We are sending you a voucher for an amount equal to that of your original purchase, and we would also like to offer you one of our popular 495-Z sweatshirts, free of charge, as an apology and a token of our appreciation.(초기 구매하신 물품가격에 해당하는 상품권을 보내드리며, 사과와 감사의 표시로 저희 인기상품 중 하나인 495-Z 운동복 상의도 무료로 드리고자 합니다.)라고 했는데, 세 번째 지문[웹 페이지], 표에서 495-Z 상품의 스타일이 Hooded(후드)임을 알 수 있으므로 (D)가 정답

TEST 04

PART 1　　　　　　　　　　　　　　P. 148

1 (D)	2 (C)	3 (B)	4 (B)	5 (C)	6 (D)

PART 2　　　　　　　　　　　　　　P. 152

7 (C)	8 (A)	9 (C)	10 (A)	11 (A)	12 (A)
13 (B)	14 (C)	15 (A)	16 (C)	17 (C)	18 (C)
19 (B)	20 (B)	21 (A)	22 (B)	23 (A)	24 (A)
25 (C)	26 (A)	27 (C)	28 (A)	29 (C)	30 (B)
31 (A)					

PART 3　　　　　　　　　　　　　　P. 153

32 (C)	33 (D)	34 (A)	35 (B)	36 (A)	37 (C)
38 (D)	39 (C)	40 (C)	41 (B)	42 (A)	43 (B)
44 (D)	45 (B)	46 (B)	47 (C)	48 (C)	49 (D)
50 (D)	51 (D)	52 (A)	53 (B)	54 (B)	55 (D)
56 (A)	57 (B)	58 (A)	59 (A)	60 (C)	61 (D)
62 (B)	63 (A)	64 (C)	65 (D)	66 (C)	67 (B)
68 (D)	69 (D)	70 (D)			

PART 4　　　　　　　　　　　　　　P. 157

71 (A)	72 (A)	73 (A)	74 (C)	75 (B)	76 (C)
77 (D)	78 (D)	79 (B)	80 (C)	81 (A)	82 (B)
83 (C)	84 (A)	85 (B)	86 (C)	87 (A)	88 (B)
89 (D)	90 (C)	91 (C)	92 (D)	93 (A)	94 (A)
95 (C)	96 (D)	97 (D)	98 (B)	99 (C)	100 (B)

PART 5　　　　　　　　　　　　　　P. 160

101 (D)	102 (C)	103 (B)	104 (A)	105 (B)	106 (C)
107 (B)	108 (B)	109 (D)	110 (D)	111 (A)	112 (B)
113 (B)	114 (C)	115 (C)	116 (B)	117 (A)	118 (A)
119 (C)	120 (C)	121 (D)	122 (B)	123 (A)	124 (B)
125 (B)	126 (B)	127 (C)	128 (D)	129 (B)	130 (C)

PART 6　　　　　　　　　　　　　　P. 163

131 (B)	132 (C)	133 (D)	134 (D)	135 (C)	136 (B)
137 (D)	138 (D)	139 (C)	140 (C)	141 (B)	142 (A)
143 (D)	144 (A)	145 (D)	146 (A)		

PART 7　　　　　　　　　　　　　　P. 167

147 (C)	148 (A)	149 (D)	150 (B)	151 (C)	152 (B)
153 (C)	154 (C)	155 (A)	156 (B)	157 (D)	158 (A)
159 (B)	160 (C)	161 (C)	162 (B)	163 (B)	164 (B)
165 (D)	166 (A)	167 (C)	168 (B)	169 (B)	170 (B)
171 (D)	172 (A)	173 (D)	174 (A)	175 (A)	176 (B)
177 (B)	178 (C)	179 (D)	180 (A)	181 (A)	182 (C)
183 (D)	184 (A)	185 (B)	186 (B)	187 (C)	188 (B)
189 (A)	190 (A)	191 (B)	192 (B)	193 (A)	194 (B)
195 (C)	196 (C)	197 (C)	198 (D)	199 (A)	200 (C)

PART 1　　　　　　　　　　　　　　P. 148

1　1인 중심　　　　　　　　　　　난이도 하

미국

(A) A woman is writing with a pen.
(B) A woman is arranging books on a shelf.
(C) A woman is setting her glasses on a desk.
(D) A woman is typing on a computer.

(A) 여자가 펜으로 글을 쓰고 있다.
(B) 여자가 책꽂이 위의 책들을 정리하고 있다.
(C) 여자가 책상 위에 안경을 놓고 있다.
(D) 여자가 컴퓨터로 타이핑하고 있다.

해설　(A) ✗ 동작 묘사 오류 (is writing)
　　　(B) ✗ 동작 묘사 오류 (is arranging)
　　　(C) ✗ 동작 묘사 오류 (is setting)
　　　(D) ◎ 여자가 컴퓨터로 타이핑하고 있는 모습을 적절히 묘사했으므로 정답

Possible Answer
She's seated in front of a laptop. 여자가 노트북 컴퓨터 앞에 앉아 있다.

어휘　**arrange** v. 정리하다, 배열하다　**set** v. (특정한 위치에) 놓다

2　2인 이상　　　　　　　　　　　난이도 중

영국

(A) Some people are packing a suitcase.
(B) Some people are looking out a window.
(C) One of the people is pulling a piece of luggage.
(D) One of the people is opening a briefcase.

(A) 몇몇 사람들이 여행 가방을 싸고 있다.
(B) 몇몇 사람들이 창 밖을 내다보고 있다.
(C) 사람들 중 한 명이 짐을 끌고 있다.
(D) 사람들 중 한 명이 서류 가방을 열고 있다.

해설　(A) ✗ 동작 묘사 오류 (are packing)
　　　(B) ✗ 동작 묘사 오류 (are looking out)

(C) ◯ 사람들 중 한 명이 짐을 끌고 있는 모습을 적절히 묘사했으므로 정답
(D) ✗ 동작 묘사 오류 (is opening)

Possible Answer
Some people are talking to each other. 몇몇 사람들이 서로 이야기를 나누고 있다.

어휘　pack v. (짐 등을) 싸다　suitcase n. 여행가방　luggage n. 짐[수하물]　set down ~을 내려놓다　briefcase n. 서류가방

3　1인 중심　난이도 중

미국

(A) He's putting some papers into a photocopier.
(B) He's holding down a book.
(C) He's plugging in a power cord.
(D) He's turning off some equipment.

(A) 남자가 복사기에 종이를 넣고 있다.
(B) 남자가 책을 누르고 있다.
(C) 남자가 전원 코드에 플러그를 꽂고 있다.
(D) 남자가 몇몇 장비를 끄고 있다.

해설　(A) ✗ 동작 묘사 오류 (is put some papers into)
(B) ◯ 남자가 책을 누르고 있는 모습을 적절히 묘사했으므로 정답
(C) ✗ 동작 묘사 오류 (is plugging in), 사진에 없는 사물 (a power cord)
(D) ✗ 동작 묘사 오류 (is turning off)

Possible Answer
A book is being photocopied. 책이 복사되고 있다.

어휘　put v. 놓다[두다]　photocopier n. 복사기　hold down 누르다　plug in 플러그를 꽂다　power cord 전원 코드　equipment n. 장비

4　1인 중심　난이도 중

호주

(A) He's using a power tool.
(B) He's removing some carpet from the floor.
(C) He's fastening a safety mask.
(D) He's installing some cables in a room.

(A) 남자가 전동공구를 사용하고 있다.
(B) 남자가 바닥에서 카펫을 제거하고 있다.
(C) 남자가 방독면을 잡아매고 있다.
(D) 남자가 방에 케이블을 설치하고 있다.

해설　(A) ✗ 사진에 없는 내용 (power tool)
(B) ◯ 남자가 바닥에서 카펫을 치우고 있는 모습을 적절히 묘사했으므로 정답
(C) ✗ 동작 묘사 오류 (is fastening)
(D) ✗ 동작 묘사 오류 (is installing)

Possible Answer
A man is wearing some gloves. 남자가 장갑을 끼고 있다.

어휘　power tool 전동공구　remove v. 제거하다, 치우다　fasten v. 매다, 채우다　install v. 설치하다

5　사물/풍경　난이도 중

미국

(A) A metal railing is being repaired.
(B) A pedestrian is crossing a street.
(C) Some bicycles are parked next to a road.
(D) Some passengers are boarding a bus.

(A) 금속 난간이 수리되고 있다.
(B) 보행자가 길을 건너고 있다.
(C) 몇몇 자전거들이 도로 옆에 주차되어 있다.
(D) 몇몇 승객들이 버스에 탑승하고 있다.

해설　(A) ✗ 동작 묘사 오류 (is being repaired)
(B) ✗ 사진에 없는 사람 (pedestrian)
(C) ◯ 자전거 몇 대가 도로 옆 난간에 놓여 있는 모습을 적절히 묘사했으므로 정답
(D) ✗ 사진에 없는 사람 (passengers)

Possible Answer
Some bicycles are against a railing. 자전거들이 난간 가까이에 있다.

어휘　metal n. 금속　railing n. 난간　repair v. 수리하다　pedestrian n. 보행자　cross v. (길을) 건너다　park v. 주차하다　next to ~옆에　passenger n. 승객　board v. 탑승하다

6　2인 이상　난이도 중

영국

(A) A woman is taking a seat at a café.
(B) A man is serving a beverage in a bottle.
(C) A patron is carrying a tray to a table.
(D) A worker is standing behind a glass counter.

(A) 여자가 카페에서 자리에 앉고 있다.
(B) 남자가 병에 담긴 음료를 서빙하고 있다.
(C) 고객이 쟁반을 테이블로 가져가고 있다.
(D) 직원이 유리 카운터 뒤에 서 있다.

해설　(A) ✗ 동작 묘사 오류 (is taking a seat)
(B) ✗ 동작 묘사 오류 (serving a beverage in a bottle)
(C) ✗ 동작 묘사 오류 (is carrying)
(D) ◯ 직원이 유리 카운터 뒤에 서 있는 모습을 적절히 묘사했으므로 정답

Possible Answer
A man has put on a pair of glasses. 남자가 안경을 착용했다.

어휘　take a seat 자리에 앉다　beverage n. 음료　patron n. (상점 등의) 고객　carry v. 나르다　tray n. 쟁반　stand v. 서 있다

TEST 04

PART 2
P. 152

7 Where 의문문 난이도 하

미국↔미국

Where can I buy a good camera?
(A) By a renowned photographer.
(B) Just as good as I had hoped.
(C) There's a place across the street.

어디서 좋은 카메라를 살 수 있을까요?
(A) 유명한 사진작가가요.
(B) 제가 바랐던 대로 좋네요.
(C) 길 건너편에 상점이 있어요.

해설 (A) ✗ 연상 어휘 함정 (camera – photographer), 유사 발음 함정 (buy – by)
(B) ✗ 동어 반복 함정 (good – good)
(C) ◯ 길 건너편 상점이 있다며 위치로 말했으므로 정답

Possible Answer
You should ask Na-Ri. 나리에게 물어보세요.

어휘 renowned adj. 유명한, 명성 있는

8 When 의문문 난이도 하

미국↔호주

When will the computer parts be shipped out?
(A) By the end of the week.
(B) Through a shipping company.
(C) For a new computer monitor.

컴퓨터 부품은 언제 발송될까요?
(A) 이번 주말까지는 될 거예요.
(B) 운송회사를 통해서요.
(C) 새 컴퓨터 모니터용이에요.

해설 (A) ◯ 이번 주말까지라며 시점으로 말했으므로 정답
(B) ✗ 유사 발음 함정 (shipped – shipping)
(C) ✗ 동어 반복 함정 (computer – computer)

Possible Answer
They've already been sent. 이미 보냈어요.

어휘 part n. 부품 ship v. 출하하다 shipping company 운송회사, 택배회사

9 Why 의문문 난이도 중

영국↔미국

Why didn't the managers report the budget update to the CEO?
(A) Yes, the financial advisors were here.
(B) No, that was last Wednesday.
(C) Because they are still working on it.

매니저들이 왜 CEO에게 개정 예산안을 보고하지 않았나요?
(A) 네, 재정 고문들이 계셨습니다.
(B) 아니요, 그건 지난 주 수요일이었습니다.
(C) 아직 작업하는 중이니까요.

해설 (A) 의문사 의문문 Yes/No 응답 불가, 연상 어휘 함정 (budget – financial)
(B) ✗ 의문사 의문문 Yes/No 응답 불가
(C) ◯ 아직 작업하는 중이라며 이유로 말했으므로 정답

Possible Answer
They're still in a meeting. 아직 회의 중이세요.

어휘 financial advisor 재정 고문

10 선택 의문문 난이도 하

호주↔영국

Are you signing up for the two-week or the three-week course?
(A) The two-week course.
(B) She'll be out of town for four weeks.
(C) Mr. Bryant took the test.

신청하실 과정이 2주 과정인가요, 아니면 3주 과정인가요?
(A) 2주 과정이요.
(B) 그녀는 4주 내내 출장 가 있을 거예요.
(C) Mr. Bryant가 그 시험을 봤어요.

해설 (A) ◯ 2주 과정이라며 선자로 말했으므로 정답
(B) ✗ 주어 불일치 함정 (you – she), 연상 어휘 함정 (two week, three week – four weeks)
(C) 연상 어휘 함정 (course – test)

Possible Answer
I'm still thinking about it. 아직 결정 못했어요.

어휘 sign up for ~을 신청[가입]하다 be out of town (출장 등으로) 도시를 떠나 있다

11 일반 의문문 난이도 하

미국↔미국

Do you have a receipt for this purchase?
(A) Yes, it's right here.
(B) I received the order.
(C) At the shopping mall.

이 구매품의 영수증 가지고 있으세요?
(A) 네, 여기 있어요.
(B) 주문품을 받았어요.
(C) 쇼핑몰에서요.

해설 (A) ◯ 'Yes'로 대답하고, 여기 있다며 적절히 덧붙여 말했으므로 정답
(B) ✗ 연상 어휘 함정 (purchase - order), 유사 발음 함정 (receipt – received)
(C) ✗ 연상 어휘 함정 (receipt, purchase - shopping mall)

Possible Answer
No, I didn't get one. 아니요, 받지 못했는데요.

어휘 receipt n. 영수증 purchase n. 구매품

12 평서문 난이도 중

미국↔호주

I have to pick up the clients from the airport tomorrow afternoon.
(A) I see. Then I'll lead the meeting for you.
(B) Thursday's delivery.
(C) Thank you for putting it up.

내일 오후에 공항에 가서 고객들을 모셔와야 해요.
(A) 그렇군요. 그럼 제가 대신 회의를 주재할게요.
(B) 목요일 배송이요.
(C) 게시해 줘서 고마워요.

해설 (A) ◯ 'I see'로 대답하고, 회의를 대신 주재하겠다며 적절히 덧붙여 말했으므로 정답
(B) ✗ 연상 어휘 함정 (pick up – delivery)
(C) ✗ 동어 반복 함정 (up – up), 유사 발음 함정 (pick up – putting it up)

Possible Answer
Didn't they postpone their flight? 비행을 연기하지 않았나요?

어휘 **pick up** ~를 (차에) 태우러 가다 **lead** v. 지휘[인솔]하다 **put up** 내붙이다[게시하다] **postpone** v. 연기하다

어휘 **celebrate** v. 축하[기념]하다 **retirement** n. (정년) 퇴직, 은퇴 **nearby** adv. 인근에, 가까운 곳에 **make a reservation** 예약하다

13 What 의문문   난이도 하

영국→미국

What time is the next shuttle to San Francisco departing?
(A) At the downtown terminal.
(B) In 30 minutes.
(C) More than 10 dollars.

San Francisco로 가는 다음 셔틀은 몇 시에 출발하나요?
(A) 시내 터미널에서요.
(B) 30분 후에요.
(C) 10달러 이상입니다.

해설 (A) ✘ 연상 어휘 함정 (shuttle – terminal)
(B) ◯ 30분 후라며 시점으로 말했으므로 정답
(C) ✘ How much 의문문에 어울리는 대답

Possible Answer
Refer to the timetable on the wall. 벽에 있는 시간표를 참고하세요.

어휘 **depart** v. 출발하다

14 선택의문문   난이도 상

호주→영국

Would you prefer having the meeting at our office or at our client's?
(A) Let's get five more chairs.
(B) New clients from last month.
(C) I'd rather stay here.

회의를 우리 사무실에서 할까요, 아니면 고객 사무실에서 할까요?
(A) 의자를 다섯 개 더 가져오도록 하죠.
(B) 지난 달에 새로 온 고객들이요.
(C) 여기 있는 게 낫겠어요.

해설 (A) ✘ 연상 어휘 함정 (meeting, office – chairs)
(B) ✘ 동어 반복 함정 (client's – clients)
(C) ◯ 여기 있겠다며 전자로 말했으므로 정답

Possible Answer
Our office is being cleaned at the moment. 우리 사무실은 지금 청소 중이에요.

어휘 **client** n. 고객 **rather** adv. 오히려, 차라리

15 Where 의문문   난이도 하

미국→미국

Where are we celebrating Barbara's retirement this Friday?
(A) At an Italian restaurant nearby.
(B) To celebrate her birthday.
(C) For 25 years.

이번 주 금요일에 어디에서 Barbara의 은퇴를 축하해줄 건가요?
(A) 인근 이탈리아 식당에서요.
(B) 그녀의 생일을 축하해 주려구요.
(C) 25년 동안이요.

해설 (A) ◯ 인근 이탈리아 식당이라며 장소로 말했으므로 정답
(B) ✘ Why 의문문에 어울리는 대답, 동어 반복 함정 (celebrating – celebrate)
(C) ✘ How long 의문문에 어울리는 대답, 연상 어휘 함정 (retirement – 25 years)

Possible Answer
I made a reservation at Spring Bistro. Spring Bistro에 예약했어요.

16 제안/요청   난이도 하

미국→호주

Could you send me a copy of the proposal?
(A) Monday afternoon.
(B) I went to the copy center.
(C) OK, I'll do that for you.

저에게 제안서 사본 한 부를 보내주시겠어요?
(A) 월요일 오후요.
(B) 제가 복사실에 갔어요.
(C) 네, 그렇게 해 드릴게요.

해설 (A) ✘ When 의문문에 어울리는 대답
(B) ✘ 동어 반복 함정 (copy – copy)
(C) ◯ 'OK'로 대답하고, 그렇게 해준다고 적절히 덧붙여 말했으므로 정답

Possible Answer
I haven't finished it yet. 아직 끝나지 못했어요.

어휘 **copy** n. 복사본 **proposal** n. 제안서

17 Who 의문문   난이도 하

영국→미국

Who are you baking the cake for?
(A) By tomorrow morning.
(B) OK, I can pick it up.
(C) A customer from Southport.

누구를 위해 케이크를 굽고 계신 거예요?
(A) 내일 오전까지요.
(B) 알겠어요, 제가 갖다 드릴게요.
(C) Southport의 고객이요.

해설 (A) ✘ When 의문문에 어울리는 대답
(B) ✘ 의문사 의문문 Yes/No 응답 불가
(C) ◯ Southport의 고객이라며 명칭으로 대답했으므로 정답

Possible Answer
It's for Meadow Farm's anniversary celebration. Meadow Farm의 기념일 행사용이에요.

어휘 **bake** v. (음식을) 굽다 **customer** n. 고객

18 When 의문문   난이도 중

호주→영국

When did they decide to move our office?
(A) To make the commute more convenient.
(B) No, I don't think we should.
(C) Weren't you at yesterday's meeting?

그들이 우리 사무실을 언제 옮기기로 결정한 건가요?
(A) 통근을 더 편리하게 하기 위해서요.
(B) 아니요, 우리가 그래야 한다고 생각하지 않아요.
(C) 어제 회의에 안 계셨어요?

해설 (A) ✘ 연상 어휘 함정 (office – commute)
(B) ✘ 의문사 의문문 Yes/No 응답 불가
(C) ◯ 어제 회의에 없었냐고 반문하며 회의에서 알려줬음을 우회적으로 말했으므로 정답

Possible Answer
At the meeting last week. 지난주 회의에서요.

어휘 **commute** n. 통근 **convenient** adj. 편리한, 간편한

19 Why 의문문 난이도 중

미국↔미국

Why did you take a day off yesterday?
(A) Not until I speak with Annie.
(B) Because I had to go see my dentist.
(C) I'll probably be back on Friday.

어제 왜 휴가를 내셨어요?
(A) Annie와 먼저 얘기해 봐야 될 걸요.
(B) 치과 진료를 받아야 했거든요.
(C) 저는 아마 금요일에 돌아올 거예요.

해설 (A) ✗ When 의문문에 어울리는 대답, 질문과 무관한 대답
(B) ○ 치과 진료를 받아야 하기 때문이라며 이유로 말했으므로 정답
(C) ✗ 연상 어휘 함정 (day off yesterday – be back on Friday)

Possible Answer
I was at my desk. 자리에 있었는데요.

어휘 take a day off 하루 휴가를 얻다 not until ~이후에야 비로소 be back (~까지는) 돌아오다 feel well 건강 상태가 좋다

20 제안/요청 난이도 중

미국↔호주

Can you send me Mr. Rashid's updated contact information?
(A) Here's my business card.
(B) Sure. I'll take care of it right away.
(C) He's been there too.

Mr. Rashid의 최신 연락처를 보내 주시겠어요?
(A) 여기 제 명함이요.
(B) 물론이죠. 지금 바로 드릴게요.
(C) 그분도 거기 가 보셨어요.

해설 (A) ✗ 연상 어휘 함정 (contact information – business card)
(B) ○ 'Sure'로 대답하고, 지금 바로 드린다며 적절히 덧붙여 말했으므로 정답
(C) ✗ 질문과 무관한 대답

Possible Answer
I already emailed it to you. 이미 이메일로 보내드렸어요.

어휘 updated adj. 최신의 contact information 연락처 business card 명함 take care of ~을 처리[해결]하다 right away 즉시[곧바로]

21 부가 의문문 난이도 중

영국↔미국

You didn't bring your laptop with you, did you?
(A) No, but Sam brought his.
(B) Around two thousand dollars.
(C) Many high-tech features.

노트북 안 가져오셨죠, 그렇죠?
(A) 네, 그런데 Sam은 가져왔어요.
(B) 2,000달러 정도요.
(C) 여러 가지 최첨단 기능이요.

해설 (A) ○ 'No'로 대답하고 Sam은 가져왔다며 적절히 덧붙여 말했으므로 정답
(B) ✗ How much 의문문에 어울리는 대답
(C) ✗ 연상 어휘 함정 (laptop – high-tech features)

Possible Answer
Melanie said I could use hers. Melanie가 본인 것을 쓰라고 했어요.

어휘 bring v. 가져오다 high-tech adj. 최첨단의 feature n. 특징, 특성

22 Who 의문문 난이도 하

호주↔영국

Who could I speak with about my ID badge?
(A) May 2nd.
(B) Ms. Song in Maintenance.
(C) The registration forms are online.

제 사원증에 대해서는 누구에게 얘기하면 되나요?
(A) 5월 2일이요.
(B) 시설관리부의 Ms. Song이요.
(C) 신청서는 인터넷에 있어요.

해설 (A) ✗ When 의문문에 어울리는 대답
(B) ○ 시설관리부의 Ms. Song이라며 사람 이름으로 말했으므로 정답
(C) ✗ 연상 어휘 함정 (ID badge – registration forms)

Possible Answer
Sorry. I'm new here. 미안해요. 저는 신입사원입니다.

어휘 speak with ~와 이야기를 나누다 ID badge 신분증 maintenance n. 유지관리 registration form 신청서

23 평서문 난이도 중

미국↔미국

Please mind the gap when you exit the airplane.
(A) Thanks. I'll watch out.
(B) No, I don't mind.
(C) I took a cab to the airport.

비행기에서 내리실 때 틈새를 조심하세요.
(A) 고맙습니다. 주의할게요.
(B) 아니요, 상관없어요.
(C) 공항까지는 택시를 타고 갔어요.

해설 (A) ○ 고맙다고 하며 주의하겠다고 적절히 덧붙여 말했으므로 정답
(B) ✗ 동어 반복 함정 (mind – mind)
(C) ✗ 유사 발음 함정 (airplane – airport, gab – cab)

Possible Answer
Thanks for letting me know. 알려주셔서 고마워요.

어휘 mind v. 조심하다, 상관하다 exit v. 나가다, 떠나다 watch out 주의하다 cab n. 택시

24 Why 의문문 난이도 중

미국↔호주

Why aren't you going to the workshop with Joe and Bonnie?
(A) Because I will be away on holiday.
(B) They work in the shop next door.
(C) No, only for directors.

왜 Joe와 Bonnie와 함께 워크숍에 가지 않으세요?
(A) 제가 휴가 중일 거라서요.
(B) 그들은 옆 건물 상점에서 일해요.
(C) 아니요, 임원만 대상이에요.

해설 (A) ○ 휴가 중이어서 워크숍에 같이 못 갈 거라고 이유를 들며 말했으므로 정답
(B) ✗ 유사 발음 함정 (workshop – work, shop)
(C) ✗ 의문사 의문문 Yes/No 응답 불가

Possible Answer
I wasn't invited. 저는 초대받지 못했어요.

어휘 on holiday 휴가 중인 next door 옆 건물[집]

25 부정 의문문 난이도 상

Don't you want to rehearse your presentation before the orientation?
(A) Thanks for the thoughtful present.
(B) At the performance center down the block.
(C) Paul is training the new recruits.

오리엔테이션 전에 프레젠테이션을 연습하고 싶지 않으세요?
(A) 정성스런 선물 감사해요.
(B) 한 블록 아래에 있는 공연장에서요.
(C) 신입직원 교육은 Paul이 하고 있어요.

해설 (A) ✗ 유사 발음 함정 (presentation – present)
(B) ✗ Where 의문문에 어울리는 정답, 연상 어휘 함정 (rehearse – performance)
(C) ○ Paul이 신입직원 교육을 한다며 본인이 프레젠테이션을 하지 않음을 우회적으로 말했으므로 정답

Possible Answer
Yes, I'll be there in five minutes. 네, 5분 내로 갈게요.

어휘 rehearse v. 리허설[예행연습]을 하다 orientation n. 예비교육 thoughtful adj. 배려심 있는, 친절한 train v. 교육하다 recruit n. (조직 등의) 새로운 구성원, 신입 사원

26 How 의문문 난이도 중

How will you get to the awards ceremony?
(A) Angela is giving me a ride.
(B) For highest number of sales this year.
(C) At the Marbella Hotel banquet room.

시상식에 어떻게 가실 건가요?
(A) Angela가 절 태워줄 거예요.
(B) 올해 최고 판매량에 대해서요.
(C) Marbella 호텔 연회장에서요.

해설 (A) ○ Angela가 태워준다며 방법으로 말했으므로 정답
(B) ✗ 연상 어휘 함정 (awards – highest number of sales)
(C) ✗ Where 의문문에 어울리는 정답, 연상 어휘 함정 (awards ceremony – banquet room)

Possible Answer
It has been canceled. 그것은 취소되었어요.

어휘 get to ~에 닿다, 도착하다 awards ceremony 시상식 give a ride 태워주다 sales n. 매출(량) banquet room 연회장

27 부가 의문문 난이도 상

Consumers seem to be pleased with our new car model, right?
(A) They'll travel by public transportation.
(B) A new company vehicle policy.
(C) I haven't read the reviews yet.

소비자들이 우리 신형 자동차 모델에 만족하는 것 같아요, 그렇죠?
(A) 그들은 대중교통으로 이동할 거예요.
(B) 새로운 회사 차량 정책이요.
(C) 아직 평을 읽어 보지 못했어요.

해설 (A) ✗ 연상 어휘 함정 (car – travel by public transportation)
(B) ✗ 동어 반복 함정 (new – new), 연상 어휘 함정 (car – vehicle)
(C) ○ 평을 읽어보지 못했다며 모르겠음을 우회적으로 말했으므로 정답

Possible Answer
Yes, it looks that way. 네, 그래 보이네요.

어휘 public transportation 대중교통 vehicle n. 차량 policy n. 방침, 정책 review n. 논평[비평] rise v. 오르다 significantly adv. 상당히

28 제안/요청 난이도 중

Can you get some milk from the supermarket?
(A) It's not open on Sundays.
(B) With cereal for breakfast.
(C) Excellent market conditions.

슈퍼마켓에서 우유 좀 사다 줄래요?
(A) 일요일엔 문을 안 열어요.
(B) 아침 식사로 시리얼에 곁들여서요.
(C) 시장 상황이 최고예요.

해설 (A) ○ 일요일엔 문을 안 연다며 우유를 사다 줄 수 없음을 우회적으로 말했으므로 정답
(B) ✗ 연상 어휘 함정 (milk, supermarket – cereal for breakfast)
(C) ✗ 유사 발음 함정 (supermarket – market)

Possible Answer
Sure. Do you need anything else? 물론이죠. 그거 말고 또 필요한 거 있어요?

어휘 cereal n. 시리얼 market n. 시장 condition n. 조건

29 부정 의문문 난이도 중

Didn't you hire the candidates you met with last week?
(A) Yes, the fee was much higher.
(B) Please confirm the date.
(C) They didn't have enough experience.

지난주에 만난 지원자들은 채용하지 않으셨나요?
(A) 아니요, 비용이 훨씬 더 비쌌어요.
(B) 날짜를 확인해 주세요.
(C) 그들은 경력이 부족했어요.

해설 (A) ✗ 유사 발음 함정 (hire – higher)
(B) ✗ 유사 발음 함정 (candidates – date)
(C) ○ 경력이 충분하지 않았다며 채용하지 않았음을 우회적으로 말했으므로 정답

Possible Answer
Yes, they will be starting next week. 아니요, 다음 주부터 근무할 예정이에요.

어휘 hire v. 고용하다 candidate n. 지원자 fee n. 요금 confirm v. 확인해 주다 enough adj. 충분한

30 일반 의문문 난이도 중

Are you going to the annual conference next month?
(A) Some product demonstrations.
(B) I won't be attending this year.
(C) She's a guest speaker.

다음 달 연례 총회에 가실 거예요?
(A) 몇 번의 제품 시연이요.
(B) 올해는 참석하지 않을 거예요.
(C) 그녀는 초청 연사입니다.

해설 (A) ✗ 연상 어휘 함정 (annual conference – product demonstrations)
(B) ○ 올해는 참석하지 않을 것이라며 질문에 적절하게 말했으므로 정답

(C) ❌ 주어 불일치 함정 (you – she), 연상 어휘 함정 (annual conference – a guest speaker)

Possible Answer
Am I supposed to go there? 제가 가야 하나요?

어휘 **annual** adj. 매년의 **conference** n. (보통 여러 날 동안 대규모로 열리는) 회의[학회] **product demonstration** 제품 시연 **attend** v. 참석하다 **guest speaker** 초청 연사

31 평서문 난이도 상

미국 ⇄ 영국

The company dinner will start in ten minutes.
(A) I'm almost done with setting the tables.
(B) Yes, the seating chart.
(C) At the hotel downtown.

회사 만찬이 10분 후에 시작해요.
(A) 테이블 세팅이 거의 마무리됐어요.
(B) 네, 좌석 배치도요.
(C) 시내 호텔에서요.

해설 (A) ⭕ 테이블 세팅이 거의 마무리됐다며 적절하게 말했으므로 정답
(B) ❌ 유사 발음 함정 (start – chart), 연상 어휘 함정 (company dinner – seating chart)
(C) ❌ Where 의문에 어울리는 정답, 연상 어휘 함정 (company dinner – hotel)

Possible Answer
But the CEO is running late. 하지만 CEO가 좀 늦으시네요.

어휘 **be done with** ~을 다 하다 **set the table** 식탁을 차리다 **seating chart** 좌석 배치도 **downtown** adv. 시내에

PART 3 P. 153

미국 ⇄ 미국

Questions 32-34 refer to the following conversation.

M: Hi, Liz. **It looks like you have created a very interesting new exercise machine.**⁽³²⁾

W: Thanks. This machine is quite unique. You can ride it like a typical stationary bicycle, but it also has special handles so you can exercise your arms and shoulders at the same time. I think our customers will like it.

M: That sounds promising. **Do you know how much it will cost?**⁽³³⁾

W: Actually, we're still working on that. **We have a general idea, but we can't seem to decide on an exact figure.**⁽³³⁾

M: Well, **you should mention it at the monthly meeting tomorrow. It could help to get feedback from people in other departments.**⁽³⁴⁾

32-34번은 다음 대화에 관한 문제입니다.

남: 안녕하세요, Liz. 아주 흥미로운 운동 기구를 새로 제작하셨나 봐요.⁽³²⁾

여: 감사합니다. 이 기구는 상당히 독특해요. 일반 고정형 자전거처럼 탈 수도 있지만, 특별한 손잡이도 있어서 팔과 어깨운동을 동시에 할 수도 있어요. 우리 고객들이 좋아할 것 같아.

남: 잘될 것 같은데요. 가격이 얼마일지 아세요?⁽³³⁾

여: 실은, 아직 고민 중이에요. 대략적인 아이디어는 있지만, 정확한 금액을 결정하기 힘든 것 같아요.⁽³³⁾

남: 음, 그걸 내일 월례 회의 때 얘기해보세요. 다른 부서에 계신 분들에게 피드백을 받는 게 도움이 될 거예요.⁽³⁴⁾

어휘 **exercise machine** 운동 기구 **quite** adv. 꽤, 상당히 **unique** adj. 독특한, 아주 특별한 **typical** adj. 보통의, 일반적인 **stationary** adj. 움직이지 않는, 정지된 **at the same time** 동시에 **promising** adj. 조짐이 좋은 **cost** v. 비용이 들다 **general** adj. 대강의, 대체적인 **exact** adj. 정확한 **figure** n. 숫자, 수치

32 주제/목적 난이도 하

해석 화자들은 어떤 상품에 대해 얘기하는가?
(A) 차량
(B) 휴대폰
(C) 운동기구
(D) 사무용 가구

해설 남자가 It looks like you have created a very interesting new exercise machine. (아주 흥미로운 운동 기구를 새로 제작하셨나 봐요.)라고 말했으므로 (C)가 정답

Paraphrasing exercise machine ➡ fitness equipment

33 세부정보 난이도 중

해석 무엇이 여전히 결정되어야 하는가?
(A) 이름
(B) 마케팅 캠페인
(C) 출시일
(D) 가격

해설 남자가 That sounds promising. Do you know how much will it cost? (잘될 것 같은데요. 가격이 얼마일지 아세요?)라고 하자, 여자가 Actually, we're still working on that. We have a general idea, but we can't seem to decide on an exact figure. (실은, 아직 고민 중이에요. 대략적인 아이디어는 있지만, 정확한 금액을 결정하기 힘든 것 같아요.)라고 말했으므로 (D)가 정답

34 요청/제의/제안 난이도 중

해석 남자는 무엇을 하라고 권하는가?
(A) 동료들과 얘기하라고
(B) 회의 일정을 잡으라고
(C) 기한을 수정하라고
(D) 몇 가지 기능들을 수정하라고

해설 남자가 you should mention it at the monthly meeting tomorrow. It could help to get feedback from people in other departments. (그걸 내일 월례 회의 때 얘기해보세요. 다른 부서에 계신 분들에게 피드백을 받는 게 도움이 될 거예요.)라고 말했으므로 (A)가 정답

Paraphrasing get feedback from people in other departments ➡ speak with coworkers

미국 ⇄ 호주

Questions 35-37 refer to the following conversation.

W: Hey, Glenn. **I finished reviewing feedback from our recent questionnaire. According to the responses, a lot of customers are dissatisfied with our online store's new payment application.**(35)

M: Really? There were some security issues with our previous version, but our development team already worked hard to fix that.

W: Well, **the main issue now is that the process is a lot more complex.**(36) Customers are complaining that they have to install unnecessary programs just to make a purchase.

M: Hmm... **I think we should post a note on our Web site to explain that these programs are required for security purposes.**(37)

W: I can do that today.

35-37번은 다음 대화에 관한 문제입니다.

여: 안녕하세요, Glenn. 최근 설문에서 얻은 의견 검토를 마무리했어요. 응답에 따르면, 많은 고객이 우리 온라인 매장의 새로운 결제 애플리케이션을 불만스러워해요.(35)

남: 정말요? 이전 버전에 보안 문제가 있었지만, 우리 개발팀에서 그걸 해결하려고 아주 열심히 작업했는데요.

여: 음, 현재 가장 큰 문제는 절차가 훨씬 더 복잡해졌다는 거예요.(36) 고객들이 결제하려면 불필요한 프로그램을 설치해야 한다고 불평하네요.

남: 흠... 이들 프로그램이 보안을 위해 필요하다는 내용을 우리 웹 사이트에 게시하는 게 좋겠어요.(37)

여: 제가 오늘 할 수 있어요.

어휘 review v. 검토하다 feedback n. 의견, 피드백 recent adj. 최근의 questionnaire n. 설문지 response n. 응답 dissatisfied adj. 불만스러워하는 security n. 보안 issue n. 문제 previous adj. 이전의 development n. 개발 fix v. 고치다 process n. 절차, 과정 complex adj. 복잡한 install v. 설치하다 unnecessary adj. 불필요한 explain v. 설명하다 required adj. 필수의 purpose n. 목적

35 주제/목적 난이도 하

해석 대화의 주제는 무엇인가?
(A) 사업 확장
(B) 설문 응답
(C) 연간 예산
(D) 채용 가능성이 있는 입사 지원자

해설 여자가 I finished reviewing feedback from our recent questionnaire. According to the responses, a lot of customers are dissatisfied with our online store's new payment application(최근 설문에서 얻은 의견 검토를 마무리했어요. 응답에 따르면, 많은 고객이 우리 온라인 매장의 새로운 결제 애플리케이션을 불만스러워해요.)라고 말했으므로 (B)가 정답

Paraphrasing feedback ➡ responses

36 세부정보 난이도 중

해석 여자는 무엇이 가장 큰 문제라고 하는가?
(A) 애플리케이션 사용이 어렵다.
(B) 팀에 인력이 부족하다.
(C) 몇몇 비용이 너무 많이 든다.
(D) 몇몇 직원들이 의욕이 없다.

해설 여자가 the main issue now is that the process is a lot more complex. (현재 가장 큰 문제는 절차가 훨씬 더 복잡해졌다는 거예요)라고 말했으므로 (A)가 정답

Paraphrasing issue ➡ problem, complex ➡ difficult

37 요청/제의/제안 난이도 중

해석 남자는 무엇을 하는 것을 추천하는가?
(A) 하드웨어를 업그레이드하는 것
(B) 보안 직원과 이야기하는 것
(C) 설명을 게시하는 것
(D) 웹 사이트를 다시 디자인하는 것

해설 남자가 I think we should post a note on our Web site to explain that these programs are required for security purposes. (이들 프로그램이 보안을 위해 필요하다는 내용을 우리 웹 사이트에 게시하는 게 좋겠어요.)라고 말했으므로 (C)가 정답

Paraphrasing note ➡ explanation

미국 ⇄ 영국

Questions 38-40 refer to the following conversation.

M: Hello, Ms. Sanchez. It's Daniel Palmer. **I spoke with you about hiring your interior design firm to remodel our office, but you haven't sent me an estimate yet.**(38)

W: Ah, I apologize for that, Mr. Palmer. **I had to go on an urgent business trip a few days ago, and I just returned late last night.**(39)

M: I see. I just wanted to make sure that you could still begin the work in March.

W: Yes. I'll send the estimate to you by the end of the day. **We do have an important workshop in the first week of March,**(40) so we would probably start the work in the second week.

38-40번은 다음 대화에 관한 문제입니다.

남: 안녕하세요, Ms. Sanchez. 저는 Daniel Palmer예요. 귀하의 인테리어 디자인 회사에 저희 사무실 개조를 의뢰하는 문제로 이야기 나눴었는데요, 아직 저에게 견적서를 보내지 않으셨네요.(38)

여: 아, 죄송합니다, Mr. Palmer. 제가 며칠 전 급히 출장을 갔다가 어제 밤 늦게 막 돌아왔습니다.(39)

남: 그렇군요. 그대로 3월에 작업을 시작하실 수 있는지 확인하고 싶었어요.

여: 네. 오늘 중으로 견적서를 보내드리겠습니다. 저희가 3월 첫 주에 중요한 워크숍이 있어서,(40) 아마 둘째 주에 작업을 시작하게 될 거예요.

어휘 hire v. 고용하다 remodel v. 개조하다 estimate n. 견적서 apologize v. 사과하다 urgent adj. 긴급한 business trip 출장 make sure 확실히 하다

38 주제/목적   난이도 중

해석 남자는 왜 전화하는가?
(A) 추가 비용을 논의하기 위해
(B) 물품을 구매하기 위해
(C) 비즈니스 학회에 등록하기 위해
(D) 개조 프로젝트에 대한 후속 조치를 취하기 위해

해설 남자가 I spoke with you about hiring your interior design firm to remodel our office, but you haven't sent me an estimate yet. (귀하의 인테리어 디자인 회사에 저희 사무실 개조를 의뢰하는 문제로 이야기 나눴었는데요, 아직 저에게 견적서를 보내지 않으셨네요.)라고 말했으므로 (D)가 정답

39 세부정보   난이도 중

해석 여자는 최근에 무엇을 했는가?
(A) 자신의 회사를 매각했다.
(B) 책을 출판했다.
(C) 여행에서 돌아왔다.
(D) 새 제품을 디자인했다.

해설 여자가 I had to go on an urgent business trip a few days ago, and I just returned late last night. (제가 며칠 전 급히 출장을 갔다가 어제 밤 늦게 막 돌아왔습니다.)라고 말했으므로 (C)가 정답

Paraphrasing an urgent business trip ➡ a trip,
returned ➡ came back

40 다음 행동/계획   난이도 중

해석 3월 첫째 주에 무슨 일이 있을 것인가?
(A) 일부 가격이 확정될 것이다.
(B) 일부 면접이 진행될 것이다.
(C) 워크숍이 열릴 것이다.
(D) 한 고객이 방문할 것이다.

해설 남자가 We do have an important workshop in the first week of March. (저희가 3월 첫 주에 중요한 워크숍이 있어서)라고 말했으므로 (C)가 정답

미국 ⇄ 미국

Questions 41-43 refer to the following conversation.

W: I'd like to welcome you all to today's managers' meeting. **This morning, Dan, our sales director, is going to go over the company's quarterly sales report.**(41) Dan, if you would…

M: Thank you. I'm sure most of you already know, but subscription numbers for our magazine's print edition have dropped considerably over the last few months. Nowadays, **people find it more convenient to read content online using new technological tools such as smartphones and tablets.**(42)

W: Hmm… **We should think about discontinuing our print edition service**(43) and just focus on promoting our online magazine.

M: Yeah, that would be a good idea. We'd also cut back on operating costs if we stopped printing the magazine.(43)

41-43번은 다음 대화에 관한 문제입니다.

여: 오늘 관리자회의에 와 주신 여러분 모두 반갑습니다. 오늘 오전에는 영업부장이신 Dan이 자사 분기별 매출보고서를 검토하실 겁니다.(41) Dan, 진행 부탁드립니다.

남: 감사합니다. 대부분 이미 아시겠지만, 우리 잡지 인쇄판 구독자 수가 지난 몇 달간 크게 감소했습니다. 요즘에는 사람들이 스마트폰이나 태블릿 같은 새로운 기술 장비를 이용해서 온라인으로 콘텐츠를 읽는 걸 더 편해 합니다.(42)

여: 음… 인쇄판 서비스 중단을 고려하고, 온라인 잡지 홍보에만 집중해야 겠어요.(43)

남: 네, 좋은 생각 같아요. 잡지 발행을 중단하면 운영비도 절감하게 될 겁니다.(43)

어휘 sales director 영업부장 go over ~을 검토하다 quarterly adj. 분기별의 sales n. 매출(액) subscription n. 구독 print n. 인쇄, 판 edition n. (간행물의) 판 drop v. 떨어지다 considerably adv. 상당히 convenient adj. 편리한 content n. 내용 tool n. 도구, 수단 discontinue v. 중단하다 promote v. 홍보하다 cut back on ~을 줄이다 operating costs 운영비

41 장소/근무지   난이도 하

해석 남자는 어느 부서에서 근무하는가?
(A) 디자인
(B) 영업
(C) 재무
(D) 편집

해설 여자가 This morning, Dan, our sales director, is going to go over the company's quarterly sales report. (오늘 오전에는 영업부장이신 Dan이 자사 분기별 매출보고서를 검토하실 겁니다.)라고 말했으므로 (B)가 정답

42 세부정보   난이도 상

해석 남자는 소비행태 변화의 원인이 무엇이라고 말하는가?
(A) 더 좋은 기술의 이용 가능성
(B) 나아진 경제 상황
(C) 더 깨끗한 환경의 필요성
(D) 증가한 연료비

해설 남자가 people find it more convenient to read content online using new technological tools such as smartphones and tablets.(사람들이 스마트폰이나 태블릿 같은 새로운 기술 장비를 이용해서 온라인으로 콘텐츠를 읽는 걸 더 편해 합니다.)라고 말했으므로 (A)가 정답

Paraphrasing using new technological tools ➡
the availability of better technology

| 43 | 세부정보 | 난이도 하 |

해석 화자들은 무엇에 관하여 동의하는가?
(A) 온라인 워크숍을 진행하는 것
(B) 서비스를 중단하는 것
(C) 새 마케팅 대행사를 이용하는 것
(D) 사무실을 개조하는 것

해설 여자가 We should think about discontinuing our print edition service (인쇄판 서비스 중단을 고려하고, 온라인 잡지 홍보에만 집중해야겠어요.)라고 하자, 남자가 Yeah, that would be a good idea. We'd also cut back on operating costs if we stopped printing the magazine. (네, 좋은 생각 같아요. 잡지 발행을 중단하면 운영비도 절감하게 될 겁니다.)라고 말했으므로 (B)가 정답

[호주 ⇄ 미국]

Questions 44-46 refer to the following conversation.

M: Hey, Shannon. It looks like some new county tax regulations will be implemented next month. **We'll have to keep these laws in mind when our accounting team handles the company's financial transactions.**(44)

W: Yes, and a few of them might be confusing. **Why don't we conduct a training workshop for our team members?**(45)

M: Good idea. Are you available this Friday to hold the session?

W: I am, but I'm not sure that day will work because **some of the accountants will be attending the Finance Expo on Friday.** (46)

44-46번은 다음 대화에 관한 문제입니다.

남: 저기, Shannon. 다음 달에 새로운 카운티 조세 규정이 시행될 것 같아요. 우리 회계팀에서 회사 금융거래를 처리할 때 이 법규들을 명심해야 해요.(44)

여: 맞아요, 그리고 그 중 일부는 헷갈릴 수 있어요. 우리 팀원들을 위한 교육 워크숍을 실시하는 게 어때요?(45)

남: 좋은 생각이에요. 이번 주 금요일에 교육할 시간 있으세요?

여: 네, 그런데 일부 회계사들이 금요일에 금융박람회에 참석할 거라서 (46) 그 날이 괜찮을지 모르겠어요.

어휘 regulation n. 규정 implement v. 시행하다 keep in mind 명심하다 accounting n. 회계 (업무) transaction n. 거래 available adj. (사람들을 만날) 시간이 있는 session n. (특정한 활동을 위한) 시간, 모임 accountant n. 회계사

| 44 | 주제/목적 | 난이도 하 |

해석 화자들은 주로 무엇에 관하여 논의하는가?
(A) 카운티 행사
(B) 최근 거래
(C) 월급
(D) 새로운 법규

해설 남자가 We'll have to keep these laws in mind when our accounting team handles the company's financial transactions. (우리 회계팀에서 회사 금융거래를 처리할 때 이 법규들을 명심해야 해요.)라고 말했으므로 (D)가 정답

| 45 | 요청/제의/제안 | 난이도 중 |

해석 여자는 무엇을 제안하는가?
(A) 공무원에게 연락하는 것
(B) 교육을 제공하는 것
(C) 초과근무를 하는 것
(D) 양식을 검토하는 것

해설 여자가 Why don't we conduct a training workshop for our team members? (우리 팀원들을 위한 교육 워크숍을 실시하는 게 어떨까요?)라고 말했으므로 (B)가 정답

Paraphrasing conduct a training workshop ➡ provide some training

---

| 46 | 다음 행동/계획 | 난이도 중 |

해석 여자는 일부 회계사들이 금요일에 무엇을 할 거라고 말하는가?
(A) 은행을 방문할 거라고
(B) 박람회에 참가할 거라고
(C) 다른 지점에 갈 거라고
(D) 고객과 만날 거라고

해설 여자가 some of the accountants will be attending the Finance Expo on Friday. (일부 회계사들이 금요일에 금융박람회에 참석할 거라서)라고 말했으므로 (B)가 정답

Paraphrasing attending the Finance Expo ➡ participating in a convention

---

[호주 ⇄ 영국 ⇄ 미국]

Questions 47-49 refer to the following conversation with three speakers.

M1: **Welcome to Genie Sports Emporium.**(47) Do you require any assistance?

W: **Yes, I'm looking for a baseball bat.**(47) I want to buy it for my nephew. Can you suggest a good brand?

M1: Actually, my coworker would probably know better. James, this customer would like a recommendation for a good baseball bat.

M2: Hmm... **I'd go for a Baton Co. bat. I'm sure you know the company. They've been operating in this city for nearly 100 years.**(48)

W: Oh yeah. I've heard of them.

M2: Also, **this bat includes a 10-percent-off voucher for any other Baton Co. product. But you can only use it online.** (49)

47-49번은 다음 세 화자의 대화에 관한 문제입니다.

남1: Genie 스포츠 백화점에 오신 것을 환영합니다.(47) 도움이 필요하신가요?

여: 네, 야구 배트를 찾고 있어요.(47) 조카에게 사 주려고요. 괜찮은 브랜드를 추천해 주시겠어요?

남1: 실은 제 동료가 더 잘 알 겁니다. James, 이 손님께서 괜찮은 야구 배트를 추천 받고 싶어 하세요.

남2: 음... 저라면 Baton사의 야구 배트로 고를 겁니다. 그 회사는 잘 아실 거예요. 이곳에서 영업한 지 거의 100년이 다 돼 가죠.(48)

여: 아, 네. 들어 봤어요.

남2: 그리고, 이 배트에는 Baton사에서 나온 다른 모든 제품에 쓸 수 있는 10퍼센트 할인쿠폰이 포함돼 있어요. 인터넷에서만 사용하실 수 있긴 하지만요.(49)

어휘 emporium n. (특정 상품을 파는) 상점 require v. 필요로 하다 assistance n. 도움 bat n. 방망이 go for ~을 택하다 Co.(=company) n. 회사 operate v. 영업하다 voucher n. 상품권, 할인권 product n. 상품

47 장소/근무지   난이도 중

해석 대화는 어디에서 일어나겠는가?
(A) 의류 액세서리 매장에서
(B) 골동품 매장에서
(C) 스포츠 용품점에서
(D) 야구 경기장에서

해설 남자가 Welcome to Genie Sports Emporium. (Genie 스포츠 백화점에 오신 것을 환영합니다.)라고 하자, 여자가 Yes, I'm looking for a baseball bat. (네, 야구 배트를 찾고 있어요.) 라고 말했으므로 (C)가 정답

48 세부정보   난이도 하

해석 Baton사는 무엇으로 알려져 있는가?
(A) 저렴한 제품을 판매하는 것
(B) 자격을 갖춘 직원을 채용하는 것
(C) 오랫동안 영업한 것
(D) 상을 받은 것

해설 남자가 I'd go for a Baton Co. bat. I'm sure you know the company. They've been operating in this city for nearly 100 years. (저라면 Baton사의 야구 배트로 고를 겁니다. 그 회사는 잘 아실 거예요. 이곳에서 영업한 지 거의 100년이 다 돼 가죠.)라고 말했으므로 (C)가 정답

Paraphrasing for nearly 100 years ➡ for a long time

49 세부정보   난이도 중

해석 제품에 어떤 추가 혜택이 있는가?
(A) 청소 도구가 포함돼 있다.
(B) 큰 운반용 가방이 딸려 있다.
(C) 10년 품질보증이 포함돼 있다.
(D) 온라인 할인 쿠폰이 딸려 있다.

해설 남자가 this bat includes a 10-percent-off voucher for any other Baton Co. product. But you can only use it online. (이 배트에는 Baton사에서 나온 다른 모든 제품에 쓸 수 있는 10퍼센트 할인쿠폰이 포함돼 있어요. 인터넷에서만 사용하실 수 있긴 하지만요.)라고 말했으므로 (D)가 정답

Paraphrasing include a 10-percent-off voucher ➡ come with a discount voucher

---

미국 ⇄ 호주

Questions 50-52 refer to the following conversation.

W: Hey, Angelo. How are you coming along with the new sneakers?

M: Pretty well. **I've completed the sketch of the running shoes, and I'm really pleased with the unique patterns.**(50) They're going to look great.

W: Glad to hear that. What about the men's formal wear? **Did you make a new design for the boots?**(51)

M: Oh, **Tina told me not to make design changes to the boots.**(51)

W: Really? Didn't we decide to revise the design? We haven't been able to sell a lot of our men's boots lately. **I'll email our recent sales figures to Tina.**(52) She'll probably want to reconsider after looking them over.

50-52번은 다음 대화에 관한 문제입니다.

여: 저기, Angelo. 새 운동화는 어떻게 진행되고 있어요?

남: 꽤 순조로워요. **운동화 스케치를 완성했는데 독특한 무늬가 아주 마음에 들어요.**(50) 아주 근사할 거예요.

여: 잘됐군요. 남성 정장은 어떤가요? **부츠 디자인을 새로 했나요?**(51)

남: 아, **Tina가 부츠는 디자인을 바꾸지 말라고 하더군요.**(51)

여: 그래요? 디자인을 수정하기로 하지 않았나요? 최근에 남성용 부츠를 많이 못 팔았잖아요. **제가 Tina에게 최근 매출수치를 이메일로 보낼게요.**(52) 살펴보고 나면 아마 재고해 볼지도 몰라요.

어휘 come along (원하는 대로) 되어 가다 sneakers n. 운동화 complete v. 완료하다 be pleased with ~이 마음에 들다 unique adj. 독특한 formal wear 정장, 예복 make changes to ~에 변화를 만들다 revise v. 변경[수정]하다 lately adv. 최근에 sales figures 매출액 reconsider v. 재고하다 look over ~을 살펴보다

50 세부정보   난이도 하

해석 남자는 신발의 어떤 특징에 만족하는가?
(A) 편안한 밑창
(B) 친환경 소재
(C) 비용
(D) 무늬

해설 남자가 I've completed the sketch of the running shoes, and I'm really pleased with the unique patterns. (운동화 스케치를 완성했는데 독특한 무늬가 아주 마음에 들어요.)라고 말했으므로 (D)가 정답

51 화자 의도 파악   난이도 상

해석 남자는 왜 "Tina가 부츠는 디자인을 바꾸지 말라고 하더군요"라고 말하는가?
(A) 예산이 한정돼 있다는 점을 언급하기 위해
(B) Tina가 스케치를 수정할 것임을 알리기 위해
(C) 제품이 잘 팔리고 있다는 점을 지적하기 위해
(D) 어떤 업무를 하지 않은 이유를 대기 위해

해설 여자가 Did you make a new design for the boots?(부츠 디자인을 새로 했나요?)라고 하자, 남자가 Oh, Tina told me not to make design changes to the boots.(아, Tina가 부츠는 디자인을 바꾸지

말라고 하더군요.)라고 말한 것이므로 (D)가 정답

52 다음 행동/계획   난이도 중

해석 여자는 Tina에게 무엇을 보낼 것인가?
(A) 매출 자료
(B) 새 디자인
(C) 초대손님 명단
(D) 프로젝트 기획안

해설 여자가 I'll email our recent sales figures to Tina. (Tina에게 이메일로 최근 매출수치를 보낼게요.)라고 말했으므로 (A)가 정답

Paraphrasing email ➡ send, sales figures ➡ some sales data

미국 ⇄ 미국 ⇄ 영국

Questions 53-55 refer to the following conversation with three speakers.

M: There's going to be an executive board meeting next Monday to decide on this year's Best Staff Member at our publishing firm.⁽⁵³⁾ We have some excellent nominees this time.⁽⁵⁴⁾ Did you read over the list?

W1: Jeremy Westfield in the Sales Department performed really well this year. He was responsible for increasing the company's sales by 15 percent last quarter.

M: And what about that editor?

W2: Ah, yes. Sally Muntz. She was in charge of the English language textbook series that received such high praise from the local high schools. I think I may vote for her.

M: Hmm… There are many factors to consider. **It's a good thing that I have some time to make my choice.**⁽⁵⁵⁾

53-55번은 다음 세 화자의 대화에 관한 문제입니다.

남: 다음 주 월요일에 우리 출판사 올해의 최우수 직원을 결정하는 이사회의가 있을 거예요.⁽⁵³⁾ 이번에는 아주 훌륭한 후보들이 몇 명 있어요.⁽⁵⁴⁾ 명단을 살펴보셨나요?

여1: 올해는 영업부의 Jeremy Westfield가 실적이 아주 좋더라구요. 지난 분기에 회사 매출을 15 퍼센트나 증가시킨 주인공이죠.

남: 그 편집자는 어때요?

여2: 아, 네. Sally Muntz요. 이 지역 고등학교에서 극찬을 한 영어 교과서 시리즈를 담당했죠. 전 그녀에게 표를 줄까 해요.

남: 음… 고려할 요인들이 많네요. **결정할 시간이 아직 좀 있어서 다행이에요.**⁽⁵⁵⁾

어휘 executive board meeting (중역) 이사회 publishing firm 출판사 nominee n. 지명[추천]된 사람, 후보 read over ~을 꼼꼼히 읽다 perform v. 수행하다, 성취하다 be responsible for ~에 책임이 있다, ~의 원인이 되다 quarter n. 사분기(1년의 4분의 1인) be in charge of ~을 맡다[담당하다] praise n. 칭찬, 찬사 vote for ~에 투표하다 factor n. 요인 make a choice 선택하다

53 장소/근무지   난이도 하

해석 화자들은 어디에서 근무하겠는가?
(A) 법률사무소에서

(B) 출판사에서
(C) 고등학교에서
(D) 방송국에서

해설 남자가 There's going to be an executive board meeting next Monday to decide on this year's Best Staff Member at our publishing firm. (다음 주 월요일에 우리 출판사 올해의 최우수 직원을 결정하는 이사회의가 있을 거예요.)라고 말했으므로 (B)가 정답

Paraphrasing firm ➡ company

54 주제/목적   난이도 하

해석 대화의 주제는 무엇인가?
(A) 수정된 계약서
(B) 수상 후보들
(C) 은퇴 직원
(D) 일부 예산수치

해설 남자가 There's going to be an executive board meeting next Monday to decide on this year's Best Staff Member at our publishing firm. We have some excellent nominees this time. (다음 주 월요일에 우리 출판사 올해의 최우수 직원을 결정하는 이사회의가 있을 거예요. 이번에는 아주 훌륭한 후보들이 몇 명 있어요.)라고 말했으므로 (B)가 정답

55 세부정보   난이도 중

해석 남자는 왜 안도하는가?
(A) 프로젝트가 추가 자금 지원을 받을 것이다.
(B) 고객이 작업에 만족한다.
(C) 업무에 더 많은 도움을 받을 것이다.
(D) 선택을 할 시간이 충분하다.

해설 남자가 It's a good thing that I have some time to make my choice. (결정할 시간이 아직 좀 있어서 다행이에요.)라고 말했으므로 (D)가 정답

Paraphrasing make my choice ➡ make a selection

영국 ⇄ 호주

Questions 56-58 refer to the following conversation.

W: Hello, Mr. Marone. **I wanted to give you an update on the office spaces you were interested in.**⁽⁵⁶⁾ Unfortunately, those downtown locations are a bit above your budget. ⁽⁵⁷⁾ There is, however, a nice building in the East District, if you're interested.

M: Hmm… **That's not good news. I really want to open an office in the downtown area.**⁽⁵⁷⁾

W: I understand, but this place is quite affordable, and it's also right across from a park.

M: Oh! The park would be a nice spot for my employees to take a break. **Can I check out the property at 2 P.M. this Thursday?**⁽⁵⁸⁾

W: Of course. I'll add you to my schedule.⁽⁵⁸⁾

56-58번은 다음 대화에 관한 문제입니다.

여: 안녕하세요, Mr. Marone. 관심 보이셨던 사무실 부지와 관련해 최신 소식을 전해 드리려고 합니다.(56) 안타깝게도 시내 소재의 해당 부지들은 귀하의 예산을 약간 초과합니다.(57) 그런데 혹시 관심 있으시다면 동부 지구에 괜찮은 건물이 하나 있긴 합니다.

남: 음… 희소식은 아니네요. 시내에 사무실을 열고 싶은 마음이 크거든요.(57)

여: 이해합니다. 그런데 이곳은 꽤 저렴한 데다 공원 바로 맞은 편이에요.

남: 아, 공원이 있으면 저희 직원들이 휴식을 취하기에 좋겠네요. 이번 주 목요일 오후 2시에 건물을 볼 수 있을까요?(58)

여: 물론이죠. 제 일정에 추가해 놓겠습니다.(58)

어휘 give an update on ~에 대한 최신 정보를 제공하다 location n. 장소, 위치 budget n. 예산 affordable adj. (가격이) 알맞은 spot n. 장소, 자리 take a break 휴식을 취하다 property n. 건물 add to ~에 더하다

56 신분/정체 난이도 중

해석 여자는 누구겠는가?
(A) 부동산업자
(B) 엔지니어
(C) 사무실 관리자
(D) 시설관리 직원

해설 여자가 I wanted to give you an update on the office spaces you were interested in. (관심 보이셨던 사무실 부지와 관련해 최신 소식을 전해 드리려고 합니다.)라고 말했으므로 (A)가 정답

57 세부정보 난이도 중

해석 남자는 왜 실망하는가?
(A) 일정을 조율할 수 없다.
(B) 몇몇 장소가 너무 비싸다.
(C) 일부 설치물들이 고장 났다.
(D) 직원이 시간이 되지 않는다.

해설 여자가 those downtown locations are a bit above your budget. (시내 소재의 해당 부지들은 귀하의 예산을 약간 초과합니다.)라고 하자, 남자가 That's not good news. I really want to open an office in the downtown area. (희소식은 아니네요. 시내에 사무실을 열고 싶은 마음이 크거든요.)라고 말했으므로 (B)가 정답

Paraphrasing a bit above your budget ➔ too pricey

58 다음 행동/계획 난이도 중

해석 화자들은 목요일에 무엇을 할 것인가?
(A) 건물을 둘러볼 것이다
(B) 마감기한을 정할 것이다
(C) 예산을 검토할 것이다
(D) 회의에 참석할 것이다

해설 남자가 Can I check out the property at 2 P.M. this Thursday? (이번 주 목요일 오후 2시에 건물을 볼 수 있을까요?)라고 하자, 여자가 Of course. I'll add you to my schedule. (물론이죠. 제 일정에 추가해 놓겠습니다.)라고 말했으므로 (A)가 정답

Paraphrasing check out ➔ view

미국 ⇄ 영국

Questions 59-61 refer to the following conversation.

M: Samantha, you've been here a long time, right? I'm having trouble putting up a vacation day request through our system.(59)

W: Did you install the computer update?(60)

M: Yes, I downloaded it yesterday.(60) I don't think that's the issue, though. Look at this... When I click the submit button, the page refreshes, and the form resets.

W: Hmm... That's strange. In that case, I don't know what the problem is. Sorry.

M: It's OK. I'll just call the IT team.(61) They'll probably know what's going on.

59-61번은 다음 대화에 관한 문제입니다.

남: Samantha, 여기서 오래 근무하셨죠? 제가 우리 시스템으로 휴가 신청서를 제출하려는데 잘 안 되네요.(59)

여: 컴퓨터 업데이트는 설치하셨어요?(60)

남: 네, 어제 다운로드했어요.(60) 그런데 그게 문제는 아닌 것 같아요. 이것 좀 보세요… 제출 버튼을 클릭하면 페이지가 새로고침 되면서 양식이 지워져요.

여: 음… 이상하군요. 이런 경우에는 뭐가 문제인지 모르겠네요. 미안해요.

남: 괜찮아요. IT팀에 전화해 보죠 뭐.(61) 그분들은 뭐가 문젠지 아실 거예요.

어휘 have trouble doing ~하는 데 애를 먹다 put up 게시하다, 내붙이다 request n. 요청서 install v. 설치하다 issue n. 문제 submit v. 제출하다 refresh v. (가장 최신정보로) 리프레시[재생]하다 form n. 양식 reset v. (컴퓨터) 지워지다, 고쳐지다

59 화자 의도 파악 난이도 상

해석 남자는 왜 "Samantha, 여기서 오래 근무하셨죠?"라고 말하는가?
(A) 도움을 요청하기 위해
(B) 동료를 칭찬하기 위해
(C) 추천을 받기 위해
(D) 승인을 요청하기 위해

해설 남자가 Samantha, you've been here a long time, right? (Samantha, 여기서 오래 근무하셨죠?) I'm having trouble putting up a vacation day request through our system. (제가 우리 시스템으로 휴가 신청서를 제출하려는데 잘 안 되네요.)라고 말했으므로 (A)가 정답

60 세부정보 난이도 중

해석 남자는 어제 무엇을 했는가?
(A) 문서를 수정했다.
(B) 워크숍에 참석했다.
(C) 업데이트를 다운로드했다.
(D) 고객과 만났다.

해설 여자가 Did you install the computer update? (컴퓨터 업데이트 설치하셨어요?)라고 하자, 남자가 I downloaded it yesterday. (어제 다운로드했어요.)라고 말했으므로 (C)가 정답

61 다음 행동/계획 난이도 하

해석 남자는 다음에 무엇을 하겠는가?
(A) 교육 과정에 등록할 것이다
(B) 웹 사이트를 확인할 것이다
(C) 회의실을 예약할 것이다
(D) IT부서에 연락할 것이다

해설 남자가 I'll just call the IT team. (IT팀에 전화해 보죠 뭐.)라고 말했으므로 (D)가 정답

Paraphrasing call ➡ contact, team ➡ department

미국 ⇄ 영국

Questions 62-64 refer to the following conversation and table of contents.

M: Irina, I just read your proposal, and I think you have some really good ideas. **This is a very unique plan for your new fitness center.**(62) I was especially impressed with the amount of research you did for where you wanted to set up your facility.

W: Thanks—that's something that my previous business undertaking has taught me. I opened my store in the same area as all my competitors, which I realize now was a bad choice. This time, I made sure to identify a place where we'd be in demand.(63)

M: Great. Now, you're looking for investors, so **you'll want to provide more details about your expected profits.**(64) The time it will take before the business starts making money needs to be especially clear. It normally takes about three years for fitness centers in this region to break even.

Business Proposal

Section 1	Description of Business
Section 2	Location and Facilities
Section 3	Industry Trends
Section 4	**Profit Forecast**(64)
Section 5	Marketing

62-64번은 다음 대화와 목차에 관한 문제입니다.

남: Irina, 지금 막 당신의 제안서를 읽었는데, 정말 좋은 아이디어가 많으신 것 같아요. **당신의 새 피트니스 센터에 맞는 매우 특별한 계획이네요.**(62) 시설을 세우실 장소에 관해 진행하셨던 연구량이 특히 인상 깊었어요.

여: 감사합니다. 이전 사업을 하면서 배운 것이에요. 경쟁업체들과 같은 지역에 제 상점을 열었었는데, 이제야 나쁜 결정이었다는 걸 알게 되었어요. 이번에는 우리를 필요로 하는 곳을 확실히 알아 봤어요.(63)

남: 좋습니다. 이제 투자자를 구하고 계시니, **예상 수익에 대한 세부 내용을 더 제공하셔야 해요.**(64) 특히 사업이 수익을 내기까지 걸리는 시간이 정확해야 해요. 이 지역의 피트니스 센터는 보통 손익분기까지 대략 3년이 걸려요.

사업 제안서	
1절	사업 설명
2절	장소 및 시설
3절	산업 동향
4절	**수익 예측**(64)
5절	마케팅

어휘 proposal n. 제안서 unique adj. 특별한 especially adv. 특별히 impressed adj. 인상 깊게 생각하는 amount n. 양 research n. 연구 facility n. 시설 undertake v. 착수하다 competitor n. 경쟁사 realize v. 깨닫다 identify v. 확인하다 in demand 수요가 많은 investor n. 투자자 expected adj. 예상되는 profit n. 이익 normally adv. 보통 break even 본전치기 하다 description n. 설명 industry trend 산업 동향 forecast n. 예측

62 세부정보 난이도 중

해석 여자는 어떤 사업을 시작하고자 하는가?
(A) 여행사
(B) 피트니스 센터
(C) 시장 조사 회사
(D) 재무 설계 회사

해설 남자가 This is a very unique plan for your new fitness center. (당신의 새 피트니스 센터에 맞는 매우 특별한 계획이네요.)라고 말했으므로 (B)가 정답

63 세부정보 난이도 상

해석 여자에 따르면, 지난 사업을 통해 무엇을 배웠는가?
(A) 이상적인 장소를 찾는 법
(B) 효과적인 광고를 디자인하는 법
(C) 단골 고객층을 만드는 법
(D) 사업자등록증을 받는 법

해설 여자가 that's something that my previous business undertaking has taught me. I opened my store in the same area as all my competitors, which I realize now was a bad choice. This time, I made sure to identify a place where we'd be in demand. (이전 사업을 하면서 배운 것이에요. 경쟁업체들과 같은 지역에 제 상점을 열었었는데, 이제야 나쁜 결정이었다는 걸 알게 되었어요. 이번에는 우리를 필요로 하는 곳을 확실히 알아 봤어요.)라고 말했으므로 (A)가 정답

Paraphrasing place ➡ location

64 시각 정보 연계 난이도 상

해석 시각 자료를 보시오. 남자에 따르면, 사업기획서에 어느 절이 수정되어야 하는가?
(A) 2절
(B) 3절
(C) 4절
(D) 5절

해설 남자가 you'll want to provide more details about your expected profits.(예상 수익에 대한 세부 내용을 더 제공하셔야 해요.)라고 말했고, 시각자료에서 Section 4 (4절)이 Profit Forecast (수익 예측)임을 확인 할 수 있으므로 (C)가 정답

Paraphrasing expected profits ➡ profit forecast

[호주 ⇄ 미국]

Questions 65-67 refer to the following conversation and computer screen.

M: You've reached Invoice Design's IT Department. How may I be of assistance?

W: Hello, I run an auto shop. **I purchased your program to create invoices for the repair and maintenance work I do on customers' vehicles. But I'm having some trouble making one.**(65) I've entered all the items, but **I don't know how to display the discount for replacing the vehicle's battery.**(65)

M: First, click on the DISCOUNT tab at the bottom of your screen. Your list will then have a box appear next to each item. Just check the ones you want to have the discount.

W: OK, **I was able to apply 15 percent to battery replacement.**(66) This should reflect the discount, right?

M: Yes. By the way, **next time, you might want to use our Web messenger service**(67) to get help more quickly.

Invoice	
Work Description	Price
Oil change	$30
Windshield repair	$70
Battery replacement (66)	$120 (66)
Tire installation	$600

65-67번은 다음 대화와 컴퓨터 화면에 관한 문제입니다.

남: Invoice Design IT 부서입니다. 어떻게 도와드릴까요?

여: 안녕하세요, 제가 자동차 정비소를 운영하는데요. **제가 고객 차량에 해 드리는 수리 및 정비 작업용 청구서를 만들려고 귀사의 프로그램을 구입했는데요. 그런데 송장을 생성하는데 문제가 좀 있어서요.**(65) 모든 항목을 입력했지만, **차량 배터리 교체에 대한 할인을 나타내는 방법을 모르겠네요.**(65)

남: 우선, 화면 아래에 DISCOUNT 탭을 클릭하세요. 그러면 목록에서 각 항목 옆에 박스가 나타날 겁니다. 할인을 적용하고 싶으신 것들에 체크하시면 됩니다.

여: 알았어요, **배터리 교체에 15퍼센트를 적용할 수 있었는데요.**(66) 이게 할인을 반영해야 하는 거 맞죠?

남: 네. 그런데, 다음 번에는 더 빠르게 도움을 받아보시려면 **저희 웹 메신저 서비스를 이용해 보세요.**(67)

송장	
작업 내역	가격
오일 교환	30달러
전면 유리 수리	70달러
배터리 교체 (66)	120달러 (66)
타이어 설치	600달러

어휘 **reach** v. 연락하다 **assistance** 도움 **run** v. 운영[경영]하다 **auto shop** 자동차 정비소 **invoice** n. 청구서 **repair** n. 수리 **maintenance** n. 정비 **item** n. 항목 **display** v. 보여주다 **replace** v. 교체하다 **apply** v. 적용하다 **reflect** v. 반영하다 **quickly** adv. 빠르게

65 주제/목적 난이도 [상]

해석 여자는 왜 전화하고 있는가?
(A) 보수점검 일정을 잡기 위해
(B) 특별 할인에 관해 문의하기 위해
(C) 비품을 구매하기 위해
(D) 어떤 프로그램에 대한 도움을 받기 위해

해설 여자가 I purchased your program to create invoices for the repair and maintenance work I do on customers' vehicles. But I'm having some trouble making one.(제가 고객 차량에 해 드리는 수리 및 정비 작업용 청구서를 만들려고 귀사의 프로그램을 구입했는데요. 그런데 송장을 생성하는데 문제가 좀 있어서요.)라고 하면서 I don't know how to display the discount for replacing the vehicle's battery.(차량 배터리 교체에 대한 할인을 나타내는 방법을 모르겠네요.)라고 말했으므로 (D)가 정답

66 시각 정보 연계 난이도 [상]

해석 시각 자료를 보시오. 어느 가격이 변경될 것인가?
(A) 30달러
(B) 70달러
(C) 120달러
(D) 600달러

해설 여자가 I was able to apply 15 percent to battery replacement.(배터리 교체에 15퍼센트를 적용할 수 있었는데요.)라고 말했고, 시각 자료에서 Battery replacement (배터리 교체)가 120달러임을 확인할 수 있으므로 (C)가 정답

67 세부정보 난이도 [중]

해석 남자가 여자에게 다음 번에 무엇을 하라고 권하는가?
(A) 신용카드로 지불하라고
(B) 온라인 커뮤니케이션 서비스를 이용하라고
(C) 동영상 설명을 보라고
(D) 고객 후기를 확인하라고

해설 남자가 next time, you might want to use our Web messenger service (다음 번에는 저희 웹 메신저 서비스를 이용해 보세요.)라고 말했으므로 (B)가 정답

Paraphrasing Web messenger service ➡
                online communication service

[호주 ⇄ 미국]

Questions 68-70 refer to the following conversation and sign.

M: Hello, Ms. Harkins. I've been expecting you. **Is that the sign you'd like to make prints of?**(68)

W: It is. I want to print this on a big banner. You can do that, right?

M: Yes. Can you show me the sign? Oh, wow… 80 years, huh? That's amazing for a small grocery store.(69)

W: It's all thanks to our loyal customers and hardworking employees. By the way, we're planning to attach the banner to a fence, so we'll need some ties to hold it in place.(70)

M: There'll be an additional fee for that,(70) but it's not much.

Geller's Grocery Store
Recognizing Achievements

- 5 years rated as Top Small Business
- 20 years run by the current owner
- 50 years in the same location
- **80 years in operation**(69)

68-70번은 다음 대화와 표지판에 관한 문제입니다.

남: 안녕하세요, Ms. Harkins. 기다리고 있었습니다. 그게 인화하시려는 게시물인가요?(68)

여: 맞아요. 이걸 큰 현수막에 인쇄하고 싶어요. 가능하시죠?

남: 네. 게시물을 좀 보여주시겠어요? 오, 와… 80년이라고요? 소규모 식료품점에서 대단하네요.(69)

여: 전부 단골고객분들과 성실한 직원들 덕분이에요. 그런데 저희가 현수막을 울타리에 붙일 거라서 자리에 고정할 끈이 좀 필요해요.(70)

남: 그러려면 추가 요금이 들긴 하지만(70) 큰 금액은 아니에요.

Geller 식료품점
그 동안의 성과를 기념합니다

- 5년간 최우수 소규모 사업체로 선정
- 20년간 현 소유주가 운영
- 50년간 현 위치에서 운영
- **80년간 영업**(69)

어휘 expect v. (오기로 한 대상을) 기다리다 sign n. 간판, 표지, 게시 make a print 인화하다 banner n. 플래카드, 현수막 thanks to ~덕분에 loyal adj. 충성스런 hardworking adj. 근면한 attach to ~에 붙이다 fence n. 울타리 hold in place 고정시키다 tie n. (물건을 묶는 데 쓰는) 끈 recognize v. (남의 수고 따위를) 인정하다, 표창하다 achievement n. 성취, 업적 current adj. 현재의 owner n. 주인 rate v. 평가하다 run v. (사업체 등을) 운영하다 in operation 운영[영업] 중인

68 장소/근무지   난이도 중

해설 남자는 어디에서 근무하겠는가?
(A) 택배회사
(B) 식료품점
(C) 컨벤션 센터
(D) 인쇄업체

해설 남자가 Is that the sign you'd like to make prints of? (그게 인화하시려는 게시물인가요?)라고 말했으므로 (A)가 정답

69 시각 정보 연계   난이도 중

해설 시각 자료를 보시오. 남자는 어떤 성과에 놀라는가?
(A) 최우수 소규모 사업체로 선정된 햇수
(B) 현 소유주가 운영한 햇수
(C) 현 위치에서의 영업 햇수
(D) 영업 햇수

해설 남자가 Oh, wow… 80 years, huh? That's amazing for a small grocery store. (오, 와… 80년이라고요? 소규모 식료품점에서 대단하네요.)라고 말했고, 시각 자료에서 80 years in operation (80년간 영업)임을 확인할 수 있으므로 (D)가 정답

70 세부정보   난이도 상

해설 여자는 무엇에 추가 요금을 지불해야 하는가?
(A) 현장 설치
(B) 빠른 배송
(C) 임대 차량
(D) 특별 비품

해설 여자가 we're planning to attach the banner to a fence, so we'll need some ties to hold it in place. (저희가 현수막을 울타리에 붙일 거라서 자리에 고정시켜 둘 끈이 좀 필요해요.)라고 하자, 남자가 There'll be an additional fee for that,(그러려면 추가 요금이 들긴 하지만)라고 말했으므로 (D)가 정답

Paraphrasing an additional fee ➡ pay extra

PART 4   P. 157

미국

Questions 71-73 refer to the following tour information.

W: Hello. I'd like to thank you all for joining us today at Twin Peaks Arts & Crafts Studio. Today, I'll be showing you around our workshop,(71) where you'll get to see how our beautiful hand-made jewelry is created by our experienced staff of designers. As we proceed through the tour, please refrain from asking questions to the designers while they are working.(72) If you have any questions, I'll be glad to answer them for you. After the tour ends, we kindly ask you complete a short survey about your experience today.(73) It'll only take a few minutes.

71-73번은 다음 여행 정보에 관한 문제입니다.

여: 안녕하세요. Twin Peaks 공예 스튜디오에서 오늘 저희와 함께 해주신 여러분 모두에게 감사 드립니다. 오늘 여러분에게 저희 작업장을 구경시켜드릴텐,(71) 저희 경험 많은 디자이너 직원들에 의해 아름다운 수공예 장신구가 만들어지는 과정을 보시게 될 것입니다. 투어가 진행되는 동안 작업 중인 디자이너들에게 질문하는 일은 삼가 주시기 바랍니다.(72) 질문이 있으시면 제가 기꺼이 대답해드리겠습니다. 투어가 끝난 후에는 오늘 여러분의 경험에 관한 짧은 설문조사를 작성해주실 것을 부탁 드립니다.(73) 몇 분밖에 걸리지 않을 겁니다.

| 어휘 | arts and crafts 공예 show ~ around ~에게 (~을) 둘러보도록 안내하다 workshop n. 작업장 get to ~하게[~가] 되다 experienced adj. 경험[경력]이 있는, 능숙한 proceed v. 진행하다 |

71 장소/근무지 난이도 하

해석 투어는 어디에서 이루어질 것인가?
(A) 공예 작업장
(B) 연구소
(C) 미술관
(D) 사진 스튜디오

해설 화자가 I'd like to thank you all for joining us today at Twin Peaks Arts & Crafts Studio. Today, I'll be showing you around our workshop (Twin Peaks 공예 스튜디오에서 오늘 저희와 함께 해 주신 여러분 모두에게 감사 드립니다. 오늘 여러분에게 저희 작업장을 구경시켜드리려고 하는데)라고 말했으므로 (A)가 정답

72 세부정보 난이도 중

해석 청자들은 무엇을 삼가야 하는가?
(A) 디자이너들에게 말 걸기
(B) 휴대전화 사용하기
(C) 음식 가져오기
(D) 그룹에서 이탈하기

해설 화자가 As we proceed through the tour, please refrain from asking questions to the designers while they are working. (투어가 진행되는 동안 작업 중인 디자이너들에게 질문을 하는 일은 삼가시기 바랍니다.)라고 말했으므로 (A)가 정답

Paraphrasing refrain from ➡ avoid,
asking questions to ➡ talking to

73 요청/제의/제안 난이도 중

해석 화자는 청자들에게 무엇을 해달라고 요청하는가?
(A) 피드백을 제공해 달라고
(B) 기념품 점을 둘러 보라고
(C) 회원으로 등록하라고
(D) 대회에 참가하라고

해설 화자가 After the tour ends, we kindly ask you complete a short survey about your experience today. (투어가 끝난 후에는 오늘 여러분의 경험에 관한 짧은 설문조사를 작성해주실 것을 부탁 드립니다.)라고 말했으므로 (A)가 정답

Paraphrasing complete a short survey ➡ provide some feedback

[미국]

Questions 74-76 refer to the following recorded message.

M: You have reached Patel and Associates Medical Clinic.(74) Our hours of operation are 9 A.M. to 7 P.M., Monday to Friday, and 10 A.M. to 6 P.M., Saturday. **This coming weekend, we will be moving to a new office at 350 Markham Road, next to Silverthorn Insurance.**(75) We will reopen on Monday, March 4. If you have an inquiry or would like to make an appointment, **please call back during our regular hours.**(76) Thank you.

74-76번 문제는 다음 녹음 메시지에 관한 문제입니다.

남: Patel and Associates 병원입니다.(74) 저희 영업시간은 월요일부터 금요일까지 오전 9시부터 오후 7시까지이며, 토요일은 오전 10부터 오후 6시까지입니다. 저희는 이번 돌아오는 주말에 Markham로 356번지에 있는 새로운 장소로 이전합니다. Silverthorn 보험사 옆입니다.(75) 3월 4일 월요일에 다시 개원합니다. 문의 사항이 있으시거나 예약을 하시려면 정상 영업시간에 다시 전화해 주시기를 바랍니다.(76) 감사합니다.

| 어휘 | medical clinic 병원 hours of operation 영업시간 coming adj. 다가오는 insurance n. 보험 reopen v. 다시 문을 열다 |

74 세부정보 난이도 하

해석 어떤 업체에서 메시지를 만들었겠는가?
(A) 직업소개소
(B) 보험회사
(C) 병원
(D) 법률사무소

해설 화자가 You have reached Patel and Associates Medical Clinic. (Patel and Associates 병원입니다)라고 말했으므로 (C)가 정답

Paraphrasing medical clinic ➡ doctor's office

75 세부정보 난이도 중

해석 업체에 대해 무엇이 언급되는가?
(A) 개조되고 있다.
(B) 이전할 것이다.
(C) 영업시간이 변경될 것이다.
(D) 연휴로 인해 문을 닫았다.

해설 화자가 This coming weekend, we will be moving to a new office at 350 Markham Road, next to Silverthorn Insurance. (저희는 이번 돌아오는 주말에 Markham로 356번지에 있는 새로운 장소로 이전합니다. Silverthorn 보험사 옆입니다.)라고 말했으므로 (B)가 정답

Paraphrasing moving ➡ relocating

76 요청/제의/제안 난이도 하

해석 화자는 청자에게 무엇을 하라고 지시하는가?
(A) 웹 사이트를 방문하라고
(B) 메시지를 남기라고
(C) 다른 시간에 전화하라고
(D) 서류를 제출하라고

해설 화자가 please call back during our regular hours (정상 영업시간에 다시 전화해주시기를 바랍니다)라고 말했으므로 (C)가 정답

[영국]

Questions 77-79 refer to the following announcement.

W: I've called this meeting to make an announcement. First, **I'd like to thank you for your prompt feedback on the survey**(77) we emailed to everyone last week. Based on your responses, **the company has decided to renovate our offices to create more workspace**(78) for all

148

employees. However, as this will be a major remodeling project, **employees will be asked to either relocate to the Middleborough branch or work from home for the next month.**⁽⁷⁹⁾ Please let your manager know what you'd like to do as soon as possible. Also, direct any questions that you may have to the HR Department.

77-79번은 다음 공지에 관한 문제입니다.

여: 공지할 사항이 있어서 이번 회의를 소집했습니다. 우선 지난주에 모든 분께 이메일로 보내드린 **설문조사에 빠르게 답변해주셔서 감사합니다.**⁽⁷⁷⁾ 여러분의 응답에 근거하여 **회사측에서는 사무실을 개조하여 전 직원을 위한 업무공간을 더 만들기로 결정했습니다.**⁽⁷⁸⁾ 그러나 이것은 대규모 리모델링 프로젝트가 될 것이기 때문에 **다음 달 한 달 동안은 직원 여러분께 Middleborough 지점으로 가시거나 재택 근무 하실 것을 부탁 드립니다.**⁽⁷⁹⁾ 여러분 매니저에게 어떻게 하고 싶으신지 가능한 한 빨리 알려주시기 바랍니다. 또한, 혹시 질문이 있으면 인사부로 직접 문의해 주시기 바랍니다.

어휘 prompt adj. 즉각적인, 지체 없는 based on ~에 근거하여 relocate v. 이전[이동]하다 direct v. ~을 (~에게) 보내다

---

77 세부정보 난이도 중

해석 화자는 왜 청자들에게 고마워하는가?
(A) 초과근무를 해줘서
(B) 영업목표를 달성해줘서
(C) 잡지를 구독해줘서
(D) 설문조사에 응답해줘서

해설 화자가 I'd like to thank you for your prompt feedback on the survey (설문조사에 빠르게 답변해주셔서 감사합니다.)라고 말했으므로 (D)가 정답

Paraphrasing feedback on ➡ responding

---

78 세부정보 난이도 중

해석 회사는 무엇을 하기로 결정했는가?
(A) 소프트웨어를 업데이트한다.
(B) 행사를 연기한다.
(C) 회사 정책을 변경한다.
(D) 사무 공간을 확장한다.

해설 화자가 the company has decided to renovate our offices to create more workspace (회사 측에서는 사무실을 개조하여 전 직원을 위한 업무공간을 더 만들기로 결정했습니다.)라고 말했으므로 (D)가 정답

Paraphrasing renovate our offices to create more workspace ➡ Expand office space

---

79 다음 행동/계획 난이도 중

해석 화자에 따르면, 청자들은 다음 달에 무엇을 하겠는가?
(A) 고과평가에 참여한다.
(B) 다른 장소에서 근무한다.
(C) 신입직원들을 만난다.
(D) 무역박람회에 참가한다.

해설 화자가 employees will be asked to either relocate to the Middleborough branch or work from home for the next month. (다음 또 한 달 동안은 직원 여러분께 Middleborough 지점으로 가시거나 재택 근무 하실 것을 부탁 드립니다.)라고 말했으므로 (B)가 정답

Paraphrasing either relocate to the Middleborough branch or work from home ➡ work from other locations

---

[호주]

Questions 80-82 refer to the following telephone message.

M: Hello, this is John Moon from City Publishing, and this message is for Ms. Rivera. **We are sorry to inform you that you were not selected for the position you applied for in our R&D Department. Although you have many years of experience, all of our researchers are required to work on a Saturday or a Sunday**⁽⁸⁰⁾ from time to time. But we do feel that your knowledge of Spanish would be an asset to our Editing Department as we publish many books in Spanish. They also have an opening, and they've already started interviewing people.⁽⁸¹⁾ The job is a little different from the R&D position, but if you're interested, I'll send them your résumé.⁽⁸¹⁾/⁽⁸²⁾ Call me back at 555-3849 if you have any questions.

80-82번은 다음 전화 메시지에 관한 문제입니다.

남: 안녕하세요, 저는 City 출판사의 John Moon이며 Ms. Rivera께 메시지를 남깁니다. **지원하신 저희 연구 개발부서 직무에 선발되지 않으셨음을 알려드리게 되어 유감입니다. 수년간의 경력이 있으시지만, 저희 연구원 모두 가끔 토요일이나 일요일에 근무해야 합니다.**⁽⁸⁰⁾ 하지만 저희가 스페인어로 된 책도 많이 출간하기 때문에 당신의 스페인어 지식이 편집부에서라면 장점이 되리라 생각합니다. 거기도 공석이 있는데 벌써 지원자 면접을 시작했습니다.⁽⁸¹⁾ 업무가 연구 개발직과 좀 다르기는 하지만 관심이 있으시다면 그쪽에 당신의 이력서를 보내겠습니다.⁽⁸¹⁾/⁽⁸²⁾ 질문이 있으시면 555-3849로 다시 전화 주세요.

어휘 inform v. 알리다, 통지하다 from time to time 가끔 asset n. 유용한 것[자질], 가치 있는 것, 이점 opening n. 빈자리[공석]

---

80 세부정보 난이도 중

해석 청자의 지원은 왜 거부되었겠는가?
(A) 업무 경력이 충분하지 않다.
(B) 특정 언어를 모른다.
(C) 주말에 일할 수 없다.
(D) 다른 도시로 이주할 수 없다.

해설 화자가 We are sorry to inform you that you were not selected for the position you applied for in our R&D Department. Although you have many years of experience, all of our researchers are required to work on a Saturday or a Sunday (지원하신 저희 연구 개발부서 직무에 선발되지 않으셨음을 알려드리게 되어 유감입니다. 수년간의 경력이 있으시지만, 저희 연구원 모두 가끔 토요일이나 일요일에 근무해야 합니다.)라고 말했으므로 (C)가 정답

Paraphrasing not selected ➡ rejected

81 화자 의도 파악 난이도 상

해석 화자가 "벌써 지원자들 면접을 시작했습니다"라고 말할 때, 그가 내비친 것은?
(A) 빨리 행동을 취해야 한다.
(B) 면접 일정을 다시 잡을 수 없다.
(C) 어떤 부서가 이미 누군가를 채용했다.
(D) 어떤 업무가 예상보다 더 어렵다.

해설 화자가 They also have an opening, and they've already started interviewing people. (거기도 공석이 있는데 벌써 지원자 면접을 시작했습니다.)라고 하면서, The job is a little different from the R&D position, but if you're interested, I'll send them your résumé. (일이 연구개발 자리와 좀 다르기는 하지만 관심이 있으시다면 그쪽에 당신의 이력서를 보내겠습니다.)라고 말했으므로 (A)가 정답

82 요청/제의/제안 난이도 중

해석 화자는 무엇을 해주겠다고 제안하는가?
(A) 방을 예약하겠다고
(B) 문서를 전달하겠다고
(C) 사무실을 방문하겠다고
(D) 지원자에게 전화하겠다고

해설 화자가 The job is a little different from the R&D position, but if you're interested, I'll send them your résumé. (일이 연구개발 자리와 좀 다르기는 하지만 관심이 있으시다면 그쪽에 당신의 이력서를 보내겠습니다.)라고 말했으므로 (B)가 정답

Paraphrasing send your résumé ➡ forward a document

[미국]

Questions 83-85 refer to the following excerpt from a meeting.

M: Now that you've been given an overview of our new electric car's functions, **we need to talk about how you're going to relay this information to car buyers.**(83) When describing electric automotive technology to customers, always keep this in mind: They probably have limited knowledge about it. Many people will especially want to learn more about the batteries that are in our vehicles.(84) Each of you will receive a diagram that will show how the battery works. Be sure to use it when explaining it to customers. **Don't forget that your goal is to sell five electric vehicles a month. Try your best to achieve this quota.**(85)

83-85번은 다음 회의 발췌록에 관한 문제입니다.

남: 우리의 신형 전기차 기능에 대한 개요를 들으셨으니, **여러분이 이 정보를 자동차 구매자에게 어떻게 전달할지에 대해 이야기를 나눠야 합니다.**(83) 전기 자동차 기술을 고객에게 설명할 때에, 항상 이 점을 명심하십시오. 그들이 이 분야에 대해 가진 지식은 한정적일 겁니다. 많은 사람들이 우리 차량에 탑재된 배터리에 대해 특히 더 알고 싶어 할겁니다.(84) 여러분 모두 배터리 작동원리를 보여주는 도표를 받으실 겁니다. 고객에게 설명할 때 꼭 사용하도록 하세요. **매달 전기차 다섯 대를 판매하는 게 목표라는 걸 잊지 마세요. 이 할당량을 맞출 수 있게 최선을 다해 주세요.**(85)

어휘 overview n. 개요 function n. 기능 relay v. 전달하다 buyer n. 구매자 describe v. 설명하다 technology n. 기술 keep ~ in mind 명심하다 limited adj. 제한된 especially adv. 특히 diagram n. 도표 achieve v. 달성하다 quota n. 할당량

83 신분/정체 난이도 하

해석 담화는 누구를 대상으로 하겠는가?
(A) 자동차 정비공
(B) 공장 직원
(C) 영업사원
(D) 컴퓨터 기술자

해설 화자가 we need to talk about how you're going to relay this information to car buyers. (여러분이 이 정보를 자동차 구매자에게 어떻게 전달할지에 대해 이야기를 나눠야 합니다.)라고 말했으므로 (C)가 정답

84 화자 의도 파악 난이도 중

해석 화자가 "그들이 이 분야에 대해 가진 지식은 한정적일 겁니다"라고 말할 때, 그가 내비친 것은?
(A) 청자들이 주제를 명확하게 설명해야 한다.
(B) 청자들이 동영상을 보여주어야 한다.
(C) 청자들이 세미나에 참석해야 한다.
(D) 청자들이 전문가와 만나야 한다.

해설 화자가 When describing electric automotive technology to customers, always keep this in mind: (전기 자동차 기술을 고객에게 설명할 때에, 항상 이 점을 명심하십시오.)라면서, They probably have limited knowledge about it. Many people will especially want to learn more about the batteries that are in our vehicles. (그들이 이 분야에 대해 가진 지식은 한정적일 겁니다. 많은 사람들이 우리 차량에 탑재된 배터리에 대해 특히 더 알고 싶어 할겁니다.)라고 말한 것이므로 (A)가 정답

85 요청/제의/제안 난이도 중

해석 화자는 청자에게 무엇을 하라고 상기시키는가?
(A) 직원들을 채용하라고
(B) 할당량을 채우라고
(C) 문서를 출력하라고
(D) 비용을 절감하라고

해설 화자가 Don't forget that your goal is to sell five electric vehicles a month. Try your best to achieve this quota. (매달 전기차 다섯 대를 판매하는 게 목표라는 걸 잊지 마세요. 이 할당량을 맞출 수 있게 최선을 다해 주세요.)라고 말했으므로 (B)가 정답

Paraphrasing achieve ➡ meet

[호주]

Questions 86-88 refer to the following excerpt from a talk.

M: Today, I have some great news in regard to our employee benefits package.(86) As you know, our company provides an extensive benefits package to all of its employees. Recently, our company has negotiated a deal with local pharmacies to give our employees a discount. **Now, you can get 10 percent off all non-prescription drugs and vitamins.**[87] Just show your business card along with a photo ID at the cash register to receive the discount. **Details about the discounts and participating stores are on this list, which I'll distribute right now.**[88]

86-88번은 다음 담화 발췌문에 관한 문제입니다.

남: 오늘은 우리의 복리후생제도와 관련된 아주 좋은 소식이 있습니다.[86] 아시다시피 우리 회사는 모든 직원들에게 폭넓은 복리후생을 제공하고 있죠. 최근 우리 회사는 지역의 약국들과의 거래를 성사시켜 우리 직원에게 할인을 해주도록 했습니다. 이제 여러분은 모든 일반의약품과 비타민 제품 가격의 10퍼센트를 할인 받을 수 있습니다.[87] 할인을 받으시려면 계산대에서 사진이 포함된 신분증과 함께 명함을 보여주시면 됩니다. 할인과 참여 매장들에 관한 세부사항은 지금 나눠드리는 이 목록에 있습니다.[88]

어휘 in regard to ~과 관련하여 employee benefits package 복리후생제도 extensive adj. 광범위한[폭넓은] non-prescription drugs (처방전이 필요하지 않은) 일반의약품 cash register 금전 등록기

86 주제/목적 난이도 하

해석 담화는 주로 무엇에 관한 것인가?
(A) 안전절차
(B) 교육일정
(C) 복리후생
(D) 휴가정책

해설 화자가 Today, I have some great news in regard to our employee benefits package. (오늘은 우리의 복리후생제도와 관련된 아주 좋은 소식이 있습니다.)라고 말했으므로 (C)가 정답

87 세부정보 난이도 중

해석 화자에 따르면, 청자들은 무엇에 대한 할인을 받을 수 있는가?
(A) 의약품
(B) 항공요금
(C) 전화요금
(D) 사무용품

해설 화자가 Now, you can get 10 percent off all non-prescription drugs and vitamins. (이제 여러분은 모든 일반의약품과 비타민 제품 가격의 10퍼센트를 할인 받을 수 있습니다.)라고 말했으므로 (A)가 정답

Paraphrasing 10 percent off ➡ discounts on, non-prescription drugs and vitamins ➡ medicine

88 다음 행동/계획 난이도 중

해석 화자는 이후에 무엇을 할 것인가?
(A) 질문에 대답할 것이다
(B) 정보를 나눠줄 것이다
(C) 손님들을 소개할 것이다
(D) 장비를 시연할 것이다

해설 화자가 Details about the discounts and participating stores are on this list, which I'll distribute right now. (할인과 참여 매장들에 관한 세부사항은 지금 나눠드리는 이 목록에 있습니다.)라고 말했으므로 (B)가 정답

Paraphrasing details about the discounts and participating stores ➡ some information, distribute ➡ hand out

[미국]

Questions 89-91 refer to the following talk.

W: Hello, and welcome to Tung Hing Chinese Buffet. Before you're seated, **let me tell you about our buffet layout. Along the wall over here is where the appetizers are. The main dishes are on the middle tables there, and desserts and beverages are on the right side by the window.**[89] And **to celebrate the opening of our restaurant, we're offering special lobster and steak dishes this weekend!**[90] You'll find those on the middle tables.[89] Umm… By the way, I think a private room might be more comfortable for your group as there are quite a few of you. **Let me quickly check to see if there is an unoccupied one.**[91]

89-91번은 다음 담화에 관한 문제입니다.

여: 안녕하세요, Tung Hing 중식 뷔페에 오신 것을 환영합니다. 자리로 안내 드리기 전에 뷔페 배치에 대해 말씀 드리겠습니다. 에피타이저는 이쪽 벽을 따라 있습니다. 주요리들은 저쪽 중앙 테이블에 있으며, 디저트와 음료는 오른쪽 창가에 있습니다.[89] 그리고 저희 식당 개업 기념으로, 이번 주말에는 특별 랍스터와 스테이크 요리를 제공하고 있습니다![90] 중앙 테이블에서 찾아보실 수 있습니다.[89] 음… 그런데, 제 생각엔 일행이 꽤 많으셔서 별도의 방이 더 편리하실 것 같습니다. 빈방이 있는지 얼른 확인해 보겠습니다.[91]

어휘 be seated 앉다 layout n. (식탁상의) 배치 quite a few 상당수 unoccupied adj. 비어 있는

89 주제/목적 난이도 중

해석 담화 주제는 무엇인가?
(A) 요리 재료
(B) 메뉴 변경
(C) 식당 개조
(D) 음식 위치

해설 화자가 let me tell you about our buffet layout. Along on the wall over here is where the appetizers are. The main dishes are on the middle tables there, and desserts and beverages are on the right side by the window. (뷔페 배치에 대해 말씀 드리겠습니다. 에피타이저는 이쪽 벽을 따라 있습니다. 주요리들은 저쪽 중앙 테이블에 있으며, 디저트와 음료는 오른쪽 창가에 있습니다.)라고 말했으므로 (D)가 정답

90 세부정보 난이도 중

해석 어떤 특별행사가 열리고 있겠는가?
(A) 환영회
(B) 시상식 만찬
(C) 개업
(D) 은퇴파티

해설 화자가 to celebrate the opening of our restaurant, we're offering special lobster and steak dishes this weekend! (저희 식당 개업 기념으로, 이번 주말에는 특별 랍스터와 스테이크 요리를 제공하고 있습니다!)라고 말했으므로 (C)가 정답

91 다음 행동/계획　　　난이도 상

해석　화자는 무엇을 확인할 것인가?
(A) 테이블의 크기
(B) 예약의 세부사항
(C) 방의 이용가능 여부
(D) 제품의 가격

해설　화자가 I think a private room might be more comfortable for your group as there are quite a few of you. Let me quickly check to see if there is an unoccupied one. (제 생각엔 일행이 꽤 많으셔서 별도의 방이 더 편리하실 것 같습니다. 빈방이 있는지 얼른 확인해 보겠습니다.) 라고 말했으므로 (C)가 정답

Paraphrasing　if there is an unoccupied one ➡ the availability of a room

---

[영국]

Questions 92-94 refer to the following news report.

W: Good evening, Daniela McAdams here with KMG 3 News. Tonight's *Your Money* segment features Landing Financial Services' new banking app for mobile devices.(92) One key aspect of the app is that users can link multiple accounts, making it easier to transfer money from their savings to checking account. Many experts have questioned the adoption of mixing banking and technology. Nevertheless, after only being released a few days ago, it has over 25,000 downloads.(93) In an effort to gain more users, everyone who signs up and completes at least two transactions within the first 72 hours of downloading the app will automatically become eligible for their electric bike sweepstakes.(94)

92-94번은 다음 뉴스 보도에 관한 문제입니다.

여: 안녕하세요, KMG 3 뉴스의 Daniela McAdams입니다. 오늘밤 <Your Money> 코너에서는 Landing Financial Services의 모바일 기기용 신규 은행 어플을 특집으로 다룹니다.(92) 이 어플의 한 가지 중요한 특징은 사용자가 여러 계좌에 접속할 수 있다는 점인데, 이는 보통 예금에서 당좌 예금으로 돈을 더 쉽게 이체할 수 있게 해줍니다. 많은 전문가들은 금융 거래와 기술을 혼합한 방식을 도입하는 것에 의문을 제기했습니다. 그럼에도 불구하고, 며칠 전에 출시되었을 뿐인데, 25,000 건 이상 다운로드 되었습니다.(93) 더 많은 사용자들을 확보하기 위한 노력의 일환으로, 어플을 다운로드한 후 첫 72시간 이내에 최소 두 건의 거래를 이행한 분들은 모두 자동으로 전기 자전거 경품행사에 응모됩니다.(94)

어휘　segment n. 부분　feature v. 특징으로 하다, 특집 기사로 싣다　key adj. 가장 중요한, 핵심적인　link v. 연결하다, 접속하다　multiple adj. 많은, 다수의　account n. 계정　transfer v. 이체하다, 옮기다　savings account 보통 예금　checking account 당좌 예금　question v. 의문을 지니하다　adoption n. 채택　mix v. 섞다, 혼합하다　nevertheless adv. 그럼에도 불구하고　release v. 출시하다　in an effort to do ~하기 위한 노력의 일환으로　gain 얻다, 쌓다　sign up 등록하다, 신청하다　at least 적어도, 최소한　automatically adv. 자동으로　eligible adj. 자격이 있는　electric bike 전기자전거　sweepstakes n. (상금이 걸린) 당첨 행사; 경주

---

92 세부정보　　　난이도 중

해석　모바일 애플리케이션은 사용자들에게 무엇을 가능하게 해줄 것인가?
(A) 업체 검색
(B) 게임 하기
(C) 사진 업로드
(D) 온라인 뱅킹

해설　화자가 Tonight's Your Money segment features Landing Financial Services' new banking app for mobile devices. (오늘밤 <Your Money> 코너에서는 Landing Financial Services의 모바일 기기용 신규 은행 어플을 특집으로 다룹니다.)라고 말했으므로 (D)가 정답

93 화자 의도 파악　　　난이도 중

해석　화자가 "25,000 건 이상 다운로드 되었습니다"라고 말할 때, 그녀가 의미한 것은?
(A) 프로그램이 인기가 있다.
(B) 마케팅 캠페인이 필요하다.
(C) 서버가 업그레이드되어야 한다.
(D) 사이트가 제대로 작동하지 않는다.

해설　화자가 Many experts have questioned the adoption of mixing banking and technology. (많은 전문가들은 금융 거래와 기술을 혼합한 방식을 도입하는 것에 의문을 제기했습니다.)라면서, Nevertheless, after only being released a few days ago, it has over 25,000 downloads. (그럼에도 불구하고, 며칠 전에 출시되었을 뿐인데, 25,000 건 이상 다운로드 되었습니다.)라고 말한 것이므로 (A)가 정답

94 세부정보　　　난이도 중

해석　일부 사용자들은 어디에 참가할 수 있는가?
(A) 추첨 대회
(B) 시범 사용기간
(C) 연구 조사
(D) 육상 경기

해설　화자가 In an effort to gain more users, everyone who signs up and completes at least two transactions within the first 72 hours of downloading the app will automatically become eligible for their electric bike sweepstakes. (더 많은 사용자들을 확보하기 위한 노력의 일환으로, 어플을 다운로드한 후 첫 72시간 이내에 최소 두 건의 거래를 이행한 분들은 모두 자동으로 전기자전거 경품행사에 응모됩니다.)라고 말했으므로 (A)가 정답

Paraphrasing　sweepstakes ➡ contest

[미국]

Questions 95-97 refer to the following excerpt from a meeting and graph.

W: Welcome to Johnson County Community College. My name is Troy Hernandez, and I am the admissions director.(95) I'd like to talk about our Workplace Learning Program. In the past, instructors would be sent out to various companies in the area, and about 1,000 students completed a class every month. But when the college's Extension Services started offering the courses online, the number of people who registered for the classes dropped to just 500. **(96)** In hopes of figuring out why we had such a large drop, **we conducted questionnaires with several hundred participants. I'm going to share that data with you now, and then, we will discuss what to do next.** **(97)**

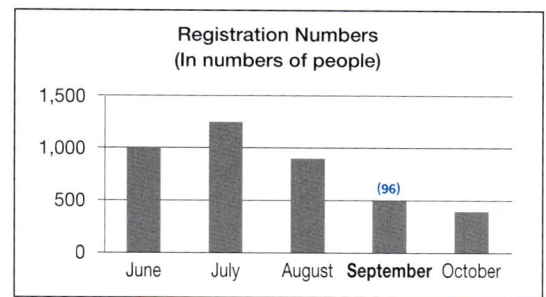

95-97번은 다음 회의 발췌록과 그래프에 관한 문제입니다.

여: Johnson 카운티 전문대학에 오신 것을 환영합니다. 제 이름은 Troy Hernandez이고 입학 처장입니다. **(95)** 저는 저희 직장 교육 프로그램에 관하여 말씀 드리려고 합니다. 과거에는 지역 내의 다양한 기업들에 강사들이 파견되었고 매달 약 1,000명의 학생이 수업을 수료했습니다. 그러나 대학의 순회교육 부서에서 온라인으로 수업을 제공하기 시작하자 수업 등록자 수가 500명으로 떨어졌습니다. **(96)** 저희는 왜 이렇게 큰 폭의 감소가 있었는지에 대해 알아내기 위해 수백 명의 참가자들을 대상으로 설문조사를 실시했습니다. 제가 지금 여러분께 그 자료를 공유해드리고 나서, 저희가 앞으로 무엇을 해야 할지 의논해 보겠습니다. **(97)**

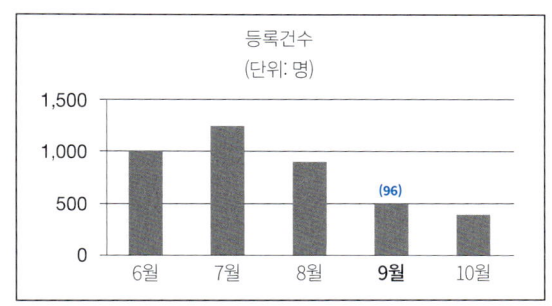

어휘 admission n. 가입, 입학 director n. 책임자, 관리자 extension service 순회교육 in hopes of ~을 바라고[~라는 희망을 갖고] figure out 알아내다 conduct v. 실시하다 questionnaire n. 설문조사

95 장소/근무지 난이도 중

해석 화자는 어디에서 근무하겠는가?
(A) 교육기관
(B) 백화점
(C) 택배사
(D) 콘퍼런스 센터

해설 화자가 Welcome to Johnson County Community College. My name is Troy Hernandez, and I am the admissions director. (Johnson 카운티 전문대학에 오신 것을 환영합니다. 제 이름은 Troy Hernandez이고 입학 처장입니다.)라고 말했으므로 (A)가 정답

Paraphrasing college ➡ educational institute

96 시각 정보 연계 난이도 중

해석 시각 자료를 보시오. 온라인 프로그램은 어느 달에 시작되었는가?
(A) 6월
(B) 7월
(C) 8월
(D) 9월

해설 화자가 But when the college's Extension Services started offering the courses online, the number of people who registered for the classes dropped to just 500. (그러나 대학의 순회교육 부서에서 온라인으로 수업을 제공하기 시작하자 수업 등록자 수가 500명으로 떨어졌습니다.)라고 말했고, 시각 자료에서 September (9월)에 500명임을 확인할 수 있으므로 (D)가 정답

97 다음 행동/계획 난이도 중

해석 이후에 어떤 일이 있겠는가?
(A) 청자들이 웹 사이트에 접속할 것이다
(B) 청자들을 여러 그룹으로 나눌 것이다
(C) 인터뷰가 실시될 것이다
(D) 설문조사 데이터가 발표될 것이다

해설 화자가 we conducted questionnaires with several hundred participants. I'm going to share that data with you now, and then, we will discuss what to do next. (저희는 수백 명의 참가자들을 대상으로 설문조사를 실시했습니다. 제가 지금 여러분께 그 자료를 공유해드리고 나서, 저희가 앞으로 무엇을 해야 할지 의논해 보겠습니다.)라고 말했으므로 (D)가 정답

Paraphrasing share ➡ present

미국

Questions 98-100 refer to the following telephone message and sign.

M: Good morning. My name is Hans Kanter. I own an accounting firm on Yosemite Road, and I need to have the place cleaned for an event I'm holding this weekend. **My neighbor gave me your number–he said he really liked your service.****(98)** **My office is about 900 square feet,****(99)** and I need it cleaned as soon as possible. **I'll be in a client meeting all morning today, so please contact me in the afternoon.****(100)** You can reach me at 555-8234. Thank you.

A-Z Commercial Cleaning Service

400 to 600 Square Feet = $45
600 to 800 Square Feet = $65
800 to 1,000 Square Feet = $85**(99)**
1,000 to 1,200 Square Feet = $105

98-100번은 다음 전화 메시지와 표지판에 관한 문제입니다.

남: 안녕하세요. 제 이름은 Hans Kanter입니다. Yosemite로에 회계 사무소를 하나 갖고 있는데, 이번 주말에 주최하는 행사 때문에 청소가 필요합니다. **제 이웃이 그쪽 번호를 알려줬는데, 서비스가 정말 좋았다고 하더군요.**(98) 제 사무실은 약 900제곱피트 정도 되고(99) 되도록 빨리 청소를 해야 합니다. 오늘은 제가 오전 내내 고객과 회의가 있어서 오후에 연락 주셨으면 좋겠습니다.(100) 555-8234로 전화하시면 됩니다. 고맙습니다.

A-Z 기업 청소서비스

400 - 600 제곱피트 = 45달러
600 - 800 제곱피트 = 65달러
800 - 1,000 제곱피트 = 85달러(99)
1,000 - 1,200 제곱피트 = 105달러

어휘 own v. 소유하다 accounting firm 회계사무소 reach v. 연락하다

98 세부 정보   난이도 중

해석 발신인은 청자의 전화번호를 어디서 구했는가?
(A) 텔레비전 광고
(B) 이웃
(C) 소식지
(D) 시 안내책자

해설 화자가 My neighbor gave me your number–he said he really liked your service. (제 이웃이 그쪽 번호를 알려줬는데, 서비스가 정말 좋았다고 하더군요.) 라고 말했으므로 (B)가 정답

99 시각정보 연계   난이도 중

해석 시각 자료를 보시오. 서비스 비용은 얼마나 들 것인가?
(A) 45달러
(B) 65달러
(C) 85달러
(D) 105달러

해설 화자가 My office is about 900 square feet,(제 사무실은 약 900제곱피트 정도 되고)라고 말했고, 시각 자료에서 800 to 1,000 Square Feet = $85 (800 - 1,000 제곱피트 = 85달러)를 확인할 수 있으므로 (C)가 정답

100 세부정보   난이도 중

해석 발신인은 왜 오늘 오전에 시간이 없는가?
(A) 병원에 간다.
(B) 고객과 만난다.
(C) 회사 워크숍에서 발표를 한다.
(D) 은행에 간다.

해설 화자가 I'll be in a client meeting all morning today, so please contact me in the afternoon. (오늘은 제가 오전 내내 고객과 회의가 있어서 오후에 연락 주셨으면 좋겠습니다.) 라고 말했으므로 (B)가 정답

Paraphrasing all morning today ➡ this morning

PART 5   P. 160

101 구조/문법 • 소유격 인칭대명사   난이도 하

해석 Silvercove 리조트는 쉽게 갈 수 있으며 자체 셔틀버스 서비스가 있습니다.

해설 빈칸은 own을 수식하는 자리. 소유 강조표현 'one's own(~자신의, ~만의)'의 형태를 완성하며, 문맥상 '리조트의 자체 셔틀버스 서비스'라는 의미가 되어야 자연스러우므로 리조트를 지칭하는 소유격 인칭대명사 (D)가 정답

Key point
형용사 own은 소유격 대명사와 함께 쓰여 소유의 의미를 강조하는 역할을 한다.

어휘 easily adv. 쉽게 accessible adj. 접근 가능한, 이용할 수 있는

102 구조/문법 • 형용사   난이도 중

해석 지역 내 중심 위치로 인해, Martenville에는 최대 규모의 열차 조차장이 있다.

해설 빈칸은 명사 location을 수식하는 자리. 문맥상 '지역 내 중심적 위치'라는 의미가 되어야 자연스러우므로 형용사 (C)가 정답

어휘 location n. 위치, 장소 province n. 지방 switch yard (열차) 조차장

103 구조/문법+어휘 • 명사   난이도 중

해석 Mr. Coulson는 새 본부의 개관을 위한 의식과 기자회견을 준비할 것이다.

해설 빈칸은 관사 the의 수식을 받는 명사자리. 문맥상 '새 본부의 개관식과 기자회견'이라는 의미가 되어야 자연스러우므로 (B)가 정답

오답보기 확인
(A) openness 솔직함
(B) opener 여는 기구
(C) open 옥외

어휘 organize v. 조직하다, 준비하다 ceremony n. 식, 의식 press conference 기자회견 opening n. 개장, 개업, 개막; 공석 headquarters n. 본사, 본부

104 어휘 • 전치사   난이도 중

해석 비상문의 잠금 장치를 풀려면 손으로 바 위를 세게 미세요.

해설 빈칸은 명사 the bar를 목적어로 하는 전치사자리. 문맥상 '문을 열려면 바(막대 모양으로 된 손잡이)를 세게 누르라'는 의미가 되어야 자연스러우므로 바 위를 누르는 그림을 완성하는 (A)가 정답

Key word
Push firmly **on the bar** with your hands to release emergency door's locking mechanism.

어휘 push v. 밀다 firmly adv. 세게 bar n. 바, 막대기(모양의 것) release v. 풀다, 풀어주다 emergency door 비상문 lock v. 잠그다 mechanism n. 기계 장치, 구조

105 구조/문법 • 부사   난이도 중

해석 이 사무실 관리인은 대학교 규정에 명백히 맞지 않는 광고를 모두 치울 것이다.

154

해설	빈칸은 주격 관계대명사와 동사 사이에서 동사를 수식하는 부사자리. 문맥상 '규정에 명백히 맞지 않는 광고를 치울 것'이라는 의미가 되어야 자연스러우므로 (B)가 정답

Key point
부사 clearly vs. clear: clearly는 '또렷하게, 분명히', clear는 '~에서 떨어져, ~에서 닿지 않게'를 의미하며, 주로 'clear of'의 형태로 쓰인다.

어휘	**administrator** n. 관리자, 행정인 **remove** v. 제거하다 **conform to** ~에 따르다, 순응하다 **regulation** n. 규정

106 구조/문법 • 부사   난이도 중

해석	Marchand 합창단이 돋보이는데, 이는 단원들이 각자의 노래 스타일을 조합하는 법을 알고 있기 때문이다.
해설	빈칸은 동사 know의 목적어자리. 빈칸 뒤 to부정사구가 있음을 고려할 때, 문맥상 '단원들이 (서로 다른) 개개인의 스타일을 잘 조합하는 법을 알기에 합창단이 돋보인다'는 의미가 되어야 자연스러우므로, 'how to V(V하는 방법)'이라는 형태를 완성하는 (C)가 정답

Key point
의문사 how는 명사절 접속사로 쓰여 'how+S+V(어떻게 S가 V하는지)'의 구조로 명사절을 이끌 수 있으며, 주절과 how절의 주어가 동일한 경우, 'how to V(~하는 법)'의 형태로 축약될 수 있다.

어휘	**choir** n. 합창단 **stand out** 눈에 띄다, 두드러지다 **blend** v. 섞다, 조합하다 **individual** adj. 개개의

107 어휘 • 형용사   난이도 중

해석	극장 카페에서 무료 음료를 받으려면, 방문객은 유효한 입장권을 제시해야 한다.
해설	빈칸은 명사구 admission ticket을 수식하는 형용사자리. 문맥상 '무료 음료를 받으려면, 유효한 티켓을 제시해야 한다'는 의미가 되어야 자연스러우므로 (B)가 정답

Key word
To receive a **complimentary** beverage at the theater café, guests must **present** a **valid** admission ticket.

오답보기 확인
(A) moderate 보통의
(C) plausible 그럴듯한
(D) determined 단호한

어휘	**complimentary** adj. 무료의 **present** v. 제시하다 **valid** a. 유효한 **admission ticket** 입장권

108 어휘 • 동사   난이도 중

해석	고객 설문조사 결과는 대부분의 사람들이 Milkmade 딸기 요거트가 매우 만족스럽다고 여긴다는 것을 보여준다.
해설	빈칸은 문장의 목적어인 that절 내 주어 most people에 대한 동사자리. 빈칸 뒤 목적어에 해당하는 명사구와 목적격 보어에 해당하는 현재분사가 있음을 고려할 때, 'find+목적어+목적격 보어(~가 ...임을 알게 되다)'의 5형식 문장구조를 완성하는 동사 (B)가 정답

Key word
The customer survey results **indicate** that most people **find** Milkmade's strawberry **drinking yogurt** very **satisfying**.

Key point
find는 일반적인 3형식 동사로 쓰일 때는 '찾다'라는 의미이지만, 5형식 동사로 쓰일 때에는 '~라고 여기다, ~임을 알게 되다'라는 의미이다.

오답보기 확인
(A) enjoy 즐기다
(C) sense 느끼다, 감지하다
(D) correspond 일치하다, 부합하다

어휘	**survey** n. 설문조사 **indicate** v. 나타내다, 보여주다 **find** v. ~라고 여기다, ~임을 알게 되다 **satisfying** adj. 만족스러운

109 구조/문법 • 종속접속사 - 명사절   난이도 중

해석	제안이 프로젝트로 선정될 지의 여부와 상관없이, 모든 제출물은 2년간 데이터베이스에 보관된다.
해설	빈칸부터 콤마(,)까지는 구전치사 regardless of의 목적어자리. 빈칸 뒤 주어+동사를 갖춘 완전한 문장이 이어짐을 고려할 때, 빈칸은 문장을 명사절로 만들어주는 접속사자리이므로 (D)가 정답. regardless of whether는 자주 출제되는 표현으로 '~인지와는 상관없이'라는 의미의 숙어적인 표현으로 외워 두자.

Key point
전치사는 명사형태(ex. 명사, 명사구, 명사절, 동명사)만을 목적어로 취할 수 있다.

어휘	**regardless of** ~에 상관없이 **proposal** n. 제안 **select** v. 선택하다 **submission** n. 제출(물)

110 구조/문법 • 부사   난이도 중

해석	Ms. Sawyer가 탄 기차는 너무 늦게 도착해서 그녀는 오찬에 참석할 수 없었다.
해설	빈칸은 부사 late을 수식하는 부사자리. 빈칸 뒤 이어지는 문장구조를 고려할 때, 'too ~ to 부정사(너무 ~해서 ...할 수 없다)'의 구조를 완성하는 부사 (D)가 정답

Key point
to부정사 관용표현 [too 형용사/부사 (for S') to부정사]는 '너무 ~해서 (S'가) ...할 수 없다'를 의미한다.

어휘	**arrive** v. 도착하다 **participate in** ~에 참여하다 **luncheon** n. 오찬

111 구조/문법 • 부정대명사   난이도 중

해석	매일 2리터의 물을 마시는 것보다 충분한 영양상태를 유지하는 데 더 필수적인 것은 없다.
해설	'There is' 유도부사 구문의 문장이므로, 빈칸은 문장의 실제 주어인 명사자리. 빈칸 뒤 주어인 명사를 후치 수식하는 형용사구가 있으므로 부정대명사 (A)가 정답

Key point
비교급 구문을 활용한 최상급 관용표현:
'부정주어(No one, Nothing 등) ~ more ... than N'은 'N보다 더 ...한 사람[것]은 없다'를 의미한다.

어휘	**essential** adj. 필수적인, 중요한 **preserve** v. 지키다, 보존하다 **nutrition** n. 영양 **liter** n. 리터 **daily** adv. 매일

112 어휘 • 명사   난이도 중

해석	Maynard 미술관은 기록장치의 사용이 로비와 접수구역으로 한정되어야 한다고 요구한다.
해설	빈칸은 문장의 목적어인 that 명사절 내 주어자리. 빈칸을 수식하는 of 전치사구의 내용을 고려할 때 문맥상 '기록장치의 사용은 일부 장소로 한정되어야 한다'는 의미가 되어야 자연스러우므로 (B)가 정답

Key word
The Maynard Fine Art Museum requires that the **usage** of recording devices be limited to the lobby and reception areas.

오답보기 확인
(A) category 범주
(C) capacity 수용력, 능력
(D) period 기간

어휘 fine art 미술 require v. 요구하다 usage n. 사용, 사용량 recording device 기록장치 limit v. 제한하다 reception n. 접수처

113 구조/문법+어휘・접속사 난이도 중

해석 계약서 최종본이 서명된 후, Ms. Cheng은 교섭자들에게 그들이 들인 시간과 노력에 대한 감사를 표했다.

해설 빈칸은 두 문장을 연결하는 접속사자리. 두 문장의 관계를 고려할 때, 문맥상 '계약서에 서명을 한 후, 교섭자들에게 감사를 표했다'는 내용으로 이어져야 자연스러우므로 (B)가 정답

Key point
'------ 문장1, 문장2'의 구조에서 빈칸은 부사절 접속사 자리이다.

어휘 final adj. 마지막의, 최종의 contract n. 계약(서) sign v. 서명하다 negotiator n. 협상가 effort n. 노력

114 어휘・전치사 난이도 중

해석 회원 리워드 프로그램에도 불구하고, Tesseract Communcations의 이용요금은 많은 사람들에게 과하다고 여겨진다.

해설 빈칸은 명사구를 목적어로 하는 전치사자리. 주절과의 관계를 고려할 때 의미가 서로 상반되므로, '리워드 프로그램이 있음에도 불구하고, 요금이 과하다고 여겨진다'는 의미로 이어져야 자연스러우므로 (C)가 정답

Key word
Despite its **membership rewards program**, Tesseract Communcations' **service rates are regarded as exorbitant** by many.

오답보기 확인
(A) thanks to ~덕분에
(B) far from 전혀 ~이 아닌
(D) during ~동안

어휘 reward n. 보상 service rate 이용요금 regard v. 간주하다 exorbitant adj. 과도한, 지나친

115 구조/문법・동사 – 현재시제 난이도 중

해석 회사 경영진은 향후 몇 달간 경영전략부서에서 예상한 이윤을 보기를 희망한다.

해설 빈칸은 주어와 목적어인 to부정사구 사이 동사자리. 문두에 미래를 나타내는 표현 over the next few months가 있으므로 과거시제는 답이 될 수 없고, 향후 몇 년간의 일을 현재 희망한다는 의미로 미래형 동사 hope의 현재시제인 (C) hopes가 정답

Key point
① 시간 부사구와 시제 일치: next, soon, shortly 등 미래 시점을 나타내는 시간 부사구는 미래시제와 함께 쓰인다.
② 미래형 동사 hope은 현재시제로 미래를 나타내는 시간 부사구와 함께 올 수 있다.

어휘 executive n. 경영진 profit n. 이윤 predict v. 예상하다 corporate strategy 기업전략, 경영전략

116 어휘・전치사 난이도 중

해석 스코틀랜드 작가 Giles Fitzpatrick의 소설 초고는 오늘 개인 수집가에게 알려지지 않은 금액에 판매되었다.

해설 빈칸은 an amount를 목적어로 취하는 전치사자리. 문맥상 '소설 초안이 알려지지 않은 금액에 판매되었다'는 의미가 되어야 하므로, 물건에 대한 교환 가치로서의 금액을 목적어로 취하는 전치사 (B)가 정답

Key word
An early **novel draft** by Scottish author Giles Fitzpatrick **was purchased** by a private collector today **for an unknown amount**.

어휘 novel n. 소설 draft n. 초안 Scottish adj. 스코틀랜드의 author n. 작가 purchase v. 구입하다 private adj. 사적인 collector n. 수집가 amount n. 양, 금액

117 어휘・부사 난이도 중

해석 Gensian 복합 오븐렌지는 Albi 주방용품에서 가장 합리적인 가격의 상품이다.

해설 빈칸은 형용사 자리의 과거분사 priced를 수식하는 부사자리. 문맥상 '합리적인 가격의 상품'이라는 의미가 되어야 자연스러우므로 'reasonably priced(합리적으로 가격이 책정된)'이라는 의미를 완성하는 부사 (A)가 정답

Key word
The Gensian range and oven combo is Albi Kitchenwares' most **reasonably priced** configuration.

오답보기 확인
(B) definitely 절대적으로
(C) sparsely 성기게, 드문드문
(D) approximately 거의

어휘 range n. (가스, 전기) 레인지 oven n. 오븐 reasonably adv. 합리적으로, 타당하게, 적정하게 priced a. 가격이 매겨진 configuration n. 배열, 형태

118 어휘・동사 난이도 상

해석 수요일에 있을 세미나는 지역 관리자들로 하여금 직원들을 효율적으로 채용하고, 관리하고, 독려하는 능력을 평가하는 데 도움이 될 것이다.

해설 빈칸은 동사 help의 목적격 보어자리. 문맥상 '세미나는 지역 관리자들이 (관리자로서) 자신들의 능력을 평가하는 데 도움이 될 것'이라는 의미가 되어야 자연스러우므로 타동사 (A)가 정답

Key word
Wednesday's seminar will **help regional managers** (to) **evaluate their ability** to efficiently hire, manage, and encourage employees.

오답보기 확인
(B) protect 보호하다
(C) assemble 조립하다
(D) progress 진행하다

어휘 regional adj. 지역의, 지방의 evaluate v. 평가하다 efficiently adv. 능률적으로 hire v. 고용하다 manage v. 관리하다 encourage v. 독려하다

119 구조/문법 • to부정사 난이도 중

해석 방문객들은 Montcrew 박물관의 최근 오픈한 고대 그리스-로마관을 관람하도록 안내 받는다.

해설 invite는 to부정사를 목적격 보어로 취하는 동사로 invite A to do 형태로 쓰이며 수동태가 되면 be invited to do 형태로 수동태 동사 뒤에 to부정사가 남는 형태가 되므로 (C)가 정답

Key point
목적격 보어자리에 to부정사를 취하는 대표적인 동사는 다음과 같다: allow, ask, expect, invite, remind 등

어휘 invite A to do A가 ~하도록 요청하다[초대하다] ancient adj. 고대의 Greek adj. 그리스의 Roman adj. 로마의 wing n. 부속건물

120 어휘 • 부사 난이도 중

해석 초청 연사는 직원 고충을 지속적으로 다루어주는 것이 직원을 유지하는 하나의 필수요소라고 주장했다.

해설 빈칸은 that 명사절 내 주어인 동명사 addressing을 수식하는 부사자리. 문맥상 '직원 고충을 지속적으로 처리해 주는 것'이라는 의미가 되어야 자연스러우므로 (C)가 정답

Key word
The guest speaker insisted that **addressing** employee complaints **consistently** was one **vital** element for **retaining** staff.

오답보기 확인
(A) largely 대개
(B) similarly 마찬가지로
(D) immensely 엄청나게

어휘 insist v. 주장하다 address v. 다루다, 처리하다 complaint n. 불평, 불만 consistently adj. 지속적으로 vital adj. 필수적인 element n. 요소 retain v. 유지하다

121 구조/문법 • 형용사 난이도 상

해석 예술가의 복제품을 원본과 함께 꼼꼼히 살펴본 후, 비평가는 양쪽의 구별되는 특성들을 구분할 수 있었다.

해설 빈칸은 관사와 명사 사이 형용사 자리. 문맥상 '양쪽을 서로 구별시켜 주는 특성들'이라는 의미가 되어야 자연스러우므로 (D)가 정답

Key point
분사형 형용사 distinguished vs. distinguishing: distinguished는 '유명한, 성공한'을, distinguishing은 '특징적인, 구별되는'을 의미한다.

어휘 careful adj. 세심한, 주의 깊은 probe n. 조사 replica n. 복제본 alongside prep. ~와 함께, ~옆에 original n. 원본 classify v. 구분하다 distinguished adj. 유명한, 성공한 distinguishing adj. 다른 것과 구별되는, 특징적인 attribute n. 자질, 속성

122 구조/문법+어휘 • 접속사 난이도 중

해석 저희가 도급업자의 측정치를 정오 전에 받는 한, 호텔 개조 견적서는 오늘 오후 발송될 것입니다.

해설 빈칸은 두 개의 문장을 연결하는 접속사자리. 문맥상 '오전에 측정치를 받는 한, 오후에 견적서가 발송될 것'이라는 내용으로 이어져야 자연스러우므로 (B)가 정답

Key point
문장과 문장 사이에는 접속사가 반드시 필요하다.

어휘 estimate n. 견적서 renovation n. 개조 보수 contractor n. 도급업자 measurement n. 치수, 측정 besides adj. 게다가 if not 그렇지 않으면, 아니면

123 구조/문법+어휘 • 명사 난이도 중

해석 이 공지는 승객들에게 국제 항공편의 휴대용 수화물에 대한 규제사항들을 알리기 위함입니다.

해설 빈칸은 전치사 of의 목적어인 명사자리. 문맥상 '승객들에게 휴대용 수화물에 대한 규제사항을 알려주는 것'이라는 의미가 되어야 자연스러우므로, 'limitations on ~(~에 대한 제약, 규제)'라는 표현을 완성하는 (A)가 정답

Key point
명사 limit vs. limitation: limit on은 '(허용한도에 대한) 제한, 허용치'를, limitation on은 '(법, 조건의) 제약, 규제'를 의미한다.

어휘 announcement n. 발표, 공지 inform v. 공지하다, 알리다 passenger n. 승객 carry-on luggage 휴대용 수화물 flight n. 항공편, 비행

124 어휘 • 구전치사 난이도 중

해석 Tyson 기업 연구센터에 따르면, 직원들에게 유연한 일정을 선택하도록 허용하는 것은 업무 성과를 향상시킨다.

해설 빈칸은 명사구를 목적어로 취하는 전치사자리. 명사구와 주절의 관계를 고려할 때, 문맥상 '연구센터에 따르면'이라는 의미가 되어야 자연스러우므로 (B)가 정답

Key word
According to the Tyson **Center** for Business Research, **allowing** employees to choose a flexible schedule improves work performance.

오답보기 확인
(A) apart from ~를 제외하고
(C) in regard to ~에 관한
(D) because of ~때문에

어휘 according to ~에 따르면 allow v. 허용하다 choose v. 고르다 flexible adj. 유연한, 융통성 있는 improve v. 향상시키다 work performance 업무성과

125 어휘 • 부사 난이도 중

해석 Ms. Fontaine은 이미 그 날에 회의에 참석해야 했기에 학회와 일정이 겹쳤다.

해설 빈칸은 since 종속절 내 수동태 동사구문을 수식하는 부사자리. 주절과 종속절의 관계를 고려할 때, 문맥상 '그 날짜에 이미 회의에 참석해야 했기에 학회와 일정이 겹쳤다'는 의미가 되어야 자연스러우므로 (B)가 정답

Key word
Ms. Fontaine **had a conflict with the conference since** she was **already required to attend a meeting on that date**.

오답보기 확인
(A) yet 아직
(C) rather 꽤, 약간
(D) not ~아니다

어휘 conflict n. 충돌 conference n. 회의, 학회 already 이미, 벌써 require v. 요구하다

126 구조/문법 • 명사 　　　　난이도 중

해석 Helvetica 사의 연구개발부서에서는 직원 혁신에 대해 보상을 제공한다.

해설 빈칸은 동사 reward의 목적어이자, 명사 employee와 복합명사를 이루는 명사자리. 동사와 명사 사이 관사가 없음을 고려할 때, 불가산 복합명사를 만들어 주는 명사 (B)가 정답

Key point
① 복합명사의 특징: 복합명사는 두 개 이상의 명사가 [명사+명사]의 형태로 하나의 단어처럼 쓰이며, 마지막 명사를 기준으로 복합명사의 성격(가산/불가산, 단/복수 등)이 결정된다.
② 가산명사는 반드시 관사(a, the)와 함께, 또는 복수형으로 와야 한다.
③ 명사 innovation vs. innovator: 불가산명사 innovation은 '혁신'을, 가산명사 innovator는 '혁신가'를 의미한다.

어휘 reward v. 보상하다　employee n. 직원

127 어휘 • 형용사 　　　　난이도 중

해석 월요일 오전의 많은 통화량을 고려해 볼 때, 고객 서비스팀과의 통화연결이 예상보다 더 오래 걸릴 수 있다.

해설 빈칸은 명사구 call volumes를 수식하는 형용사자리. 문맥상 '월요일 오전의 상당히 많은 통화량을 고려할 때, 통화연결에 시간이 오래 걸릴 수 있다'는 의미가 되어야 자연스러우므로, '양, 정도가 보통보다 많다'는 의미를 전달하는 (C)가 정답

Key word
Considering the heavy call volumes on Monday mornings, contacting our customer services may take longer than expected.

오답보기 확인
(A) multiple 다수의, 다양한
(B) noisy 시끄러운
(D) extended 길어진, 늘어난

어휘 considering prep. ~을 고려하면　heavy a. 많은, 심한; 무거운　call volume 통화량

128 구조/문법 • 명사 　　　　난이도 중

해석 Houston에서 열리는 컨벤션에 참석하는 직원들은 교통비를 결제하고, 영수증을 보관하고, 복귀 후 상환신청서를 제출하라고 안내 받았다.

해설 빈칸은 동사 make의 목적어인 명사자리. 'make a payment (결제하다)'의 표현을 완성하는 명사 (D)가 정답

어휘 attend v. 참석하다　direct v. 안내하다, 지시하다　transportation n. 교통, 수송　receipt n. 영수증　file v. 제출하다　reimbursement n. 상환, 환급　request n. 신청　return v. 돌아오다

129 어휘 • 부사 　　　　난이도 중

해석 웹 디자인 워크숍 이후, 참가자들은 자신들의 사이트 접속량이 상당히 많아졌다고 말했다.

해설 빈칸은 비교급 형용사 higher를 수식하는 부사자리. 문두의 following 전치사구의 내용을 고려할 때, 문맥상 '웹 디자인 워크숍 이후, 사이트 접속량이 상당히 많아졌다'는 의미가 되어야 자연스러우므로 비교급 강조부사 (B)가 정답

Key point
대표적인 비교급 강조부사들은 다음과 같다: considerably, significantly (상당히), even, far, still(훨씬)

오답보기 확인
(A) severely 심하게, 혹독하게
(C) necessarily 어쩔 수 없이
(D) willingly 자진해서, 기꺼이

어휘 participant n. 참가자　state v. 말하다, 진술하다　traffic n. (전산망을 통한 정보의) 소통(량)　considerably adj. 상당히

130 구조/문법 • 동사 - 현재완료 　　　　난이도 중

해석 Flagstone 카페는 지난 10년간 일요일에 조식 판촉행사를 제공해오고 있다.

해설 빈칸은 주어와 목적어 사이 동사자리. 문장 끝에 기간을 나타내는 표현 'for the last decade' 가 있으므로 현재완료시제 (C)가 정답

Key point
① 시간 부사구와 시제 일치: 기간을 나타내는 시간부사구는 완료시제와 함께 쓰인다.
② '조동사+have p.p.'는 가정법 과거완료 구문으로 과거사실에 대한 반대를 표현한다.

어휘 promotion n. 홍보(활동)　decade n. 10년

PART 6　　　　P. 163

131-134번은 다음 편지에 관한 문제입니다.

오랜 고객님께 드리는 메시지:

Bullseye 가정용품점은 저렴한 가격에 고품질의 상품을 **131. 제공해 드리기 위해** 노력합니다. 경쟁력 있는 비용과 더불어, 엄청난 고객서비스로 저희는 지역 내 가장 신뢰받는 가정용품 체인점이 되었습니다. Bullseye 내 5곳의 지점은 도합 60년 **132. 동안** 온타리오 주민들에게 서비스를 제공해 왔습니다.

최상의 서비스를 제공해 드리기 위해, 저희는 5월 8일부터 5월 29일까지 리모델링으로 Kitchener 지점의 문을 닫습니다. **133. 이로 인해 생겨나는 모든 불편에 미리 사과 드립니다.** 이 기간 동안, 인근의 Cambridge 매장이 정규 영업 **134. 시간 동안** 계속 영업할 것입니다. 문의사항이나 의견이 있으시면 저희에게 알려주세요. 저희는 항상 귀하의 시간과 거래를 소중히 여깁니다.

감사드리며,

Pablo Guaido
소유주 겸 창립자, Bullseye 가정용품점

어휘 loyal adj. 충실한　appliance n. (가정용) 기기　strive v. 매진하다, 노력하다　high-quality adj. 고품질의　affordable adj. (가격이) 알맞은　competitive adj. 경쟁력 있는, 뒤지지 않는　tremendous adj. 엄청난, 굉장한　chain n. 체인점　retailer n. 소매업자　province n. 지방　location n. 위치, 장소　serve v. (상품, 서비스를) 제공하다　collective adj. 집단의, 단체의　a total of 총　enable v. ~를 할 수 있게 하다　remodel v. 개조하다, 리모델링하다　neighboring adj. 근처의, 인접한　value v. 가치 있게 여기다

131 구조/문법 • to부정사 난이도 중

해설 빈칸은 동사 strive의 목적어자리. 빈칸 뒤 명사구가 있음을 고려할 때, 목적어를 취하는 준동사 자리이므로 능동형의 to부정사 (B)가 정답

Key point
일부 동사는 목적어 자리에 to부정사 또는 동명사만을 취할 수 있다. to부정사만을 목적어로 취하는 대표적인 동사는 다음과 같다: strive, intend, decide, choose 등

132 어휘 • 전치사 난이도 중

해설 빈칸은 기간 표현을 목적어로 취하는 전치사자리. 문맥상 '60년 동안 서비스를 제공해왔다는 의미가 되어야 자연스러우므로 (C)가 정답

Key point
기간 전치사 for vs. within: for는 '~동안'을, within은 '~이내'를 의미하며, for는 현재완료 시제와 함께 주로 사용된다.

133 문맥이해 • 문장삽입 난이도 중

해석 (A) 매장은 5월 31일까지 한 시간 더 영업을 할 것입니다.
(B) 모든 의견에는 48시간 내 답변을 드립니다.
(C) 이 보증은 제한된 시간 동안만 이용할 수 있습니다.
(D) 이로 인해 생겨나는 모든 불편에 미리 사과 드립니다.

해설 빈칸 앞 문장의 '리모델링으로 Kitchener 지점의 문을 닫는다'는 내용과 빈칸 뒤 문장의 '그 동안 인근지역의 지점은 정상영업을 할 것'이라는 내용을 고려할 때, 문맥상 '지점 리모델링으로 불편을 드려 미리 사과 드린다'는 내용이 들어가야 자연스러우므로 (D)가 정답

Key word
To enable us to provide you with the best possible service, we will close the Kitchener location from May 8 to May 29 for remodeling. We would like to apologize in advance for any bother this causes. Throughout this time, the store in neighboring Cambridge will remain open during regular business hours.

134 어휘 • 명사 난이도 하

해설 빈칸은 명사 business와 함께 복합명사를 이루는 명사자리. 문맥상 '영업 시간 동안'이라는 의미가 되어야 자연스러우므로 (D)가 정답

Key word
Throughout this time, the store in neighboring Cambridge will remain open during regular business hours.

135-138번은 다음 정보에 관한 문제입니다.

<The Natural World>의 많은 135. **기고가들**은 오랜 기간 동안 저희 출판물과 함께 작업해온 베테랑 생물학자들입니다. 136. **그렇지만**, 저희는 항상 미래 과학자들의 작품을 알리는 데 관심이 있습니다. 저희는 모든 호에 새로운 연구자의 제출작을 적어도 1~2개 싣는 것을 목표로 하고 있지만, 저희의 분기별 출판 일정으로는 모든 훌륭한 글을 싣는 것이 어렵습니다. 작품을 제출하시기 전에, 저희 출판물 지침을 숙지하시는 것이 매우 중요한데(naturalworld.com/submissions에서 보실 수 있습니다), 여기에 인용 및 서식 규칙이 자세히 나와 있습니다. 137. **이는 귀하의 작품이 선택될 가능성을 높여줄 것입니다.**

저희는 수령하는 모든 서신에 답하기 위해 최선의 노력을 다하고 있다는 것을 기억해 주십시오. 하지만 많은 양의 제출물로 인해, 저희는 항상 빠르게 답을 드릴 수 없습니다. 이로 인해, 저희는 여러분께 138. **참을성 있게 기다려 주시기**를 요청 드립니다.

어휘 veteran n. 전문가, 베테랑 biologist n. 생물학자 collaborate v. 공동으로 작업하다, 협력하다 publication n. 출판물 extended period 장기간 promote v. 홍보하다 aspiring adj. 장차~가 되려는 issue n. (정기 간행물의) 호 aim v. 목표하다 feature v. 특별히 포함하다 at least 적어도, 최소한 submission n. 제출 researcher n. 연구원, 조사원 quarterly adj. 분기별의 publishing n. 출판 worthy adj. ~를 받을만한, (~을 받을) 자격이 있는 article n. 글, 기사 submit v. 제출하다 essential adj. 필수적인, 극히 중요한 familiarize ~ with ... ~가 …에 익숙[친숙]해지다 guidelines n. 지침, 가이드라인 available adj. 이용할 수 있는 detail v. 상세히 알리다, 열거하다 citation n. 인용 formatting rule 서식설정 규칙 keep in mind 명심하다 respond v. 답장을 보내다, 대답하다 correspondence n. 편지, 서신 volume n. 양

135 구조/문법 • 명사 난이도 하

해설 빈칸은 문장의 주어인 명사자리. Many of의 한정을 받고 있으므로 복수명사 (C)가 정답

Key point
한정사 many는 가산 복수명사와 함께 쓰인다.

136 어휘+문맥이해 • 연결어 난이도 중

해설 빈칸 앞 문장의 '많은 기고자들은 오랜 기간 동안 함께 작업해온 베테랑 생물학자들'이라는 내용과 빈칸 뒷 부분의 '미래 과학자들의 작품을 알리는 데에도 관심이 있다'는 내용을 고려할 때, 빈칸에 '그렇지만'을 의미하는 연결어가 들어가야 문맥상 자연스러우므로 (B)가 정답

Key word
Many of the contributors to The Natural World are veteran biologists who have collaborated with our publication over an extended period. Even so, we are always interested in promoting the work of aspiring scientists.

137 문맥이해 • 문장삽입 난이도 중

해석 (A) 저희 구독자 대부분은 대학교수 및 대학원생들입니다.
(B) 이번 달 출간호는 앞으로 2주 내 발송될 것입니다.
(C) 귀하의 접근법에 깊은 인상을 받았습니다만, 저희는 더 많은 통계적인 증거를 필요로 합니다.
(D) 이는 귀하의 작품이 선택될 가능성을 높여줄 것입니다.

해설 빈칸 앞 문장의 '작품 제출 전, 출판물 지침을 숙지하는 것이 매우 중요한데, 여기에 인용 및 서식 규칙이 자세히 나와 있다'는 내용을 고려할 때, 문맥상 '출판물 지침을 숙지하는 것이 작품이 선택될 가능성을 높여줄 것'이라는 내용으로 연결되어야 자연스러우므로 (D)가 정답

Key word
Before you submit your work, it is essential to familiarize yourself with our publication guidelines (available at naturalworld.com/submissions), which detail our citation and formatting rules. This will improve the chances that your work is chosen.

138 어휘+문맥이해•형용사　난이도 중

해설 빈칸은 빈칸 앞 문장의 '많은 양의 제출물로 인해, 항상 빠르게 답을 드릴 수 없다'는 내용을 고려할 때, 문맥상 '이로 인해 참을성 있게 기다려 주길 요청 드린다'는 내용으로 이어져야 자연스러우므로 (D)가 정답

Key word
but **due to the high volume of submissions, we cannot always do so quickly. Because of this**, we have to **ask you to be patient**.

139-142번은 다음 광고에 관한 문제입니다.

TBD 금융의 새로운 Endeavor 카드는 귀하의 투자에 대한 보상을 제공합니다.

TBD 금융은 재고주문에서 신규 사무용 가구 구입에 이르기까지 일상적인 사업비용으로 포인트를 적립할 수 있는 사업용 리워드 신용카드를 제공해 드리게 되어 기쁩니다. 이제, 일하면서 다음 휴가를 위한 저축을 시작하실 수 있습니다. 왜 레스토랑에서 식사를 하거나 영화를 보는 것으로만 혜택을 주는 카드에 139. 만족하시나요? Endeavor 카드는 매 구매의 1.5%를 포인트로 전환해주 140. 지만, 사무용품, 가스, 모바일 서비스와 같은 주요 사업비용에 대해서는 두 배로 제공해드립니다. 이는 자신의 사업을 최우선 순위에 놓는 141. 개인들에게 최고의 선택입니다. 오늘 TBD 금융에 가입하시고 500달러의 특별 선지급 보너스 혜택을 받으세요. 142. 이 굉장한 혜택은 3월 1일에 끝나니, 지체하지 마세요.

어휘 reward v. 보상[보답]하다　invest in ~에 투자하다　accrue v. 누적되다　day-to-day adj. 그날그날의, 매일의　expense n. 돈, 비용　range from A to B (범위가) A에서 B에 이르다　inventory n. 물품 목록, 재고품　furniture n. 가구　dine out 외식하다　office supplies 사무용품　priority n. 우선(권), 우선사항　take advantage of ~을 이용[활용]하다　signing bonus 계약 선지급금, 사이닝 보너스

139 구조/문법•동사　난이도 중

해설 빈칸은 의문사와 전치사 사이 자리. 문맥상 '왜 레스토랑에서 식사를 하거나 영화를 보는 것으로만 혜택을 주는 카드에 만족하시나요?'라는 내용이 되어야 자연스러우므로 'Why (do you) settle for ~(왜 ~에 만족하시나요)'의 의문문에서 '의문문 조동사+주어'가 생략된 구조를 완성하는 동사원형 (C)가 정답

140 구조/문법•접속사　난이도 중

해설 빈칸은 두 개의 문장을 연결하는 접속사자리. 문맥상 '매 구매의 1.5%를 포인트로 전환해 주지만, 주요 사업구매비용에 대해서는 2배로 제공해 준다'는 내용으로 이어져야 자연스러우므로 (C)가 정답

Key point
① '------ 문장1, 문장2'의 구조에서 빈칸은 부사절 접속사 자리이다.
② 접속사 while은 '~하는 동안(동시 동작), ~반면(대조), ~이긴 하지만(양보)'의 의미를 갖는다.

141 구조/문법•지시대명사　난이도 중

해설 빈칸은 복수명사 individuals를 수식하는 자리. 수식하는 대상과 수일치를 이뤄야 하므로 복수형의 지시형용사 (B)가 정답

Key point
지시형용[대명]사 those는 [those (명사) who~]의 형태로 쓰여 불특정 다수를 지칭하며, '~한 사람들'로 해석된다.

142 문맥이해•문장삽입　난이도 중

해석 (A) 이 굉장한 혜택은 3월 1일에 끝나니, 지체하지 마세요.
(B) Endeavor 카드는 레스토랑 사용액에 대해 보너스 포인트를 제공하지 않습니다.
(C) 교통 관련 비용에는 포인트가 발생하지 않습니다.
(D) 당신이 추천하는 사람들도 각각 가입 선물을 받게 됩니다.

해설 빈칸 앞 문장의 '오늘 TBD 금융에 가입하시고 500달러의 특별 선지급 보너스 혜택을 받으세요'라는 내용을 고려할 때, 문맥상 '이 혜택은 3월 1일에 끝나니, 지체하지 마세요.'라는 내용으로 이어져야 자연스러우므로 (A)가 정답

Key word
Sign up with TBD Financial **today to take advantage of our special $500 signing bonus. This amazing offer expires March 1, so don't wait**.

143-146번은 다음 이메일에 관한 문제입니다.

발신: Amanda Nguyen
수신: staff@hbcentertainment.com
제목: Jakob Bernal의 새로운 일자리
일자: 11월 21일

안녕하세요,

저는 여러분께 Jakob Bernal이 HBC Entertainment를 떠나 Etten Media에 운영담당 부사장으로 합류한다는 소식을 전하게 되어 매우 자랑스러우면서도 약간 아쉽습니다. 그의 143. 마지막 날은 1월 31일 목요일입니다.

Jakob은 우리 회사에서 근무하는 동안, 생산부서에서 큰 역할을 해왔습니다. 특히 지난 2년 동안, 그는 가장 크고 성공적인 프로젝트 몇 건을 이끌었습니다. 그 당시, 그는 HBC Entertainment의 많은 사람들과 돈독하고 지속적인 우정을 144. 쌓았습니다. 그의 열정과 리더십은 우리가 의지할만한 것이었습니다. 145. 저는 우리 모두가 그의 재치와 유머, 헌신을 그리워할 것이라고 확신합니다.

앞으로 며칠 간 시간 나시면, Jakob에게 연락해 주세요. 우리 모두 그의 새로운 업무에 행운과 146. 지속적인 성공을 빌어줬으면 합니다.

Best,

Amanda Nguyen
CEO

어휘 position n. 일자리, 직위　deeply adv. 깊이　inform v. 알리다　move on (새로운 일로) 넘어가다　join v. 합류하다, 가입하다　operation n. 영업, 사업　especially adv. 특히　guide v. (특정한 방향으로) 인도하다, 이끌다　lasting adj. 지속적인　passion n. 열정　leadership n. 지도력, 리더십　count on ~를 믿다　reach out to ~에게 연락하다

160

143 어휘+문맥이해•형용사 난이도 중

해설 빈칸은 명사 day를 수식하는 자리. 빈칸 앞 문장의 'Jakob Bernal이 HBC Entertainment를 떠나 Etten Media에 운영담당 부사장으로 합류한다'는 내용을 고려할 때, 문맥상 '그의 마지막 날'이라는 의미가 되어야 자연스러우므로 (D)가 정답

Key word
I'm both deeply proud and a little sad to inform you all that Jakob Bernal will be moving on from HBC Entertainment to join Etten Media as Vice President of Operations. His last day here will be Thursday, January 31.

144 구조/문법•동사 난이도 중

해설 빈칸은 주어와 목적어 사이 동사 자리. 빈칸 앞 문장의 내용을 고려할 때, 문두의 In that time이 지난 2년의 기간을 의미한다는 것을 알 수 있으므로, 과거시제 (A)가 정답

Key word
Especially **over the course of the last two years**, he has guided some of our biggest and most successful projects. **In that time**, he formed strong and lasting friendships with so many of us at HBC Entertainment.

145 문맥이해•문장삽입 난이도 중

해석
(A) 그는 Khepri Faried와 협력하여 프로그램을 개발했습니다.
(B) 인사팀은 자격을 갖춘 후보자를 광범위하게 검색했습니다.
(C) 그는 이전에 DeBrunye사의 미디어 디자인팀에서 근무했습니다.
(D) 저는 우리 모두가 그의 재치와 유머, 헌신을 그리워할 것이라고 확신합니다.

해설 빈칸 앞 문장들의 '그는 많은 사람들과 돈독하고 지속적인 우정을 쌓았고, 그의 열정과 리더십은 우리가 의지할만한 것이었다'는 내용을 고려할 때, 문맥상 '우리 모두 그를 그리워할 것'이라는 내용으로 이어져야 자연스러우므로 (D)가 정답

Key word
In that time, **he formed strong and lasting friendships with so many of us** at HBC Entertainment. **His passion and leadership have been something we could count on**. I'm sure we'll all miss his quick wit, good humor, and dedication.

146 구조/문법•분사 난이도 하

해설 빈칸은 명사 success를 수식하는 자리. 문맥상 '새로운 업무에서도 계속 이어지는 성공'이라는 의미가 되어야 자연스러우므로 과거분사 (A)가 정답

Key point
분사(현재분사, 과거분사)는 형용사처럼 명사를 수식할 수 있다.

PART 7

147-148번은 다음 정보에 관한 문제입니다.

> 모든 Electric Avenue 청취자 여러분!
>
> 이제 저희 청취자 여러분은 모든 주요 온라인 스트리밍 플랫폼에서 프로그램에 접속하실 수 있습니다.(147)
>
> • 언제든지 저희 콘텐트를 스트리밍하세요(148)
> • 전 목록을 무료로 재생하세요.
>
> 당신의 음악 구독서비스에서 'Electric Avenue'를 검색하거나
>
> WCCRB에 채널 고정하셔서 오후 8시부터 자정까지 생방송으로 청취하세요.

어휘 access n. 접속하다 major adj. 주요한 streaming platform 스트리밍 플랫폼(인터넷 상 실시간으로 서비스를 제공하는 플랫폼) stream v. 데이터 전송을 이어서 하다 content n. 콘텐츠 entire adj. 전체의 catalogue n. 목록 free of charge 무료로 subscription n. 구독 tune in to (채널을) ~에 맞추다 live adv. 생방송으로 midnight n. 자정

147 주제/목적/대상 난이도 중

해석 정보의 주요 목적은 무엇인가?
(A) 새로운 스트리밍 플랫폼을 알리는 것
(B) 특별 생방송 행사를 홍보하는 것
(C) 팬들을 위한 새로운 옵션을 광고하는 것
(D) 라디오 방송에 신규 청취자를 유치하는 것

해설 첫 번째 줄에서 Now, our listeners can access the show on all major online streaming platforms.(이제 저희 청취자 여러분은 모든 주요 온라인 스트리밍 플랫폼에서 프로그램에 접속하실 수 있습니다.)라고 했으므로 (C)가 정답

148 사실확인 난이도 중

해석 스트리밍 서비스에 관하여 언급된 것은?
(A) 청취자는 하루 24시간 프로그램을 들을 수 있다.
(B) 청취자는 월 이용료를 지불해야 한다.
(C) 일부 청취자만 이용할 수 있다.
(D) 청취자는 이메일을 통해 계정을 활성화해야 한다.

해설 두 번째 줄에서 Stream our content any time(언제든지 저희 콘텐트를 스트리밍하세요)라고 했으므로 (A)가 정답

Paraphrasing any time ➡ 24 hours a day

149-150번은 다음 기사에 관한 문제입니다.

> Turner 연구소에서 당신을 원합니다.
>
> Turner 연구소에서는 농업과학에 조예가 깊고 농장 운영 경험이 있는 보조 연구원을 찾고 있습니다.(149) 프로젝트 자격요건에 대해 더 자세히 알아보고 온라인으로 지원하시려면 www.turnercropinitiative.org를 방문해 주세요. 또는 방문 지원을 원하시면, Lyndale로 2425번지에 있는 연구소로 오셔서, Nicole Sessions를 찾으시기 바랍니다.(150)

Dr. Jackson Sparrow에 의해 설립된 연구소는 건강에 좋고 해충에 강한 작물을 재배하는 오픈 소스 종자를 개발 및 시험, 홍보함으로써 전세계에 식량을 공급하는 것을 목표로 합니다.

어휘 institute n. 기관 knowledge n. 지식 agricultural adj. 농업의 background n. 배경, 경력 requirement n. 필수요건 in person 직접 locate v. ~에 위치시키다 found v. 설립하다 aim v. 목표로 하다 feed v. 먹을 것을 주다, 먹여 살리다 promote v. 홍보하다 open-source adj. 오픈 소스의 seed n. 씨앗, 종자 grow v. (식물을) 재배하다 wholesome adj. 건강에 좋은 pest-resistant adj. 해충에 강한 crop n. 농작물

149 주제/목적/대상 | 난이도 하

해석 기사의 목적은 무엇인가?
(A) 재배 방식을 설명하는 것
(B) 시장성 테스트를 위해 자원봉사자들을 요청하는 것
(C) 과학자의 은퇴를 축하하는 것
(D) 일자리를 공지하는 것

해설 제목에서 Turner Institute Wants You(Turner 연구소가 당신을 권합니다.)라고 하며, 첫 번째 단락에서 The Turner Institute is looking for research assistants who have a deep knowledge of agricultural sciences and a background in farm management. (Turner 연구소가 농업과학에 대한 깊이 있는 지식과 농장 경영이 대한 경험을 갖춘 보조 연구원을 찾고 있습니다.)라고 했으므로 (D)가 정답

150 암시/추론 | 난이도 중

해석 Ms. Sessions는 누구겠는가?
(A) 대학원생
(B) 연구소 직원
(C) 농업대학 교수
(D) 지역 언론인

해설 첫 번째 단락에서 Or, if you want to apply in person, visit the Institute, located on 2425 Lyndale Road, and ask for Nicole Sessions.(방문 지원을 원하시면, Lyndale가 2425번지에 있는 연구소로 오셔서 Nicole Sessions를 찾으시기 바랍니다.)라고 하여 Ms. Sessions가 연구소에 근무하는 사람임을 알 수 있으므로 (B)가 정답

151-152번은 다음 설명서에 관한 문제입니다.

Rison전자를 선택해주셔서 감사합니다! 귀하의 상품을 등록하려면,(151) 다음의 단계를 따라 주시기 바랍니다.

1. 저희 웹 사이트 www.risonelectronics.com/product_registration 을 방문하십시오.
2. 제품 상자에 포함된 임시 ID와 비밀번호로 로그인 하십시오.(152)
3. 귀하의 이름과 이메일 주소를 포함하여 양식을 작성하세요. 구입일자와 최초 구입한 국가 역시 입력하셔야 합니다. 그 다음, 귀하가 구입한 제품의 시리얼넘버를 입력하세요. 시리얼넘버는 설명서 마지막 페이지에 있습니다.
4. 그리고 나면, 개인 ID와 비밀번호를 만들라는 안내를 받게 되실 다.(151) 귀하의 계정에 접속할 때마다 이 정보를 이용하십시오.

5. 작성이 모두 완료되면, "제출" 버튼을 클릭하십시오. 귀하의 상품은 이제 저희 보증서비스에 등록되었습니다.

RISON 전자

어휘 instruction n. 설명 choose v. 선택하다, 고르다 register v. 등록하다 complete v. 완료하다 adj. 완전한 temporary adj. 임시의 input v. 입력하다 n. 투입 purchase n. 구입 original adj. 원래의 afterward adv. 그 후에, 나중에 enter v. 입력하다, 들어가다 personal adj. 개인의 access v. 접속하다, 접근하다 fill out 작성하다 submit v. 제출하다 warranty n. 보증

151 암시/추론 | 난이도 중

해석 설명은 누구를 대상으로 하겠는가?
(A) Rison전자 직원
(B) 제품 개발자
(C) 신규 고객
(D) 품질 관리관

해설 첫 번째 단락에서 Thank you for choosing Rison Electronics! To register your product,(Rison전자를 선택해주셔서 감사합니다! 귀하의 상품을 등록하려면,)라고 하여 Rison 전자의 상품을 새로 구입하여 등록하려는 사람들을 대상으로 한다는 것을 알 수 있으므로 (C)가 정답

152 상세정보 | 난이도 중

해석 읽는 사람은 무엇을 하라고 요청 받는가?
(A) 보증기간을 연장하라고
(B) 로그인 정보를 갱신하라고
(C) 몇몇 파일을 다운로드 하라고
(D) 설문조사를 완료하라고

해설 두 번째 단락, 2번에서 Log in using the temporary ID and password included inside the product box.(제품 상자에 포함된 임시 ID와 비밀번호로 로그인 하십시오.)라고 했는데, 4번에서 You will then be asked to make your own personal ID and password.(그리고 나면, 개인 ID와 비밀번호를 만들라는 안내를 받게 되실 겁니다.)라고 하여 로그인 정보를 업데이트하라고 요청하고 있음을 알 수 있으므로 (B)가 정답

Paraphrasing ID and password ➡ log-in details

153-154번은 다음 문자 메시지 대화에 관한 문제입니다.

Andre Lawrence [오후 1시 55분]
저기, 식당에서 벌써 나오셨나요?

Olga Furtak [오후 1시 57분]
주차장을 찾느라 애먹었어요. **지금 막 들어왔어요.**(153)

Andre Lawrence [오후 1시 58분]
그럼 잘됐네요. Griggs 지점 직원 2명이 아니라 5명이 저희와 함께 점심식사를 할 거라는 걸 방금 알았어요.(153)/(154)

Olga Furtak [오후 1시 59분]
문제없어요. 참석자들이 모두 먹을 수 있게 샌드위치를 충분히 가져갈게요.[(154)] 더 사야 할 게 있나요?

Andre Lawrence [오후 2시 00분]
그거면 될 거예요. 접시와 식기류는 사무실에 충분히 있으니까요.

어휘 | **branch** n. 지점 **attend** v. 참석하다 **plate** n. 접시 **utensil** n. 식기류

---

153 화자 의도 파악   난이도 ●

해설 | 오후 1시 58분에, Mr. Lawrence가 "그럼 잘됐네요"라고 할 때 무엇을 의미하겠는가?
(A) 메뉴 종류에 만족한다.
(B) 식당이 좋은 만남의 장소라고 생각한다.
(C) Ms. Furtak에게 정보를 제공하기에 적당한 때에 연락했다.
(D) Ms. Furtak가 Griggs지점으로 전근간다는 것에 만족한다.

해설 | 오후 1시 57분~ 오후 1시 58분 대화에서 Olga Furtak가 I just walked in.(지금 막 들어왔어요.)라고 하자, Andre Lawrence가 Actually, that's good to hear. I just found out that five employees from the Griggs branch will be joining us for lunch, not two.(그럼 잘됐네요. Griggs 지점 직원 2명이 아니라 5명이 저희와 함께 점심식사를 할 거라는 걸 방금 알았어요.)라고 말한 것이므로 (C)가 정답

---

154 암시 / 추론   난이도 ●

해설 | Ms. Furtak는 이후에 무엇을 하겠는가?
(A) 접시와 식기구를 살 것이다
(B) 다른 사업체를 방문할 것이다
(C) 음식을 추가로 주문할 것이다
(D) 상사에게 연락할 것이다

해설 | 오후 1시 58분~ 오후 1시 59분 대화에서 Andre Lawrence가 Actually, that's good to hear. I just found out that five employees from the Griggs branch will be joining us for lunch, not two.(그럼 잘됐네요. Griggs 지점 직원 2명이 아니라 5명이 저희와 함께 점심식사를 할 거라는 걸 방금 알게 됐어요.)라고 하자, Olga Furtak이 No problem. I'll pick up enough sandwiches for everyone attending.(문제없어요. 참석자들이 모두 먹을 수 있게 샌드위치를 충분히 가져갈게요.)라고 말한 것이므로 (C)가 정답

155-157번은 다음 이메일에 관한 문제입니다.

발신: JohnRothko@updikehomestore.com
수신: JiwooP@flash.net
제목: 배송 문제
날짜: 3월 15일

Ms. Park께,

고객님의 Updike 홈스토어 가을 카탈로그가 지난주에 발송되었습니다. 그러나 '발신인에게 반송'이라는 메모와 함께 저희에게 돌아왔습니다.

올 가을 독점 제공 혜택들을 놓치지 않도록 카탈로그를 받아보시기 바랍니다. **고객님의 과거 구매이력으로 볼 때, 신규 테라스 의자 및 테이블 제품군에 관심 있으실 것 같습니다.**[(156)] 저희가 50달러 상당의 할인쿠폰과 함께 카탈로그를 다시 보내드릴 수 있도록 현 주소지를 알려주시기 바랍니다.[(155)]

아울러, 저희 고객지원 서비스가 개선되었습니다. 이제 전화통화 대신, 신규 온라인 채팅 기능을 통해서도 저희 직원과 상담하실 수 있습니다.[(157)] 물론, 주문관련 문제에 대해 저희 지원센터에 555-3093번으로 전화주셔도 됩니다.

연락 기다리겠습니다.

John Rothko
총지배인, Updike 홈스토어

어휘 | **package** n. 소포 **note** n. 메모 **miss out** 놓치다 **exclusive** adj. 독점적인 **offer** n. 할인 **given** prep. ~을 고려해 볼 때 **range** n. 범위, 종류 **patio** n. 테라스 **current** adj. 현재의, 지금의 **voucher** n. 상품권, 할인권 **feature** n. 특성, 기능 **representative** n. 직원

---

155 주제 / 목적 / 대상   난이도 ●

해설 | 이메일은 왜 발송되었는가?
(A) 새 연락처를 요청하기 위해
(B) 입사지원에 대한 후속논의를 하기 위해
(C) 파손품에 대해 사과하기 위해
(D) 개정된 환불정책에 관해 설명하기 위해

해설 | 두 번째 단락에서 Please provide us with your current home address so that we can mail you the catalog again as well as a discount voucher worth $50.(저희가 50달러 상당의 할인쿠폰과 함께 카탈로그를 다시 보내드릴 수 있도록 현 주소지를 알려주시기 바랍니다.)라고 했으므로 (A)가 정답

Paraphrasing current home address ➡ new contact information

---

156 사실확인   난이도 ●

해설 | Ms. Park에 관하여 언급된 것은?
(A) 최근에 다른 도시로 이사했다.
(B) 이전에 Updike 홈스토어에서 가구를 구입한 적이 있다.
(C) 할인쿠폰을 요청했다.
(D) 예전 카탈로그를 보고 제품을 구매했다.

해설 | 두 번째 단락에서 Given purchases you've made in the past, you may want to know about our new range of patio chairs and tables.(고객님의 과거 구매이력으로 볼 때, 신규 테라스 의자 및 테이블 제품군에 관심 있으실 것 같습니다.)라고 했으므로 (B)가 정답

---

157 상세정보   난이도 ●

해설 | 최근 Updike 홈스토어에서 무엇을 변경했는가?
(A) 이제 고객지원센터를 24시간 내내 이용할 수 있다.
(B) 가정 설치비가 인하되었다.
(C) 일부 비인기 제품군이 단종되었다.
(D) 고객 문의사항이 채팅서비스를 통해 처리될 수 있다.

해설 | 세 번째 단락에서 In addition, we have improved our customer support services. Now, instead of calling, you have the option of using our new online chat feature to talk with our representatives.(아울러, 저희 고객지원 서비스가 개선되었습니다.

이제 전화통화 대신, 신규 온라인 채팅 기능을 통해서도 저희 직원과 상담하실 수 있습니다.)라고 했으므로 (D)가 정답

Paraphrasing online chat feature ➡ chat service

158-160 번은 다음 이메일에 관한 문제입니다.

제목: 주문번호 234-19887
날짜: 4월 2일
수신: emacpherson@naismith.org
발신: Carl@customizedcookwarehouse.com

Mr. Macpherson께,

이 이메일은 귀하의 최근 주문에 관한 것입니다. —[1]—. 안타깝게도, 아래 나열된 상품이 이미 품절되었습니다.(158)

"맞춤형 주방" 전문가용 세라믹 논스틱 프라이팬 세트, 150달러

이로 인해 발생할 수 있는 혼란에 사과 드립니다. —[2]—. 저희는 완벽한 사용자 경험을 제공해 드리기 위해 노력하지만, 가끔 문제가 발생합니다.(160) —[3]—. 마지막 남은 세트를 몇 시간 전 다른 고객이 구매했습니다. 결제 처리가 지연되어, 저희 재고 시스템에 해당 상품이 품절임을 반영하는 업데이트가 제대로 이루어지지 않았습니다. 이는 드물지만 당혹스러운 오류로, 저희는 이를 해결하기 위해 노력하고 있습니다.

저희는 귀하의 Cookwarehouse.com계정으로 구매에 사용하신 포인트를 환불해 드렸습니다. 저희 웹 사이트에서 보이는지 확인해 주시되,(159) 환불이 처리되는데 2시간에서 6시간 정도 걸린다는 것을 감안해 주시기 바랍니다. —[4]—.

Best Regards,

Carl Weizen
Customized Cookwarehouse, 고객 관리부

어휘 in reference to ~와 관련하여 list v. 목록을 작성하다 sell out 매진되다 customized adj. 주문제작한, 맞춤형의 professional adj. 전문가의 non-stick adj. 눌어붙지 않는 apologize v. 사과하다 confusion n. 혼란 strive v. 분투하다 seamless adj. 아주 매끄러운, 원활한, 완벽한 occasionally adv. 때때로 run into 만나다, 겪다 issue n. 문제 remaining adj. 남은 purchase v. 구입하다 delay n. 지연 process v. 처리되다 payment n. 지불, 납입 inventory n. 재고 properly adv. 제대로 update v. 업데이트하다 reflect v. 반영하다 out of stock 재고가 떨어진 rare adj. 드문 unfortunate adj. 운이 나쁜, 불행한 error n. 실수, 오류 address v. 처리하다 refund v. 환불하다 verify v. 확인하다 appear v. 나타나다 allow for ~를 감안하다 reimbursement n. 상환, 환급 warehouse n. 창고 customer relations 고객 관리

158 주제/대상/목적 난이도 중

해설 이 이메일의 주요 목적은 무엇인가?
(A) 상품을 구매할 수 없다는 것을 말하려고
(B) 주문이 지연될 것임을 알리려고
(C) 특정 상품에 대한 판매를 촉진하려고
(D) 물품이 배송되었는지 확인하려고

해설 첫 번째 단락에서 Unfortunately, the item listed below has already sold out(안타깝게도, 아래 나열된 상품이 이미 품절되었습니다)라고 했으므로 (A)가 정답

159 상세정보 난이도 중

해설 Mr. Macpherson은 무엇을 하라고 요청 받는가?
(A) 새로운 결제방식을 제공하라고
(B) 온라인 계정을 확인하라고
(C) 고객 관리팀에 이메일을 보내라고
(D) 특별 할인쿠폰을 사용하라고

해설 네 번째 단락에서 We have refunded the points used to make the purchase to your Cookwarehouse.com account. Please verify that that these appear on our Web site.(저희는 귀하의 Cookwarehouse.com계정으로 구매에 사용하신 포인트를 환불해 드렸습니다. 저희 웹 사이트에서 보이는지 확인해 주시되)라고 했으므로 (B)가 정답

Paraphrasing verify ➡ check

160 문장 삽입 난이도 중

해설 [1], [2], [3], [4]로 표시된 곳 중, 다음 문장이 들어갈 위치로 가장 적절한 것은?
"이것이 귀하의 사례에서 발생했습니다."
(A) [1]
(B) [2]
(C) [3]
(D) [4]

해설 세 번째 단락에서 We strive to provide a seamless user experience; however, we do occasionally run into issues.(저희는 완벽한 사용자 경험을 제공해 드리기 위해 노력하지만, 가끔 문제가 발생합니다.)라고 하여 주어진 문장이 이어지기에 자연스러우므로 (C)가 정답

161-163번은 다음 이메일에 관한 문제입니다.

수신: mailinglist@topmall.com
발신: Top Mall
날짜: 10월 12일
제목: 공지

Top Mall은 온라인 소매업의 선두주자로, 전 세계에 광범위한 제품을 제공합니다. 사이트의 높은 접속량으로 인해, 즐거운 쇼핑경험을 보장해 드릴 수 있도록 저희는 지속적으로 서버를 업그레이드 해야 합니다.(161)

따라서 10월 15일 그리니치 표준시 기준 오전 3시부터 11시까지 이 업그레이드 작업을 수행하기 위해 웹 사이트가 접속이 차단됩니다.(161) 이 시간 동안 상품 둘러보기, 장바구니 접속, 주문 변경 등을 하실 수 없습니다. 그러나 저희 고객서비스 직원들이 문의 및 우려사항에 대해 영어와 중국어, 스페인어로 답변해드릴 것입니다.(162) 유감스럽게도 이 과정을 진행하는 동안 일부 계정정보는 이용하지 못하실 수도 있습니다. 여러분의 이해에 감사 드립니다.

10월 15일 이후에는 고객 여러분의 쇼핑에 필요한 모든 것들을 훨씬 더 잘 도와드릴 수 있게 됩니다. 또한 Top Mall은 고객들에게 특가품과 판촉행사에 관한 정보를 담은 주간 회보 제공을 시작합니다. 이메일로 바로 받아보시도록 온라인으로 신청하시면, 다음 구매시 15 퍼센트 할인받을 수 있는 쿠폰도 보내드립니다.(163)

어휘 mailing list 메일 수신자 명단(메일을 동시에 보낼 수 있도록 모아 놓은 수신자 이메일 주소 목록) retailing n. 소매업 a wide range of 광범위한, 다양한 traffic volume 접속량 continuously adv. 지속적으로, 계속하여 GMT 그리니치 표준시(Greenwich Mean Time) down adj. (컴퓨터시스템이) 작동이 안 되는 perform v. 수행하다 browse v. 둘러보다 inventory n. 물품 목록 access v. 접속하다 available adj. 이용할 수 있는 account n. (서비스) 이용계정 special offer 특가 판매 promotion n. 홍보[판촉] (활동) voucher n. 할인권, 쿠폰 good adj. 유효한

161 주제/목적/대상   난이도 중

해석 이메일은 왜 발송되었는가?
(A) 주문을 확인하기 위해
(B) 신제품을 소개하기 위해
(C) 시스템 업그레이드를 공지하기 위해
(D) 최신 배송정보를 제공하기 위해

해설 첫 번째 및 두 번째 단락에서 Because of the high traffic volume our site receives, we must continuously upgrade our servers to ensure a pleasant shopping experience. Therefore, on 15 October, from 3 A.M. to 11 A.M. GMT, our Web site will be down to perform these upgrades.(사이트의 높은 접속량으로 인해, 즐거운 쇼핑경험을 보장해 드릴 수 있도록 저희는 지속적으로 서버를 업그레이드 해야 합니다. 따라서 10월 15일 그리니치 표준시 기준 오전 3시부터 11시까지 이 업그레이드 작업을 수행하기 위해 웹 사이트 접속이 차단됩니다.)라고 했으므로 (C)가 정답

162 사실확인   난이도 중

해석 Top Mall에 관하여 알 수 있는 것은?
(A) 웹 사이트 이용이 편리하다.
(B) 직원들이 여러 언어를 구사할 수 있다.
(C) 여러 국가에 지점이 있다.
(D) 고객들로부터 높은 평가를 받았다.

해설 두 번째 단락에서 Our customer service agents, however, will be available to answer your questions and concerns in English, Chinese, and Spanish.(그러나 저희 고객서비스 직원들이 문의 및 우려사항들에 대해 영어와 중국어, 스페인어로 답변해드릴 것입니다.)라고 했으므로 (B)가 정답

163 상세정보   난이도 중

해석 독자들은 어떻게 쿠폰을 받을 수 있는가?
(A) 온라인 서비스를 업그레이드해서
(B) 회보를 구독해서
(C) 일정금액 이상을 써서
(D) 고객서비스 직원과 통화해서

해설 세 번째 단락에서 Top Mall will also start offering our customers a weekly newsletter with information on special offers and promotions. Sign up online to have it sent directly to your e-mail, and we will also send you a discount voucher good for 15 percent off your next purchase.(또한 Top Mall은 고객들에게 특가품과 판촉행사에 관한 정보를 담은 주간 회보 제공을 시작합니다. 이메일로 바로 받아보시도록 온라인으로 신청하시면, 다음 구매시 15 퍼센트 할인받을 수 있는 쿠폰도 보내드립니다.)라고 했으므로 (B)가 정답

Paraphrasing sign up ➡ subscribe, a discount voucher ➡ a coupon

164-167번은 다음 기사에 관한 문제입니다.

NEW YORK (4월 2일) – 어제 오후, 판사 John Reinsdorf는 일부 전문가들의 반대에도 불구하고 국내 시장을 선도하는 두 회계법인의 합병이 진행되어도 좋다고 판결했다. 이는 Markkanen & Associates와 Donovan ELX가 이제 자유롭게 30만명 이상의 직원을 보유한 국내 최대 회계법인을 구성할 수 있다는 것을 의미한다.[164]

Markkanen의 Spencer Mitchell은 "이 두 회사가 힘을 합칠 때 일어날 일이 기대됩니다."라고 말했는데, 그는 Markkanen-Donovan으로 알려질 새로운 회사의 CEO가 될 가능성이 높다. "우리는 엄청난 양의 노하우와 놀라울 정도로 다양한 고객 포트폴리오를 2개나 가지고 있습니다. 이 변화는 New York과 Los Angeles 지점을 유지시켜줄 뿐만 아니라, 우리의 영향력을 전 세계로 넓혀 나갈 수 있도록 해줄 것입니다.[167] 우리는 내년에 미국을 벗어나 싱가포르에 새 지사를 설립하는 것을 검토 중입니다."[165]

Mitchell은 자선사업, 특히 소액 대출을 통해 개발도상국의 영세기업을 지원해주는 활동으로 전국 언론사의 관심을 끌었다.[166]

Mitchell은 Markkanen-Donovan이 각 회사의 전 직원을 유지할 계획이라고 밝혔다. 그는 "모든 부서가 회사에 기여할 필수 기술을 가지고 있습니다,"라고 설명했다.

어휘 judge n. 판사 rule v. 판결을 내리다 merger n. 합병 leading adj. 선두의 accounting n. 회계 go ahead 진행되다, 일어나다 objection n. 이의, 반대 expert n. 전문가 form v. 구성[형성]하다 join forces 힘을 합치다, 협력하다 firm n. 회사 tremendous adj. 엄청난 know-how n. 노하우, 실제 지식 및 경험 diverse adj. 다양한 reach n. (영향력 등의) 범위 look at ~에 대해 고려[검토]하다 set up ~을 (새로) 시작[설립]하다 draw v. 끌다 press agency 언론사 charity work 자선사업 effort n. 노력, 활동 promote v. 촉진하다, 육성하다 developing country 개발도상국 micro loan 소액 융자 retain v. 유지하다 vital adj. 필수적인 bring to the table (단체의) 이익에 기여하다

164 주제/목적/대상   난이도 중

해석 이 기사의 주요 목적은 무엇인가?
(A) 새로운 조세규정을 설명하는 것
(B) 두 회사의 결합에 관해 보도하는 것
(C) 법률 소송에 대해 논의하는 것
(D) 회계 서비스를 광고하는 것

해설 첫 번째 단락에서 Yesterday afternoon, Judge John Reinsdorf ruled that a merger between the nation's two leading accounting firms could go ahead, despite objections from some experts. This means that Markkanen & Associates and Donovan ELX are now free to form what will be the country's largest accounting company, with over 300,000 employees.(어제 오후 판사 John Reinsdorf는 일부 전문가들의 반대에도 불구하고 국내 시장을 선도하는 두 회계법인의 합병이 진행되어도 좋다고 판결했다. 이는 Markkanen & Associates와 Donovan ELX가 이제 자유롭게 30만명 이상의 직원을 보유한 국내 최대 회계법인을 구성할 수 있다는 것을 의미한다.)라고 했으므로 (B)가 정답

Paraphrasing merger ➡ combining

165 상세정보   난이도 중

해석 Markkanen-Donovan은 무엇을 할 계획인가?
(A) 자금을 빌릴 계획이다
(B) 이사회 선거를 할 계획이다
(C) New York 지점 중 한 곳을 닫을 계획이다
(D) 다른 나라로 확장할 계획이다

해설 두 번째 단락에서 We're looking at setting up a new office outside of the U.S. in Singapore in the next year.(우리는 내년에 미국을 벗어나 싱가포르에 새 지사를 설립하는 것을 검토 중입니다.)라고 했으므로 (D)가 정답

Paraphrasing set up a new office ➡ expand

166 암시/추론   난이도 중

해석 Mr. Mitchell에 관하여 알 수 있는 것은?
(A) 전국적으로 알려져 있다.
(B) 은행원이었다.
(C) Los Angeles에서 근무한다.
(D) 작은 사업체를 소유하고 있다.

해설 세 번째 단락에서 Mitchell has drawn the attention of the press agencies around the country for his charity work, especially his efforts to promote small businesses in developing countries through micro loans.(Mitchell은 자선사업, 특히 소액 대출을 통해 개발도상국의 영세기업을 지원해주는 활동으로 전국 언론사의 관심을 끌었다.)라고 하여 그가 전국에 알려진 인물임을 알 수 있으므로 (A)가 정답

Paraphrasing around the country ➡ nationally

167 동의어   난이도 중

해석 두 번째 단락, 열한 번째 줄의 단어 "reach"와 의미상 가장 가까운 것은?
(A) 길이
(B) 도착
(C) 영향력
(D) 연장

해설 두 번째 단락의 This move will not only let us keep our New York and Los Angeles branches, but also make it possible to increase our reach worldwide.(이 변화는 New York과 Los Angeles 지점을 유지시켜줄 뿐만 아니라, 우리의 영향력을 전 세계로 넓혀 나갈 수 있도록 해줄 것입니다.)에서 'reach'는 '영향력'이라는 의미로 쓰였으므로 보기 중 같은 의미를 갖는 (C)가 정답

168-171번은 다음 기사에 관한 문제입니다.

Herbert McGraw는 다른 음악강사들과 비교하면 정말 독특하다. 그는 **경력의 대부분을 Roth & Stein Associates에서 성공한 변호사로 보낸 후,**(168) 갑자기 음악으로 관심을 돌렸다. ―[1]―. McGraw는 초등학교 때 학교 공부를 따라가느라 애를 먹었다. 그러나 중학교 시절부터 학교 음악 프로그램이 그의 흥미를 끌었다. 음악에 대한 그의 열정은 학업에 대한 집중력을 향상하는 데 도움을 주기도 했다. 그래서 자신의 고향 학군에서 모든 음악 프로그램 예산을 삭감했다는 것을 알았을 때, 자신이 무언가를 해야 한다고 생각했다. ―[2]―. 그 '무언가'는 음악 스튜디오 To the Beat가 되었다.

음악 스튜디오는 도시 중심부에 위치하여, 지역 학생들이 쉽게 이용할 수 있다. 무엇보다 좋은 것은 McGraw가 학생들에게 모든 것을 무료로 제공한다는 점이다.

―[3]―. McGraw의 스튜디오에는 상상할 수 있는 거의 모든 종류의 악기가 갖춰져 있으며, 학생들이 가져다 연주하도록 권장된다. To the Beat는 매일 학생들에게 자신의 재능을 발견하고 음악을 통해 자신을 표현할 기회를 제공한다. "고향의 학교들이 음악 프로그램들을 없앤다는 말을 듣고 화가 났어요,"라고 McGraw는 말했다.(169) "저는 음악이 학업과 인생에서 중요한 기능을 한다는 것을 경험으로 알고 있어요. 단지 이 일에 장기적으로 자금을 댈 방법을 찾을 수 있길 바랄 뿐인데, 그 부분이 쉽지 않을 듯 해요."(171) ―[4]―.

수상 경력이 있는 밴드 The Jamming Camels는 이 아이들을 도우려는 McGraw의 노력에 대한 이야기를 들었다. 그들은 지지를 표하기 위해 McGraw와 To the Beat 음악 스튜디오에 금액을 비공개로 기부했다.(170)

어휘 compared to ~와 비교하여 instructor n. 강사 career n. 경력, 사회생활 attorney n. 변호사 attention n. 주의, 주목 struggle v. 애쓰다, 고투[분투]하다 keep up (~의 진도·증가 속도 등을) 따라가다 passion n. 열정 focus n. 집중, 주목 school district 학군 accessible adj. 접근[입장/이용] 가능한 be stocked with ~으로 채워지다, 구비되다 instrument n. 악기 imaginable adj. 상상할 수 있는 opportunity n. 기회 get rid of ~을 제거하다 finance v. 자금[재원]을 대다 for the long term 장기간 undisclosed adj. 밝혀지지 않은

168 상세정보   난이도 중

해석 Herbert McGraw는 어디에서 직장생활을 시작했는가?
(A) 광고회사
(B) 법률 분야
(C) 음악산업
(D) 교육 분야

해설 첫 번째 단락에서 After spending most of his career as a successful attorney with Roth & Stein Associates,(경력의 대부분을 Roth & Stein Associates에서 성공한 변호사로 보낸 후,)라고 했으므로 (B)가 정답

169 상세정보   난이도 중

해석 Herbert McGraw의 고향에서 무엇이 변화했는가?
(A) 관광객의 수
(B) 학교 프로그램의 수
(C) 일부 부동산의 가격
(D) 지역의 인구 규모

해설 세 번째 단락에서 "I was upset when I heard that the schools in my hometown were getting rid of their music programs," said McGraw.("고향의 학교들이 음악 프로그램들을 없앤다는 말을 듣고 화가 났어요." McGraw는 말했다.)라고 했으므로 (B)가 정답

170 사실확인   난이도 중

해석 To the Beat에 관하여 사실인 것은?
(A) 최근 Roth & Stein Associates를 고용했다.
(B) The Jamming Camels로부터 자금지원을 받았다.

(C) 지역 학군에 물품을 기부할 것이다.
(D) 수상경력이 있는 밴드와 함께 앨범을 녹음할 것이다.

해설 네 번째 단락에서 The award-winning band, The Jamming Camels, heard about McGraw's efforts to help these kids. To show their support, they have donated an undisclosed amount to McGraw and To the Beat music studio.(수상 경력이 있는 밴드 The Jamming Camels는 이 아이들을 도우려는 McGraw의 노력에 대한 이야기를 들었다. 그들은 지지를 표하기 위해 McGraw와 To the Beat 음악 스튜디오에 금액을 비공개로 기부했다.)라고 했으므로 (B)가 정답

Paraphrasing an undisclosed amount ➡ some funding

171 문장 삽입 난이도 중

해석 [1], [2], [3], [4]로 표시된 곳 중, 다음 문장이 들어갈 위치로 가장 적절한 것은?

"그러나 지금 예상치 못했던 곳으로부터 도움이 왔다."

(A) [1]
(B) [2]
(C) [3]
(D) [4]

해설 세 번째 단락에서 I just hope that I can find a way to finance this for the long term—that part won't be easy.(단지 이 일에 장기적으로 자금을 댈 방법을 찾을 수 있길 바랄 뿐인데, 그 부분이 쉽지 않을 듯 해요.")라고 하여 접속부사 however로 시작하는 문장과 서로 상반되는 내용으로 주어진 문장이 이어지기에 자연스러우므로 (D)가 정답

172-175번은 다음 온라인 채팅 대화문에 관한 문제입니다.

Kevin Johnson [오전 10시 33분]
모두들, 좋은 아침입니다. Harper 마케팅 대행사에서 만들고 있는 광고캠페인과 관련해 우리가 몇 가지 세부사항들을 검토해야 하는 걸로 알고 있어요. 그런데 제가 방금 굉장한 소식을 들었습니다. 우리 남성복 봄 라인이 다음달 있을 Global 패션쇼에 오를 거에요.(172)

Aviva Feldman [오전 10시 35분]
대단해요! 저는 우리가 그 프로젝트를 위해 한 일이 정말 자랑스러워요.

Udom Haslam [오전 10시 36분]
저도요. 이건 분명 다음 분기 매출 증가에 도움이 될 거에요.(173)

Aviva Feldman [오전 10시 38분]
저도 그렇게 생각해요.(173) 이 쇼에 많은 잠재 고객들이 있을 거에요.

Kevin Johnson [오전 10시 40분]
Fodesi에게 이번 일도 잘 해준 것에 대해 감사 드려야겠어요.

Udom Haslam [오전 10시 41분]
맞아요, 그들 덕분에 우리가 이렇게 성공할 수 있었어요.

Kevin Johnson [오전 10시 43분]
우리가 새로운 직물을 사용해 달라고 요청한 걸 감안하면, Fodesi는 이번에 특히 협조적이었어요. 우리는 전통적인 면 대신 망사원단을 적용했고, 셔츠는 딱 우리가 원한 대로 나왔어요.(174)

Aviva Feldman [오전 10시 44분]
품질도 여전히 훌륭하고요.

Kevin Johnson [오전 10시 45분]
자, 그럼 오늘의 주요 주제로 넘어갑시다. Udom, Harper사 Amit Mathur가 광고캠페인에 대해 제안한 내용이 있었나요?(175)

Udom Haslam [10:45 A.M.]
있었습니다. 지금 바로 이메일로 보내드릴게요.(175)

어휘 go over 검토하다 detail n. 세부사항 regarding prep. ~에 관하여 on display 전시된 definitely adv. 분명히, 확실히 generate v. 발생시키다, 창출하다 revenue n. 수익 quarter n. 분기 potential adj. 잠재적인 client n. 고객 especially adv. 특히 cooperative adj. 협조적인 considering prep. ~을 고려하면 material n. 직물, 재료 opt v. 적용하다 mesh n. 망사, 그물망 fabric n. 직물, 천 cotton n. 면 come out 나오다, 생산되다 quality n. 품질 continue v. 계속하다 suggestion n. 제안, 의견 email v. 이메일을 보내다 right now 즉시, 지금 바로

172 상세정보 난이도 중

해석 Kevin Johnson은 동료들과 무엇을 공유했는가?
(A) 회사의 흥미로운 행사
(B) 회사 합병에 관한 발표
(C) 판매 보고서의 내용
(D) 최근 설문조사의 결과

해설 오전 10시 33분, Kevin Johnson의 메시지에서 I just received some big news. Our spring line of men's clothes will be on display at next month's Global Fashion Show.(그런데 제가 방금 굉장한 소식을 들었습니다. 우리 남성복 봄 라인이 다음달 있을 Global 패션쇼에 오를 거에요.)라고 했으므로 (A)가 정답

173 화자 의도 파악 난이도 중

해석 오전 10시 38분에, Ms. Feldman이 "저도 그렇게 생각해요"라고 할 때 무엇을 의미하겠는가?
(A) 동료들과 논의하는 것이 필요하다.
(B) 재능 있는 사람들과 일할 수 있어 좋았다.
(C) 회사 제품이 많은 국가에서 인기가 있다.
(D) 회사가 더 많은 돈을 벌 것이다.

해설 오전 10시 36분 ~ 10시 38분 대화에서 Udom Haslam이 Me, too. This will definitely help generate more revenue next quarter.(저도요. 이건 분명 다음 분기 매출 증가에 도움이 될 거에요.)라고 한 말에, Aviva Feldman이 I think so, too.(저도 그렇게 생각해요.)라고 하며 그의 말에 동의하고 있음을 알 수 있으므로 (D)가 정답

Paraphrasing generate more revenue ➡ earn more money

174 암시/추론 난이도 중

해석 Fodesi는 무엇이겠는가?
(A) 직물 생산업체
(B) 패션잡지
(C) 광고회사
(D) 법률사무소

해설 오전 10시 43분, Kevin Johnson의 메시지에서 Fodes' was especially cooperative this time considering that we asked them to use new materials. We opted for mesh fabrics rather than traditional cotton, and the shirts came out just the way we wanted them.(우리가 새로운 직물을 사용해 달라고 요청한 걸 감안하면, Fodesi는 이번에 특히 협조적이었어요. 우리는 전통적인 면 대신 망사원단을 적용했고, 셔츠는 딱 우리가 원한 대로 나왔어요.)라고 한 것으로 미루어, Fodesi가 직물을 생산하는 업체라는 것을 알 수 있으므로 (A)가 정답

175 상세정보   난이도 중

해석 Mr. Haslam은 다음으로 무엇을 할 것인가?
(A) 마케팅 대행사에서 제안한 내용을 전송할 것이다
(B) Mr. Mathur에게 전화해서 광고 캠페인 일정을 조정하라고 할 것이다
(C) Global 패션쇼 티켓을 예약할 것이다
(D) 셔츠를 몇 장 더 구입할 것이다

해설 오전 10시 45분 대화에서 Kevin Johnson이 Alright, let's continue on to today's main topic. Udom, did Amit Mathur from Harper have any suggestions on the ad campaign?(자, 그럼 오늘의 주요 주제로 넘어갑시다. Udom, Harper사 Amit Mathur가 광고캠페인에 대해 제안한 내용이 있었나요?)라고 한 말에, Udom Haslam이 "He did. I'll email them to you right now.(있었습니다. 지금 바로 이메일로 보내드릴게요.)라고 대답했으므로 (A)가 정답

176-180번은 다음 전단지와 이메일에 관한 문제입니다.

**Idalou 도시 마켓에서
모든 공예가들을 초대합니다**

Idalou 도시 마켓이 6월 12일부터 15일까지 Skyline 공원으로 돌아옵니다. 공예가는 자신들의 재능과 제품을 뽐낼 기회를 갖게 됩니다. 매년 방문객의 수가 증가해왔고, 올해도 마찬가지일 것이라 예상합니다. **예년에는 Texas에 사는 장인들만 참여할 수 있었지만,(179)** 저희는 거주하는 주에 상관없이 모두 수용하는 걸로 규칙을 바꿨습니다.

지원하시려면, 다음을 따라주세요:

1. www.idaloumarket.com/register로 가셔서 양식을 작성해 주세요. **가판대를 공유할 예정인 분들의 경우, 양측이 하나의 양식을 사용할 수 있습니다. 하지만, 등록비 35달러는 여전히 두 판매자에게 모두 적용됩니다.(178)**

2. 마켓에서 전시할 예정인 품목의 사진을 10장 이하로 업로드해 주세요. 파일이름을 다음과 같이 지정해 주세요: 품목 설명_판매자 이름.

필수 서류 제출 마감일은 4월 20일입니다. **승인 받으셨으면, 5월 2일까지 이메일이 전송될 것입니다.(176)** 해당자는 5월 16일까지 나머지 525달러의 가판대 관리비를 지불하셔야 합니다. 이 요금에는 원하는 대로 사용하실 수 있는 5피트 길이의 테이블 4개가 포함됩니다. 제공해주신 사진은 귀하의 홈페이지 링크와 함께 저희 웹 사이트 "출품자" 탭에 게재될 것입니다.(177)

어휘 urban adj. 도시의 craftspeople n. 공예가, 장인 show off ~를 자랑하다 talent n. 재능, 재주 artisan n. 장인 eligible ~를 할 수 있는 participate v. 참여하다 modify v. 수정하다 regardless of ~에 상관없이 state n. 주 apply v. 지원하다 fill out 작성하다 plan v. 계획하다 share v. 공유하다 stand n. 가판대 party n. (계약의) 당사자 registration n. 등록 fee n. 요금 apply to ~에 적용되다 seller n. 판매자 upload v. 업로드하다 display v. 전시하다 name v. 명명하다 submit v. 제출하다 document n. 서류 approve v. 찬성하다 pay v. 지불하다 remaining adj. 남아있는 management n. 운영, 관리 exhibitor n. 전시자, 출품자 tab n. 탭, 색인표 along with ~와 함께 link n. 링크

발신: rin.takai@takaisupply.com
수신: e.orville@idaloumarket.com
참조: henry.reiss@reissphotos.net
제목: 도시 마켓
날짜: 5월 9일

안녕하세요.

저의 가판 파트너인 Henry Reiss와 저는 승인 이메일을 받았고, 저희는 올해 축제에 참여하게 되어 매우 기쁩니다. 저희는 웹 사이트에 있는 계좌 번호로 계좌 이체해서 공유 가판대에 대한 비용을 지불했습니다.(178) 올해 행사에 관해 더 많이 듣고 싶습니다.

저는 작년에 행사에 참여할 기회가 있었고,(179) 몇몇 장인들이 제공한 개별 지도 시간이 정말 좋았어요. 올해도 그와 유사한 무언가가 있을까요? 저는 관객에게 저희가 공예품을 어떻게 만드는지 보여주고 싶어서요, 만약 있다면 저에게 알려주세요.(180)

Sincerely,

Rin Takai

어휘 stall n. 가판대, 좌판 approval n. 승인 thrilled adj. 신이 난 festivity n. 축제행사 payment n. 지불 via prep. ~를 통해 bank transfer 계좌이체 account n. 계좌 partake in ~에 참가하다 tutorial n. 개별 지도 (시간) similar to ~과 비슷한 audience n. 관객 craft n. 공예품

176 상세정보   난이도 중

해석 승인 이메일은 언제 발송되는가?
(A) 4월 20일
(B) 5월 2일
(C) 5월 16일
(D) 6월 12일

해설 첫 번째 지문[전단지], 다섯 번째 단락에서 If you have been approved, an e-mail will be sent to you by May 2.(승인 받으셨으면, 5월 2일까지 이메일이 전송될 것입니다.)라고 했으므로 (B)가 정답

177 사실확인   난이도 중

해석 전단지에서는 Idalou 도시 마켓에 관해 무엇을 언급하는가?
(A) 모든 참가자들에게 무료 주차를 제공한다.
(B) 온라인 페이지에서 참여하는 공예가들을 홍보한다.
(C) 처음으로 개최될 것이다.
(D) 입장료를 받지 않는다.

해설 첫 번째 지문[전단지], 다섯 번째 단락에서 The images that

you provide will be displayed on our Web site under the "Exhibitors" tab along with a link to your homepage.(제공해주신 사진은 귀하의 홈페이지 링크와 함께 저희 웹 사이트 "출품자" 탭에 게재될 것입니다.)라고 했으므로 (B)가 정답

178 암시/추론   난이도 중

해석 Ms. Takai와 Mr. Reiss에 관하여 알 수 있는 것은? (연계질문)
(A) 서로 다른 양식을 작성했다.
(B) 테이블이 더 필요할 것이다.
(C) 둘 다 35달러의 요금을 지불했다.
(D) 비디오 사용 지침서를 제공한다.

해설 첫 번째 지문[전단지], 세 번째 단락에서 For those planning to share a stand, one form can be used for both parties. However, the $35 registration fee still applies to both sellers.(가판대를 공유할 예정인 분들의 경우, 양측이 하나의 양식을 사용할 수 있습니다. 하지만, 등록비 35달러는 여전히 두 판매자에게 모두 적용됩니다.)라고 했는데, 두 번째 지문[Ms. Takai가 보낸 이메일], 첫 번째 단락에서 I, along with my stall partner, Henry Reiss, received the approval e-mails, and we are thrilled to be a part of this year's festivities. We have sent the payment for our shared stand via bank transfer using the account number on your Web site.(제 가판 파트너인 Henry Reiss와 저는 승인 이메일을 받았고, 저희는 올해 축제에 참여하게 되어 매우 기쁩니다. 저희는 웹 사이트에 있는 계좌번호로 계좌이체해서 공유 가판대에 대한 비용을 지불했습니다.)라고 하여 Ms. Takai와 Mr. Reiss가 각각 등록비를 지불했음을 알 수 있으므로 (C)가 정답

179 암시/추론 [연계문제]   난이도 상

해석 Ms. Takai에 관하여 무엇이 사실이겠는가?
(A) 그녀의 공예품이 작년에 인기 있었다.
(B) 그녀의 작품이 잡지에 실렸다.
(C) 온라인 페이지를 갖고 있지 않다.
(D) Texas에 거주한다.

해설 첫 번째 지문[전단지], 첫 번째 단락에서 In previous years, only Texas-based artisans were eligible to participate,(예년에는 Texas에 사는 장인들만 참여할 수 있었지만,)이라고 했는데, 두 번째 지문[Ms. Takai가 보낸 이메일], 두 번째 단락에서 I had the chance to partake in the event last year,(저는 작년에 행사에 참여할 기회가 있었고)라고 하여 그녀가 Texas에 거주한다는 것을 알 수 있으므로 (D)가 정답

180 상세정보   난이도 중

해석 이메일에서, Ms. Takai는 무엇에 대해 물어보는가?
(A) 기술을 보여줄 가능성
(B) 가판 규격
(C) 다른 예술가들 연락처
(D) 허용되는 결제 수단

해설 두 번째 지문[Ms. Takai가 보낸 이메일], 두 번째 단락에서 I really enjoyed the tutorials that some artisans provided. Will there be something similar to that this year? Please let us know if there is because I would love to show the audience how we produce some of our crafts.(몇몇 장인들이 제공하는 개별 지도 시간이 정말 좋았어요. 올해도 그와 유사한 무언가가 있을까요? 저는 관객에게 저희가 공예품을 어떻게 만드는지 보여주고 싶어서요, 만약 있

다면 저에게 알려주세요.)라고 했으므로 (A)가 정답

Paraphrasing show ➡ demonstrate

181-185번은 다음 공고와 이메일에 관한 문제입니다.

QMC 건설 솔루션 주식회사
Contreras 체험학습 프로그램

Rancho Cucamonga에 본사를 둔 QMC 건설 솔루션 주식회사는 Contreras 체험학습 프로그램(CWSP)에 참여할 15명의 전도유망한 학생들을 모집하고 있습니다.[181] 프로그램 참가자들은 San Bernardino, Riverside, 또는 Rancho Cucamonga에 있는 3곳의 QMC 시설들 중 한 곳에서 근무하게 될 것입니다. 검토를 원할 경우, 학생들은 CWSP@qmcconstruction.com로 자기소개서와 이력서를 보내야 합니다. 프로그램에 선발된 사람들은 다음 달 발행되는 <Inland Empire 비즈니스 저널>의 특집 기사에 실립니다.

프로그램 소개:
CWSP는 Anthony Contreras가 창설한 것으로, 그는 QMC 건설 솔루션의 원 소유자인 Guillermo M. Contreras의 업적을 기리고자 하였습니다. **이 프로그램은** Guillermo Contreras의 정신을 받아들여 **젊은 건축학도를 양성하기 위해 만들어져,**[184] 디자인과 건축 문제에 보다 효과적인 해결책을 모색하고 개발합니다. 건축학 석사학위 취득 후, Guillermo Contreras는 자신의 형인 Edwin과 공동으로 QMC 건설 솔루션 주식회사를 설립했습니다. 해를 거듭하며 그는 소규모 회사를 남부 캘리포니아에서 가장 훌륭한 건설회사들 중 하나로 성장시켰습니다. **그는 35년간 경영 일선에 있다 올해 초 자리에서 물러났고, 자신의 조카 Anthony에게 자리를 물려줬습니다.**[182]

어휘 base v. 근거지[본사]를 두다   promising adj. 유망한, 촉망되는   participant n. 참가자   facility n. 시설   consideration n. 고려   cover letter 자기소개서   CV(curriculum vitae) 이력서   select v. 선택하다   feature v. 특별히 포함하다   article n. 기사   creation n. 창조, 창작(품)   commemorate v. 기념하다   original adj. 원래의, 본래의   owner n. 소유주   design v. 설계하다   foster v. 양성[육성]하다   architecture n. 건축   example n. 예, 본보기   explore v. 탐험하다   develop v. 개발하다   effective adj. 효과적인   solution n. 해결책   construction n. 건설   complete v. 완료하다   partnership n. 동반자 관계, 동업   pass v. 통과하다, 지나가다   grow v. 키우다; 증가하다   respect v. 존경하다   lead v. 이끌다   step down 내려오다, 물러나다   nephew n. 조카   take charge 책임지다, 떠맡다

수신: Jerry Skakal <JSkakal@desertcollege.edu>
발신: Deanna Rogers <rogers@qmcbuilders.com>
날짜: 7월 14일
제목: 세부사항

Mr. Skakal께,

Contreras 체험학습 프로그램을 수락하신 것에 축하 드립니다.[184] 귀하는 앞으로 수일 내 합격통지서 및 계약서를 받게 됩니다. **숙소에 대해 문의 주신 것과 관련하여, 저는 귀하가 매일 San Diego의 자택에서 두 시간씩 운전하여 통근하는 것을 원치 않으실 것에 전적으로 동감합니다만, 아쉽게도 저희는 프로그램 참가자들께 숙소를 제공해드릴 수가 없습니다.**[183] 하지만, Riverside 사무실에 있는 프로그램 담당자 Rodrigo Carvalho와 이 문제에 대해 상의해 보세요. 그는 Riverside에서 태어나고 자라서, 아마 그곳의 저렴한 숙소에 대한 정보를 알고 있을 거예요.[185]

다시 한번 축하 드리며, 저희는 귀하와 함께 일하기를 기대하고 있겠습니다.

Best Regards,

Deanna Rogers
HR 전문가
QMC 건설 솔루션 주식회사

어휘 acceptance n. 수락, 승인 official adj. 공식적인, 공인된 contract n. 계약서 concerning prep. ~에 관한 accommodation n. 숙소, 거처 certainly adv. 분명히, 틀림없이 prefer v. 선호하다 arrange v. (일을) 주선하다, 처리하다 housing n. 주택 (공급) coordinator n. 진행자, 조정자 raise v. 키우다 probably adv. 아마도 suggestion n. 제안, 의견 lodging n. 임시숙소, 하숙

181 주제/목적/대상   난이도 중

해석 공지는 왜 게시되었는가?
(A) 회사 프로그램을 홍보하기 위해
(B) 새로운 사장을 구하기 위해
(C) 건축 프로젝트에 대해 보고하기 위해
(D) 잡지 기사를 광고하기 위해

해설 첫 번째 지문[공지], 첫 번째 단락에서 QMC Construction Solutions, Inc., based in Rancho Cucamonga, is looking for 15 promising students for the Contreras Work Study Program (CWSP).(Rancho Cucamonga에 본사를 둔 QMC 건설 솔루션 주식회사는 Contreras 체험학습 프로그램(CWSP)에 참여할 15명의 전도유망한 학생들을 모집하고 있습니다.)라고 했으므로 (A)가 정답

182 상세정보   난이도 중

해석 Anthony Contreras는 누구인가?
(A) 대학교 행정직원
(B) 회사 설립자
(C) 기업 대표
(D) 학생 인턴

해설 첫 번째 지문[공지], 두 번째 단락에서 After leading the company for 35 years, he stepped down earlier this year to let his nephew, Anthony, take charge.(그는 35년간 경영 일선에 있다 올해 초 자리에서 물러났고, 자신의 조카 Anthony에게 자리를 물려줬습니다.)라고 했으므로 (C)가 정답

183 주제/목적/대상   난이도 중

해석 Ms. Roger가 보낸 이메일의 목적에 해당하는 것은?
(A) Mr. Skakal의 계약서에 대해 논의하려고
(B) 부동산 중개업소를 추천하려고
(C) 문제에 대해 물어보려고
(D) 문의에 답하려고

해설 두 번째 지문[Ms. Rogers가 보낸 이메일], 첫 번째 단락에서 Concerning your question about accommodations, I certainly understand that you'd prefer not to make a 2-hour drive from your home in San Diego every day, but I'm afraid that we are unable to arrange housing for program participants.(숙소에 대해 문의주신 것과 관련하여, 저는 귀가가 매일 San Diego의 자택에서 두 시간씩 운전하여 통근하는 것을 원치 않으실 것에 전적으로 동감합니다만, 아쉽게도 저희는 프로그램 참가자들께 숙소를 제공해드릴 수가 없습니다.)라고 했으므로 (D)가 정답

Paraphrasing question ➡ inquiry

184 사실확인 [연계문제]   난이도 중

해석 Mr. Skakal에 관하여 사실인 것은?
(A) 건축학을 공부한다.
(B) 전에 Mr. Carvalho를 만난 적이 있다.
(C) 다른 사무실로 이동할 것이다.
(D) QMC 건설 솔루션을 고용하고 싶어한다.

해설 첫 번째 지문[공지], 두 번째 단락에서 The program is designed to foster young architecture students(이 프로그램은 젊은 건축학도들을 양성하기 위해 만들어져,)라고 했는데, 두 번째 지문[Mr. Skakal에게 전송된 이메일], 첫 번째 단락에서 Congratulations on your acceptance to the Contreras Work Study Program.(Contreras 체험학습 프로그램을 수락하신 것에 축하 드립니다.)라고 하여 그가 건축학도임을 알 수 있으므로 (A)가 정답

185 상세정보   난이도 중

해석 Mr. Skakal는 어디서 일할 것인가?
(A) San Bernardino에서
(B) Riverside에서
(C) Rancho Cucamonga에서
(D) San Diego에서

해설 두 번째 지문[Mr. Skakal에게 전송된 이메일], 첫 번째 단락에서 Rodrigo Carvalho, the program coordinator for the Riverside office, would be a good person to talk to about this. He was born and raised in Riverside, and he will probably have some suggestions for low-cost lodging there.(프로그램 담당자 Rodrigo Carvalho와 이 문제에 대해 상의해 보세요. 그는 Riverside에서 태어나고 자라서, 아마 그곳의 저렴한 숙소에 대한 정보를 알고 있을 거에요.)라고 했으므로 (B)가 정답

186-190번은 다음 이메일, 광고, 메모에 관한 문제입니다.

발신: Lew Burns (영국 Flotech)
수신: Ashraf Bhagat (파키스탄 Flotech)
날짜: 12월 5일
제목: Awad 엔지니어링

Ashraf, 안녕하세요.

Awad 엔지니어링의 방문을 맞이할 준비를 하고 계시다고 들었어요. Flotech 컨설팅 영국지사가 이곳 London에서 수년째 Awad 엔지니어링과 협력해 와서, 그들은 Flotech 파키스탄 팀과도 좋은 관계를 맺을 거라 매우 기대하고 있어요.(186)/(189) 상대하기 매우 편한 사람들이라는걸 알게 되실 거에요.

1월 12일로 준비하고 계신 식사에 관해서는,(189) 엔지니어들 중 몇 명이 다소 엄격한 식이 제한사항이 있다는 걸 말씀 드려야겠네요.(187) 준비하실 때 이 점을 염두에 두시는 게 좋을 거에요.

물어보실 게 있으시면 전화주세요.

고맙습니다.

-Lew

어휘 | **branch** n. 지점, 지사 **concerning** prep. ~에 관한 **rather** adv. 좀, 약간 **strict** adj. 엄격한 **dietary restriction** 식사 제한 사항 **make arrangements** 준비하다

Darbar 출장뷔페
Karachi

완벽한 행사를 계획하고 싶으실 때는, Darbar 출장뷔페를 찾아주세요. 저희 회사는 1955년부터 Karachi 지역에서 영업해 왔는데, 기업과 가족모임 모두에 최상의 음식과 음료를 제공합니다.

왜 Darbar여야 하냐구요? 저희를 돋보이게 하는 점은 다음과 같습니다:
*회사 로고를 포함한 맞춤제작 장식물
*양식, 남아시아식 및 중식 인기 품목을 포함하는 국제적인 메뉴
*다양한 음식기호에 맞춰 만들어드리는 특별 메뉴(187)
*요청 시 이용 가능한 무도장 설치 및 음악 공연 서비스

저희 서비스는 매일 정오부터 오후 10시까지 이용하실 수 있습니다.(188)

더 자세한 내용은 (92) 0213-555-1212로 전화주세요.

어휘 | **catering** n. 음식공급(업체) **at one's service** 마음대로 사용할 수 있는 **delight** v. 즐겁게 하다 **corporate** adj. 기업[회사]의 **gathering** n. 모임 **stand out** 두드러지다 **customized** adj. 개인의 요구에 맞춘 **feature** v. 특별히 포함하다 **suit** v. (…에게) 맞다 **setup** n. 설치, 설정

Bilal 리조트
Avaricor 그룹 호텔(190)

1월 12일(189)

Mr. Opfel께,(189)

파키스탄에 오신 걸 환영합니다! London에서부터 즐거운 여행이었길 바랍니다. 오후 12시 30분에 이 리조트 2층 Rainbow 홀에서 있을 특별 오찬에 저희와 함께 해주신다면 저희 팀과 저는 영광이겠습니다.(189)/(190) 공사 현장으로 나가기 전에, 좋은 음식을 먹으면서 당신에 대해 조금 알게 되길 기대하고 있습니다.

그 동안, 제가 도와드릴 일이 있다면 (92) 0304-551-2522로 저에게 전화주세요.

Yours Faithfully,

Ashraf Bhagat

어휘 | **head** v. (특정 방향으로) 향하다 **in the meantime** 그 동안에 **be of assistance** 도움이 되다

---

186 주제/목적/대상   난이도 중

해석 | 이메일은 왜 발송되었는가?
(A) 신규 계약 조항을 논의하기 위해
(B) 고객 문제로 다른 지점과 협력하기 위해
(C) 엔지니어 자리의 후보자를 추천하기 위해
(D) 고객과의 오찬회의 일정을 다시 잡기 위해

해설 | 첫 번째 지문[이메일], 첫 번째 단락에서 I've just heard that you are preparing for a visit from Awad Engineering. The UK branch of Flotech Consulting has been working with Awad Engineering for many years here in London, and they are looking forward very much to a good relationship with the Flotech Pakistan team as well.(Awad 엔지니어링의 방문을 맞이할 준비를 하고 계시다고 들었어요. Flotech 컨설팅 영국지사가 이곳 London에서 수년째 Awad 엔지니어링과 협력해와서, 그들은 Flotech 파키스탄 팀과도 좋은 관계를 맺을 거라 매우 기대하고 있어요.)라고 했으므로 (B)가 정답

187 상세정보 [연계문제]   난이도 상

해석 | Darbar 출장뷔페의 어떤 특징이 행사에 가장 적합한 업체로 만들어주는가?
(A) 저렴한 서비스
(B) 넓은 장소
(C) 주문제작 메뉴
(D) 공연 옵션

해설 | 첫 번째 지문[이메일], 두 번째 단락에서 Concerning the meal you are planning for them on January 12, I should mention that several of the engineers have rather strict dietary restrictions.(1월 12일로 준비하고 계신 식사에 관해서는, 엔지니어들 중 몇 명이 다소 엄격한 식이 제한사항이 있다는 걸 말씀 드려야겠네요.)라고 했는데, 두 번째 지문[광고], 두 번째 단락에서 Special menus that can be created to suit a variety of food preferences(다양한 음식 기호에 맞춰 만들어드리는 특별 메뉴)라고 하여 업체 특징 중에 주문제작 메뉴가 있음을 알 수 있으므로 (C)가 정답

Paraphrasing created to suit a variety of food preferences ➡ customized

188 암시/추론   난이도 중

해석 | 광고에 따르면, Darbar 출장뷔페는 어떤 유형의 행사에 도움이 되지 않겠는가?
(A) 시상식 만찬
(B) 기업 조찬행사
(C) 연휴 기념행사
(D) 졸업 파티

해설 | 두 번째 지문[광고], 세 번째 단락에서 Our services are available daily, Noon to 10 P.M.(저희 서비스는 정오부터 오후 10시까지 매일 이용하실 수 있습니다.)라고 하여 정오 이후의 행사부터 진행한다는 것을 알 수 있으므로 (B)가 정답

189 암시/추론 [연계문제]   난이도 상

해석 | Mr. Opfel은 어디서 근무하겠는가?
(A) Awad 엔지니어링
(B) Darbar 출장뷔페
(C) Flotech 컨설팅
(D) Avaricor 그룹

해설 첫 번째 지문[이메일], 첫 번째 단락에서 I've just heard that you are preparing for a visit from Awad Engineering. The UK branch of Flotech Consulting has been working with Awad Engineering for many years here in London, and they are looking forward very much to a good relationship with the Flotech Pakistan team as well.(Awad 엔지니어링의 방문을 맞이할 준비를 하고 계시다고 들었어요. Flotech 컨설팅 영국지사가 이곳 London에서 수년째 Awad 엔지니어링과 협력해와서, 그들은 Flotech 파키스탄 팀과도 좋은 관계를 맺을 거라 매우 기대하고 있어요.)라고 하면서, 두 번째 단락에서 Concerning the meal you are planning for them on January 12,(1월 12일로 준비하고 계신 식사에 관해서는,)이라고 했는데, 세 번째 지문[1월 12일 Mr. Opfel에게 보낸 메모], 첫 번째 단락에서 I hope you had a pleasant flight from London—welcome to Pakistan! My team and I would be honored if you would join us at 12:30 P.M. for a special luncheon in Rainbow Hall on the second floor of this resort.(London에서부터 즐거운 여행이었길 바랍니다. 파키스탄에 오신 걸 환영합니다! 오후 12시 30분에 이 리조트 2층 Rainbow 홀에서 있을 특별 오찬에 저희와 함께 해주신다면 저희 팀과 저는 영광이겠습니다.)라고 하여 Mr. Opfel이 London에서 온 Awad Engineering 직원임을 알 수 있으므로 (A)가 정답

190 암시/추론 난이도 중

해석 Mr. Opfel은 어디에서 메모를 전달받았겠는가?
(A) 리조트 프론트데스크에서
(B) Flotech에서 주최하는 사교모임에서
(C) London 공항의 출발게이트에서
(D) Awad 엔지니어링 본사에서

해설 세 번째 지문[메모], 제목에서 Bilal Resort, An Avaricor Group Hotel(Bilal 리조트, Avaricor 그룹 호텔)라고 했고, 첫 번째 단락에서 I hope you had a pleasant flight from London—welcome to Pakistan! My team and I would be honored if you would join us at 12:30 P.M. for a special luncheon in Rainbow Hall on the second floor of this resort.(London에서부터 즐거운 여행이셨길 바랍니다. 파키스탄에 오신 걸 환영합니다! 오후 12시 30분에 이 리조트 2층 Rainbow 홀에서 있을 특별 오찬에 저희와 함께 해주신다면 저희 팀과 저는 영광이겠습니다.)라고 하여 리조트측에서 메모를 전달했을 것임을 알 수 있으므로 (A)가 정답

191-195번은 다음 이메일들과 행사정보에 관한 문제입니다.

발신:	XiaoHui Huang
수신:	Joseph Lucchese
날짜:	7월 12일
제목:	8월 12일 포스터
첨부파일:	포스터 내용

안녕하세요, Joseph.

말씀 나눴던 대로, 포스터에 실릴 내용 보내드립니다. 각 지점의 다양한 곳에 게시하려면 최소 100부는 필요합니다. 제공해주신 템플릿을 검토해보니, 배경은 '핫핑크', 글자 대부분은 '연하늘색'으로 해야 할 것 같습니다. 그리고 연사들의 이름은 사람들의 시선을 끌 수 있게 화려한 폰트를 쓰는 걸로 합시다.(191)

경영진도 이 부분에 대해 이해할 수 있도록, **반드시 기념행사보다 훨씬 전에 샘플을 보여드릴 수 있도록 합시다.**(192) 다음 주까지 한 부 준비해줄 수 있겠어요?

고맙습니다.

XiaoHui Huang,
프로그램 준비위원

어휘 per prep. ~에 따라 content n. 내용 display v. 보여주다, 전시하다 post v. 게시하다 review v. 검토하다 template n. 견본 background n. 배경 majority n. 다수 lettering n. (특정한 서체로 인쇄된) 글자 fancy adj. 장식이 많은, 화려한 lecturer n. 강연자 catch v. (주의, 관심 등을) 끌다 management n. 경영[운영]진 on the same page 생각이 같은, 동의한 in advance of ~보다 앞서

ErgoBuff 연구소
35회 연례 공로표창

8월 12일, 오후 7시-10시, Overlook 호텔(193)

오후 7시 ~ 오후 7시 15분 – CEO Tony Bibbo의 개회사
오후 7시 15분 ~ 오후 8시 15분 – 만찬 및 Juan Talavera의 음악 공연
오후 8시 15분 ~ 오후 8시 45분 – 특별 강연 1: <생활양식으로서의 체육관>(Silver 체육관, 마케팅 담당 부사장 Roger Severen)
오후 8시 45분 ~오후 9시 15분 특별 강연 2: <영양제 산업의 미래>(Tamaulipas 대학교, Ernest Jung 교수)(191)
오후 9시 15분 ~ 오후 9시 45분 시상
오후 9시 45분 ~ 오후 10시 폐회사

수상자:(193)
Philip Bain – 우수 사업모델 개발(193)
Shruti Chandrashekar – 최우수 영업(193)
Rebecca Wilson – 25년 근속(193)
Eileen Vogel – 최우수 신규 아이디어(193)

어휘 recognize v. 인정하다, 공인하다 excellence n. 우수성, 뛰어남 opening[closing] remarks 개[폐]회사 musical performance 음악 공연 nutritional supplement 영양(보조)제 outstanding adj. 우수한, 뛰어난 silver anniversary 25주년 기념일

발신:	Eric Eilenberger
수신:	XiaoHui Huang
날짜:	7월 19일
제목:	8월 12일 포스터 내용

안녕하세요, XiaoHui.

제안하신 포스터 디자인을 검토했는데, 전체적으로 좋습니다. 배경과 폰트 색상이 밝아서, 확실히 예년에 내걸었던 포스터들보다 더 발랄한 느낌입니다! 연사들도 직함에서부터 확실히 인상적이네요.

한 가지만 참고해 주세요. 25년 근속상 수상자는 회사에서 25년 이상 근무한 사람입니다.(194) 대부분의 경우, 고위 관리직에 있죠. 그 부분을 제외하면, 현재의 순서가 좋습니다. 하지만 뭐든지 마무리하기 전에는, 반드시 Mr. Bibbo의 승인을 받으세요. 그리고 포스터에 있는 모든 이름이 제대로 적혀 있는지도 확인하세요. 특별 행사이니까요.(195)

우리가 이용하는 인쇄소는 보통 일 년 중 이맘때 아주 바쁩니다. 그래서 자주 연락을 취하는 것이 중요합니다. 2년 전에는 프로그램 준비자가 주문을 너무 늦게 해서, 포스터가 행사 당일에 나왔답니다.

Eric Eilenberger
인사부장

어휘 certainly adv. 틀림없이, 분명히 cheerful adj. 발랄한, 쾌활한 feel n. 느낌, 분위기 put up 게시하다 job title 직위, 직책 recipient n. 받는 사람 impressive adj. 인상적인 as well 또한 aside from ~외에는 current adj. 현재의 finalize v. 마무리 짓다 approval n. 승인, 인정 correctly adv. 정확하게 crucial adj. 중대한 maintain v. 유지하다 back adv. 전에 place v. (주문을) 하다

191 암시/추론 [연계문제] 난이도 상

해석 누구의 이름이 포스터에 특별한 스타일로 나오겠는가?
(A) Tony Bibbo
(B) Ernest Jung
(C) Juan Talavera
(D) Eileen Vogel

해설 첫 번째 지문[첫 번째 이메일], 첫 번째 단락에서 But also, let's use a fancy font for the lecturers' names so that they catch people's attention.(그리고 연사들의 이름은 사람들의 시선을 끌 수 있게 화려한 폰트를 쓰는 걸로 합시다.)라고 했는데, 두 번째 지문[행사 정보], 8:45-9:15분 일정에서 Special Lecture 2: The Future of the Nutritional Supplement Industry by Professor Ernest Jung of Tamaulipas University.(오후 8시 45분~오후 9시 15분 특별 강연 2: <영양제 산업의 미래>(Tamaulipas 대학교, Ernest Jung 교수))라고 했으므로 (B)가 정답

Paraphrasing fancy font ➡ special style

192 동의어 난이도 중

해석 첫 번째 이메일에서 두 번째 단락, 첫 번째 줄의 단어 "far"와 의미상 가장 가까운 것은?
(A) 거리가 먼
(B) 오래
(C) 깊이
(D) 늘어진

해설 첫 번째 지문[첫 번째 이메일], 첫 번째 단락의 let's make sure to show them a sample far in advance of the celebration.(반드시 기념행사보다 훨씬 전에 그들에게 샘플을 보여줍시다.)에서 'far'는 '(시간상) 훨씬'라는 의미로 쓰였으므로 보기 중 '(시간상) 길게, 오래'를 뜻하는 (B)가 정답

193 상세정보 난이도 중

해석 8월 12일에 어떤 행사가 열리는가?
(A) 시상식
(B) 관리자 회의
(C) 지점 개업
(D) 상품 출시

해설 두 번째 지문[행사정보]에서 Overlook Hotel, August 12, 7-10 P.M.(8월 12일, 오후 7시-10시, Overlook 호텔)라고 했고, Recipients(수상자)에서 Philip Bain – Outstanding Business Development(우수 사업모델 개발), Shruti Chandrashekar - Top Sales(최우수 영업), Rebecca Wilson – Silver Anniversary(25년 근속), Eileen Vogel - Best New Idea(최우수 신규 아이디어)라고 수상자들이 열거되어 있어 8월 12일에 시상식이 있음을 알 수 있으므로 (A)가 정답

194 암시/추론 [연계문제] 난이도 상

해석 Ms. Wilson에 관하여 알 수 있는 것은?
(A) 8월 12일 행사에서 공연을 제공할 것이다.
(B) ErgoBuff에서 25년 이상 근무했다.
(C) 행사 준비자로 일했었다.
(D) 인사부를 감독한다.

해설 두 번째 지문[ErgoBuff Laboratories의 행사정보], Recipients(수상자)에서 Rebecca Wilson – Silver Anniversary(25년 근속)이라고 했고, 세 번째 지문[두 번째 이메일], 두 번째 단락에서 The recipient for the Silver Anniversary is typically given to someone who has been with the company for more than 25 years.(25년 근속상의 수상자는 보통 회사에서 25년 이상 근무한 사람입니다.)라고 하여 Ms. Wilson이 ErgoBuff에서 25년 이상 근무했음을 알 수 있으므로 (B)가 정답

195 상세정보 난이도 중

해석 Mr. Eilenberger는 Ms. Huang에게 무엇을 하라고 요청하는가?
(A) 다른 판매업체를 선택하라고
(B) 용품을 더 주문하라고
(C) 정보가 맞는지 확인하라고
(D) 배경색을 변경하라고

해설 세 번째 지문[두 번째 이메일], 두 번째 단락에서 Before you finalize anything though, be sure to get Mr. Bibbo's approval. In addition, confirm that every name on the poster is written correctly. It is a special event after all.(하지만 뭔가를 마무리하기 전에는, 반드시 Mr. Bibbo의 승인을 받으세요. 그리고 포스터에 있는 모든 이름이 제대로 적혀 있는지도 확인하세요. 특별 행사이니까요.)라고 했으므로 (C)가 정답

Paraphrasing confirm ➡ check

196-200번은 다음 송장과 이메일들에 관한 문제입니다.

Ronzone's Suppliers

435 Harrison Avenue
Elkhart, IN 46516

(574) 555-1212

www.ronzonesuppliers.com

날짜: 5월 15일
주문자: Michele's 이탈리아 식당

제품번호	제품명	수량	가격/단위	계
255X	올리브 오일	30	5.25달러/병	157.50달러
136B	텃밭 채소 믹스 피클	25	3.15달러/병	78.75달러
119Z(197)	적포도주(197)	50	10.60달러/병	530달러
364D	토마토 페이스트	100	2.25달러/캔	225.00달러

총액(991.25달러)은 상품 인도 시 결제하시기 바랍니다.

어휘 supplier n. 공급업체 quantity n. 양 amount n. 총액; 액수 pickled adj. 식초에 절인 jar n. 병 paste n. 반죽, 페이스트 due adj. (돈을) 지불해야 하는 delivery n. 배달

발신: Michele Ciaramitaro
수신: Greg Ronzone
날짜: 5월 18일
제목: 5월 15일 주문

안녕하세요, Greg.

5월 15일 주문에 몇 가지 문제가 있는 것 같아요.**(196)** 텃밭 채소 믹스는 15병밖에 안 왔고, 와인 10병은 눈에 띄게 긁힌 자국이 있습니다.**(197)** 주문처리 방식에 변화가 있었나요?

저는 당신이 20년 전 사업을 시작했을 때부터 당신의 서비스에 매우 만족해와서,**(199D)** 이런 일이 있을 거라고는 전혀 예상하지 못했어요. 게다가 제 친구인 Beaugard 요리학교장 Sanjiv Saini도 이번 달 당신에게 주문했을 때 비슷한 문제를 겪었다는 걸 말씀 드려야 할 것 같네요.**(199B)**

어쨌든 이 문제를 어떻게 해결해 주실 건지 알려주세요. 저희가 바쁜 시기라서, 이 물품들이 꼭 필요합니다.**(196)**

감사합니다.

Michele Ciaramitaro

어휘 issue n. 문제 visibly adv. 눈에 띄게, 분명히 scratch v. 긁다 operation n. 작업, (시스템의) 운용 culinary adj. 요리의 institute n. 기관, 협회 as well 또한, 마찬가지로 in any case 어쨌든 correct v. 바로잡다 supplies n. 용품, 비품

발신: Greg Ronzone
수신: Michele Ciaramitaro
날짜: 5월 18일
제목: 회신: 5월 15일 주문

안녕하세요, Michele.

배송건은 정말 죄송합니다. Sanjiv Saini건은 말할 것도 없고요. **즉시 Sanjiv에게 연락해서 그분의 상황도 처리하겠습니다.(198)** 당신은 여러 해 동안 좋은 고객이었고, 당신에게 형편없는 서비스를 제공하는 것은 제가 절대 하고 싶지 않은 일입니다. 저희가 최근 다른 배송업체를 이용하기 시작했는데,**(199C)** 그곳의 작업 수행이 저희의 기대치에 미치지 못했습니다. 그렇더라도, 저희는 문제를 즉시 바로잡도록 하겠습니다. 누락물품과 교체물품을 포함한 새 배송품을 익일 배송으로 보내드리겠습니다. 추가로 다음 번 주문 시 20 퍼센트 할인을 제공해 드리고자 합니다. 결제하실 때 판촉코드 "20RR"을 입력해 주세요.**(200)**

그 외 필요하신 것이 있으면, 언제든지 저에게 연락주세요.

Sincerely,

Greg Ronzone

어휘 shipment n. 수송, 배송 not to mention ~는 말할 것도 없고 get in touch with ~와 연락하다 address v. (문제·상황 등을) 고심하다, 다루다 firm n. 회사 performance n. 수행, 실행 be that as it may 그렇다고 하더라도 set ~ straight ~을 바로잡다 overnight delivery 익일배송 checkout n. (슈퍼마켓의) 계산대

---

196 주제/목적/대상 난이도 중

해석 첫 번째 이메일의 목적은 무엇이었는가?
(A) 주문을 갱신하는 것
(B) 고객을 소개하는 것
(C) 문제의 해결을 요청하는 것
(D) 설문조사에 응하는 것

해설 두 번째 지문[첫 번째 이메일], 첫 번째 단락에서 I'm afraid there are a few issues with my May 15 order.(5월 15일 주문에 몇 가지 문제가 있는 것 같아요.)라고 했고, 세 번째 단락에서 In any case, please let me know what you will do to correct this situation. It's our busy season, so I really need these supplies.(어쨌든 이 문제를 어떻게 해결해 주실 건지 알려주세요. 저희가 바쁜 시기라서, 이 물품들이 꼭 필요합니다.)라고 했으므로 (C)가 정답

Paraphrasing situation ➡ issue, correct ➡ resolve

197 상세정보 [연계문제] 난이도 중

해석 어느 제품이 손상된 채로 배송되었는가?
(A) 255X
(B) 136B
(C) 119Z
(D) 364D

해설 두 번째 지문[첫 번째 이메일], 첫 번째 단락에서 10 of the wine bottles were visibly scratched.(와인 10병은 눈에 띄게 긁힌 자국이 있습니다.)라고 했는데, 첫 번째 지문[송장], 표에서 와인 물품에 해당하는 항목이 Red Wine(적포도주)이므로 (C)가 정답

Paraphrasing scratched ➡ damaged

198 동의어 난이도 중

해석 두 번째 이메일에서 첫 번째 단락, 두 번째 줄의 단어 "address"와 의미상 가장 가까운 것은?
(A) (특정 위치에) 두다
(B) 총괄하다
(C) 처리하다
(D) (우편으로) 보내다

해설 세 번째 지문[두 번째 이메일], 첫 번째 단락의 I'll get in touch with Sanjiv right away and address his situation as well.(즉시 Sanjiv에게 연락해서 그분의 상황도 처리하겠습니다.)에서 'address'는 '처리하다'라는 의미로 쓰였으므로 보기 중 같은 의미를 갖는 (C)가 정답

199 상세정보 [연계문제] 난이도 상

해석 Ronzone Suppliers에 관하여 언급되지 않은 것은?
(A) 제품 목록을 업데이트하고 있다.
(B) 요리학교에 상품을 판매하고 있다.
(C) 최근 새로운 업체를 이용했다.
(D) 20년 동안 영업해왔다.

해설 지문의 단서와 보기를 매칭시키면, 두 번째 지문 [첫 번째 이메일], 두 번째 단락에서 I've been very happy with your services since you got started 20 years ago,(저는 당신이 20년 전 사업을 시작했을 때부터 당신의 서비스에 매우 만족해와서,) → (D) They have been in business for 20 years./ I think I should mention that my friend Sanjiv Saini, general manager of Beaugard Culinary

Institute, had similar problems when he ordered from you this month as well.(제 친구인 Beaugard 요리학교장 Sanjiv Saini도 이번 달 당신에게 주문했을 때 비슷한 문제를 겪었다는 걸 말씀 드려야 할 것 같네요.) → (B) They sell their items to cooking schools. / 세 번째 지문[두 번째 이메일], 첫 번째 단락에서 We just started using a different delivery firm,(저희가 최근 다른 배송업체를 이용하기 시작했는데,) → (C) They recently hired a new company.와 일치하지만, 제품 목록을 업데이트한다는 내용은 언급된 바 없으므로 (A)가 정답

200 상세정보   난이도 중

해석   Ronzone Suppliers는 Mr. Ciaramitaro에게 무엇을 줄 것인가?
(A) 올리브 오일병 추가분
(B) 신상품 샘플
(C) 향후 구매에 대한 할인
(D) 배송비 면제

해설   세 번째 지문[두 번째 이메일], 첫 번째 단락에서 we would like to give you 20 percent off on your next order. Simply enter promo code 20RR during the checkout process.(다음 번 주문 시 20 퍼센트 할인을 제공해 드리고자 합니다. 결제하실 때 판촉코드 "20RR"을 입력해 주세요.)라고 했으므로 (C)가 정답

Paraphrasing   20 percent off on your next order ➡ A discount on a future purchase

TEST 05

PART 1 — P. 190
1 (A) 2 (C) 3 (B) 4 (B) 5 (B) 6 (D)

PART 2 — P. 194
7 (A) 8 (A) 9 (B) 10 (B) 11 (C) 12 (A)
13 (C) 14 (C) 15 (A) 16 (C) 17 (C) 18 (B)
19 (B) 20 (C) 21 (B) 22 (A) 23 (B) 24 (A)
25 (C) 26 (B) 27 (B) 28 (A) 29 (C) 30 (C)
31 (B)

PART 3 — P. 195
32 (D) 33 (A) 34 (C) 35 (B) 36 (D) 37 (C)
38 (B) 39 (A) 40 (C) 41 (C) 42 (A) 43 (B)
44 (A) 45 (C) 46 (B) 47 (A) 48 (C) 49 (A)
50 (D) 51 (C) 52 (A) 53 (C) 54 (B) 55 (A)
56 (A) 57 (C) 58 (B) 59 (D) 60 (A) 61 (B)
62 (A) 63 (D) 64 (B) 65 (B) 66 (B) 67 (A)
68 (C) 69 (A) 70 (A)

PART 4 — P. 199
71 (A) 72 (B) 73 (D) 74 (B) 75 (D) 76 (C)
77 (B) 78 (D) 79 (A) 80 (D) 81 (B) 82 (C)
83 (A) 84 (D) 85 (D) 86 (B) 87 (A) 88 (B)
89 (A) 90 (B) 91 (B) 92 (C) 93 (C) 94 (A)
95 (C) 96 (B) 97 (A) 98 (A) 99 (A) 100 (B)

PART 5 — P. 202
101 (D) 102 (D) 103 (C) 104 (D) 105 (C) 106 (D)
107 (C) 108 (D) 109 (C) 110 (D) 111 (B) 112 (A)
113 (A) 114 (C) 115 (C) 116 (C) 117 (D) 118 (C)
119 (B) 120 (C) 121 (C) 122 (B) 123 (D) 124 (D)
125 (C) 126 (D) 127 (D) 128 (D) 129 (A) 130 (C)

PART 6 — P. 205
131 (D) 132 (D) 133 (C) 134 (B) 135 (B) 136 (D)
137 (B) 138 (C) 139 (D) 140 (A) 141 (B) 142 (B)
143 (C) 144 (D) 145 (C) 146 (A)

PART 7 — P. 209
147 (C) 148 (D) 149 (A) 150 (C) 151 (B) 152 (A)
153 (C) 154 (B) 155 (D) 156 (D) 157 (B) 158 (C)
159 (B) 160 (B) 161 (D) 162 (B) 163 (D) 164 (D)
165 (A) 166 (D) 167 (D) 168 (D) 169 (A) 170 (D)
171 (B) 172 (C) 173 (D) 174 (A) 175 (B) 176 (C)
177 (A) 178 (D) 179 (D) 180 (B) 181 (C) 182 (A)
183 (B) 184 (B) 185 (B) 186 (C) 187 (B) 188 (C)
189 (A) 190 (C) 191 (B) 192 (A) 193 (B) 194 (C)
195 (D) 196 (D) 197 (C) 198 (B) 199 (D) 200 (B)

PART 1 — P. 190

1 1인 중심 난이도 하

미국

(A) A woman is examining some products.
(B) A woman is wiping off her sunglasses.
(C) A woman is filling a shopping cart.
(D) A woman is placing a basket on a counter.

(A) 여자가 몇몇 제품들을 살펴보고 있다.
(B) 여자가 선글라스를 닦고 있다.
(C) 여자가 쇼핑 카트를 채우고 있다.
(D) 여자가 계산대에 바구니를 놓고 있다.

해설 (A) ◯ 여자가 제품을 살펴보고 있는 모습을 적절히 묘사했으므로 정답
(B) ✗ 동작 묘사 오류 (is wiping off)
(C) ✗ 사진에 없는 사물 (a shopping cart)
(D) ✗ 동작 묘사 오류 (is placing)

Possible Answer
A woman is holding some bottles. 여자가 병 몇 개를 들고 있다.

어휘 examine v. 조사하다 product n. 제품 wipe off 닦아내다 fill v. 가득 채우다 place v. 놓다, 두다 counter n. 계산대

2 1인 중심 난이도 하

영국

(A) He's raking some leaves.
(B) He's watering some plants.
(C) He's picking up some wood.
(D) He's cutting some tree branches.

(A) 남자가 갈퀴로 나뭇잎들을 긁어 모으고 있다.
(B) 남자가 화초에 물을 주고 있다.
(C) 남자가 나무를 집어 들고 있다.
(D) 남자가 나뭇가지를 자르고 있다.

해설 (A) ✗ 동작 묘사 오류 (is raking)
(B) ✗ 동작 묘사 오류 (is watering)
(C) ◯ 남자가 나무를 집고 있는 모습을 적절히 묘사했으므로 정답
(D) ✗ 동작 묘사 오류 (is cutting)

Possible Answer
A man is working outdoors. 남자가 야외에서 일하고 있다.

어휘 rake v. 갈퀴로 긁어 모으다 water v. (화초 등에) 물을 주다

3 2인 이상 난이도 중

미국

(A) A woman is pointing at a door.
(B) A woman is holding some documents.
(C) A man is drawing a chart on a whiteboard.
(D) A man is distributing some handouts at a meeting.

(A) 여자가 문쪽을 가리키고 있다.
(B) 여자가 서류를 들고 있다.
(C) 남자가 화이트보드에 도표를 그리고 있다.
(D) 남자가 회의에서 유인물을 나눠주고 있다.

해설 (A) ✗ 동작 묘사 오류 (is handing)
(B) ○ 여자가 서류를 들고 있는 모습을 적절히 묘사했으므로 정답
(C) ✗ 동작 묘사 오류 (is drawing)
(D) ✗ 동작 묘사 오류 (is distributing)

Possible Answer
The people are standing in front of a whiteboard. 사람들이 화이트보드 앞에 서 있다.

어휘 hand v. 건네주다, 넘겨주다 hold v. 잡고 있다 distribute v. 나누어 주다, 분배하다 handout n. 배포자료, 유인물

4 1인 중심 난이도 중

호주

(A) A woman is adjusting a shelf.
(B) A woman is hanging up a skirt.
(C) A woman is trying on a shirt.
(D) A woman is opening a closet door.

(A) 여자가 선반을 조절하고 있다.
(B) 여자가 치마를 걸고 있다.
(C) 여자가 셔츠를 입어보고 있다.
(D) 여자가 벽장 문을 열고 있다.

해설 (A) ✗ 동작 묘사 오류 (is adjusting)
(B) ○ 여자가 치마를 걸고 있는 모습을 적절히 묘사했으므로 정답
(C) ✗ 동작 묘사 오류 (is trying on)
(D) ✗ 동작 묘사 오류 (is opening)

Possible Answer
She's organizing some clothes. 여자가 옷을 정리하고 있다.

어휘 adjust v. 조정[조절]하다 hang up 걸다 try on 입어보다 closet n. 벽장

5 1인 중심 난이도 중

영국

(A) Some vehicles are being inspected in the garage.
(B) Some boxes are stacked in the warehouse.
(C) A man is packing a crate with merchandise.
(D) A man is loading a delivery truck.

(A) 차량들이 차고에서 점검 받고 있다.
(B) 상자들이 창고에 쌓여있다.
(C) 남자가 상품이 들어있는 상자를 포장하고 있다.
(D) 남자가 배달 트럭에 짐을 싣고 있다.

해설 (A) ✗ 동작 묘사 오류 (are being inspected)
(B) ○ 상자들이 창고에 쌓여있는 모습을 적절히 묘사했으므로 정답
(C) ✗ 동작 묘사 오류 (is packing)
(D) ✗ 동작 묘사 오류 (is loading)

Possible Answer
A worker is transporting some boxes. 작업자가 상자를 옮기고 있다.

어휘 inspect v. 점검하다 stack v. 쌓다 warehouse n. 창고 pack v. 포장하다 crate n. 상자 load v. 싣다

6 사물/풍경 난이도 상

미국

(A) A carpet has been rolled up against the window.
(B) A painting is positioned on a wall.
(C) Some light fixtures are hanging from the ceiling.
(D) Some cushions have been set on a sofa.

(A) 카펫이 창문에 기대어 말려 있다.
(B) 그림 한 점이 벽에 배치되어 있다.
(C) 몇몇 조명기구들이 천장에 매달려 있다.
(D) 몇몇 쿠션들이 소파 위에 놓여 있다.

해설 (A) ✗ 상태 묘사 오류 (has been rolled up)
(B) ✗ 사진에 없는 사물 (a painting)
(C) ✗ 상태 묘사 오류 (are hanging)
(D) ○ 쿠션들이 소파 위에 놓여있는 모습을 적절히 묘사했으므로 정답

Possible Answer
Some flowers have been arranged in a vase. 꽃이 꽃병에 꽂혀있다.

어휘 roll up 둘둘 말다 position v. 배치하다 light fixture 조명기구 ceiling n. 천장

PART 2

P. 194

7 Where 의문문 난이도 하

미국↔영국

Where do you usually have lunch?
(A) At Hopewell Shopping Center.
(B) Around 12.
(C) I'll have the daily special.

보통 점심을 어디서 드세요?
(A) Hopewell 쇼핑센터에서요.
(B) 12시쯤에요.
(C) 저는 일일 특선으로 할게요.

해설 (A) ⓞ 쇼핑센터라며 장소로 말했으므로 정답
(B) ✘ When 의문문에 어울리는 대답
(C) ✘ 연상 어휘 함정 (lunch – daily special)

Possible Answer
I bring a packed lunch. 저는 도시락을 싸와요.

어휘 **have lunch** 점심을 먹다 **around** adv. ~쯤, 경 **daily special** 일일 특선

8 How 의문문 난이도 중

미국↔미국

How do I update my personal information?
(A) Didn't you check the online guide?
(B) No, it's up to date.
(C) Here is my business card.

제 개인정보를 어떻게 업데이트 하나요?
(A) 온라인 가이드 안보셨나요?
(B) 아니요, 그것은 최신이에요.
(C) 여기 제 명함이요.

해설 (A) ⓞ 온라인 가이드를 보지 않았냐고 반문하며 질문에 적절하게 말했으므로 정답
(B) ✘ 의문사 의문문 Yes/No 응답 불가, 유사 발음 함정 (update – up to date)
(C) ✘ 연상 어휘 함정 (personal information – business card)

Possible Answer
You should check with Human Resources. 인사부에 확인해 보셔야 해요.

어휘 **personal information** 개인정보 **up to date** adj. 최신(식)의 **business card** 명함

9 Who 의문문 난이도 하

영국↔호주

Who should I ask for when I get to the office?
(A) In the waiting room.
(B) Ask for Jason.
(C) Yes, the reception desk.

사무실에 도착하면 누구를 찾아야 할까요?
(A) 대기실에서요.
(B) Jason을 찾으세요.
(C) 네, 접수 데스크요.

해설 (A) ✘ Where 의문문에 어울리는 대답
(B) ⓞ Jason을 찾으라며 질문에 적절하게 답했으므로 정답
(C) ✘ 의문사 의문문 Yes/No 응답 불가, 연상 어휘 함정 (office – desk)

Possible Answer
You can just call me. 저에게 전화 주시면 돼요.

어휘 **ask for** ~를 찾다 **waiting room** 대기실, 대합실 **reception desk** 접수 데스크

10 평서문 난이도 중

호주↔미국

I'm having a hard time printing out the evaluation form.
(A) My supervisor evaluated me.
(B) Let me give you a hand with that.
(C) A form of identification.

제가 평가 서식을 인쇄하는 데 고생하고 있어요.
(A) 제 관리자가 저를 평가했어요.
(B) 제가 도와드릴게요.
(C) 신분증이요.

해설 (A) ✘ 유사 발음 함정 (evaluation – evaluated)
(B) ⓞ 도와준다며 적절하게 말했으므로 정답
(C) ✘ 동어 반복 함정 (form – form)

Possible Answer
Try using the printer downstairs. 아래층에 있는 프린터를 써보세요.

어휘 **have a hard time ~ing** ~하는데 고생하다 **supervisor** n. 관리자 **evaluation** n. 평가, 사정 **evaluate** v. 평가하다 **give ~ a hand** 도와주다 **identification** n. 신분 증명(서)

11 부정 의문문 난이도 하

미국↔영국

Weren't you supposed to speak with the IT Department?
(A) The company's Web site.
(B) Yes, a keynote speaker.
(C) The manager is too busy.

IT 부서와 이야기하기로 하지 않았어요?
(A) 회사 웹 사이트요.
(B) 네, 기조 연설자요.
(C) 관리자가 너무 바빠요.

해설 (A) ✘ 연상 어휘 함정 (IT – Web site)
(B) ✘ 유사 발음 함정 (speak – speaker)
(C) ⓞ 관리자가 너무 바빴다며 이야기하지 못했음을 우회적으로 말했으므로 정답

Possible Answer
Yes, but the meeting was delayed. 네, 그런데 회의가 연기되었어요.

어휘 **be supposed to** ~ 하기로 되어 있다 **keynote speaker** 기조 연설자 **busy** adj. 바쁜

12 선택의문문 난이도 중

미국↔미국

Are you a resident of the city or a visitor?
(A) I'm from out of town.
(B) The vice president.
(C) I've never visited there.

시 주민이신가요 아니면 방문객이신가요?
(A) 저는 타지에서 왔어요.
(B) 부사장님이요.
(C) 저는 그곳을 가본 적이 없어요.

해설 (A) ⭕ 타지에서 왔다며 후자로 말했으므로 정답
(B) ❌ 유사 발음 함정 (resident – president)
(C) ❌ 유사 발음 함정 (visitor – visited)

Possible Answer
I'm here on business. 업무 차 이곳에 왔어요.

어휘 **resident** n. 주민, 거주자 **visitor** n. 방문객 **from out of town** 다른 지역에서 온 **vice president** 부사장

13 When 의문문 난이도 하

When did you start taking exercise classes?
(A) I usually listen to classical music.
(B) It starts early.
(C) Sometime last spring.

운동 수업 듣는 건 언제 시작했어요?
(A) 저는 보통 클래식 음악을 들어요.
(B) 일찍 시작해요.
(C) 지난 봄에요.

해설 (A) ❌ 유사 발음 함정 (classes – classical)
(B) ❌ 동어 반복 함정 (start – starts)
(C) ⭕ 지난 봄이라며 시점으로 말했으므로 정답

Possible Answer
Not too long ago. 얼마 안됐어요.

어휘 **exercise** n. 운동 **usually** adv. 보통, 대개

14 일반 의문문 난이도 중

Did you organize the office supplies in the storage closet?
(A) Some extra printer paper.
(B) They were purchased last month.
(C) No, Stanley sorted it out.

비품 창고에 있는 사무 용품을 정리하셨어요?
(A) 여분의 인쇄 용지요.
(B) 지난달에 구입한 거예요.
(C) 아니요, Stanley가 정리했어요.

해설 (A) ❌ 연상 어휘 함정 (office supplies – printer paper)
(B) ❌ 연상 어휘 함정 (office supplies – purchased)
(C) ⭕ 'No'로 대답하고, Stanley가 정리했다며 적절히 덧붙여 말했으므로 정답

Possible Answer
Yes, it was too full. 네, 너무 꽉 차 있더라고요.

어휘 **organize** v. 정리하다 **office supplies** 사무용품 **storage closet** 비품창고 **extra** adj. 여분의, 가외의 **sort out** ~을 정리하다

15 Who 의문문 난이도 하

Who can help set up some chairs for the seminar?
(A) Daniel said he would.
(B) We'll both be attending.
(C) She was just promoted.

세미나용 의자배치를 누가 도와줄 수 있나요?
(A) Daniel이 하겠다고 했어요.
(B) 저희 둘 다 참석할 거예요.
(C) 그녀는 막 승진되었어요.

해설 (A) ⭕ Daniel이 하겠다고 했다며 사람 이름으로 말했으므로 정답
(B) ❌ 연상 어휘 함정 (seminar – attending)
(C) ❌ 질문과 무관한 대답

Possible Answer
I can give you a hand. 제가 도와드릴 수 있어요.

어휘 **set up** 놓다[세우다] **attend** v. 참석하다 **promote** v. 승진[진급]시키다

16 제안/요청 난이도 중

Should I send the package tomorrow morning?
(A) The brown box by the door.
(B) He's not available.
(C) That might be too late.

소포를 내일 아침에 보내야 할까요?
(A) 문 옆에 갈색 상자요.
(B) 그는 시간이 없어요.
(C) 그건 너무 늦을 지도 몰라요.

해설 (A) ❌ 연상 어휘 함정 (package – brown box)
(B) ❌ 주어 불일치 함정 (I – he)
(C) ⭕ 너무 늦을 지도 모른다며 우회적으로 거절한 대답이므로 정답

Possible Answer
The items aren't ready yet. 물품이 아직 준비되지 않았어요.

어휘 **package** n. 소포 **available** adj. 시간이 있는, 이용 가능한 **late** adj. 늦은

17 평서문 난이도 중

I'm not sure how to get to the conference hall from the hotel.
(A) We'll be staying for three nights.
(B) The room has a great view.
(C) Carl will send you the directions.

호텔에서 회의장까지 어떻게 가는지 잘 모르겠어요.
(A) 저희는 3박을 할 거예요.
(B) 그 방은 전망이 아주 좋아요.
(C) Carl이 당신에게 약도를 보내줄 거예요.

해설 (A) ❌ 연상 어휘 함정 (hotel – staying for three nights)
(B) ❌ 연상 어휘 함정 (hotel – room, great view)
(C) ⭕ Carl이 약도를 보내줄 거라며 질문에 적절하게 대답했으므로 정답

Possible Answer
Let's just call a cab. 그냥 택시를 부르죠.

어휘 **get to** ~에 도착하다 **conference hall** 회의장 **directions** n. 길 안내

18 Why 의문문 난이도 중

Why did you upload the job posting?
(A) Sure, I can do that right away.
(B) Because Barbara is retiring.
(C) No, not since last week.

왜 구인공고를 올리셨나요?
(A) 그럼요, 바로 할 수 있어요.
(B) Barbara가 은퇴하거든요.
(C) 아니요, 지난주 이후로 아니에요.

해설 (A) ❌ 의문사 의문문 Yes/No 응답 불가
(B) ⭕ Barbara가 은퇴하기 때문이라며 이유를 들어 말했으므로 정답
(C) ❌ 의문사 의문문 Yes/No 응답 불가

Possible Answer
We're looking for a new accounting manager. 저희가 새로운 회계부장을 찾고 있어요.

어휘 **job posting** 구인공고 **right away** 바로, 즉시 **retire** v. 은퇴하다

19 How 의문문 난이도 하

호주↔미국

How much do you estimate we'll use for car rental?
(A) For three days.
(B) About 500 dollars.
(C) I usually drive.

자동차 대여 비용은 얼마를 예상하고 있어요?
(A) 3일 동안이요.
(B) 500달러 정도요.
(C) 저는 보통 운전해서 가요.

해설 (A) ✗ How long 의문문에 어울리는 대답
(B) ○ 500달러 정도라며 금액으로 말했으므로 정답
(C) ✗ 연상 어휘 함정 (car – drive)

Possible Answer
I'll call and ask the agency. 업체에 전화해서 물어볼게요.

어휘 **estimate** v. 어림[추정]하다 **rental** n. 대여 **agency** n. 대리점

20 일반 의문문 난이도 중

미국↔영국

Have you watched the new documentary film?
(A) A movie theater.
(B) OK. Let's have some.
(C) Yes, it was very informative.

새 다큐멘터리 영화 보셨나요?
(A) 극장이요.
(B) 좋아요. 좀 갖죠.
(C) 네, 아주 유익했어요.

해설 (A) ✗ 연상 어휘 함정 (documentary film – movie theater)
(B) ✗ 동어 반복 함정 (have – have)
(C) ○ 'Yes'로 대답하고, 아주 유익했다며 적절히 덧붙여 말했으므로 정답

Possible Answer
I haven't had the time yet. 아직 그럴 시간이 없었어요.

어휘 **watch** v. 보다 **movie theater** 극장 **informative** adj. 유익한, 유용한 정보를 주는

21 Where 의문문 난이도 하

미국↔미국

Where's the subway station?
(A) I stopped taking the bus.
(B) Down the block from the museum.
(C) I like that radio station.

지하철역이 어디에 있나요?
(A) 저는 버스를 안타요.
(B) 박물관에서 한 블록 더 가면 있어요.
(C) 저는 그 라디오 방송국을 좋아해요.

해설 (A) ✗ 연상 어휘 함정 (subway - bus)
(B) ○ 박물관에서 한 블록 내려가면 있다며 위치로 말했으므로 정답
(C) ✗ 동어 반복 함정 (station - station)

Possible Answer
I'm not familiar with this area. 제가 이 곳이 익숙지 않아서요.

어휘 **subway station** 지하철역 **block** n. (도로로 나눈) 구역, 블록 **radio station** 라디오 방송국

22 부가 의문문 난이도 중

영국↔호주

You'll be at Ruth's birthday party, won't you?
(A) Yes, I'll be joining.
(B) A room for 20 people.
(C) She is the finance director.

Ruth의 은퇴식에 계실 거죠, 그렇죠?
(A) 네, 참석할 거예요.
(B) 20명이 들어갈 방이요.
(C) 그녀는 재무 이사예요.

해설 (A) ○ 'Yes'로 대답하고, 참석할거라며 적절하게 덧붙여 말했으므로 정답
(B) ✗ 연상 어휘 함정 (party – a room for 20 people)
(C) ✗ 연상 어휘 함정 (Ruth – she)

Possible Answer
When is it going to be? 언제인가요?

어휘 **birthday party** 생일 파티 **join** v. 함께 하다

23 선택 의문문 난이도 중

호주↔미국

Should I contact the shipping company or the retailer?
(A) Ship it to my home address.
(B) Try the store first.
(C) Do you have an express option?

제가 택배사에 연락해야 할까요 아니면 소매점에 연락해야 할까요?
(A) 그것을 저희 집 주소로 보내주세요.
(B) 먼저 매장에 연락해봐요.
(C) 속달 옵션이 있나요?

해설 (A) ✗ 유사 발음 함정 (shipping – ship it)
(B) ○ 먼저 매장에 연락해보라며 후자로 말했으므로 정답
(C) ✗ 연상 어휘 함정 (shipping – express)

Possible Answer
Call the shipping company. 택배사에 전화해보세요.

어휘 **shipping company** 운송 회사, 택배회사 **retailer** n. 소매점 **ship** v. 수송[운송]하다 **express** adj. 속달의

24 When 의문문 난이도 중

미국↔영국

When can I buy tickets to the jazz concert?
(A) They go on sale tomorrow.
(B) At the box office.
(C) Yes, I heard about it last week.

재즈 콘서트 티켓들을 언제 살 수 있나요?
(A) 내일 판매를 시작해요.
(B) 매표소에서요.
(C) 네, 지난주에 이야기 들었어요.

해설 (A) ○ 내일 판매를 시작한다며 시점으로 말했으므로 정답
(B) ✗ 연상 어휘 함정 (buy tickets – box office)
(C) ✗ 의문사 의문문 Yes/No 응답 불가

Possible Answer
In two weeks. 2주 후에요.

어휘 go on sale 판매에 들어가다 box office 매표소 hear v. 듣다

25 제안/요청 난이도 중

미국↕호주

Would you like to make an appointment for another time?
(A) I have another laptop.
(B) No, the clock's broken.
(C) Sure. What are the available times?

다른 시간으로 예약하시겠어요?
(A) 저는 노트북이 하나 더 있습니다.
(B) 아니요, 시계가 고장 났어요.
(C) 그러죠. 가능한 시간이 언제인가요?

해설 (A) ✗ 동어 반복 함정 (another – another)
(B) ✗ 연상 어휘 함정 (time – clock)
(C) ○ 'Sure'로 대답하고, 가능한 시간이 언제냐며 적절히 덧붙여 말했으므로 정답

Possible Answer
Yes, I'd appreciate that. 네, 그렇게 해 주시면 고맙겠습니다.

어휘 make an appointment (진료·상담 등을) 예약하다 laptop n. 노트북 컴퓨터 broken adj. 고장 난 available adj. 구할[이용할] 수 있는 appreciate v. 고맙게 생각하다

26 부가 의문문 난이도 상

영국↕미국

The project due date has been pushed back, hasn't it?
(A) On the projection screen.
(B) I'm done, actually.
(C) A little more to the left.

그 프로젝트 마감일이 미뤄졌죠, 그렇지 않나요?
(A) 영사 스크린에요.
(B) 사실, 저는 다 했어요.
(C) 왼쪽으로 조금 더요.

해설 (A) ✗ 유사 발음 함정 (project – projection)
(B) ○ 사실 다 했다며 마감일이 미뤄지는 것이 상관없음을 우회적으로 말했으므로 정답
(C) ✗ 연상 어휘 함정 (pushed back – more to the left)

Possible Answer
Yes, to next spring. 네, 내년 봄으로요.

어휘 due date 마감일, 예정일 push back (날짜 등을) 미루다 done adj. 다 된, 완료된

27 부정 의문문 난이도 중

호주↕영국

Didn't a new grocery store open nearby?
(A) For some fruits and vegetables.
(B) Not that I know of.
(C) A seven percent growth.

인근에 새 식료품점이 문을 열지 않았나요?
(A) 과일과 채소를 좀 사려고요.
(B) 제가 알기로는 아니에요.
(C) 7퍼센트 성장이요.

해설 (A) ✗ 연상 어휘 함정 (grocery – fruits and vegetables)
(B) ○ 제가 알기로는 아니라며 질문에 적절히 말했으므로 정답
(C) ✗ 유사 발음 함정 (grocery – growth)

Possible Answer
Yes, Sherry told me about it. 맞아요. Sherry가 말해줬어요.

어휘 grocery store 식품점 vegetable n. 채소 nearby adv. 인근에, 가까운 곳에

28 Which 의문문 난이도 상

미국↕영국

Which candidate are you going to hire?
(A) I need to talk to the director first.
(B) A higher number of applications.
(C) I went to the café downstairs.

어느 지원자를 고용하실 건가요?
(A) 먼저 이사님께 말씀 드려봐야 해요.
(B) 더 많은 수의 지원서들이요.
(C) 저는 아래층에 있는 카페에 갔어요.

해설 (A) ○ 먼저 이사님께 말씀 드려야 한다며 질문에 적절하게 말했으므로 정답
(B) ✗ 유사 발음 함정 (hire – higher), 연상 어휘 함정 (candidate, hire – appliations)
(C) ✗ 연상 어휘 함정 (going to – went to)

Possible Answer
The one with the most experience. 경력이 가장 많은 사람이요.

어휘 candidate n. 지원자 hire v. 고용하다 application n. 지원[신청](서) downstairs adj. 아래층에

29 제안/요청 난이도 상

미국↕미국

Could I get your opinion on this design?
(A) Tom has an extra one.
(B) No, with the computer software.
(C) I was just about to leave.

이 디자인에 대한 당신의 의견 좀 얻을 수 있을까요?
(A) Tom이 여분을 하나 가지고 있어요.
(B) 아니요, 컴퓨터 소프트웨어로요.
(C) 저는 막 퇴근하려던 참이었어요.

해설 (A) ✗ 질문과 무관한 대답
(B) ✗ 연상 어휘 함정 (design - computer software)
(C) ○ 막 퇴근하려던 참이었다며 우회적으로 거절한 대답이므로 정답

Possible Answer
Sorry, but I have to attend a meeting. 죄송하지만, 제가 회의에 참석해야 해요.

어휘 opinion n. 의견 extra adj. 여분의, 추가의 be about to ~ 막 ~하려는 참이다

30 Why 의문문 난이도 상

영국↕호주

Why do you think customers will like this product?
(A) They're at the checkout counter.
(B) From an online store.
(C) That's what the survey said.

왜 고객들이 이 제품을 좋아할 것이라고 생각하세요?
(A) 그것들은 계산대에 있어요.
(B) 온라인 상점에서요.
(C) 설문 조사에 그렇게 나왔어요.

해설 (A) ✗ 연상 어휘 함정 (customer, product – checkout counter)
(B) ✗ 연상 어휘 함정 (customer, product – store)
(C) ○ 설문 조사에 그렇게 나와있다며 이유를 들어 말했으므로 정답
Possible Answer
It's much faster than the previous one. 예전 것보다 훨씬 더 빠르거든요.

어휘 **checkout counter** 계산대 **previous** adj. 이전의 **survey** n. 설문조사

31 평서문 난이도 상

호주 ↔ 미국

The filing cabinets in the reference room are all full.
(A) Yes, the file has been deleted.
(B) We'll have to order more then.
(C) It's on the bottom shelf.

자료실에 있는 서류 정리함이 다 꽉 찼어요.
(A) 네, 파일이 삭제되었어요.
(B) 더 주문해야겠네요.
(C) 맨 아래 칸에 있어요.

해설 (A) ✗ 유사 발음 함정 (filing – file), 연상 어휘 함정 (full –deleted)
(B) ○ 더 주문해야겠다며 적절히 대답했으므로 정답
(C) ✗ 연상 어휘 함정 (cabinets – shelf)
Possible Answer
We should reorganize them. 다시 정리해야겠어요.

어휘 **filing cabinet** 서류 정리함 **reference room** 자료실 **full** adj. 가득한 **delete** v. 삭제하다 **order** v. 주문하다 **shelf** n. 칸, 선반

PART 3 P. 195

미국 ⇄ 미국

Questions 32-34 refer to the following conversation.

W: Hello, Dillon. **Roy's room is locked, and I'm supposed to give him some receipts**(32) from my recent business trip before noon. Would you mind taking them?

M: Not at all. I'll give them to him when he gets back. **He's been with the vice president all morning going over next quarter's budget.**(33)

W: I really appreciate it! OK, **I need to go show some investors around our office now.**(34)

32-34번은 다음 대화에 관한 문제입니다.

여: 안녕하세요, Dillon. **Roy의 사무실이 잠겨있는데, 제가 정오 전에 최근 다녀온 출장 영수증을 드려야 하거든요.**(32) 받아주실 수 있나요?

남: 네, 그럼요. 그가 돌아오면 제가 전달하도록 할게요. **그는 오전 내내 부사장님과 다음 분기 예산을 검토하고 있어요.**(33)

여: 정말 감사 드려요! 좋아요, **저는 이제 투자자 분들께 우리 사무실을 구경시켜드리러 가야 해요.**(34)

어휘 **lock** v. 잠그다 **be supposed to** ~하기로 되어 있다 **receipt** n. 영수증 **business trip** 출장 **noon** n. 정오 **mind** v. 상관하다, 개의하다 **go over** 검토하다 **quarter** n. 분기 **budget** n. 예산 **appreciate** v. 고마워하다 **show ~ around** ~에게 구경시켜 주다

32 주제/목적 난이도 하

해석 여자는 왜 Roy의 사무실을 방문했는가?
(A) 물건을 반납하기 위해
(B) 장비를 고치기 위해
(C) 예산제안서를 논의하기 위해
(D) 서류를 제출하기 위해

해설 여자가 Roy's room is locked, and I'm supposed to give him some receipts (Roy의 사무실이 잠겨있는데, 제가 정오 전에 최근 다녀온 출장 영수증을 드려야 하거든요)라고 말했으므로 (D)가 정답

Paraphrasing give ➡ submit, receipts ➡ documents

33 세부정보 난이도 중

해석 Roy는 왜 부재중인가?
(A) 임원과 회의 중이다.
(B) 곧 공항으로 갈 것이다.
(C) 고객 설문조사를 진행 중이다.
(D) 컨벤션에 참석 중이다.

해설 남자가 He's been with the vice president all morning going over next quarter's budget. (그는 오전 내내 부사장님과 다음 분기 예산을 검토하고 있어요.)라고 말했으므로 (A)가 정답

Paraphrasing vice president ➡ executive

34 다음 행동/계획 난이도 중

해석 여자는 다음에 무엇을 할 것인가?
(A) 매니저에게 연락할 것이다
(B) 사용 설명서를 읽을 것이다
(C) 사무실을 구경시켜줄 것이다
(D) 프로그램을 다운로드할 것이다

해설 여자가 I need to go show some investors around our office now. (저는 이제 투자자분들께 우리 사무실을 구경시켜 드리러 가야 해요.)라고 말했으므로 (C)가 정답

Paraphrasing show ~ around ➡ give an ~ tour

호주 ⇄ 미국

Questions 35-37 refer to the following conversation.

M: Tabitha, I'd like to go over your annual performance evaluation. I'm sure you're aware of this, but **you wrote many of our newspaper's most popular articles this year.** (35) Your attention to detail is very impressive.

W: Thank you. **I believe producing high-quality materials is the most important thing.**(36)

M: **I agree.**(36) Anyway, I was thinking of making you a team manager. Would you be interested?

W: Really? This is a big surprise! Do I have to decide now?

M: No. Just tell me your decision by next Monday. Also, **I'll email you a document that lists the duties of the position.**(37)

W: Alright. Thank you so much.

182

35-37번은 다음 대화에 관한 문제입니다.

남: Tabitha, 당신의 연례 고과를 좀 검토하고 싶은데요. 알고 있겠지만, 올해 우리 신문에서 가장 인기 있는 기사 대부분은 당신이 쓴 거예요.(35) 세심한 주의력이 정말 인상적이에요.

여: 감사합니다. 저는 고품질 자료를 생산하는 것이 가장 중요한 일이라고 생각합니다.(36)

남: 동의해요.(36) 그건 그렇고, 당신한테 팀장 자리를 맡길 생각인데요, 관심 있어요?

여: 정말이요? 생각지도 못한 일인데요! 지금 결정해야 하나요?

남: 아니에요. 다음 주 월요일까지 결정해서 알려주세요. 그리고 제가 그 직책의 직무가 나와 있는 문서를 이메일로 보내줄게요.(37)

여: 알겠습니다. 정말 감사합니다.

어휘 go over ~을 검토하다 annual adj. 연례의 performance evaluation 고과평가 be aware of ~을 알다 article n. 기사 attention to ~에 대한 주의[주목] impressive adj. 인상적인 produce v. 생산하다 materials n. 자료, (읽을) 거리 list v. (특정한 순서로) 열거하다 duty n. 직무 position n. 직책, 직위

35 장소/근무지 난이도 중

해석 화자들은 어디에서 근무하겠는가?
(A) 직물 매장에서
(B) 신문사에서
(C) 도서관에서
(D) 공장에서

해설 남자가 you wrote many of our newspaper's most popular articles this year. (올해 우리 신문에서 가장 인기 있는 기사 대부분은 당신이 쓴 거예요.)라고 말했으므로 (B)가 정답

36 세부정보 난이도 중

해석 화자들은 무엇이 가장 중요하다고 생각하는가?
(A) 해박한 직원을 고용하는 것
(B) 제품군을 확대하는 것
(C) 좋은 고객관계를 유지하는 것
(D) 고품질의 자료를 만들어 내는 것

해설 여자가 I believe producing high-quality materials is the most important thing. (저는 고품질 자료를 생산하는 것이 가장 중요한 일이라고 생각하고 있어요.)라고 하자, 남자가 I agree. (동의해요.)라고 말했으므로 (D)가 정답

Paraphrasing producing ➡ creating

37 요청/제의/제안 난이도 중

해석 남자는 여자에게 무엇을 보낼 것인가?
(A) 보너스 급여
(B) 계약서 견본
(C) 업무 요약서
(D) 제품 목록

해설 남자가 I'll email you a document that lists the duties of the position. (제가 그 직책의 직무가 나와 있는 문서를 이메일로 보내줄게요.)라고 말했으므로 (C)가 정답

Paraphrasing email ➡ send, a document that lists the duties of the position ➡ a job summary

미국 ⇄ 영국

Questions 38-40 refer to the following conversation.

M: Welcome to the Crestfall Art Museum. I oversee this wing of the museum.(38)

W: Hi, I was interested in joining a guided tour of the Asian sculpture exhibits.(39) Do you know how long it usually takes? I have another appointment later.

M: It should take about two hours. Please be aware that you are not allowed to take photos or record videos of the exhibits.

W: OK. By the way, is there some place I can store my backpack?(40)

M: Yes, you can leave it here at the front desk.

38-40번은 다음 대화에 관한 문제입니다.

남: Crestfall 미술관에 오신 것을 환영합니다. 저는 이 미술관 별관을 관장하고 있습니다.(38)

여: 안녕하세요, 아시아 조각 전시회의 가이드 인솔 프로그램에 참여하고 싶은데요.(39) 보통 얼마나 걸리는지 아시나요? 이따 다른 약속이 있거든요.

남: 두 시간 정도 걸릴 겁니다. 전시물에 대한 사진이나 동영상 촬영은 허용되지 않으니 유의해 주세요.

여: 알겠습니다. 그런데 제 배낭을 보관할 수 있는 곳이 있나요?(40)

남: 네, 여기 안내데스크에 맡기시면 됩니다.

어휘 oversee v. 감독하다 wing n. (건물의) 부속건물 guided tour 안내원이 딸린 (관광) 여행 exhibit n. 전시품, 전시회 aware adj. 알고[의식하고] 있는 allow v. 허용하다 record v. 녹음[녹화]하다 store v. 보관하다 leave v. 맡기다

38 정체/신분 난이도 중

해석 남자는 누구겠는가?
(A) 대학교수
(B) 박물관 관리자
(C) 유명 미술가
(D) 회의 주최자

해설 남자가 Welcome to the Crestfall Art Museum. I oversee this wing of the museum. (Crestfall 미술관에 오신 것을 환영합니다. 저는 이 미술관 별관을 관장하고 있습니다.)라고 말했으므로 (B)가 정답

39 주제/목적 난이도 하

해석 대화의 주제는 무엇인가?
(A) 조각 전시회
(B) 교통 상황
(C) 회원 혜택
(D) 사진 제출물

해설 여자가 I was interested in joining a guided tour of the Asian sculpture exhibits. (아시아 조각 전시회의 가이드 인솔 프로그램에 참여하고 싶은데요.)라고 말했으므로 (A)가 정답

40 세부정보 　　　　　　　　　　　　　난이도 하

해석　여자는 무엇에 관하여 묻는가?
　　　(A) 선물 구매
　　　(B) 장비 대여
　　　(C) 가방 보관
　　　(D) 요금 납부

해설　여자가 is there some place I can store my backpack? (제 배낭을 보관할 수 있는 곳이 있나요?)라고 말했으므로 (C)가 정답

호주 ⇌ 영국 ⇌ 미국

Questions 41-43 refer to the following conversation with three speakers.

M:　Hello, Kristie. Hello, Tiffany. **I heard you wanted to talk to me about our chocolate mixing machine.**(41) What's going on?

W1: **The mixing unit keeps shutting down every 30 minutes.** (42) Tiffany called a technician about the problem.

W2: Yes. The technician checked it out and found that the motor is overheating. He said that we will have to get a new one.

M:　Alright. **Why don't we place an order today for a new motor?**(43)

41-43번은 다음 세 화자의 대화에 관한 문제입니다.

남:　안녕하세요, Kristie. 안녕하세요, Tiffany. 초콜릿 혼합 기계에 대해 저와 이야기하고 싶으시다고 들었어요.(41) 무슨 일이신가요?

여1: 혼합 장치가 30분마다 꺼지네요.(42) Tiffany가 이 문제로 기술자에게 연락했어요.

여2: 네. 기술자가 확인했는데, 모터가 과열되었다고 해요. 새것을 사야 한다고 하더라고요.

남:　알았어요. 오늘 새 모터를 주문하는 건 어때요?(43)

어휘　mix v. 혼합하다　unit n. 장치　shut down (기계가) 멈추다, 정지하다　technician n. 기술자　check ~ out ~을 확인하다　overheat v. 과열하다　place an order 주문하다

---

41 장소/근무지 　　　　　　　　　　　　난이도 중

해석　화자들은 어느 산업에 종사하겠는가?
　　　(A) 가전제품 판매
　　　(B) 자동차 생산
　　　(C) 식품 제조
　　　(D) 컴퓨터 프로그래밍

해설　남자가 I heard you wanted to talk to me about our chocolate mixing machine. (초콜릿 혼합 기계에 대해 저와 이야기하고 싶으시다고 들었어요.)라고 말했으므로 (C)가 정답

Paraphrasing　chocolate ➡ food

---

42 세부정보 　　　　　　　　　　　　　난이도 중

해석　어떤 문제가 논의되고 있는가?
　　　(A) 장비가 계속 꺼진다.
　　　(B) 매니저가 부재중이다.
　　　(C) 몇몇 고객들이 불만을 표했다.
　　　(D) 물품 재고 목록이 정확하지 않다.

해설　여자가 The mixing unit keeps shutting down every 30 minutes. (혼합 장치가 30분마다 꺼지네요.)라고 말했으므로 (A)가 정답

Paraphrasing　unit ➡ equipment, shutting down ➡ turning off

---

43 요청/제의/제안 　　　　　　　　　　　난이도 중

해석　남자는 무엇을 추천하는가?
　　　(A) 새로운 판매처 선택
　　　(B) 대체부품 주문
　　　(C) 쿠폰 제공
　　　(D) 배송 지연

해설　남자가 Why don't we place an order today for a new motor? (오늘 새 모터 주문을 하는 건 어때요?)라고 말했으므로 (B)가 정답

Paraphrasing　place an order ➡ order,
　　　　　　　　new motor ➡ replacement part

미국 ⇌ 미국

Questions 44-46 refer to the following conversation

W:　Hi, Nobuhiko. How do you like this year's food technology convention?

M:　I'm really impressed. **There's a lot of new technology I could use in my restaurants' kitchens.**(44) And this location is so much nicer than the last year's. **The auditorium is just a short drive from the airport!**(45)

W:　I agree. **I flew in this morning, and it was so easy to get here.**(45) By the way, at the convention last year, you were planning to install a new computer network for your service staff. How has that been going?

M:　Very well. It helps the service staff stay organized, and they love it. **It's a lot easier to get customer orders right during busy times.**(46)

44-46번은 다음 대화에 관한 문제입니다.

여:　안녕하세요, Nobuhiko. 올해 음식 기술 대회는 어때요?

남:　정말 인상 깊었어요. 제 식당 주방에서 사용할 만한 신기술이 많더라고요.(44) 그리고 이번 장소가 작년보다 훨씬 더 좋았어요. 강당이 공항에서 조금만 운전해서 가면 있어요!(45)

여:　맞아요. 제가 오늘 아침에 비행기를 타고 왔는데, 이곳에 아주 쉽게 왔어요.(45) 그런데, 작년 대회 때, 당신의 서비스 직원들을 위해 컴퓨터 네트워크를 새로 설치하려고 했었잖아요. 그건 어떻게 돼가고 있어요?

남:　아주 잘 되고 있어요. 계속 체계적으로 일할 수 있게 도와줘서 서비스 직원들이 아주 좋아해요. 바쁜 시간대에 고객 주문을 제대로 받기가 훨씬 더 수월해졌어요.(46)

어휘　convention n. 대회, 집회　impressed adj. 인상 깊게 생각하는, 감명을 받은　auditorium n. 강당　organized adj. 체계화된, 조직적인

44 장소/근무지   난이도 중

해석　남자는 어떤 사업체를 소유하는가?
　　　(A) 식당
　　　(B) 무역 회사
　　　(C) IT 회사
　　　(D) 택시업

해설　남자가 There's a lot of new technology I could use in my restaurants' kitchens. (제 식당 주방에서 사용할만한 신기술이 많더라고요.)라고 말했으므로 (A)가 정답

45 세부정보   난이도 중

해석　화자들은 강당의 어떤 점을 좋아하는가?
　　　(A) 음식을 살 곳이 있다.
　　　(B) 공간이 넓다.
　　　(C) 여행객들에게 편리하다.
　　　(D) 경치 좋은 곳에 있다.

해설　남자가 The auditorium is just a short drive from the airport! (강당이 공항에서 조금만 운전해서 가면 있어요!)라고 하자, 여자가 I agree. I flew in this morning, and it was so easy to get here. (맞아요. 제가 오늘 아침에 비행기를 타고 왔는데, 이곳에 아주 쉽게 왔어요.)라고 말했으므로 (C)가 정답

46 세부정보   난이도 중

해석　남자의 사업체에서 컴퓨터 네트워크는 어떻게 사용되는가?
　　　(A) 비용을 계산하기 위해
　　　(B) 주문을 처리하기 위해
　　　(C) 일정을 생성하기
　　　(D) 상품을 점검하기 위해

해설　남자가 It's a lot easier to get customer orders right during busy times. (바쁜 시간대에 고객 주문을 제대로 받기가 훨씬 더 수월해졌어요.)라고 말했으므로 (B)가 정답

Paraphrasing get customer orders right ➡ process orders

미국 ⇄ 미국

Questions 47-49 refer to the following conversation.

M: Ms. Kern, it's Matthew Weimer from Cyan Florist Co. calling about your recent order of white rose arrangements. We may not be able to deliver all 70 centerpieces to the wedding hall by this Saturday.(47)

W: Hmm… That's not good. I really need them to arrive then. The wedding is on Sunday, and the centerpieces have to be set on the tables the day before.

M: I see. The thing is, we're running very short of white roses at the moment. What if we use both pink and white roses for the centerpieces then?(48)

W: I'm afraid the client made a specific request for this.(48)

M: OK, here's what I'll do: I'll call some other flower shops in the city(49) and try to get some more white roses.

W: I'd appreciate that. Please keep me updated.

47-49번은 다음 대화에 관한 문제입니다.

남: Ms. Kern, 저는 Cyan 화훼회사의 Matthew Weimer라고 하는데요, 최근 주문하신 흰 장미 꽃장식건과 관련하여 전화드립니다. 이번 토요일까지 웨딩홀로 센터피스 70개 전체를 배송해드리지 못할 수도 있어서요.(47)

여: 흠… 안 되는데요. 그때까지 꼭 도착해야 해요. 결혼식이 일요일이고, 그 전날 테이블에 센터피스가 세팅되어 있어야 해요.

남: 그렇군요. 문제는, 현재 흰 장미가 매우 부족하다는 건데요. 그러면 센터피스에 분홍 장미와 흰 장미를 함께 사용하는 건 어떨까요?(48)

여: 고객이 이걸 특별 요청한 거라서요.(48)

남: 네, 그럼 이렇게 할게요. 제가 시내 다른 꽃집에 전화해서(49) 흰 장미를 더 구해보겠습니다.

여: 그렇게 해주시면 감사합니다. 상황을 계속해서 알려주세요.

어휘　**florist** n. 꽃집 **recent** adj. 최근의 **order** n. 주문 **arrangement** n. 배치, 배열 **centerpiece** n. (테이블의) 중앙 장식물 **arrive** v. 도착하다 **the thing is** 실은, 문제는 **run short of** ~이 부족하다 **specific** adj. 명확한 **request** n. 요청 **appreciate** v. 고마워하다

47 주제/목적   난이도 중

해석　남자는 무엇 때문에 전화했는가?
　　　(A) 주문을 완료하는 것
　　　(B) 단기 직원을 채용하는 것
　　　(C) 가구를 배열하는 것
　　　(D) 더 큰 장소를 찾는 것

해설　남자가 it's Matthew Weimer from Cyan Florist Co. calling about your recent order of white rose arrangements. We may not be able to deliver all 70 centerpieces to the wedding hall by this Saturday. (저는 Cyan 화훼회사의 Matthew Weimer라고 하는데요, 최근 주문하신 흰 장미 꽃장식건과 관련하여 전화드립니다. 이번 토요일까지 웨딩홀로 센터피스 70개 전체를 배송해드리지 못할 수도 있어서요.)라고 말했으므로 (A)가 정답

48 화자 의도 파악   난이도 중

해석　여자가 "고객이 이걸 특별 요청한 거라서요"라고 말할 때, 그녀가 내비친 것은?
　　　(A) 남자가 고객에게 연락해야 한다.
　　　(B) 가격이 이미 책정되어 있다.
　　　(C) 변경을 할 수 없다.
　　　(D) 남자가 오류를 수정해야 한다.

해설　남자가 What if we use both pink and white roses for the centerpieces then? (센터피스에 분홍 장미와 흰 장미를 함께 사용하는 건 어떨까요?)라고 하자, 여자가 I'm afraid the client made a specific request for this.(고객이 이걸 특별 요청한 거라서요.)라고 말한 것이므로 (C)가 정답

49 요청/제의/제안   난이도 중

해석　남자는 무엇을 하겠다고 제안하는가?
　　　(A) 지역 업체들에 연락하겠다고
　　　(B) 할인을 제공하겠다고
　　　(C) 배송을 신속히 처리하겠다고

(D) 장비를 설치하겠다고

해설 남자가 here's what I'll do: I'll call some other flower shops in the city (그럼 이렇게 할게요. 제가 시내의 다른 꽃집들에 전화해서)라고 했으므로 (A)가 정답

Paraphrasing call ➡ contact, shop ➡ businesses

미국 ⇄ 미국

Questions 50-52 refer to the following conversation.

W: You've reached Maxicar Fitness Club. How can I be of assistance?

M: Hello. **I'm a member of your club, and I wanted to extend for another year.**(50) I heard that you're taking 40 percent off the one-year membership rate.

W: Ah, **unfortunately, that discount is only valid for new members—I'm so sorry.**(51) We do, however, offer a free sports bag if you decide to renew for a year.

M: Oh, if that's the case, I'll just extend for six more months. I'm on a tight budget.

W: I understand. **I'll still give you a complimentary T-shirt**(52) to show our appreciation for your continued business.

50-52번은 다음 대화에 관한 문제입니다.

여: Maxicar 헬스클럽입니다. 무엇을 도와드릴까요?

남: 안녕하세요. 저는 클럽회원인데요, 1년 더 연장하고 싶어서요.(50) 1년 회원가에서 40퍼센트를 할인해준다고 들었어요.

여: 아, 유감스럽게도 그 할인가는 신규 회원에게만 유효합니다. 정말 죄송해요.(51) 하지만 1년을 연장하시면 스포츠백을 무료로 드립니다.

남: 오, 그러면 6개월만 더 연장할게요. 예산이 빠듯하거든요.

여: 알겠습니다. 그래도 계속 이용해 주시는 것에 대한 감사의 표시로 무료 티셔츠를 드릴게요.(52)

어휘 fitness club 헬스클럽 assistance n. 도움 extend v. 연장하다 take ~ off (금액에서) ~을 빼다 rate n. 요금 unfortunately adv. 유감스럽게도 valid adj. 유효한 renew v. 연장하다 budget n. 예산 complimentary adj. 무료의 appreciation n. 감사 continued adj. 지속적인 business n. (고객의) 애용

50 주제/목적 난이도 하

해설 남자가 전화한 목적은 무엇인가?
(A) 일자리에 지원하기 위해
(B) 환불을 요청하기 위해
(C) 문제점을 보고하기 위해
(D) 회원권을 연장하기 위해

해설 남자가 I'm a member of your club, and I wanted to extend for another year. (저는 클럽회원인데요, 1년 더 연장하고 싶어서요.)라고 말했으므로 (D)가 정답

51 세부정보 난이도 중

해설 여자가 왜 사과하는가?
(A) 남자는 잘못된 설명을 받았다.

(B) 청구서에 추가 요금이 포함되었다.
(C) 남자는 할인 대상이 아니다.
(D) 신용카드가 처리되지 않는다.

해설 여자가 unfortunately, that discount is only valid for new members—I'm so sorry. (유감스럽게도 그 할인가는 신규 회원에게만 유효합니다. 정말 죄송해요.)라고 말했으므로 (C)가 정답

Paraphrasing valid for ➡ qualify

52 요청/제의/제안 난이도 중

해설 여자가 무엇을 하겠다고 제안하는가?
(A) 연락처를 업데이트하겠다고
(B) 주문을 수정하겠다고
(C) 무료 상품을 제공하겠다고
(D) 다른 지점에 전화하겠다고

해설 남자가 I'll still give you a complimentary T-shirt (무료 티셔츠를 드릴게요)라고 말했으므로 (C)가 정답

Paraphrasing complimentary ➡ free, T-shirt ➡ item

호주 ⇄ 영국

Questions 53-55 refer to the following conversation.

M: OK, here are your keys. Just make sure to return the car this Friday before noon.(53) Are you here on business?

W: Yes, that's right. I'm attending the local sales conference, but I'm free all afternoon today. I've never been to this city.(54)

M: Well then, I suggest checking out Merkville National Park.(54) It has some of the most beautiful hiking trails.

W: Thank you. I do enjoy outdoor activities.

M: You should purchase your entrance pass through the park's Web site. Doing that can save you $10.(55)

W: I appreciate the tip!

53-55번은 다음 대화에 관한 문제입니다.

남: 자, 열쇠 여기 있습니다. 금요일 정오 전에 차를 꼭 반납해 주세요.(53) 업무차 오신 건가요?

여: 네, 맞아요. 제가 이 지역에서 열리는 영업 콘퍼런스에 참석하는데, 오늘 오후 내내 자유시간이라서요. 제가 이 도시에는 처음이에요.(54)

남: 음, 그러면, Merkville 국립공원에 가보시는 걸 추천 드려요.(54) 정말 아름다운 등산로가 몇 군데가 있어요.

여: 감사해요. 제가 야외활동을 정말 좋아하거든요.

남: 공원 웹 사이트에서 입장권을 구입하도록 하세요. 그렇게 하시면 10달러를 절약하실 수 있어요.(55)

여: 조언 감사해요!

어휘 return v. 반납하다 noon n. 정오 on business 업무차 attend v. 참석하다 check out 살펴보다 purchase v. 구입하다 appreciate v. 고마워하다

| 53 | 장소/근무지 | 난이도 중 |

해석 화자들은 어디에 있겠는가?
(A) 차량 대여점
(B) 콘퍼런스 홀
(C) 관광 안내소
(D) 도시버스 터미널

해설 남자가 here are your keys. Just make sure to return the car this Friday before noon (열쇠 여기 있습니다. 금요일 정오 전에 차를 꼭 반납해 주세요)라고 말했으므로 (A)가 정답

Paraphrasing car ➡ vehicle

| 54 | 화자 의도 파악 | 난이도 중 |

해석 여자는 왜 "제가 이 도시에는 처음이에요"라고 말하는가?
(A) 여행 가이드를 요청하기 위해
(B) 제안을 요청하기 위해
(C) 문제를 설명하기 위해
(D) 교통수단에 대해 문의하기 위해

해설 여자가 I'm free all afternoon today. I've never been to this city. (오늘 오후 내내 자유시간이라서요. 제가 이 도시에는 처음이에요.)라고 하자, 남자가 I suggest checking out Merkville National Park. (Merkville 국립공원에 가보시는 걸 추천 드려요.)라고 말한 것이므로 (B)가 정답

| 55 | 세부정보 | 난이도 중 |

해석 남자는 여자에게 왜 온라인으로 주문하라고 권하는가?
(A) 할인을 받을 수 있어서
(B) 추가 비용이 없어서
(C) 대기시간이 없어서
(D) 웹 사이트에 제품이 더 많아서

해설 남자가 You should purchase your entrance pass through the park's Web site. Doing that can save you $10(공원 웹 사이트에서 입장권을 사도록 하세요. 그렇게 하시면 10달러를 절약하실 수 있어요.)라고 말했으므로 (A)가 정답

미국 ⇄ 미국

Questions 56-58 refer to the following conversation.

W: Glad I ran into you, Gerald. As you know, **we did a pretty good job with Haxwell Apparel's ad campaign.**(56) And apparently, they recommended us to other businesses.

M: That's wonderful! More people have been showing interest in our services recently. We just secured four new contracts last week.

W: With our company growing so rapidly, **we need to look into working with a corporate lawyer who can advise us on legal matters.**(57)

M: Well, I've read good things about Millerson & Associates. **Why don't I arrange a meeting with them?**(58) Does Friday work for you?

56-58번은 다음 대화에 관한 문제입니다.

여: 마침 잘 만났네요, Gerald. 아시다시피, **우리가 Haxwell 의류 광고 캠페인을 아주 잘 해냈어요.**(56) 그리고 듣자 하니, 그들이 다른 기업들에 우리를 추천해줬다고 해요.

남: 정말 잘 됐네요! 최근에 더 많은 사람들이 우리가 제공하는 서비스에 관심을 보이고 있어요. 지난주에 신규 계약을 4건이나 땄어요.

여: 우리 회사가 빠르게 성장하고 있으니, **법적인 문제를 상담해줄 수 있는 법인 고문변호사와 함께 일하는 것을 알아봐야 해요.**(57)

남: 음, 제가 Millerson & Associates에 대한 좋은 평가를 읽었어요. **제가 그들과 회의자리를 마련해 볼까요?**(58) 금요일 괜찮으세요?

어휘 pretty adv. 아주, 꽤 apparel n. 의류 apparently adv. 듣자 하니 recommend v. 추천하다 interest n. 관심 recently adv. 최근에 secure v. 얻어내다, 확보하다 contract n. 계약 rapidly adv. 빨리 corporate lawyer 법인 고문 변호사 advise v. 조언하다 legal adj. 법률과 관련된 matter n. 문제, 사안 arrange v. 마련하다

| 56 | 장소/근무지 | 난이도 중 |

해석 화자들은 어디에서 일하겠는가?
(A) 마케팅 회사
(B) 의류 소매점
(C) 법률사무소
(D) 제작사

해설 여자가 we did a pretty good job with Haxwell Apparel's ad campaign. (우리가 Haxwell 의류 광고 캠페인을 아주 잘 해냈어요)라고 말했으므로 (A)가 정답

Paraphrasing ad ➡ marketing

| 57 | 제의/제안/요청 | 난이도 중 |

해석 여자는 무엇을 제안하는가?
(A) 더 큰 장소로 이전하는 것
(B) 세미나를 신청하는 것
(C) 변호사와 상담하는 것
(D) 추가 근무를 하는 것

해설 여자가 we need to look into working with a corporate lawyer who can advise us on legal matters. (법적인 문제를 상담해줄 수 있는 법인 고문변호사와 함께 일하는 것을 알아봐야 해요.)라고 말했으므로 (C)가 정답

Paraphrasing working with ➡ consulting

| 58 | 요청/제의/제안 | 난이도 중 |

해석 남자는 무엇을 하겠다고 제의하는가?
(A) 납입금을 처리하겠다고
(B) 회의 일정을 잡겠다고
(C) 고객을 데리러 가겠다고
(D) 입사 지원서를 검토하겠다고

해설 남자가 Why don't I arrange a meeting with them? (제가 그들과 회의자리를 마련해 볼까요?)라고 말했으므로 (B)가 정답

Paraphrasing arrange ➡ schedule

영국 ⇄ 미국 ⇄ 미국

Questions 59-61 refer to the following conversation with three speakers.

W1: Hello, Mr. Almeda. I'm Rose Figueroa. **I'm the HR manager at Watscorp Publishers.**(59) And this is one of our senior editors, Nicole Lane.

W2: Thanks for coming in, Mr. Almeda. Why don't you start by talking about your previous work experience?(59)

M: Sure. I've been in the R&D field for many years. This is a list of my past projects.

W1: Oh, the list is quite extensive. **What would you say is your biggest accomplishment?**(60)

M: **I'm proudest of my work on the South American history textbook series for local universities.**(60)

W2: Why would you leave your current company? You've been there so long.

M: I enjoy the work, but the benefits aren't great. **Watscorp provides quarterly incentives, and that shows that you care about your staff. I really like that.**(61)

59-61번은 다음 세 화자의 대화에 관한 문제입니다.

여1: 안녕하세요, Mr. Almeda. Rose Figueroa예요. **저는 Watscorp 출판사의 인사 매니저입니다.**(59) 그리고 여기는 선임 편집자 중 한 명인 Nicole Lane이에요.

여2: 와주셔서 감사해요, Mr. Almeda. 이전 경력에 관한 얘기로 시작해볼까요?(59)

남: 네. 저는 수년간 연구개발 업계에 종사했습니다. 이게 제가 몸담았던 지난 프로젝트 목록입니다.

여1: 오, 이 목록은 꽤 광범위하네요. **가장 큰 업적은 무엇이라고 생각하세요?**(60)

남: **지역 대학용으로 작업한 남미 역사 교과서 시리즈가 제일 자랑스럽습니다.**(60)

여2: 왜 현재 회사를 그만두시려고 하시나요? 꽤 오래 계셨는데요.

남: 업무를 즐기지만, 복리후생이 그다지 좋지 않습니다. **Watscorp는 분기마다 인센티브를 제공해서 직원들에 대해 신경 쓴다는 걸 보여줍니다. 그 부분이 정말 마음에 듭니다.**(61)

어휘 publisher n. 출판사 senior adj. 선임의 editor n. 편집자 previous adj. 이전의 work experience 경력 R&D 연구개발 field n. 업계 past adj. 이전의, 지난 quite adv. 꽤, 상당히 extensive adj. 광범위한 accomplishment n. 업적 proud adj. 자랑스러워하는 current adj. 현재의 benefits n. 복리후생 provide v. 제공하다 quarterly adj. 분기별의 incentive n. 장려금 care about ~에 관해 신경을 쓰다

59 주제/목적   난이도 중

해석 남자는 왜 Watscorp 출판사에 있는가?
(A) 새로운 도서 프로젝트를 논의하기 위해
(B) 회사 워크숍을 진행하기 위해
(C) 점검을 실시하기 위해
(D) 일자리 면접을 보기 위해

해설 여자1이 I'm the HR manager at Watscorp Publishers. (저는 Watscorp 출판사의 인사 매니저입니다.)라고 하자, 여자2가 Thanks for coming in, Mr. Almeda. Why don't you start by talking about your previous work experience? (와주셔서 감사해요, Mr. Almeda. 이전 경력에 관한 얘기로 시작해볼까요?)라고 말한 것이므로 (D)가 정답

60 세부정보   난이도 중

해석 남자에 따르면, 그의 가장 큰 업적은 무엇인가?
(A) 교육 자료를 만든 것
(B) 자영업을 시작한 것
(C) 국가 상을 받은 것
(D) R&D 매니저가 된 것

해설 여자1이 What would you say is your biggest accomplishment?(가장 큰 업적은 무엇이라고 생각하세요?)라고 하자, 남자가 I'm proudest of my work on the South American history textbook series for local universities.(지역 대학용으로 작업한 남미 역사 교과서 시리즈가 제일 자랑스럽습니다.)라고 말한 것이므로 (A)가 정답

Paraphrasing textbook series ➡ educational materials

61 세부정보   난이도 중

해석 남자는 Watscorp의 어떤 면을 마음에 들어 하는가?
(A) 유명한 소설을 출판한다.
(B) 직원들을 신경 쓴다.
(C) 업계 리더이다.
(D) 최근에 사옥을 확장했다.

해설 남자가 Watscorp provides quarterly incentives, and that shows that you care about your staff. I really like that. (Watscorp는 분기마다 인센티브를 제공해서 직원들에 대해 신경 쓴다는 걸 보여줍니다. 그 부분이 정말 마음에 듭니다.)라고 말했으므로 (B)가 정답

Paraphrasing staff ➡ workers

미국 ⇄ 미국

Questions 62-64 refer to the following conversation and schedule.

M: Hey, Britney. You're at the station, right? **I'm stuck in traffic right now, so it'll take me another 20 minutes to get there.**(62) There's a chance I won't be able to board the train.

W: You'll be fine. **I just checked, and our train's departure has been delayed by 45 minutes.**(63) So don't worry.

M: Ah, OK. **But please message Mr. Riley.**(64) He needs to be aware that we won't be there for the opening speech of the company awards ceremony.

Train Number	Destination	Departure Time/Status
230	Rochester	8:20 A.M. On Schedule
231	Buffalo	9:15 A.M. Delayed 60 minutes
232	Albany	10:30 A.M. On Schedule
233	Syracuse	11:00 A.M. **Delayed 45 minutes**(63)

188

62-64번은 다음 대화와 일정표에 관한 문제입니다.

남: 안녕하세요, Britney. 지금 역에 계시죠, 그렇죠? **제가 지금 차가 막혀서, 도착하려면 20분이 더 걸릴 거예요.**(62) 제가 기차에 못 탈 수도 있어요.

여: 괜찮으실 거예요. **지금 막 확인해봤는데, 우리 기차가 출발이 45분 지연됐어요.**(63) 그러니까 걱정하지 마세요.

남: 아, 그래요. 그래도 **Mr. Riley에게 메시지를 보내주세요.**(64) 우리가 회사 시상식 개회사에 참석하지 못할 거라는 걸 알고 계셔야 해요.

기차 번호	목적지	출발 시각/상태
230	Rochester	오전 8시 20분/정시 출발
231	Buffalo	오전 9시 15분/60분 지연
232	Albany	오전 10시 30분/정시 출발
233	Syracuse	오전 11시/**45분 지연**(63)

어휘 stuck in traffic 교통이 막힌 board v. 탑승하다 departure n. 출발 delay v. 지연시키다 aware adj. 알고 있는 opening speech 개회사 awards ceremony 시상식

---

62 세부정보 난이도 중

해석 남자의 문제는 무엇인가?
(A) 늦게 도착할 것이다.
(B) 표를 예약하지 못했다.
(C) 노트를 집에 두고 왔다.
(D) 주차공간을 못 찾고 있다.

해설 남자가 I'm stuck in traffic right now, so it'll take me another 20 minutes to get there. (제가 지금 차가 막혀서, 도착하려면 20분이 더 걸릴 거예요.)라고 말했으므로 (A)가 정답

63 시각 정보 연계 난이도 중

해석 시각 자료를 보시오. 화자들은 어떤 기차에 탑승할 것인가?
(A) 230
(B) 231
(C) 232
(D) 233

해설 여자가 I just checked, and our train's departure has been delayed by 45 minutes. (지금 막 확인해봤는데, 우리 기차가 출발이 45분 지연됐어요.)라고 말했고, 시각 자료에서 Delayed 45 minutes (45분 지연)된 열차 번호가 233임을 확인할 수 있으므로 (D)가 정답

64 요청/제의/제안 난이도 중

해석 남자는 여자에게 무엇을 요청하는가?
(A) 연설을 해 달라고
(B) 메시지를 전송해 달라고
(C) 발표를 검토해 달라고
(D) 납부를 해 달라고

해설 남자가 But please message Mr. Riley. (그래도 Mr. Riley에게 메시지를 보내주세요.)라고 말했으므로 (B)가 정답

Paraphrasing message ➔ send a message

호주 ⇄ 미국

Questions 65-67 refer to the following conversation and storage racks.

M: Cindy, have you checked out the canned foods section? **We're all out of the beans and corn. So we'll have to get some more from this storage room.**(65)

W: OK. I'll get to that once I finish unpacking these crates of oranges.(66) By the way, do you have another scanning device I can use? This one is running low on battery power.

M: Yeah, I'll grab you one from the office. Also, once you've finished both tasks, **please pick up any unused boxes and put them in the recycling bin.**(67)

Rack 1	Apples
Rack 2	**Oranges**(66)
Rack 3	Peaches
Rack 4	Strawberries

65-67번은 다음 대화와 저장고에 관한 문제입니다.

남: Cindy, 통조림식품 구역을 확인하셨나요? **콩과 옥수수가 다 떨어졌어요. 그래서 이 창고에서 좀 가져가야 해요.**(65)

여: 네. **오렌지 상자들을 풀고 난 후 바로 시작할게요.**(66) 그런데, 혹시 제가 사용할 수 있는 다른 스캐너가 있나요? 이건 배터리가 거의 없어요.

남: 네, 사무실에서 하나 가져다 드릴게요. 그리고, 두 가지 업무를 끝내면, **사용하지 않는 상자를 가져다가 재활용품 통에 넣어주세요.**(67)

선반 1	사과
선반 2	**오렌지**(66)
선반 3	복숭아
선반 4	딸기

어휘 canned food 통조림 식품 storage room 창고 unpack v. 풀다 crate n. 상자 by the way 그런데 device n. 장치 run low 고갈되다, 떨어져 가다 task n. 일 unused adj. 사용하지 않는 rack n. 선반

65 세부정보 난이도 중

해석 남자는 어떤 문제를 보고하는가?
(A) 창고가 청소되어야 한다.
(B) 물품을 다시 채워야 한다.
(C) 식품의 유통기한이 만료되었다.
(D) 배송품에 하자가 있다.

해설 남자가 We're all out of the beans and corn. So we'll have to get some more from this storage room. (콩과 옥수수가 다 떨어졌어요. 그래서 이 창고에서 좀 가져가야 해요.) 라고 말했으므로 (B)가 정답

66 시각 정보 연계 난이도 중

해석 시각 자료를 보시오. 여자는 어떤 선반에서 작업하고 있는가?
(A) 선반 1
(B) 선반 2

(C) 선반 3
(D) 선반 4

해설 여자가 I'll get to that once I finish unpacking these crates of oranges. (오렌지 상자들을 풀고 난 후 바로 시작할게요.)라고 답했고, 시각 자료에서 Rack 2 (선반 2)가 Oranges (오렌지)임을 확인할 수 있으므로 (B)가 정답

67 요청/제의/제안 난이도 상

해석 남자는 여자에게 무엇을 하라고 지시하는가?
(A) 상자를 폐기하라고
(B) 장치를 수리하라고
(C) 업체에 전화하라고
(D) 고객 문의에 대응하라고

해설 남자가 please pick up any unused boxes and put them in the recycling bin. (사용하지 않는 상자를 가져다가 재활용품 통에 넣어주세요.)라고 말했으므로 (A)가 정답

Paraphrasing put ~ in the bin ➡ discard

영국 ⇄ 미국

Questions 68-70 refer to the following conversation and seating chart.

W: Hello. According to your Web site, **the performing arts center was remodeled last week**[68] and offers wider seats now.

M: Yes. But that's not all. The seats are also cushioned for comfort. Just remember to try to purchase tickets in advance to ensure a good view.

W: Alright. Actually, I want to purchase four seats for the Wingding Orchestra concert next Friday. Can I do that right now?

M: Of course. OK, **it looks like the gold section is the only area with four seats together.**[69] If you're fine with that, I'll go ahead and reserve them now.

W: Yes.[69] And one more thing: **I have a 20-percent-off voucher I want to use.**[70]

M: Sure. Just read me the 12-digit number on the voucher.

```
        MAIN STAGE
       (GOLD SECTION)
Row A  ■ ■ ■ ■ ■ ■ ■  Row A
Row B  □ □ □ ■ ■ ■ ■  Row B
Row C  ■ ■ ■ ■ ■ ■ □  Row C
Row D  ■ ■ ■ □ □ □ ■  Row D
                  Open Seals □
```

68-70번은 다음 대화와 좌석 배치도에 관한 문제입니다.

여: 안녕하세요. 귀사의 웹 사이트를 보니, **공연 예술 센터가 지난주에 개조되어**[68] 이제 더 넓은 좌석을 제공한다고 나오네요.

남: 네. 그런데 그게 다가 아닙니다. 안락할 수 있게 좌석들에 쿠션도 덧대어 있습니다. 좋은 시야를 확보할 수 있게 미리 티켓을 구매하시는 것만 기억하세요.

여: 알겠습니다. 실은 제가 다음 주 금요일 Wingding 오케스트라 콘서트에 네 좌석을 구매하고 싶은데요. 지금 할 수 있을까요?

남: 물론이죠. 자, **골드 섹션이 좌석 4개가 붙어있는 유일한 구역인 것 같네요.**[69] 괜찮으시면, 제가 지금 예약해드리겠습니다.

여: 네.[69] 그리고 한 가지 더 있는데요. **20퍼센트 할인쿠폰을 사용하고 싶습니다.**[70]

남: 그럼요. 쿠폰에 있는 12자리 숫자를 저에게 알려주세요.

```
          중앙 무대
         (골드 섹션)
A열  ■ ■ ■ ■ ■ ■ ■  A열
B열  □ □ □ ■ ■ ■ ■  B열   (69)
C열  ■ ■ ■ ■ ■ ■ □  C열
D열  ■ ■ ■ □ □ □ ■  D열
                공석 □
```

어휘 performing arts 공연 예술 cushion v. 쿠션을 깔다[대다] comfort n. 안락함 in advance 미리, 사전에 voucher n. 할인권, 쿠폰 digit n. 숫자

68 세부정보 난이도 중

해석 최근에 공연 예술 센터에서 무슨 일이 있었는가?
(A) 새로운 매니저가 채용되었다.
(B) 공연의 날짜가 변경되었다.
(C) 시설의 개조가 마무리되었다.
(D) 주차장이 건설되었다.

해설 여자가 the performing arts center was remodeled last week (공연예술센터가 지난주에 개조되어) 라고 말했으므로 (C)가 정답

Paraphrasing was remodeled ➡ the renovation ~ was finished

69 시각 정보 연계 난이도 상

해석 시각 자료를 보시오. 여자는 어느 열의 티켓을 사겠는가?
(A) A열
(B) B열
(C) C열
(D) D열

해설 남자가 it looks like the gold section is the only area with four seats together. (골드 섹션이 좌석 4개가 붙어있는 유일한 구역인 것 같네요)라고 말했고, 시각 자료에서 좌석 4개가 붙어있는 공간은 Row B (B열)임을 확인할 수 있으므로 (B)가 정답

70 세부정보 　　난이도 하

해석　여자는 무엇을 하고 싶다고 말하는가?
(A) 쿠폰을 사용하고 싶다고
(B) 회원으로 가입하고 싶다고
(C) 전자 티켓을 받고 싶다고
(D) 좌석을 업그레이드 하고 싶다고

해설　여자가 I have a 20-percent-off voucher I want to use. (20퍼센트 할인쿠폰을 사용하고 싶습니다.)라고 말했으므로 (A)가 정답

PART 4　　P. 199

[영국]

Questions 71-73 refer to the following introduction.

W: Hello, and welcome to the 10th Annual Renewable Energy Convention.(71) Our first speaker is the renowned scholar Jonathan Matthews, who all of us know quite well. He has been one of the strongest advocates of our industry for the past decade. Earlier this year, Mr. Matthews was given the Washburn Medal for his recent work on biodiesel production.(72) Mr. Matthews will share with us the latest on his research. But before he takes the stage, I want to remind you to keep your name badge on at all times.(73)

71-73번은 다음 소개에 관한 문제입니다.

여: 안녕하세요, 제 10회 연례 재생 가능 에너지 컨벤션에 오신 것을 환영합니다.(71) 첫 번째 연사는 우리 모두가 잘 아는 분이죠, 저명한 학자이신 Jonathan Matthews이십니다. 그 분은 지난 10년 간 우리 업계의 가장 강력한 지지자 중 한 분이셨습니다. 올해 초, Mr. Matthews는 바이오 디젤 생산에 대한 그의 최근 연구로 Washburn 메달을 수상했습니다.(72) Mr. Matthews는 그의 가장 최근 연구들을 우리에게 공유해 주실 겁니다. 하지만, 그를 무대로 모시기 전에 여러분께 다시 한 번 말씀드리면 명찰을 항시 착용해주길 바랍니다.(73)

어휘　renewable adj. 재생 가능한　convention n. 대회, 협의회　renowned adj. 저명한, 명성 있는　scholar n. 학자　advocate n. 지지자, 옹호자　decade n. 10년　biodiesel n. 바이오디젤 (폐식용 기름을 원료로 만든 차량용 연료)　remind v. 상기시키다　name badge 명찰　at all times 항상

71 주제/목적 　　난이도 하

해석　컨벤션의 주제는 무엇인가?
(A) 재생 가능 에너지
(B) 컴퓨터 공학 기술
(C) 쓰레기 재활용
(D) 직물 생산

해설　화자가 Hello, and welcome to the 10th Annual Renewable Energy Convention. (안녕하세요, 제 10주년 재생가능 에너지 컨벤션에 오신 것을 환영합니다.)라고 말했으므로 (A)가 정답

72 세부정보 　　난이도 중

해석　화자에 따르면, Jonathan Matthews는 올해 무엇을 했는가?
(A) 기계를 발명했다.
(B) 상을 받았다.
(C) 회사를 설립했다.
(D) 새로운 책을 썼다.

해설　화자가 Earlier this year, Mr. Matthews was given the Washburn Medal for his recent work on biodiesel production. (올해 초, Mr. Matthews는 바이오 디젤생산에 대한 그의 최근 연구로 Washburn 메달을 수상했습니다.)라고 말했으므로 (B)가 정답

Paraphrasing　was given the Medal ➡ received an award

73 요청/제의/제안 　　난이도 하

해석　화자는 청자들에게 무엇을 하라고 상기시키는가?
(A) 질문 거리를 적으라고
(B) 제품을 써보라고
(C) 시연회에 참석하라고
(D) 명찰을 착용하라고

해설　화자가 I want to remind you to keep your name badge on at all times. (여러분께 다시 한 번 말씀드리면 명찰을 항시 착용해주시길 바랍니다.)라고 말했으므로 (D)가 정답

Paraphrasing　keep your name badge on ➡ wear a name tag

[호주]

Questions 74-76 refer to the following recorded message.

M: You have reached Hello Telecommunications' support line.(74) We understand that many of our customers are experiencing difficulties connecting to the Internet right now due to last night's heave rainfall.(75) We hope to restore all connection issues by 3 P.M. Saturday afternoon. If you continue to have problems after this time, please speak to one of our representatives directly by dialing this number again and then pressing "0".(76)

74-76번은 다음 녹음 메시지에 관한 문제입니다.

남: Hello 텔레콤 지원팀입니다.(74) 어젯밤 폭우로 인하여 현재 많은 고객이 인터넷 연결에 어려움을 겪고 계신걸 알고 있습니다.(75) 저희는 토요일 오후 3시까지 모든 연결 문제들을 복구하기를 바라고 있습니다. 이 시간 이후에도 계속 문제를 겪으신다면, 이 번호로 다시 전화하신 다음 0번을 누르셔서 저희 직원에게 직접 말씀해 주세요.(76)

어휘　reach v. (전화로) 연락하다　telecommunications n. 통신　experience v. 겪다, 경험하다　heavy rainfall 폭우　restore v. 복구하다　issue n. 문제, 사안　representative n. 담당자　dial v. 전화를 걸다

74 장소/근무지 　　난이도 하

해석　화자는 어디에서 일하겠는가?
(A) 컴퓨터 제조업체
(B) 인터넷 서비스 공급업체
(C) 집수리 회사
(D) 방송국

해설 화자가 You have reached Hello Telecommunications' support line. (Hello 텔레콤 지원팀입니다.)라고 말했으므로 (B)가 정답

75 세부정보 난이도 중

해석 문제의 원인은 무엇인가?
(A) 기술적인 오류가 있었다.
(B) 작업 일부가 마무리되지 않았다.
(C) 일부 기계들이 파손되었다.
(D) 날씨가 안 좋았다.

해설 화자가 We understand that many of our customers are experiencing difficulties connecting to the Internet right now due to last night's heavy snowstorm. (어젯밤 폭우로 인하여 현재 많은 고객이 인터넷 연결에 어려움을 겪고 계신걸 알고 있습니다.)라고 말했으므로 (D)가 정답

Paraphrasing heavy snowstorm ➡ inclement weather

76 세부정보 난이도 하

해석 청자들은 문제가 계속될 경우에 무엇을 해야 하는가?
(A) 서류를 제출해야 한다
(B) 장비를 교체해야 한다
(C) 나중에 다시 전화해야 한다
(D) 업체에 방문해야 한다

해설 화자가 If you continue to have problems after this time, please speak to one of our representatives directly by dialing this number again and then pressing "0". (이 시간 이후에도 계속 문제를 겪으신다면, 이 번호로 다시 전화하신 다음 0번을 누르셔서 저희 직원에게 직접 말씀해 주세요.)라고 말했으므로 (C)가 정답

Paraphrasing dial ➡ call

미국

Questions 77-79 refer to the following announcement.

W: Thank you everyone for attending the grand opening of the latest addition to our theater, the memorabilia showroom.(77) I'm thrilled to share this moment with the movie fans in our city. The showroom will display props from some of the most popular films ever made. Before you enter, we'd like you to fill out this survey letting us know your movie preferences.(78) Also, to show our appreciation for your support, everyone here will be getting a $10 voucher to our concession stand.(79)

77-79번은 다음 안내에 관한 문제입니다.

여: 최근 저희 극장의 수집품 전시실 증축의 개장 행사에 참석해 주신 모든 분들께 감사드립니다.(77) 우리 시의 영화팬분들과 이 시간을 함께하게 되어 무척이나 기쁩니다. 전시실에는 지금껏 만들어온 가장 인기있는 일부 영화들의 소품들을 전시할 것입니다. 입장하시기 전에, 여러분이 선호하는 영화들을 저희가 알 수 있도록 이 설문을 작성해 주시기 바랍니다.(78) 또한, 여러분의 지원에 대한 감사의 표시로, 여기 계신 모든 분들은 저희 구내매점에서 사용하실 수 있는 10달러 할인권을 받게 됩니다.(79)

어휘 grand opening 개장 addition n. 추가된 것, 부가물 memorabilia n. 수집품, 기념품 showroom n. 전시실 thrilled adj. 아주 흥분한 prop n. (연극, 영화 등에 쓰이는) 소품 fill out 작성하다 preference n. 선호(되는 것) appreciation n. 감사 voucher n. 할인권, 상품권 concession stand 구내매점

77 세부정보 난이도 하

해석 극장은 무엇을 기념하고 있는가?
(A) 영화 개봉
(B) 전시실 개장
(C) 건물 개조
(D) 기념일

해설 화자가 Thank you everyone for attending the grand opening of the latest addition to our theater, the memorabilia showroom. (최근 저희 극장의 수집품 전시실 증축의 개장 행사에 참석해주신 모든 분들께 감사 드립니다.)라고 말했으므로 (B)가 정답

78 세부정보 난이도 중

해석 청자들은 처음에 무엇을 할 것인가?
(A) 영상을 시청할 것이다
(B) 투어를 할 것이다
(C) 사진을 찍을 것이다
(D) 질문에 답할 것이다

해설 화자가 Before you enter, we'd like you to fill out this survey letting us know your movie preferences. (입장하시기 전에, 여러분이 선호하는 영화들을 저희가 알 수 있도록 이 설문을 작성해 주시기 바랍니다.)라고 말했으므로 (D)가 정답

Paraphrasing fill out ~ survey ➡ answer some questions

79 세부정보 난이도 하

해석 청자들은 무엇을 받을 것인가?
(A) 구내매점 할인권
(B) 영화전시 소품
(C) 무료입장 티켓
(D) 상영시간 일정표

해설 화자가 everyone here will be getting a $10 voucher to our concession stand (여기 계신 모든 분들은 저희 구내매점에서 사용하실 수 있는 10달러 할인권을 받게 됩니다.)라고 말했으므로 (A)가 정답

영국

Questions 80-82 refer to the following telephone message.

W: Hello. My manager, Vince, was praising your company after returning from his holiday.(81) I need your company's help preparing for my own travel this spring.(80) I was researching the Grand Mediterranean Cruises Web site and saw a 5-city package for $670 during the month of May. I understand that this is one of the busier months, which explains why it's so expensive. But, I'm told that the Mediterranean is breathtaking during that season. That's why I wanted to get in touch with you before I finalize my plans.(82) You can contact me at 555-9328.

80-82번은 다음 전화메시지에 관한 문제입니다.

여: 안녕하세요. 제 매니저이신 Vince가 휴가를 다녀오신 후에 귀사에 대해 칭찬해 주셨는데요.(81) 제가 올 봄에 저 혼자 가는 여행을 준비하는데 귀사의 도움이 필요해서요.(80) 제가 그랜드 지중해 크루즈 웹 사이트를 조사했는데 5월 한 달 동안 670달러에 5개 도시 패키지를 보았어요. 이게 비싼 극성수기 중 한 때라는 건 알고 있습니다. 하지만 지중해는 그 시기에 숨막힐 듯 아름답다고 들었어요. 그래서 제가 계획을 확정하기 전에 연락 드리고 싶었습니다.(82) 555-9328번으로 저에게 연락주세요.

어휘 praise v. 칭찬하다 research v. 연구하다, 조사하다
Mediterranean adj. 지중해의 breathtaking adj. 숨이 멎는 듯한
get in touch 연락을 취하다 finalize v. 마무리 짓다, 완결하다

80 세부정보 난이도 하

해석 화자는 무엇을 준비하고 있는가?
(A) 연구조사 발표
(B) 고객 방문
(C) 기념일 파티
(D) 휴가

해설 화자가 My manager, Vince, was praising your company after returning from his holiday. I need your company's help preparing for my own travel this spring. (제 매니저이신 Vince가 휴가를 다녀오신 후에 귀사에 대해 칭찬해 주셨는데요. 제가 올 봄에 저 혼자 가는 여행을 준비하는데 귀사의 도움이 필요해서요.)라고 말했으므로 (D)가 정답

81 정체/신분 난이도 중

해석 청자는 누구겠는가?
(A) 선장
(B) 여행사 직원
(C) 리조트 매니저
(D) 전시회 코디네이터

해설 화자가 My manager, Vince, was praising your company after returning from his holiday. (제 매니저이신 Vince가 휴가를 다녀오신 후에 귀사에 대해 친찬해 주셨는데요.)라고 말했으므로 (B)가 정답

82 화자 의도 파악 난이도 중

해석 화자가 "지중해는 그 시기에 숨막힐 듯 아름답다고 들었어요"라고 말할 때, 그녀가 의미한 것은?
(A) 서비스에 만족하지 않는다.
(B) 추천에 동의한다.
(C) 그 가격에 구매할 가치가 있다고 생각한다.
(D) 청자가 그녀와 동행하기를 원한다.

해설 화자가 I understand that this is one of the busier months, which explains why it's so expensive. (이게 비싼 극성수기 중 한 때라는 건 알고 있습니다.)라면서, But, I'm told that the Mediterranean is breathtaking during that season. That's why I wanted to get in touch with you before I finalize my plans. (하

지만 지중해는 그 시기에 숨막힐 듯 아름답다고 들었어요. 그래서 제가 계획을 확정하기 전에 연락 드리고 싶었습니다.)라고 말한 것이므로 (C)가 정답

[미국]

Questions 83-85 refer to the following telephone message.

M: Hello. I'm calling for Barbara Loggins. I was driving through the Glenmoore community because I'm looking to buy a house there, and I came across your real estate ad. I really like the fact that there is a recreation center nearby, as health and fitness are very important to me.(83) Concerning the kind of house I want, I need a place with a basement that has enough room for my music equipment—I have quite a lot.(84) I'm leaving the country tonight to do some business overseas, so I'll give you another call when I get back.(85)

83-85번은 다음 전화 메시지에 관한 문제입니다.

남: 안녕하세요. Barbara Loggins께 메시지 남깁니다. Glenmoore 지역에 집을 사려고 알아보고 있는데요, 차를 타고 지나가다 당신의 부동산 광고를 우연히 발견했어요. 저에게는 건강과 운동이 매우 중요해서 인근에 레크리에이션 센터가 있다는 사실이 정말 마음에 들어요.(83) 원하는 집의 종류에 관해 말씀 드리자면, 음악 장비를 위한 공간이 충분한 지하실이 있는 곳이 필요합니다–꽤 많거든요.(84) 제가 오늘 밤 업무차 해외로 출국해서요, 돌아와서 다시 전화 드리겠습니다.(85)

어휘 come across ~을 우연히 발견하다 nearby adv. 인근에, 가까운 곳에 concerning prep. ~에 관한 basement n. (건물의) 지하층 overseas adv. 해외로

83 세부정보 난이도 하

해석 화자는 왜 Glenmoore 지역에 관심이 있는가?
(A) 레크리에이션 센터 근처에 있다.
(B) 보안 출입문이 있다.
(C) 학군이 좋다.
(D) 가격이 알맞다.

해설 화자가 I was driving through the Glenmoore community because I'm looking to buy a house there, and I came across your real estate ad. I really like the fact that there is a recreation center nearby, as health and fitness is very important to me. (Glenmoore 지역에 집을 사려고 알아보고 있는데요, 차를 타고 지나가다 당신의 부동산 광고를 우연히 발견했어요. 저에게는 건강과 운동이 매우 중요해서 인근에 레크리에이션 센터가 있다는 사실이 정말 마음에 들어요.)라고 말했으므로 (A)가 정답

84 세부정보 난이도 하

해석 화자는 자신의 집에 무엇을 원하는가?
(A) 홈 시어터
(B) 정원
(C) 가구가 비치된 거실
(D) 넓은 지하실

해설 화자가 Concerning the kind of house I want, I need a place with a basement that has enough room for my music equipment—I have quite a lot. (원하는 집의 종류에 관해 말씀 드리자면 음악 장비를 위한 공간이 충분한 지하실이 있는 곳이 필요합니다-꽤 많거든요.)라고 말했으므로 (D)가 정답

Paraphrasing a basement that has enough room for ~ ➡ a large basement

85 다음 행동/계획 난이도 하

해석 화자는 오늘 저녁에 무엇을 할 거라고 말하는가?
(A) 악기를 구매할 거라고
(B) 밴드와 만날 거라고
(C) 집주인과 이야기할 거라고
(D) 출장을 갈 거라고

해설 화자가 I'm leaving the country tonight on some business, so I'll give you another call when I get back. (제가 오늘밤 업무차 해외로 출국해서요, 돌아와서 다시 전화 드리겠습니다.)라고 말했으므로 (D)가 정답

Paraphrasing leaving the country on some business ➡ go on a business trip

[호주]

Questions 86-88 refer to the following announcement.

M: This announcement is for all passengers taking the 11:30 A.M. train to Seoul.(86) The departure time has been delayed one hour due to the heavy snow.(87) Crew members are currently doing their best to clear the tracks. All passengers with tickets for this train will be given a coupon for a free lunch set at the cafeteria.(88) You may pick these up at any service counter. We apologize for the inconvenience.

86-88번은 다음 안내방송에 관한 문제입니다.

남: 오전 11시 30분 서울행 열차에 탑승하시는 승객 여러분께 안내말씀 드립니다.(86) 폭설로 인해 출발 시각이 1시간 지연되었습니다.(87) 작업반이 현재 선로 제설 작업에 최선을 다하고 있습니다. 이 열차 탑승권을 소지하신 모든 승객 여러분께 구내식당에서 무료 점심을 드실 수 있는 쿠폰을 드릴 예정입니다.(88) 모든 안내 카운터에서 받으실 수 있습니다. 불편을 끼쳐드려 죄송합니다.

어휘 passenger n. 탑승객 departure time 출발 시각 delay v. 지연시키다 due to ~때문에 crew n. 팀, 반, 조 currently adv. 현재, 지금 do one's best 최선을 다하다 clear v. 치우다 cafeteria n. 구내식당 pick up (어디에서) ~을 찾다 apologize for ~에 대해 사과하다 inconvenience n. 불편

86 장소/근무지 난이도 하

해석 안내 방송은 어디에서 나오고 있는가?
(A) 버스 터미널에서
(B) 기차역에서
(C) 선박에서
(D) 비행기에서

해설 화자가 This announcement is for all passengers taking the 11:30 A.M. train to Seoul. (오전 11시 30분 서울행 열차에 탑승하시는 승객분께 안내 말씀 드립니다.)라고 말했으므로 (B)가 정답

87 세부정보 난이도 하

해석 문제의 원인은 무엇인가?
(A) 궂은 날씨
(B) 고장난 장비
(C) 늦게 온 승객들
(D) 직원 부족

해설 화자가 The departure time has been delayed one hour due to the heavy snow. (폭설로 인해 출발 시각이 1시간 지연되었습니다.)라고 말했으므로 (A)가 정답

Paraphrasing heavy snow ➡ inclement weather

88 다음 행동/계획 난이도 하

해석 청자들은 무엇을 받을 것인가?
(A) 주차권
(B) 식권
(C) 잡지
(D) 환불

해설 화자가 All passengers with tickets for this train will be given a coupon for a free lunch set at the cafeteria. (이 열차 탑승권을 소지하신 모든 승객 여러분께 구내식당에서 무료 점심을 드실 수 있는 쿠폰을 드릴 예정입니다.)라고 말했으므로 (B)가 정답

Paraphrasing be given ➡ receive, a coupon for a free lunch ➡ a meal voucher

[미국]

Questions 89-91 refer to the following telephone message.

M: Hello, Katherine. This is Scott from the Administration Department. I'm calling regarding the company's anniversary celebration next month.(89) I know we were considering having it at the same place as last year, but the thing is, the employees from the overseas branch are also coming. They won't be having a separate event at their own branch this year. So let's have a meeting to figure out how much money we have for the venue. (91) Then, we'll report to the CEO with some alternative options.(90) Call me back and let me know what time would be good for you.

89-91번은 다음 전화 메시지에 관한 문제입니다.

남: 안녕하세요, Katherine. 총무부의 Scott이에요. 다음 달에 있을 회사 창립기념 행사 때문에 전화 드렸어요.(89) 작년과 같은 장소에서 하는 걸 고려하고 있다고 알고 있는데요, 문제는 해외 지점의 직원들도 온다는 거예요. 올해는 자기들 지점에서 별도의 행사를 하지 않을 거라더군요. 그러니까 회의를 해서 우리가 장소 마련에 쓸 돈이 얼마나 있는지 알아보도록 해요.(91) 그리고 나서 CEO께 대안들을 보고하기로 하죠.(90) 전화 주셔서 몇 시가 좋은지 알려주세요.

어휘 administration department 총무부 regarding prep. ~에 관하여 figure out 알아내다 venue n. 장소 alternative adj. 대체 가능한, 대안이 되는

89 세부정보 | 난이도 하

해석 화자는 무엇을 준비하고 있는가?
(A) 기념일 행사
(B) 교육
(C) 영업 콘퍼런스
(D) 자선기금마련

해설 화자가 I'm calling regarding the company's anniversary celebration next month. (다음 달에 있을 회사 창립기념 행사 때문에 전화 드렸어요.)라고 말했으므로 (A)가 정답

Paraphrasing celebration ➡ event

90 화자 의도 파악 | 난이도 상

해석 화자가 "해외 지점의 직원들도 온다는 거예요"라고 말할 때, 그가 내비친 것은?
(A) 음식을 더 주문해야 한다.
(B) 더 큰 장소가 필요할 것이다.
(C) 초대손님 명단이 갱신되어야 한다.
(D) 문서가 번역될 것이다.

해설 화자가 I know we were considering having it at the same place as last year (작년과 같은 장소에서 하는 걸 고려하고 있다고 알고 있는데요)라고 하면서, but the thing is, the employees from the overseas branch are also coming. (문제는 해외 지점의 직원들도 온다는 거예요.)라고 했고, 이어서 They won't be having a separate event at their own branch this year. So let's have a meeting to figure out how much money we have for the venue. Then, we'll report to the CEO with some alternative options. (올해는 자기들 지점에서 별도의 행사를 하지 않을 거라는군요. 그러니까 회의를 해서 우리가 장소 마련에 쓸 돈이 얼마나 있는지 알아보도록 해요. 그러고 나서 CEO께 대안들을 보고하기로 하죠.)라고 말한 것이므로 (B)가 정답

91 세부정보 | 난이도 중

해석 화자는 왜 여자와 만나고 싶어하는가?
(A) 메뉴 옵션을 선택하기 위해
(B) 예산에 관하여 의논하기 위해
(C) 계약을 검토하기 위해
(D) 발표자를 선발하기 위해

해설 화자가 So let's have a meeting to figure out how much money we have for the venue. (그러니까 회의를 해서 우리가 장소 마련에 쓸 돈이 얼마나 있는지 알아보도록 해요.)라고 말했으므로 (B)가 정답

Paraphrasing figure out how much money we have for the venue ➡ discuss a budget

---

[미국]

Questions 92-94 refer to the following tour information.

W: Good afternoon. I'll be your guide today here at the Fremont Museum. **This museum is one of the largest in California. In fact, it covers an area of nearly 70,000 square meters.** (92) We are proud to offer free admission, but the museum does rely on financial donations from our guests. (93) Alright, let's start with the Ancient Egypt exhibit. We ask that you not use your cameras in this exhibit. Thank you in advance for your kind understanding. (94)

92-94번은 다음 여행 정보에 관한 문제입니다.

여: 안녕하세요. 저는 오늘 여러분께 이곳 Fremont 박물관을 소개해 드릴 가이드입니다. 이 박물관은 캘리포니아에서 가장 큰 박물관 중 하나인데요. 실은 거의 7만 제곱 미터 면적을 차지하고 있습니다.(92) 저희는 무료 입장 시행을 자랑스럽게 생각하고 있습니다만, 박물관이 방문객의 재정 기부에 의존하는 것도 사실입니다.(93) 그럼, 고대 이집트 전시관부터 시작하죠. 이 전시관에서는 카메라 사용을 삼가 주시길 바랍니다. 양해에 미리 감사 드립니다.(94)

어휘 cover v. (언급된 지역에) 걸치다 nearly adv. 거의 admission n. 입장 rely on v. ~에 의존하다 financial adj. 재정적인 exhibit n. 전시회, 전시품 revise v. 변경[수정]하다 in advance 미리, 사전에

92 세부정보 | 난이도 중

해석 화자는 박물관에 대해 무엇을 강조하는가?
(A) 직원
(B) 역사
(C) 규모
(D) 위치

해설 화자가 This museum is one of the largest in California. In fact, it covers an area of nearly 70,000 square meters. (이 박물관은 캘리포니아에서 가장 큰 박물관 중 하나인데요. 실은 거의 7만 제곱 미터 면적을 차지하고 있습니다.)라고 말했으므로 (C)가 정답

93 화자 의도 파악 | 난이도 상

해석 화자는 왜 "박물관이 방문객의 재정 기부에 의존하는 것도 사실입니다"라고 말하는가?
(A) 방문객의 불만 사항에 대응하려고
(B) 회원제에 대해 설명하려고
(C) 기부금을 요청하려고
(D) 개정된 정책을 발표하려고

해설 화자가 We are proud to offer free admission, but the museum does rely on financial donations from our guests.(저희는 무료 입장 시행을 자랑스럽게 생각하고 있습니다만, 박물관이 방문객의 재정 기부에 의존하는 것도 사실입니다.) 라고 말했으므로 (C)가 정답

Paraphrasing donations ➡ contributions

94 세부정보 | 난이도 중

해석 화자에 따르면, 무엇이 금지되는가?
(A) 사진을 찍는 것
(B) 그룹을 이탈하는 것
(C) 가방을 소지하는 것
(D) 유물을 만지는 것

해설 화자가 We ask that you not use your cameras in this exhibit. Thank you in advance for your kind understanding. (이 전시관에서는 카메라 사용을 삼가 주시길 바랍니다. 양해에 미리 감사 드립니다.)라고 말했으므로 (A)가 정답

Paraphrasing use your cameras ➡ taking photographs

[호주]

Questions 95-97 refer to the following talk and table.

M: Welcome to this week's sales team meeting, everyone. I'm sure you're all excited because today marks the end of the first month of our new sales incentive program. **Remember, we are offering rewards to all staff members based on their clothing and accessories sales.**(95) During this past month, **nearly everyone sold between $2,000 and $3,000 worth of items.**(96) If you were in this group, you may pick up your gift card after this meeting. Now, only one employee, Henry Manning, was able to sell over $3,000 worth of clothes. **Henry is planning to take a week off next month to visit his parents in Vermont, so the flight tickets come at a good time.**(97) Good work, Henry!

Reward Tier	Amount of Sales	Reward
Tier A	Over $3,000	Free round-trip airfare
Tier B	**$2,000 to $3,000**(96)	**$300 Gift Certificate**
Tier C	$1,000 to $2,000	Set of Steak Knives
Tier D	Under $1,000	Pair of Headphones

95-97번은 다음 담화와 표에 관한 문제입니다.

남: 모두 이번 주 영업팀 회의에 오신 것을 환영합니다. 오늘은 새 영업 인센티브 프로그램 시행 첫 달의 마지막 날이므로 여러분 모두 분명히 기대하고 있을 겁니다. 의류 및 액세서리 판매량에 근거하여 전직원에게 포상이 이루어진다는 점을 기억하시기 바랍니다.(95) 지난 한 달 동안 거의 모든 분이 2,000달러에서 3,000달러 상당의 제품을 판매했습니다.(96) 이 그룹에 속하신다면 회의가 끝난 후에 상품권을 받아 가시면 되겠습니다. 자, 오직 한 명의 직원 Henry Manning만이 3,000달러 이상에 상당하는 의류를 판매했습니다. Henry는 Vermont에 계신 부모님을 뵈러 다음달에 일주일 간 휴가를 가는데요, 그러면 항공권이 적기에 나오는 것이군요.(97) 수고하셨습니다, Henry!

포상 단계	판매 금액	보상책
A 단계	3,000달러 이상	무료 왕복 항공료
B 단계	2,000달러 - 3,000달러(96)	300달러 상품권
C 단계	1,000달러 - 2,000달러	스테이크 나이프 세트
D 단계	1,000달러 미만	헤드폰

어휘 mark v. (중요 사건을) 기념하다 reward n. 보상 based on ~에 근거하여 worth n. ~의 값어치만큼의 양, ~에 상당하는 양 take ~ off ~(동안)을 쉬다 tier n. 단계 round-trip adj. 왕복 여행의 airfare n. 항공 요금 gift certificate 상품권

95 장소/근무지   난이도 하

해석 화자는 어떤 종류의 사업체에서 근무하겠는가?
(A) 휴대폰 회사
(B) 자동차 대리점
(C) 의류 매장
(D) 광고 대행사

해설 화자가 Remember, we are offering rewards to all staff members based on their clothing and accessories sales. (의류 및 액세서리 판매량에 근거하여 전직원에게 포상이 이루어진다는 점을 기억하시기 바랍니다.)라고 말했으므로 (C)가 정답

96 시각 정보 연계   난이도 중

해석 시각 자료를 보시오. 대부분의 직원들은 어느 포상단계를 달성했는가?
(A) A 단계
(B) B 단계
(C) C 단계
(D) D 단계

해설 화자가 nearly everyone sold between $2,000 and $3,000 worth of items. (거의 모든 분이 2,000달러에서 3,000달러 상당의 제품을 판매했습니다.)라고 말했고, 시각자료에서 Tier B(B 단계)가 $2,000 to $3,000 (2,000달러 - 3,000달러)임을 확인할 수 있으므로 (B)가 정답

Paraphrasing nearly everyone ➡ most of the staff members

97 세부정보   난이도 하

해석 화자는 Henry Manning이 왜 다음 달에 Vermont에 갈 거라고 말하는가?
(A) 가족을 만나러
(B) 마케팅 세미나에 참석하러
(C) 상을 받으러
(D) 대회에 참가하러

해설 화자가 Henry is planning to take a week off next month to visit his parents in Vermont, so the flight tickets come at a good time. (Henry는 Vermont에 계신 부모님을 뵈러 다음달에 일주일 간 휴가를 가는데요, 그러면 항공권이 적기에 나오는 것이군요.)라고 말했으므로 (A)가 정답

Paraphrasing visit his parents ➡ see his family

[미국]

Questions 98-100 refer to the following announcement and catalogue.

M: If we could have your attention for a moment, we have a few announcements to make before our **overnight flight to Honolulu takes off.**(98) First of all, complimentary bottled water is available at all times during this flight. If you are thirsty, simply tell me or one of the other cabin crew members, and we will be glad to bring you a bottle. (99) And don't forget, we have all kinds of gifts available for purchase to delight your friends and family. Shop from the catalog now! **Just one thing—I'm afraid that Product #82 has sold out.**(100) But there are plenty of other great choices!

Product #75
Chocolate Box ($25)

Product #82(100)
Wallet ($55)

Product #79
Sunglasses ($70)

Product #95
Wireless Charger ($40)

98-100번은 다음 안내와 카탈로그에 관한 문제입니다.

남: 잠시 주목해주시면, Honolulu로 가는 야간 비행편이 이륙하기 전, 몇 가지 안내 말씀 드리겠습니다.⁽⁹⁸⁾ 먼저, 비행하시는 동안 생수를 언제든 무료로 이용하실 수 있습니다. 목이 마르시면, 저나 다른 승무원에게 말씀만 해주시면 고객님께 가져다 드리겠습니다.⁽⁹⁹⁾ 그리고 기억해주세요. 승객 여러분의 친지분들을 기쁘게해드릴 모든 종류의 선물을 구매하실 수 있습니다. 지금 카탈로그를 보시면서 쇼핑하세요! 하나만 더 말씀 드리면, 아쉽게도 82번 제품은 매진되었습니다.⁽¹⁰⁰⁾ 하지만 그 밖에도 선택하실 좋은 물건들이 많이 있습니다.

75번 제품
초콜릿 상자 (25달러)

82번 제품⁽¹⁰⁰⁾
지갑 (55달러)

79번 제품
선글라스 (70달러)

95번 제품
무선 충전기 (40달러)

어휘 attention n. 주의집중 announcement n. 안내, 공지 overnight adj. 야간의 flight n. 비행, 항공 takes off 이륙하다 complimentary adj. 무료의 at all times 항상 thirsty adj. 목마른 cabin crew 승무원 purchase n. 구입 delight v. 즐겁게 하다 shop v. 쇼핑하다, 사다 catalog n. 카탈로그 sell out 매진되다

98 정체/신분 · 난이도 하

해석 청자들은 누구겠는가?
(A) 항공기 승객
(B) 콘서트 참석자
(C) 리조트 고객
(D) 쇼핑몰 방문객

해설 화자가 If we could have your attention for a moment, we have a few announcements to make before our overnight flight to Honolulu takes off. (잠시 주목해주시면, Honolulu로 가는 야간 비행편이 이륙하기 전, 몇 가지 안내 말씀 드리겠습니다.)라고 말했으므로 (A)가 정답

99 요청/제의/제안 · 난이도 하

해석 화자는 무엇을 해주겠다고 하는가?
(A) 음료를 제공해주겠다고
(B) 불을 꺼주겠다고
(C) 소지품을 보관해주겠다고
(D) 돈을 환불해주겠다고

해설 화자가 First of all, complimentary bottled water is available at all times during this flight. If you are thirsty, simply tell me or one of the other cabin crew members, and we will be glad to bring you a bottle. (먼저, 비행하시는 동안 생수를 언제든 무료로 이용하실 수 있습니다. 목이 마르시면, 저나 다른 승무원에게 말씀만 해주시면 고객님께 가져다 드리겠습니다.)라고 말했으므로 (A)가 정답

Paraphrasing bring a bottle ➡ provide a beverage

100 시각 정보 연계 · 난이도 하

해석 시각 자료를 보시오. 어떤 물건을 더 이상 구할 수 없는가?
(A) 초콜릿 상자
(B) 지갑
(C) 선글라스
(D) 무선 충전기

해설 화자가 Just one thing—I'm afraid that Product #82 has sold out. (하나만 더 말씀 드리면, 아쉽게도 82번 제품은 매진되었습니다.)라고 말했고, 시각 자료에서 Product #82(82번 제품) - Wallet ($55)(지갑 (55 달러))을 확인할 수 있으므로 (B)가 정답

Paraphrasing sold out ➡ no longer available

PART 5

101 구조/문법+어휘 • 전치사 · 난이도 중

해석 회사 임원들은 전 직원의 모든 수고와 노력에 감사해 한다.

해설 빈칸은 형용사와 명사구 사이의 자리. 빈칸 앞 형용사를 고려할 때, 'be grateful for(~에 감사하다)'라는 표현을 완성하는 전치사 (D)가 정답

어휘 executive n. 임원 grateful adj. 감사하는 hard work 수고, 노고 effort n. 노력 staff n. 직원

102 구조/문법 • 부사 · 난이도 하

해석 Lisa Chen은 보도자료를 발표하기 전에 신중히 교정을 보았다.

해설 빈칸은 주어, 동사, 목적어를 갖춘 완전한 문장과 전치사구 사이의 수식어 자리이므로 동사를 수식하는 부사 (D)가 정답

Key Point
부사는 부사(구), 형용사, 동사, 문장 등을 수식하며, 문장 내 가장 다양한 위치에 올 수 있는 품사이다.

어휘 proofread v. 교정을 보다 press release 보도자료 publication n. 발표

103 어휘 • 명사 · 난이도 중

해석 겨우 일주일 전에 일을 시작한 Ms. LaPointe는 다른 간호사들과 보조를 맞추는 데 어려움을 겪었다.

해설 빈칸은 동사 keep의 목적어인 명사자리. 문맥상 '다른 간호사들과 보조를 맞춘다'는 의미가 되어야 자연스러우므로 'keep pace with(~와 보조를 맞추다, ~에 따라가다)'의 관용표현을 완성하는 명사 (C)가 정답

Key word
Having started only a week ago, Ms. LaPointe had a difficult time **keeping** pace **with** the other physician's assistants.

오답보기 확인
(A) line 선, 경계
(B) track 길, 진로
(D) control 통제(력)

어휘 **pace** n. 속도; 걸음 **physician** n. 의사 **assistant** n. 조수, 보조

---

104 구조/문법 • 형용사 　　난이도 중

해설 수십 년 동안 Margate 대학은 연례 기금마련 행사를 통해 지역의 청소년 단체들을 후원하는 데 적극적이었다.

해설 빈칸은 be동사 뒤 주격보어자리. 문맥상 'Margate 대학이 후원에 적극적'이라는 의미가 되어야 자연스러우므로 'active in(~에 적극적인)'이라는 표현을 완성하는 형용사 (D)가 정답

Key Point
주격보어 자리에는 명사 또는 형용사가 올 수 있으며, 문맥상 주어와의 관계 및 빈칸 앞, 뒤의 관사, 전치사 등의 유무를 고려하여 판단한다.

어휘 **decade** n. 10년 **support** v. 후원[지원]하다 **youth organization** 청소년단체 **fundraising** n. 모금

---

105 어휘 • 동사 　　난이도 중

해설 Kaiser 미디어와 Gaulish 신문사는 회계연도 초에 합병한다는 합의에 도달했다.

해설 빈칸은 주어와 목적어 사이 동사자리. 문맥상 '합의에 도달했다'는 의미가 되어야 자연스러우므로, 'reach an agreement(합의에 도달하다)'라는 표현을 완성하는 (C)가 정답

Key Point
reach와 관련된 기출 표현

reach an agreement	합의에 이르다
reach a conclusion	결론에 이르다
reach a decision	결정에 이르다
reach a compromise	타협에 이르다

Key word
Kaiser Media and Gaulish Press have **reached an agreement** to merge at the beginning of the fiscal year.

오답보기 확인
(A) emerge 드러나다, 부상하다
(B) criticize 비판하다
(D) acclaim 찬사를 보내다

어휘 **press** n. 신문, 언론 **reach** v. ~에 이르다 **agreement** n. 합의(서), 계약(서) **merge** v. 합병하다 **fiscal year** 회계연도

---

106 어휘 • 전치사 　　난이도 중

해설 Devon사는 동부 훈련 센터의 확장을 발표하게 되어 기쁘다.

해설 빈칸은 명사 center를 목적어로 취하는 전치사자리. 문맥상 '기숙사의 확장을 발표하게 되어 기쁘다'는 의미가 되어야 자연스러우므로 (D)가 정답

Key word
Devon **University** is pleased to announce the **expansion of** its east **campus dormitory**.

어휘 **announce** v. 발표하다 **expansion** n. 확장

---

107 어휘 • 형용사 　　난이도 중

해설 식당손님들은 새로 문을 연 Merchant Bistro에서 일년 내내 이례적인 요리를 경험해볼 수 있다.

해설 빈칸은 문장의 목적어인 dishes를 수식하는 형용사 자리. 문맥상 '새로운 식당에서 이례적인 요리를 경험해볼 수 있다'는 의미가 가장 자연스러우므로 (C)가 정답

Key word
Diners can **try exceptional dishes** all year round **at the newly opened** Merchant **Bistro**.

오답보기 확인
(A) dominant 우세한
(B) abundant 풍부한
(D) excessive 과도한

어휘 **diner** n. 식당 손님 **exceptional** adj. 이례적일 정도로 우수한, 뛰어난 **dish** n. 요리 **all year around** 일년 내내 **newly** adv. 새로

---

108 구조/문법 • 부사 　　난이도 상

해설 Van Tassel Media는 다른 제작사들에 비해 상당히 작지만, 다큐멘터리 영화로는 거의 틀림없이 국내 최고에 속한다.

해설 빈칸은 be동사와 among 전치사구 사이의 자리. 접속사 but으로 연결된 두 문장 관계를 고려할 때, 빈칸을 제외하고 '업체의 규모는 작지만, 다큐멘터리 영화로는 국내 최고에 속한다'라는 의미가 되어 문맥상 자연스러우므로 <among+the 최상급+전치사구>를 수식하는 부사 (D)가 정답

Key Point
부사 arguably는 최상급 표현을 수식해 그 의미를 더욱 강조하는 역할을 한다.

어휘 **rather** adv. 상당히, 약간 **in comparison to** ~와 비교하여 **production** n. 생산 **documentary film** 다큐멘터리 영화 **arguably** adj. 틀림없이

---

109 어휘 • 동사 　　난이도 중

해설 Duoyi의 가장 인기 있는 건강 추적기는 최신 GPS 시스템이 특징이다.

해설 빈칸은 주어와 목적어 사이 동사자리. 문맥상 '건강 추적기는 최신 GPS시스템을 특징으로 한다'는 의미가 되어야 자연스러우므로 (C)가 정답

Key word
Duoyi's most popular **fitness tracker features** a state-of-the-art GPS system.

오답보기 확인
(A) exercise 행사하다
(B) challenge 도전하다
(D) contend 주장하다

어휘 **popular** adj. 인기 있는 **fitness tracker** 건강 추적기 **feature** v. ~을 특징으로 하다, ~을 특별히 포함하다 n. 특징 **state-of-the-art** adj. 최신의

110 구조/문법 • 종속접속사 - 부사절   난이도 중

해석 사무실 공간은 작업자들이 가구를 치우는 대로 청소될 것이다.

해설 빈칸은 두 개의 완전한 문장을 연결하는 접속사자리. 문맥상 '가구를 치우는 대로, 공간이 청소될 것'이라는 의미로 연결되어야 자연스러우므로 부사절을 만들어주는 접속사 (D)가 정답

> **Key Point**
> 부사 once vs. 접속사 once: 부사일 때는 '한 번, 한때'를, 접속사일 때는 '일단 ~하면, ~하자마자'를 의미한다.

어휘 space n. 공간, 자리 clean v. 청소하다 remove v. 치우다 furniture n. 가구

111 구조/문법 • to부정사   난이도 중

해석 Harper 벽지는 어떤 가정에든 어울리도록 매우 다양한 패턴으로 판매된다.

해설 빈칸은 수동태 구조의 완전한 문장과 명사구를 연결하는 준동사자리. 문맥상 '어느 가정에든 어울리도록 하기 위해 다양한 패턴으로 판매된다'는 의미가 되어야 자연스러우므로 부사적용법의 to부정사 (B)가 정답

어휘 wallpaper n. 벽지 a wide variety of 매우 다양한 sell v. 팔다(sell-sold-sold)

112 어휘 • 형용사   난이도 중

해석 Strom 스마트폰은 작은 디자인 덕분에 사용자의 주머니에 쉽게 들어갈 수 있다.

해설 빈칸은 명사 design을 수식하는 형용사자리. 주절의 내용을 고려할 때, 문맥상 '작은 디자인 덕분에, 주머니에 쉽게 들어간다'는 의미가 되어야 자연스러우므로 (A)가 정답

> **Key word**
> Thanks to its **compact design**, the new Strom smartphone can **comfortably fit in** the user's **pocket**.

> **오답보기 확인**
> (B) vague 모호한
> (C) rigid 엄격한
> (D) significant 중요한

어휘 thanks to prep. ~덕분에 compact adj. 소형의 comfortably adv. 수월하게, 편안하게 fit v. (어느 장소에 들어가기에) 맞다

113 구조/문법 • 소유격 관계대명사   난이도 중

해석 재정적 지원으로 새로운 시립공원 건립을 가능하게 했던 Hiroko Mifune가 개관식에서 연설을 할 것이다.

해설 문장의 콤마(,) 사이 Hiroko Mifune을 선행사로 하는 관계절이 삽입된 구조. 빈칸 뒤 삽입된 문장이 주어, 동사, 목적어, 목적격보어를 갖춘 완전한 문장을 이루고 있으므로 소유격 관계대명사 (A)가 정답

> **Key Point**
> ① 주격 관계대명사 뒤에는 주어가 없는 불완전한 절이, 목적격 관계대명사 뒤에는 목적어가 없는 불완전한 절이 오지만, 소유격 관계대명사 뒤에는 완전한 문장이 온다. 단, 소유격 관계대명사 바로 뒤에 오는 명사는 어떤 한정사도 붙어 있지 않다.
> ② 복합관계대명사는 '선행사+관계대명사' 역할을 하므로, 별도의 선행사를 필요로 하지 않다: whoever = anyone who ~ (~하는 사람은 누구나)

어휘 dedication ceremony (새 건조물의) 개관식

114 구조/문법 • 주격 인칭대명사   난이도 하

해석 Ms. Kitigoe는 조립 라인을 점검한 후, 그녀는 더 효율적으로 운영할 방법을 제안할 것이다.

해설 빈칸은 동사 앞 문장의 주어자리. 빈칸 앞 after 부사절의 내용을 고려할 때, Ms. Kitigoe를 지칭하는 주격 대명사가 와야 문맥상 자연스러우므로 (C)가 정답

어휘 inspect v. 점검하다 assembly line 조립 라인 run v. 작동하다

115 구조/문법 • 과거분사   난이도 중

해석 연례 취업박람회 참석에 관심 있는 학생들은 등록 양식을 작성해야 한다.

해설 이 문장에는 이미 should complete라는 동사가 있으므로 동사 (A), (B)는 탈락. 따라서 빈칸은 주어 students를 후치 수식하는 분사자리. 수식을 받는 대상이 사람명사인 students이며, interest '~에게 관심을 끌다'는 의미의 감정동사로 감정동사의 분사는 사람을 수식할 때 과거분사를 쓴다는 점과, 형태상 빈칸 뒤에 목적어 없이 전치사구가 연결되어 있다는 점에서도 수동의 의미로 과거분사 (C)가 정답

> **Key Point**
> interest(관심을 끌다), disappoint(실망시키다), embarrass(당황시키다), surprise(놀라게 하다)와 같은 감정동사가 명사를 꾸며주는 분사로 쓰일 때, 수식 받는 명사가 사람일 때는 과거분사를, 사물일 때는 현재분사를 쓴다.

어휘 attend v. 참석하다 job fair 취업박람회 complete v. 작성하다 registration n. 등록

116 어휘 • 부사   난이도 중

해석 자연사 박물관의 방문자수는 신규 공룡 전시 개장 이후 급속히 증가했다.

해설 빈칸은 동사 increased를 수식하는 부사자리. 이어지는 following 전치사구를 고려할 때, 문맥상 '신규 전시 개장 이후 방문자수가 급속히 증가했다'는 내용으로 이어져야 자연스러우므로 (C)가 정답

> **Key word**
> Visitor numbers at the Natural History Museum **increased rapidly following** the **opening** of the new dinosaur exhibit.

> **오답보기 확인**
> (A) strictly 엄격히
> (B) exactly 정확히
> (D) closely 밀접히

어휘 number n. 수 increase v. 증가하다 rapidly adj. 급속히, 빠르게 following prep. ~후에 dinosaur n. 공룡 exhibit n. 전시

117 구조/문법 • 종속접속사 - 부사절   난이도 중

해석 건설자재가 늦게 배송됐음에도 불구하고, 공사직원들은 신속히 작업했고, 프로젝트 일정을 지켰다.

해설 빈칸은 두 개의 완전한 문장을 연결하는 접속사자리이므로 (D)가 정답

> **Key Point**
> '------ 문장1, 문장2'의 구조에서 빈칸은 부사절 접속사 자리이다.

어휘 supplies n. 용품, 물품 deliver v. 배달하다 construction n. 공사 staff n. 직원 on schedule 예정대로

TEST 05 199

118 구조/문법 • 동사 – 수동태 난이도 중

해석 Kraven 로스쿨에서는 대학원생으로서의 자격 취득을 위해 6개월 간의 법률 관련 인턴십이 요구된다.

해설 빈칸은 주어 뒤 동사자리. 주어가 six months로 복수이므로 (D)는 수 일치에서 탈락. 빈칸 뒤에 목적어가 없고 문맥상 '법률 인턴십이 요구된다'는 의미가 되어야 하므로 수동태 동사 (C)가 정답

어휘 certification n. 증명(서 교부) graduate student 대학원생

119 어휘 • 명사 난이도 중

해석 그래픽 디자이너는 광고캠페인을 위해 회사 로고를 수정했다.

해설 빈칸은 동사 made의 목적어자리. 빈칸 뒤 전치사 to가 있으며 문맥상 '회사 로고를 수정했다'는 의미가 되어야 자연스러우므로, 'make revisions to(~를 수정하다)'라는 표현을 완성하는 (B)가 정답

Key Point
전치사 to와 같이 쓰이는 명사 어휘

access to ~의 이용기회, 접근권한	adjustment to ~에 대한 조정
subscription to ~의 구독	reaction to ~에 대한 반응
commitment to ~에 대한 전념	response to ~에의 응답, 대응
resolution to ~에 대한 해결책	attention to ~에 대한 관심, 집중
contribution to ~에 대한 공헌	alternative to ~에 대한 대체방안
correction to ~에 대한 수정	objection to ~에 대한 반대
revision to ~에 대한 수정	

Key word
The graphic designer **made revisions to** the company's **logo** for the ad campaign.

오답보기 확인
(A) duplication 복사품
(C) installation 설치, 장치
(D) complication 문제

어휘 logo n. 로고 revision n. 수정 ad campaign 광고캠페인

120 어휘 • 명사 난이도 중

해석 Rotherton 박물관을 개조하겠다는 Calumet 건설의 제안서가 오늘 오전 경영진의 승인을 받았다.

해설 빈칸은 동사 received의 목적어자리. 빈칸 앞에 관사가 없으며, 문맥상 '제안서가 경영진의 승인을 받았다'는 의미가 되어야 자연스러우므로 불가산명사 (C)가 정답

Key word
Calumet Construction's **proposal** to remodel the Rotherton Museum **received approval** by the management this morning.

오답보기 확인
(A) obedience 복종
(B) decision 결정
(D) reaction 반응

어휘 proposal n. 제안(서) approval 승인 management n. 경영진

121 구조/문법+어휘 • 전치사 난이도 중

해석 당신의 의류 상품은 48시간 이내에 배송되어야 하지만, 최대 4 영업일까지 걸릴 수도 있다.

해설 빈칸은 기간을 나타내는 명사구를 목적어로 취하는 전치사자리이므로 (C)가 정답

Key Point
전치사 within은 기간, 범위, 한도 등을 나타내는 표현을 목적어로 취하며, '~이내에'라는 의미를 갖는다.

어휘 clothing n. 의복, 옷 deliver v. 배달하다 business day 영업일

122 구조/문법 • 부사 난이도 하

해석 공기업들은 절차를 더 편리하게 하기 위해 온라인 요금납부 서비스를 점점 더 많이 제공해오고 있다.

해설 빈칸은 현재완료 진행 동사구문(have been V-ing)의 사이에서 동사를 수식하는 부사자리이므로 (B)가 정답

어휘 utilities company (전기, 수도 등) 공익 기업 bill n. 청구서 convenient adj. 편리한

123 구조/문법+어휘 • 형용사 난이도 중

해석 Stowaway 보관센터는 임차인들이 전자 잠금장치로 인해 가끔 겪는 어려움에 대해 사과했다.

해설 빈칸은 명사 difficulties를 수식하는 자리. 문맥상 '전자 잠금장치로 인해 가끔씩 겪는 어려움'이라는 의미가 되어야 자연스러우므로 형용사 (D)가 정답

Key Point
명사 앞 자리에는 형용사, 형용사 역할을 하는 분사, 복합명사를 이루는 명사가 올 수 있으므로, 문맥을 통해 파악한다. 복합명사는 앞 명사가 뒤 명사의 용도나 목적을 나타낸다. 예를 들어 safety regulations는 '안전을 위한 규정'이란 의미이다. 참고로, 일반 형용사와 분사가 보기에 함께 있을 때, 일반 형용사의 정답 확률이 높다.

어휘 apologize v. 사과하다 renter n. 임차인, 대여하는 사람 locking system 잠금 장치

124 구조/문법+어휘 • 명사 난이도 중

해석 Dr. Rangit은 짧은 상담을 위해 목요일에 오후 1시부터 6시까지 사무실에 있을 것이다.

해설 빈칸은 전치사 for의 목적어인 명사자리. 문맥상 '상담을 위해 사무실에 있을 것'이라는 의미가 되어야 자연스러우므로 (D)가 정답

Key Point
명사 consulting vs. consultant vs. consultations: consulting은 '자문(업)'을, consultant는 '상담사(사람)'를, consultation은 '상담, 협의, 참조'를 의미한다.

125 어휘 • 형용사 난이도 중

해석 최근 고무업계의 불확실성에도 불구하고, 자동차 타이어에 대한 수요는 꽤 안정적으로 유지되었다.

해설 빈칸은 주어 demand에 대한 주격보어자리. 문두의 in spite of 전치사구의 내용을 고려할 때, 문맥상 '고무업계의 불확실성에도 불구하고, 타이어에 대한 수요는 안정적인 편'이라는 의미가 되어야 자연스러우므로 (C)가 정답

Key word
In spite of recent **uncertainty** in the rubber industry, **demand** for vehicle **tires has remained** fairly **stable**.

오답보기 확인
(A) unpredictable 예측할 수 없는

(B) complacent 현실에 안주하는
(D) strict 엄격한

어휘 uncertainty n. 불확실성 rubber n. 고무 demand n. 수요, 요구 vehicle n. 차량 stable adj. 안정적인

126 구조/문법・동사 - 3인칭 단수 능동태 　난이도 중

해석 Feder사의 새 가전제품군의 시연은 기술 박람회에서 많은 관심을 불러일으켰다.

해설 동사가 없는 문장으로, 빈칸은 동사자리이므로 (B) 탈락. 주어가 3인칭 단수명사 expansion이므로 (A)는 수일치에서 탈락. 뒤에 목적어가 있어 능동태 동사가 와야 하므로 수동태 (C) 탈락. 따라서 (D)가 정답

어휘 demonstration n. 시연 consumer electronics 가전제품 line n. 제품군 attention n. 주목, 관심 technology expo 기술 박람회

127 구조/문법・명사 　난이도 중

해석 Duratek 노트북 Titanium 시리즈는 2미터 높이에서 떨어뜨려도 기능을 잃지 않는다.

해설 빈칸은 동명사 losing의 목적어인 명사자리이므로 (D)가 정답

> **Key Point**
> 타동사의 동명사는 목적어를 필요로 한다.

어휘 drop v. 떨어뜨리다 lose v. 잃다

128 구조/문법+어휘・등위접속사 　난이도 상

해석 판촉행사 이후에 판매량이 급증해서, 매장 관리자는 특가 상품을 더 제공하는 방안을 고려할 것이다.

해설 빈칸은 완전한 두 개의 문장을 연결하는 접속사자리. 문맥상 두 문장이 '판매가 급증해서 특가상품 제공을 더 고려할 것'이라는 인과 관계로 이어져야 자연스러우므로 (D)가 정답

어휘 soar v. 급증[급등]하다 promotional adj. 홍보[판촉]의 consider v. 고려하다 special deal 특가 상품

129 어휘・부사 　난이도 상

해석 주차장은 독립적으로 소유 및 운영되고 있으나, 컨벤션 방문객들은 그 공간을 이용할 수 있는 티켓을 받는다.

해설 빈칸은 동사를 수식하는 부사자리. 접속사 but으로 연결된 두 문장관계를 고려할 때, '주차장은 독립 운영되고 있지만 방문객은 이용권을 받는다'는 의미가 되어야 자연스러우므로 (A)가 정답

> **Key word**
> The parking garage is owned and regulated **independently**, **but** convention **visitors receive tickets to use** the space.

> **오답보기 확인**
> (B) unintentionally 고의 아니게, 무심코
> (C) steadily 착실하게, 꾸준히
> (D) automatically 자동적으로

어휘 own v. 소유하다 regulate v. 규제[통제]하다, 조절하다 independently adj. 독립적으로

130 구조/문법・동사 　난이도 중

해석 접수 담당자가 막 퇴근하려고 할 때 사무용품 배송품이 도착했다.

해설 빈칸은 as 종속절 내 주어 뒤 동사자리. 주절의 시제가 과거이므로 종속절은 보기 중 과거진행 시제 (C)가 정답

> **Key Point**
> 종속절의 시제는 주절의 시제보다 미래가 될 수 없다.

어휘 package n. 소포 office supplies 사무용품 receptionist n. 접수담당자

PART 6 P. 205

131-134번은 다음 메모에 관한 문제입니다.

수신: drivers@canberratransport.gov.au
발신: Harold Strahan
제목: 차량 평가
날짜: 5월 7일

운전사 여러분,

지난 주 말씀 드린 것처럼, 시장실에서 나온 대표단이 저희 버스에 대해 평가를 **131.** 실시할 예정입니다. 그들은 내년에 **132.** 어떤 장거리버스와 운송용 화물차가 교체되어야 하는지 결정할 계획입니다.

이 **133.** 문제에 대해 저희를 도와주시면, 도움이 될 것입니다. 시간 있으실 때, 차량을 운행하면서 지속적으로 발생했던 문제들을 저희에게 알려주세요. 이 정보를 관리팀에 mgmt@canberratransport.gov.au으로 이메일을 보내주세요. **134.** 정확한 기술적 설명은 필요하지 않습니다. 저희는 단지 차량 등록번호, 모델연도, 문제에 대한 간략한 요약만 있으면 됩니다.

여러분의 헌신에 항상 감사 드립니다.

어휘 vehicle n. 차량 assessment n. 평가 mention v. 언급하다 representative n. 대표자, 대리인 mayor n. 시장 bus fleet (한 기관이 소유한) 전체 버스 determine v. 결정하다 motor coach (장거리) 버스 transport n. 운송, 수송 van n. 화물차, 밴 replace v. 교체하다 assist v. 돕다, 지원하다 inform v. 알리다 persistently adv. 끊임없이, 지속적으로 occur v. 발생하다 operate v. (기계를) 가동[조작]하다 management n. 관리, 운영 registration n. 등록 summary n. 요약 issue n. 문제 dedication n. 헌신

131 구조/문법+문맥이해・동사 　난이도 중

해설 빈칸은 주어 representatives와 목적어 an assessment 사이 동사자리. 빈칸 뒷 문장의 '그들이 정할 계획이다'라는 내용을 고려할 때, 문맥상 '평가를 실시할 예정'이라는 의미를 완성하는 미래시제 (D)가 정답

> **Key word**
> As I mentioned last week, **representatives** from the mayor's office **will be administering** an assessment of our bus fleet. **They plan** to determine...

> **Key point**
> 미래진행시제(will be V-ing)는 '미래의 어느 시점에 진행될 일'을, 미래완료시제(will have p.p.)는 '과거 또는 현재에 시작된 일이 미래의 어느 시점까지 계속되어 완료되는 일'을 가리킬 때 사용된다.

132 구조/문법 • 명사절 접속사　　　난이도 중

해설　빈칸은 동사와 완전한 문장 사이의 자리. 동사 determine은 목적어를 필요로 하는 타동사이므로, 빈칸은 뒤에 나오는 문장을 명사절로 만들어 줄 접속사자리. 빈칸 뒤 문장이 목적어가 필요 없는 수동태임을 고려할 때, '어떤 버스 및 운송용 화물차가 교체되어야 하는지를 결정할 계획'이라는 내용이 되어야 문맥상 자연스러우므로 의문형용사 (D)가 정답

Key point
의문형용사(what, which, whose)는 '의문사+주어+동사~'의 형태로, 명사절을 이끄는 접속사 역할을 할 수 있다.

133 어휘+문맥이해 • 명사　　　난이도 중

해설　빈칸은 this의 수식을 받는 명사자리. this가 가리키는 내용을 앞 단락에서 찾으면, '시장실에서 방문해 교체가 필요한 차량을 살펴보는 것'이므로, 문맥상 '이 문제에 도움을 달라'는 의미가 되어야 자연스러우므로 (C)가 정답

Key word
As I mentioned last week, **representatives from the mayor's office will be administering an assessment of our bus fleet. They plan to determine which motor coaches and transport vans should be replaced in the coming year.**
It would be **helpful if you assist us in this matter.** When you have time, inform us of any problems that have persistently occurred when operating your vehicle.

134 문맥이해 • 문장삽입　　　난이도 중

해석　(A) 저희는 보고된 피해 수준에 깜짝 놀랐습니다.
(B) 정확한 기술적 설명은 필요하지 않습니다.
(C) 수리는 가능한 한 빨리 실시될 것입니다.
(D) 당신이 추천한 사람이 고용되면, 100달러의 보너스를 받게 됩니다.

해설　빈칸 앞 문장의 '정보를 이메일로 보내달라'는 내용과 빈칸 뒷 문장의 '차량등록번호, 모델연도, 문제에 대한 간략한 요약만 있으면 된다'는 내용을 고려할 때, 문맥상 '정확한 기술적 설명은 필요 없다'는 내용이 들어가야 자연스러우므로 (B)가 정답

Key word
Please send this information to the management team via e-mail at mgmt@canberratransport.gov.au. **An exact technical explanation is not necessary.** We need only the vehicle's registration number, model year, and a short summary of the issue.

135-138번은 다음 이메일에 관한 문제입니다.

발신: Curtis Branson <branson@edental.com>
수신: Dominic Powell <dpowell@iu.edu>
제목: 환자 알림 서비스
날짜: 10월 27일

Mr. Powell께,

최대한 효율적이고 편리하게 환자분들을 135. 모시려는 바람으로, 저희는 휴대폰 앱을 이용하여 알림과 공지를 받아보실 수 있는 혜택을 제공하기 시작했습니다. 현재 저희는 이메일 주소로 귀하께 최신정보를 보내드리고 있습니다. 136. 이 방식에 만족하신다면, 그 어떤 변경도 없을 것입니

다. 귀하께서 앱을 사용해보고 싶거나, 저희가 드리는 알림 서비스의 137. 선택사항들에 대해 의의하고 싶으시면, 858-555-1212번으로 전화해 주시기 바랍니다.

138. 저희의 목표는 환자분들께 치과치료와 관련된 모든 것에 관한 시기적절하고 유용한 정보를 제공하고 항상 최상의 치료 경험을 받도록 보장해 드리는 것입니다.

Curtis Branson
사무장
Lenexa Elite 치과

어휘　alert n. 경고, 경계　efficiently adv. 효율적으로　conveniently adv. 편리하게　offer v. 제공하다　opportunity n. 기회　notification n. 알림, 통지　reminder n. 상기시켜주는 것　currently adv. 현재　aim n. 목적　timely adj. 시기 적절한　aspect n. 측면　dental adj. 치과의　ensure v. 보장하다　optimal adj. 최선의, 최적의

135 어휘 • 동사　　　난이도 중

해설　빈칸은 our patients를 목적어로 취하는 동명사 자리. 문맥상 '환자들에게 가능한 한 효율적이고도 편리하게 서비스를 제공하려는 바람으로'라는 내용이 되어야 자연스러우므로 (B) 가 정답

Key word
In hopes of **serving** our patients as efficiently and conveniently as possible, we have started offering the opportunity to receive notifications and reminders by using a mobile application.

136 문맥이해 • 문장삽입　　　난이도 중

해석　(A) 저희는 저희 병원이 이 지역에서 최고라고 믿습니다.
(B) 적어도 일년에 한 번 방문 일정을 잡는 것을 기억하십시오.
(C) 이메일 알림 서비스는 작년에 처음 시작됐습니다.
(D) 이 방식에 만족하신다면, 그 어떤 변경도 없을 것입니다.

해설　빈칸 앞 부분의 '신규 앱 알림 서비스를 시작했는데, 현재는 이메일로 최신정보를 알려준다'는 내용을 고려할 때, 문맥상 '현재 방식에 만족하면 변경되지 않을 것'이라는 내용이 이어져야 자연스러우므로 (D)가 정답

Key word
we have started offering the opportunity to receive notifications and reminders by using a mobile application. Currently, we send you updates to your e-mail address. **No changes will be made if you are satisfied with this arrangement.**

137 구조/문법 • 명사　　　난이도 하

해설　빈칸은 소유격 대명사 your의 수식을 받는 명사자리이므로 (B)가 정답

138 문맥이해 • 인칭대명사　　　난이도 중

해설　빈칸은 문장의 주어 aim을 수식하는 자리. 이메일에서 서비스를 제공하는 병원을 We로 지칭하고 있으므로, 문맥상 '저희의 목표는 환자에게 유용한 정보를 제공하는 것'이라는 의미가 되어야 자연스러우므로 (C)가 정답

Key word
In hopes of **serving our patients** as efficiently and conveniently as possible, **we have started offering** the opportunity to receive notifications and reminders by using a mobile application. Currently, **we send you** updates to your e-mail address. No changes will be made if you are satisfied with this arrangement. If you would like to try using the app or wish to discuss your options for notifications **from us**, please give us a call at 858-555-1212.
Our aim is to provide patients with timely and helpful information

Key word
I would like to **inquire about the engineering manager opening** recently posted on your Web site. I am confident that I would be **a valuable addition to** Milltek Systems' engineering **team** as a supervisor.

139-142번은 다음 편지에 관한 문제입니다.

7월 16일

Derek Hunter
인사부
Milltek Systems, Inc.

Mr. Hunter께,

최근 귀하의 웹 사이트에 올라온 엔지니어 매니저 직무에 관해 문의 드리고 싶습니다. 저는 Milltek Systems의 엔지니어링 **139. 팀** 관리자로 귀중한 인재가 될 것이라 자신합니다.

140. 저는 관련 분야에서 수 년의 경험을 가지고 있습니다. 현재는 Tappco Machinery에서 프로젝트 매니저로 근무하고 있는데, 거의 10년 간 농업 및 산업 분류 기계류를 설계해왔습니다. 이 **141. 전**에는 AgroTec Engineering에서 근무했었는데, 그곳에서 제분 및 제빵 애플리케이션을 위한 전산화 과정을 개발했습니다.

제 이력서를 첨부해 드리며, 이력서에는 제 경력과 자격증들에 대한 더 많은 정보가 **142. 담겨** 있습니다. 이 내용이 귀사와 잘 맞는다고 생각하신다면, 만나뵙고 더 심도있게 이야기를 나누고 싶습니다.

Best Regards,

Edwin Dearing
동봉물재중

어휘 inquire v. 문의하다 opening n. 공석 recently adv. 최근 post v. 게시하다 confident adj. 자신 있는, 확신하는 valuable adj. 귀중한 addition n. 부가물 engineering n. 공학 supervisor n. 관리자, 감독관 presently adv. 현재 employ v. 고용하다 design v. 설계하다, 고안하다 agricultural adj. 농업의 industrial adj. 산업의 sort v. 분류하다 machinery n. 기계(류) nearly adv. 거의 decade n. 10년 develop v. 개발하다 computerize v. 전산화하다 mill v. 으깨다 application n. 애플리케이션, 응용 장치 attach v. 첨부하다 CV(curriculum vitae) 이력서 qualification n. 자격, 자질 match n. 잘 어울리는 것 organization n. 조직, 기관 further adv. 더 enclosure n. 동봉된 것

139 어휘+문맥이해 • 명사   난이도 하

해설　빈칸은 'Milltek Systems' engineering'의 수식을 받는 명사자리. 빈칸 앞 문장의 '엔지니어링 매니저 직무에 관해 문의하고 싶다'는 내용을 고려할 때, '엔지니어링팀의 관리자로서'라는 의미가 되어야 자연스러우므로 (D)가 정답

140 문맥이해 • 문장삽입   난이도 중

해석　(A) 저는 관련 분야에서 수 년의 경험을 가지고 있습니다.
(B) 당신은 이 직무에 공학 학위가 필수라고 하셨습니다.
(C) 저의 예전 직장동료들로부터 이메일 몇 통을 받으셨을 겁니다.
(D) 좀 더 적합한 자리가 생기면 저에게 알려주세요.

해설　빈칸 뒷 문장들에서 현 직장 및 전 직장에서 맡은 업무를 구체적으로 설명하고 있으므로, 문맥상 '관련 업계에 경력이 많다'는 내용이 들어가야 자연스러우므로 (A)가 정답

Key word
I have many years of experience in relevant industries. I am presently employed as a project manager at Tappco Machinery, where I have designed agricultural and industrial sorting machinery for nearly a decade. 137. ------ to this, **I worked at AgroTec Engineering, where I developed computerized processes for milling and baking applications.**

141 어휘+문맥이해 • 구전치사   난이도 중

해설　빈칸은 전치사 to와 함께 구전치사를 완성하는 자리. 빈칸 앞 문장에서는 현 직장에서의 담당 업무를, 빈칸 뒷 부분에서는 전 직장에서 맡았던 업무를 설명하고 있음을 고려할 때, 두 문장 사이에는 '이 곳(현 직장) 이전에는'이라는 전치사구가 들어가야 연결이 자연스러우므로 시간 전치사구 'prior to(~이전에는)'를 완성하는 (B)가 정답

Key word
I am presently employed as a project manager at Tappco Machinery, where I have designed agricultural and industrial sorting machinery for nearly a decade. **Prior to this, I worked at AgroTec Engineering,**

142 구조/문법 • 동사   난이도 중

해설　빈칸은 which 주격 관계절 내 동사자리. 선행사가 3인칭 단수형 명사구 'a copy of my CV'이며, 관계절에서 첨부된 이력서의 특징에 대한 부가설명을 제공하고 있으므로 현재시제 (B)가 정답

Key point
관계대명사의 계속적 용법:
「선행사+콤마(,)+관계대명사」의 형태로 「접속사+대명사」의 의미로 해석하며, 선행사에 대한 정보를 추가할 때 사용된다.

143-146번은 다음 기사에 관한 문제입니다.

Yuccaville (8월 9일) – 옥상에 나란히 줄지어있는 태양 전지판들은 Yuccaville이 재생 가능한 에너지에 관심을 가지고 있다는 사실을 증명한다. 사실, 오늘날 Yuccaville에서 생산되는 전력의 5%는 태양열에서 비롯되고, 그 수치는 **143. 꾸준한** 속도로 증가하고 있다. 이는 어느 정도 태양열 전지판 소유주들에게 주어지는, 마을의 상당한 세금 **144. 감면** 때문이다. Yuccaville Renewable Energy Solutions의 CEO인 Brian Alvarez에 따르면, 보다 효율적인 배터리와 설치가 용이한 판 **145. 또한** 이 기술을 더 매력적으로 만들어주었다. Mr. Alvarez는 Yuccaville에 있는 태양 전지판

의 수는 미래에 엄청나게 증가할 것으로 예상한다. ¹⁴⁶·사실, 그는 10년 내 거의 모든 건물들이 태양 전지판을 보유하게 될 것이라고 믿는다.

어휘 row n. 열, 줄 rooftop n. 옥상 solar panel 태양 전지판 attest v. 증명하다 renewable adj. 재생 가능한 generate v. 발생시키다 rate n. 속도 degree n. 정도 significant adj. 중요한, 상당한 tax n. 세금 grant v. 주다, 수여하다 owner n. 소유주 efficient adj. 효율적인 easy-to-install adj. 설치하기 쉬운 technology n. 과학기술 attractive adj. 매력적인 anticipate v. 예측하다 dramatically adv. 극적으로

143 어휘 + 문맥이해 · 형용사   난이도 중

해설 빈칸 앞 부분의 '재생 가능한 에너지에 관심을 가지고 있다'는 내용을 고려할 때, 문맥상 태양열로 생산되는 전력의 비중이 꾸준한 속도로 증가하고 있다'는 내용으로 이어져야 자연스러우므로 (C)가 정답

Key word
the fact that Yuccaville has taken an interest in renewable energy. In fact, 5 percent of the power generated in the Yuccaville comes from solar energy these days, and that number is rising at a steady rate.

144 구조 / 문법 · 명사   난이도 중

해설 빈칸은 because of 전치사구의 목적어인 명사자리이므로, 빈칸 앞 명사 tax와 함께 복합명사를 완성하는 명사 (D)가 정답

Key word
To a certain degree, this is because of the town's significant tax reduction granted to solar panel owners.

145 어휘 + 문맥이해 · 부사   난이도 중

해설 빈칸은 현재완료 동사구조 have p.p. 사이에 위치하여 동사를 수식하는 부사자리. 빈칸 앞 부분의 '태양열 에너지 비중이 증가하는 데에는 세금 감면의 이유가 있다'는 내용을 고려할 때, '효율적인 배터리와 설치가 용이한 판 또한 (태양열) 기술을 더 매력적인 것으로 만들어준다'는 첨가 내용으로 이어져야 자연스러우므로 (C)가 정답

Key word
In fact, 5 percent of the power generated in the Yuccaville comes from solar energy these days, and that number is rising at a steady rate. To a certain degree, this is because of the town's significant tax reduction granted to solar panel owners. According to Brian Alvarez, CEO of Yuccaville Renewable Energy Solutions, more efficient batteries and easy-to-install panels have also made the technology more attractive.

146 문맥이해 · 문장삽입   난이도 중

해석 (A) 사실, 그는 10년 내 거의 모든 건물들이 태양 전지판을 보유하게 될 것이라고 믿는다.
(B) 그는 이것이 Yuccaville에서 장사를 시작하려는 업체들이 점점 더 줄어드는 이유 중 하나라고 생각한다.
(C) 그는 증가된 비용이 판매에 어떤 영향을 미칠지에 관해 염려한다.
(D) 게다가, 그는 작년에 구입한 전지판의 품질에 매우 만족해왔다.

해설 빈칸 앞 문장의 '태양 전지판의 수가 증가할 것'이라는 내용을 고려할 때, 문맥상 '10년 내 거의 모든 건물들에 태양 전지판이 설치되어 있을 것'이라는 내용으로 이어져야 자연스러우므로 (A)가 정답

Key word
Mr. Alvarez anticipates that the number of solar panels in Yuccaville will increase dramatically in the future. As a matter of fact, he believes that within a decade, almost all buildings will have solar panels.

PART 7 P. 209

147-148번은 다음 쿠폰에 관한 문제입니다.

> **Luigi Angelo's**
>
> Luigi Angelo's는 Chester 공원 지점의 리모델링이 이제 완료되었음을 알려드리게 되어 기쁩니다. 다시 문을 열어 여러분을 맞이하오니 Yosemite가 196번지로 방문해 주세요. 3월 3일에서 9일 사이에 아무 때나 이 쿠폰을 가져오시면⁽¹⁴⁸⁾ 일반 음료와 수제 파스타 요리 중 하나⁽¹⁴⁷⁾ 주문 시 가든 샐러드를 무료로 드실 수 있습니다. 데이블당 한 장의 쿠폰만 사용하실 수 있습니다.

어휘 voucher n. 상품권, 쿠폰 announce v. 알리다, 발표하다 location n. 장소, 위치 complete adj. 완료된 reopen v. 다시 문을 열다 complimentary adj. 무료의 fountain drink (식당) 기계에서 나오는 음료 homemade adj. 수제의 dish n. 요리 limit v. 제한[한정]하다 per prep. ~당

147 사실확인   난이도 중

해석 Luigi Angelo's에 관하여 사실인 것은?
(A) 채소밭이 있다.
(B) 3월에 새 지점을 열 것이다.
(C) 직접 파스타를 만든다.
(D) 최근에 제공 메뉴를 확장했다.

해설 네 번째 줄에서 one of our homemade pasta dishes.(수제 파스타 요리 중 하나)라고 했으므로 (C)가 정답

148 암시 / 추론   난이도 중

해석 쿠폰에 관하여 알 수 있는 것은?
(A) 배달 주문에 적용할 수 있다.
(B) Luigi Angelo's 전 지점에서 사용할 수 있다.
(C) 손님들이 그것으로 무료 음료를 받을 수 있다.
(D) 일주일 동안만 유효하다.

해설 세 번째 줄에서 Bring this voucher anytime between March 3 and March 10(3월 3일에서 9일 사이에 아무 때나 이 쿠폰을 가져오시면)이라고 했으므로 (D)가 정답

149-150번은 다음 웹 페이지에 관한 문제입니다.

> www.kilkennyperformingartscentre.ie
>
> <Street Wildlife> 공개오디션
> Kilkenny 음악원

204

저희는 Saoirse Kilpatrick이 연출하는 **클래식 뮤지컬 <Street Wildlife>**[150]의 코러스에서 노래할 재능 있는 지역 청년들(12세에서 16세 사이)을 찾고 있습니다.[149]

공연 일정:
Waterford의 Avalon 극장, 10월 12-18일[150]

예선:
3가지 옵션 중에 선택할 수 있습니다: 2월 25, 26, 그리고 28일 오후 4-6시, Church가 174번지 Kilkenny 음악원 스튜디오. 최고의 참가자들을 위한 콜백 오디션은 3월 2일 토요일에 있을 것입니다. 다과가 제공됩니다. "Streetlight People (반복부분)"를 부를 준비를 해주세요.

지원:
kmurphy@kilkennyconservatory.ie로 Keira Murphy에게 오디션 가능한 날짜(들)과 사진을 보내주세요.[149]

어휘 open adj. 공개되어 있는 audition n. 오디션 conservatory n. 음악학교 talented adj. 재능 있는 local adj. 지역의 youth n. 청년 chorus n. 코러스 production n. 제작 classic musical 클래식 뮤지컬 direct v. 감독하다, 연출하다 performance n. 공연 schedule n. 일정 tryout n. 예선 studio n. 연습실, 작업실 callback n. (면접 등을 위한) 통보, 회신 전화 refreshment n. 다과 perform v. 연주하다 reprise n. (음악에서) 반복 부분 application n. 지원 available adj. 시간이 있는

149 상세정보 난이도 중

해석 웹 페이지에 따르면, 누가 Ms. Murphy에게 연락해야 하는가?
(A) 가수
(B) 모델
(C) 감독
(D) 예술가

해설 첫 번째 단락에서 We are looking for talented local youths (from ages 12 to 16) to sing in the chorus(코러스에서 노래할 재능 있는 지역 청년들(12세에서 16세 사이)을 찾고 있습니다.)라고 했는데, 네 번째 단락에서 Send a photo and the date(s) you are available to audition to Keira Murphy(Keira Murphy에게 오디션 가능한 날짜(들)과 사진을 보내주세요.)라고 했으므로 (A)가 정답

150 암시/추론 난이도 중

해석 <Street Wildlife>에 관하여 알 수 있는 것은?
(A) Ms. Kilpatrick이 썼다.
(B) 원래 Waterford에서 공연되었다.
(C) 10월에 공연될 것이다.
(D) 3회 공연될 것이다.

해설 첫 번째 단락에서 our production of the classic musical Street Wildlife(클래식 뮤지컬 <Street Wildlife>)라고 하면서, 두 번째 단락에서 Performance Schedule: Avalon Theatre in Waterford, 12-18 October(공연 일정: Waterford의 Avalon 극장, 10월 12-18일)라고 하여 <Street Wildlife>가 10월에 공연 예정임을 알 수 있으므로 (C)가 정답

151-152번은 다음 문자메시지 대화에 관한 문제입니다.

(오전 11시 12분) Michelle Pouncey
저기, Neusha, 점심 회의하러 출발했나요?

(오전 11시 13분) Neusha Mansoori
아직이요. 몇 가지 일을 마무리 지어야 해서요. 무슨 일 있어요?

(오전 11시 15분) Michelle Pouncey
사무실 나서기 전에 보험증서 챙기는걸 깜박했어요.[151] 저 대신 그 서류들 좀 챙겨줄 수 있으세요?

(오전 11시 16분) Neusha Mansoori
그럼요. 그게 어디에 있는지 아세요?

(오전 11시 18분) Michelle Pouncey
제 테이블 위 폴더 안에 있을 거예요.[152]

(오전 11시 20분) Neusha Mansoori
테이블에 폴더가 여러 개 있네요.[152]

(오전 11시 21분) Michelle Pouncey
오, 맞아요! 초록색 폴더예요.[152] 제일 위에 있는 걸 거예요.

(오전 11시 24분) Neusha Mansoori
찾았어요! 다른 필요한 거 있으세요?

(오전 11시 27분) Michelle Pouncey
없어요. 그게 다예요. 곧 만나요!

어휘 leave v. 떠나다, 출발하다 finish up 마무리 짓다 grab v. 붙잡다 insurance paper 보험증서 folder n. 폴더

151 상세정보 난이도 중

해석 Ms. Pouncey는 어떤 문제를 언급하는가?
(A) 그녀는 위치를 찾는데 도움이 필요하다.
(B) 그녀는 어떤 문서를 가져오지 않았다.
(C) 그녀는 회의에 늦는다.
(D) 그녀는 보험료를 지불하는 것을 깜박했다.

해설 오전 11시 15분, Michelle Pouncey의 메시지에서 I forgot to grab the insurance papers before I left the office.(사무실 나서기 전에 보험증서 챙기는걸 깜박했어요.)라고 했으므로 (B)가 정답

Paraphrasing grab ➡ bring, papers ➡ documents

152 화자 의도 파악 난이도 중

해석 오전 11시 20분에, Ms. Mansoori가 "테이블에 폴더가 여러 개 있네요"라고 할 때 무엇을 의미하겠는가?
(A) 그녀는 추가 정보를 필요로 한다.
(B) 그녀는 사무용품을 좀 더 주문해야 한다.
(C) Ms. Pouncey는 더 큰 테이블이 필요하다.
(D) Ms. Pouncey는 그녀의 업무공간을 정리해야 한다.

해설 오전 11시 18분 ~ 11시 21분 대화에서 Michelle Pouncey가 They should be in a folder on my table.(제 테이블 위 폴더 안에 있을 거예요.)라고 한 말에, Neusha Mansoori가 You have a few folders on the table.(테이블에 폴더가 여러 개 있네요.)라고 하자, Michelle

Pouncey가 다시 Oh, right! It's the green one.(오, 맞아요! 초록색 폴더에요.)라고 했으므로 (A)가 정답

153-154번은 다음 이메일에 관한 문제입니다.

수신: Maureen Wakehouse
발신: Brad Splitter
제목: 베를린 기술회담
날짜: 5월 14일
첨부: Wakehouse_docs

Ms. Wakehouse께,

이 이메일은 귀하가 올해 베를린 기술 회담(BTS)의 초청 명단에 포함되셨음을 알려드리기 위함입니다. 첨부파일에서 숙박정보 및 영수증을 찾아보실 수 있습니다.⁽¹⁵³⁾ 귀하는 또한 행사 마지막 날 열리는 저녁 축하연도 신청하셨습니다. 저희는 귀하께 첨부문서에 들어있는 선호 식사 양식을 작성하셔서 5월 30일 전까지 이메일로 보내주시길 요청 드립니다.⁽¹⁵⁴⁾ 제출하시면 선택을 변경할 수 없다는 것을 유념해주시기 바랍니다. 귀하가 참석하길 기대하고 있겠습니다.

염려되는 점이 있으시면, 언제든 저에게 연락 주십시오.

Sincerely,

Brad Splitter
행사 주최자
베를린 기술 회담

어휘 summit n. 정상회담 successfully adv. 성공적으로 lodging n. 숙소 attached adj. 첨부된 sign up 등록하다 gala n. 축하행사 request v. 요청하다 fill out 작성하다 meal n. 식사 preference n. 선호 form n. 서식, 유형 locate v. (특정 위치에) 두다 document n. 문서 aware adj. 의식하고 있는 submit v. 제출하다 look forward to 고대하다, 기대하다 attendance n. 참석 contact v. 연락하다 concern n. 걱정, 염려

153 주제/목적/대상   난이도 중

해석 Mr. Splitter는 왜 이메일을 보냈는가?
(A) Ms. Wakehouse에게 일정 변경을 알리려고
(B) BTS의 업적을 강조하려고
(C) 등록을 확인시켜 주려고
(D) 호텔을 추천하려고

해설 첫 번째 단락에서 This e-mail is to let you know that you have been successfully added to the guest list for this year's Berlin Tech Summit (BTS). You'll find your receipt, as well as lodging information, in the attached files.(이 이메일은 귀하가 올해 베를린 기술 회담(BTS)의 초청 명단에 포함되셨음을 알려드리기 위함입니다. 첨부파일에서 숙박정보 및 영수증을 찾아보실 수 있습니다.)라고 했으므로 (C)가 정답

154 상세정보   난이도 중

해석 Ms. Wakehouse는 무엇을 하라고 권장 받는가?
(A) 연락정보를 업데이트하라고
(B) 특정 날짜까지 답변을 보내달라고

(C) 저녁파티에 일찍 도착하라고
(D) 지도를 출력하라고

해설 첫 번째 단락에서 We request that you fill out the meal preference form located in the attached documents and email it to us no later than May 30.(저희는 귀하께 첨부문서에 들어있는 선호 식사 양식을 작성하셔서 5월 30일 전까지 이메일로 보내주시길 요청 드립니다.)라고 했으므로 (B)가 정답

155-157번은 다음 양식에 관한 문제입니다.

계약 청구서
PABLO'S 전문 간판 서비스 (PPSS)

전화: 613-555-7899
이메일: pablo@ppss.ca
홈페이지: http://www.ppss.ca

의뢰인: Raphael Boucher⁽¹⁵⁶⁾
작업 장소: 1350 Golden Line Road, Ottawa, Ontario⁽¹⁵⁶⁾
작업 유형: 상점 간판⁽¹⁵⁶⁾
설치 예정일: 8월 21일, 오전 11시⁽¹⁵⁷⁾
예상 완료 시간: 오후 4시⁽¹⁵⁷⁾

작업 및 서비스 내용	금액
주문제작 간판 설계 및 제작	499.99달러
간판 배송 및 설치	245.95달러
분기별 유지보수 방문⁽¹⁵⁵⁾	150.50달러

총액: 896.44달러
계약금 (8월 2일 수령): 300.00달러
잔액 (완공 시): 596.44달러⁽¹⁵⁷⁾

어휘 contractor n. 계약자 invoice n. 송장, 청구서 bill v. 청구서를 보내다 n. 청구서 work site 작업 장소 installation n. 설치 estimated adj. 견적의, 추측의 completion n. 완료, 완성 design v. 설계하다 create v. 만들다 custom adj. 주문 제작의 delivery n. 배송 quarterly adv. 분기별로 maintenance n. 유지보수 visit n. 방문 down payment 계약금 due adj. (돈을) 지불해야 하는

155 사실확인   난이도 중

해석 프로젝트에 관하여 언급된 것은?
(A) 이틀에 걸쳐 완료될 것이다.
(B) 정기적으로 서비스를 제공한다.
(C) 한 번에 전액 지불되었다.
(D) 특정 조명기구를 필요로 한다.

해설 표의 DESCRIPTION OF WORK AND SERVICES(작업 및 서비스 내용)의 마지막 항목에서 Quarterly maintenance visits(분기별 유지보수 방문)라고 하여 정기적으로 방문하여 서비스를 제공한다는 것을 알 수 있으므로 (B)가 정답

Paraphrasing quarterly ➡ periodically

156 상세정보   난이도 중

해석 프로젝트는 어디서 일어날 것인가?
(A) 스포츠 경기장에서

(B) 버스 정류장에서
(C) PPSS의 본사에서
(D) Mr. Boucher의 사업장에서

해설 청구서에서 BILL TO(의뢰인)이 Raphael Boucher이고, WORK SITE(작업 장소)가 1350 Golden Line Road, Ottawa, Ontario, TYPE OF WORK(작업유형)이 Store Sign(상점간판)이라고 하여 Mr. Boucher의 사업장에서 프로젝트가 진행된다는 것을 알 수 있으므로 (D)가 정답

157 상세정보 난이도 중

해설 PPSS는 8월 21일에 얼마를 받을 것인가?
(A) 245.95달러
(B) 300.00달러
(C) 499.99달러
(D) 596.44달러

해설 청구서에서 SCHEDULED INSTALLATION DATE(설치 예정일)이 21 August, 11:00 A.M.(8월 21일, 오전 11시), ESTIMATED COMPLETION TIME(예상 완료 시간)이 4:00 P.M.(오후 4시)라고 하여 8월 21일 하루 만에 설치 완료 예정임을 알 수 있으며, 청구서 마지막 항목인 AMOUNT DUE(upon completion)(잔액(완공 시))이 $596.44(596.44달러)라고 하여 8월 21일에 설치완료 후 잔액을 수령할 예정임을 알 수 있으므로 (D)가 정답

158-160번은 다음 구인광고에 관한 문제입니다.

미술관 큐레이터 채용공고

직무
Montreal 국립 미술 고대 예술 파트에서 경력자를 찾고 있습니다. 큐레이터의 업무에는 방문객들을 교육하고 전시에 관해 알려주는 일뿐만 아니라 미술품 수집, 소장품 관리 및 전시가 포함됩니다.

자격조건
지원자는 박물관이나 갤러리에서 최소 2년의 근무경험이 있어야 합니다. **또한 성공적인 지원자는 프랑스어를 유창하게 구사합니다.**(158) 지원자는 또한 미술 또는 미술사 같은 전공으로 학사 학위나 그에 준하는 자격을 갖춰야 합니다. **석사학위는 필수사항은 아니나, 추가 이점이 됩니다.**(159)

지원방법
지원서를 작성하시려면 웹 사이트 www.montrealart.com/jobs/ancientart를 방문해 주십시오.

연락
문의사항이 있거나 직무에 관해 더 자세히 알아보시려면, HR매니저에게 janlopez@montreal.com으로 이메일을 보내주시기 바랍니다.(160)

어휘 in need of ~을 필요로 하는 experienced adj. 경험 있는 individual n. 개인 ancient adj. 고대의 responsibility n. 책임, 맡은 일 curator n. 큐레이터 acquire v. 얻다, 획득하다 artifact n. 공예품, 인공물 display n. 전시, 진열 inform v. 알리다 exhibit n. 전시회, 전시품 qualification n. 자격조건 candidate n. 지원자 fluently adv. 유창하게 hold v. 보유하다 equivalent adj. 동등한 subject n. 주제, 과목 graduate degree 석사학위

158 상세정보 난이도 중

해설 그 직무에 필요한 자격조건은 무엇인가?
(A) 석사 학위
(B) 커뮤니케이션 능력
(C) 특정 언어에의 유창함
(D) 미술을 가르쳐본 경험

해설 두 번째 단락 [QUALIFICATIONS(자격조건)]에서 In addition, successful candidates will have the ability to speak French fluently.(또한, 성공적인 지원자는 프랑스어를 유창하게 구사합니다.)라고 했으므로 (C)가 정답

159 동의어 난이도 중

해설 두 번째 단락, 네 번째 줄의 단어 "bonus"와 의미상 가장 가까운 것은?
(A) 상
(B) 장점
(C) 수수료
(D) 보상금

해설 두 번째 단락 [QUALIFICATIONS(자격조건)]의 Although a graduate degree is not necessary, it is an added bonus.(석사학위는 필수사항은 아니나, 추가 이점이 됩니다.)에서 'bonus'는 '이점, 장점'이라는 의미로 쓰였으므로 보기 중 같은 의미를 갖는 (B)가 정답

160 상세정보 난이도 중

해설 직무에 대한 추가 정보는 어떻게 얻을 수 있는가?
(A) 직업박람회에 참석해서
(B) 직원에게 연락해서
(C) 박물관에 가서
(D) 홈페이지들 방문해서

해설 네 번째 단락 [CONTACT(연락)]에서 If you have any questions, or would like to learn more about the position, please email our HR manager at janlopez@montrealart.com.(문의사항이 있거나 직무에 관해 더 자세히 알아보시려면, HR매니저에게 janlopez@montrealart.com으로 이메일을 보내주시기 바랍니다.)라고 했으므로 (B)가 정답

161-163번은 다음 보도자료에 관한 문제입니다.

보도 자료
Leonard Osgard
홍보이사, Windermere Partners
losgard@windermerep.com

Marina (2월 15일) – **Windermere Partners는 자사 신규 쇼핑구역, Marina Square의 개장을 자랑스럽게 발표합니다.** —[1]—. 대부분의 점포가 판매되었지만, 10곳의 소매 점포가 아직 판매 중입니다.(161)

모든 소매 공간은 선반, 작업대, 그리고 파티션과 같은 추가 요소들을 추가할 옵션이 있어 여러분이 취향에 맞게 설계할 수 있도록 개방형 평면도로 제공됩니다. —[2]—. 또한, 모든 상점은 쇼핑센터에서 제공하는 무료 무선 인터넷과, 사업장을 밤낮으로 안전하게 지켜줄 보안순찰대, 그리고 현장 청소 및 유지보수 지원 혜택을 비롯해 기타 다른 편의 사항들을 누릴 수 있을 것입니다.(162)

Marina Square는 단순한 쇼핑센터 그 이상입니다. 훌륭한 복합 오락 공간이기도 합니다. —[3]—. 다수의 훌륭한 식사공간과 온 가족이 참여할 수 있는 다양한 액티비티를 갖춘 Marina Square는 도시 내 새로운 명소가 될 것입니다.

Marina Square에 들러서 부담 없이 한 번 둘러보세요. —[4]—. 개별 상담을 원하시면, 710-555-6214로 전화하셔서 상담예약을 하시기 바랍니다.(163)

어휘 proudly adv. 자랑스럽게 announce v. 발표하다 opening n. 개장 brand new adj. 완전히 새로운 commercial adj. 상업적인, 상업의 n. 광고 unit n. 구성 단위 retail space 소매점 for sale 판매중인 floor plan 평면도 design v. 설계하다 liking n. 좋아함, 취향 option n. 옵션, 선택사항 extra adj. 추가의 feature n. 특성, 특징 shelving n. 선반 countertop n. 작업대, 조리대 partition n. 파티션 take advantage of ~을 이용하다 security n. 보안, 경비 patrol n. 순찰(대) on-site adj. 현장의, 현지의 maintenance n. 유지보수 assistance n. 지원, 도움 convenience n. 편리 destination n. 목적지 multiple adj. 다수의 fine adj. 고급의, 질 높은 plenty n. 풍부한 양 hot spot 활기 넘치는 곳, 명소 consultation n. 상담 arrange v. 주선하다, 마련하다 appointment n. 약속

161 암시/추론 난이도 중

해석 Windermere Partners는 어떤 종류의 사업체이겠는가?
(A) 홍보 회사
(B) 건축 자재 제조사
(C) 사설 보안회사
(D) 상업 부동산 개발회사

해설 첫 번째 단락에서 Windermere Partners proudly announces the opening of its brand new shopping area, at Marina Square. Although many of the commercial units have been sold, 10 retail spaces are still up for sale.(Windermere Partners는 자사 신규 쇼핑구역, Marina Square의 개장을 자랑스럽게 발표합니다. 대부분의 점포가 판매되었지만, 10곳의 소매 점포가 아직 판매 중입니다.)라고 했으므로 (D)가 정답

162 사실확인 난이도 중

해석 소매 공간에 관하여 언급된 것은?
(A) 창고 공간을 포함한다.
(B) 몇몇 서비스를 이용 가능하다.
(C) 환경친화적으로 설계된다.
(D) 단기로 임대될 수 있다.

해설 두 번째 단락에서 In addition, all stores will be able to take advantage of the shopping center's free wireless Internet, security patrols to keep your business safe day and night, and on-site cleaning and maintenance assistance, along with many other conveniences.(또한, 모든 상점은 쇼핑센터에서 제공하는 무료 무선인터넷과, 사업장을 밤낮으로 안전하게 지켜줄 보안순찰대, 그리고 현장 청소 및 유지보수 지원 혜택을 비롯해 기타 다른 편의사항들을 누릴 수 있을 것입니다.)라고 했으므로 (B)가 정답

Paraphrasing take advantage of ➡ have access to

163 문장 삽입 난이도 중

해석 [1], [2], [3], [4]로 표시된 곳 중, 다음 문장이 들어갈 위치로 가장 적절한 것은?
"저희는 공개를 매일 오전 11시에 시작하여 오후 5시까지 합니다."
(A) [1]
(B) [2]
(C) [3]
(D) [4]

해설 네 번째 단락에서 Feel free to stop by Marina Square and have a look around.(Marina Square에 들러서 부담 없이 한 번 둘러보세요.)라고 했고, 이어 For an individual consultation, call 710-555-6214 to arrange an appointment.(개별 상담을 원하시면, 710-555-6214로 전화하셔서 상담예약을 하시기 바랍니다.)라고 하여 주어진 문장이 두 문장 사이에 들어가기 자연스러우므로 (D)가 정답

164-167번은 다음 온라인 채팅 대화문에 관한 문제입니다.

> **David Villa** [오후 1시 02분]
> 여러분. 부탁할 게 있어요. 제가 원래 오늘 야간근무인데, 몸 상태가 별로 좋지 않네요. 누구 저와 근무시간을 좀 바꿔주실 수 있을까요?
>
> **Allison Costello** [오후 1시 04분]
> 제가 바꿔드리고 싶은데, 호텔에 9시는 되어야 도착할 거예요.(164) Haverford 시내에서 7시에 저녁 약속이 있거든요. 제가 약간 늦게 근무를 시작하는 걸 Ms. Wahlberg가 괜찮다고 하신다면,(165) 제가 대신 할게요.
>
> **Lamar Jackson** [오후 1시 06분]
> David, 제가 도와드리고 싶은데, 새 영화 <Halfway There>의 저녁 상영 티켓을 이미 사놔서요. 누군가 다른 분이 도와드릴 수 있으면 좋겠네요.
>
> **David Villa** [오후 1시 08분]
> Allison, 그거 나쁘지 않은 생각인데요, Ms. Wahlberg가 거절하실까 봐 걱정되네요.(165) 안내 데스크에 항상 충분한 수의 직원이 있는 걸 정말 중요하게 생각하시거든요.
>
> **Allison Costello** [오후 1시 09분]
> 맞아요. David, Ms. Wahlberg에게 연락해서 지금 근무 중인 사람 중에 잠깐 더 일할 수 있는 사람이 있는지 알아보는 게 어때요?(166)
>
> **Jessica Choi** [오후 1시 12분]
> 모두 안녕하세요. 더 일찍 답변을 드렸어야 했는데, 너무 바빴어요. 제가 좀 더 있으면서 Allison이 올 때까지 기다릴게요.(166)/(167)
>
> **Allison Costello** [오후 1시 14분]
> 좋은 계획인 것 같아요. Ms. Wahlberg도 괜찮다고 하실 것 같나요?(166)
>
> **David Villa** [오후 1시 18분]
> 방금 그 분과 통화했어요. Ms. Walhberg도 전혀 상관없으시대요.(166) 모두 도와줘서 고마워요.
>
> **Allison Costello** [오후 1시 19분]
> 별 말씀을요. 이따 봐요, Jessica.

어휘 favor n. 부탁 shift n. 교대근무 (시간) feel well 건강 상태가 좋다 swap v. 맞바꾸다 make it to ~에 이르다 cover for ~대신 근무하다 showing n. 상영 reject v. 거부[거절]하다 at all times 항상 get off the phone 전화통화를 마치다 mind v. 상관하다, 개의하다 support n. 지원, 지지

164 상세정보 　　　　　　　　　　난이도 중

해석 작성자들은 어디에서 근무하는가?
(A) 극장
(B) 병원
(C) 식당
(D) 호텔

해설 오후 1시 04분, Allison Costello의 메시지에서 but I won't be able to make it to the hotel until 9.(호텔에 9시는 되어야 도착할 거예요.)라고 했으므로 (D)가 정답

165 암시/추론 　　　　　　　　　난이도 중

해석 모든 작성자들에 관해 무엇이 사실이겠는가?
(A) 같은 상사 밑에서 일한다.
(B) 함께 저녁을 먹을 것이다.
(C) 정기적으로 영화를 본다.
(D) 모두 Haverford에 산다.

해설 오후 1시 04분, Allison Costello의 메시지에서 If Ms. Wahlberg is fine with me starting the shift a bit later,(제가 약간 늦게 근무를 시작하는 걸 Ms. Wahlberg가 괜찮다고 하신다면,)이라고 했고, 오후 1시 08분, David Villa가 I'm worried Ms. Wahlberg would reject it.(Ms. Wahlberg가 거절하실까 봐 걱정되네요.)라고 하여 그들의 상사가 Ms. Wahlberg임을 알 수 있으므로 (A)가 정답

166 화자 의도 파악 　　　　　　　난이도 중

해석 오후 1시 18분에, Mr. Villa가 "Ms. Walhberg도 전혀 개의치 않으시대요"라고 할 때 무엇을 의미하는가?
(A) 계획이 맘에 들지 않는다.
(B) 그를 데리러 올 수 있다.
(C) 일주일 동안 그를 대신해 근무할 것이다.
(D) 일정 변경에 개의치 않는다.

해설 오후 1시 09분 ~ 1시 18분 대화에서 Allison Costello가 David, why don't you contact Ms. Wahlberg and check if someone who is already there can work a little longer?(David, Ms. Wahlberg에게 연락해서 지금 근무 중인 사람 중에 누군가가 잠깐 더 일할 수 있는지 알아보는 게 어떠세요?)라고 물었을 때 Jessica Choi가 I would've replied earlier, but we got really busy. I'll be happy to stay later and wait until Allison gets here.(더 일찍 답변을 드렸어야 했는데, 너무 바빴어요. 제가 좀 더 있으면서 Allison이 올 때까지 기다릴게요.)라고 하자, Allison Costello가 Do you think it will be OK with Ms. Wahlberg?(Ms. Wahlberg도 괜찮다고 하실 것 같나요?)라고 한 말에 David Villa가 Ms. Walhberg doesn't mind at all.(Ms. Walhberg도 전혀 개의치 않으시대요.)라고 대답한 것이므로 (D)가 정답

Paraphrasing doesn't mind ➡ is fine with

167 상세정보 　　　　　　　　　난이도 중

해석 오늘 저녁에 누가 원래 계획보다 늦게 근무를 마치겠는가?
(A) David Villa
(B) Lamar Jackson
(C) Allison Costello
(D) Jessica Choi

해설 오후 1시 12분, Jessica Choi의 메시지에서 I would've replied earlier, but we got really busy. I'll be happy to stay later and wait until Allison gets here.(더 일찍 답변을 드렸어야 했는데, 너무 바빴어요. 제가 좀 더 있으면서 Allison이 올 때까지 기다릴게요.)라고 했으므로 (D)가 정답

168-171번은 다음 이메일에 관한 문제입니다.

발신: n.sullivan@raiden.com
수신: Raiden 직원
제목: 파이프 건 진행상황
날짜: 11월 15일, 일요일
첨부: 워크샵 문서

모두 안녕하세요.

기술자가 손상된 수도관을 교체하는 작업이 계획보다 오래 걸려 화요일에도 건물을 이용할 수 없을 예정입니다.(168)/(169) 새로운 소식이 있는지 이 메일을 정기적으로 확인해주십시오. 또한 **여러분은 고객들과 정기적인 연락을 유지하고, 그 밖의 다른 업무들을 자택에서 처리하셔야 합니다.**(169)

반면, 저희는 화요일 워크숍을 다음주로 옮겨야 할 것입니다. **워크숍에서는 분기별 매출 및 수익에 대해 논의할 것입니다. 이와 관련된 자세한 내용은 이메일에 첨부된 문서에 있으니, 자세히 읽어주시기 바랍니다.**(170) 논의 후에는, 세탁기 및 건조기 신규 라인의 성공적인 출시를 축하하는 전사 차원의 저녁식사 자리가 있을 예정입니다.(171)

마지막으로, 저는 여러분 모두의 인내와 헌신에 감사 드립니다. 이번 수리가 예측하지 못한 어려움을 야기시켰다는 것을 잘 알고 있습니다만, 저는 우리가 그것을 잘 헤쳐나갈 것이라고 믿습니다.

Sincerely,

Nancy Sullivan
Raiden사

어휘 progress n. 진행, 진척 inaccessible adj. 접근할 수 없는 technician n. 기술자 replace v. 교체하다, 대신하다 damaged adj. 손상된, 하자가 생긴 water pipe 수도관 check v. 확인하다 regularly adv. 정기적으로 further adj. 더 이상의 require v. 요구하다 maintain v. 유지하다 regular adj. 정기적인 contact n. 연락 v. 연락을 취하다 take care of 처리하다 assignment n. 과제, 임무 move v. 옮기다 quarterly adv. 분기별로 sales n. 매출 earnings n. 수익, 소득 attach v. 첨부하다 detailed adj. 자세한 document n. 문서 regarding prep. ~에 관하여 afterwards adv. 나중에, 후에 company-wide adj. 회사 전반의 celebrate v. 축하하다 launch n. 개시, 출시 v. latest adj. 최신의 final adj. 마지막의 note n. 메모, 어조 patience n. 인내 dedication n. 헌신 repair n. 수리 cause v. 야기하다 unforeseen adj. 예측하지 못한 challenge n. 도전 confident adj. 자신 있는 get through ~를 끝내다, 완료하다

168 사실확인 　　　　　　　　　난이도 중

해석 수도관에 관하여 언급된 것은?
(A) 수리하는데 비용이 많이 든다
(B) 초반에 Ms. Sullivan이 점검했다
(C) 몇 주간 누수가 있었다
(D) 교체하는데 시간이 더 걸릴 것이다

해설 첫 번째 단락에서 The building will still be inaccessible on

Tuesday because it's taking technicians longer than expected to replace the damaged water pipes.(기술자가 손상된 수도관을 교체하는 작업이 예상보다 오래 걸려 화요일에도 건물을 이용할 수 없을 예정입니다.)라고 했으므로 (D)가 정답

Paraphrasing take longer than expected ➡ take more time

169 상세정보 　　　　　　　　　　　　　　난이도 중

해석　직원들은 화요일에 무엇을 할 예정인가?
(A) 다른 장소에서 근무할 것이다
(B) 몇몇 사업체를 방문할 것이다
(C) 휴가를 쓸 것이다
(D) 사무실에 늦게 올 것이다

해설　첫 번째 단락에서 The building will still be inaccessible on Tuesday because it's taking technicians longer than expected to replace the damaged water pipes.(기술자가 손상된 수도관을 교체하는 작업이 예상보다 오래 걸려 화요일에도 건물을 이용할 수 없을 예정입니다.)라고 하며, 이어 In addition, you are still required to maintain regular contact with your clients and take care of any other assignments while at home.(또한 여러분은 고객들과의 정기적인 연락을 유지하고, 그 밖의 다른 업무들을 자택에서 처리하셔야 합니다.)라고 하여 직원들이 화요일에 회사 건물이 아닌 다른 곳에서 업무를 할 것임을 알 수 있으므로 (A)가 정답

170 상세정보 　　　　　　　　　　　　　　난이도 중

해석　Nancy Sullivan은 이메일에 무엇을 첨부했는가?
(A) 저녁식사 메뉴
(B) 고객 연락 명단
(C) 행사일정 달력
(D) 재무 보고서

해설　두 번째 단락에서 During the workshop, we'll be discussing our quarterly sales and earnings. Attached to the e-mail, you'll find a detailed document regarding this, so please read it over carefully.(워크숍에서는 분기별 매출 및 수익에 대해 논의할 것입니다. 이와 관련된 자세한 내용은 이메일에 첨부된 문서에 있으니, 자세히 읽어주시기 바랍니다.)라고 했으므로 (D)가 정답

Paraphrasing attach to the e-mail ➡ include with the email, detailed document ➡ report

171 암시/추론 　　　　　　　　　　　　　　난이도 중

해석　Raiden사는 어떤 종류의 업체겠는가?
(A) 자산관리 회사
(B) 가전제품 제조사
(C) 수도배관회사
(D) 회계사무소

해설　두 번째 단락에서 Afterwards, we will be having a company-wide dinner to celebrate the successful launch of our latest line of washers and dryers.(논의 후에는, 세탁기 및 건조기 신규 라인의 성공적인 출시를 축하하는 전사차원의 저녁식사 자리가 있을 예정입니다.)라고 하여 Raiden사가 가전제품 제조사라는 것을 알 수 있으므로 (B)가 정답

Paraphrasing washers and dryers ➡ home appliance

172-175번은 다음 기사에 관한 문제입니다.

Sindri, Manitoba에 오다

(3월 19일)—개인 가전제품을 만드는 것으로 유명한 캐나다 생산업체 Sindri가 주요 생산 시설을 옮길 예정이다.(172) 내년 7월 신규 첨단공장이 Manitoba에 오픈하면 Quebec에서 이루어지는 생산 대부분이 중단될 것이다. —[1]—. 이전은 태블릿 PC를 포함해 Sindri의 다양한 새로운 모델들의 발표와 맞물려 있다.

"저희 최초 모델인 Sindri Book 노트북 컴퓨터는 7년 전 출시됐을 때 인기가 엄청났습니다.(173)"라고 회사 창립자이자 CEO인 Claude McCleod가 말했다. "저희가 3년 전 일체형 데스크탑 판매를 시작하면서 좀 더 휴대하기 좋은 것에 관심이 있다는 고객들의 피드백을 받았습니다."라고 덧붙였다. 기존 모델들 판매가 여전히 강세를 보이지만, McCleod는 새로운 태블릿이 새로운 고객층을 회사 제품으로 끌어들일 것이라고 확신한다.(175) —[2]—.

Sindri는 일반적인 비싼 가격표가 붙지 않은 고품질 상품을 내놓으며 두각을 나타냈다. —[3]—. Sindri는 적당한 가격대의 소비자 가전제품에 대한 수요가 증가하면서 성장했으며, 특히 개발도상국가들에서 강세를 보였다. 회사의 사내 여론조사에서는 고객들이 경쟁사대비 Sindri를 선택한 가장 큰 이유로 품질보증과 신뢰성에 대한 평판, 그리고 전 모델의 높은 가성비라고 보여준다.(174) —[4]—. 회사의 신규 상품라인에 대한 자세한 내용은 웹 사이트 sindri.com에서 확인할 수 있다.

어휘　**manufacturer** n. 제조사　**personal** adj. 개인의, 개인적인　**electronics** n. 전자제품　**production** n. 생산　**facility** n. 시설　**cease** v. 중지하다　**state-of-the-art** adj. 최신의　**plant** n. 공장　**relocation** n. 이전, 재배치　**coincide with** ~과 동시에 일어나다, ~과 일치하다　**announcement** n. 발표, 소식　**a range of** 다양한　**including** prep. ~를 포함해　**original** adj. 원래의　**laptop** n. 노트북　**tremendously** adv. 엄청나게, 대단히　**come out** 생산되다　**founder** n. 설립자　**all-in-one** adj. 일체형　**feedback** n. 피드백　**portable** adj. 휴대용의　**sale** n. 판매, 매출　**existing** adj. 기존의　**remain** v. 여전히 ~이다　**confident** adj. 자신감 있는, 확신하는　**demographics** n. 인구통계　**distinguish** v. 구별하다　**high-quality** adj. 고품질의　**steep** adj. 너무 비싼　**price tag** 가격표　**grow** v. 성장하다　**demand** n. 요구　**affordable** adj. 가격이 알맞은　**take off** 급히 인기를 얻다　**particularly** adv. 특히　**country with developing economies** 개발 도상국　**internal** adj. 내부의　**polling** n. 여론조사, 투표　**competitor** n. 경쟁자　**warranty** n. 품질보증서　**reputation** n. 명성, 평판　**reliability** n. 신뢰도, 확실성　**price-performance ratio** 가격 성능비　**find out** 알아내다, 알게 되다

172 암시/추론 　　　　　　　　　　　　　　난이도 중

해석　기사는 Manitoba에 관해 무엇을 암시하는가?
(A) 여러 국가에 제조공장이 있다.
(B) Manitoba에 2개의 공장을 운영할 것이다.
(C) 개인용 기기를 만든다.
(D) 영업한지 10년이 넘었다.

해설　첫 번째 단락에서 Sindri, the Canadian manufacturer known for making personal electronics, is moving its main production facility.(개인 가전제품을 만드는 것으로 유명한 캐나다 생산업체 Sindri가 주요 생산시설을 옮길 예정이다.)라고 했으므로 (C)가 정답이다.

Paraphrasing personal electronics ➡ personal devices

173 상세정보   난이도 하

해석 Sindri에서 판매한 최초의 상품은 무엇이었는가?
(A) 스마트 워치
(B) 데스크톱 컴퓨터
(C) 태블릿
(D) 노트북 컴퓨터

해설 두 번째 단락에서 Our original model, the Sindri Book laptop, was tremendously popular when it came out seven years ago,(저희 최초 모델인 Sindri Book 노트북 컴퓨터는 7년 전 출시됐을 때 인기가 엄청났습니다.)라고 했으므로 (D)가 정답

Paraphrasing first ➡ original

174 사실확인   난이도 중

해석 Sindri 고객들에 관하여 언급된 것은?
(A) 가격에 관심이 있다.
(B) 환경을 의식한다.
(C) 다른 제품들보다 태블릿을 선호한다.
(D) 대부분 선진국에 산다.

해설 세 번째 단락에서 The company's internal polling suggests that the top reasons customers chose Sindri over their competitors were its warranty and reputation for reliability, and their high price-performance ratio across all models.(회사의 사내 여론조사에서는 고객들이 경쟁사대비 Sindri를 선택한 가장 큰 이유로 제품 품질보증과 신뢰성에 대한 평판, 그리고 전 모델의 높은 가성비라고 보여준다.)라고 하여 고객들은 품질보증, 신뢰성, 가격에 관심이 있다는 것을 알 수 있으므로 정답은 이 세 가지 중 하나를 언급한 (A)이다.

175 문장삽입   난이도 중

해석 [1], [2], [3], [4]로 표시된 곳 중, 다음 문장이 들어갈 위치로 가장 적절한 것은?
"젊은 사람들, 특히 학생들이 고객일 가능성이 높다."
(A) [1]
(B) [2]
(C) [3]
(D) [4]

해설 두 번째 단락에서 new demographics of customers to the company's products.(새로운 고객층을 회사 제품으로 끌어들일 것이라고 확신한다.)이라고 하여 주어진 문장이 이어지기에 자연스러우므로 (B)가 정답

176-180번은 다음 이메일과 공지에 관한 문제입니다.

발신: Petra Stojakovic <petras@bellingercorp.com>
수신: employees@bellingercorp.com
제목: 주차공간 재배정
날짜: 4월 22일 (179)

직원 여러분께 알려드립니다.

Bellinger사의 신규 R&D 시설공사가 4월 29일에 시작됨을 다시 알려드립니다. (176)

4월 27일부터, J와 K 주차장은 완공 예정일인 7월 9일까지 이용하실 수 없습니다. (176)/(179) J와 K 주차장에 배정된 직원 여러분은 방문자 주차장에 주차할 수 있는 임시 '방문자' 주차증을 받게 됩니다. (177) 시설관리부에서 내일 정오까지 이 허가증을 자리로 가져다 드릴 것입니다. 주차증을 차량 조수석 앞 유리에 놓아주십시오.

J와 K 주차장으로 이어지는 도로는 공사장 출입로 제작으로 인해 폐쇄될 것입니다. 또한, 보안 사무실과 화원 출입구도 폐쇄됩니다. 두 장소에 모두 대체 출입구를 사용하실 수 있을 것입니다. (178)

유입되는 차량 수를 줄일 수 있도록 급한 용무가 아니면 이들 구역을 피해 줄 것을 요청 드립니다. (178) 명심하세요! 임시 출입구를 사용하실 때는 페인트로 표시된 통로만을 이용해 주시기 바랍니다.

협조해 주셔서 감사합니다.

Best regards,

Petra Stojakovic
시설관리부

어휘 reallocation n. 재할당, 재분배 commence v. 시작되다 inaccessible adj. 접근할 수 없는 estimate v. 추산[추정]하다 completion n. 완성, 완료 allocate v. 배정하다 temporary adj. 임시의 parking permit 주차증 garage n. 차고, 주차장 place v. 놓다 passenger n. 승객 windshield n. (자동차의) 앞 유리 lead up to ~로 통하다 close off ~를 차단시키다, 폐쇄하다 creation n. 창조, 창작 access n. (장소로의) 입장, 접근 v. 접근하다; 이용하다 security office 경비실 alternate adj. 대체 가능한, 대안이 되는 entry point 입구 reduce v. 줄이다 incoming adj. 도착하는, 들어오는 urge v. 강력히 권고[촉구]하다 urgent adj. 긴급한 entrance n. 입구 walkway n. 보도 cooperation n. 협조, 협력

BELLINGER사 빌딩 안내데스크에 오신 것을 환영합니다.

중요 공지:
J와 K 주차장은 8월 1일까지 폐쇄됩니다. (179)

이들 주차장으로 배정되었는데 임시 주차증을 받지 못한 직원은 가급적 조속히 보안사무실을 방문해야 합니다. 사원증과 자동차 등록증이 필요합니다.

공사현장이나 적하 구역과 같은 지정 작업구역 근처에 주차된 차량은 견인 대상입니다. (180) 적절한 허가증 없이 주차장에 세워진 차량에는 하루 30달러의 벌금이 부과됩니다.

직원들이 여러분을 도와드립니다.

어휘 lot n. 주차장 loading area 적하 구역 be subject to ~의 대상이다 tow v. 견인하다 proper adj. 적절한 issue v. 발부하다 penalty n. 벌금 on hand (특히 도움을) 구할 수 있는

176 상세정보   난이도 중

해석 왜 일부 주차장이 폐쇄되는가?
(A) 방문자만 이용할 수 있게 된다.
(B) 청소 및 다시 페인트칠하는 작업이 진행 중이다.
(C) 곧 공사가 시작된다.

(D) 회사가 그 곳을 행사에 사용할 것이다.

해설 첫 번째 지문[4월 22일에 발송된 이메일], 첫 번째 단락에서 This e-mail is to remind you that construction of the new Bellinger Corp. R&D Facility will commence on 29 April. Starting 27 April, parking lots J and K will be inaccessible until 9 July, the estimated date of completion.(Bellinger사의 신규 R&D 시설공사가 4월 29일에 시작됨을 다시 알려드립니다.)라고 하여 7일 후 공사가 시작됨을 알 수 있으므로 (C)가 정답

Paraphrasing commence ➡ start, inaccessible ➡ closed

177 상세정보 난이도 중

해설 이메일에 따르면, 누가 임시 주차증을 받는가?
(A) 평소 J와 K 주차장에 주차하는 사람들
(B) R&D시설을 견학하는 사람들
(C) Bellinger사 입사 면접을 보는 사람들
(D) 시설관리부에 신청한 사람들

해설 첫 번째 지문[이메일], 두 번째 단락에서 Employees allocated to lots J and K will receive a temporary "visitor" parking permit allowing them to park their vehicles in the visitor garage.(J와 K 주차장에 배정된 직원 여러분은 방문자 주차장에 주차할 수 있는 임시 '방문자' 주차증을 받게 됩니다.)라고 했으므로 (A)가 정답

178 상세정보 난이도 중

해설 직원들은 왜 보안사무실 방문을 피하려고 해야 하는가?
(A) 방문객이 안내데스크를 이용할 수 있도록
(B) 보안직원들이 점검을 실시할 수 있도록
(C) 정원을 즐길 수 있도록
(D) 교통량을 줄일 수 있도록

해설 첫 번째 지문[이메일], 세 번째 단락에서 In addition, the main entrance to the security office and flower garden will be closed. An alternate entry point will be available for both locations.(또한, 보안 사무실과 화원 출입구도 폐쇄됩니다. 두 장소에 모두 대체 출입구를 사용하실 수 있을 것입니다.)라고 하면서, 이어 네 번째 단락에서 In order to reduce the number of incoming cars, we urge everyone to avoid these areas unless you have urgent business.(유입되는 차량 수를 줄일 수 있도록 급한 용무가 아니면 이들 구역을 피해줄 것을 요청 드립니다.)라고 했으므로 (D)가 정답

Paraphrasing the number of incoming cars ➡ traffic

179 상세정보 [연계문제] 난이도 중

해설 4월 22일에 이메일이 발송된 이후 무엇이 바뀌었는가?
(A) 이용할 수 없는 주차장
(B) 일부 주차장을 이용할 수 없는 기간
(C) 직원들이 주차증을 받는 시점
(D) 주차증이 놓여야 하는 위치

해설 첫 번째 지문[이메일], 두 번째 단락에서 Starting 27 April, parking lots J and K will be inaccessible until 9 July,(4월 27일부터, J와 K 주차장은 완공예정일 7월 9일까지 이용하실 수 없습니다.)라고 했는데, 두 번째 지문[공지], 첫 번째 단락에서 IMPORTANT NOTICE: PARKING LOTS J & K WILL BE CLOSED UNTIL 1 AUGUST(중요 공지: J와 K 주차장은 8월 1일까지 폐쇄됩니다.)라고 하여 주차장을 이용할 수 없는 기간이 더 늘어났음을 알 수 있으므로 (B)가 정답

180 상세정보 난이도 하

해설 공지에 따르면, 직원 차량은 왜 견인될 수 있는가?
(A) 7월 9일 이후에 주차장에 세워진 경우
(B) 적하 구역 옆에 주차된 경우
(C) 주차증이 없는 경우
(D) 방문자 주차장에 주차된 경우

해설 두 번째 지문[공지], 세 번째 단락에서 Vehicles parked near designated work zones, such as the construction site or loading areas, are subject to be towed.(공사현장이나 적하구역과 같은 지정 작업구역 근처에 세워진 차량은 견인 대상입니다.)라고 했으므로 (B)가 정답

181-185번은 다음 설문지와 이메일에 관한 문제입니다.

설문지

시간을 내어 설문지를 작성해주셔서 감사 드립니다. 설문에 응해주시면, 이곳 Barkley's에서 귀하께 더 나은 서비스를 제공해 드리는 데 도움을 주시게 됩니다. 아래 양식에서 항목별 만족도를 나타내는 칸에 표시해주시기 바랍니다.

(1=매우 나쁨, 2=나쁨, 3=보통, 4=좋음, 5=매우 좋음)

	1	2	3	4	5
매장 분위기와 청결을 어떻게 평가하시겠습니까?	□	□	□	■	□
요리에 사용된 재료의 신선도를 어떻게 평가하시겠습니까?(181)	□	□	□	□	■
음식 값으로 지불한 금액 대비 귀하의 만족도를 어떻게 평가하시겠습니까?(181)/(182)	□	□	□	■	□
받으신 서비스의 속도를 어떻게 평가하시겠습니까?	□	□	□	□	■
문의사항에 응답하는 직원들의 능력을 어떻게 평가하시겠습니까?(184)	■	□	□	□	□
Barkley's에 대한 전체적인 인상을 어떻게 평가하시겠습니까?	□	□	□	■	□

• 오늘 얼마를 지불하셨습니까? : 75 달러
• 나이(선택사항)
  14-21 □/22-29 ■/30-37 □/38-45 □/46-54 □/55+ □
• 이름(선택사항): Miguel Nunez
• 이메일(선택사항): mnunez1@penmail.co.nz

어휘 questionnaire n. 설문지 fill out 작성하다 serve v. (서비스) 제공하다 indicate v. 나타내다 satisfaction n. 만족 aspect n. 부문, 항목 average adj. 평균의 rate v. 평가하다 atmosphere n. 분위기 cleanliness n. 청결 freshness n. 신선 ingredient n. 재료 dish n. 요리 compared to ~과 비교하여

수신: Miguel Nunez <mnunez1@penmail.co.nz>
발신: Support Services <ss@ Barkleys.co.nz>
제목: 설문지
날짜: 8월 4일 화요일, 오전 11시 25분
첨부파일: 쿠폰

Mr. Nunez께,

시간을 내어 Barkley's에 관한 설문지를 작성해주셔서 감사 드립니다. 저희는 **많은 분들께 피드백을 받았고, 여러분 모두의 의견을 소중하게 생각합니다.** (183)/(185) 이 정보는 저희에게 배움과 더 나은 서비스를 제공할 기회를 줍니다.

Barkley's에 대한 귀하의 전체적인 평가가 만족이었다는 사실에 기쁩니다. 하지만, 저희가 받은 응답 중 대다수에서 귀하가 만족하지 못했던 것과 동일한 항목에 관해 부정적인 인상을 표현했다는 점에서 실망스러웠습니다. 저희는 이 문제를 바로잡는 데 필요한 조치를 취하고 있음을 귀하께 확실히 말씀 드리고 싶습니다. 조만간 새로운 직원교육 프로그램이 시작됩니다.(184)

응답에 대한 감사의 표시로, 다음 번 구매 시 Barkley's 전국 어느 지점에서든 할인 받을 수 있는 20 퍼센트 할인 쿠폰(이메일에 첨부)을 드리고자 합니다. 항상 이용해주셔서 감사 드립니다.

Best,

Yasiel Sanders

어휘 value v. 소중하게 여기다 rating n. 순위, 평가 satisfactory adj. 만족스러운 disappointed adj. 실망한 the majority of 대다수의 express v. 표현하다, 나타내다 impression n. 인상 regarding prep. ~에 관하여 aspect n. 측면 assure v. 장담하다, 확언하다 take steps 조치를 취하다 correct v. 바로잡다 appreciation n. 감사

---

181 암시/추론   난이도 중

해석   Barkley's는 어떤 종류의 사업체이겠는가?
(A) 전자제품 매장
(B) 슈퍼마켓
(C) 식당
(D) 마케팅 대행사

해설   첫 번째 지문[설문지], 표의 두 번째 질문에서 How would you rate the freshness of the ingredients used in your dish?(요리에 사용된 재료의 신선도를 어떻게 평가하시겠습니까?)라고 했고, 세 번째 질문에서 How would you rate your satisfaction compared to how much you paid for the food?(음식 값으로 지불한 금액 대비 귀하의 만족도를 어떻게 평가하시겠습니까?)라고 하여 식당에 대한 설문조사임을 알 수 있으므로 (C)가 정답

---

182 암시/추론   난이도 중

해석   Mr. Nunez는 Barkley's에 관한 어떤 진술에 동의하겠는가?
(A) 가격이 합리적이다.
(B) 서비스가 다양하다.
(C) 위치가 편리하다.
(D) 직원들이 노련하다.

해설   첫 번째 지문[설문지], 표의 세 번째 질문 How would you rate your satisfaction compared to how much you paid for the food?(귀하의 만족도를 음식 값으로 지불한 금액과 비교하여 어떻게 평가하시겠습니까?)에 대해 4 Good(좋음)이라고 평가하여 음식값으로 지불한 비용에 비교적 만족한다는 것을 알 수 있으므로 (A)가 정답

---

183 동의어   난이도 중

해석   이메일에서 첫 번째 단락, 두 번째 줄의 단어 "value"와 의미상 가장 가까운 것은?
(A) 계산하다
(B) 진가를 알아보다
(C) 이익을 얻다
(D) 강조하다

해설   두 번째 지문[이메일], 첫 번째 단락의 We received feedback from a lot of people, and we value all of your opinions.(저희는 많은 분들께 피드백을 받았고, 여러분 모두의 의견을 소중하게 생각합니다.)에서 'value'는 '소중히 여기다'라는 의미로 쓰였으므로 보기 중 '진가를 알아보다'를 뜻하는 (B)가 정답

---

184 암시/추론 [연계문제]   난이도 상

해석   Barkley's는 무엇을 하려고 계획하고 있겠는가?
(A) 사업장을 더 자주 청소할 것이다
(B) 일부 상품의 가격을 낮출 것이다
(C) 설문조사에 참여하는 모든 고객에게 쿠폰을 제공할 것이다
(D) 직원들이 제품에 대해 더 잘 알도록 교육할 것이다

해설   첫 번째 지문[설문지], 표의 다섯 번째 질문 How would you rate the staff's ability to answer your questions?(문의사항에 응답하는 직원들의 능력을 어떻게 평가하시겠습니까?)에 대해 1 Poor(매우 나쁨)으로 평가하였는데, 두 번째 지문[이메일], 두 번째 단락에서 We were, however, disappointed to see that the majority of the responses we received expressed negative impressions regarding the same aspect that you were unhappy with. I want to assure you that we are taking the necessary steps to correct this problem. A new employee education program will be starting in the near future.(하지만, 저희가 받은 응답 중 대다수에서 귀하가 만족하지 못했던 것과 동일한 항목에 관해 부정적인 인상을 표현했다는 점에서 실망스러웠습니다. 저희는 이 문제를 바로잡는 데 필요한 조치를 취하고 있음을 귀하께 확실히 말씀 드리고 싶습니다. 조만간 새로운 직원교육 프로그램이 시작됩니다.)라고 하여 직원들을 대상으로 교육을 할 것임을 알 수 있으므로 (D)가 정답

---

185 암시/추론   난이도 중

해석   설문지에 관하여 알 수 있는 것은?
(A) 인터넷으로 작성되어야 한다.
(B) 많은 고객들이 작성했다.
(C) 2년마다 업데이트된다.
(D) Mr. Sanders가 설계했다.

해설   두 번째 지문[이메일], 첫 번째 단락에서 We received feedback from a lot of people, and we value all of your opinions.(저희는 많은 분들께 피드백을 받았고, 여러분 모두의 의견을 소중하게 생각합니다.)라고 했으므로 (B)가 정답

186-190번은 다음 계획 안내서, 정보지, 의견카드에 관한 문제입니다.

San Lorenzo: 방문기간 최대한 즐기기

몇 시간 들르시거나 잠시 머물러보세요. 어느 쪽이든 San Lorenzo시에 마음을 뺏기실 겁니다. 아래와 같은 방문일정을 추천해 드립니다.

반일 투어

Main가 113번지에 있는 San Lorenzo 관광 안내소에 가셔서 도시의 역사에 관한 짧은 강연을 들어보세요.⁽¹⁸⁶⁾/⁽¹⁸⁸⁾ 그리고 나서 시내 명소들에 방문객들을 태우고 내려주는 투어버스에 타세요.

종일 투어

반일 투어의 모든 활동 외에,⁽¹⁸⁸⁾ 관광 안내소 바로 건너편에 있는 Phoenix 궁전에 가보세요.⁽¹⁸⁶⁾ 매일 정오부터 일몰 시까지 궁전과 궁전 식물원에서 가이드와 함께 하는 투어를 이용하실 수 있습니다. 아름다운 기념품을 위해 기념품점도 꼭 방문해주세요.

수일 투어(하루 이상)

위에 열거한 모든 활동을 하신 후,⁽¹⁸⁸⁾ 시내 및 주변지역에서 도보 관광을 하시면서 San Lorenzo에 관해 더 알아보세요.

어휘 **get the most out of** ~을 최대한으로 활용하다 **drop in** (~에) 들르다 **partial** adj. 부분적인 **brief** adj. 짧은 **hop** v. ~에 타다 **pick up** ~를 (차에) 태우다 **landmark** n. 역사적인 장소 **on top of** ~외에 **botanical garden** 식물원 **sundown** n. 일몰 **souvenir** n. 기념품 **list** v. 열거하다 **surrounding** adj. 주변의

San Lorenzo의 산책로

Rainbow 산마루 (10.3km)
대부분 오르막인 이 10.3km의 하이킹은 항만에서 출발하여 시내를 지나 Rainbow 산마루 공원의 경치 좋은 절벽까지 이어집니다. 시내 최고 전경을 보기에 안성맞춤이지만, 초보 등산객들에게는 부담스럽습니다.⁽¹⁸⁹⁾

Borges 반도(6.1km)
이 6.1km 산책로는 Borges 야생보호구역 근처의 완만한 언덕들을 통과하여 지나갑니다. 두꺼운 나뭇잎은 산책로에 빛이 많이 들지 않는다는 것을 의미하므로, 일몰 전에 돌아오세요.⁽¹⁸⁷⁾

옛 교회 경로 (1.7km)
성 Catherine 교회에서 성 Jessica 교회까지의 자갈이 깔린 길을 따라 경치에 감상하면서 걸어보세요. 1.7km의 수월한 평지길입니다.

Brilliant대로(2.1km)
박물관 구역에서 Crimson 타워에 이르는 인기 경로입니다. 거리를 따라 쇼핑과 식사를 즐겨 보세요. 이 2.1km 경로는 밤에 약간 붐빌 수 있습니다.

어휘 **walking trail** 산책로 **ridge** n. 산등성이 **uphill** adj. 오르막의 **hike** n. 하이킹 **harbor** n. 항구 **scenic** adj. 경치가 좋은 **bluff** n. 절벽 **demanding** adj. 부담이 큰, 힘든 **novice** n. 초보자 **peninsula** n. 반도 **rolling** adj. 완만하게 경사진 **wildlife reserve** 야생보호구역 **foliage** n. 나뭇잎 **head** v. 가다 **stroll** v. 거닐다, 산책하다 **cobbled** adj. 자갈을 깐 **admire** v. 감탄하며 바라보다 **sight** n. 광경, 모습 **flat** adj. 평평한 **easy going** adj. 마음 편한 **boulevard** n. 대로 **hectic** adj. 정신 없이 바쁜

San Lorenzo 관광 안내소
의견 카드

이름: Scottie Fitzgerald⁽¹⁸⁸⁾
방문일: 8월 1일-2일⁽¹⁸⁸⁾

메시지:

우리 가족은 San Lorenzo 여행이 정말 좋았습니다. 그 도시를 방문해본 적이 없어서, 관광 안내소에서 받은 계획 안내서에 나온 추천사항들을 그대로 따랐는데, 정말 도움이 되었습니다. 토요일과 일요일 모두 시내에서 보내면서 구경을 많이 했습니다.⁽¹⁸⁸⁾ 투어버스는 돈이 아깝지 않더군요. 저희가 가보지 않은 유일한 산책로는 가장 길고 가장 어려운 코스였습니다. 저희 아이들이 아직 그런 것을 하기에는 너무 어리거든요. 하지만 조만간 가보고 싶습니다.⁽¹⁸⁹⁾ 물론 제가 첫날 구매한 San Lorenzo 교통카드가 8월 말일에 만료되기 전에 갈 수 있다면 좋겠네요.⁽¹⁹⁰⁾

어휘 **try out** 시험적으로 사용해보다 **transit card** 교통카드

---

186 사실확인   난이도 중

해석 계획 안내서에서는 Phoenix 궁전에 관하여 무엇을 언급하는가?
(A) 주민에게 할인을 제공한다.
(B) 입장료를 받지 않는다.
(C) Main가에 위치한다.
(D) San Lorenzo에서 가장 오래된 장소이다.

해설 첫 번째 지문[계획 안내서], 두 번째 단락 Partial Day(반일 투어)에서 Go to the San Lorenzo Visitor Center at 113 Main Street for a brief lecture on the city's history.(Main가 113번지에 있는 San Lorenzo 관광 안내소에 가셔서 도시의 역사에 관한 짧은 강연을 들어보세요.)라고 했고, 세 번째 단락에서 On top of all the partial-day activities, check out Phoenix Palace right across from the Visitor Center.(반일 투어의 모든 활동 외에, 관광 안내소 바로 건너편에 있는 Phoenix 궁전에 가보세요.)라고 했으므로 (C)가 정답

---

187 사실확인   난이도 중

해석 산책로 정보에 따르면, Borges 반도 산책로에 관하여 사실인 것은?
(A) 도시 전경을 볼 수 있다.
(B) 그늘진 구역이다.
(C) 밤에 매우 아름답다.
(D) 초보자가 사용하면 안 된다.

해설 두 번째 지문[정보지]. 두 번째 단락에서 The thick foliage means that the trail doesn't get much light, so head back before sundown.(두꺼운 나뭇잎들은 산책로에 빛이 많이 들지 않는다는 것을 의미하므로 일몰 전에 돌아오세요.)라고 했으므로 (B)가 정답

Paraphrasing doesn't get much light ➡ shaded

---

188 암시/추론 [연계문제]   난이도 상

해석 Mr. Fitzgerald는 도시를 방문했을 때 무엇을 처음으로 했겠는가?
(A) 투어버스를 탔을 것이다
(B) 궁전을 방문했을 것이다
(C) 강연을 들었을 것이다
(D) 하이킹을 갔을 것이다

해설 세 번째 지문[Scottie Fitzgerald가 작성한 의견 카드]에서 Date(s) of Visit(방문일): August 1-2(8월 1-2일)이고, Message(메시지)에서 Since we'd never visited the city, we followed the recommendations in the Visitor Center's planning guide exactly, and it really helped. We spent both Saturday and Sunday in town, and we saw a lot.(그 도시를 방문해본 적이 없어서, 관광 안내소에서 받은 계획 안내서에 나온 추천사항들을 그대로 따랐는데, 정말 도움이 되었습니다. 토요일과 일요일 모두 시내

에서 보내면서 구경을 많이 했습니다.)라고 했는데, 첫 번째 지문[계획 안내서], 두 번째 단락 Partial Day(반일투어)에서 Go to the San Lorenzo Visitor Center at 113 Main Street for a brief lecture on the city's history.(Main가 113번지에 있는 San Lorenzo 관광 안내소에 가셔서 도시의 역사에 관한 짧은 강연을 들어보세요.), 세 번째 단락 Complete Day(종일 투어)에서 On top of all the partial-day activities,(반일 투어의 모든 활동 외에), 네 번째 단락 Multi-Day (More than one day)(수일 투어(하루 이상))에서 After doing all the activities listed above,(위에 열거한 모든 활동을 하신 후에)라고 하여 가장 먼저 도시 역사에 관한 짧은 강연을 들었을 것임을 알 수 있으므로 (C)가 정답

189 상세정보 [연계문제] 난이도 상

해석 Mr. Fitzgerald는 나중에 어느 산책로에서 하이킹을 할 계획인가?
(A) Rainbow 산마루
(B) Borges 반도
(C) 옛 교회 경로
(D) Brilliant대로

해설 세 번째 지문[의견 카드], Message(메시지)에서 The only walking trail we didn't try out was the longest and most difficult one. Our children are still too young for something like that. However, I wish to try it soon(저희가 가보지 않은 유일한 산책로는 가장 길고 가장 어려운 코스였습니다. 저희 아이들이 아직 그런 것을 하기에는 너무 어리거든요. 하지만 조만간 가보고 싶습니다.)라고 했는데, 두 번째 지문[정보지], 첫 번째 단락에서 Rainbow Ridge (10.3km) This 10.3-kilometer, mostly uphill hike takes you from the harbor side, through downtown, to all the way up to the scenic bluffs of Rainbow Ridge Park. Perfect for the best views of the city, but demanding for novice hikers.(Rainbow 산마루 (10.3km): 대부분 오르막인 이 10.3km의 하이킹은 항만에서 출발하여 시내를 지나 Rainbow 산마루 공원의 경치 좋은 절벽까지 이어집니다. 시내 최고 전경을 보기에 안성맞춤이지만, 초보 등산객들에게는 부담스럽습니다.)라고 하여 그가 다음에는 Rainbow 산마루를 하이킹할 것임을 알 수 있으므로 (A)가 정답

190 암시/추론 난이도 중

해석 Mr. Fitzgerald는 의견 카드에서 무엇을 암시하는가?
(A) 계획 안내서가 매우 유용했다고 생각하지 않는다.
(B) 전문 등산가이다.
(C) 한 달짜리 교통카드를 구입했다.
(D) 관광 안내소 근처의 호텔을 예약했다.

해설 세 번째 지문[의견 카드]에서 Date(s) of Visit(방문일): August 1-2(8월 1-2일)이고, Message(메시지)에서 hopefully before my San Lorenzo transit card I bought on my first day expires on the last day of August.(물론 제가 첫날 구매한 San Lorenzo 교통카드가 8월 말일에 만료되기 전에 갈 수 있다면 좋겠네요.)라고 하여 그가 구매한 교통카드가 한 달간 유효하다는 것을 알 수 있으므로 (C)가 정답

Paraphrasing transit card ➡ transportation card,
bought ➡ purchased

191-195번은 다음 기사, 일정, 이메일에 관한 문제입니다.

Johnson 카운티, 수도관 보수작업 실시

(3월 12일) – 4월 한달 동안, Johnson 카운티 수자원 공사는 자치주의 수도시스템이 최적의 방식으로 계속 작동할 수 있도록 수 마일의 구리관을 폴리염화비닐(PVC)관으로 업그레이드할 계획입니다.

"더 강한 수압에도 견딜 수 있는 PVC 수도관은 세탁기, 식기세척기 및 다른 다양한 종류의 소비자 가전제품들이 더 잘 작동할 수 있게 해줍니다."[191]라고 Johnson 카운티 상수지구 감독관인 Mr. Sohel Khan은 말합니다. "또한 새로운 수도관은 예전의 구리 수도관보다 더 적은 잠재 환경 오염원을 내포합니다."

카운티에 있는 몇몇 도로들은 보수작업이 진행되는 24시간 동안 전면 봉쇄될 것입니다.[193] 수자원 공사 담당자들은 업체들에 불필요한 문제 야기를 방지할 일정표에 동의를 얻으려는 희망으로 지역 상인들과 협의 중에 있습니다.[195] 일정은 계속 변경될 것이며, 이는 County Clerk 웹 사이트에서 확인하실 수 있습니다.[192] 주민들은 또한 County Clerk에 의견 및 우려사항들을 올릴 수 있습니다.

어휘 county n. 자치주, 카운티 renovate v. 개조하다, 보수하다 water pipe 배수관, 수도관 network n. 망, 네트워크 throughout prep. ~동안, 내내 district n. 지구, 지역 several adj. 몇몇의 copper n. 구리 polyvinyl chloride(PVC) 폴리염화비닐 ensure v. 보장하다 function n. 기능 v. 기능하다 optimal adj. 최적의, 최상의 manner n. 방식 withstand v. 견디다 pressure n. 압력 allow v. 허용하다 operation n. 작업, 작전 laundry machine 세탁기 dishwasher n. 식기세척기 variety n. 여러 가지, 다양성 consumer n. 소비자 device n. 장치, 기구 pose v. (문제 등을) 제기하다 potential adj. 잠재적인 environmental adj. 환경의 hazard n. 위험 (요소) completely adv. 완전히 inaccessible adj. 접근하기 어려운 renovation n. 개조, 수리 take place 일어나다 official n. 공무원 consult v. 상의[상담]하다 local adj. 지역의 in hopes of ~의 희망을 가지고 agree upon ~에 동의하다 timetable n. 일정표 avoid v. 방지하다, 피하다 cause v. 야기시키다, 유발하다 unnecessary adj. 불필요한 constant adj. 거듭되는, 끊임없는 revision n. 수정(사항), 변경 schedule n. 일정 resident n. 주민 address v. 다루다, 언급하다 comment n. 언급, 논평 concern n. 걱정, 염려

---

www.johnsoncountyclerk.gov

수도관 보수 일정:

4월 4일, 토요일	Antioch Street[193]
4월 5일, 일요일	Corinth Avenue
4월 11일, 토요일	Jameson Lane[194]
4월 12일, 일요일	Cherokee Drive

보수작업이 마무리된 후, Johnson 카운티 수자원 공사 직원이 수압 확인을 위해 귀하의 자택 또는 사업장을 방문할 것입니다.

어휘 complete v. 완료하다 employee n. 직원 check v. 확인하다

수신: Ed Haber <eddie@eddiesbakery.com>
발신: **Anita Quackenbush**
       <quackenbush@johnsoncountyclerk.gov> (195)
제목: 점검
날짜: 4월 1일

Mr. Haber께,

아시다시피, 저희는 4월 11일 토요일 귀하의 점포를 지나는 도로 수도관에 보수공사를 진행합니다.(194) 그날 오전 약 4시간 동안 수돗물이 공급되지 않음을 예상하셔야 합니다. 이 작업으로 불편을 드려 죄송합니다. **상수지구 기술자는 수압이 적절한지를 확인하기 위해 다음날 오전 9시에서 11시 사이 귀하의 사업장을 방문할 예정입니다. 다른 시간으로 일정을 잡으셔야 한다면, 저희에게 555-1212번으로 알려주시기 바랍니다.**(195)

Best Regards,

Anita Quackenbush

어휘   inspection n. 점검   anticipate v. 예상하다   running water 수돗물   apologize v. 사과하다   inconvenience n. 불편   technician n. 기술자   following adj. (시간상) 다음의   confirm v. 확인하다   proper adj. 적절한, 제대로 된   arrange v. 정하다, 주선하다   notify v. 알리다, 통지하다

---

191   사실확인   난이도 중

해석   기사에 따르면, 새로운 수도관에 관하여 언급된 것은?
(A) 구리관보다 더 저렴하다.
(B) 일부 기기가 더 잘 작동하게 해 줄 것이다.
(C) 오전에 설치될 것이다.
(D) 자주 점검될 것이다.

해설   첫 번째 지문[기사], 두 번째 단락에서 The ability of PVC pipes to withstand greater water pressure will allow for better operation of laundry machines, dishwashers, and a variety of other consumer devices.(더 강한 수압에도 견딜 수 있는 PVC 수도관은 세탁기, 식기세척기 및 다른 다양한 종류의 소비자 가전제품들이 더 잘 작동할 수 있게 해줍니다.)라고 했으므로 (B)가 정답

Paraphrasing   allow for better operation of ~ ➡ make ~ function better

---

192   사실확인   난이도 중

해석   기사에서 프로젝트 일정에 관하여 언급한 것은?
(A) 정기적으로 업데이트될 것이다.
(B) Mr. Khan이 만들었다.
(C) 일부 주민들이 찬성하지 않는다.
(D) 몇 가지 문제가 있다.

해설   첫 번째 지문[기사], 세 번째 단락에서 Water District officials are consulting with local store owners in hopes of agreeing upon a timetable that will avoid causing unnecessary problems for businesses. Constant revisions will be made to the schedule, which can be found on the County Clerk's Web site.(수자원 공사 담당자들은 영업에 불필요한 문제야기를 피할 일정표에 동의를 얻으려는 희망으로 지역 상인들과 협의 중에 있습니다. 일정은 계속 변경될 것이며, 이는 County Clerk 웹 사이트에서 확인하실 수 있습니다.)라고 했으므로 (A)가 정답

---

193   상세정보 [연계문제]   난이도 중

해석   4월 4일에 무슨 일이 일어날 것인가?
(A) 새로운 카운티 서기 관리자가 임명될 것이다.
(B) 도로가 봉쇄될 것이다.
(C) 비즈니스 컨벤션이 열릴 것이다.
(D) 도시 퍼레이드가 있을 것이다.

해설   첫 번째 지문[기사], 세 번째 단락에서 Several roads in the county will be completely inaccessible for 24-hour periods while the renovation is taking place.(카운티에 있는 몇몇 도로들은 보수작업이 진행되는 24시간 동안 전면 봉쇄될 것입니다.)라고 했는데, 두 번째 지문[일정], 표에서 Saturday, April 4(4월 4일, 토요일)에 Antioch Street의 보수작업이 예정되어 있어 도로가 봉쇄될 것임을 알 수 있으므로 (B)가 정답

Paraphrasing   completely inaccessible ➡ blocked

---

194   암시/추론 [연계문제]   난이도 중

해석   Mr. Haber의 매장에 관하여 알 수 있는 것은?
(A) 일주일 동안 영업을 하지 않았다.
(B) 하루 24시간 영업한다.
(C) Jameson Lane에 위치한다.
(D) 최근 문을 열었다.

해설   세 번째 지문[Mr. Haber에게 보낸 이메일]에서 As you may know, we will be renovating water lines on the street that runs along your store on Saturday, April 11.(아시다시피, 저희는 4월 11일 토요일 귀하의 점포를 지나는 도로 수도관에 보수공사를 진행합니다.)라고 했는데, 두 번째 지문[일정], 표에서 Saturday, April 11(4월 11일, 토요일)에 Jameson Lane의 보수작업이 예정되어 있어 Mr. Haber의 매장이 Jameson Lane에 있음을 알 수 있으므로 (C)가 정답

---

195   암시/추론 [연계문제]   난이도 중

해석   Ms. Quackenbush는 누구겠는가?
(A) 지역 상인
(B) 건설 노동자
(C) 상수지구 기술자
(D) 공무원

해설   첫 번째 지문[기사], 세 번째 단락에서 Water District officials are consulting with local store owners in hopes of agreeing upon a timetable that will avoid causing unnecessary problems for businesses.(수자원 공사 담당자들은 업체들에 불필요한 문제 야기를 방지할 일정표에 동의를 얻으려는 희망으로 지역 상인들과 협의 중에 있습니다.)라고 했는데, 세 번째 지문[Ms. Quackenbush이 보낸 이메일]에서 A Water District technician is scheduled to visit your business the following day between 9 a.m. and 11 a.m. to confirm proper water pressure. If you need to arrange a different time, please notify us at 555-1212.(상수지구 기술자는 수압이 적절한지를 확인하기 위해 다음날 오전 9시에서 11시 사이 귀하의 사업장을 방문할 예정입니다. 다른 시간으로 일정을 잡으셔야 한다면, 저희에게 555-1212번으로 알려주시기 바랍니다.)라며 사업장 방문일정을 협의하고 있어 수자원 공사 소속직원임을 알 수 있으므로 (D)가 정답

Paraphrasing   official ➡ government employee

196-200번은 다음 브로셔와 이메일들에 관한 문제입니다.

Nevardo's

Palm Springs 바로 외곽의 Cathedral City의 사막 지역에 있는 Nevardo's는 그 어떤 종류의 세미나, 파티, 또는 행사에도 완벽한 장소를 제공합니다.(196) 매우 아름다운 Indian Canyon 자연보호구역의 끝자락에 위치한 이곳은 넓찍한 파티오 라운지에서 바라보면 숨막히는 전망을 선사합니다.

내부에는 Coachella Room이 150명까지 수용할 수 있고, Agua Caliente 홀은 250명을 거뜬히 수용할 수 있습니다.(198) 콘퍼런스의 경우, Joshua Tree Room은 최대 75명의 단체까지 소화하며, 그 이상의 참여 인원은 새롭게 복원된 Lucille Ball 강당을 이용하면 되는 데, 이곳은 100석이 마련되어 있습니다. 뒤의 두 곳에는 성공적인 프레젠테이션이 가능하도록 최고급 시청각장비가 완비되어 있습니다.

저희의 수상경력에 빛나는 뷔페인 Nopalitos Grill에서는 환상적이고 다양한 멕시코 및 남서부지역 요리를 제공합니다. 5월 5일에 저희의 스페셜 Cinco de Mayo 메뉴를 꼭 확인해 주세요!

자세한 내용은 저희 웹 사이트를 참조해 주시기 바랍니다: www.nevardos.com.

저희는 일부 날짜에 Coachella Valley 업체들에게 30퍼센트 지역 협력업체 특별 할인을 제공합니다. 자세한 내용은 760-555-1212로 전화주세요.

어휘 desert n. 사막 community n. 지역사회, 공동체 provide v. 제공하다 location n. 위치, 장소 situate v. 위치시키다 edge n. 가장자리, 모서리 gorgeous adj. 아주 멋진, 아름다운 feature v. 특징으로 삼다 n. 특징, 특성 breathtaking adj. 숨이 막히는, 숨이 멎는 듯한 spacious adj. 넓찍한 patio n. 테라스, 파티오 lounge n. 라운지 host v. 주최하다 comfortably adv. 편안하게, 수월하게 fit v. (장소에) 맞다 attendee n. 참석자 participant n. 참가자 turnout n. 참가자 수 accommodate v. 수용하다 newly adv. 새로, 최근에 restore v. 복원하다, 회복시키다 seat v. 앉히다, 좌석이 있다 latter adj. 후자의, 마지막의 fully adv. 완전히 equip v. 장비를 갖추다 top-quality adj. 최고 품질의 audio-visual adj. 시청각의 equipment n. 장비 award-winning adj. 상을 받은 serve up (요리를) 제공하다 array n. 무리, 집합체 dish n. 요리, 접시 check out 확인하다 local adj. 지역의, 현지의 certain adj. 어떤, 확실한 detail n. 세부사항

수신: Dan Chan <dchan@charpentierfinancial.com>
발신: Fadila Boumaza <fboumaza@charpentierfinancial.com>
날짜: 1월 4일
제목: 합병 축하행사 계획

Mr. Chan께,

저는 당신이 월요일 회의 때 언급한 식당 Nevardo's를 확인해봤습니다. 저희 기업합병 파티장소로 안성맞춤인 것 같습니다. 식당이 있는 장소의 경치가 너무 좋고, 타지에서 참석하는 분들까지 현재 200명이 넘는 참석자가 있어,(198) 방문하시는 분들께 사막의 아름다움을 보여드릴 수 있는 좋은 기회입니다. 그곳에는 5월 11일, 5월 25일, 5월 27일에 이용 가능한 적당한 공간이 있습니다. 첫 번째 날짜는 저희 같은 지역업체들에 상당한 할인을 제공하는 날입니다.(200)

회계팀에 확인해주시고, 그 쪽에서 예약을 해도 좋다고 하면 저에게 알려주세요.(197) 하지만 너무 지체하지 않는 게 좋을 거에요. 그 곳은 이미 4월까지 예약이 찼고, 5월 빈자리들도 곧 마감될 것 같습니다.(199)

감사합니다,

-Fadila

어휘 merger n. 합병 celebration n. 축하, 기념 (행사) mention v. 언급하다 corporate adj. 기업의 scenic adj. 경치가 좋은 attend v. 참석하다 fine adj. 좋은, 괜찮은 opportunity n. 기회 appropriate adj. 적절한, 적당한 space n. 공간, 자리 available adj. 이용할 수 있는 substantial adj. 상당한 confirm v. (사실임을) 확인해주다 reservation n. 예약 book up 예약하다 opening n. 빈자리, 공석 fill up 가득 차다, 마감되다 quickly adv. 빨리, 곧

수신: Fadila Boumaza <fboumaza@charpentierfinancial>
발신: Dan Chan <dchan@charpentierfinancial>
날짜: 1월 4일
제목: 회신: 합병 축하행사 계획

Fadila께,

Nevardo's에 관한 세부내용들을 보내주셔서 감사합니다. 회계담당자와 논의한 후, 저희는 할인금액을 적용 받을 수 있는 날짜로 하는 걸로 결정했습니다.(200) 이는 저희 예산에 도움이 될 거에요. Nevardo's에 전화해서 장소를 예약해 주세요.

Dan Chan
인사총괄임원, Charpentier 금융

어휘 regarding prep. ~에 관하여 go with (제의 등을) 받아들이다, 따르다 reduce v. 줄이다, 감소하다 rate n. 요금, 비율, 속도 budget n. 예산 book v. 예약하다 venue n. 장소

---

196 사실확인 난이도 중

해석 브로셔에 따르면, Nevardo's에 관하여 무엇이 사실인가?
(A) 강당을 리모델링할 계획이다.
(B) 레스토랑 메뉴를 최근 업데이트했다.
(C) Palm Springs 시내에 위치한다.
(D) 다양한 종류의 행사에 적합하다.

해설 첫 번째 지문[브로셔], 첫 번째 단락에서 Just outside Palm Springs, in the desert community of Cathedral City, Nevardo's provides a perfect location for any seminar, party, or ceremony.(Palm Springs 바로 외곽의 Cathedral City의 사막 지역에 있는 Nevardo's는 그 어떤 종류의 세미나, 파티, 또는 행사에도 완벽한 장소를 제공합니다.)라고 했으므로 (D)가 정답

Paraphrasing any seminar, party, or ceremony ➡ various kinds of events

---

197 사실확인 난이도 중

해석 Ms. Boumaza는 기업합병 파티에 관하여 무엇을 언급하는가?
(A) 여러 날짜에 열릴 것이다.
(B) 다른 사람들의 승인을 필요로 한다.

(C) 비디오 프레젠테이션을 포함할 것이다.
(D) 연기될 지도 모른다.

해설   첫 번째 지문[첫 번째 이메일], 두 번째 단락에서 Please confirm with Accounting and let me know when they say it's okay to make the reservation.(회계팀에 확인해주시고, 그 쪽에서 예약을 해도 좋다고 하면 저에게 알려주세요.)라고 했으므로 (B)가 정답

198   암시/추론 [연계문제]   난이도 중

해석   기업합병 파티는 어디서 열리겠는가?
(A) Coachella Room에서
(B) Agua Caliente 홀에서
(C) Joshua Tree Room에서
(D) Lucille Ball 강당에서

해설   첫 번째 지문[첫 번째 이메일], 첫 번째 단락에서 since we've got a lot of guests, now over 200, from out of town attending(타지에서 참석하는 분들까지 현재 200명이 넘는 참석자가 있어,)라고 했는데, 첫 번째 지문[브로셔], 두 번째 단락에서 the Agua Caliente Hall can comfortably fit 250 attendees(Agua Caliente 홀은 250명을 거뜬히 수용할 수 있습니다.)라고 했으므로 (B)가 정답

199   상세정보   난이도 중

해석   Ms. Boumaza는 왜 걱정하는가?
(A) 행사장 비용이 인상될 수 있어서
(B) 장소가 너무 불편할 수 있어서
(C) 다수의 손님들이 참석을 확정하지 않아서
(D) 가장 알맞은 공간을 이용할 수 없을까 봐

해설   두 번째 지문[첫 번째 이메일], 두 번째 단락에서 But we shouldn't wait too long—the place is already booked up through April, and these openings in May will probably fill up quickly, too.(하지만 너무 지체하지 않는 게 좋을 거예요. 그 곳은 이미 4월까지 예약이 찼고, 5월 빈자리들도 곧 마감될 것 같습니다.)라고 하여 해당 장소가 예약 마감될 것을 걱정하고 있음을 알 수 있으므로 (D)가 정답

200   암시/추론 [연계문제]   난이도 중

해석   Charpentier 금융의 파티는 언제 열리겠는가?
(A) 5월 5일
(B) 5월 11일
(C) 5월 25일
(D) 5월 27일

해설   세 번째 지문[두 번째 이메일]에서 After talking with the accounting manager, we decided to go with the date where we can receive a reduced rate.(회계담당자와 논의한 후, 저희는 할인금액을 적용 받을 수 있는 날짜로 하는 걸로 결정했습니다.)라고 했는데, 두 번째 지문[첫 번째 이메일], 첫 번째 단락에서 They have an appropriate space available on May 11, May 25, and May 27. The first date is when they offer a substantial discount for local companies like ours.(5월 11일, 5월 25일, 5월 27일에 이용 가능한 적당한 공간이 있습니다. 첫 번째 날짜는 저희 같은 지역업체들에 상당한 할인을 제공하는 날입니다.)라고 하여 할인이 적용되는 5월 11일로 결정할 것임을 알 수 있으므로 (B)가 정답

파고다
토익 LC RC
실전 1000제 해설서